THE LEGACY OF THE ANCIENT WORLD

BY

W. G. DE BURGH, M.A.

Late Professor Emeritus of Philosophy, in the University of Reading ;
Fellow of the British Academy.

NEW EDITION
REVISED AND ENLARGED

𝕷𝖔𝖓𝖉𝖔𝖓
MACDONALD & EVANS
8 JOHN STREET, BEDFORD ROW, W.C.1
1947

First Edition . . . 1923
Second Impression . . 1926
New and Revised Edition . 1947

PRINTED IN GREAT BRITAIN BY RICHARD CLAY AND COMPANY, LTD.,
BUNGAY, SUFFOLK

PREFACE

THIS book is designed as an introduction to the study of ancient civilization for those unacquainted with its history. There is a growing desire, among men and women of all classes and callings in life, for whom Israel, Greece and Rome are little more than names, to learn something of the nature of their achievements. This demand cannot be satisfied by elementary manuals. Those who have minds, and wish to use them, need no bare summary of facts, but a guide to the best thought of antiquity on man and his relations to the world and to God. It is an error to suppose that the public is indifferent to, or unable to understand, the problems of religion and philosophy. There are many, not only in universities and schools, but in the larger world outside, and especially among the workers in industrial towns, who are keenly alive to such questions and determined to think them out for themselves. They are turning towards the legacy of the past, in the belief that here they will gain enlightenment for the solution of their own difficulties. It is primarily for such as these that this book has been written.

There are many, again, who have received a classical education, yet have never formed a coherent view of ancient civilization as a whole. They have studied portions of the Old Testament, selected books of certain Greek and Latin authors, and the outlines of Greek history to Alexander and of Roman history to Augustus. But they possess the vaguest notions of the connexions and relationships that gave structure to the life of antiquity, or of the manner in which its several civilizations combined to influence the mediæval and the modern world. How few there are, even among those who have graduated in Arts in our universities, who could tell within a century the dates of Constantine, Augustine, Justinian, Mahomet and Charles the Great; or could give an intelligent account of their historical significance! How few have even a shadowy conception of the results of Alexander's empire on the early life of Christianity, or of the place of Constantinople in world-history! How few, again, have ever learnt that Amos and Hosea played as memorable a part in the religious development

of humanity, as Copernicus and Galileo in that of modern
science ! The study of antiquity is still overmuch confined
within water-tight compartments. Courses in universal history
should surely form part of the ordinary curriculum in our colleges
and schools.[1]

The fact that the present is an age of historical specialism
is a further reason why a book of this kind should prove of
service. Historical knowledge is advanced, mainly, by work in
two directions : by minute research in highly specialised fields,
embodied in learned periodicals; and by publications, based
directly on these researches, which cover a wider ground and
treat of the several periods and aspects of history. These tasks
fall to trained experts, whose writings are addressed to professed students rather than to the general reader. But there
is a real danger, at the present time, not only in history but
in all branches of knowledge, of a divorce between the learning
of the specialist and the mind of the non-academic public.
History itself can teach us that, if the breach remains unbridged,
the issue will prove disastrous. Such, for instance, was the
outcome of the clerical monopoly of theological learning in the
age preceding the Reformation. In this country, at all events,
scientific and philosophical thinking has always striven to keep
in contact with that of the larger world. As knowledge grows
more specialised and the reading public more democratic, this
honourable tradition must not be suffered to fall into abeyance.

Bearing these needs in mind, I have tried to convey an
impression of the living continuity of ancient civilisation. I
felt that there was an advantage in presenting the whole sequence
of development, however imperfectly, in a single view. The
history of antiquity is no mere aggregate of periods and peoples,
but a whole of parts, linked together in internal cohesion. When
the parts are studied in isolation, the unity is apt to elude the
grasp.

> Dann hat er die Theile in seiner Hand,
> Fehlt leider nur das geistige Band.

I have taken the term " history " with something of the broad
meaning that it bore to its first authors, the Greeks, i.e., as
the whole record of man's life in relation to the world surrounding him, and as including interpretation as well as narrative

[1] Such courses should prove invaluable to university students in
Science and in Faculties other than that of Arts.

description.[1] The attempt to cover so wide a field has necessitated both compression and elimination. General views had
often to be stated without the evidence supporting them. A
multitude of details would only confuse the reader's mind. If
illustrations have been drawn from leading personalities rather
than from the average level of achievement, it is because the
aim has been, not to sketch the life of ancient peoples in its
whole compass, but to indicate their legacy to the modern
world. In no part of the book has any previous knowledge of
the facts been presupposed. It is designed to leave the reader
unsatisfied, and to inspire him with the desire to study more
thoroughly, with the aid of the original sources, the civilizations
of Israel, Greece and Rome.

Two omissions require brief explanation.

(i) In treating of the Hellenic legacy, I have touched but
lightly on art and poetry, though these are the aspects of
Hellenism which appeal most directly to the reading public.
But I confess to a deep mistrust of talk *about* art and poetry
addressed to those who are unacquainted with the originals.
The masterpieces of Greek literature are accessible to all in
English translations. Let the beginner begin with these. As
regards Greek art, let him visit the Elgin room and the galleries
of our national museum. I have, therefore, given only so
much introductory explanation as will indicate the historical
and intellectual context amid which the Greek poets and artists
produced their work.

(ii) In the ninth chapter, on Christianity, it may seem that
undue emphasis has been laid on the institutional history of
the Church and on the development of theological dogma. I
have expressly stated that these were but the external embodiments of the inward spiritual life which inspired the Christian
community. But I have said little or nothing about the nature
of that inward principle, or its source in the personality and
teaching of Jesus of Nazareth. The task demands qualifications,
not only of scholarship but of religious insight, which I cannot
claim to possess. While affirming my conviction that the
history of Christianity can only be accounted for by the unique

---

[1] See the striking fragment of Euripides (*fr.* 902, Dindorf); "Happy
is he who has laid hold of the lore of history (*historia*) . . . seeking to
behold the ageless order (*kosmos*) of deathless nature (*physis*), the manner
of its structure, and whence it arose, and how." On the meaning of
physis for the Greeks, see below, pp. 108 ff.

personality of its founder, I have confined attention to its basis in Judaism and its contacts with Rome and Hellenism.

The notes are intended, partly, to give references to such sources as are easily available in translations, e.g. to the Old and New Testaments and the best-known Greek and Latin authors; partly, to qualify statements which require to be taken with reservations; partly, to suggest, more discursively, analogies to modern developments and problems. The appended bibliography makes no claim to be exhaustive; it is merely a provisional selection of good English works, as a guide to further study.

I wish to express my thanks to all who have helped me in the preparation of this book. I am specially indebted to my colleague, Professor P. N. Ure, who read and commented on the whole work in proof; to Mr. Vernon Rendall, who not only rendered me a like service, but placed freely at my disposal his wide knowledge of classical and modern literature; and to my wife, whose help and criticism have been from first to last my chief encouragement.

W. G. de B.

Ashmore,
August 1923.

NOTE

The preparation of this new edition of *The Legacy of the Ancient World* was completed by my husband shortly before his death in August, 1943. He left on record that he wished to thank the Editor of the Aristotelian Society's Proceedings and the Editor of the Hibbert Journal for permission to print matter that has appeared in their publications ; also he wished to say that in revising the earlier chapters he had received much help from Sir John Myres, and, in Chapter III, from Dr. Wheeler Robinson. While for what is printed he is solely responsible, he felt that he owed very much to their kind interest and aid. He desired also to acknowledge his appreciation of the suggestions of Sir Richard Livingstone, President of Corpus ; of Professor Fordyce of Glasgow, and Professor Knox of St. Andrews, and to express his indebtedness to reviewers of the first edition, and to correspondents thereupon, more particularly to the late Professor A. E. Taylor, and the late Rev. P. H. Wicksteed. He felt encouraged in the work of preparation for the reissue of this book by the knowledge that it had been appreciated and recommended by men whose judgment cannot lightly be passed over : especially John Burnet, Samuel Alexander, and Professor Taylor.

It will be noticed that in addition to sundry small changes in the text and the insertion here and there of new matter, there are three appendices at the end of this new edition designed to amplify the argument and conclusions of the book.

E. DE B.

READING,
January 1947.

CONTENTS

CHAPTER V

CHAPTER VI

CHAPTER IX

CHAPTER X

CHAPTER XI

CHAPTER XII

CHAPTER I

INTRODUCTION

§ 1. AMONG the peoples of the ancient world there are three who bequeathed a legacy that is a living power at the present day. These three peoples are the Hebrew, the Greek and the Roman. The creations of their genius, Hebrew prophecy, the philosophy, poetry and sculpture of Greece, the law and political organisation of Rome, constitute a heritage of lasting inspiration to mankind. They have borne a memorable part in shaping the civilization of after-time. *Civilization*, like many words in common speech, is hard to define, and suggests now a wider, and now a more restricted, meaning. A formal definition, such as is appropriate at the outset of a mathematical or scientific treatise, if it is to be of service in a work like this, must come not at the beginning but at the close; when the reader has become familiarised with varied types of civilization in their chequered course of growth, maturity and decay, and has learnt that a cultured achievement never perishes, but even in its apparent disintegration bears what is often its richest fruit in fostering the life of its successor. " That which thou thyself sowest is not quickened, except it die " ; these words are true of peoples and cultured epochs as well as of individuals. So the Roman Empire declined but did not fall; like Hellenism and mediæval Christianity, it persists with ever-renewed vitality in the civilization of the modern world. In these pages we mean by civilization the character of the life exhibited by the higher races at different periods of their history. It embraces at once a world of ideals and a world of accomplished facts. It covers the entire body of social custom and enacted law, of religious, moral and political institutions, of industry and commerce, arts and sciences, literature and philosophy, which represent the cumulative achievement of a people. But it covers more than this. Man is an ideal-forming animal, stirred at every stage of his development by aspirations which transcend the level of his actual attainment; and his civilization, at any given epoch, comprises also the world of his religious, moral and economic values, his intellectual outlook upon life, his personal beliefs as to his function and destiny, his standards of moral goodness and social welfare. It is in the light of such ideals, determining our conception of human progress, that we

B

distinguish civilization from barbarism.[1] Applying this distinction to the history of antiquity, we find that long before our Celtic, Germanic and Scandinavian forefathers had emerged from barbarism, the three races above mentioned had attained to a high plane of civilization. Thus they were enabled, when the hour of contact arrived, to influence profoundly the less-cultured peoples who have grown into the leading nations of to-day. When, for instance, the rude barbarians accepted Christianity, they accepted therewith the legacy of Jewish religious and moral traditions, of Greek philosophy and of the Roman legal and political system. The purpose of this book is to trace the story of that inheritance. We shall begin with a brief indication of the special service rendered by each of these three peoples to the civilization of the modern world.

§ 2. *The Hebrews.*—The debt which modern civilization owes to the Hebrews lies almost wholly in the field of religion. Their poetry, the surest guide to the thought and feeling of a people, is essentially religious poetry. Its value lies not so much in literary form or in speculative argument as in the deep spiritual insight to which it gives expression. The Hebrew race was but little distinguished in war or politics; save for a brief period of empire under King David, its secular achievements would pass almost unnoticed in world-history. It was the spiritual genius of prophets, such as Amos and Hosea in Israel and Isaiah in Judah in the eighth century B.C., which first transformed an exclusive tribal faith into a religion of universal meaning for the world. Jehovah was revealed no longer as a jealous tribal God leading his people to victory over equally real tribal gods of their enemies, but as the divine ruler of the universe, who punished Israel through their enemies for sin, desired mercy and not sacrifice, and claimed the worship, not of personal gift, but of righteous dealing between man and man. This transformation of Hebrew religion contributed, it is true, to break up the political unity of the Hebrew state. But the seed sown by the early prophets ripened, during the bitter experience of national humiliation and captivity, into a purified religion, which in due season gave birth to the faith that conquered the civilized world. The Hebrews were the first of historic peoples to attain to the belief in one God, the creator and ruler of the universe, and the Father of all mankind. Christ, born of a Jewish mother and bred in the strict observance of the Jewish law, came not

[1] See below, Appendix I., pp. 465–474.

to destroy that law but to fulfil. The influence of Greece and Rome on the growth of Christianity, of which we shall speak later in this book, has obscured but has never obliterated the hall-mark of its Hebrew origin. We have only to think of the Puritans of the seventeenth century to realise how deeply modern Christianity has been permeated by the Hebraic spirit.

§ 3. *The Greeks.*—It is more difficult to indicate in a few words the work of the Greeks, or *Hellenes*, as they styled themselves, in history. They influenced modern religion not so much through their religion as through their philosophy. The Olympian deities were fashioned in the likeness of men, with human passions and interests. Though stronger, more beautiful, more jealous and more amorous, though immortal and enjoying a richer life than mortals, in all essentials they felt and acted as Greek men and women felt and acted. We shall see how philosophers strove to spiritualise the popular faiths and how the effort resulted in a breach between the reasoned conclusions of the few and the religious beliefs of the many. Greek religion has afforded in all times a rich field for art and poetry, and its tales are still a delight to the imagination; but it could not satisfy the intellectual or the moral aspirations of a more reflective age. On the other hand, our debt to the Greeks embraces the whole domain of secular culture. In philosophy and science, in art and literature, the Greek genius achieved results which for their range and value are without comparison in the history of mankind. "The period which intervened between the birth of Pericles and the death of Aristotle," i.e. the fifth and fourth centuries B.C. in Greek history, " is undoubtedly, whether considered by itself or with reference to the effects which it produced upon the subsequent destinies of civilized man, the most memorable in the history of the world." So wrote Shelley; and all thinkers and poets are witnesses to the truth of his words. Freedom and individuality are present everywhere in the life of the ancient Greeks. What strikes us most is their wonderful energy. Their whole history is a record of bold experiment in thought and practice. They were at once eager and courageous in intellectual inquiry and full of delight in life and action. Their intellectual genius was the fountain-head of philosophy and science; their practical genius found expression alike in political activity, in war and commerce, in literary and artistic creation. Almost every type of poetry and speculation was initiated by the Greeks and carried far on the path towards perfection. Their ideal was

that of a gifted and harmonious personality, controlled by inward
principle and reason; of energy, not wild and ungoverned,
but ruled by self-knowledge and clear judgement. No race has
been so free from other-worldliness or has striven to embody
aims and values so entirely in the actual conditions of human
experience. Resisting every craving after the impossible, they
set themselves resolutely to understand the nature of man and
the world in which he lives, and, with a clear grasp of the truth
of things, to use that world as a field for the realisation of their
ideals of life. The characteristic gifts of the race bore with
them their curse. The individuality and freedom that made
the Greeks supreme in art and science proved the ruin of their
political independence. It is true, as we shall see later on, that
Greek culture found its stimulus and its scope in the atmosphere
of free discussion which prevailed in the city-state, and that the
Greek genius was manifested alike in their political theory and
in their political practice. But there is another side to the picture.
The political life of the Greek cities presents a dark scene of restless ambition, personal jealousy and party faction, aversion from
federal solidarity, continual revolution and civil strife. It was
this lack of national unity that left Greece so easy a prey to the
armies, first of the Macedonian kings, and afterwards of the
Roman republic. But the Greek spirit had its revenge; as under
Alexander it leavened the culture of the East, so, later, it permeated the Roman conquerors and through Rome moulded the
thought and culture of the modern world.

§ 4. *The Romans.*—Rome was the imperial state of antiquity,
and the Roman people were the great empire-builders of world-
history. Their religion was strictly subordinate to the political
authority. An instance may serve to bring this home. Cæsar,
a frank sceptic, whose private life was certainly not above
suspicion, staked all at a critical moment of his career on his
election as supreme pontiff : it was merely a step on the ladder
of political ambition. The influence of Rome on Christianity is
most evident in the field of ecclesiastical organisation. By nature
the Roman had little appreciation either of art or science; in
early days he regarded a poet as a vagabond and philosophy
as a danger to morality. Far otherwise was it with the Greeks
in Homer; for them the blind poet had been bereft by the gods
of sight, but in its stead had received the gift of godlike song.
The impulse to poetry and art came to Rome from Greece;
though, when once they had learnt their lesson, the Romans

expressed their national spirit with no servile imitation in imperishable verse. Their poets knew and recognised wherein lay the true genius of the race. " Others may mould in softer lines the breathing bronze—ay, and cause living features to start from the marble; they may plead their lawsuits better, and trace the motions of the heavens and the rising of the stars; be it thine, O son of Rome, to rule the nations : these shall be thy arts, to impose the habit of peace, to spare the vanquished, and to crush the haughty by the sword." [1] Like all empire-builders whose work has stood the stress of time, the Romans had no wild thirst for conquest. They were a race not so much of warriors as of lawgivers and administrators. " To lay down the law of peace," the *pax Romana,* to repress anarchy and disorder around their ever-expanding dominion was their peculiar mission. Children beside the Greeks in culture, with a marked vein of inhumanity and coarseness in their nature, the Romans were strong precisely where the Greeks were weak, in racial solidarity, in political union, in subjection of individuality to the service of the state. To " do at Rome as Rome does " was the virtue of the Roman citizen. Greek history is the history of cities and individuals : Roman history is the history of a people. Governed by no deliberate policy of conquest, but by the logic of hard fact, the fortune of the Roman people led them to incorporate in their empire the whole civilized world, as it stood at the time of Christ's birth. To gather up in one vast organisation the peoples and civilizations of antiquity, to police the Mediterranean and ordain peace over a disordered world, to hand on to the barbarians of the north and west of Europe the culture of the past, tempered by their own genius for law and government; these were the functions and the destiny of Rome. Thus " all roads lead to Rome." As the great military highways of the Romans radiated from Rome over the empire, so the currents of ancient and modern history alike find their meeting-point in Rome. The nations of to-day owe a great part of their law, their language and their institutions to the genius of Imperial Rome.

§ 5. These three peoples had all of them their home by the shores of the Mediterranean ; the Mediterranean and its coastlands formed their world. Trained as we are from childhood to think in terms of two hemispheres with their continents and oceans, it is hard to appreciate a time when the world meant merely a

[1] Virgil, *Æneid,* vi. 847–53.

narrow ring of countries converging upon an inland sea. Behind
these coastlands in all directions lay a mysterious and illimitable
waste, in the west the impenetrable Atlantic, to north and south
the abodes of wild barbarians, who brought down their wares
for barter to the dwellers on the Mediterranean shore. Only
towards the east was the veil lifted, as far as the line where the
plateau of Irân (Persia) rose high above the Mesopotamian and
Babylonian plains. Within these limits there was civilization.
Hence, to the peoples of antiquity, the distinction of three
continents, Europe, Africa and Asia, seemed artificial and
irrelevant.[1] Long before the Hebrews, Greeks and Romans
began to play their part in history, the Mediterranean had been
the meeting-place of the world's trade. Through all ages commerce and civilization have developed hand in hand; commercial highways, the links of international intercourse, aid the
distribution not merely of material products, but of ideas and
habits of life. Thus from earliest recorded time the history of
civilization has been the history of the Mediterranean area,
and such it remained, until the discoveries of great navigators
at the close of the fifteenth century bore fruit in the Oceanic
civilization amidst which we live to-day.[2] The voyages of Diaz,
da Gama and Columbus did more than disclose new markets
and fields for empire in the Indies and the New World. They
changed the centre of gravity of human culture. The Oceanic
civilization that has arisen upon their foundations is even yet
scarcely ripe for history. If what Lancashire thinks to-day,
England will think to-morrow; if our island is no longer an
outwork on the north-western frontier of civilization, but
holds a central position in the economic and intellectual intercourse of the nations; if the life of the world pulses in lands
unknown to the ancients, in America, in the British Dominions
beyond the seas; this is due to changes initiated only four or
five centuries ago, the issues of which, enlarging from hour to
hour before our eyes, form material for the journalist rather

[1] Herodotus, iv. 45. " I am unable to understand why it is that to
the earth, which is one, three different names have been given, all derived
from women . . .; nor can I find out who they were who fixed the
boundaries, or from whom they gave the names."

[2] " The grand object of travelling," said Dr. Johnson, " is to see the
shores of the Mediterranean. On those shores were the four great empires
of the world, the Assyrian, the Persian, the Grecian and the Roman. All
our religion, almost all our law, almost all our arts, almost all that sets us
above savages, has come to us from the shores of the Mediterranean "
(Boswell, vi. 154).

than for the historian. The days when Rome's empire over the Mediterranean area brought the whole civilized world under her sway seem indeed remote. Yet such is the solidarity of history through the successive epochs of its development, that even this momentous revolution received its stimulus from the inheritance of Græco-Roman culture. There is no impassable breach of continuity between the Oceanic civilization of the present and that moulded more than twenty centuries ago by the peoples of the Mediterranean world.

§ 6. The Hebrews, Greeks and Romans, though sharing in a common Mediterranean habitation, were sundered by a difference of origin, which goes far to account for the distinctive character of their civilizations. The Hebrews were a branch of the Semitic stock, whose home was Arabia, one of the great nurseries of the human race. In the next chapter we shall meet with other nations, Babylonians and Assyrians, and the dwellers in Phœnicia and Syria, who were members of the same Semitic family. The Greeks and the Romans, on the contrary, belonged, at all events in the main, to the Indo-European family, whose home was probably in the steppe-lands north of the Caucasus. Already in remote antiquity this family had parted into two great branches. One of these passed westwards into Europe; from it sprang not only the Greeks and Italians, but also our Celtic, Germanic and Scandinavian ancestors. The other branch struck south-east, part settled on the tableland of Irân, and gave birth to the Medes and Persians of ancient history; while part passed the mountains into the valleys of the Indus and the Ganges, and colonised northern India. All these migrations took place in remote ages; the historic peoples of antiquity were rarely, if ever, free from racial intermixture.

§ 7. The divergence in the life and character of the three peoples was not such as to preclude an ultimate fusion. The truth is rather the reverse; each created and bequeathed to after-ages one of the essentials in the idea of a complete civilization. The Greeks were the first to realise, in their practice as in their theory, the worth of individual liberty, as the soil wherein alone man's imagination and intellect can flourish and bear fruit. In the domains of art and philosophy the human spirit is its own law. But man is called upon also to act, and the effective realisation of his practical purposes demands their accommodation to the hard facts of human nature and of the world of circumstance. The adjustment can be accomplished only by aid of external authority and government. This disciplinary function in the history of civilization was fulfilled by Rome. But, alike in the field of thought and in that of action, the spirit of man is doomed to waste in anarchy or bondage, unless inspired by the knowledge of its ideal goal. "Where there is no vision, the people perish." [1] The Hebrews had seen the vision; and they transmitted it, through a faith that had its roots in the spiritual life of Israel, to the Aryan peoples of the West. Freedom, law, and the kingdom of God; these form the threefold legacy of antiquity to the modern world.

§ 8. The historian, looking back upon the past from a distance of twenty centuries, is bound to throw into relief the outstanding and distinctive features of these civilizations. But we must not think of them as cast in rigid moulds or exaggerate the clearness of their outlines. The sequel will show how the life of the Hebrew, Greek and Roman peoples, like that of the individuals composing them, was ever on the move, shaping itself as it grew, and changing from moment to moment in relation to its physical and social context. It is a far cry from the Israel that gathered round Elijah on mount Carmel to the Israel which nine centuries later clamoured before a Roman governor for the release of Barabbas. The Pharisee of Jerusalem at the time of Christ moved in a different world from the Hellenised Jew of Alexandria. The gulf between the Greek merchant-princes of the sixth century and St. Paul's auditors at Corinth or Athens was as wide as that which parted the former from the wild sea-rovers, who, forsaking the tombs of their forefathers and their ancestral gods, sought new homes in the Ægean at the close of the second millennium B.C. Hellenic culture meant one thing at Syracuse, another at Miletus; the Rome which tamed the Spaniard in the days of Cato would have scarcely been recognised as Rome by the Slav and the Bulgar who knew only the Christian and Byzantine empire of the early Middle Ages. We can best appreciate this constant variability of civilization if we think of the world as it is to-day. All the resources of modern ingenuity for facilitating swift communication and the diffusion of ideas, such as the printing press, steam, electricity, the aeroplane and radio, have not availed to break down the barriers which sever even contemporaries of a common stock. The Dorset peasant and the Northumbrian miner live in alien worlds. The Oxford scholar's outlook upon life has little in common with that of his fellow-countryman in

[1] Prov. xxix. 18 (R.V. " cast off restraint ").

Manitoba or New Zealand. Wider still is the chasm that parts any one of these twentieth-century Englishmen from his ancestor in the thirteenth. If we think of the difference between the England that we know and the England of the Plantagenets, we can form some measure of the difficulty of gathering into a single view the ever-changing phases of the civilization of antiquity. Further, we shall see as we go forward how the legacy was modified in the course of transmission to the modern world. The fruits of the Hebrew, Greek and Roman genius have been fused with one another and with elements derived from Teutonic and Scandinavian sources. Their significance has been altered by their entry into new forms of combination. The present, in assimilating the past, clothes it with a meaning, richer it may be or poorer than it once bore, but always new. The clearest illustration of this is furnished by language. A man need not be an expert in philology to recognise the origin of many of our English words. Some, e.g. *law, order, state, colony, responsibility, person,* are obviously derived from the Latin; others, e.g. *dogma, atom, history, biology, logic,* from the Greek; others again, e.g. *friend, body, king, God,* betray a Norse or Germanic ancestry. The forms of these words have been modified in the process of reception; *lex* has become *law, atomon,* atom; in some cases the change is more radical, and it requires some experience to detect the Latin *metipsimum* beneath its modern French derivative *même.* What is true of the verbal forms is true also of their meanings. Our examples show how words signifying legal and political ideas have often been inherited from the Romans, who were the world's masters in those fields, while scientific terminology tends to preserve the speech of the creators of science, the ancient Greeks. Yet, despite this unimpeachable lineage, such terms as *responsibility* and *law* are fraught to us with a meaning drawn not merely or mainly from the experience of Roman jurists, but from that of the generations which have inherited and enriched their legacy during some two thousand years. The historian and the physicist of the twentieth century conceive of *history* and of the *atom* very differently from Herodotus and Democritus. What we have said of language applies to every aspect of civilization; the past, in passing into the present, changes its character as past, and dies phœnix-like to be reborn in a new form.

§ 9. This process of continuity amid ceaseless change is hard to unravel. The task may be approached in two different ways. We may take present-day civilization as our starting-point and work backwards, step by step, to its sources in the past. Or we may begin at the beginning, with the races of antiquity, and trace the effects on subsequent generations till we reach the confines of modern history. The latter is the course we propose to follow. Its treatment will, however, be subject to two restrictions. In the first place, we must select, from the wealth of available material, those features in the life of the Hebrews, Greeks and Romans which impressed themselves most markedly on after-times. There is always the danger that we may fail to see the wood for the trees. Thus we shall concentrate attention on the religion of Israel, on the science and philosophy of Greece, and on the mission of Rome in mediating the transition from ancient to mediæval civilization; touching but lightly on other aspects of their history, however great their intrinsic interest. The second restriction has reference to the other races which peopled the ancient world. Among these we may draw a three-fold distinction. There are (i) races, such as the primitive inhabitants of a large part of Africa, who never succeeded in emerging from a state of barbarism. Full of interest for the anthropologist and the student of primeval religious and social custom, they left no distinctive trace on the higher civilizations of antiquity, and therefore call for no mention in this book. The same is true of (ii) the civilized peoples of the Farther East, in India, China and Japan. These were almost wholly precluded by geographical barriers from active intercourse with the culture of the Mediterranean area.[1] Now, when contact has been established through the opening of Oceanic highways and facilitated by the aeroplane and wireless, the art of China and Japan and the religious thought of the higher Indian peoples evoke an increasing interest among Europeans. The historian of five centuries hence may have much to say on the issues of this intercourse alike in East and West; but as yet they lie hidden from our view. The grant of autonomy, in conjunction with the growth of commerce and industrialisation, are bound to prove disintegrating influences

[1] The obvious exception to this very general statement is furnished by Alexander the Great's conquest of the Punjâb. The contact thus established between the West and India was of brief duration, and memorable rather for Greek influence upon India than for Indian influence upon Greece. Trade by overland caravan routes from the Far East persisted throughout antiquity, but the effects on Western civilization were secondary and indirect. Nor have the Tartar invasions of the West in post-Christian times, from the Huns of the fifth century onwards, contributed anything positive to Western culture.

on the traditional outlook upon life among the peoples of India, and this not merely in the domains of economics and politics. Whether a closer familiarity with their religious and meta-physical inheritance will affect our Western civilization to a like extent is more disputable. The cleavage between the mind of the West and that of the East cuts very deep; the West takes for granted much that is alien and even antagonistic to Indian thought, which finds itself faced by almost insuperable obstacles to a reciprocal understanding. For one thing, Indian thinkers have never taken time seriously. The temporal process that forms the material of history has seemed to them to be little more than an illusion (*Máya*), veiling the changeless reality of the Absolute. That is why India, which has given birth to great philosophers and religious mystics, has produced no historians.[1] So, again, Indian political leaders seem to find difficulty in realising what to the Western mind is a matter of course, that self-govern-ment can only prove of lasting benefit if achieved as the fruit of a gradual process of political education. If, as is admitted on all sides, it is good, and therefore desirable, what ground is there in reason for delaying its fulfilment? Why not complete the good work, here and now, by a stroke of the pen? The mind of the West, on the contrary, for all its faith in an eternal other-worldly reality, has rarely, if ever, denied a measure of genuine actuality to the temporal process.[2] There is a further cleavage to be noted. A conviction of the indefeasible worth of human personality is deeply rooted in the Western mind, which has hardly been touched by the desire for absorption in the Absolute, which has won possession of the hearts of Indian sages. Here lies the radical difference between Christian and Hindu mysticism.[3] These reflections lead to the suggestion that if the spiritual barriers parting Western from Indian cultures are ever to be

[1] In our own day, she produced in Ramanujan a mathematician of genius; but mathematics, like metaphysics, is unconcerned with the course of temporal events. Even modern historians of Indian philosophy, like Radakrishnan and Dasgupta, while successful in exposition of the several systems, fail to display their historical sequence as arising one from the other in a natural order of development.

[2] Spinoza, for instance, who held time to be a product of low-grade thinking (*auxilium imaginationis*) never questioned the actuality of temporal occurrences. He simply denied that, as temporal, they were fully real. Christian thought has always attached a high significance to the spatio-temporal world as the scene of man's probation. His vocation is " so to pass through things temporal as not to lose finally the things eternal." This implies that the " things temporal " are anything but illusory.

[3] Christian mystics aspire after direct communion, not after fusion of being, with God.

broken down, it will be through the spread in India of historical studies and of Christianity. However this may be, the future of the Indian, as of other Oriental peoples, lies beyond the scope of this volume. It is otherwise with a third group (iii), the civilizations that arose in very early times on the banks of two great rivers, the Nile and the Euphrates, and in Crete. These arrest our attention, not only by the intrinsic value of their culture, but as furnishing the historical antecedents to the story of Israel, Greece and Rome. They form part of the life of the Mediterranean world. This is obvious in the case of Crete; but the civilization of Egypt also gravitated northwards to the shores of the Delta, while that of the Babylonian plain expanded ever westwards towards the Ægean and the Levant. It is true that their influence on later ages was indirect, and mediated by the three peoples who form the chief subject of our study. But they left their mark on the life-work of Israel, Greece and Rome; and they formed the historical context amid which these nations arose and played their part. We shall therefore attempt a brief survey of these earlier civilizations in the ensuing chapter. This will help us to realise the essential solidarity of the ancient world, and to think of its several peoples, not as isolated atoms which can be studied piecemeal, but as members of a community of nations, with mutual relationships of hostility or of co-operation which conditioned their distinctive contributions to the march of human history.

CHAPTER II

THE EARLY CIVILIZATIONS OF THE EAST

I. Introductory (§ 1).

§ 1. The early civilizations which claim our notice as a preparation for the study of Israel, Greece and Rome, are those (i) of Egypt, (ii) of the nations who successively dominated the Euphrates–Tigris valley—the Babylonians and Assyrians, (iii) of the peoples who inhabited the lands between the last-mentioned and the Mediterranean sea-board, Syria, Canaan and eastern Asia Minor, (iv) of Crete, which permeated the Ægean and a large portion of the Mediterranean area. We shall carry our brief survey of these civilizations forward to the time when they were, for the most part, absorbed in the mighty world-empire of Persia (sixth century B.C.). Finally (v) we shall indicate the character of the Persian empire and its civilization, up to the Græco-Macedonian conquest by Alexander the Great (334–323). The subsequent history of Egypt and the Middle East, under Græco-Macedonian and Roman sovereignty, belongs naturally to the later chapters, dealing with Greece and Rome.

II. Egypt [1] (§§ 2–5).

§ 2. "Egypt," wrote the Greek historian Herodotus, who visited the land in the fifth century B.C., "is the gift of the Nile." [2] Soil, products, vegetation, animals and human life are alike determined by the great river, which, long before man's advent, widened a limestone fracture into a gorge, filled the gorge with debris from the southern highlands, and encroaching upon the Mediterranean formed the Delta. The country is a long narrow oasis stretching for 750 miles from the First Cataract, the ancient southern boundary, to the Delta; the valley, ten to thirty miles in breadth, is imprisoned by desert-barriers to

[1] In the matter of early Egyptian chronology, as in much else in this section, I have followed Breasted's conclusions, as given in his *History of Egypt* (2nd edition, 1919). While the majority of Egyptologists are in substantial agreement with Breasted's chronology of the earlier dynasties, it must be borne in mind that the dates are still a subject of controversy prior to the eighteenth dynasty (1580 B.C.). The reader should consult the synchronistic tables in the earlier volumes of the *Cambridge Ancient History* on all questions of chronology that arise in connexion with this chapter.

[2] Her., ii. 5.

east and west. Its prosperity depends, now as seventy centuries
ago, on one great natural phenomenon, the annual inundation
of the Nile, caused by the spring rains and the melting of the
snows in the far highlands of the south. The uniformity of
these simple physical conditions is paralleled by a like uniformity
in the life and habits of the people. The fellaheen under
Mehemet Ali in the nineteenth century of our era plied the
same monotonous tasks of tilling the soil and forced labour as
the nameless serfs who built the pyramids in the third millennium B.C. The economic wealth of Egypt has always been
agricultural. The Egyptians called their country " the Black
land," contrasting the " Red " desert on either side, and the
black alluvial soil of the Nile valley, which, under an efficient
system of irrigation, proved of extraordinary fertility. The
river was the highway down which the corn-trade passed to
the Delta ports, and the link of communication between Egypt
and the outside world. The irregularity of the Nile's overflow
early evoked human effort to ward off the periodic danger of
famine. Nowhere has man's cunning fought so persistently
with nature. The land was permeated by canals, dykes and
reservoirs, in the construction of which the engineers of ancient
Egypt displayed a mastery of mechanical art. The vast reservoir
of lake Moeris, the work of Theban Pharaohs of the twelfth
dynasty (early second millennium), bears witness to the same
energy of purpose as the Assouan dam completed by British
engineers under the direction of Lord Cromer.

§ 3. Our knowledge of the early history of Egypt originated
during the invasion by Napoleon (1798). In 1799 a French
officer discovered near Rosetta a stone, now in the British Museum,
bearing an inscription in three scripts, hieroglyphic, demotic or
popular, and Greek. The proper names, which were the same in
the Greek as in the hieroglyphics, gave after long study the key
to the hieroglyphic writing on Egyptian monuments. The last
century has witnessed the gradual unveiling of the shroud that
hid the remote past. Imagination is dazzled as scholars have
revealed cycle upon cycle of past history, stretching back at least
into the fourth millennium B.C.; a history not merely of the
wars and conquests of kings, but of beliefs and customs, art and
culture, comprising a series of rich civilizations hitherto unsuspected by mankind.

§ 4. The story of Egypt from its first union under a single
government in the fourth millennium to the Persian conquest in

525 B.C. presents a succession of cycles of civilization, each with its periods of rise and fall, and parted one from the other by intervals of stagnation and decadence. Recent archæological research has carried the record yet farther back, to a time when tribes of African origin, but modified by Semitic immigrations, dwelt in local centres under separate chieftains. These pre-dynastic Egyptians had already mastered the arts of workmanship in clay and stone, and framed the calendar year of 365 days, adopted more than three thousand years later by Julius Cæsar, and in current use at the present day.[1] Early in the fourth millennium we find two kingdoms, one in the Delta, the other in Upper Egypt, which were consolidated into a single state by Menes, the first king of the first dynasty (c. 3400). From this point onwards Egyptian history may be gathered round the rise and fall of three great cycles of development : the Old Kingdom, the Middle Kingdom and the New Empire.[2]

(I) *The Old Kingdom* (Dynasties I–VI).[3]—This epoch, lasting a thousand years, reached its climax under the kings of the fourth dynasty at Memphis (from 2900 B.C.), who extended their sovereignty westwards over Libya and southwards over Nubia, worked the mines of Sinai, and traded with their fleets over the Red Sea and the Levant. They were great administrators and great builders, who organised an elaborate fiscal system and ruled Egypt with an army of officials, brought the irrigation of the country to a high state of perfection, and erected as their tombs the mighty pyramids of Gizeh. The mastery of mechanical contrivance and the vast resources of labour necessary for these constructions may be gathered from the fact that the pyramid of Khufu was built of more than two million

[1] The calendar was introduced in 4241 B.C., the earliest fixed date in history. Breasted, *Ancient Records, Egypt*, i. 25 ff., argued that the calendar began with the commencement of the inundation of the Nile, which from time to time coincided approximately with the feast of the rising of Sirius (*Sothis*) at sunrise on the eastern horizon on July 19. But the Sothic year (i.e. the interval between the two successive risings of Sirius) was a quarter of a day longer than the calendar year of 365 days. The Sothic and calendar years began on the same day in 4241, 2780, 1320 B.C., and 140–41 to 143–44 A.D. It has, however, been questioned whether the cycle was observed as early as 4241 B.C. More likely there was a subsequent back-reckoning.

[2] Egypt has never known any form of government save despotism. The foundations of political liberty are being laid, for the first time, in our own day.

[3] Manetho, an Egyptian priest who wrote under the first Ptolemies (third century B.C.), grouped the kings of Egypt in 31 dynasties. His grouping is frequently inaccurate, but is still in general use for purposes of historical reference.

blocks of masonry, each of an average weight of 2½ tons. The art of the same period, especially in portrait-sculpture and reliefs on tombs and temples, was of a beauty unequalled in any subsequent epoch of Egyptian culture.

(II) *The Middle Kingdom* (Dynasties XI–XII).—The Old Kingdom fell, in the middle of the third millennium, at the hands of the landed nobility, which it had fostered at its peril. There followed some three centuries of disintegration, power resting, as in the pre-dynastic age, with the local chieftains, until a second centralised monarchy, known as the Middle Kingdom, arose at Thebes in Upper Egypt, under the powerful Pharaohs [1] of the eleventh and twelfth dynasties (2150–1780). Commerce was restored on an extended scale with Punt (Somaliland) to the south by the Red Sea, with the Semites of Syria and Canaan, and with the maritime peoples of the eastern Mediterranean. Minoan pottery of the epoch is found in Egypt, and Minoan art shows signs of Egyptian influence.[2] Under the Middle Kingdom, the industrial arts reached their highest development; literature flourished; the sculptures, if more conventional, rival those of the fourth and fifth dynasties.

(III) *The New Empire* (Dynasties XVIII–XIX).—The close of the twelfth dynasty was followed by an obscure period, in which a divided Egypt lay at the mercy of foreign invaders. Semitic nomads (the *Hyksos* or so-called shepherd-kings), among them possibly an Israelite tribe,[3] ruled in the land. Unity was again restored by Theban princes, and the most brilliant epoch, if not of Egyptian culture at least of Egyptian political power, opens with the eighteenth dynasty (1580 B.C.). The Egyptians were by nature an unwarlike people; but internal disorder had led to the formation of an organised professional army, and the Pharaohs of the New Empire were the military rulers of a military state. They conquered Syria and Phœnicia, fought the Mitanni (a tribe with Aryan chiefs) and the Hittites on the upper Euphrates, and reigned supreme from that river to the Libyan desert and the confines of Ethiopia. They received tribute from beyond the Mediterranean; Egypt was open to the merchants of the Ægean (Keftiu), her products were in use at

---

[1] *Pharaoh (Per-O)*, meaning literally "the great house," was a title originally applied to the seat of government, and afterwards to the person of the monarch.

[2] See below, § 16.

[3] Scarabs of a king of this period bear the name of *Jacob-her* or *Jacob-et* (Breasted, p. 220).

Cnossus and her own decorative art influenced that of the Mycenæan craftsmen.[1] The Empire was administered by a huge body of state-officials and the state-religion by an organised priestly class. This was the greatest age of Egyptian architecture; the temple of the god Ammon at Karnak was one of the most splendid religious monuments of antiquity. A commemorative obelisk, erected by the most brilliant conqueror of the eighteenth dynasty, Thothmes (Thutmose) III, stands to-day on the Thames Embankment. After two centuries of imperial grandeur the inevitable signs of dissolution began to appear; the strange effort of the religious reformer, Ikhnaton (Amenhotep IV, 1375–1358), to establish a spiritual monotheism outraged priestly and popular feeling;[2] the nineteenth dynasty failed to maintain the prestige of Egypt abroad, and well before the close of the second millennium Syria and Canaan had passed from Egyptian hands and the sea-peoples of the Ægean were harrying the Delta.[3] It was during this period of incipient decline that the children of Israel sojourned in the land of Goshen; the exodus to the Sinaitic desert took place at latest under one of the Pharaohs of the nineteenth dynasty (c. 1320–1200).

In the centuries of disintegration that followed the fall of the New Empire, we find Libyan mercenary-chiefs ruling in the Delta and Ethiopian princes in upper Egypt.[4] Late in the seventh century (670) the Assyrians, who had for some time menaced Egyptian independence, conquered the Delta under Esarhaddon and made Egypt a vassal-state.[5] The age of foreign domination had begun. As the power of Assyria waned before that of Babylon, there came one more chance of

[1] For the Hittites, see below, § 12; for Cnossus and Mycenæ, §§ 15–16.

[2] The Tell-el-Amarna letters, the archives of Ikhnaton's foreign correspondence, discovered in 1885, throw much light on the diplomacy of the New Empire. Tell-el-Amarna is the site of the capital, Akhetaton, which Ikhnaton founded as the centre of the monotheistic worship of Aton. For this monotheistic religion, see Ikhnaton's hymn to Aton, translated in Breasted, pp. 371 ff.

[3] The Keftiu (Minoans) vanish from Egyptian monuments about 1350; a century and a half later the Akaiuasha (Achæans) make their appearance. See below, § 15.

[4] Sheshonk I (the *Shishak* of the Old Testament) was one of the former; he had been Solomon's ally, gave shelter to Jeroboam the founder of the northern (Ephraimite) kingdom, and attacked Rehoboam, the ruler of the southern kingdom (Judah), c. 926 (1 Kings ix. 15–17; xi. 40; xiv. 25).

[5] The Assyrian armies had reached the frontier of Egypt twice in the eighth century; Sennacherib's abortive invasion occurred in 701. The weakness of Egypt is clearly realised by Isaiah, who denounced the policy of alliance between Judah and Egypt against Assyria (Is. xxx. 1–7; xxxi. 1–3).

independence; under the kings of the twenty-sixth dynasty (at Sais in the Delta, 663–525) we witness a brief and somewhat artificial revival of culture, and an abortive reassertion of imperial aspirations. Egypt was allied with Lydia and the Asiatic Greeks; Greek mercenaries were enlisted in the royal service; a settlement was allotted to Greek traders at Naucratis (= " Sea-power ") in the Delta. Necho (609–593) conquered Canaan, and fought Nebuchadrezzar of Babylon on the Euphrates. His offering of the cloak that he wore when he defeated Josiah at Megiddo to the temple of the Milesian Apollo at Branchidæ is a significant illustration of historical contact between Egypt, Judah, Babylon and Greece.[1] But the restoration of inde-pendence was short-lived; when Babylon fell before the Persians, the doom of Egypt was already imminent. In 525 Cambyses conquered Egypt, and the land remained subject to the Persian empire, save for fitful and transitory revolts, till the advent of Alexander of Macedon (332–330).

§ 5. It remains to ask, how far the civilization of the ancient Egyptians affected that which developed during the last millen-nium B.C. in the Mediterranean world. Looking first (a) to religion, which in Egypt, as among all early races, was the focus of culture, we find a multitude of local faiths and worships unified by the Pharaohs of the early dynasties in a state-religion with certain central deities, whose tales and ritual were moulded, as time went on, into systematic and stereotyped form by priestly scribes. They contain little of speculative or spiritual value, with the solitary exception of Ikhnaton's attempt, referred to above, to replace the established cults by the monotheistic worship of the sun-god Aton. His revolution seems to have been provoked by a genuine speculative idealism; but it proved abortive and without influence even in his own land. The religious writings, such as *The Book of the Dead*, concerning the fortunes of the soul in a future life, a collection originating under the Middle Kingdom and shaped into definite form at the time of the eighteenth dynasty, were dominated by magic and reveal a thoroughly materialist conception of the soul. The belief in a moral judgement after death, associated with

---

[1] Necho was defeated at Carchemish in 604 : the Babylonian conquest of Judah followed quickly on this victory. See 2 Kings xxiii. 29 and Herodotus, ii. 159. Megiddo was in the plain of Jezreel or Esdraelon, the scene of the battle between the Israelites and Sisera (Judges iv, v) and the Armageddon (R.V. Harmagedon = mountains of Megiddo) of Rev. xvi. 16. The text of the latter passage is, however, open to doubt.

the cult of Osiris, had a certain ethical value. In the early " pyramid texts " the conception of a moral order in the world may be seen arising out of popular judgements on conduct " according to rule " in family and village. But there is no evidence that Egyptian religion seriously influenced the outside world. The worship of Jehovah had its home in the desert of Sinai, not in Egypt. At a later epoch, when East and West met under Macedonian princes at Alexandria, native Egyptian worships, such as those of Isis and Sarapis, together with the beliefs in immortality and faith-healing associated with those deities, and the practice of moral allegorism that marked Egyptian priestly teaching, spread widely over the Græco-Roman world. But before this date the religions of Israel, Greece and Rome had already developed to their maturity.

(b) The so-called " wisdom " of the Egyptians, again, was a thing of little scientific value. Their intellectual interests were utilitarian, and they displayed slight aptitude for pure science or philosophy. They devised ingenious rules for measuring fields and buildings, but geometry meant for them land-surveying and nothing more. Neither here nor in their astrology did they evidence any grasp of scientific method. When awkward remainders appeared in their calculations, they simply left them out. Plato was entirely justified when he criticised Egyptian mathematics as restricted to purely practical ends.[1] Their medicine, again, was a medley of rule-of-thumb recipes and magical incantations. Early medical writings show close observation of the human body, common-sense treatment of injuries and speculations on the physiological functions that may have reached the Greeks and served as a stimulus to the first Hellenic men of science. But, until illuminated by the search for causes and reasons, they remained little more than collections of pre-scientific data.[2] When the Greeks visited the land under the twenty-sixth dynasty, their imagination was naturally impressed by

---

[1] *Laws*, 747. See the account of the Rhind papyrus in Burnet's *Early Greek Philosophy*, 3rd edition, pp. 18 ff., and his remarks on the alleged scientific attainments of the Egyptians. On Egyptian medicine, contrasted with that of the Greeks, see Brett : *History of Psychology*, pp. 219 ff.

[2] See the Edwin Smith *Surgical Papyrus* (ed. Breasted). Treatment is prescribed according to rule (" Thou shalt say, etc. "). A study of this interesting document leaves the reader with the impression that the modern medical practitioner, though fortified by a vastly extended groundwork of facts, has preserved not a little of the mentality of his primitive forerunners.

its antiquity. " You Greeks are always children : there is not
an old man among you "; so the Egyptian priest is said to have
told Solon ; reverence for the age-long monuments, strengthened
by the dignified reserve of the priestly interpreters, led the
northern travellers to idealise, in terms of their own intellectual
achievement, the learning of a people with so remote a past.[1]
On the other hand, in the mechanical arts, the influence of Egypt
was considerable in after-times.[2] Westminster Public Libraries

(c) Egyptian culture was artistic rather than literary, though
popular tales and a religious drama arose under the Middle
Kingdom, and the papyrus, a gift of the Nile marshes, made
correspondence and written record portable and easy. But it was
the art of Egypt which impressed its influence on the outside
world, as is evident from the traces discernible in the pottery and
reliefs of Minoan and Mycenæan workmanship. This was prior
to the dawn of Hellenic culture; when that day came, the art of
Egypt had degenerated. A single exception lay in architecture.
The Egyptians built immense temples and tombs, and used columns
and colonnades to admit light to interiors, while limiting themselves to the simplest constructions and relying for decoration
on low relief and colour. Their later sculpture influenced that
of the Greeks in its early stages, but its rigid conventions were
soon outgrown. The Macedonian rulers of Egypt fostered a
revival of native art, but Greek copies were tasteless and inaccurate. To-day, thanks to the archæologists, it is otherwise.
The great works of the sculptors of the early dynasties have been
revealed in their beauty, to serve as a fresh source of inspiration
to the artists of the modern world.

III. BABYLONIA AND ASSYRIA [3] (§§ 6–10).

§ 6. The second great fluvial civilization of antiquity was
that of Babylon. The alluvial plain of Chaldæa, between the
lower waters of the Euphrates and the Tigris, was, like Egypt,
capable under proper irrigation of great fertility, and supported
in ancient times a vast population. To-day, after centuries of

[1] Plato, Timœus, 22.
[2] They could move heavy objects and pile them together, but not
more. The fact that they never attempted a barrage of the Nile shows
how limited was their proficiency as engineers.
[3] Here again the early chronology is unsettled. Where there is
division of opinion among scholars, lower dates rather than higher have
been preferred, e.g. for Sargon of Akkad and the first Babylonian dynasty.
See the tables in the Cambridge Ancient History.

misrule have blighted its prosperity, it requires an effort of imagination to realise that Babylonia was once, like Egypt, one of the chief granaries of the world, where the crops bore fruit two and even three hundred-fold, and the land, even after the second reaping, furnished abundant pasture.[1] The capital city that arose on the banks of the Euphrates and became from the dawn of the second millennium a great seat of empire, was from its huge size a marvel to antiquity; the inner wall was nearly forty miles in circuit. Babylon, says Aristotle, is more like a nation than a city.[2] To its agricultural resources was added the wealth derived from textile industries and a great trade.[3] From the second millennium Babylon was the market of the East, a cosmopolitan centre, which drew to its bazaars and wharves the produce of India and Irân, and formed the terminus of the traffic along the desert-routes to the Euphrates from the Mediterranean countries in the west. The natural course of Babylonian expansion lay up-stream, for the Chaldæan plain was enclosed to the south and west by the desert, and to the east by the plateau of Irân; already in the third millennium we find that Sargon of Akkad, the founder of the first Semitic kingdom, had overrun Assyria and Mesopotamia and penetrated round the north of the desert as far as Syria and Canaan.[4] Thus early did the Babylonians develop beyond the limits of a fluvial into a Mediterranean civilization, though when they reached the sea, they made little use of it. For two thousand years the rulers of the Euphrates–Tigris valley looked westwards to the Mediterranean waters as the goal of their ambition.

§ 7. The historic culture of Babylonia and Assyria was Semitic, though, prior to the descent of Semites from Arabia, native

[1] Mesopotamian civilization was wrecked by the Mongols, and the Turks failed to effect a restoration. Theophrastus, the most celebrated of Aristotle's pupils, wrote in his *History of Plants* : " In Babylon the wheat fields are regularly mown twice, and then fed off with beasts to keep down the luxuriance of the leaf; otherwise the plant does not run to ear. When this is done the return in lands that are badly cultivated is fiftyfold; while in those that are well farmed it is a hundredfold " (quoted by Rogers, i. 419); compare Herodotus's yet more generous estimate, i. 193.

[2] Arist., *Pol.*, iii. 3, 1276a. Herodotus's description (i. 178–87) should be read; but his estimate of the circuit has been criticised by Rogers (i. 438) in the light of recent excavations.

[3] Hence it was not necessary to limit the population by infanticide. But the climate of the Chaldæan plain ensured a high death rate.

[4] Rogers dates Sargon c. 3000 B.C., but this date errs by being too high. See the tables in *Cambridge Ancient History*. It may be noted that Babylonia was more accessible to invasion, even from the mountainous side, than Egypt.

tribes had developed a civilization known as Sumerian (*Sumer* = S. Chaldæa), laying the foundations of religion, language, law, irrigation and urban life, which persisted long after the Semites had established their supremacy. Gem-cutting, an art in which the Babylonians excelled, had in Sumerian times been carried to high perfection; inscriptions were engraved in pictographic and later in cuneiform (arrow-headed) characters; we read already of astronomical observations, the composition of grammars and dictionaries and the formation of a royal library. Late in the third or early in the second millennium we find a dynasty, known as the first Babylonian dynasty, with its seat at Babylon, henceforward the capital of western Asia. Religion is all-important in Babylonian history; the priesthood possessed immense wealth and power; the kings were frequently dependent on their favour, and, even in the days of Assyrian overlordship, the conqueror could secure his authority in Babylon only by doing homage to Marduk. It was Khammurabi, the greatest sovereign of this dynasty, who centralised the local cults of Chaldæa in the worship of Marduk, the patron-deity of Babylon. Khammurabi organised the administrative system of the empire, subdued Elam to the east and Assyria to the north, and extended his sovereignty to the coasts of the Mediterranean.[1] The culture of his age is evidenced by numerous literary remains, including contract-tablets and royal correspondence. But the chief monument of his reign is the code of laws, discovered in the first years of this century by French archæologists at Susa.[2] This code—" the judgements of righteousness, which Khammurabi, the great king, set up "—regulated with precision the civil law of Babylon, including property and contracts, agriculture, trade and banking, marriage, adoption and bequest, as well as the machinery of judicial administration, and testifies to the central position which Babylon had already attained in the commerce of the nations. It forms an elaborate system of state law; though traces survive of earlier custom, e.g. ordeal and the *lex talionis*, it represents an enormous advance on the customary law of early societies. Blood-revenge is prohibited; the *lex talionis* can only be applied through the established courts; all classes, the stranger as well

[1] Khammurabi (Hammurabi, Hammurapi) is *possibly* the Amraphel of Gen. xiv. 1. Rogers dates the first Babylonian dynasty from 2232 to 1932, and Khammurabi from 2130 to 2087.

[2] Fragments have also been discovered in the library of Assur-bani-pal at Nineveh. The code is translated by the Rev. C. H. W. Johns, *The Oldest Code in the World*.

as the home-born, are under the protection of the law. It is extraordinarily interesting to read how such modern problems as exemption from military service, fixity of tenure, compensation for agricultural improvements, control of the liquor traffic, banking deposits, liability for a wife's debts, and the legal rights of women and children, were regulated by this Babylonian sovereign at the close of the third millennium B.C. As Babylonian civilization spread over Syria and Palestine, the code of Khammurabi and the later law which rested on it set their mark on the legislation of the western Semites.[1] The code itself remained in force well on into the Christian era, and influenced subsequently the laws of the Mohammedan conquerors of the East. The Babylonians already stand forth as a civilizing force in western Asia; their language, currency and measures of weight prevailed over all the East; their women enjoyed a legalised status of dignity, and a man could ride in safety from the Persian Gulf to the Mediterranean under the protection of the laws of Khammurabi.

§ 8. As the second millennium wore on, the Babylonian kingdom grew weak; and to the north a new race rose to greatness on the banks of the river Tigris round Nineveh. This people, the children of Asshur, or Assyrians, Semitic colonists from Babylonia and at first subject to its rulers, became its conquerors about 1300 B.C. The Babylonians were a nation of agriculturists and traders : religion counted for more in their public economy than the art of war. The Assyrians, on the contrary, were from first to last a warrior race; their kings were generals who commanded a military nobility; ferocious and cruel beyond all other eastern peoples, their history is a record of war and conquest. Such culture as they acquired was borrowed from Babylonia : their sole advance was to build in stone as well as brick. The huge winged bulls and the inscribed slabs in the British Museum record a continuous tale of savage warfare. " I filled with their corpses the ravines and summits of the mountains," wrote one of the earlier Assyrian princes of his enemies, " I cut off their heads and crowned with them the walls of their cities; I brought away slaves, booty, treasure, innumerable." The Assyrians were fanatically devout; and all their victories were in the name and to the glory of their

---

[1] On the interesting question of the relation between the Mosaic law and the Babylonian code, see S. A. Cook, *The Laws of Moses and the Code of Hammurabi*. Analogies are due rather to common Semitic origin than to direct influence : Babylonian influence on Hebrew law probably dates from the exile (sixth century B.C.).

god Asshur; but the priesthood had little influence in their councils. Their princes were the first to replace annual conscription by a standing army; and their military triumphs were largely due to the introduction of cavalry to supplement chariots. Their capacity for organising empire is evidenced by an elaborate hierarchy of officials, and the imposition of fixed annual tribute upon the provinces. Their power was at its height at three periods of their history, in the twelfth, and again during the ninth and in the later eighth and early seventh centuries.[1] It was in the ninth century that the scourge of the Assyrian armies descended upon Syria and Canaan, overthrew the kingdom of Israel, and reached the shores of the Mediterranean. Samaria, the capital of the northern (Ephraimite) monarchy, besieged by Shalmaneser IV, fell before Sargon in 721. We have seen how, twenty years later, Sargon's son, Sennacherib, overran Judah and threatened Egypt with invasion; and how the conquest was achieved a generation later by his successor, Esarhaddon, whose empire extended from the plateau of Irân to the Libyan desert and the Levant, including also the highlands of Media and the island of Cyprus. His death (668) was followed by the decay of Assyrian power; before the close of the century it succumbed to a coalition between the Medes and the Babylonians, who had regained their independence under Nabopolassar.[2] With the fall of Nineveh (612) the empire of Assyria vanished from history; her records were soon buried beneath the Mesopotamian sand,

> Her glory mouldered and did cease
> From immemorial Nineveh;

till, in the nineteenth century of our era, Botta and Layard unearthed the stones that tell the story of her ferocity and her conquests.[3]

[1] The third and latest period of Assyrian greatness was inaugurated by Tiglath-Pileser III (746–727), the conqueror of Babylonia and Damascus, and continued by Shalmaneser IV (727–722), Sargon (721–705), Sennacherib (704–682), and Esarhaddon (680–668), the last great monarch. Under Esarhaddon's son, Assur-bani-pal (668–626), who cast a thin veil of culture over the savagery of Assyrian rule, the power of the state rapidly declined. Assur-bani-pal's great library is a main source of our knowledge of Babylonian and Assyrian history.

[2] The Scythian (Cimmerian) invasions assisted this decline; see § 17, below.

[3] Rossetti: *The Burden of Nineveh*. Her fall was hailed with exultation by the surrounding peoples. " All that hear the bruit of thee " (i.e. of thy fall), we read in Nahum iii. 19, " clap the hands over thee; for upon whom hath not thy wickedness passed continually? " The city fell before the Medes, who took possession of Assyria proper; Mesopotamia and the Syro-Phœnician lands went to the Babylonians.

§ 9. The victors apportioned the spoils between them, with the exception of Egypt, who recovered her independence, after four years of subjection, in 664; but their triumph was short-lived. The power of Media decayed swiftly after the death of its founder, Cyaxares. That of Babylon reached its climax under Nebuchadrezzar (605–562), who conquered Syria and Jerusalem and bore away the inhabitants of Judah to captivity in Babylonia (586).[1] His buildings, temples and palaces and terraced gardens, made Babylon one of the marvels of the world. But ere long his dynasty suffered the fate that sooner or later befell every oriental empire. Hardy warriors descend from the neighbouring highlands upon the fertile plains, win and consolidate a new dominion, to yield in its turn, when luxury has sapped the strength of rulers and people, to a fresh race of conquerors. So now (553) the Persians, a vigorous and martial peasantry of Indo-European stock, dwelling in the mountainous region to the east of the Persian Gulf, rose against their Median overlords under their chieftain, Cyrus (*Kourush*). Fourteen years later (539) they conquered Babylon. After two thousand years of sovereignty the Semitic empires had fallen, and a new type of civilization, of Aryan origin, bore sway over the East.[2]

§ 10. The wide sweep of Babylonian empire and her commercial supremacy in western Asia led to the diffusion of her culture over a larger area than in the case of Egypt. That culture was literary rather than artistic; though gem-cutting, copper-work, embroidery and kindred arts flourished at Babylon, and " Babylonian garments " were proverbial throughout the ancient world. The native architecture was of brick and comparatively formless; the temples, their chief buildings, stood on rectangular platforms, rising in successive stories to a considerable height. Later, the Assyrians worked their native stone, and adorned their palaces with the colossal figures and bas-reliefs familiar to every visitor to the British Museum. Three questions

[1] The dynasty in question was, strictly, Chaldæan. The Chaldæans were more warlike than the Babylonians, yet equally capable of a high plane of culture. Greek writers applied the name Chaldæa to Babylonia generally; it properly means the land of the Kaldi, Semites who dwelt round the mouths of the Euphrates and the Tigris, between Babylonia and the Persian Gulf.

[2] Cyrus, king of Anshan in Elam, belonged to the Persian clan of the Achæmenids; in 553, after his conquest of Media, he called himself King of the Persians. In 546 Crœsus of Lydia, who had attacked him, was crushed, and all Asia Minor lay in Cyrus's hands. Rogers dates the fall of Babylon in 539.

arise in regard to the influence of Babylonian culture upon the chief civilizations of antiquity. First, there is a close resemblance between the religious traditions of the Babylonians and those of the Hebrews, as recorded in the early chapters of Genesis. In both we read of the garden of Eden, of the deluge and the ark, of the tower of Babel and the confusion of tongues. The Hebrews told how their forefathers in a nomadic stage had sojourned in Chaldæa. It is hard to determine how far this affinity of tradition was due to direct intercourse with Babylonia in remote times, how far to later association with the peoples of Canaan, who had certainly assimilated Babylonian religion, how far, again, to direct contact during the captivity.[1] However this may be with details of Hebrew religious tradition and observances, the fact remains that the development of the religion of Israel, in the hands of the prophets, into a spiritual monotheism was as original and distinctive a creation of the Hebrew religious genius, as the philosophies of Plato and Aristotle were of the intellectual genius of Greece. Secondly, there is the question of the influence of Chaldæan astronomy upon Greek scientific thought. The Chaldæans recorded minute observations of the positions of the heavenly bodies for a period of more than two thousand years, distinguished and named the planets, determined empirically the cyclical recurrence of eclipses, and invented a sexagesimal system of numeration.[2] They constructed the gnomon, an instrument indicating by its shadow the solstices and equinoxes. These data became known to the Greeks, and, like the empirical geometry of the Egyptians, stimulated them to scientific investigation. But here again, mere observation is not science. This is clear when we inquire as to the use which the Babylonian astronomers made of their records. Whereas the Greeks in a single century discovered the true cause of eclipses, the

---

[1] Scholars are divided in opinion on this question. The stories in question are contained in the portion of the book of Genesis compiled in Judæa probably in the ninth century, and known as the Jehovistic narrative (J). They are certainly pre-exilic, and must be accounted for on one of the two first alternatives mentioned in the text. During the exile Babylon again influenced Hebrew culture, both in religion and law. At a yet later date, the fusion of East and West under Macedonian rule led to a further influence of Babylonian religious thought on that of the Jews, traceable, e.g. in Jewish apocalyptic literature of the last two centuries B.C., and also in Gnostic ideas in the early days of Christianity.

[2] See Burnet, *Early Greek Philosophy*, pp. 21 ff. and notes. The researches of Father Kugler have established the limits of their astronomical knowledge. Both in Babylonia and in Egypt, the so-called " science " was a monopoly of the priestly caste.

Babylonians never even attempted to find a rational explanation. They employed their data for purely astrological purposes. If an eclipse had once been followed by a war with Elam, a war with Elam was foretold from its recurrence. Observations, however accurate, which are utilised solely as a basis for fantastic inferences do not constitute scientific knowledge.[1] Finally, Babylonian civilization exerted a real influence on the industrial and commercial life of the western world. The highway that led round the north of the Syrian desert through Asia Minor to Sardis and the coast of the Ægean was the channel of communication between the East and Greece. In particular, Babylonian currency and measures obtained in the first millennium a wide circulation over Asia and the Mediterranean world; Indians and Greeks alike employed the Babylonian *manah* (Greek *mnâ*) as the standard of weight. Thus early, in eastern Babylon as in western Carthage, did the Semite enter upon his historic rôle in the economic history of mankind.

IV. THE HITTITES AND THE WESTERN SEMITES (§§ 11–14).

§ 11. We have seen how Semitic culture set its mark upon the civilization of Egypt, and absorbed that of the earlier Sumerians in the Euphrates–Tigris valley. It was the same in the intervening lands between Mesopotamia and the Mediterranean. The language, religion and culture of Syria and Canaan were Semitic from very early times. We can distinguish various branches of the stock, the southern Semites of Arabia and Ethiopia, the middle Semites of Canaan, the northern (Aramaic) of Syria, the eastern of Babylonia and Assyria; but all alike were children of one Arabian home, and their mutual affinities are as clearly marked as those of the several Teutonic groups in mediæval and modern Europe. It is of the northern and middle branches that we have now to speak; the former comprising the peoples of Syria, the latter, the Phœnicians and dwellers in Canaan, and among them the Hebrews. These all, because of their geographical position between two great empires, play the rôle of buffer states; intermediaries in trade and pawns in the political game for their more powerful neighbours, their

---

[1] We must draw a distinction between the unscientific astrology of the early Chaldæans and (1) the later influence of that astrology on popular Greek religion, and (2) the scientific development of astronomy *under Greek influence* in Babylonia, both subsequent to the Macedonian conquest (see below, c. vii).

history is determined, for welfare or for ruin, by their relationship to Assyria and Egypt.

§ 12. Among these intermediaries was a nation, almost certainly non-Semitic, which ranked for many centuries as a leading power in western Asia. The records of the second millennium show the Egyptians (under the eighteenth dynasty) and, somewhat later, the Assyrians contending on the upper Euphrates against a people known as the Kheta or Hittites.[1] Their origin is obscure, the pictographic script of their inscriptions still undeciphered and their history full of problems that await solution. It seems probable that some, if not all, spoke an Indo–European language, entered Asia Minor from the lower Danube and brought with them a culture and language of their own, modified subsequently by the Semitic influences which were dominant throughout the Middle East.[2] The first centre of their dominion was the tableland of Cappadocia, where many Hittite monuments have been discovered; thence it extended over Cilicia and northern Syria, and over the peoples of western Asia Minor (Phrygia and Lydia).[3] This was between 1700 and 1200; towards the latter date they appear to have lost their sovereignty over Asia Minor and the avenues to Mediterranean and Ægean commerce, events probably connected with the northern incursions into the Ægean area and the fall of the maritime ascendancy of Crete. From this time forward the Syrian Hittites and the new masters of Asia Minor (probably Phrygian) turned their energy to the east and south-east attracted by the rich Mesopotamian resources. From their new headquarters at Carchemish on the upper waters of the Euphrates they commanded the overland highways between east and west. They treated on equal terms with both Egypt and Assyria, and for several generations headed a coalition which blocked the westward

[1] They appear as *Kheta* in Egyptian records, as *Khatti* in Assyrian, in the book of Genesis as " *sons of Heth* " (Gen. xxiii), and elsewhere in the O.T. as *Hittites*.

[2] Some of the cuneiform inscriptions from Boghaz-Keui (their Cappadocian capital) are Semitic, others not so. Semitic was the current tongue of international intercourse in the East. The hieroglyphic inscriptions have been found both in Asia Minor and in North Syria and seem to be later than the cuneiform. The serious study of Hittite remains has made great advances in the last half-century : the pioneers were Wright (1872) and Sayce. See Cowley, *The Hittites* (Schweich Lectures, 1918).

[3] Hittite remains have been found from Eyuk in N. Asia Minor to Hamath in Syria, from the Euphrates in the east to the Ægean coast lands in the west.

expansion of the Mesopotamian Semites.[1]   In the ninth and eighth centuries their power succumbed to the Assyrian armies, and received a final blow from Crœsus of Lydia in the west, shortly before the advent of the Persians.

§ 13. Passing over the Syrian states, indisputably Semitic, which lay on the caravan routes from Assyria to the Mediterranean and received their culture partly from Egypt but in the main from the Babylonians, we come to the coast lands of northern Canaan, where dwelt, at least from the third millennium, the Phœnician Semites. Their whole life centred in maritime trade. Possessed of a small stretch of territory at home, they planted forts and commercial stations along the inland highways, especially around the shores of the Mediterranean. Sidon was in early times the chief Phœnician city; about the twelfth century she yielded place to Tyre. We read in the Old Testament of the alliance, in the tenth century, between David and Solomon and the Tyrian prince Hiram. The Phœnicians dwelt in city-states, under monarchical government, anticipating thus, though to very different issues, the city-states of Hellenism. The great age of Phœnician sea-power and commercial enterprise was between 1200 and 800, subsequent to the fall of Minoan sea-power in the Mediterranean, and prior to the rise of Greece. The argosies of Phœnicia sailed westwards beyond the pillars of Melkarth (the straits of Gibraltar) into the open Atlantic, settled Tarshish (Tartassus, near Cadiz), navigated the Morocco coast, and penetrated also northwards on the Euxine (Black Sea). Wherever they sailed, they planted colonies, in Sicily, Spain and Africa; the oldest on record was Utica in northern Africa (c. 1100), the most famous was Carthage. In course of time Carthage threw off her dependence on the mother-city of Tyre, made herself suzerain of the surrounding lands in Africa, planted colonies of her own, and established a monopoly of trade in western Mediterranean waters. A Greek version of the fifth-century voyage of the Carthaginian Hanno to the west coast of Africa is still extant. From the seventh century onwards Carthage was engaged in ceaseless commercial conflict with the Greek cities of Sicily and the West, which lasted till the third century, when she was called on to face the rising power of Rome. We shall return to the story

---

[1] Carchemish is first mentioned in Egyptian records, c. 1480; it was the centre of Hittite power between the twelfth and ninth centuries. We should think of the Hittites primarily as a barrier between Babylonia and Assyria on the one side, and Asia Minor and the Ægean on the other.

of this struggle in a later chapter. The silver mines of Spain proved a source of immense wealth to the Phœnicians. One result of their discovery was the depreciation of silver against gold, which had hitherto been hardly obtainable in Asia and Africa, as the metal of highest value. The Phœnicians also had for a while a monopoly of the purple dye, extracted from sea-molluscs. After the eighth century Phœnicia lost her independence. At a later date she furnished the navy of her new Persian overlords. We would gladly know more of the internal economy of these great cities, where the clash of interests was a constant source of unrest. With all their skill in mining and metal work and their daring on the sea, the Phœnicians were not originators. They were the great middle-men of their time; their work was simply to diffuse the products of other lands among the peoples of the Mediterranean world.

§ 14. The Semitic inhabitants of Canaan, to the south of Phœnicia, owe their historical importance to a close connexion with the children of Israel. After their sojourn on the borders of Egypt, and deliverance by Moses, under the nineteenth dynasty, the Israelites roved the desert of Sinai, until we find them settled at Kadesh in southern Canaan. We shall see later how Moses had already brought into being a Hebrew nation, by his establishment of the worship of Jehovah as the exclusive religion of the Israelite tribes. When, some generations afterwards the Israelites entered Canaan, they absorbed the culture of the earlier inhabitants and, under Canaanite influence, exchanged the habits of the nomad for a settled agricultural life. At the close of the second millennium, the struggle with the Philistines, a non-Semitic people, probably immigrants from Crete, brought about the institution of kingship under Saul the Benjamite, and ushered in a brief epoch of secular prosperity. David subdued the kindred nations of Moab, Edom and Ammon, and the Syrian kingdoms to the north. Under his successor, Solomon, commerce was developed, and the Hebrews came into closer contact with Egyptian and Babylonian culture; life became more luxurious, and the old simplicity of manners was over-shadowed by the urban civilization of the court. On Solomon's death (c. 933), the northern Israelites, led by the tribe of Ephraim, declared their independence of the south (Judah). The divided monarchy persisted with varying fortunes for more than two hundred years; the northern kingdom, the more powerful of the two, played a considerable part in international politics under the house of Omri, of which we have record in Assyrian tablets; but it was manifestly only a question of time before they succumbed to the armies of the east. In 721 Samaria fell to the Assyrian Sargon, and the Ephraimite kingdom ceased to exist. Judah was saved for a season by the timely homage of her sovereigns, and by the failure of Sennacherib in Egypt (701), till Babylonia had replaced Assyria as the dominant power in the East. Then, at the hand of Nebuchadrezzar, the hour of her doom struck (586), and the Jewish people lingered in exile by the waters of Babylon, till Cyrus, the founder of the Persian empire, suffered them to recolonise their old home (538). It was at this epoch that, with a religious faith purified by suffering and a law renovated under the influence of the prophetic teachers, Israel, though of little moment in the secular comity of nations, entered upon her spiritual mission to mankind. Of the Hebrew genius in religion, and of its influence on world-civilization, we shall speak in the next chapter.

V. CRETE (§§ 15–17).

§ 15. We have carried our survey of Egypt, Babylonia and Assyria, Canaan and Syria to the latter half of the sixth century B.C., when they were absorbed in the mighty empire of Persia. But we have yet to speak of another series of civilizations which arose in Crete, and the islands and shores of the Ægean sea. We have already alluded to the inroads made by sea rovers into Egypt in the time of the nineteenth and twentieth dynasties. Who were these sea-peoples, who bear on Egyptian monuments names (Dardenui, Akaiuasha) akin to the Dardanians (= Trojans) and Achæans of Homer? There is a special interest in these early Ægean races, over and above that of the wonderful discoveries revealed by archæologists in recent years, in that they were the forerunners of the Greeks. Some seventy years ago little or nothing was known for certain of their life and history. The pioneer of Ægean archæology was Heinrich Schliemann. As an errand-boy in a tradesman's shop in Germany his imagination was stirred by the stories in the poems of Homer; he taught himself Greek, won success in business, and amassed wealth, with the single aim of verifying by researches on the site of the Homeric Troy the truth of the narrative in the *Iliad*. At Hissarlik in the Troad (north-west of Asia Minor), the reputed site of Troy, at Mycenæ and Tiryns in the Peloponnesus, he unearthed traces of a great civilization dating from the second millennium B.C.[1] Scholars of all nations followed in his steps, and every year is adding to the rich stores of knowledge thus revealed about the early life and culture of the Ægean area. We can only outline here some of the chief results that have been disclosed.

§ 16. In the course of the third millennium there arose in the island of Crete a rich and varied civilization, which spread in the event over the islands of the Ægean, Rhodes and Cyprus, the Greek peninsula, and the Ionian islands, with later offshoots in North Syria, Sicily, and the western Mediterranean, and led to intercourse with Palestine and Egypt. It has been called " Minoan," after Minos, the lawgiver and friend of Zeus, of Greek tradition, the memory of whose sovereignty of the seas has been preserved in the pages of Thucydides.[2] The race that inhabited Crete in pre-Hellenic times was not Asiatic, but Mediterranean, belonging, in all probability, to the dark, long-headed, short and slender stock that had its original home in northern Africa. Crete is a natural link between Europe, Asia and Africa, and became in time the centre of a powerful commercial and maritime empire. Her civilization was distinct in type from those of Egypt and of Babylonia, and reached its height, first, at the opening of the second millennium (second Middle Minoan period), when the twelfth dynasty ruled in Egypt, and again, a few centuries later (second Late Minoan period), contemporary with the eighteenth Egyptian dynasty. Thus it flourished continuously for some six hundred years. Recent excavations have brought to light, at Cnossus, Phæstus and elsewhere, splendid royal palaces adorned with sculptured reliefs and paintings, containing treasures of metal work in gold, bronze and copper, figures of ivory, porcelain, engraved gems and pottery of rare excellence, that furnish ample evidence of a high plane of culture and refinement. The palace at Cnossus, with its storied maze of chambers, passages and courts, is a town in itself, the veritable labyrinth through which, as in the legend, now shown to record the truth of history, captives were led

[1] Schliemann identified the Homeric Troy with the second (from the bottom) in the series of cities discovered at Hissarlik. In fact, this city proved to be of much earlier date (c. 2000), and the Homeric Troy was the sixth city or perhaps the earlier seventh, in the series (c. 1450–1200).

[2] Thuc., i. 4; cf. Herod., i. 171, 173. The ancient Greeks ascribed much of their law (e.g. Lycurgus' legislation at Sparta), art (the legend of the craftsman Dædalus, the first aeronaut, who made the Labyrinth for Minos, and statues that moved of themselves), and religion (Zeus was born in the cave of Dicte) to Cretan origin.

to the bull-ring, as offerings to the sacred beast of Cretan worship. The drainage-system and sanitary arrangements were worthy of the twentieth century A.D. When a French scholar was shown the costumes of the women in the wall-paintings, he exclaimed, "*Mais ce sont des Parisiennes!*" They are portrayed in close-fitting attire, with zouave jackets and bishops' sleeves, bodices cut low in front, small-waisted, flounced or bell-shaped skirts, and high collars like those of the court-ladies of Elizabethan England. They were curled and *frisées*, tight-laced, and wore shady hats ornamented with ribbons and rosettes. The men were close-shaven, with their long hair coiled in twists, and with curls over their shoulders, clad in kilts and strong top-boots, belted at the waist, and, like the women, adorned with necklaces and armlets. The Cretan architects and stonemasons rivalled those of Memphis and of Thebes. The Cretans were the first-known of European peoples to use writing; inscriptions, both in hieroglyphic and in linear characters, have been found in abundance; when the efforts to decipher them have proved successful, we shall know more of the detailed history of the early Mediterranean world. This much, however, is already certain; that, by the middle of the second millennium, a uniform culture had been diffused far beyond the limits of the Ægean area. To its later phases belong the discoveries of Schliemann at Tiryns and Mycenæ; and it is possible that, as Crete declined from her greatness, Mycenæ, the home of the Homeric Agamemnon, inherited a portion of her sea-power. However this may be, there is clear evidence that, at a date somewhere about 1400, the Minoan civilization in Crete suffered a catastrophic overthrow. The charred ruins of the palace at Cnossus tell their own tale. Earthquakes account for much; but barbarian invaders from the north were pressing in successive hordes over the Ægean world; rude fighters with superior weapons and eventually knowledge of iron, who recked little of the brilliant culture that they overthrew. These men, speaking an Indo-European language, were very possibly ancestors of the Greeks of history. An epoch of darkness ensued, which lasted until the relics of the old civilization, in fusion with the temper and genius of new masters, gave birth to the culture of historic Greece.[1]

[1] See below, c. iv. § 1. Some authorities hold that the Greeks inherited their culture, and even their language, from the Minoans (see Burnet, *Early Greek Philosophy*, pp. 2 ff). The revival of popular religion (as distinct from the Olympian cults) in the seventh and sixth centuries points to the survival of the old Minoan religious tradition, which centred

§ 17. The Ægean shores of Asia Minor, as we shall see presently, were Greek from very early times. When rich commercial cities arose in the eighth and seventh centuries B.C., they were a natural object of envy to the princes of the interior. Asia Minor is a table-land from which valleys descend to the west coast, isolated by mountain ridges. The relief of the land has determined its history. The maritime cities, cut off one from the other by mountains, were an easy prey to conquerors from the inland plateau. In the second millennium the Hittites and those who followed them on the plateau had extended their power to the coasts of the Ægean. In the eighth century the roving Cimmerians [1] from the steppes north of the Black Sea swept over Asia Minor, and devastated the Greek cities by the sea. They ruined the ancient monarchy of Phrygia, and dealt a rude blow to the younger power of Lydia. Lydia was at this time (eighth to sixth century B.C.) the buffer state between the Greek world and the great empires of the East. A new Lydian dynasty arose, whose princes assimilated Greek culture and in return gave the Greeks what is usually assigned as the one original invention of the Lydians, a stamped coinage, which replaced the unstamped weighed metal of the Babylonian and other early cultures.[2] About 560 B.C. Crœsus became king of Lydia. While he subjugated the Greeks on the Ægean coasts of Asia, he ruled them liberally and was a patron of Greek religion and culture. When Cyrus the Persian had conquered Media (549), Crœsus, without waiting for the support of Egypt and other allies, attacked Cyrus, and his defeat cost him his kingdom (546). The fall of Lydia carried with it the submission of the Asiatic Greeks and the empire of Persia stretched from the Hindu-Kush to the Ægean.

VI. THE PERSIAN EMPIRE (§§ 18–20).

§ 18. In prehistoric times a branch of the Indo-European family had left their primeval home in the steppe-lands north

---

in the worship of a goddess of the underworld. The discoveries in Crete during the present century will always be associated with the name of Sir Arthur Evans.

[1] These Cimmerians were probably nomads from north of the Black Sea. It was a period of incursions from the north; in the seventh century the Scythians, who expelled the Cimmerians, also overran Syria and Canaan (see Herod., i. 103 f., and the prophecies of Jeremiah and Zephaniah referred to in the next chapter, § 9).

[2] It is possible that stamped coinage is of even earlier date. It may have arisen in Phrygia; in any case, its origin is connected with the great caravan route which came down from the interior plateau of Asia Minor to the Ægean coast and, in tradition, with the gold-field of Sardis.

of the Caspian, and migrated in a south-easterly direction, some passing through the Khyber pass into the Punjâb, while others settled in the east of the great Iranian plateau. Early in the second millennium, these Iranian tribes (they called themselves Aryans, whence the local names Aria and Irân are derived) moved westwards to the highlands that fringed the Mesopotamian and Chaldæan plains. A thousand years later we find Medes to the south of the Caspian, Parthians in Khorassan, Bactrians on the northern slopes of the Hindu-Kush, and Persians in the mountains that overhang the Persian gulf on the north-east. The Hindu-Kush and Soliman ranges formed their barrier towards India.. These Aryans brought with them the horse, a product of the steppe, unknown to the Babylonians of the days of Khammurabi, but utilised by the Assyrians as an instrument of war.[1] They brought with them also a distinctive religion, which contrasts strikingly with that of their Semitic neighbours on the plain. It differed also, despite a common groundwork that has maintained itself with astonishing persistence among the Persians to the present day, from that of their Aryan kinsmen in India.[2] While the Indian faith subordinated all other divinities to a single supreme God, Iranian religion presented dualistic features;[3] their pantheon grouped itself round two sovereign powers; one of good, a positive creative force, the source of light and life, the other of evil, the negative force of darkness and death, who were called respectively Ahura-mazda (Ormuzd) and Ahriman. The supernatural conflict of these two divine forces was reflected in the course of human history. Between the two stood man, endowed with moral freedom, on the use of which depended his fate in the world beyond the grave. Iranian religion was strongly ethical; its deities were not, like those of the Indian Aryans, speculative abstractions, but moral persons; the goal of human striving was no mystic absorption in a pantheistic Absolute, but eternal felicity in the heaven where Ahuramazda reigned. Human life, its social

[1] As is evidenced by the Babylonian name for the horse, " the ass of the East."

[2] Among the common elements are the cult of Mithra, the sun-god and dragon-slayer (the Indian Indra), fire-worship, and the belief in a law of destiny superior to gods and man. See F. Cumont, *Les Mystères de Mithra*, pp. 1–3, and below, c. ix. § 8. Varuna, the most ethical deity in the Vedic pantheon, was a parallel development to Ahuramazda from a common Aryan original.

[3] But the supreme Brahma of Hindu monotheism (*sic*) was inaccessible and men were driven to propitiate lower deities (Siva, Vishnu).

obligations, its joys and its sorrows, were no illusion, but the
field for energetic action and the fulfilment of moral duty.   In
its recognition of the worth of secular culture, and in its direction
to the end of individual rather than national salvation, the
religion of Irân differed from that of Israel, to which its lofty
ethical teaching presents a certain resemblance.   The Persians
tolerated local religions when not hostile to their own, yet their
faith spread westwards with the expansion of their empire.   In
its purity, as developed by the prophet Zoroaster, it was doubtless
the faith of a few rather than of the many; it tended in the
hands of the Magi (the priestly caste) to degenerate into formal
observances, while the masses interpreted its teaching in terms of
the old pre-Zoroastrian religion.[1] Its real strength lay in insistence on moral responsibility.   The Persians of history present
a noble type of character; they were born rulers of men, proud
and stately in demeanour, lovers of the banquet and the chase,
humane in war, magnanimous to their subject-peoples, ready
to tolerate and even to absorb foreign ideas.   When in the fourth
century Alexander's Macedonians conquered their empire, they
could recognise in the Persian nobles, what in fact was the
truth, their ancient kinsmen.   In art and architecture the
Persians showed little originality, and copied from Babylonian
models.   Commerce they scorned as unworthy of a free man;
arms, agriculture and husbandry were their traditional tasks.
The most heinous of crimes was falsehood; and the training
of their youth is thus summed up by Herodotus, "to ride, to
shoot with the bow, and to speak the truth."[2]

§ 19. The drama of the Persian empire took the course that
has become familiar in Oriental history.   Conquest, organisation,
stationary maintenance of power, decadence and fall, follow in
logical sequence.   Cyrus, the founder, and one of the great

---

[1] Zoroaster (*Zarathustra*) lived probably about 650 B.C.   The Persian
sacred books, collectively entitled the *Avesta*, contain the Gathas, hymns
probably written by the prophet himself.   Zoroastrianism is almost
monotheistic.   Fire-worship was strongly emphasised; fire being the
purest manifestation of Ahuramazda.   The early Magi seem to have been
anti-Zoroastrian.   Herodotus' informant had little use for them.   Like
those of Egypt and Babylonia, Persian cults influenced western religion
first in the age succeeding Alexander's conquests.   In the Roman period,
as we shall see later, Mithra worship was very popular in the Mediterranean
world, and Persian dualism influenced eastern Christianity.   It is the
source of the belief in a personal Satan.   See Cumont, *Les Mystères de
Mithra*, Intr., pp. vi–viii, and the article "God" (*Iranian*) in Hastings'
Dictionary of the Bible.

[2] Her., i. 136.   Compare the prayer in i. 132.   The Persian prayed
for the King and all the Persians, never for himself alone.

empire-builders of history, represents the period of conquest. At his death in 528, his dominions stretched from the Ægean in the west to the Hindu-Kush in the east, from the Caspian in the north to the desert of Arabia in the south. The Persian monarch styled himself " King of Kings "; nor was the claim to world-empire, thus asserted, without foundation. It was Cyrus's son, Cambyses, who conquered Egypt (525) and the Greek colony of Cyrene. Never before had the civilizations of the Nile and the Euphrates been gathered into a single state. The second epoch, of organisation, centres in the person of Darius, son of Hystaspes (521–486). Darius is the type for all time of the Oriental administrator. His vast empire, a medley of all peoples, nations and languages, with no unity of race, religion or common interest, was divided into twenty satrapies or vice-royalties. To guard against the ever-present danger of revolt, the civil and military powers in each satrapy were entrusted to different hands; and a high personage at Susa, the official capital, who bore the title of " the King's Eye," had for his special function the supervision of the satraps. A magnificent system of roads and posts aided to centralise control.[1] As was the general practice in Oriental empires, subject peoples preserved their local religions, customs and institutions in entire freedom from interference by the central government; the two marks of subjection were the payment of a fixed annual tribute, and the levy for service in the field. The Persian nobility lived in close personal relations with the sovereign; Persians settled through the provinces formed, together with representatives of the native inhabitants, the council of the satrap. The satrap was thus controlled at once by his council, by the general of the army and by the central government. The system thus established by Darius became the model for succeeding Oriental monarchies.[2] Darius also added the Punjâb and Arabia to the empire, passed the Hellespont into Europe and received the homage of Thrace and Macedonia.

[1] The royal road from Susa to Sardis (in Lydia) secured for the first time in history the control of Asia Minor by a Mesopotamian power. An army could advance along it at the rate of 20 miles a day, a fact that goes far to explain the successes of Alexander. There were also Persian roads across Asia Minor from N. to S., from Babylon by Ecbatana to Bactria and from Mesopotamia through Phœnicia to Egypt. The highlands of the peninsula, however, were virtually unpoliced till Rome appeared upon the scene.

[2] Darius was a great builder, and sought to conciliate his subjects by lavish honours paid to their religions. He employed the same policy beyond the borders of the empire; e.g. in gifts to the oracle at Delphi, which favoured at the outset the Persian attack on Greece.

At the close of his long reign he was gathering a great host to effect the subjugation of free Greece. Like other Oriental powers, Persia strove to expand westwards; it was from the West that she met her doom. But the story of the Greek conflict with Persia belongs to a later chapter of this book.

§ 20. The successors of Darius, throughout the next century and a half (486–338) were chiefly concerned to maintain the empire which he had consolidated. Enervation in the ruling house, constant revolts in outlying provinces and especially in Egypt, and the long struggle with Greece, combined to foster its degeneration. The centre of gravity in world-politics had shifted to the shores of the Ægean. By the middle of the fourth century, Persian prestige rested on the support of Greek mercenaries and their captains. The death of the last capable ruler, Artaxerxes III (Ochus), in 338 was followed by an interval of anarchy, which furnished a unique opportunity to the enemy. King Philip of Macedon had already planned a war of revenge for the Persian invasion of Greece in the preceding century, and in 334 his son Alexander crossed the Hellespont and made himself master of Asia Minor. In 331 he won his crowning victory at Gaugamela, and a year later, on the death of the last successor of Darius, both the title and the empire passed to the Macedonian conqueror. Henceforward the history of the Middle East becomes part of that Hellenic civilization.

VII. Conclusion (§ 21).

§ 21. The various civilizations that have passed before us in this chapter, though rich in intrinsic interest, were, with one notable exception, of secondary importance for the future of the western world. Viewed from this angle, it might be said that nothing became them better than their eventual absorption into Hellenism. We shall see presently how, when the fusion of East and West became a living reality under the successors of Alexander, the religious ideas of Egypt, Babylonia and Persia evoked a response from within the sphere of Græco-Roman culture. But that culture had arisen and developed on its own lines, in contrast to, rather than by the aid of, the thought and customs of the East. The solitary exception, referred to above, is, of course, the religion of Israel. In this field, and in that of morals, the debt of after ages to the Semitic race is incalculable. A Jew of Tarsus, trained in the strictest school of Pharisaic orthodoxy, became the apostle of the Gentiles. The following chapter, therefore, will be devoted to a study of the chief constructive epoch in Hebrew religious history.   We shall then turn westwards to Greece and Rome.   Even the religion of Israel did not seriously influence the West, until Greece and Rome had fashioned the structure of their civilization.   Hellenism had reached its zenith long before the first missionaries of the gospel set themselves to accommodate Jewish tradition to the temper and habits of the Græco-Roman world.   In all its highest expressions, in art, philosophy and civic life, Hellenism was the original creation of the Greek genius.   Other races contributed materials to its economic substructure, and a stimulus to its intellectual curiosity; here and there, as in architecture, they left their traces upon some detail of its achievement.   But the Greeks knew what they meant, when they contrasted their own culture with the welter of barbarism that surged around their small communities on every side.[1]   That culture arose, as if by magic, amid an alien world, as the goddess Athene in the legend sprang from the head of Zeus;   the history of the surrounding peoples serves merely to point the contrast, and to furnish the framework for its expression.[2]

[1] Bury (*Hellenistic Age*, pp. 24 ff.) suggests that the doctrine of barbarian inferiority was the product of the Persian Wars.   Later it was questioned by philosophers;   Plato conjectured that a philosopher-king might be found among barbarians, and the Stoics went so far as to conceive one brotherhood of all mankind.   See below, p. 195.

[2] Grote, in the preface to his *History of Greece* (1846), spoke of "the spontaneous movement of Grecian intellect, sometimes aided but never borrowed from without, and lighting up a small portion of the world otherwise clouded and stationary."   Much has been discovered since Grote's day, but his assertion of the originality of Greek science remains unshaken.

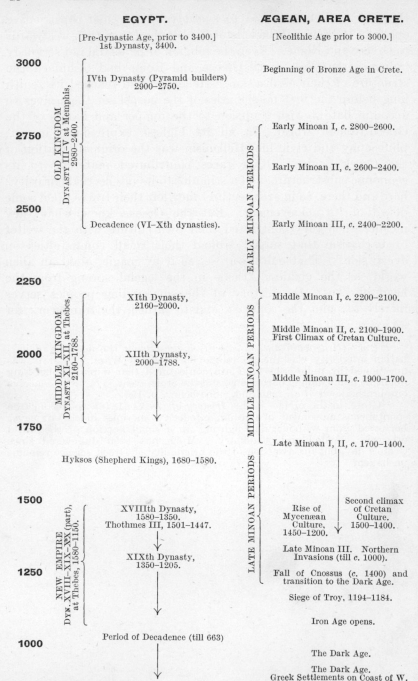

	EGYPT.	ÆGEAN, AREA CRETE.
	[Pre-dynastic Age, prior to 3400.] 1st Dynasty, 3400.	[Neolithic Age prior to 3000.]
3000	IVth Dynasty (Pyramid builders) 2900–2750.	Beginning of Bronze Age in Crete.
2750	OLD KINGDOM DYNASTY III–V at Memphis, 2980–2400.	Early Minoan I, *c.* 2800–2600.
		Early Minoan II, *c.* 2600–2400.
2500	Decadence (VI–Xth dynasties).	Early Minoan III, *c.* 2400–2200.
2250	XIth Dynasty, 2160–2000.	Middle Minoan I, *c.* 2200–2100.
	MIDDLE KINGDOM DYNASTY XI–XII, at Thebes, 2160–1788.	Middle Minoan II, *c.* 2100–1900. First Climax of Cretan Culture.
2000	XIIth Dynasty, 2000–1788.	Middle Minoan III, *c.* 1900–1700.
1750		Late Minoan I, II, *c.* 1700–1400.
	Hyksos (Shepherd Kings), 1680–1580.	
1500	XVIIIth Dynasty, 1580–1350. Thothmes III, 1501–1447.	Rise of Mycenæan Culture, 1450–1200. / Second climax of Cretan Culture. 1500–1400.
	NEW EMPIRE DYN. XVIII–XIX–XX (part), at Thebes, 1580–1150.	Late Minoan III. Northern Invasions (till *c.* 1000).
1250	XIXth Dynasty, 1350–1205.	Fall of Cnossus (*c.* 1400) and transition to the Dark Age.
		Siege of Troy, 1194–1184.
		Iron Age opens.
1000	Period of Decadence (till 663)	The Dark Age.
		The Dark Age. Greek Settlements on Coast of W. Asia Minor.

WESTERN ASIA.   **BABYLONIA AND ASSYRIA.**

Sumerians (prior to 3000).

3000

Sargon
(a little later)

2750

Sumerian revival.

2500

Assyrian Kings
at Asshur, from
c. 2400.

2250

FIRST BABYLONAIN
DYNASTY,
2232–1932.

Khammurabi,
2130–2087.

2000

Aryans to Persia,
c. 2000–1600.

Series of Babylonian
Dynasties.

The Exodus of Israel (?).

1750

Aryans to India,
c. 1600.

Hittite power in Asia Minor,
1700–1200.

1500

Rise of Assyrian
power, from 1380.

Shelmaneser I (1276).

Exodus of Israel from Egypt,
c. 1230 (?).
Phœnician Sea-power : Tyre re-
places Sidon : first African Colonies
(12th century).
Hittites and their successors at
Carchemish, c. 1200.

Babylon under
Assyrian rule.

1250

Tiglath-Pileser I,
c. 1120.

Kingship in Israel { Saul, c. 1025.
{ David, c. 1010.

1000

Decline of Assyrian
power (to c. 900).

EGYPT.

ÆGEAN AREA AND

The Dark Age, to c. 800.

1000   Period of Decadence (till 663).

Libyan and   Sheshonk (Shishak),
Ethiopian rulers.   945–924, invades
      Palestine.

Growth of the Greek Epic.

900

800

Decline of Phœnician Commercial
Power.
Epoch of Greek commercial
expansion and colonisation
(to c. 600).

Phœnician Colonies in Africa and the West.

700

670. Esarhaddon conquers Egypt.
663. Egypt independent, under XXVIth
    Dynasty at Sais, to 525.

Rise of
Tyranny.

Greek   Necho (609–593).
600   Settlements
in Egypt.

Solon : Thales and the birth of
science.

Pisistratus.

525. Cambyses' conquest of Egypt.
   Egypt under Persian rule to 332.

Clisthenes.

500

The Persian Wars (490 : 480).

Pericles and the Athenian Empire.

400

Peloponnesian War.

Rise of Macedon.

332–330. Alexander's conquest of Egypt.

Battle of Chæronea (338).

Greece under Macedonian rule.

300

WESTERN ASIA.	ISRAEL.	BABYLONIA AND ASSYRIA.	
	David, c. 1010–970. Solomon, c. 970–933. Division of N. (Ephraimite) Kingdom from S. (Judah) (933).	Decline of Assyrian power to c. 900.	**1000**
		Recovery of Assyria.	**900**
Decline of the post-Hittite power. Cimmerian Invasion.	Ahab (d. 854) : Elijah.		**800**
	Amos; Hosea; JE.	746. Assyrian Empire at its height.	
Lydian power in Western Asia.	721. Fall of Samaria (N. King- dom) before Assyria. Isaiah.	Sennacherib invades Judah.	**700**
		668. Death of Esarhaddon; de- cline of Assyria.	
	621. Deuteronomic code. Jeremiah. 597. Babylonian conquest of Judah, first deportation. 586. Final captivity of Judah; Ezekiel.	612. Fall of Nineveh. Chaldæan empire at Babylon. Nebuchadrezzar (605–562).	**600**
546. Cyrus conquers Lydia. Western Asia under Persian rule to 334.	The Second Isaiah. 538. Restoration under Cyrus.	553. Cyrus conquers Media. 539. Cyrus conquers Babylon. 529. Cambyses King of Persia. 522. Darius I King of Persia.	**500**
		485. Xerxes. 465. Artaxerxes I.	
		423. Darius II. 404. Artaxerxes II.	**400**
	397. Ezra's Restoration.		
Alexander conquers Western Asia (334).	332. The Jews under Mace- donian rule.	359. Artaxerxes III (Ochus), to 338. 333. Alexander conquers Persia.	**300**

CHAPTER III

THE RELIGION OF ISRAEL [1]

I. INTRODUCTORY (§§ 1, 2).

§ 1. THE three great religions of the Mediterranean world, Judaism, Islam and Christianity, are all of Semitic origin. That they are still of living power among men testifies to the enduring value of the religious genius of the Semites. The appeal of the two former has been almost wholly confined to the Semitic stock. The third, Christianity, early broke the barriers of race, and claimed as a world-religion the allegiance of the Gentile as of the Jew. But its gospel was preached to the Jew first; it arose among the Jews as the historical fulfilment of Hebrew law and Hebrew prophecy. The question confronts us : how did it come about that the tribal faith of an insignificant Semitic people furnished, in the course of its historical development, the basis of a spiritual message for mankind ? Where, amid the particularism of the faith and worship of ancient Israel, lay the seeds of universality ? In its early phases, the religion of Israel had little to distinguish it from that of the surrounding peoples of Canaan. How was it that, while their gods vanished with the political ruin of the states that worshipped them, the God of Israel survived the captivity and dispersion of his people, and is still reverenced by millions of all races at the present day ? The answer to this question is to be found in the study of the Hebrew prophets. As the intellectual genius of Greece, working on methods of universal validity for human thought, transformed the crude data of experience into a structure of reasoned knowledge; as the political genius of Rome moulded the laws of an Italian city into principles of jurisprudence for a world-state : so the religious genius of Israel, manifested through the vision of her prophets, purified the cult of a tribal deity, whose office was to fight his people's battles against the rival gods of other lands, into that of

---

[1] The Hebrews of Old Testament days called themselves " the sons of Israel " (*B'ne Isra'el*). The name *Israel* is of obscure origin and has been interpreted " God (*El*) strives " or " persists." The name *Hebrew* is of later application, and, on the traditional view, means " the people from the other side of " (Heb. *'ibhrim*) the river Euphrates (or the Jordan ?). The name *Jew* (*Y'hudi*) means " man of Judah," and applies strictly to the dweller in southern Palestine. Possibly *Israel* and *Hebrew* were originally clan-names.

the one God, the creator of the universe, who displayed his spiritual fatherhood in the righteous government of all nations of the earth.

§ 2. When Moses, in the latter half of the second millennium before Christ, united a group of Semitic clans into a single community, he founded not merely a nation but a national religion.[1] It was as the bearer of a religious revelation that, like Mahomet two thousand years later, he was enabled to initiate a far-reaching transformation in the otherwise so persistent tribal customs of Semitic nomads. He fixed the worship of Jehovah (*Yahweh*) as that of a people, and thereby called a nation into being.[2] Henceforward Yahweh was the God of Israel, who had freed their fathers from bondage and led them through the perils of the wilderness into the promised land. To Moses also can be assigned the institution of a ritual and a priesthood; and his oral judgements formed the nucleus for the development of a Law (*Torah*).[3]

[1] The date of the Exodus is uncertain. Some authorities regard it as coinciding with the expulsion of the *Hyksos* or Semitic shepherd-kings (early sixteenth century); others date it under the eighteenth dynasty (Amenhotep II, *c.* 1445); others under Merneptah (nineteenth dynasty), *c.* 1220 or a generation later.

[2] The Jews, from fear of abusing the sacred name *Yahweh*, wrote it with the vowels of the words *Adonai* (= my lord) or *Elohim* (= my God), as an indication that these words were to be read aloud in its place. This practice dates from the introduction of vowel signs, some centuries after the Christian era. Hebrew writing was originally consonantal. Hence arose the quite misleading form *Jehovah*, referred to early in the sixteenth century A.D. by a certain Petrus Galatinus (*de arcanis Catholicae veritatis*, 1518). The meaning of the name *Yahweh* is uncertain. Some scholars hold that Yahweh was worshipped by Israel before the time of Moses; the O.T. is ambiguous on this point, the Jehovist writer (J, see next note) stating that his worship was pre-Mosaic (Gen. iv. 26), the Elohist (E) and Priestly (P) writers that it was introduced by Moses (Exod. iii. 11–14, vi. 2–3), perhaps from Midian. The pre-Mosaic history is very uncertain and obscure.

[3] The Pentateuch (i.e. Gen., Exod., Lev., Num., Deut.) and Joshua represent a compilation of early history and law, which reached its present form after the Exile. The compilation can be traced to three main sources, designated respectively JE, D and P.

(*a*) Two narratives of early history, written, one in the northern (Ephraimite) kingdom, the other in the southern (Judah), probably between 850 and 750, and combined in a single historical work *c.* 750. The former is called E, from the use of the name *Elohim* for God; the latter is called J, from the use of the name *Jahweh* (*Yahweh*). The combined work is called JE.

(*b*) The Deuteronomic law, called D, dating from the middle of the seventh century (see below, § 8).

(*c*) The Priestly history and code, called P, probably composed at the time of the captivity (see below, §§ 10, 11).

Gen., Exod., Num. represent the fusion of JE and P; Lev. belongs to P; Deut. to D; Joshua to JE, a Deuteronomic editor, and P.

The reader must understand that the successive editors were com-

This religion of Yahweh, as brought by the Israelites into Canaan, was assuredly primitive and anthropomorphic. Yahweh was conceived as possessing bodily form and a local habitation, and as moved by human passions of jealousy and anger. He was a warrior deity, " a man of war," who fought ruthlessly for his own people against their enemies, and, like an Oriental potentate, required in return homage and gifts. His concern was not with the individual but with the nation, and with the nation especially in times of war. Yet already in this primitive form of national faith can be detected the germs of an ethical religion. It was, if not monotheistic, avowedly monolatrous; the command had gone forth to Israel, " Thou shalt have none other gods but me." [1] Yahweh had no mythology, no pantheon of associated deities, no goddess-consort, such as marked the Canaanite worships.[2] He was the source of right and justice, and his sanctuary the recognised depository of law. " The great merit of Moses," writes an eminent modern scholar, " lies in the fact of his connexion of the religious idea with the moral life." [3] Yahweh stood to his people in the personal relationship of a father to his children, a relationship that rested not on the natural tie of blood-kinship, but on choice and will. Yahweh had chosen Israel, and Israel had accepted Yahweh; we have here the germ of the later doctrine of the Covenant. It was this moral conviction, exemplified for the Hebrews of that age in Yahweh's championship of Israel against her foes, that preserved the new-born nation from being absorbed by the older civilisation of the Canaanites. The settlement in Canaan was

pilers rather than original authors, and incorporated in their work preexisting documents, adding only what was necessary to fit the extracts together. Thus many of the laws and narratives in these books were based on customs, traditions and songs of much earlier date, and some of them on written records (e.g. Num. xxi. 14 f.; Joshua x. 12 f). The ancient nucleus of law, called the *Book of the Covenant* (Exod. xx. 22–xxiii. 33), and the *Older Decalogue* (Exod. xxxiv. 17–26), existed in writing before E was compiled. So, too, the latest compilation (P) contains some very ancient law in the *Book of Holiness* (Lev. xvii–xxvi), referred to as H, and probably pre-exilic. While the Law *as we have it* is later than the older prophecy, much of its contents dates back to pre-prophetic times.

On the whole subject, see Driver, *Introduction to the Literature of the O.T.*, pp. 82 ff., 116 ff.

[1] Monolatry means that, though many gods may exist, only one is to be worshipped; monotheism that there is only one god.

[2] The Elephantine papyri indicate a goddess-consort. But they present the religion of Israel in a debased form. See Cowley, *Aramaic Papyri* (Introduction).

[3] Kuenen, *Religion of Israel*.

a slow process of fusion, which incidentally left traces on Israel's religion. As the nomadic immigrants learnt from their neighbours the habits of agricultural life, they appropriated therewith the cults of the Canaanite deities (*Baalim* = lords of the land). These Baalim were not, as was Yahweh, warrior gods, but peaceful nature-divinities, impersonations of the productive powers of fertility and life, associated in pairs of male (*Baal*) and female (*Ashtōreth*), with varying local cults, which were accompanied by gross sensuality.[1] Had the process of fusion been wholly pacific, the religion of Israel might easily have sunk to the Canaanitish level, Yahweh been merged in the Baalim, and Israel have left no impress on the spiritual history of mankind. But the invaders had to fight for their inheritance; and the fact of constant war preserved their national and religious individuality. Yahweh remained, amid all assimilation of Canaanite worships, such as high places, groves or sacred pillars, the God of his chosen people. The Song of Deborah, one of the oldest fragments of Hebrew poetic literature, survives to show how the faith of Yahweh inspired the clans of Israel in these early struggles with the surrounding peoples.[2] The consciousness of a distinctive nationality was intensified by the wars with the Philistines in the eleventh and tenth centuries, which brought about the institution of the kingship in the person of Saul the Benjamite. The king was the embodiment at once of national and religious independence. Henceforward the worship of Yahweh, despite a multitude of Canaanite accretions, became the avowed symbol of Israel's distinctive destiny.

§ 3. Leaving on the one side the obscure problems of the origin of the cult of Yahweh, and on the other deferring consideration of the development of the religion of Israel under prophetic influence to pure ethical monotheism, we note the following persistent characteristics of that religion from the times of its inauguration by Moses until Judaism attained its final form as a world-religion in the first two centuries of the Christian era. They will indicate to the reader the wide gulf that separates the Hebraic religious tradition, both before and after its appropriation

---

[1] That the sensuality referred to was the outcome of ritual requirement only makes the difference more remarkable. The *Ras Shamra* tablets (fifteenth to thirteenth century B.C.), discovered in 1929, illustrate the full Canaanite mythology (see Jack, *The Ras Shamra Tablets*), and furnish evidence of literary activity in Palestine some centuries prior to the establishment of the Israelite monarchy.

[2] Judges v., cf. the ancient invocation in Num. x. 35, 36, "Let Jehovah arise and let his enemies be scattered," etc.

by Christianity, and that which has its source in Hellenic speculation, whether on metaphysics or on theology. In the first place
(a), it rested on the unquestioned conviction of God's existence
rather than on any inferential conclusions as to his existence or
his nature and essence. The only answer vouchsafed to Moses'
enquiry as to his name was the affirmation of his self-existence :
" I am that I am." [1] As self-existent, he is the cause as creator
of the existence of all that is : " In the beginning God created
the heavens and the earth." [2] These opening words of the
Pentateuch express no philosophical hypothesis but a primary
datum of the Hebrew religious consciousness. From the first,
Yahweh proclaimed himself a living God, to be accepted by faith,
transcending the utmost reach of speculative enquiry.[3] Unlike
the God of Plato and Aristotle, the God of Abraham, Isaac and
Jacob is for the human intellect a hidden God (Deus absconditur).
Secondly (b), Hebrew religion is revelational, deriving its authority
and its claim on man's obedience, not from reason, but solely
from its divine authorship. The revelation is one, as God is one ;
the conception of an anti-God, by means of which Persian
religion escaped the problem of the origin of evil, was wholly
alien to the Hebrew mind. Moreover, it was final and complete
as God Himself is perfect and immutable. " The whole of
religion was revealed and the whole content of revelation was
religion." [4] It constituted the Torah or Law of God, comprising
both the written Law (The Pentateuch) and, as time went on, its
oral interpretation as eventually formulated and systematised in
the Jewish schools. So it is also with the prophets, who speak not
their own words, uttered in their own authority, but the words
revealed to them by Yahweh. Thirdly (c), the religion of Israel
is pragmatic, being the expression of the divine will, addressed to
man as a volitional and active being. It is a body of commands
regulative of human conduct, and enforced by sanctions of weal
or woe, consequential on man's acceptance or rejection. " The
fear of the Lord, that is wisdom " ; [5] in so far as God makes
his nature known to Israel in his self-revelation, it is as energy
of operation. The universe is brought into being by his free act
of power ; and the whole record of his dealings with Israel is
the embodiment of his initial purpose. Though ineffably

---

[1] Ex. iii. 14.   [2] Gen. i. 1.
[3] As Dr. Whitehead has put it (Adventures of Ideas, p. 132), the question
" Canst thou by searching find out God ? " is good Hebrew but it is bad Greek.
[4] G. F. Moore, Judaism, i. 112.   [5] Job xxviii. 28.

transcendant of all processes of time and change, his presence is imminent and his will made manifest in every detail of nature and human history. Not the chosen people only, but the whole universe and all the nations who inhabit it form the scene for his activity. " Have I not brought up Israel out of the land of Egypt, and the Philistines from Caphtor, and the Syrians from Kir ? " [1] Hence the consummation of God's purpose, though, like its inauguration, an act of supernatural intervention into the course of history, is conceived as a catastrophic event in the historical future. The thought of eternal life, congenial to Greek philosophers, was foreign to the Hebrew religious outlook. Yahweh transcended time, not by his timelessness, but by his unending duration : he was " from everlasting to everlasting." [2] Finally, it is obvious (a) that a religion inspired by these convictions was pregnant with rich potency of ethical development. Yahweh was a God of righteousness and mercy, who enjoined acts of righteousness and mercy on his servants. The former of these attributes was exemplified in his rigorous exaction of retributive punishment for sin, i.e., in Johannine phrase, for " transgression of the Law " ; [3] the latter in his never-failing readiness to forgive sin, on the sole condition of repentance in the sinner. There is here no consciousness of the distinction between ethical and religious obligation; every act, whether of the individual or of the community falls within the field of moral responsibility, and also implies obedience or disobedience to the divine command. For the community, the " house of Israel," too, stood in a personal relationship to Yahweh, as a real " corporate person," to be distinguished as ethical from the pre-moral and instinctive herd-consciousness, and as a real entity from the artificial society which is the product of contract on the part of the individuals who are its members.

II. Pre-Exilic Prophecy (§§ 4–10).

§ 4. It is at this moment that we first hear of prophets (nebi'im) in Israel. King Saul himself on one occasion figured among their number.[4] But these prophets were scarcely distinguishable from the prophets of Baal found among other Canaanite peoples, companies of ecstatic dervishes, who under stimulus of music and dancing experienced possession by their deity. They were men of a type very different from the great

---

[1] Amos ix. 7.
[2] Ps. xc. 2.
[3] 1 John iii. 4; cf. St. Paul in Rom. c. iv.
[4] 1 Sam. xix. 20–24.

teachers who came forward a few generations later as the champions of a purified faith. These latter appear first at the time of the dismemberment of Solomon's monarchy, in the northern or Ephraimite kingdom, in opposition to the spread of alien religious cults and secular civilization.[1] Solomon had already opened the door to foreign trade and fostered dynastic alliances with foreign courts, a policy which led to innovations in time-honoured social custom and to the introduction of foreign worships. Wealth and luxury brought in their train class distinctions and a growing cleavage between rich and poor; forced labour, after the Egyptian model, was required for the building of kings' palaces, fortified towns and religious sanctuaries; a court, a harem and a swarm of military and priestly officials became part of the new order of life. These and similar features of Solomon's monarchy were reproduced in the northern kingdom under the dynasty of Omri (from c. 887). When Ahab, Omri's son, legitimised the worship of the Tyrian Baal and stretched the royal prerogative at the expense of traditional custom, Elijah, clad in nomad's garb and voicing the spirit of primitive nomadic simplicity, denounced both the religious and the secular policy of the court.[2] His successor, Elisha, in close association with the prophetic gilds, compassed the overthrow of the dynasty, and guided, as acknowledged adviser, the counsels of Jehu and his son.[3] Prophecy had triumphed in the northern kingdom and established itself as a moral force in the community. It was no mere political victory. Elijah and Elisha stood for the exclusive claim of Yahweh to the allegiance of Israel, and for his law as a law of righteousness, requiring moral service from his chosen children. To worship any other god was sin : to worship Yahweh meant to realise his moral prescripts in the life of the community. This recognition of Yahweh's ethical personality, anticipating the voice of written prophecy, is witnessed to not only by the recorded narratives, but by the older portions of the Pentateuch, composed probably under the influence of Elijah's prophetic mission.

§ 5. The earliest written prophecy, that of Amos, dates

[1] The revolt of Jeroboam I and the establishment of a separate Ephraimite kingdom (933) were probably due to dislike of forced labour, and were supported by the prophet Ahijah. See 1 Kings xi. 28 ff.

[2] Ahab's infringement of social custom in the matter of Naboth's vineyard stirred popular feeling more than any other feature in his policy. Ahab's reign may be dated after 853.

[3] "The chariots of Israel and the horsemen thereof " : so he is styled by the king (2 Kings xiii. 14).

from the reign of Jeroboam II in northern Israel (783–745).[1] The Ephraimite kingdom presented a scene of apparent prosperity. But beneath the surface the nation was sick unto death. Court, nobles and priesthood were alike corrupt; luxury and sensuality, injustice and oppression of the poor, abounded; the worship at the great sanctuaries, such as Bethel, furnished occasion not only for sumptuous revelry and splendid ceremonial, but for acts of violence and wrong.[2] The old brotherly-kindliness was vanishing with the spread of wealth and self-indulgence. The free peasantry, hitherto the strength of the nation in peace and war, were falling into decay. Beyond the border, the decline of the buffer-state of Damascus had brought the terrible Assyrian menace to the very doors of Israel.[3] King and people alike were blind to the impending doom; yet to a clear vision ruin was as imminent and certain as it would have been to Belgium in 1914, had she been confronted, without an ally, by the onset of the German armies. It was at such a crisis that Amos, a keeper of flocks and dresser of scyamores from Tekoa in the southern highlands bordering on the Dead Sea, appeared among the careless revellers at Bethel to utter the word of judgement which Yahweh had revealed to his servant. Amos's message, like that of all the earlier prophets, was one of unrelieved gloom. Israel had sinned, and Yahweh's righteous judgement would be manifested in the utter ruin of the nation. Men looked for the "day of Yahweh," by which they meant the day when by Yahweh's aid Israel would triumph in battle over her enemies. Amos, heralding the Assyrian conqueror as Yahweh's instrument, invested the old catchword with a new and terrible significance. "Woe unto you that desire the day of Yahweh! wherefore would ye have the day of Yahweh? It is darkness and not light."[4] For Amos, Yahweh is never "the God of Israel"; He is "Yahweh of hosts" (seba'oth), Lord, not of the national armies, but of the hosts of heaven and earth. The popular

---

[1] Amos' prophecy falls between 765 and 750; Hosea's, also in northern Israel, between 750 and 734. Next in order come Micah and Isaiah, both in Judah, during the last third of the century.

[2] See Amos and Hosea generally : on injustice and decay of old social bonds, Amos ii. 6–8, iii. 10, v. 11, viii. 4–6; Hos. iv. 1, 2 : on licentious worship and idolatry, Amos ii. 7, 8; Hos. iv. 13, 14 : on corruption of prophets and priests, Hos. iv. 5, 6; vi. 9.

[3] Jeroboam II had recovered all eastern Palestine up to the north of Lebanon, 2 Kings xiv. 25. The Assyrians conquered Damascus in 803; Jeroboam probably paid allegiance to Assyria.

[4] Amos v. 18.

religion saw in defeat a sign that Yahweh had forsaken his people; to Amos the impending downfall was the clearest vindication of Yahweh's justice upon his people who had forsaken him. It was because he had chosen them to be the recipients of his knowledge that their moral disobedience had provoked his righteous punishment. " You only have I known of all the families of the earth : therefore will I visit upon you all your iniquities." " For three transgressions of Israel, yea, for four, I will not turn away the punishment thereof; because they have sold the righteous for silver and the needy for a pair of shoes." " The virgin of Israel is fallen; she shall no more rise : she is cast down upon her land; there is none to raise her up." [1]

§ 6. The prophecies of Amos and Hosea claim attention not merely as representing the dawn of a new epoch in the spiritual history of Israel but also as embodying the essential characteristics both in manner and substance, of pre-exilic prophetic teaching. The mission of the prophet was to declare Yahweh's " word " to his people. The prophecy was the communication of a personal revelation. Its essence does not lie in prediction of future happenings. The prophet is " one who speaks on behalf of " Yahweh, in conscious opposition to the world of secular rulers, the official priesthood, popular opinion, and even the prophetic gilds. " I was no prophet," says Amos, " neither was I a prophet's son." [2] His voice is that of one crying in the wilderness, in passionate denunciation of public immorality and the injustice of the social order. The word which he declares is not his own, but Yahweh's. The prophetic office is none of his choosing; he has felt the compelling mastery of Yahweh's hand and utters only what Yahweh has put into his mouth. " The lion hath roared, who will not fear ? The Lord God hath spoken, who can but prophesy ? " [3] Hence the intensity of his personal conviction, his absolute certainty of the truth of the message. But his utterance was no mere ecstatic rhapsody, nor was it dependent on artificial stimulation; few traces of physical or mental derangement can be detected in the prophetic writings. The abnormal vision and conditions that accompany the prophetic experience (most frequently in Ezekiel, least frequently in Jeremiah) are accepted as

[1] Amos iii. 2; ii. 6; v. 2.
[2] Amos vii. 14; cf. Hos. ix. 7. The narrative passage, Amos vii. 10–17, brings out clearly this opposition to the policy of the rulers and priesthood.
[3] Amos iii. 8; cf. Amos vii. 14 f., Is. vi, Jer. i and xxiii. 9, Ezek. i. 3.

objective and referred to direct inspiration by Yahweh.[1] Yahweh's word approves itself to his understanding and his conscience. The revelation may be by vision, or, more frequently, by spoken word; it may be sanctioned by sign and enforced by analogy and symbolism; but it is invariably lucid and incisive.[2] Further, the message is addressed to the nation, rarely to an individual. The individual counted as yet but lightly in the religion of Israel. Moral retribution, for weal or woe, was dispensed to the community in the course of its earthly history. We shall see in the sequel, how at a later day the claim of the individual Israelite on the divine justice, and the hope of felicity after death, won expression in Hebrew religion. But the theme of the early prophets is the obligation to national righteousness and Yahweh's judgements on national sin. Once more, the message, as the revelation of Yahweh's purpose, is its own warrant and needs no support of argument. If proof be sought, it is furnished not by abstract inference, but by a sign, that is, by a concrete sensible indication of its divine origin. We find no trace of speculative reasoning in Hebrew prophecy. The prophet's teaching was concerned with practice, not with theory, and his appeal is not to the intellect, but to the will.[3] It was stimulated, at each stage, by a practical crisis in the fortunes of the nation. The Assyrian menace evoked the messages of Amos, Hosea and Isaiah, the Babylonian that of Jeremiah. Herein Hebrew prophecy furnishes a striking contrast to Greek philosophy. Whereas the Greek thinker required rational explanation for every fact and rational grounds for every judgement, the Hebrew prophet found full assurance in the immediate intuition of Yahweh's will, and prefaced his utterance with the simple declaration, "thus spake Yahweh." The one was the flower of secular culture, the other its uncompromising foe. Both claimed to know the truth, the one by knowledge of reasoned science, the other by that of moral faith.

§ 7. The guarantee of truth lay not only in the manner, but in the substance of the prophetic revelation. The temper

---

[1] See Wheeler Robinson in *The People and the Book*, pp. 371 ff. "The prophet is conscious of the import of the inspiration; like the poet, he 'half creates and half perceives.'"

[2] Only one vision is recorded by Isaiah during forty years of prophetic mission. The prophecies are throughout free from any touch of rhapsody.

[3] The implication of the term *lēb*, usually translated "heart," is volitional rather than emotional. See below, p. 75 (1).

of the pre-exilic prophets is one of austere reprobation of Israel's sin, and tragic despair of Israel's repentance. The way of salvation is open, " Seek good and not evil, that ye may live; " [1] but the prophet has little hope of its adoption. It is the false prophet that cries peace when there is no peace, and, to please men, proclaims an illusory security.[2] When the blow had fallen and Israel was carried away into captivity, the tone changes and Yahweh's message is a promise of blessing and restoration.[3] Already in Isaiah we read of a just remnant of the people who shall be saved in the hour of desolation to form the nucleus of a renovated Israel. But despair of Israel's repentance never clouds for an instant the prophet's faith in Yahweh's righteous government. Let Israel perish, if thereby Yahweh's justice be made manifest. The Assyrian conqueror was but the instrument of his omnipotent and holy will. Yahweh, for Amos and Hosea, is the God of all nations and of the whole earth. His power extends over nature, over the hosts of heaven, even over the realm of the departed (*Sheol* = Hades).[4] He was a moral person, whose unique and universal sovereignty left no place for any divine power but himself. It was his living presence, in active operation, not his essence, that filled the minds of the prophets; and they interpreted his activity of will in terms that precluded the recognition of any other deity. His moral government was manifested in his dealings with all peoples, and primarily with his chosen people. Heathen nations, like Israel, were to be punished for their sins.[5] In the phrase of a great modern scholar, the prophets conceive a divine drama, with the earth as the stage, the nations the *dramatis personae*, Israel the hero of the plot, and Yahweh

[1] Amos v. 14.
[2] 1 Kings xxii, Is. xxx. 9–11, Jer. xxviii, and (esp.) Ezek. xiii. Deut. xviii. 21, 22 places the criterion of truth in fulfilment; but cf. Deut. xiii. 1–4. False prophecy may be fulfilled; true prophecy may not. See Charles, *Eschatology*, p. 185 *n*.
[3] Such passages as Amos ix. 8–15 and Hos. xiv, predicting a future restoration, are possibly of later date though the latter is probably genuine. They are accepted by Robertson Smith and by Driver (*Introduction*, pp. 306, 307), who urges that the prophets, guided rather by feeling than by logic, may well have expressed the hope of an ideal restoration at the close of their denunciatory warnings.
[4] Amos ix. 2; Is. vii. 11. Yet the primitive conception of Sheol as outside Yahweh's sway persisted for centuries, alongside of monotheism; the speculative inconsistency was not felt as such (see Is. xxxviii. 18; Ps. lxxxviii. 5).
[5] Amos i, ii and ix. 7. It is for wrongs committed against *Israel* that five of the six nations referred to in cc. i and ii are to be punished. The later universalism is still far off. In Is. x. 5–15, Assyria is within the domain of Yahweh's sovereignty.

the author of the tragedy.[1] The advent of the Assyrian opened
their eyes to a larger world; this enlargement of their imaginative horizon furthered an advance of spiritual insight. The
faith in Yahweh's moral government sufficed for the greater
world as for the less. Once more, this conception of Yahweh's
moral personality carried with it the requirement of moral
service from his worshippers. Formal observances and empty
ceremonial counted for nothing in his sight. " I desired mercy
[Hesed = love] and not sacrifice; and the knowledge of God
more than burnt-offerings." " I hate, I despise your feast-days,
and I will take no delight [I will not smell—A.V.] in your solemn
assemblies: though ye offer me burnt-offerings and meat-offerings,
I will not accept them. . . . But let judgment run down as
waters and righteousness as a mighty stream." [2] It is under
the form of knowledge that the prophets express the moral
relationship between Yahweh and his people. Yahweh knew
Israel, and Israel has refused to know Yahweh. " There is no
truth, nor mercy (love), nor knowledge of God in the land. . . .
My people are destroyed for lack of knowledge; because thou
hast rejected knowledge, I will also reject thee." [3] For
Amos, this knowledge lies in the practical recognition of
social justice, in the observance of humanity and fair dealing
between man and man. For Hosea, its essential note is love,
the love of the child for its father, of the bride for her husband.
His own bitter experience of the unfaithfulness of the wife he
loved lends a unique pathos to Hosea's picture of Yahweh's
unfailing tenderness to Israel, and of Israel's desertion of Yahweh
to gratify a carnal desire for the Canaanitish Baalim. She has
broken the bond of her betrothal; and in anguish of heart Yahweh
is driven to pronounce her doom. " And now will I discover her
lewdness in the sight of her lovers, and none shall deliver her out
of mine hand." [4]

§ 8. We have dwelt in some detail on the prophetic message
of Amos and Hosea, because it initiated a new era of incalculable
significance in the development of the religion of Israel. The
essential features of their teaching were unfolded with varied

[1] Wellhausen, who points out further how the prophets absorbed
into their religion the new conception of world-power (i.e. Assyria), which
was destroying other nations and their religions.

[2] Hos. vi. 6, Amos. v. 21–4; cf. Is. i. 11–17, xxii. 12–13.

[3] Hos. iv. 1, 6; cf. Amos iii. 2, 10, and Hos. ii. 19–20, v. 3, viii. 2.
Amos insists on Yahweh's knowledge of Israel, Hosea on Israel's failure
to know Yahweh.

[4] Hos. ii. 10; cf. i, iii, xi. 1–8, and the final denunciation in xiii.

application to the changing course of Hebrew history by the prophets of the succeeding age. With the fall of the northern kingdom (721), the centre of interest shifts southwards to Judah. Here, under kings of the lineage of David, government was centralised and stable. Social life, save in the court at Jerusalem, was simpler and less luxurious. Hitherto the Assyrian menace had been more remote. But now the conquest of Samaria brought the enemy to the very gate. The national crisis provided, as always, the occasion for prophetic revelation, in the persons of Micah, a peasant from the Philistine border, and Isaiah of Jerusalem, the grandest figure in Hebrew prophecy. The work of Isaiah was spread over the last forty years of the eighth century and culminated under king Hezekiah in 701, when Sennacherib's Assyrians invaded Judah and appeared before the walls of the capital. His prophecies are contained in the first thirty-nine chapters of the book which bears his name.[1] In substance they strike the note already sounded by Amos and Hosea, of stern denunciation of national sin and of Yahweh's impending judgement at the hand of Assyria. Isaiah's governing conception is that of holiness, a term current in the popular religion, to which he gives a new spiritual meaning; Yahweh is not only the " Lord of hosts " but " the Holy One of Israel," and Israel a holy people consecrated to his service. It was Yahweh's holiness, in contrast with his own uncleanness and that of Israel, which smote the prophet with shame and terror in the magnificent vision that called him to the prophetic ministry.[2] The law of holiness is exemplified, as in Amos, by the requirement of social justice, as in Hosea, by that of personal devotion. " The Lord of hosts shall be exalted in judgment, and God that is Holy shall be sanctified in

[1] Esp. in cc. i–xii, xiv. 24–xxiii, xxviii–xxxii. The present form of the book of Isaiah is post-exilic. Any discussion of the problems raised by modern criticism lies beyond our province. The reader should consult Robertson Smith, *Prophets of Israel*, lecture v. (esp. *note* 7, p. 422), and Driver's *Introduction to the Literature of the O.T.* For more drastic views see Cheyne's *Introduction to Isaiah* and his article (Isaiah) in the *Encyclopaedia Biblica*. For the Second Isaiah, see § 15, below.

[2] Is. vi : the vision should be carefully studied. In the traditional religion, the "holy " thing was *taboo*, i.e. prohibited to human use, as " charged " with supernatural properties; see Robertson Smith, *Religion of the Semites*, lecture iv (and *note* B) and Joshua vii (story of Achan), 1 Sam. xv (Saul and Agag), 2 Sam. vi (Uzzah and the ark). In Isaiah, the word has a purely inward and spiritual reference, to consecration and purification of the heart. The fact that the same word is used as the title of the temple-prostitutes, set apart for the sensual rites of the sanctuary, which were not suppressed till the Deuteronomic reformation, will serve as a measure of the gulf between the higher prophecy and the popular religion of the day.

righteousness." The sin of the people is that "they have cast away
the law of the Lord of hosts and despised the word of the Holy
One of Israel." [1] Isaiah is distinguished from his predecessors by
the long stretch of his prophetic activity, and by his position as
a recognised political adviser of the king.[2] Within the state
he preached justice towards the peasantry who formed, as in
northern Israel, the backbone of the nation, and the need of
realising religious obligations as an integral part of ordinary
life.[3] In foreign policy, he urged that Judah should steer clear
of international entanglements, especially of alliance with Egypt
and other powers against Assyria.[4] "Take heed and be quiet"
was his early counsel to Ahaz, repeated years afterwards to
Hezekiah in face of Sennacherib's onset, "in quietness and confidence shall be your strength." [5] The ruin of the Assyrian
army established Isaiah's authority in the eyes of the king and
of the people. It did more than this, for it gave Judah a
breathing-space to absorb the lesson of the prophetic teaching.
In the northern kingdom, disaster had followed swiftly on the
warnings of Amos and Hosea. Neither among the captives in
Assyria nor among the relics in Palestine did any trace of the
religion of Yahweh survive. Had Judah suffered a like fate
at the hand of Sennacherib, before the religious life of her people
had won new power from Isaiah's message, the faith in a purely
national God would have perished with the nation's downfall.
But Isaiah's confidence was justified by the event; the danger
passed, and the rapid decline of the Assyrian power staved off
the fall of Judah for a century. When that fall came at the
hands of Babylon, Isaiah's message had taken root. Already
in his lifetime a faithful remnant gathered round him and formed
the nucleus of a religious community within and, distinct from,
the nation. In this band of disciples [6] the prophet saw the

[1] Is. v. 24.
[2] Cf. his relations with Ahaz at the time of the Syro-Ephraimitish
invasion (735–4), Is. vii. 1–16, and with Hezekiah at the time of Sennacherib's invasion (701), 2 Kings xviii. 13–xx (from which source Is. xxxvi–
xxxix is mainly derived).
[3] Condemnation of injustice and luxury, Is. i. 21–3, iii. 16–23, v. 8–23,
x. 1–3; cf. Mic. ii. 2, iii. 2–3, 11.
Condemnation of sorcery and witchcraft, Is. ii. 6, viii. 19.
Condemnation of idolatry, Is. i. 29–30, ii. 8, 18, 20; cf. Mic. i. 7.
Condemnation of priests and prophets, Is. xxviii. 7 f., xxx. 8 f.; Mic. ii.
11, iii. 5–7, 11.
[4] The Egyptian alliance is denounced in Is. xxx–xxxi.
[5] Is. vii. 4, xxx. 15.
[6] Is. viii. 16, which means probably "I will tie up the testimony and
seal the teaching in the heart of my disciples"; cf. Jer. xxxi. 33. The
Jewish papyri at Assouan (fifth century B.C.) were found tied up and sealed.

promise of an eventual restoration, after Yahweh had visited his judgement upon the existing state; of a purified Zion, under a prince of the old Davidic line and with a sovereignty over the surrounding peoples; of an Israel made holy by suffering and living its national life in perfect accordance with Yahweh's law. " Therefore, saith the Lord, the Lord of hosts, the Mighty One of Israel, Ah, I will ease me of mine adversaries and avenge me of mine enemies; and I will turn my hand upon thee, and purely purge away thy dross, and take away all thy tin; and I will restore thy judges as at the first, and thy counsellors as at the beginning; afterward thou shalt be called the city of righteousness; the faithful city." [1] The note of hope had been sounded, and henceforward the faith in a restoration of Israel persisted, with ever-growing intensity, as an essential feature in Hebrew prophecy.

§ 9. Isaiah's influence bore fruit, possibly in his own lifetime, and certainly, after a period of reaction under Manasseh, in the religious reformation under king Josiah (639–608). The Deuteronomic code, officially promulgated in 621, was the work of his school and is pervaded throughout by the spirit of his teaching.[2] Its aim was intensely practical, to bring the actual daily life of the Hebrews into conformity with the prophetic ideal. All idolatry and image-worship were forbidden, together with other survivals of Canaanitish cults; social relations and religious observances alike were regulated in the spirit of the prophets.[3] Above all, the local sanctuaries were ruthlessly

[1] Is. i. 24–6; cf. vii. 3, xxviii. 16 f. Isaiah, the native of Jerusalem and royal adviser, has none of the prejudice against the city, and in favour of a reversion to nomadic life, that is characteristic of his prophetic predecessors. If c. ix. 1–7 and c. xi are Isaianic, as many authorities hold them to be, they afford the most striking expressions of the hope of restoration. The passage in c. xi has had a memorable history. The fourth Eclogue of the Roman poet Virgil contains lines that are closely analogous; cf. Ecl. iv. 21 f., v. 60 and Is. xi. 6–8. This resemblance in Virgil to a prophecy which was interpreted as referring to Christ goes far to account for the peculiar reverence felt towards Virgil in early Christian and in mediæval times. Cheyne notes (Religious Life, p. 103 note) that in the cathedral of Zamora in Spain Virgil is represented among the Hebrew prophets. Probably both Virgil and the Hebrew prophet gave independent expression to a common oriental idea.

[2] It is contained in Deut. v–xxvi, and is a republication of older law, modified by the prophetic teaching. For the story of the reformation, see 2 Kings xxii–xxiii.

[3] Isaiah had condemned the worship of images and of spirits in trees (i. 29 f., xvii. 10). Image-worship had already been condemned by Hosea (viii. 4–6, x. 5, xiii. 2), whose influence on Deuteronomy was greater than that of any other of the eighth-century prophets. Deuteronomy enjoins humanity and justice towards the widow and the orphan, the slave, the foreign settler, and even dumb animals.

abolished, and the purified religious worship centralised in the temple at Jerusalem. Had the mass of the nation proved capable of following in the path thus marked out for them, the Deuteronomic legislation might have furnished an efficient instrument of reformation. But this was not to be; the prophetic ideal remained an ideal, impotent to change the hearts, save of a small minority. The contrast between precept and practice is as evident on the eve of the ruin of Jerusalem, as it had been on the eve of the ruin of Samaria.

§ 10. It was this obstinate rejection of Yahweh's declared will that branded itself upon the soul of Jeremiah.[1] Once again, the enemy was at the gates; not the Assyrians, whose day of empire had passed, but Nebuchadrezzar of Babylon. The hour of captivity was at hand, and the death-throes of Judah found utterance in the prophet's cry of despairing anguish. Jeremiah, the priest from Anathoth, had in his youth championed the Deuteronomic reformation; but now it seemed a hollow mockery, and its watchword " the temple of Yahweh " a shibboleth of lying priests and prophets. The temple of Zion, the sanctuary of the renovated ritual, would share the doom of that of Shiloh. " How do ye say, we are wise and the law of the Lord with us ? Lo, certainly in vain made he it; the pen of the scribes is in vain." " A wonderful and horrible thing is come to pass in the land; the prophets prophesy falsely, and the priests bear rule by their means; and my people love to have it so : and what will ye do in the end thereof ? " [2] Jeremiah's call was to a worship

---

[1] Jeremiah first came forward as a prophet in 626, at the time of the Scythian invasion, described by Herodotus (i. 103 f.), which called forth the prophecies in Jer. iv–vi. Zephaniah, possibly a prince of the blood royal, prophesied at the same crisis (see Zeph. ii. 3 f.). The Scythians helped to weaken the declining power of Assyria; they annihilated the Philistines and reached the borders of Egypt, but Judah seems to have been spared. Zephaniah saw in their coming the " day of Yahweh," see Zeph. i. 14 f., a passage which inspired the Christian hymn *Dies irae, dies illa.* Jeremiah survived the final capture of Jerusalem by Nebuchadrezzar in 586. The chief of his prophecies are contained in cc. i–xxiv; the restoration-prophecies in cc. xxx–xxxiii have been questioned by some recent critics, but are accepted by Wellhausen, Driver and Cornill, as substantially the work of Jeremiah (except xxxiii. 14–26). We are told (c. xxxvi) that the earlier prophecies were republished *with additions* by Baruch at Jeremiah's command many years after their delivery. The prophecies of Nahum (c. 612, the date of the fall of Nineveh) and Habakkuk (shortly before 600) belong to the same epoch. Habakkuk gives a new turn to the conception of " the day "; as in the popular view, it is a day of Israel's triumph over Assyria, but interpreted ethically is a triumph of the *righteous* nation over the *wicked.*

[2] Jer. viii. 8, v. 30, 31. On Jeremiah's early preaching of the Deuteronomic law, see c. xi. 1–8; on the temple worship, see c. vii; on the

resting not on the formalities of the temple-service, but on inward purity of heart. He appealed from external ordinance and book-religion to a spiritual temple and spiritual sacrifices. In clearer tones than any preceding prophet, he gave utterance to the claims of personal religion. Those of a later age who pleaded against legalism in the name of inward piety looked back with good reason to Jeremiah as a source of inspiration.[1] This tragedy of a sensitive and retiring nature, compelled by an imperious call to denounce the disobedience of rulers and people, and to foretell their impending ruin, appealed with compelling force to the imagination of after-times. Fearless, amid continual risk to life, in the discharge of his vocation, "like a lamb or an ox that is brought to the slaughter," a hero, as a sympathetic writer has said, not by nature but by grace, Jeremiah was keenly conscious of his isolation. There was not one that doeth justly, that seeketh truth, in all Jerusalem.[2] He longed in vain to be freed from the agony of his mission : " Oh, that I had in the wilderness a lodging-place of wayfaring men ; that I might leave my people and go from them ! for they be all adulterers, an assembly of treacherous men." [3] Jeremiah is the pioneer of the religious lyric and the inspirer of many of the Psalms ; some have even seen in him the model for Isaiah liii. Despairing of national repentance, " Can the Ethiopian change his skin, or the leopard his spots ? then may ye also do good, that are accustomed to do evil," [4] he found refuge in the thought of a new covenant, not as of old between Yahweh and the nation, but between Yahweh and the individual Israelite. " In those days they shall say no more, the fathers have eaten a sour grape and the children's teeth are set on edge. But every one shall die for his own iniquity : every man that eateth the sour grape, his teeth shall be set on edge. . . . This shall be the covenant that I will make with the house of Israel after those days, saith the Lord ; I will put my law in their inward

---

false prophets, c. xiv. 13–16, xxiii. 9 ff., and c. xxviii, where Hananiah, Jeremiah's adversary, stands for the political faith that inspired Josiah's reformation.

[1] Cf. Jeremiah's spiritual conception of the new covenant, xxxi. 31–4, quoted below in the text, with, e.g. Ps. xl. 6–8. It is noteworthy that Jeremiah is the forerunner of a religion that is both inward personal communion of the individual with God and universal in its appeal not only to the Jew but to all mankind. In both respects he heralded the spirit of Christianity, as Ezekiel heralded that of later Judaism.

[2] Jer. xi. 19 : the writer quoted is Cheyne ; Jer. v. 1. On the attempts to take his life, see xi. 18 ff. (the men of his native Anathoth), xviii. 18, xxvi. 8 ff., xxxviii. 4.

[3] Jer. ix. 2 ; cf. Ps. lv. 5–8.   [4] Jer. xiii. 23.

parts, and write it in their hearts; and will be their God and they shall be my people : and they shall teach no more every man his neighbour, and every man his brother, saying, know the Lord : for they shall all know me, from the least of them unto the greatest of them, saith the Lord : for I will forgive their iniquity and I will remember their sin no more." [1] This utterance strikes a new note in the spiritual education of Israel. The vision of earlier prophets had been dimmed by the absorption of the individual in the life and destiny of the nation. It was not till Jeremiah realised that the true Israel was narrowed to himself that this prejudice could be overcome. Henceforward a consciousness of the worth of personal religion in Yahweh's sight was an abiding possession of Hebrew prophecy. Judah indeed passed into captivity before Jeremiah's eyes, and the gulf that severed the ideal from the actual seemed more impassable than at any previous moment of history. The chief of the people were deported to Babylon in 597; eleven years later Jerusalem was laid in ruins and the Jewish state ceased to exist (586). But Jeremiah's faith in Yahweh as the living God of Israel was unshaken by the political dissolution of the nation. Nebuchadrezzar was Yahweh's servant, and Yahweh had delivered Israel into his hand.[2] The prophet's mission was destined to a richer fulfilment than he dreamed of. If, to all appearance, his words had failed to save the nation's soul, the reverse was literally the truth. Borne away by the captives into exile, they were pregnant with vitalising energy for the coming time. The hour of secular downfall furnished the occasion for Israel to enter upon her spiritual mission to mankind.

III. The Exile and After (§§ 11–16).

§ 11. The captivity in Babylonia made a profound impression on the original history of the exiles. The temple at Jerusalem, where religious worship had been centralised under the Deuteronomic reformation, lay in ruins.[3] The chosen people lay, as it were, under an interdict. The hope of the old popular religion, that Yahweh would save Israel from her enemies, had been rudely shattered; the "day," as Amos and Isaiah had predicted, had proved a day of darkness and not of light. Had it not been for the seed of a higher faith implanted by the teaching of the prophets,

---

[1] Jer. xxxi. 29–34.   [2] Jer. xxvii.

[3] The site was, however, not inaccessible (see Jer. xli. 5) and a continuous life seems to have gone on among those left in Judaea, though they lacked sufficient energy to effect any restoration.

the exiles might well have been absorbed, in accordance with the intention of their conquerors, in the religious and national life of Babylonia. But in fact it was otherwise; the very circumstance of their isolation gave fresh vitality to what was highest and most distinctive in their faith. It proved, first, a powerful stimulus to the religion of personal piety, which had found expression in the prophecies of Jeremiah. The individual soul sought consolation and refuge in personal communion with Yahweh. Secondly, in sharp contrast to this devotion of the heart, the exiles recalled with loyal attachment the traditions of the old temple-worship; and they gathered, in close and loving study, the inheritance of ceremonial lore. Priestly scribes interpreted and developed the law; sabbath-meetings were held for prayer and the reading of the prophets; fasting and corporate humiliation became the practice; and the congregation began to take the place of the vanished nation. The age of the exile was that of the foundation of the Jewish church. Priestly authority and ecclesiastical institutions acquired a new value. The conviction grew that the religion of Yahweh could be preserved only by strict fulfilment of legal precept. The same symptoms were repeated in later times, both after the restoration in the fifth century, and again in the legalism of Rabbinic teaching, after the destruction of the second temple by the Romans and the final dispersion of the Jewish people. In the third place, the exiles turned for comfort and hope to the vision of a restored Zion, when Israel should once more dwell in his own land, and princes of the lineage of David rule in righteousness as ministers of Yahweh's will. This is the predominant note of exilic and post-exilic prophecy. The word of Yahweh was no longer one of anger and impending doom. Now that the judgment had fallen on Israel's sin, Yahweh revealed himself in loving-kindness, as the gracious deliverer and redeemer of his people. These three characteristics of the exilic epoch are already manifest in the prophecy of Ezekiel, a Hebrew priest deported to Babylonia in 597, whose prophetic work belongs to the opening years of the captivity (592–570). His book leaves on the reader a strong impression of the unity of its structure, and it may be that it exists to-day very nearly as Ezekiel wrote it by the banks of the Chebar five and twenty centuries ago. Yet it is possible that, as some critics hold, part of the work was written in Jerusalem, and that portions (e.g. of the closing chapters) were added by a later hand. Unlike earlier prophecy, it is largely a literary composition rather than a collection of spoken utterances, though it contains some oral prophecies,[1] and comprises a sequence of discourses arranged in methodical order by his own hand. It abounds in vision and symbolism, and reflects throughout the temper of the priestly theologian.[2] Ezekiel (a) was uncompromising in his assertion of individual responsibility and retribution. He broke once and for all with the traditional conception of Yahweh as a jealous God, visiting the sins of the fathers upon the children. Each man stands or falls in Yahweh's sight by his own acts. " The son shall not bear the iniquity of the father, neither shall the father bear the iniquity of the son; the righteousness of the righteous shall be upon him, and the wickedness of the wicked shall be upon him." [3] There is no thought yet of retribution in a future life. Earthly prosperity and misfortune are apportioned in accordance with moral desert. We shall see in a later section how this exaggerated individualism failed to satisfy the developed moral consciousness of the Hebrew people. But, in view of the exclusive insistence of the earlier religious teaching on the claims of the community, it was necessary and natural for Ezekiel to stress, with an equally one-sided emphasis, the complementary claim of the individual, that Yahweh's judgement should be determined by reference to his acts and to his alone. The prophet was confronted with the murmur of the exiles that God's ways were not equal, and his answer, in that it recognised the worth of individual personality, represents an ethical advance. No real progress was possible in moral reflection till the doctrine of personal retribution had been affirmed and found wanting. Again (b), the closing chapters of Ezekiel's book contain the promise of Israel's restoration. Yahweh will gather his scattered sheep out of all lands : " I will make them one nation in the land, upon the mountains of Israel . . . and David my servant shall be king over them . . . My tabernacle also shall be with them; yea, I will be their God and they shall be my people. And the heathen shall know that I the Lord do sanctify Israel, when my sanctuary shall be in the midst of them for evermore." [4] Ezekiel's horizon is limited to the

[1] Ezek. xxxiii. 30, 31.   On these disputed questions see the Introduction to Cooke's *Ezekiel* in the International Critical Commentary.

[2] In Ezekiel we can trace the origin of the apocalyptic literature which later took the place of prophecy; see § 15 below.   Unlike preexilic prophecy, that of the captivity and after assumes a literary form; it was written down by the prophet himself and not necessarily spoken at all.

[3] Ezek. xviii. 20; see the whole chapter and xiv. 12–30, xxxiii. 1–20.

[4] Ezek. xxxiii–xlviii, esp. xxxvi; the quotation is from xxxvii. 21–8.

future of the chosen people; the Gentiles have no place in the
Messianic kingdom, but survive the triumph of Israel only to
perish in the moment of their acknowledgement of Yahweh's
omnipotence.[1] Zeal for Yahweh's honour dominates the whole
sequence of Ezekiel's prophecies. Yahweh is bound to restore
Israel, so runs his thought, for thus only will his honour be
vindicated and his power be made manifest in the sight of all the
earth. Hence he dwelt on the immeasurable gulf that parted man's
impurity from the holiness of Yahweh. The restored Israel will
be made clean. The priest in Ezekiel is clearly manifest in (c)
this ideal of ceremonial purity. In the nine concluding chapters,
he sketches the ideal constitution for the restored community.
The formalism of his outlook and his conception of ritual holiness
are obvious on every page. The governing idea was that of a
priestly hierarchy, championed by Messianic princes of the
house of David, and regulating the religious life of Israel from a
renovated temple. The measurements of the new sanctuary
were prescribed in minute detail. Circumcision was commanded
not as a national custom, but as a divine ordinance. Ezekiel
was the forerunner of the theocratic ideal actually embodied in the
institutions of the restoration epoch, and the true father of the
Priestly code. Legalism and the conception of a church-nation
had come to stay. The age of the prophets was about to give place
to that of the law.

§ 12. As it is our purpose, not to review the history of Hebrew
religious life in its varied manifestations, but rather to illustrate
its bequest to modern civilization, we shall not trace the growth
of legalism in the exilic and post-exilic periods, or dwell on the
crust of pedantry and formalism which at times obscured the
larger teaching of the great prophets.[2] Yet the influence of the

[1] Ezek. xxxviii, xxxix. But these eschatological chapters and considerable parts of chapters xl to xlviii may have been added later.

[2] After the law had established its autocracy as the complete system
of divine commands in the restored community, there was no longer room
for *personal* inspiration. Hence no new writer could come forward without the *imprimatur* of the law. Additions to the prophetic writings were
ascribed to prophets (e.g. Daniel) anterior to the law. Pride of authorship
was foreign to the Semitic temper and to the spirit of Hebrew prophecy;
the titles ascribing prophecies to their authors are additions of later date.
The apocalyptic that took the place of prophecy (see below, § 16) was
pseudonymous. Rabbinical Judaism, which was legalistic, turned its
back on apocalyptic in the first century A.D., leaving the field to Christian
writers of apocalypses. Christian apocalyptic, freed from bondage to the
law, threw over pseudonymity, but Jewish apocalyptic retained it through
the early centuries of our era and the middle age. See Charles, *Eschatology*,
pp. 196 ff., 403 f.

prophets on the religion of Israel was never greater than in the centuries succeeding the restoration. "The view that Ezra's lawbook turned Judaism into an arid ritualism and legalism is refuted by the whole literature of the following time." So writes Dr. Moore,[1] having in mind many of the finest of the Psalms, Proverbs, Job, and additions to the prophetic writings that date from the Persian and Greek periods. It was only very gradually that the prophetic inspiration was choked; it remained a living force until the ascendancy of Pharisaism. The centuries which followed the restoration were of crucial significance for the subsequent history of Judaism. In them were determined the essential lines of its religious and moral practice for after-time. When Cyrus conquered Babylon, he granted leave to the exiles to return to their homes (538–7). A century later (458) the restored community was joined by a priestly company under Ezra, who brought with him a renovated law, the work of Babylonian Jews. This law, promulgated by Ezra in 397, served henceforward as the guiding rule of the community. The Deuteronomic law was transformed into the Priestly code and the traditions of the past were re-edited as the Priestly history. The Pentateuch assumed a form virtually identical with that in which we read it in our Bibles to-day. The note of Ezra's reconstruction was that already sounded by Ezekiel, of sacerdotalism. An artificial Israel, a congregation rather than a state, inspired by the ideal of Levitical holiness, gathered under the presidency of the high priest around the temple-worship at Jerusalem.[2] Everything in Israel, so run the post-exilic teaching, is Yahweh's by right; if the prescribed dues are paid, he will send his blessing on the remainder. The principle was a noble one; but its application by the casuists became well-nigh unbearable.[3] The breach of ritual prescriptions, often devoid of ethical significance, came to be regarded as sin of equal gravity with violations of the moral law; for both alike, as commands

[1] *Judaism*, I. 16.
[2] The second temple was built in 516; the tone of this period is reflected in Haggai and Zechariah, i–viii. On external holiness, see Lev. xii.; xiv, 1–18, 33–53; xv. 16–30. It is well, however, to remember Kuenen's remark (*Religion of Israel*, ii. 285): "We cannot but own that they were grand and beautiful designs which the lawgiver" (of the Priestly code) "had in view. He formed broadly the idea of a holy people dedicated to Yahweh, and tried to realise it on a large scale."
[3] See Inge: *Outspoken Essays, St. Paul*, pp. 211, 215–16, on the "seminary education" under the Rabbis in apostolic times.

D

of Yahweh, were of unconditional obligation.[1] In course of time the authority of the scribes, whose task was to edit and expound the law, tended to replace that of the priestly corporation.[2] Judaism became more and more the religion of a sacred book.[3] From this source sprang the oral law, with its ever-growing burden. Above all, the bar of separation between the Jew who observed the reconstituted law, on the one hand, and the heretic Samaritan and heathen Gentile, on the other, was made absolute. The rite of circumcision, the hall-mark of national particularism, was presented in the Priestly history as an integral part of the religion of Yahweh, the sign of his everlasting covenant with Abraham. We can see the reason that prompted the Jews of the restoration to prescribe this rigorous exclusiveness. Under the Persian, and especially under the Macedonian empires, contact between East and West grew more intimate, racial barriers were gradually broken down, and the pious worshippers of Yahweh might easily have lost their identity and been merged in the heathen world around them, had they not fenced in their distinctive faith, and therewith their distinctive nationality, with a ring-wall of ceremonial law. They alone were holy to Yahweh, all others were uncircumcised and profane. This consciousness of a peculiar vocation, and the unswerving resolve to be loyal to its obligations, were intensified in the second century by the persecution of Antiochus Epiphanes (175–164), and subsequently by the conquest by Rome. We can trace to this period the origin of the astonishing persistency that marks Jewish religion and Jewish racial character through all succeeding history. There is unquestionably a grandeur in the spectacle of a small and despised people, bereft of the natural and political bulwarks of unity, thus forging artificial stanchions, which availed to preserve their nationality as a rock amid the storms that beat on every side. The price paid was heavy, the imposition of a burden too grievous to be borne, and the final closing of the door to spiritual fellowship with the Gentile world.

[1] See, for example, Exod. xxx. 33, Lev. x. 1–16, xiv. 33–53, and Lev. generally.
[2] After the close of the Persian period in 332, the scribes appear as a class distinct from the priesthood.
[3] The canon of scripture was not yet fixed even in the first century A.D. Christianity took over the Jewish scriptures and therewith the doctrine of literal inspiration; adding the N.T., which was much more homogeneous in contents and in plane of spiritual teaching than the O.T. With the effects of a book-religion on pre-Christian Judaism we may compare those of its revival after the Reformation, still discernible to-day.

Henceforward, it was only by a revolutionary breach with Jewish orthodoxy that the spirit of the religion of the prophets could permeate western civilisation. We must look elsewhere than to the law for the main legacy of Israel to mankind.[1] The law was the shell rather than the kernel of post-exilic religious life. Side by side with ceremonial formalism developed a religion of inward piety and devotion. Side by side with the particularism of the orthodox congregation broke the vision of an ideal kingdom in Zion which should embrace all nations, and bring salvation not only to the Israelite, but to the Gentile.[2]

§ 13. It was entirely natural that this twofold expression of religious faith, the ideals of a personal communion with God and of his universal kingdom, should arise coincidently with the particularism of the law. An illustration of this tendency

[1] This statement must not be taken as a denial of the obvious influence exercised by the Mosaic law on the history of Christianity. For example, the moral precepts contained in the Pentateuch left a deep mark on Christian ethics. Christianity, when fused with Hellenism, preserved the lofty moral code which it inherited from Judaism. It is only necessary to mention the Decalogue. Again, the history of the priesthood and of Christian sacerdotalism was influenced by the Jewish priestly code and the Jewish conception of the priestly office. The epistle to the Hebrews is an early illustration of this influence, which left its mark also on the Christian doctrine of atonement. Yet the Christian priesthood, unlike the Jewish, was never hereditary and often celibate. Christian juridical thought was also influenced by the Mosaic law, as is evident from Aquinas' tractate *de legibus* (S. Th. ii. 1. qq. 90–108). The Mosaic law served as a model for modifications introduced by Constantine and his Christian successors in the empire into the criminal law of Rome. "The laws of Moses," wrote Gibbon (c. 44), "were received as the divine original of justice, and the Christian princes adapted their penal statutes to the degrees of moral and religious turpitude": e.g. adultery was made a capital offence. This juridical influence of the Jewish law received a strong impetus at the time of the Reformation. Prior to that time, it did not seriously affect the actual laws of western peoples. Alfred refers to Moses in the prologue to his Anglo-Saxon code, but the laws that follow show no trace of the influence. On the other hand, Protestant communities frequently embodied Mosaic precepts in their legislation. In a manifesto issued by the German peasantry in 1525, we find the demand "that all doctors of laws should be abolished and that justice should be administered according to the law of Moses, because it is not good for man to get better law than that proclaimed by God" (Vinogradoff, *Roman Law in Mediæval Europe*, p. 129.) The early colonists in Massachusetts refused to adopt trial by jury on the ground that it was not authorised in "Moses his judicials." The death penalty for witchcraft and for sabbath-breaking, there and elsewhere in Puritan communities, was justified by reference to Mosaic authority. Of Luther's teaching, J. N. Figgis writes (*From Gerson to Grotius*, p. 209): "law is for Luther, whether natural, moral, or civil, all embodied in the ten commandments, and anything else is mere administrative regulation, whether in state or church."

[2] See Additional Note at the close of this chapter, on post-exilic Jewish history.

of the extremes of individualism and universalism to meet in intimate conjunction is afforded by contemporary Hellenism, where, on the decay of the free city-state after the Macedonian conquest, the Stoic philosophers insisted equally on the claims of individual virtue and on membership of a cosmopolitan society. Both ideals are prominent in Jewish religious literature of the exilic and post-exilic epochs. In regard to the former, it is very necessary to observe, especially after what has been said about the formalism that marked the institution of the Priestly code, how the rule of the law fostered in the Jewish community a lofty moral standard and a rich vein of piety. The strength of the religion of Israel was, in part, rooted in its very weakness.[1] The local synagogue, with its meetings for public prayer and for the reading and interpretation of scripture, proved a powerful stimulus to individual religion. Still more noteworthy is the fact that the temple-worship itself nurtured a spirit of fervent piety, which won enduring expression in the Psalter. The product of many successive compilations, ranging in date from the period of the captivity to the second century, these songs of unknown authorship, comprising the Psalter, have been called with good reason " the hymn-book of the second temple." [2] They testify on every page how the heart of the individual Jew beat in unison with that of his religious community. He lived and moved and had his being in the life of the spiritual Israel. If Yahweh is no remote divinity, but " a very present help in trouble," it is because he " watches over Israel." If his soul panteth after Yahweh " as the hart panteth after the water brooks," it is because he is parted from the temple-sanctuary, where the God of heaven and earth has his peculiar dwelling in the midst of his

[1] Mr. Claude Montefiore, in the Hibbert Lectures for 1892 on *Hebrew Religion*, has shown clearly how the law fostered the higher moral and spiritual life of the post-exilic community. The ethical results of " legalism " were not what might *a priori* have been expected. " One needs," he says, " to be very cautious in writing about the law " (p. 478, *note* 1). Chastity, benevolence and, above all, joy in loving service marked the life of the orthodox followers of the law. It was not felt as a burden by the Jew; though from the point of view of universalism it was a burden. In this chapter the religion of Israel is treated exclusively from this standpoint; its value within the pale of Judaism lies beyond our scope. On Judaism in the first century A.D. see Mr. Montefiore's chapter, entitled *The Spirit of Judaism*, in Jackson and Lake's *The Beginnings of Christianity*, vol. i.

[2] Though, unlike our hymn-books, they were never in the hands of the congregation. It is possible that some of the Psalms are pre-exilic, but improbable that any are of Davidic authorship. See Driver, *Introduction*, and Cheyne, *Origin of the Psalter*.

chosen people.[1] When the Psalmist speaks in the first person, it is not in his own name but in that of the spiritual corporation in which his private personality is absorbed. Some of the Psalms are inspired directly by devotion to the law; others, in a narrower vein, express the aspirations and the sufferings of the champions of rigid orthodoxy, the *Chasîdim* (Asidæans or "pious," the forerunners of the Pharisees), who laid down their lives in resistance to Hellenism in the days of Antiochus Epiphanes.[2] Side by side with the utterance of faith in Yahweh and of joy in his presence, we hear the voice of ancient national memories, of hopes for national deliverance, and of delight in the worship of the temple. But the interest of the Psalter for us lies rather in its embodiment of a spirit of religious devotion transcending the narrow bounds of the priestly worship and the law. The sway that these poems have exercised over the human heart for more than two thousand years bears witness to the intensity and breadth of feeling that inspired their nameless authors by the waters of Babylon and in the restored community of Palestine. In certain Psalms personal piety consciously breaks through the barriers of external prescript, and appeals from the written law to that inscribed upon the heart.[3] It is this variety and wealth of religious emotion, embracing all the moods in which the human spirit turns towards God, alike in good and evil days, that has made the Psalter the hymn-book, not merely of the second temple, but of Judaism in all ages, and also of the Christian church.

§ 14. If the pious Israelite found satisfaction for his aspirations in the practical religion of the temple-service and in observance of the law, he was at the same time confronted with an ethical and theological problem which caused grave searchings of heart. The doctrine of Ezekiel, echoed in certain of the Psalms,[4] that each man is duly rewarded or punished for his deserts in the course of his earthly life, could not maintain its hold in the face of facts. The fortunes of the individual were manifestly dependent on those of his fellows; nor was the meed of outward happiness proportioned to his merit. It was this practical contradiction, rather than any speculative inconsistency, that

---

[1] Ps. xlii.

[2] Devotion to the law, esp. Ps. cxix. Ps. i. expresses the feelings of the "pious" or "righteous," in contrast with the "wicked," "sinners," "the scornful" (cf. xii. 1). Reference to the temple is conspicuous in Pss. xxiv, xxvii, lxv, cxxxviii. For an outline classification of the themes of the Psalter, see Driver, *Introduction*, pp. 368–9.

[3] E.g. Pss. xl, l, li.

[4] E.g. Ps. i. 3; xxxiv. 19–21; Prov. xi. 31.

stirred men to question the divine justice.[1] Some minds took
refuge in the distinction between external prosperity and inward satisfaction; others in the thought that the sufferings of
the righteous were not punitive, but disciplinary, while the
good fortune of the wicked served only to heighten the eventual
catastrophe of his ruin.[2] But the conception of suffering as retributive for sin was too deeply rooted in the Hebrew mind for such
solutions to be acceptable. The problem which thus arose forms
the theme of the dramatic poem of Job. Why do the wicked
prosper and the righteous suffer unmerited misery? The writer
feels that it is unanswerable in terms of personal sin; but, while
formulating the difficulty, he offers no adequate solution. The
Prologue seems to give grounds for the suggestion that Job
suffered as a martyr-witness to God's justice while himself
remaining unconscious of the purpose of his sufferings, viz., the
vindication of disinterested piety. His final appeal is from the
facts of outward circumstance to the dictates of moral faith;
his practical assurance of Yahweh's righteousness remains unshaken at the close.[3] In a single passage he gives a momentary
suggestion of the hope, which was destined, from the second
century onwards, to gain ground among the Jews, in a resurrection
of the righteous to enjoy the personal vision of Yahweh.[4] We
shall return presently to this belief, merely noting here that it
emerges not as an inference from speculative premisses, but as a

---

[1] Job xxi. 1–15.   [2] Ps. xxxiv. 19; xxxvii. esp. 35, 36.

[3] See Dr. Robinson's booklet entitled *The Cross of Job* (Religion and
Life Books), pp. 64–69, and Charles, *Eschatology*, pp. 69–73. In the
volume on Job in the *International Critical Commentary* (Driver and Gray),
the fifth century is suggested as the probable date of the poem.

[4] Job xix. 25–7 : see Charles, p. 71, and Driver, *Introduction*, p. 418
("The thought of a future beatific life is *nascent* in the book of Job").
In the volume on Job in the *International Critical Commentary*, the passage
is thus rendered by Gray :

v. 25.	But I know that my vindicator liveth,
	And that hereafter he will stand up upon the dust.
v 26.	And . . . .
	And away from my flesh I shall behold God.
v. 27.	Whom *I* shall behold (to be) on my side,
	And mine eyes shall see (to be) unestranged.

The first half of v. 26 presents almost hopeless difficulty. The word
translated "redeemer" in A.V. means a vindicator from undeserved
wrong (see R.V. *marg.*). The *I* in v. 27 is emphatic. In his commentary,
Gray interprets the passage as expressing Job's conviction, not of a
continued life of blessedness after death, but of a momentary vision of
God after death, revealing that God is with him. On the belief in a
resurrection, see below, § 15.

conclusion forced upon the mind by the practical difficulties of life. This fact is sufficient of itself to rule out the suggestion that the appearance of the new belief was due to Hellenic influence. Despite the subjection of the Jews to Macedonian rule from 332 onwards, the policy of fusion between West and East fostered by Alexander's successors left little trace on Jewish thought, save at Alexandria, where the Jewish colony enjoyed a position of peculiar privilege. The most striking exception in the Old Testament is offered by the book of Ecclesiastes, written probably towards the close of the third century, where religious individualism takes, under Hellenic stimulus, the form of sceptical enquiry. The words, " I applied my heart to seek and to search out by wisdom concerning all that is done under heaven " reflect the temper of Herodotus.[1] The writer's facile cynicism, " I have seen all the works that are done, under the sun; and, behold, all is vanity and a striving after wind," and his lack of speculative earnestness merely show how uncongenial a medium was the Hebrew mind for the reception of Greek philosophy. The views he affected were the prudential ethics of the Epicureans, the one of all the later Hellenic schools which attached least weight to metaphysical enquiry. The problem of Job is cursorily dismissed by the denial of moral retribution.[2] Ecclesiastes is an isolated figure in Jewish " wisdom " literature. The sufferings of the martyred *Chasîdim* under Antiochus Epiphanes and the fierce patriotism of the Maccabæan revolt, provoked by his efforts to impose Hellenism by force, quenched the spirit of intellectual liberty in Palestine, and secured the victory of Jewish particularism.

§ 15. During the captivity the hope of the kingdom became a dominant force in the religious life of Israel. It was of gradual growth and took a variety of specific forms, now narrowed to square with the most rigid nationalism, now enlarged so as to break down every barrier that parted Israel from the Gentile world. It is often associated, especially in the years immediately

[1] Eccles. i. 13, 14; cf. Prov. xxx. 2–4, for a similar scepticism. Greek influence is traceable also in (possibly) Prov. i–viii and in the book of Ecclesiasticus, where the ideal of the wise man is sketched, and the doctrine of the mean and of the value of leisure for the life of wisdom are insisted on (e.g. Ecclus. xxxviii. 24). The name *Ecclesiastes* is the Greek translation of the Hebrew *Qohéleth*, which means a public teacher of wisdom. On the *Wisdom* literature, to which the book of Proverbs belongs, see Driver, *Introduction*, pp. 392 ff.

[2] Eccles. viii. 14, ix. 2. Chance rules the world (ix. 11). Epicurean ethics of the less elevated type, akin to Cyrenaicism (iii. 12 f., v. 18 f., ix. 7–10). These and many other passages recall the tone of the *Rubáiyát* of Omar Khayyám.

preceding the birth of Christ, with the belief in the advent of a Messiah, the king of David's line who should deliver Israel and inaugurate Yahweh's kingdom.[1] But this feature is unessential; the core of the conception is the institution of " a regenerated community, in which the divine will should be realised." [2] The ancient expectation of " the day of Yahweh " interpreted no longer as a visitation of wrath upon Israel but as a promise of redemption, was absorbed in the hope of the kingdom, heralded by Isaiah and Jeremiah, and explicitly developed by Ezekiel.[3] In Ezekiel's prophecy the conception is presented in its most exclusive form, as the establishment of a priestly church, preceded by a merciless judgement on the Gentiles and unfaithful Jews. The blessings of the kingdom are reserved for the righteous in Israel, and for them alone.[4] That this narrow interpretation eventually triumphed among the Jews of the restoration was due, in part to the fatal persecution under Antiochus, in part to their inability to grasp the full bearings of their monotheistic faith. They could not else have failed to draw the inference that the God of the whole earth did not restrict his providential care to a single privileged people, but willed that his knowledge should, through Israel, be a light for all nations upon earth. This larger conception of the kingdom did, in fact, receive expression in exilic and post-exilic prophecy. There was that in the spiritual life of Israel which would not brook confinement within the bounds prescribed by Ezekiel. Such was the vision of the kingdom that inspired the message of the Second Isaiah.[5] He opens with the

[1] *Messiah* means "anointed"; its Greek equivalent is *Christos* (Christ). "Yahweh's anointed" was a term frequently applied to the pre-exilic kings.

[2] Charles, *Eschatology*, p. 84. The ideal kingdom is conceived by pre-Christian Judaism sometimes as the rule of a secular prince of Davidic lineage, sometimes as a theocracy under sacerdotal government. There is no mention of the Messiah in Amos, Zephaniah, Nahum, Habakkuk, Joel; nor in Daniel, nor in the late passages, Is. xxiv–xxvii, lxv–lxvi. The kingdom is often conceived as directly under the rule of Yahweh.

[3] On the " day," see above, § 4; for Is., see above, § 7; Jer. xxiii. 5, 6, Ezek. xxxiv. 23 ff., xxxvii. 24 ff. But there is no Messianic hope in Ezekiel (see Cooke, op. cit., *Introduction*, p. xxx).

[4] Contrast Jer. iv. 2, xii. 14–17, xvi. 19, where the nations are incorporated in the kingdom. The narrower view is reflected in, e.g., Is. lxvi, and in the prophecy of Joel (c. 400 B.C.).

[5] The prophecies of the Second Isaiah are found in cc. xl–lv. They date from the time of Cyrus's conquest of Babylon (538). Included in these chapters are the four *Songs of the Servant of Yahweh*, possibly by another writer; cc. xlii. 1–4, xlix. 1–6, l. 4–9, lii. 13–liii. 12. The last eleven chapters of the book of Isaiah (lvi–lxvi) are probably by different authors and of later date. In any case, it may be taken as established that cc. xl–lxvi contain no prophecies of Isaiah himself.

voice of consolation, " Comfort ye, comfort ye my people,"
and of assurance of coming redemption, when " the glory of
Yahweh shall be revealed and all flesh shall see it together."
Though the hope of speedy deliverance at the hand of Cyrus the
Persian is coupled with remembrance of Israel's past infidelity
and reproach for her present lack of faith,[1] the dominant note is
that of confidence in Yahweh's mercy; He is the gracious
Saviour who " shall feed his flock like a shepherd " and has
freely pardoned the transgressions of his people. " In a little
wrath I hid my face from thee for a moment; but with everlasting kindness will I have mercy on thee, saith the Lord thy
redeemer." [2] The call of the Second Isaiah is to faith rather
than to repentance. His theology is more conscious and reflective than that of earlier prophets; he enforces his monotheistic convictions as speculative truths, not by dogmatic
assertion, but by persuasive argument. Yahweh is the acknowledged creator and sustainer of the universe, the one eternal
and infinite God, whose almighty hand is manifest throughout
all nature and all history. " Who hath wrought and done it,
calling the generations from the beginning ? I, the Lord, the first
and with the last, I am he." [3] The last traces of monolatry, as
distinct from monotheism, have vanished. The gods of the
heathen are idols, things of nought and vanity; " beside me
there is no God." [4] In full accordance with this clear grasp
of the divine unity, the prophetic vision pierces beyond the
narrow bounds of nationalism, and sees the salvation of all
peoples within the restored kingdom.[5] Jerusalem is conceived
as the destined metropolis of a universal church; " the Gentiles
shall come to thy light and kings to the brightness of thy rising." [6]
It is in the four *Songs of the Servant of Yahweh* that Israel's catholic
mission receives its noblest affirmation. There is here no thought

[1] Is. xl. 27 f., xlii. 18–25, xlix. 14–21.
[2] Is. xl. 11, xliii. 25, liv. 8.
[3] Is. xli. 4, cf. xl. 12–end, xlv. 5–8, xliv. 24, li. 13.
[4] Is. xliv. 6, cf. xliv. 9–20, xlvi, 1–7.
[5] The relationship of the Gentiles to the kingdom is presented in
various forms in the last twenty-six chapters of Isaiah. At one time,
Israel appears as an imperial power to which all nations owe allegiance,
Is. xlv. 14–17 (retribution visited upon the nations), xlix. 7, 22–3, liv. 3.
At another, the nations accept Yahweh's kingdom of their own free will,
Is. ii. 2–4 (= Mic. iv. 1–3), a post-exilic passage; xxv. 6, 7 (probably
c. 300 B.C.).
[6] Is. lx. 3; cf. Pss. xxii. 27–31, xlv, lxxxvi, lxxxvii and Is. xix. 18–25,
a late and very striking passage, in which Assyria and Egypt are incorporated in the kingdom in complete equality with Israel. See also the
allegorical narrative of Jonah.

of political domination or human sovereignty. Righteous
Israel is portrayed as a servant, suffering not for his own sin but
for that of his people, " despised and rejected of men, a man of
sorrows and acquainted with grief," sent forth into alien lands to
deliver those who are in bondage and to herald the coming of the
kingdom. It is no exaggeration to say that these and similar
passages from the later chapters of Isaiah left on men's vision
an impress of an ideal order of society, that has endured through
all after-time. Christians from the first saw in them the closest
anticipation of the gospel-kingdom. It was on the *Songs of the
Servant* that the Ethiopian eunuch was pondering in his chariot
when the deacon Philip met him on the road from Jerusalem to
Gaza. The song of Simeon, recorded by St. Luke, is evidence that,
despite the victory of particularism in the religion of orthodox
Judaism, there were those at the time of Christ's coming who
cherished the larger hope of the kingdom, as " a light to lighten
the Gentiles and the glory of thy people Israel." [1] Moreover, it
is surely possible that Christ, who took a passage akin to the
Servant songs as his text when preaching in the synagogue,
should have been consciously influenced by them in His own
redemptive mission.

§ 16. The doctrine of the kingdom was transformed in a
striking manner in the two centuries preceding the birth of
Christ, through fusion with the belief, foreign to earlier Jewish
thought, in the resurrection from the dead.[2] Alike in popular

[1] Acts viii. 26 ff., Luke ii. 32.
[2] See Charles, *Eschatology,* cc. v and vi. The Jewish belief in a
resurrection to life, when it appeared thus late in the day, was in no
sense a recrudescence of primitive ideas. It arose out of moral and
religious problems that belong to the maturity of Jewish civilization.
The religion of Yahweh had gradually killed ancestor-worship, with the
associated belief in the continued life of the ghost in *Sheol.* Centuries
elapsed before the new ethical faith in a resurrection arose, as explained
in the text, out of the developed religion of Yahweh. The conception
of a future life was closely connected in Judaism with that of a resurrection from the grave. Among the Greeks, on the other hand, it took
shape as the belief in the deathlessness of the soul, whose immortality
was intrinsic; there was no question of a resurrection. But the Platonic
doctrine of the soul's immortality had this in common with the Jewish
doctrine of resurrection, that it was independent of primitive survivals
(though it utilised materials drawn from popular religious beliefs). Plato's
conviction rested on scientific grounds (and in this stands in sharp contrast with that of the Jews). See below, c. iv. § 17, c. v. §§ 20, 21. The
Christian belief in immortality, combined with that in the resurrection
of the dead to eternal life, rests on a twofold basis, (*a*) on post-exilic
Judaism (resurrection), (*b*) on Platonic philosophy (immortality). See
C. C. J. Webb, Gifford Lectures (Second Course) on *Divine Personality and
Human Life,* pp. 257–64.

tradition and in the teaching of the prophets, the kingdom of Yahweh had been conceived as a deliverance of Israel to be realised in the future history of the nation upon earth. It was late in the day and under the overmastering stimulus of personal suffering that the Jews were led to associate the hope of the kingdom with that of a resurrection of the righteous to share in its felicity, and, subsequently, with a belief in the immortality of the soul. The traditional view of the soul, for the Hebrews as for other races, was crude and material, closely associated with the cult of ancestors, and devoid of ethical significance. At death the wraith passed to *Sheol*, where it persisted in quasi-bodily form; while the spirit or breath of life, which was distinguished later as the source of the higher psychical faculties, returned to God who gave it. There is here no question of personal immortality or of moral retribution after death.[1] It took long, as we have seen, for the Hebrew mind to grasp the thought of individual responsibility; until the eve of the exile, the nation was accountable for the sins of its

[1] On the interesting and too much neglected subject of Hebrew psychology, see the Essay (XI) under that title by Principal Wheeler Robinson in *The People and the Book* (ed. Peake), pp. 353–382. For the Hebrews the individual human being (the self) is " the body as a complex of parts drawing their life and activity from a breath-soul which has no existence apart from the body " (p. 366). The life-principle, including conscious powers, is assigned both to the bodily substance as a whole and to its several members (heart, reins, flesh, bones, eye, hand, etc.). Hebrew psychology knows no dichotomy of soul and body, and *a fortiori* no trichotomy of body, soul and spirit. The body is the man; personality is animated body, not incarnate soul. The Hebrew word for the life-principle is *néphesh*, usually mistranslated " soul " in A.V. and R.V. Another term *rūach* (normally translated " spirit," which originally meant " wind," regarded as the " breath " of God) is frequently used with an inspirational implication, to indicate the life-principle as an afflatus or in-breathing of the divine energy acting on man from without, esp. in prophetic inspiration and other exceptional manifestations of life-power. Of man's conscious activities, feeling and emotion are commonly referred to *néphesh*; intellect and (esp.) will (conscience) to *lēb* (lit. " heart "); will being primary in Hebrew ethics, both in God and in man (see above, p. 48, *n.* 1). The ghost or wraith passed to Sheol as a replica of the whole man and continued his existence in a ghostly state. To regard Sheol as the *habitat* of " departed spirits " is therefore a grave error; Sheol was peopled solely by these " shades " (*nephaim*). When, as in the case of Samuel at Endor, the dead are supposed, quite exceptionally, to return, the bodily guise borne when living is continued. So in Homer (Od. xi), the wraiths in Hades need to drink blood in order to recover consciousness and converse with Odysseus. Consequently, when the Hebrews came to conceive a future life, it was as a true resurrection of the body, to provide a renewal of bodily life on earth. The Christian doctrine of the resurrection of the body is strictly faithful to the Hebraic tradition, though it was fortified by opposition to Manichean dualism (the view that matter, and especially the human body, is inherently evil and due to a superhuman evil creator).

members, and innocent and guilty alike suffered from the retribution which befell the community. Then, with the exile, came a change; the claims of the individual on Yahweh's justice pressed more and more urgently for satisfaction. We have seen how thinkers like the author of Job struggled vainly to find an answer to the problem. It was the stress of persecution under Antiochus that forced the belief in resurrection upon the mind of the Jewish people. Prior to that time it had been confined to a small minority, influenced possibly by contact with Zoroastrian ideas during the epoch of Persian rule. The passages in the Old Testament that allude to it are few and late.[1] When the conviction took root among the Jews, it was in a distinctively Jewish form, in close alliance with the national expectation of the kingdom. The righteous Israelites would rise from *Sheol* to share in the realisation of the kingdom upon earth. Thus a solution was reached which vindicated Yahweh's justice towards the individual sufferer, and satisfied the cherished aspiration for the eventual deliverance of Israel. The apocalyptic writings of the second and first centuries show that this belief was no stereotyped dogma, but appeared in a diversity of forms in dependence on the changing course of Jewish history.[2] Many questions were stirring, which

---

[1] The two passages in the O.T. where the belief appears are in the remarkable (late) prophecy in Is. xxiv–xxvii (esp. xxvi. 1–19, resurrection of righteous Israelites, c. 300 B.C.), and the apocalyptic book of Daniel (c. 165 B.C.). In Dan. xii. 2 we find resurrection of (*a*) the eminently righteous, (*b*) the eminently wicked (i.e. apostates from Judaism). In neither passage is there mention of a *general* resurrection. The resurrection is viewed as the return of the ghost to renewed bodily life on earth, the only kind of life conceivable by the Hebrew mind. They never entertained the idea of a disembodied soul.

[2] On the nature of apocalyptic (Greek *apocalypsis* = revelation) and its distinction from prophecy, see Charles, *Eschatology*, pp. 173 ff., 387–8. The main differences are that apocalyptic is later in date, pseudonymous, and more comprehensive in range. It essayed a philosophy of religion and of history, seeking to penetrate behind events to their divine purpose, and embracing past, present, and future in a single supernatural scheme, culminating in the advent of the divine kingdom, that last judgement, and the resurrection of the righteous to a blessed future life. It showed a taste for fixing the dates of coming events with chronological precision. Millennarianism is the product of Jewish apocalyptic. It furnished an imaginative outlet for the patriotic spirit among the Jews, who were too weak to realise their national aspirations in action. The numerous Jewish apocalyptic writings are translated by Charles in his great work : *The Apocrypha and Pseudepigrapha of the O.T.*; on Christian apocalyptic, see the same writer's edition of the Book of Revelation in the *International Critical Commentary*; and, for a brief survey of the whole subject, his volume entitled *Between the Old and the New Testaments* in the Home University Library. The importance of Jewish apocalyptic for an understanding of the religious environment under which Christianity appeared

admitted of varying answers. Was it the righteous Israelites only who rose, or did the wicked and the heathen share in the resurrection? In the latter case, what was the fate of the unfaithful Jew and the Gentile at the judgement preceding the institution of the kingdom? Were the Gentiles admitted to its privileges or reduced to bondage to Israel? These problems were met normally in a spirit of rigorous particularism. Again, of what nature was the intermediate state, between death and the advent of the kingdom? Was the resurrection of the soul only or of the embodied spirit, and what was the form of the resurrection body? Was the kingdom eternal on earth, or of limited duration? What was the function of the Messiah in relation to its institution and to the judgement? As the first century drew on, a further and far-reaching development made its appearance. The conviction grew that this earth was unworthy to be the scene of the consummation of the kingdom, that at the coming of the Messiah, or at the close of his earthly reign, Yahweh would create a new heaven and a new earth, and that, after a final judgement, the soul of the righteous Israelite would pass to an eternal life in the heavenly kingdom. Moreover, the Messiah is sometimes figured as a supernatural " Son of Man," sometimes as a prince sprung from the lineage of David, who should deliver the Jewish people from the Roman yoke, and inaugurate the earthly kingdom as a prelude to the heavenly and eternal.[1] It would be interesting to follow out these conceptions in Jewish apocalyptic literature after the coming of Christ; but enough has been said to show how decisively the spirit of national exclusiveness had triumphed by that date over the larger outlook of earlier prophecy. Rarely in the Jewish writings of the first century B.C. or the first century A.D. is any trace discoverable of the admission of the Gentiles to the kingdom.[2] Monotheism and particularism persist henceforward, despite their essential inconsistency, in the faith of the Jewish community.

---

is very great, and its influence on Christian eschatology proved deep and lasting; e.g. the conceptions of the final judgement, of heaven, and of everlasting punishment have their source in apocalyptic literature.

[1] The supernatural Messiah is to be clearly distinguished from the Davidic. Christ's adoption of this title " Son of Man " gives a peculiar importance to its history. There is no supernatural implication in its frequent use by Ezekiel (cf. Ps. viii, where it stands for humanity in general). In Dan. vii. 13, it is used of Israel as the ideal type of humanity, in contrast to the beasts = heathen kingdoms. In the apocalyptic Enoch i (second century B.C.) it is applied to the supernatural Messiah.

[2] But IV Esdras is an exception.

IV. Conclusion (§§ 17, 18).

§ 17. We have traced the course of the prophetic teaching and its issues to the eve of the foundation of Christianity. Two conclusions can be gathered from our survey. In the first place, the religious life of Israel, even in its highest developments, is inseparably blended with characteristic limitations. The strength of Hebrew religion lay in the belief in one sole God and in his moral government of the world. Its besetting weakness was the ineradicable presupposition that the divine purpose was concentrated on a single people, chosen out of all the nations to be the peculiar recipients of Yahweh's favour, and that the whole course of nature and of human history revolved, by Yahweh's will, around the life and destiny of Israel. That the policy of artificial isolation intensified religious loyalty, and fostered a moral elevation that forms a contrast to the prevalent laxity of Græco-Roman and Græco-Oriental practice, is undeniable; but it excluded the Gentile from any share in the spiritual inheritance. Jewish religious history is full of these strange anomalies and paradoxical contrasts. The humility which springs from the sense of personal sin was coupled with a fierce and intolerant pride in membership of a righteous community, the spirit of inward piety with a meticulous scrupulosity in regard to external observances. The faith in God's continual presence and in his providential ordering of every incident of common life gave rise to an equal respect for the essentials of moral duty and for the puerile regulations of a ritual code.[1] Thus the Hebrew people failed to realise effectively the larger hope of the prophets, or to complete their appointed mission in the spiritual education of mankind. If we seek the underlying reason of this failure, if we ask why it was that they never grasped the incompatibility of particularism with the faith in a single moral ruler of the universe, we must point in answer to their intellectual limitations. Unlike the Greek, the Hebrew did not think things out. He never attained to the plane of intellectual development at which reason claims a voice in the determination of religious

---

[1] So also God's transcendence and his immanence as indwelling in the heart of the righteous, his justice and his mercy, the doctrine of strict retribution and that of free forgiveness, the hope of future reward for meritorious acts and the pursuit of goodness for its own sake, determinism and freedom, the wrath and the love of God, are combined in Jewish religious thought, though the *speculative* difficulties are never thoroughly grasped.

and ethical beliefs.[1] This is why the noblest utterances of Hebrew piety defy systematisation in a coherent body of theological truth, and are riddled with inconsistencies and contradictions, of which their authors remain entirely unaware. Thus again we can explain what may be termed the contingency of Hebrew religious thought, the fact, noted frequently above, that its utterances are determined by the sequence of historical incidents which happened to affect the Hebrew nation. These incidents suggested not only the occasion, but in large measure the content, of Hebrew prophecy. The more bitter the humiliation, the more intense the sufferings, of the chosen people, the stronger grew their certainty of eventual redemption. The spiritual vision of Israel expanded in inverse ratio to her secular achievement. The logic, for a logic it needs must have, was in part that of historic circumstance, in part the inward logic of the conscience. Only it was never, from first to last, the logic of the intellect. Thus, finally, it was granted to the prophets to see truths, now one and now another, in their isolation and independence; it was not granted them to know the truth. This is the reason why, even apart from the restrictions of the law, the Hebrews were incapable of conveying the import of their spiritual vision to the peoples of the West. For this to be possible, the several truths needed to be moulded into a coherent whole, the essential to be distinguished from the irrelevant, the implications unfolded, and the relative validity of each truth defined, by a process at once of clarification and of enlargement. Thus only could the prophetic teaching issue in a religious faith that appealed not merely to the heart, but to the mind. Was it credible that so

[1] When the intellect did come into play, it tended towards casuistry, formalism and the barren logic of the schools. At the same time, continuity was preserved between the highest spiritual teaching and the religion of the people. The Jewish prophets succeeded here, where the Greek philosophers failed (see Webb, Gifford Lectures, First Series, on *God and Personality*, pp. 85, 86). The personal relationship of Yahweh to his Jewish worshipper was unimpaired at all levels of religious apprehension. We may note also that while the close connexion between Hebrew prophecy and the historic crises of the nation tied Yahweh's purposes and will down to temporal events, it gave the Jews a strong sense of the moral significance of history. They were never tempted, as Greek philosophers were often tempted, to divorce ideal values from the course of facts. "The whole of history is an unfolding of the divine purpose; and so history as a whole has for the Jew an importance which it never had for the Greek thinker, nor for the Hellenised Jew, Philo. The Hebrew idea of God is dynamic and ethical; it is therefore rooted in the idea of time" (Inge, *Outspoken Essays*, St. Paul, p. 215). This sense for the value of historic fact impressed itself strongly on Christian thought; see below, c. ix.

radical a transformation should take effect save at the cost of a
breach with Judaism ?

§ 18. In the second place, the religious life of Israel furnished
the historical antecedents of Christianity. Christ himself recognised this affiliation when he declared that he came not to
destroy the law, but to fulfil. For St. Paul, the apostle of the
Gentiles, the law was a schoolmaster to lead men to Christ.
It was through the mediation of Christianity that the spiritual
inheritance of Israel was transmitted to the western world. In
the process of transmission it was remoulded and transformed;
much that was distinctive of Judaism was dropped, and what
was assimilated became the groundwork of a new structure.
Henceforward the two religions went their several ways; the
consciousness of historical relationships served but to widen the
chasm that parted them. The continuity is most apparent in the
conception of the divine kingdom. It was natural that the
disciples of the new faith should turn for anticipations of the
gospel to the prophets rather than to the law. For to the prophets
had been revealed the vision of " the day of Yahweh," when
justice shall prevail and oppression and wrong shall vanish, when
men " shall beat their swords into plowshares and their spears into
pruning-hooks : nation shall not lift up sword against nation,
neither shall they learn war any more," when " they shall not hurt
nor destroy in all my holy mountain; for the earth shall be full
of the knowledge of the Lord, as the waters cover the sea." [1]
Their reception of these truths had been trammelled by limitations,
by their prejudice for the prerogatives of the peculiar people, their
failure to reconcile the spiritual claim of the individual with
that of the community, their imperfect realisation of divine
immanence, and their relegation of the ideal society to future
time. In the teaching of the gospel, the thought of the kingdom
was freed, once and for all, from these restrictions. The individual could find salvation and win eternal life only through
incorporation in the divine society, whose members were bound
one to another in their personal relationship to its head. The
barriers of nationalism were at length and for ever broken down;
the doors of the kingdom were opened to Jew and Gentile, Greek
and barbarian, bond and free; and a faith that bridged the gulf
which had severed the divine from the human united all mankind
in the bonds of universal brotherhood. Once more, the institution
of the kingdom was conceived as no remote event, but as a present

[1] Is. ii. 4 = Mic. iv. 3; Is. xi. 9 = Hab. ii. 14.

fact, a living reality, actual in the hearts of men, " on earth as it is in heaven." [1] But the seeds of this doctrine, so fruitful for the spiritual regeneration of humanity, were planted in the soil of Hebrew prophecy. It is for this reason that not the Jew only, but the Christian, can admit the claim of Israel to the title of the chosen people. " You only have I known of all the families of the earth." To Israel alone of the peoples of the pre-Christian world was vouchsafed the vision of the kingdom of God; and her record of that vision constitutes her legacy to mankind.[2]

[1] On the kingdom as present fact : Mark iv. 11, 30 ff. (the grain of mustard seed), x. 14, xii. 34; also Matt. v. 3 = Luke vi. 20, Matt. vi. 33 = Luke xii. 31.

On the kingdom as not yet come : Mark i. 15 ("at hand "); also Matt. viii. 11, xxii. 2 ff., and the parables of the treasure hid in a field and the pearl of great price.

On the kingdom as eternal life in the age to come : Mark ix. 43 ff., x. 17 ff.; also Matt. vii. 21 ff.

See Jackson and Lake, *Prolegomena* I. to the *Acts of the Apostles*, pp. 278 ff., whence the above references are taken. They all occur either in Mark or in the portions of Matthew and Luke that can be assigned to a common source, styled Q, co-ordinate in value with Mark. Charles (*Eschatology*, pp. 364 ff.) cites Matt. xii. 28, Luke iv. 18–21 (kingdom as present), Mark ix. 1 (future, in heaven), Matt. xviii. 3, 4 and Luke xviii. 17 (both present and future).

[2] A further difference between Christianity and contemporary Judaism must be indicated. Christ came to preach " good tidings of great joy," and it was as such that his message appealed to the peoples of the Mediterranean world. But in the Jewish apocalyptic writings of the period 200 B.C.–A.D. 100, the dominant thought is that of the divine vengeance. For the world at large, and even for the ungodly among the Jews, the message was one of terror, not of hope. The Jews believed in the efficacy of fear and punishment, and taught God's implacable enmity to unrepentant sinners. Even the *Testament of the Twelve Patriarchs* (second century B.C.), which contains the nearest approach to the Christian doctrine of forgiveness, falls short of the Christian ideal of love towards enemies. Mr. Montefiore (in Jackson and Lake's *Acts*, i. 79) notes that contemporary Judaism lacks the distinctively Christian precept of a love that seeks out the sinner and the fallen. If this be man's duty, it must be as the expression of divine love, extending even to the unthankful and the evil. The apocalyptic writers came to marvel why God created the mass of men for eternal punishment; but they never questioned the fact. Doubtless, Christian theology absorbed much of this Jewish tradition. In Dante's poem, we read that shoals of spirits are driven into hell before the poet's eye, while only one (Statius) passes, during his journey, from Purgatory into Paradise. Yet this baneful legacy has never obliterated Christ's new and essential teaching of the universal love of God, as enshrined, e.g. in the parables of the lost sheep and the prodigal son.

ADDITIONAL NOTE

ON POST-EXILIC JEWISH HISTORY.

It will be useful to summarise briefly the salient facts of post-exilic history. It falls into three periods.

(i) The restored exiles were subject to the mild sovereignty of Persia from the middle of the fifth century till the conquest by Alexander the Great of Macedon (332).

(ii) For nearly two centuries they were ruled by Macedonian overlords. Palestine was once more the bone of contention between the Ptolemies in Egypt and the Seleucid kings of Asia. The gates were thrown open to Hellenism. Under the Seleucid Antiochus Epiphanes, civil tumult broke out (168) between Hellenising Jews, supported by the Greek king, and the orthodox party, leading to Antiochus' forcible intervention, the violation of the temple, and frequent martyrdoms. The "godly" found a champion in Judas Maccabæus, of the priestly tribe of the Hasmonæans (*Hashmūnai*), who secured national independence and established a theocratic state, which lasted till Rome appeared on the scene.

(iii) In 63–61, Pompey, having conquered Mithradates of Pontus, Rome's great enemy in the East, reorganised that part of the Mediterranean area. The Jews were placed under Roman suzerainty, with a considerable measure of self-government under the high priests. In 40, the government passed into the hands of Herod the Great, an Idumæan ruler of exceptional ability, who consistently supported, and was supported by, Rome. He rebuilt the temple with great splendour and founded Cæsarea. Among the mass of the Jews he was unpopular as an alien. On his death (4 B.C.) the kingdom, always under Roman suzerainty, was divided; in A.D. 6, Judæa became a province of the second rank, administered by a *procurator*, who was responsible to the *legatus* of Syria. This mode of government lasted (except during the three years 41–44 A.D., when Herod Agrippa I ruled Judæa as king) till the great revolt of 66 and the destruction of Jerusalem by Titus in 70. Pontius Pilate was one of the series of *procurators* in the reign of Tiberius. Lastly, after the second rising of the Jews against Rome in the time of Hadrian (132–135), the community received its final blow :

the name Judæa was suppressed, and the subsequent history of the Jews is that of the Dispersion.

It should further be noted : (a) that Jewish national patriotism grew in intensity and exclusiveness with the increasing stringency of foreign sovereignty, Persian, Greek and Roman. Every attempt to impose western ideas provoked a passionate outburst of resistance. The nationalist party gained strength under Roman rule, despite the studied respect of the imperial government for Jewish religious sentiment, and the wide judicial and administrative powers granted to the Sanhedrin (Greek *synedrion* = council). The Jewish people were always on the verge of revolt throughout this period : Galilee was the chief storm-centre. (b) That the Jewish communities of the *Diaspora* (= Dispersion) grew steadily in numbers and importance during the Macedonian and Roman periods. There was always a large and very important Jewish colony in Babylon; Jews settled in the towns of Asia Minor, Syria and Egypt, especially at Alexandria, where they occupied two of the five quarters of the city and enjoyed extensive privileges. There the Greek version of the O.T., known as the *Septuagint*, was compiled in the second century B.C. Alexandria was the chief meeting-ground of Judaism and Hellenic thought; we find Judaism bending to western influence, but never breaking under the strain (see below, c. vi. § 8 and c. ix. § 2). The Jews made many proselytes (also half-proselytes, who accepted the Jewish faith without circumcision and other Mosaic observances) in the Hellenised provinces. Acts ii. 9–11 conveys some idea of the range of the *Diaspora*; the presence, there indicated, of Jews in Parthia and other eastern lands outside of the Roman empire accounts for the preaching of Christianity in those parts in early times (though very little is known about these missions). The desire expressed by St. Paul to preach in Spain (Rom. xv. 28) suggests that Jews had penetrated to the extreme west of the Roman world. (c) That it was in the Greek, Persian and Roman periods that Judaism, as distinct from the pre-exilic religion of Israel, developed as a religion to the complete and definitive form in which it has persisted ever since the latter half of the second century and the beginning of the third. This process, which, as we have seen, began with the promulgation of the Law by Ezra, and which, through the prophetic influence in its earlier phases, preserved unbroken continuity with pre-Judaic religion, was marked by the increasing dominance of the traditional *Torah*, as interpreted in the schools and synagogues by the " scribes " and subsequent professional expositors, whose work was eventually embodied in the *Mishnah*, the body of traditional law as promulgated at the close of the second century and later in the *Talmud* (" Learning ") compiled in Galilee (late fourth century) and Babylonia (late fifth century). The *Torah*, thus codified, provided a catholic Jewish faith, based on community of observance, penetrating to every detail of the communal life of the Jews, secular as well as religious, personal and domestic as well as national. Particularism had replaced universalism ; legalism had triumphed, and living prophecy had ceased ; but the creation of Judaism in its final and permanent shape remains a truly notable achievement of the religious genius of the chosen people.[1]

---

[1] See Moore, *Judaism*, Vol. I, Introduction; Chap. I, Vol. IX.

CHAPTER IV

THE RISE OF HELLENISM

I. INTRODUCTORY (§ 1).

§ 1. THE origins of the Greek people are hard to trace. We have seen how, far back in the third millennium, Crete was the home of a rich civilization, which reached continental Greece, the Ægean islands and the Mediterranean. It is generally thought that the makers of this civilization differed from the Greeks of later history in race, character and language. Further, the evidence both of ancient tradition and of modern archæology points to a catastrophic overthrow of Cretan power, some time towards the close of the second millennium, and to a subsequent period of anarchy and chaos, analogous to that which intervened between the downfall of the Roman empire in the west and the emergence of a new order of society in the Middle Ages. Antiquity too had its Dark Ages; and from it issued the Greece of history. In Crete, for example, the great Minoan buildings were destroyed by conflagration; then, after centuries of which but slight record is left, we find Dorian Greeks in occupation of the island. Greek religious story told of conflicts between older and younger gods, and of the victory of the latter; Greek poets and historians have preserved memories of migrations by land and sea, of struggle and of fusion between Achæan and Dorian invaders on the one hand, and pre-Achæan "Pelasgians" on the other. The little that we know of this age of transition suggests problems rather than conclusions. But this much at least is certain, that late in the second millennium tall, yellow-haired, fair-complexioned warriors of Indo-European stock descended in successive waves upon the Ægean world from the inland regions of the north. Some, bearing with them their families and chattels, like the Goths and Franks of a later time, forced their way southwards by land into Thrace and Macedonia, Thessaly and Epirus, and on into central Greece and the Peloponnesus. Others, possibly at an earlier date, crossed the Hellespont into Asia Minor. Others, again, like the ninth-century Northmen, raided by sea the coasts and islands of the Ægean. We may picture these rude northerners as not dissimilar, in their manners and culture, to the Macedonians of the age of Philip and Alexander, or to the Albanians of the present day. It was not wholly as destroyers that they mastered, in the course of centuries, the ancient civilization of Crete. It left its traces on their development; and it is possible that the superiority of Greek culture as compared with that of the Romans was due in part to this fact of early contact with Minoan civilization. In any case, the Greeks of history were the product of gradual fusion between Achæan and other intruders from the north and the older inhabitants of the Ægean world. It is natural that the latter, being far more numerous, should have impressed their culture upon the conquerors. The settlements of the invaders in European Greece were accompanied or followed by migrations of Greek colonists to the islands and Asiatic shores of the Ægean, and by conflicts with their own kinsmen, who had earlier passed thither by another route. Very possibly it is the memory of such struggles that is preserved in the story of the Trojan war.[1] One of these groups of colonists, the Æolian, sailed from Thessaly to the north-west of Asia Minor and the islands that lay off the coast. Other settlers, farther to the south, united in a federation, called the Ionian league, round the sanctuary of Apollo at Delos. It was by the name Ionians (*Javan* in the Old Testament) that the early Greeks were known to the peoples of the East. We may date these maritime migrations across the Ægean between 1300 and 1000 B.C.; they are very probably connected with the troubles which Egypt suffered from sea-rovers under the twentieth dynasty.[2] Finally, at the very close of the second millennium, the last wave of northern invasion broke upon European Greece, when the Dorians, a hardy warlike stock, the forefathers of the Spartans of later history, occupied parts of Central and Western Greece, and, pressing southwards, gradually mastered the greater part of the Peloponnesus. Dorian emigrants also crossed the Ægean, colonizing Crete, Rhodes and the south-western shores of Asia Minor. As the outcome of these movements, which covered several centuries and terminated about 900 B.C., the Greek race and the Greek language were established on both sides of the Ægean.

---

[1] The traditional date of the Trojan war is B.C. 1184. The opinion of scholars at the present day is more conservative than a generation ago. These commotions in the Ægean and eastern Mediterranean world may have caused the Hittites to lose their influence in western Asia Minor. See above, c. ii. § 12, and Cowley's Schweich Lectures on *The Hittites*.

[2] See above, c. ii. § 4. Some of the later invaders carried iron swords of improved design, against which the bronze rapiers of their Cretan antagonists could avail little.

II. The Hellenic City-States (§§ 2-6).

§ 2. The life of the Greek people during the early centuries of the first millennium, as in the preceding period of the migrations, is veiled in obscurity, and our knowledge of its character consists largely of general conclusions, based upon inference from the succeeding age. This, at all events, is clear, that from the dawn of its history Hellenic civilization extended beyond the limits of continental Greece. We shall see presently how in the eighth and seventh centuries it spread beyond the Ægean area round the Euxine (Black Sea), and over the coast-lands of northern Africa, southern Italy and Sicily. Southern Italy came to be known to the Greeks as " Great Hellas." Wherever in the Mediterranean world we find Greek cities and the Greek speech, there for purposes of history is Greece. But the fact of cardinal importance for Hellenic civilization is that, when the veil is partially drawn in the eighth century, the Greeks, with the exception of backward inland communities, are already grouped in city-states. The patriarchal monarchies of which we read in the Homeric poems have mostly given place to hereditary aristocracies; and in the more advanced of the civic communities laws and constitutions are beginning to appear. Each of these small cities enjoyed complete political independence and developed its own distinctive institutions and rule of life. It is essential to realise that free Greece was never united in a single state. The national bond was that of common race and language, not that of political union. We must think of Greek history as the record of hundreds of independent cities scattered over the islands and shores of the Mediterranean, each possessed of a small tract of civic territory. That of Athens, for example, which was exceptionally large, comprised the peninsula of Attica, with an area equal to that of an average English county. Its citizen-levy in the age of Pericles was 30,000, representing a free population of about 250,000, including women and children, to whom must be added many slaves and resident aliens.[1] Like the Italian republics of the later Middle Ages, these Greek cities were passionately jealous of their independence. Whenever any one of them, such as Athens or Sicilian Syracuse, acquired sovereignty

---

[1] See note to c. v. § 5. Sparta, a strictly limited conquest-state, had some 8,000 citizens able to bear arms at the time of the Persian war; this number had declined to about 1200 to 1500 by 371, and in Aristotle's day to less than 1000. Argos and Thebes had about 20,000 citizen-soldiers at the end of the fifth century.

over others, the empire was invariably transient and, while it lasted, provoked deep resentment among its subjects. Greek patriotism was civic rather than national. This does not mean that they were insensible to the common bond of Hellenic kinship; on the contrary, they realised clearly the gulf that parted their own standards of morality and civilization from those of the " barbarians " who surrounded them; but the tie was one of feeling, speech and culture.[1] It found peculiar expression in the great athletic festivals, held under religious auspices, and open to all Hellenes, and to them alone.   Of these the oldest and most celebrated was that which took place every four years at Olympia on the borders of Elis in honour of Zeus; from the early sixth century others were instituted at Nemea, near Argos, on the isthmus of Corinth, and—the Pythian—on the plain of Crisa, near Apollo's shrine of Delphi. The religion of the Greeks, despite a multitude of local variations, constituted a common inheritance; the chief Olympian deities, such as Zeus, Poseidon, Athene and Apollo, were reverenced throughout the Hellenic area, and in the epoch of commercial expansion the oracle at Delphi developed into a pan-Hellenic religious institution. Thanks to easy communication by sea between all parts of the Hellenic world, the art, the poetry and the science, that arose in various centres of culture, became rapidly a common possession of them all.   Thus the need of political union as an instrument of civilization was not felt by the Greeks through the great creative period of their history ; even when, in the fourth century, the cities of central and eastern Greece were dominated by the Macedonian kingdom, those of Italy and Sicily retained their independence, and the Macedonian overlordship was won and held by force.

§ 3. The *Polis* or city-state was the peculiar creation of the Hellenic people.[2]   Its significance for the future of civilization

[1] Professor Gilbert Murray points out (*Five Stages of Greek Religion,* p. 81) that the consciousness of Hellenism takes its rise among the Ionian Greeks in Asia Minor, where the contrast with the surrounding barbarism was most evident, " Hellenic " means " like the Hellenes," not " descended from Hellenes " (*ibid.,* pp. 58 f.).

[2] The Phœnicians, both at home and in their colonies, especially Carthage, founded city-states; but nowhere do we find the free public life associated with the institution as in the case of the Greek cities or of Rome.   Fowler (*City-State,* p. 5) sees in the *Polis* the key to the sense of a common inheritance of civilization left by Greeks and Romans (e.g. by the Greek historian Polybius in the second century B.C.).   It may be questioned whether the Italian urban communities were fully-formed city-states.   The towns of Latium and Campania were rather urban centres within a tribal group.   On Rome, described by Polybius as " a state most like the Hellenic," see below, ch. VII.

is incalculable. In the first place, in its life and structure are presented, in a simpler form than in the large states of modern times, the data and problems, both moral and economic, which confront man in all ages as the member of a social community. As, in their philosophy, the Greeks formulated in comparatively simple terms the essential issues of human thought, obscured to our later view beneath a complex mass of material, so, in the field of public action in the *Polis*, they set themselves to realize the essential conditions of a worthy civic life. Again, the problems of civilized society were worked out by the Greeks to the full solution possible under that form of organization; the history of the Hellenic *Polis* can be followed from its beginnings until its decline and fall. Thirdly, the Greeks furnished their own theory of politics; they not only created the *Polis*, but reflected upon it; in their philosophy we find both the ideal and the speculative analysis of their public action. The Hellenic city-state stands in contrast, on the one hand, to the early empires of the East, on the other hand, to the states of modern times. The modern state is the fatherland, not its capital town; the capital may be changed, as in Russia from Moscow to St. Petersburg, and later from Leningrad to Moscow, while the state remains the same. A state may come into being, like the Australian Commonwealth, even before the site of its future capital has been fixed. But in Greece, and in Rome under the republic, the capital city was itself the state. In distinction from Oriental kingdoms, the city-states of Greece achieved the union of civilized life and political liberty. In the East, freedom of government is found, but only among rude tribes living in small communities. Advance in culture is possible only through the formation of large aggregates of such communities under despotic rule, and is therefore purchased at the cost of liberty. So the Israelites, struggling against their neighbours, placed themselves voluntarily under a monarch, as the only hope of national salvation. " And they said, Nay; but we will have a king over us, that we also may be like all the nations, and that our king may judge us, and go out before us, and fight our battles." [1] Throughout antiquity, a large state meant despotism. Till the Greeks appeared, progress in civilization meant the creation of a large

[1] See Bevan, *House of Seleucus*, vol. i. c. i, whence the illustration from 1 Sam. viii. is taken. The passage was appealed to frequently by political writers of the Middle Ages, to support the doctrines of the popular basis of sovereignty and of the social contract.

state. They were the first to solve the problem of uniting culture
with freedom in a small community, and solved it through the
city-state. They willed to resemble one another and achieved
a unique result, realizing in the free public life of the *Polis* a
history that contrasts dramatically with the monotonous tale
of despotism, caste-privilege and servitude recounted in the
records of the East.

§ 4. The *Polis* furnished at once the basis and the ideal of
Hellenic civilization. We know little of the process by which
the primitive settlements developed into city-states. We can
picture the northern invaders, dwelling as conquerors amid a
hostile population, in days when the sea was thronged with freebooters, and erecting rude forts at points of vantage on hills a
little distance from the shore, whither they might take refuge
with their herds in moments of danger. At Athens in historic
times the citadel of the Acropolis was still the " City." Village
communities may have come together for self-defence or have
united round a common sanctuary for religious worship. In
Homer the *Polis* was first and above all else a defensible fortress.[1]
We must think ourselves back into a time when, among the
Greeks as among other early races, gods, men and even their
animals were bound together by a tie of kinship. With the
migrations, the bond weakened, and family attachments began to
give way to devotion to the group. The *Polis* became the concrete symbol of this loyalty ; it stood there visible to the naked
eye of every clansman as he farmed his holding in the outskirts,
or foregathered with his fellows for barter and for worship within
its walls. In the precincts of the city everything that met his
view was intimate and familiar. In the little community of
a few hundred citizens, grouped in families and clans, with the
sense of kinship still alive within them, there prevailed a real
equality of comradeship.[2] Everyone knew everyone by sight;
rich and poor, rulers and ruled, stood in direct personal relationships one to another. Kings and nobles were not hemmed in,
as at eastern courts, by etiquette and state-ceremony ; no
formalities of introduction served as a barrier to human inter-

---

[1] It is "sacred" (*hieros*) in Homer; e.g. *Il.*, i. 366. The earliest
temples were, naturally, on the rocky citadel, hard by the chieftain's
palace; later, as commercial activities developed, temples arise around
the *agora*, or market-place.

[2] So, in the *Odyssey* (Book VI. 1–109), Nausicaa, a king's daughter,
washes ' the ' clothes with her maidens; Herodotus (iii. 42) represents
the pirate-despot Polycrates as asking a fisherman to dine with him.

course. The Greek lived his life in the open, under the sun; lounging in the market-place (*agora*) or wrestling-ground (*palaestra*), as the southerner still loves to lounge, in leisurely conversation with his neighbours.[1] The Greeks were an agricultural people, cultivators of corn, vine and olive; their occupation and the climate rendered possible a life spent largely out of doors, with stretches of leisure for social intercourse.[2] No contrast more complete can be imagined to the life of a modern industrial city, where everyone is hustling to his business, and moments of relaxation are few and regular, than the free informal life oi the Greek *Polis*. But leisure meant to the Greek anything rather than idleness; it furnished an escape from the pressure of material claims, and an occasion for the display of intellect and talent. We must think of the Greeks as men of action, even more than as artists or thinkers; their art and their science were closely bound up with the interests of practical life. Sculpture and architecture arose naturally among them out of the need of houses for gods and men; and their philosophy out oi the need for intelligent control of the world in which they lived The Greek admired efficiency above all things; his word for virtue (*areté*) covers not only moral excellence, but intellectual talent and the capacity to win success in every field of public life.[3] The ideal of the strong man, who knows what he wants from the world, and has the power to get it, was ever luring him away from the path of moderation. For this restless energy of mind and body the *Polis* provided a natural field. The only life worth living in the eyes of the Greek was that of citizen service. The family possessed little interest and no serious moral value. The son, when of age, left his father and mother; in his own household, the wife had no soul and did not count. Hence the inferior status of women and children, and the failure of Greek education.

[1] See Zimmern, *Greek Commonwealth*, c. i. The Greek of to-day likes to overwhelm a stranger with eager questions. The ancient Greek prided himself on his " boldness of speech " (*parrhêsia*): he was free from all shyness or reserve. Plato (*Rep.*, viii. 557) indicates *parrhêsia* as a symptom of extreme democracy. Zimmern suggests that the short question and answer attending the entry of a new character in the Attic drama reflects this national characteristic.

[2] The Greek word for leisure was *scholé*, whence our " school." For leisure meant to them opportunity for pursuits of intrinsic worth, such as a man would choose for their own sake (e.g. the pursuit of knowledge). This idea is at the root of their distinction between " liberal " pursuits and " necessary." This distinction is of fundamental importance in Aristotle's *Politics*. See below, ch. xii. § 9.

[3] The Greeks would have regarded Napoleon as a man of pre-eminent *areté*. Themistocles possessed *areté* in a remarkable degree.

The *Polis* and, in the *Polis*, the *agora* with its surrounding
porticos and public buildings, formed his home and his world.
Hence, as the intellectual and moral horizon of the Greeks expanded, the culture in which it found expression was at every
point associated with the city. The tone of public opinion,
which determines insensibly and yet so powerfully men's character
and habits, was the distinctive tone or *êthos* of the *Polis*.[1] To
play his part worthily in its life formed the highest ambition
of the citizen and the measure by which he gauged his success
and his happiness. *Spartam nactus es ; hanc exorna*. To be
born into a mean *Polis* was accounted a grievous misfortune.
Moreover, the *Polis* determined the content not only of his moral,
but of his religious, obligations. The Greeks knew no distinction
between church and state; from Homeric times onwards, the
magistrate presided over the religion of the community, while
the priesthood was confined to the discharge of ceremonial
duties.[2] The *Polis* furnished also the stimulus to intellectual
progress. Alike in the formal assemblies of the people and in the
daily intercourse of the market-place or the dinner-table, it gave
opportunity for freedom of thought and speech. Such liberty
of criticism is something quite independent of democratic institutions and the machinery of political self-government. Soldiers
canvass the acts and characters of their officers behind the scenes,
juniors those of their seniors at school or college, without possessing
any right of voting for their election. Democracy in Greece
was the effect, not the cause, of free discussion. The Greeks
were a nation of talkers, and their talk was often childish and
insincere, such as to rouse scorn in the breast of the Roman,
who was wont to act in silence. What distinguished the Greeks
above other nations who have loved talking is that they talked
also about what was most worth discussion : law and freedom,
moral duty and the end of government, the nature and causes of
things, art and poetry, virtue and the good for man. Above all,
their talk was reasoned and logical, the expression of clear thinking and grasp of fact. No people have ever thought so deeply
or talked so well on these high subjects as did the Greeks. No
people have ever drawn with so firm a hand the line between

---

[1] We may bear in mind the moral atmosphere of a school, college,
club or regiment. Plato (*Rep.*, vi. 492) asserted that no individual,
however gifted, could resist the force of the public tone of his *Polis*.

[2] As the gods could not compel, but only warn and punish, so the
priest could only warn and protest. He was the housekeeper and watch-
man (ὑπηρέτης) of his god, and only occasionally his spokesman. When
a χρησμός is given, it is because a man Ἐχρῆτο, i.e. accepted the god's help.

illusion and reality, or set themselves so resolutely to understand and master the world of nature. And all this was the outcome of the free play of mind with mind, fostered by common intercourse as citizens of the city-state.

§ 5. The Greek ideal of life was conceived in terms of the *Polis*. Alike for statesmen and for philosophers, happiness (*eudaimonia*) lay in the honourable discharge of civic duty.[1] The dramatists and historians of the fifth century reflect on almost every page of their writings their sense of the value of the *Polis* as furnishing scope for the realization of the good life.[2] The philosophers who sought to determine by scientific reasoning the nature and standard of human goodness, were unswerving in their conviction that the only life worth living was that of the citizen in the Hellenic city-state. When Socrates after his condemnation by the Athenians was offered escape from prison, he replied that to evade the law of the *Polis*, even when unjustly exercised, was as morally wrong as for a son to do violence to an aged parent. Plato condemned all existing Greek states as hopelessly corrupt, yet sketched in his *Republic* the ideal community as a reformed Hellenic *Polis*.[3] For him, as for Aristotle in the succeeding generation, the good city afforded at once the condition and the complement of the good life for its members. Aristotle defined the *Polis* as " an association formed for maintenance of complete and self-sufficient life "; other forms of association enabled man to live, but the *Polis* alone enabled him to live well.[4] Man he defined as " a political animal," a living creature whose nature marked him out for the life of civic activity.[5]

---

[1] *Eudaimonia* (lit. having a good " dæmon " or guardian-spirit) was the Greek term for " happiness " or felicity," i.e. the *summum bonum* or ideal of human life. For the interpretation of this ideal by a cultured Greek of the fifth century, see Herodotus's tale of Solon's conversation with Crœsus (i. 30 ff.). To the popular mind happiness consisted in good fortune (*eutychia*); the philosophers consciously rejected the view that the chief good depended on external circumstances, or on the arbitrary caprice of the gods, or on luck.

[2] Compare especially Herodotus, *loc. cit.* and iii. 80 ff. In the latter passage the Persian grandees are represented as debating the merits of democracy, aristocracy and monarchy respectively. The speeches, of course, reflect Greek sentiments, just as Shakespeare's Romans are really Elizabethan Englishmen. See also the conversation of Xerxes with Demaratus, vii. 101 ff.

[3] Plato, *Rep.*, v. 470. For Socrates' refusal, see Plato's *Crito*.

[4] Arist., *Pol.*, iii. 9, 1280 *b*; i. 2, 1252 *b*.

[5] Arist., *Pol.*, i. 2, 1253 *a*. Writing as late as the middle of the second century, the Greek historian of Rome, Polybius, insists that a constitution is good or bad according as it produces citizens of good or bad moral character (*Polyb.*, vi. 47).

The main function of the lawgiver and the statesman was the development of moral goodness in the citizen, his education to the complete achievement of the capacities of his nature in the city-state. Even the Stoics, writing amid the shattered fragments of Greek political independence, strove to reconstruct the fabric of moral duty by teaching men to live as citizens of a cosmopolitan republic, a *Polis* grounded in pure reason, the city of God.[1]

§ 6. Thus the civilization of the Greek people was rooted deep in the soil of the city-state. It was "the rock whence they were hewn," "the hole of the pit whence they were digged." Architecture and sculpture, the dramatic festivals and lyric song, science and philosophy, religion and morals, craft-gilds and the arts of peace and war, the structure of the constitution and the maxims of public policy, the forms of social intercourse, speech and manners, were branches of a single organism, the *Polis*. But there is another side to the picture. Freedom has a two-edged sword; and the life of the *Polis* gave play alike to the temper of civic patriotism and to that of personal ambition. In ancient Greece, as two thousand years afterwards in Dante's Florence, the disintegrating forces of party faction and individual self-seeking seethed close beneath the surface. *Stasis*, civil discord, was the chronic malady of the Hellenic *Polis*. Both the forms which it assumed, the inability of cities to combine in political union even in face of a common foe, and the internal strife of men, families and parties within the walls of a single town, worked for the eventual dissolution of Greek independence. We read continually, it is true, of confederations of cities for purposes of religion or of defence. Greek history is largely the history of Leagues, from the Amphiktyonic league of the seventh century to the Achæan and Ætolian leagues of the fourth and third. But these combinations lacked permanence and solidarity; they were effective only for transient purposes and within the narrow bounds of Hellenism, and proved wholly unavailing when matched against the forces of Macedon and Rome.[2] In the event, excess of liberty issued in bondage to an alien power. The Greeks, with their keen sense of the facts of life, were not slow to diagnose their own disorder, but they were powerless to cure it. Plato's unerring insight into human

---

[1] Cosmopolis means "the city (*polis*) of the universe (*cosmos*)."
[2] Federations and empires alike appeared to the Greeks to mark a retrograde step from the independent *Polis*.

nature traced the source of public tyranny in the state to the tyranny of lawless passion within the individual. He saw that it was the most gifted of the citizens, a Themistocles or an Alcibiades, who, because of their great possessions, were the most tempted to fall victims to the lust for power, and to shatter, first, the economy of their own souls, and then that of the community.[1] For all its splendour of achievement, Greek history is full of tragedy. Its pages are strewn with the wreckage of ruined lives. They represent the sacrifice by which the mind of man purchased its freedom to think and act. But they must not deceive us into thinking for an instant that the triumph was not worth the sacrifice.

III. The Expansion of Greece (§§ 7–8).

§ 7. The influence of the city-state, for good and for evil, becomes clearer as we study its development in Greek history. The eighth and seventh centuries saw its rapid diffusion over the islands and coast-lands of the Mediterranean. This expansion of the Greek race was favoured by geographical and climatic conditions. The cities of the Ægean area were situated either on islands or in valleys parted by high mountain ridges, and were thus protected from aggression on land. But they were not shut off from mutual intercourse; else, like the Swiss of modern history, they would have preserved their independence at all costs. The bond of union was the sea. The gulf of Corinth and numberless bays and inlets secured for the European Greeks a great length of coast-line; there was hardly any Greek state that had not easy access to the sea. The Greeks were a maritime race from early days; intercourse in trade both among themselves and with other peoples combined with the freedom and individuality of their cities to promote a rich and varied culture. Rarely has any race been so lavishly endowed by nature with the physical conditions of civilization.[2] Mountains and sea, a temperate and bracing climate, a soil that called forth and rewarded energy and skill, fostered the qualities of love of adven-

---

[1] See *Rep.*, vi. 490 ff. (where the reference is undoubtedly to Alcibiades), and viii. 562 ff. (where tyranny is shown to arise out of excess of democratic liberty).

[2] But they had no resources of natural power (hence the necessity of slave-labour on a large scale), no glass (hence no chemistry or optical instruments), no coal (hence no boiler-plates or steam).

ture and free action that the northern invaders brought with them when they descended into the Ægean world.[1]

§ 8. The eighth and seventh centuries were marked by commercial enterprise, great activity in colonization, the growth of wealth and social refinement and widespread political unrest. By 600 B.C. the Greeks had planted commercial colonies on the shores of the Propontis (Sea of Marmora) and the Euxine (Black Sea), on the northern coast of Africa, round the south of Italy, and over the whole Sicilian coast-line, save where the Carthaginian strongholds commanded the extreme west of the island. We saw how, early in the sixth century, Greek traders secured from the friendly princes of the twenty-sixth dynasty a permanent foothold at Naucratis in the Egyptian Delta. The trade of the Mediterranean from Sicily to the Levant had passed from the Phœnicians to the Greeks. In the extreme west Carthage enjoyed an unchallenged monopoly. But elsewhere the Greek trader and colonist, with a natural genius for making himself at home amid new conditions and alien peoples, ousted earlier races from the markets of the Mediterranean. This commercial expansion carried with it far-reaching effects on social and political life. Splendid cities arose, such as Miletus in Ionia, Syracuse in Sicily, and Sybaris in southern Italy; a " Sybarite " is to this day a term for the lover of luxurious ease. A class of merchant princes sprang into existence, who were liberal patrons of art and poetry. In the field of politics there seethed perpetual ferment and revolution. The new plutocracy struggled for power and privilege against the monopoly of the old nobility. Keen party struggles proved a stimulus to fresh colonization. Not infrequently, and often under the guidance of the Delphic oracle, which rose to importance in this epoch, the malcontents were despatched as colonists to some unoccupied region favourable to trade, where they founded a self-governing *Polis*. The Greek colony was politically independent of the mother-city; such bonds as existed were those of religion, of sentiment or of commercial alliance.[2] Thus the age was one of rapid political transition. The rivalry of birth and wealth, of land and trade,

---

[1] But the Minoans as well as the Northerners showed maritime enterprise.

[2] Yet we read of colonies that were bitter commercial rivals of the parent-city, e.g. Corinth and her colony Corcyra. See Thucydides, iii. 82 ff., where the revolutions at Corcyra are described as an illustration of the moral and political effects of party struggles in the Hellenic world of the later fifth century. On the Delphic oracle and colonisation, see Her., iv. 150–8 (Cyrene).

prepared the way, now for democracy, now for despotism. The most remarkable phenomenon of the times was the rise of the form of government known to the Greeks as " tyranny." Though short-lived in any single city, it is henceforward a standing feature in the commercial centres of Greece. Often, as in the days of the Italian renaissance, a rich merchant would overthrow the oppressive nobles with popular aid, and establish himself as despot. The " tyrants " were frequently enlightened and humane rulers, e.g. Pisistratus at Athens in the sixth century, but they deeply offended the Greek love of freedom, and their rule excited bitter resentment. They set themselves above the law, and thereby renounced all claim to its protection. Their authority was a violation of the *êthos* of the Hellenic city-state. Moreover, the Greeks shared to the full the dislike, felt in all ages by free people, towards power based on possession of wealth. " To lay low a tyrant who consumes the people is no sin and will not be punished by the gods," wrote Theognis of Megara. The poet Simonides celebrates the praise of the murderers of Pisistratus' son in these words : " A great light broke upon the Athenians when Harmodius and Aristogiton slew Hipparchus." The issues of this epoch in the public life of Greece are seen also in the development of law and political institutions, and in the advance towards democracy through the breaking-down of hereditary privilege.[1] Of still greater moment was the expansion of culture in the domain of poetry, art and science.

IV. EARLY POETIC LITERATURE (§§ 9–12).

§ 9. The literature of Greece, like that of many nations, opens with song; and the earliest poems that we possess are two epics ascribed to Homer, the *Iliad* and the *Odyssey*. The *Iliad* tells the story of battles " on the ringing plains of windy Troy," of the wrath and prowess of Achilles, and his slaying of Trojan Hector. The *Odyssey* narrates the ten years' wandering of Odysseus over sea and land after Troy had fallen, his return to Ithaca, and his slaughter of the suitors who had wasted his home.[2] They are the two survivals of many early epics, and

[1] The intervention of Persia, which could always co-operate with oligarchies, cut sharply across the normal development to democracy. This accounts for the persistence of oligarchy into the fourth century.

[2] In neither epic is the sequence of incidents presented as the fulfilment of a single large design. As Mr. C. S. Lewis has recently pointed out in his illuminating *Preface to Paradise Lost*, it is characteristic of the early heroic epic, in Greece, as among the peoples of northern Europe,

E

represent the ripe fruit of a long period of poetic creation. The first Greek settlers in Asia Minor, of Æolian stock, brought with them from southern Thessaly ballads and lays in praise of gods and tribal ancestors, composed in hexameter verse—" the stateliest measure ever moulded by the lips of man." [1] These were wrought into great epics in the island of Lesbos or on the shores of north-western Asia between about 1200 and 800, and brought into their present form, with later modifications, accretions and expurgations among the Ionian settlers further south.[2] We can trace in them changes of language, thought and custom, and the growth of moral ideas; the *Odyssey*, which on the whole is the later of the two, perhaps reflects the romantic temper of the age of maritime adventure. We cannot enter here upon the disputed problems, how far the two epics or either one of them was the work of a single poet, and merely note that to-day scholars are more disposed to take a conservative view on these questions than they were half a century ago. The view that Homer was an actual individual and that the *Iliad* and the *Odyssey* are to be ascribed to his authorship can no longer be ruled cavalierly out

---

that unlike the later " secondary " epic it has no great subject, such as the founding of Rome (Virgil) or the fall of man (Milton). " That kind of greatness," he writes (pp. 28–29), " arises only when some event can be held to effect a profound and more or less permanent change in the history of the world. . . . The mere endless up and down, the constant aimless alternations of glory and misery, which make up the terrible phenomenon called a Heroic Age, admit no such design. No one event is really very much more important than another. . . . Nothing 'stays put,' nothing has a significance beyond the moment. Heroism and tragedy there are in plenty, therefore good stories in plenty; but no ' large design. . . .' The total effect is not a pattern, but a kaleidoscope."

[1] Tennyson, *To Virgil*. The verse of ancient poetic literature was unrhymed; Dante was the first great world-poet to use rhyme. Greek (and Latin) metres rest on the quantity of the syllables rather than on stress. Hence modern imitations of, e.g., hexameter verses give a very inadequate impression of the metre as used by the ancients. The following from Clough's *Bothie of Tober-na-vuolich*, may serve as an imperfect illustration:

" So in the | golden | morning they | parted and | went to the | westward."

" There hath he | farmstead and | land, and | fields of | corn and | flax fields."

The normal scheme of the six feet line is:

$$-\,\smile\,\smile \;|\; -\,\smile\,\smile \;|\; -\,\smile\,\smile \;|\; -\,\smile\,\smile \;|\; -\,\smile\,\smile \;|\; -\,\smile$$
$$-\;-\quad|\quad -\;-\quad|\quad -\;-\quad|\quad -\;-\quad|\quad -\;-\quad|\quad -\;-$$

the long-syllable having double the value of the short (♩ and ♪) and being reckoned as replacing two short syllables.

[2] They are in the Ionic dialect, but were originally composed in the Æolic. On the Homeric theology, see Nilsson, *History of Greek Religion*.

of court. For us, as for the Greeks, Homer stands as the personification of the whole body of epic saga. The marvel is that the race could thus early give birth to a school of consummate poets. No extant literature opens so gloriously as that of Greece with these two poems. Alike in content and in form, they reign in unquestioned sovereignty over the epic poetry of every race and time. Their significance for the after civilization of Greece and of the world is threefold. Their beauty and splendour have been a perennial source of poetic inspiration. We can trace their influence through the whole course of Greek literature and art. Roman poetry, and especially the *Æneid* of Virgil, is shaped in large measure on the model of the *Iliad* and the *Odyssey*; and the spirit of Homer still breathes in the poetry of the modern world. Æschylus is said to have called his tragedies " fragments from the great banquet of Homer "; poets of all ages might echo his words. The parting of Hector and Andromache; Helen's remembrance of her dead brothers as she watches the Achæan host from the walls of Troy; the supplication of Priam to Achilles for Hector's corpse, when the aged king " dared what none other man on earth has dared before, to stretch forth my hand toward the face of the slayer of my sons "; stir a like emotion in readers of every nation and language, in the unlettered peasant as in the scholar or the poet.[1] From the dawn of Greek poetry its theme is what is most universal in human life and feeling. Secondly, as time went on, the Homeric poems came to be read and taught as a storehouse of moral and religious truth. Lines such as the words of Achilles to the envoys, " hateful to me as the gates of hell is he who speaketh one thing with his lips but hideth another in his heart," or Odysseus' " endure, my heart : far worse hast thou endured," served as texts, which Greek children learnt much as those of modern England learn verses from the scriptures.[2] The Homeric poems did much to shape and

---

[1] *Il.*, vi. 390 ff., iii. 234 ff., xxiv. 505–6 (*tr.* Lang, Leaf and Myers).

[2] *Il.*, ix. 312–13, *Od.*, xx. 18. On the other hand, there were many passages which struck the developed moral sense of later Greeks as ill-suited for the education of the young. Such were the incidents from the *chronique scandaleuse* of the gods, which were probably late additions, reflecting the *persiflage* and religious scepticism of the seventh-century Ionians ; e.g. the tricking of Zeus by Hera (*Il.*, xiv. 153 ff.) ; the surprise of the amours of Hephæstus and Aphrodite (*Od.*, viii. 266 ff.), condemned by Plato (*Rep.*, iii. 390) ; and the fight of Athena with Ares and Aphrodite (*Il.*, xxi. 391 ff.), which might be paralleled with the parody in *Tom Jones* (Bk. IV. c. 8—Molly Segrim's encounter with the village women), " a battle sung," Fielding tells us, " by the Muse in the Homerican style." On these later additions, see Murray, *Rise of the Greek Epic*, Lect. X. They

fix the religious and moral ideas of subsequent generations.[1]
Thirdly, these poems have a value for history. They depict
with substantial fidelity the life of the chieftains and warriors
of the Ægean world in the later centuries of the second millennium.
We cannot indeed affirm that the persons actually lived or that
the incidents actually took place, though a siege of Troy is no
historic improbability. The poets, it is true, are singing of a past
age, and the picture is coloured by an infusion of later custom.
Yet we learn much of early usage, of marriage and religious
worships, of modes of house-building and habits of domestic
life, of the manner of warfare, of agriculture and faring on the
sea. When we read the description of the institutions of king,
council and assembly of the folk (e.g. in the second book of the
Iliad), of the shield of Achilles (in the eighteenth book), of the
palaces, the armour and the dress, we find striking confirmation
of their accuracy in the discoveries of Schliemann and his successors. The world of Homer was a real world. Two features,
among others, stand out in prominent relief. The life portrayed
is that of a feudal aristocracy. We hear but little of the common
people; they bear no part in the action, and the very slaves are
captives of princely birth. The poetry before us was not popular
poetry, any more than its religion was popular religion; it was
composed for noble chieftains by minstrels who sang to the honour
of their families and clans. Yet, despite this undemocratic
character, we breathe an air of freedom in the Homeric world.
There is no political despotism, no priestcraft; intrigue and
magic alike are rare; women live on an equality with men to a
degree unknown in later Greece, and enjoy high dignity in the
household; slaves speak to their masters, and are spoken to,
as men to men.[2] Common humanity reaches nearer to the surface
in Homeric society than in our more complex modern world.

§ 10. The early epics were tales of heroic action, of the deeds

---

have their value for history, e.g. Hera's toilet (*Il.*, xiv. 170 ff.) is highly
instructive. Plato's strictures on Homer and the poets generally in his
Republic (ii. 377–iii. 392) are directed not against their merits as poetry
(which he fully recognised: *Rep.*, x. 607), but against their claim to be a
bible of religious and moral instruction. He expressly singles out for
approval (*Rep.*, iii. 390) the words of Odysseus quoted in the text.

[1] Herodotus (ii. 53) recognises this: the passage is quoted in § 11
below. The Olympian religion, as distinct from more primitive popular
worships, owed its enduring triumph largely to Homer.

[2] On women, see the *Odyssey*. The relations between the sexes are
handled with delicacy and restraint. On slaves, see Eumæus in the
Odyssey; he is of noble birth, captured in war, and is treated as an honoured
retainer of the family. See later, c. v, Additional Note.

of famous men. Later poets struck a new subjective note, and in a more romantic spirit uttered their passion in lyric verse. Their interest was centred, not on the past, but on the present, on the poets' personal experience of life. The age of commercial expansion saw the birth of lyric and elegiac poetry, richly varied in subject and metrical form, comprising poems of love and war, sorrow and *ennui*, the dirge and the marriage-song, choric odes, and political and personal satire. "Age cannot wither" the imperishable beauty of these poems. They defy translation, but an echo of their charm may be caught in Rossetti's adaptation from Sappho—

1.

" Like the sweet apple that reddens upon the topmost bough,
  A-top on the topmost twig—which the pluckers forgot
    somehow—
  Forgot it not, nay, but got it not, for none could get it till now."

2.

" Like the wild hyacinth flower which on the hills is found,
  Which the passing feet of the shepherds for ever tear and
    wound,
  Until the purple blossom is trodden into the ground."

The elegiac vein may be illustrated by the famous couplet inscribed by Simonides early in the fifth century on the tomb of the Spartan dead at Thermopylæ : " Go, stranger, and tell the men of Lacedæmon that we lie here, obedient to their charge." Lyric poetry, as the name implies, was written to be sung to music. The choric ode, developed to great perfection in this same age, was accompanied both by music and dancing. The chorus celebrated the praises of gods or heroes or victors in the games ; the extant odes of Pindar (early fifth century), one of the glories of Greek poetry, are mainly in honour of athletic victories. In the next chapter we shall see how the lyric genius of the Greeks was interwoven with the epic in the Attic drama.

  § 11. Side by side with these forms of lyric verse, the growing interest in moral reflexion gave rise to gnomic poetry (*gnômê* = a maxim), expressive of naïve criticism of life, counsels of policy or prudence, and precepts of private and public action. Didactic poetry had arisen in yet earlier times among the peasantry of central Greece, as the counterpart of the Homeric epics among the Æolian and Ionian aristocracy ; it survives in the poems ascribed to the Bœotian Hesiod.[1] The gnomic poetry of the later seventh and sixth centuries may be compared with the works of Piers Plowman, or of the " moral " Gower, in English literature. Theognis of Megara voiced in elegiac metre the Dorian noble's scorn for the vile demos who had robbed his class of wealth and power; the Athenian statesman, Solon, sang of loyal service to the city, and of the duty of restraint in the use of power, to a people ever prone to overstep the bounds of moderation. This new type of poetry is of special significance, when we remember how in the Greek view poets rather than priests were the recognized teachers of moral and religious truth. This does not mean that the Greeks failed in piety ; the Athenians of Solon's day, like their descendants at the time of St. Paul's visit, were if anything too " god-fearing," [2] and their attachment to the worships of the *Polis* broke out on occasion into frenzied extravagance.[3] It was part of the poets' function to narrate and interpret the tales of gods and heroes, and considerable latitude was allowed them in selection and reconstruction. Herodotus said that the early epic poets, Homer and Hesiod, " gave the gods their titles and distributed among them honours and arts and set forth their forms." He meant that they brought some measure of system and co-ordination into the multitude of local cults, and thus helped to crystallize the leading outlines of religious tradition for after times. No one can realize the part that poetry played in the life and education of the Greeks, who does not keep in view its intimate association with their religion.[4]

[1] The *Works and Days* of Hesiod give an interesting picture of life in the later part of the dark age that followed on the northern immigrations into the Ægean. See Ure, *The Greek Renaissance*, c. ii.

[2] Acts xvii. 22. The Greek term, translated " superstitious " in A.V. and R.V., means literally " dæmon-fearing." Dæmons were divine beings, like Heracles and other children of the gods in Greek religious story.

[3] E.g. on the occasion of the mutilation of the statues of Hermes, on the eve of the sailing of the Armada to Sicily in 415 : see Thuc., vi. 27 f. The effect on the populace may be compared to that which a desecration of the images of the Madonna would have produced in a Spanish town at the time of the Armada of 1588. On the Homeric theology, see Nilsson, *History of Greek Religion*. The society of the Olympian gods was feudal in character, after the fashion of human societies in the heroic age. The gods were conceived anthropomorphically, as differing from men only in *degree* of knowledge and power, but as immortal. They were not omniscient nor omnipotent ; yet everything in human life was regarded as subject to their influence.

[4] See Plato, *Rep.*, ii, iii, on the place of poetic tales about gods and dæmons and men in the moral instruction of the young rulers of the ideal city.

§ 12. The gnomic poets heralded the work of Pindar and the fifth-century dramatists, in that they attempted to adjust poetic teaching to the growing moral consciousness of the time. The prevalent unrest led inevitably, among a people endowed with rare powers of intellect, to changes in men's views of life, and to the substitution of new moral values for the old. A symptom of this reflective temper was the circulation in this epoch of proverbial maxims, such as " know thyself," " nothing in excess," " rule will reveal the man," which represent popular inductions from moral experience. The conception of an ethical standard took shape in the ideal of *sôphrosynê*, a term which defies translation by any single English word, and means literally " keeping the mind safe," or, as we might say, " the head clear." [1] Its primitive nucleus is the Homeric *aidôs* or respect, the inner feeling which in the days of barbaric warfare stayed a man's hand from outrage of the orphan, the aged, the suppliant or a fallen foe; checked his impulse to cowardice or to disloyalty, and kept him dutiful towards parents, rulers, and the gods.[2] The essential meaning of *sôphrosynê*, as it developed in the Greek mind, was self-restraint and obedience to law, whether of the state or of inward principle, in face of the besetting temptation to abuse wealth and power, and to subordinate civic loyalty to the claims of personal ambition. Over and above this negative obligation, it implied the positive quality of clear vision, born of self-knowledge, that enables an individual or a community to act with a balanced judgement in the critical moments of their history. The well-known phrase, " a right judgement in all things," furnishes perhaps the closest expression of its meaning.[3] The antithesis to this saving wisdom was *hubris*. The term is found already in the early epics; its root-meaning is the violent overstepping of the mark, the insolence of triumph, and the pride

[1] Aristotle (*Ethics*, vi. c. 5) interprets the term as meaning literally the virtue " which keeps safe practical wisdom (*phronêsis*)." *Phronêsis* means the power of right judgement in matters of human conduct.

[2] See Murray, *Rise of the Greek Epic*, pp. 78 ff. In the *Iliad* (iv. 402 ff.), when Agamemnon chides Diomedes for slowness in gathering his men to battle, the latter answers not back " from *aidôs* for the voice of the reverend (*aidoios*) king "; and when Sthenelus answers angrily in his stead, Diomedes rebukes him, " For I do not feel *nemesis* at Agamemnon, shepherd of the people, when he urges the well-greaved Achæans to the fight."

[3] See especially the analysis of *sôphrosynê* in Plato, *Rep.*, iv. 430 ff., and Aristotle, *Ethics*, bk. III. In these philosophers the term represents the reflective outcome of *aidôs*, the primitive feeling developed into a clearly defined form of moral excellence. The phrase quoted in the text is from the collect for Whitsunday in the English *Book of Common Prayer*.

of life that tramples under foot the unwritten law of gods and men. *Hubris* is the closest Greek equivalent for " sin." Its most characteristic application was to the insatiable thirst for power which drives a man or a nation headlong, as though possessed by a demon, on the path of unbridled self-assertion. This blinding passion, outraging alike personal liberty and public law, lures the victim in a frenzy of self-confidence towards destruction. · It provokes *nemesis*, the feeling of righteous indignation, in the gods and in his fellow-men. " An ancient *hubris* ever breeds a fresh and living *hubris* to add to human woes "; [1] so the Greek poet, striving to give their due both to inherited fatality and individual desert, pictured the gathering cloud of doom that visited the sins of the fathers upon the children, through successive generations of a sinful race. When tyranny made its appearance, it was regarded as the crowning manifestation of *hubris* in the public life of the city-state.[2] Later on, the conception is applied to the collective action of a nation uplifted by pride of empire to menace Hellenic independence, as in the case of the Persian invasion and the maritime sovereignty of Athens.[3] The Greek knew full well his weakness and the evil passions that were ever on the watch to lure him to assert his individuality beyond the bounds prescribed by reason and law. . It was hard for him, with his great possessions, to enter on the kingdom of his own soul. Of temptress-passions the chief were Persuasion (*Peithô*), Hope (*Elpis*) and Passion (*Erôs*). They were conceived as personal agents rather than as abstract motives. " Miserable Persuasion wreaks her might, the insufferable child of fore-counselling Doom (*Atê*) ; and all cure is vain." [4] " Hope,"

[1] Æsch., *Agam.*, 760 ff. In this play, when Clytemnestra bids her lord Agamemnon tread the purple on entering his home on his return from Troy, preparatory to the doom she has prepared for him, he does so with fear : " As I tread these sea-stuffs, may no jealousy (*phthonos*) from a god's far eyes strike me. For I have much *aidôs* in wasting substance, ruining by my tread riches and textures bought with silver " (*Ag.*, 946–9).   [2] Soph., *O.T.*, 873, " *hubris* begets a tyrant."
[3] For Persian *hubris* and its resulting *nemesis*, see Æschylus' " Persians " and the history of Herodotus, esp. Her., vii. 7–18 (conversation of Xerxes and Artabanus). On Athenian *hubris* in the closing third of the fifth century towards her subjects, see Thucydides, i. 75, 76, iii. 37 ff., and especially the Melian dialogue, v. 89 ff., followed immediately by the Sicilian expedition (*nemesis*). A Greek would have readily interpreted the rapid development of German nationalism into a policy of Germanising the world by force as an example of national *hubris*. On *nemesis*, see Murray, *op. cit.* The idea is definitely ethical. While *aidôs* expresses my sense of the inconceivability of such behaviour, *nemesis* expresses my conviction that I (or another person) *should* not act thus.
[4] Æsch., *Agam.*, 385.

wrote Hesiod, " is an ill guide for a needy man " ; and Sophocles,
" Far-roving Hope, though many have comfort of her, is to
many a delusion, that wings the dream of Love; and he whom
she haunts knows naught till he burn his feet against hot fire." [1]
Poets and philosophers alike hold Love to be a tyrant, who
enslaves his blinded victims to wild passion. " Love rules even
gods at will, and me also," cries the hapless Deianira, "how then
rules he not others such as I ? "

> " For mad is the heart of Love,
>   And gold the gleam of his wing ;
> And all to the spell thereof
>   Bend, when he makes his spring." [2]

A later age came to see in these three powers, Faith, Hope and
Love, a triad of graces, the crowning glory of man's spiritual
pilgrimage. But to the Greek of the great days they were evil
dæmons, luring the gambler in the game of life to stake his all
blindly on one fatal throw, and to rouse thereby the *nemesis* of
heaven. For the Olympian gods were jealous, and visited their
wrath on the insolent mortal who dared to outrage their prerogative.[3] Greek poetic literature is full of reflexions which
centre round these conceptions of *sôphrosynê* and *hubris* ; they
form the Hellenic counterpart to the ethical teaching of the
Hebrew prophets, and exemplify the conscious recognition by
the poets of their function as the moral educators of the Greek
people. But already in the sixth century another voice was
audible ; philosophy was asserting in opposition to poetry a
rival claim to teach the truth about the world and human life.

[1] Hesiod, *Works and Days*, 494; Soph., *Antig.*, 616; cf., on Hope,
Æsch., *Agam.*, 990 ff., Soph., *Trach.*, 666, Thucydides, iii. 45, v. 103, and
Cornford, *Thucydides Mythistoricus*.

[2] Soph., *Trach.*, 443–4; Eur., *Hipp.*, 1268 ff. (*tr.* Murray). See also
Plato's picture of the soul mastered by a tyrant *Erôs* in *Rep.*, ix. 572–3,
and the opening of the choric song in Soph., *Antig.*, 781 ff., thus rendered
by Swinburne (*Ode to Athens*) :

" Love in fight unconquered, love with spoils of great men laden,
    Never sang so sweet from throat of woman or of dove ;
Love whose bed by night is in the soft cheeks of a maiden,
    And his march is over seas and low roofs lack not love ;
Nor may one of all that live, ephemeral or eternal,
    Fly nor hide from love ; but whoso clasps him fast goes mad."

[3] On the jealousy (*phthonos*) of the gods, see Her., iii. 40–43 (the tale
of Polycrates) and vii. 10 (Artabanus' speech). Plato's passionate denial
that God is jealous, echoed by Aristotle and all later philosophers, marks
one of the great advances made by scientific thought on popular religion
(Plato, *Phaedr.*, 247; Aristotle, *Met.*, i. 2).

V. The Birth of Philosophy (§§ 13–18).

§ 13. " The desire of knowledge," wrote Aristotle, " is natural to all men "; and, again, voicing Plato, " It was wonder that first led men to philosophy." [1] The desire he has in mind is the disinterested love of truth, the impulse to think for thinking's sake, not merely as a means to practical ends. " The man who is puzzled and wonders is conscious of his ignorance; therefore, since they philosophised in order to escape from ignorance, it is clear that they studied science for the sake of knowledge, and not for any utilitarian end." To the Greeks the curiosity to know the causes of things and to probe their inner nature came naturally; already in the childhood of their history they had all the child's desire to know how and why. " At first they wondered at the obvious puzzles; little by little they advanced to enquiry into the larger problems, the phenomena of the moon and sun and the stars, and the origin of the universe." [2] In this disinterested curiosity, as Aristotle was aware, science and philosophy had their birth. The Greeks drew no distinction between the two, for knowledge had not yet been mapped out into provinces; the world of human experience, in its entirety and in its detail, formed the common theme of their enquiry. The speculative impulse, thus grounded in the Greek genius, was stimulated to effective exercise by the age of expansion. Miletus, a great centre of Ionian commerce and colonial enterprise, was the birthplace of Greek philosophy. [3] The unrest, which we have noted in the field of politics, seethed also in the minds of thinking men. A larger world had been unfolded to view, traditional customs were seen to vary with local and temporal conditions, and old tales were disproved by wider experience—the Scylla and Charybdis of the *Odyssey* were found to be mere natural phenomena, a rock and a whirlpool. The frequent migrations of the period broke down the links that bound early faiths to special localities. For the first time in the history of human civilization the scientific spirit swung free from entanglement with popular religious beliefs.

§ 14. The attempts of the first Milesian philosophers to ex-

---

[1] Aristotle, *Met.*, i. 1, 980 *a* 21 and i. 2, 982 *b* 11 ff., *tr.* Ross (with very slight alteration); cf. Plato, *Theaet.*, 155 d. Plato illustrates by the tale that Iris, the messenger of the gods, was the child of Thaumas (Wonder).   [2] Aristotle, *Met.*, i. 2.

[3] Miletus was in contact with Mesopotamian civilization by the great road that led from the Ægean coast eastwards through Asia Minor, and with Egypt by the recently established Milesian settlement at Naucratis.

plain the universe were distinguished by three features from
any that had gone before. In the first place, they bore, like all
other creations of the Hellenic genius, the stamp of individuality.
Eastern science, if we may dignify it with that name, was, in the
main, anonymous, the inherited achievement and possession of
a caste or gild.[1] But Thales, Anaximander and Anaximenes,
the first philosophers of Miletus in the sixth century, stand forth
as personalities, each with his distinctive contribution to the
development of thought.[2] Like Plato and Aristotle at a later
day, they founded schools; but the corporate tradition was based
on the creative work of individual thinkers, whose names have
survived, and whose personality dominated, in an increasing
degree, the course of intellectual progress. In the second place
their procedure was thoroughly scientific; observation was
broadened by experiment [3] and illumined by hypothesis; limited
as were the range of accessible facts and the instruments of
research, their aim was the discovery of principles of necessary
connexion amid the changing diversity of phenomena. " Nothing can arise out of nothing "; " naught happens for nothing,
but everything from a ground and of necessity." [4] Unlike the
Chaldæan astronomers, who merely utilised their store of observed
facts as a basis for fantastic interpretation, the Greek thinkers
set themselves to understand the world as a world of rational law,
with system and unity of structure. They pursued this path
with unswerving confidence and courage, displaying rare genius
alike for scientific hypothesis and for logical procedure. " No
sooner," writes Professor Burnet, " did an Ionian philosopher
learn half-a-dozen geometrical propositions, and hear that the
phenomena of the heavens recur in cycles, than he set to work
to look for law everywhere in nature, and with an audacity

[1] See Burnet, *Early Greek Philosophy*, pp. 28 ff. The Hebrew prophets,
as has been shown in the previous chapter, were in no sense scientific
thinkers. The remark in the text applies to the wise men in Egypt and
Babylonia, and also to the annalists and codifiers of the law among the
Hebrews. Even prophecy became anonymous as it became reflective,
e.g. in Is. xl–lxvi, while the later apocalyptic was either anonymous or
attached itself to earlier teachers (e.g. Enoch); see above, c. iii. § 11, *note*
and § 15, *note*.

[2] Thales flourished *c.* 585, Anaximander, *c.* 565, Anaximenes *c* 550–
545.

[3] Cf. Anaximander's observations in marine biology and Empedocles'
experiment with the water-clock to prove that air is a physical body;
Burnet, *Early Greek Philosophy*, 71, 229.

[4] Parmenides, *fr.* 8, Empedocles, *fr.* 12, Leucippus (Burnet, *Early
Greek Philosophy*, p. 340). The fragments are referred to according to
the numbering in the translations given by Burnet.

almost amounting to *hubris*, to construct a system of the universe."
Thus it was that they were enabled to discover, in the course of
two or three generations, the true theory of eclipses, the sphericity
of the earth, and the fact of its revolution, like the other planets,
round the centre of its system.[1] Such were the firstfruits harvested
by the spirit that took to itself two watchwords, to " save the
phenomena " and to " give a reason." Thirdly, the scientific
genius of the Greek philosophers is evident in their clear conception of the problem they set themselves to solve. Renouncing
once and for all the fruitless quest after a first beginning of the
universe in primeval chaos, which in Greece as elsewhere had
tortured the ingenuity of earlier generations, they sought for
the underlying reality of that which *is*. What, they asked, is
the bottom truth of the world as we know it now ? The desire
to find unity and principle amid the restless variety of nature
took the form of the search for a primary substance which remains permanent amid change, for an active energising matter
whose motions, determined in accordance with necessary law,
give birth to the phenomena of sense-experience. Such a
primary substance, called by them *physis* (nature), formed the
theme of their enquiry and the title of their treatises.[2] Thales
held it to be water, others found it in vapour or in fire or in a
combination or harmony of opposite principles. They differed
also in their explanations of the process by which our world
arises from this ultimate reality. But all alike start from
observed facts and advance by logical reasoning towards the
conception of an ordered universe, wherein, by operation of
necessary law, the One Generates the Many and the Many are
resolved into the One.[3]

[1] *Early Greek Philoosphy*, pp. 23, 25.
[2] To translate *physis* by " nature " may be misleading, since it
transfers attention from process to origin. *Physis* is always a verbal
substantive, meaning a process like the growth of a plant.
[3] Our knowledge of these early thinkers is derived from scattered
fragments of their writings and from notices in later Greek authors.
Thales alone left no writing behind him. Anaximander, his successor,
held that *physis* was a boundless material substance containing in fusion
all the opposite principles (moist and dry, hot and cold), which were
separated out from the boundless mass by a sifting process, and thus
gave rise to innumerable worlds of which ours is one. Anaximander
was the first to realise that the earth swings free in space, needing no
material support. Early Greek medicine (Alcmæon, see below, p. 111,
n. 1) was based on Anaximander's opposites; health was conceived as
the *isonomy* or equilibrium of the hot and the cold, the moist and the
dry, disease as the despotism of one of the opposites over the other.
Anaximenes, the third in time of the Milesian philosophers, held that

§ 15. We cannot do more than indicate the trend of these early speculations, in order to show how they present an ordered sequence of scientific thought.

(i) The first efforts of the Ionian thinkers referred to in the preceding section led, at the beginning of the fifth century, to the philosophy of Heraclitus of Ephesus,[1] whose central doctrine was that the life of nature consisted in a strife of opposite forces, in tension one against the other, and constituting by their reciprocal action the harmonious unity of the world. Fire, the most active element, passes into air and is fed by moisture in equal measures; summer and winter, waking and sleeping, day and night, life and death all exemplify the ceaseless and universal conflict of the " way up " and the " way down." " War is the father of all and the king of all " ; " the way up and the way down is one and the same " ; " men do not know how what is at variance with itself agrees with itself. It is an attunement of opposite tensions, like that of the bow and the lyre." Heraclitus realised that nature's law is one of ceaseless change, that the world as it appears to sense is ever a becoming and a ceasing to be, nowhere a *being*, nowhere a thing of which we can say " it *is*." " You cannot," he said, " step into the same river twice " ; " No," added one of his followers, " nor even once." The issues of this thought of the ceaseless flux of the sense-world are apparent, as we shall see later, in the philosophy of Plato.

(ii) Coincidently with this development among the Ionian Greeks, the impulse to scientific enquiry had been stirring in the west. (a) Already in the sixth century Pythagoras and his followers in southern Italy had founded the study of mathematics, both in the field of pure geometry and in the application of mathematics to other branches of science, especially to the theory of musical sounds, and to philosophy in general.[2] Their doctrine

---

physis was vapour, from which our world arises by condensation and rarefaction. For details on these and the other early thinkers, see Burnet, *Early Greek Philosophy*, and *Thales to Plato*.

[1] Heraclitus flourished between 500 and 480; he was influenced also by early Pythagorean science. The quotations that follow are from *Fr*. 44, 69, 45, 41 (cf. 81).

[2] Pythagoras flourished about 530; he was a native of Ionian Samos who settled in Italy. Little is known of his life or of his personal teaching apart from that of his school. The Pythagoreans combined scientific research with a religious rule of life, and played an active part in south Italian politics. Henceforward Greek philosophy is never merely intellectualist; it directs *praxis* as well as *theoria*. The school continued its work well on into the fourth century. In contrast to the eastern Greek philosophers, their enquiries were predominantly mathematical. See

that " things were numbers " was no fantastic analogy, but the reasoned conclusion of thinkers, who in their analysis of experience found themselves confronted at every turn by laws admitting of mathematical formulation. They were feeling their way towards a system like that of Descartes, who determined the independent reality of the physical universe, in terms of its geometrical properties, as figured extension. This was precisely the position taken up by Plato in the *Timaeus*, under the influence of his Pythagorean predecessors.[1] (*b*) Another school of thought, the Eleatic, founded by Parmenides of Elea, also had its home in southern Italy.[2] Parmenides unfolded with inexorable logic the conclusions that follow from the assumptions which previous thinkers had accepted without question. All had taken for granted not only that *physis* or reality was one, but also that it was corporeal; all moreover had conceived this one body as possessed of inherent motion, and had thus derived from it the manifold phenomena of experience. Parmenides showed that, if the real is one and is corporeal, the many and motion are alike illusory. He accepted this refutation of the reality of the changing world of sense, but in effect his logic proved the *reductio ad absurdum* of the received assumptions. Henceforward the unity of *physis* was sacrificed by all thinkers who retained their faith in the other Parmenidean tenet, viz., that the real was of the nature of body.[3]

Sir T. Heath, *History of Greek Mathematics*, especially pp. 2, 166 ff., where the mathematical achievements of the Pythagoreans are summarised (covering Euclid, books I, II, IV, VI and probably III).

[1] The Pythagoreans interpreted numbers in terms of geometry, the unit being a point having position in a spatial field; hence arose the term (mathematical) "figures." See Burnet, *Early Greek Philosophy*, pp. 99 ff., and *Thales to Plato*, pp. 51 ff. Burnet shows how the discovery that the notes of the lyre depend on mathematical ratios influenced mathematical speculations. Pythagorean science also stimulated the study of medicine and of rhetoric in southern Italy and Sicily. Its importance was thus very great. The thought that the physical world is built up of spatial (or spatio-temporal) elements and that its nature can be explained in terms of mathematical equations, is prominent in modern physics and philosophy. The most recent metaphysical system in this country, that of Professor S. Alexander (*Space, Time and Deity*, Gifford Lectures at Glasgow, 1916–18) interprets the universe as generated from pure spatio-temporal elements, viz. point-instants. The scientific studies of the Pythagoreans led them, in the very dawn of scientific development, to conceptions that were extraordinarily fruitful.

[2] Parmenides flourished between 480 and 450; about the latter date he visited Athens, see Plato, *Parm.* 127. Burnet's view of his place in Greek philosophy is followed in the text.

[3] Zeno's famous paradoxes, e.g. that of Achilles and the tortoise, were put forward in support of his master Parmenides' denial of motion.

(iii) As a result of Parmenides' philosophy, there arose in the middle of the fifth century a number of pluralist systems. Empedocles of Agrigentum in Sicily, Anaxagoras of Clazomenæ in Asia (the first philosopher to take up his abode at Athens) and Leucippus of Miletus (the teacher of Democritus and founder of the Atomic school), all agree with the later Pythagoreans in holding two positions, the traditional view that reality is corporeal, and the new view, to which they were driven by Parmenides, that it is not one but many.[1] Empedocles and Anaxagoras further sought for a cause of motion; the latter found it in *nous* or mind, though he interpreted its action mechanically as that of an external physical agent.[2] The entire course of speculative development was summed up by the Atomists, who were the first to affirm the reality of empty space, and who reduced the universe to a congeries of innumerable atoms, homogeneous, and differing only in size, shape and position, drifting through infinite space in ceaseless motion.[3] With the publication of this system, the effort to conceive the world in terms of its material elements had worked itself out to fulfilment.

§ 16. It was entirely natural that the problems as to the nature of reality, and whether it is one or many, should have been answered by these early philosophers in physical terms. By *physis* they meant either one body or a plurality of bodies,

There was, of course, another way out of the quandary, viz. to maintain that reality was one, but that it was a spiritual, not a material, unity. This view appears first with Socrates and Plato, see c. v. §§ 17, 20.

[1] Empedocles flourished c. 460, Anaxagoras and Leucippus c. 450; Democritus belongs to the next generation and was influenced by the Sophists, on whom see c. v. §§ 13–15. The middle of the fifth century was a time of great creative activity in Greek thought. It should be observed also that the biological sciences were assuming increasing importance during the fifth century. Schools of medicine also flourished, at first, in close connexion with philosophy, as that of Alcmæon of Croton in southern Italy, who dedicated his work to the Pythagorean community, but later, in independence, as in the case of the fifth-century Hippocratean school in the island of Cos. Alcmæon was the real founder of psychology (see on this and generally on early Greek psychology, Beare, *Greek Theories of Elementary Cognition*, and Brett, *History of Psychology*, esp. pp. 24, 25 and c. v). Later Greek sculpture (the school of Pergamos) shows some knowledge of anatomy. See Burnet, *Early Greek Philosophy*, pp. 26, 193 ff.

[2] For Socrates' dissatisfaction with the concept of mind as a mechanical force, to the exclusion of purposive action, see the remarkable account of his early intellectual history in Plato, *Phaedo*, pp. 96 ff.

[3] Leucippus' more famous successor, Democritus of Abdera in Thrace, wrote in the last third of the fifth century, when the new ideas of the Sophists, raising problems of the theory of knowledge and of ethics, were abroad. The Atomism of Epicurus (see c. vi. § 18) is based on Democritus's system.

and, in the latter case, bodies either limited or unlimited in number, and either differing in quality or homogeneous. A time would come when the thought of a spiritual reality would arise in the mind of Greek thinkers, but for this the hour was not yet ripe. Each successive phase of Greek philosophy appears in order of logical development, in obedience to a law imposed, not by external circumstance, but by the intrinsic nature of human reason. We must not suppose that these physical enquirers ignored the facts of man's mental and moral life. The distinction, so familiar and yet so puzzling to modern thought, between the material and the spiritual had not yet been clearly drawn. Anaximenes of Miletus, for example, held that the soul is vapour.[1] To call this materialism in the modern sense would be less true than to say that his vapour was something not merely physical. So, again, Heraclitus spoke of fire convicting all things and of the sun as observing the bounds of justice;[2] while love and strife, the motive forces of Empedocles, were conceived as corporeal masses, and the *nous* of Anaxagoras as filling space. But it was not till well on in the fifth century that men's thinking and conduct claimed equal attention with the problems of physical nature. Then first the question arose: since moral standards, religious beliefs and the laws and institutions of the *Polis* present, like physical nature, a scene of instability and change, are they in consequence only of local and transitory value, " conventions " artificially set up by human ordinance ? Or is there some *physis* or natural morality, some unchanging law of God or man, of which the changing conventions are the passing embodiment ? Such questions were inevitable in a time of political unrest, when men's minds had already been disciplined by more than a century of intellectual enquiry. They were asked by the Greeks of the middle years of the fifth century, and, when once asked, gave birth, as we shall see in a later chapter, not only to moral and political philosophy, but to a new and enlarged conception of the nature of reality, and of man's place and destiny in the universe.

§ 17. It remains for us to notice the double relationship, of hostility and of fusion, between the new-born philosophy and the

[1] The " air " of Anaximenes included the " breath " of life, wind and vapour.

[2] *Fr.* 27; cf. *fr.* 29. " The sun will not overstep his measures; if he does, the Erinyes, the handmaids of justice, will find him out." So Anaximander : things " make reparation and satisfaction to one another for their injustice in an order of time " (Burnet, *Early Greek Philosophy,* p. 52).

old religion.[1] On the one hand, the broadening of men's range
of experience, the growth of the critical temper, and the awakening of higher moral aspirations were bound to provoke scepticism.
But this effect was confined to the few who thought seriously
about such matters, or, at most, to the cultured public. Anaxagoras might proclaim that the sun was not a god, but a stone
" about as large as the Peloponnese "; the fifth-century Athenian
felt a shock to his devotion, and condemned the philosopher for
impiety. Such hostility was due, not to any distaste for speculation, but to inbred loyalty to the traditional worships of the city.
This was the main reason for the distrust of science and philosophy
that found brilliant expression in the satire of the Old Attic
comedy. One of the charges brought against Socrates by his
accusers was that of introducing new divinities, and teaching
men to disbelieve in those whom the city worshipped. It is
thoroughly significant of Greek life that the opposition to philosophy was led, not by priests, but by poets and politicians.
The philosophers, on their side, were uncompromising in condemnation of the traditional beliefs. Especially in Ionia, the
birthplace both of science and history, where the merchant-
princes formed a cultivated public, the spread of the sceptical
spirit was rapid and general. " Homer and Hesiod," wrote
Xenophanes of Colophon, " have ascribed to the gods all things
that are a shame and a disgrace among men, thefts and adulteries
and deception of one another." " Homer," said Heraclitus,
" should be turned out of the lists and whipped, and Archilochus
likewise." The " quarrel between poetry and philosophy " was
referred to by Plato in the *Republic* as of long standing; he

[1] In conformity with our purpose of concentrating attention on those
factors which have most directly influenced later times, we have omitted
the interesting subject of Greek religion, save in so far as it bears on the
history of Greek philosophy. Recent investigations have done much to
throw light on this field, which is important not only for an understanding
of Greek poetry, law and daily life, but also, of course, for the comparative
study of early religions. A point of special interest to readers of this book
is the distinction between the Olympian gods, represented by Apollo, and
the Mystery gods, represented by Dionysus. The former were idealised
superhuman beings, dwelling in remote transcendence, with whom anything of the nature of personal communion was hardly conceivable; the
latter were directly accessible to the initiated in the state of emotional
ecstasy, and through sacramental food and drink. The mystery-religions
furnished materials to the philosophers (see below, § 17 and c. v. § 21);
that of the Olympians provoked only hostility. See C. C. J. Webb, Gifford
Lectures on *Personality, Human and Divine*, i. 77 ff. Nietzsche's *Birth of
Tragedy* should be read; see also Gilbert Murray, *Five Stages of Greek
Religion*, and other works mentioned in the bibliography appended to this
book.

meant the quarrel, not of art and knowledge, for these have no ground of conflict, but between the rival claims of religious tradition and scientific reason to teach the truth.[1]

§ 18. In the matter of the relationship of the new science to the established faiths of the *Polis* there was thus from the first a clear issue. The case was different and less simple in regard to the wave of revival of primitive popular religion that swept over Greece in the sixth century. Beneath the cult of the Olympian deities, fostered by the Homeric poets and the aristocracy of the Dark Ages, there may have persisted in the minds of the common people a mass of ancient belief, the survival probably of pre-Hellenic Minoan religion.[2] These primitive faiths, traces of which appear in the Hesiodic and even in the Homeric poems, were associated with the cult of the dead, with the divinities of the under-world, and especially with the incarnation of the non-Homeric god, Dionysus. Dionysus and Orpheus were alike associated closely with Thrace. They received official recognition in the mystic rites of Eleusis in Attica, which consisted of dramatic representations of sacred incidents, and of initiatory ceremonies to purify the soul of the worshipper from guilt. Purification was the essence of the sixth-century revival. Prophets and purifiers of cities, such as the Cretan Epimenides, who was called in to cleanse Athens, appear in the Hellenic world, as do also organised confraternities, analogous to churches, and detached from the bonds, of kinship or of the *Polis*, which formed the basis of the established worships. They possessed sacred poetic writings, ascribed to the legendary hero Orpheus, and containing distinctive theological doctrines, especially in regard to the destiny of. the soul in the world beyond the grave. The Orphic brotherhoods taught the soul's pre-existence and inherent immortality, resting upon its kinship with the divine, its successive incarnations in the bodily forms of men and animals, and its purification from guilt through ecstatic union with the god.[3] For the initiated

[1] Plato, *Rep.*, x. 607. Xenoph., *fr.* 11. Heracl., *fr.* 119; cf. *fr.* 16, 35, 43.

[2] The worship of Apollo and the Olympian religion generally were probably introduced by the northern (Achæan) invaders, though the new cult may have been coloured by assimilation of the beliefs of older Ægean peoples. The close association of the tyrants of the sixth century, both with the religious revival and with the early development of the drama (which arose in connexion with the worship of Dionysus), is explicable, if we regard their power as that of wealthy capitalists resting on popular support against the feudal aristocracy. The latter were naturally attached to the traditional Olympian religious cults.

[3] The belief in immortality depends on that in the kinship of man

they held out the hope of everlasting felicity; in this life the soul suffers imprisonment and the body is its tomb; through the series of incarnations it works out its cycle of destiny. In practice, these doctrines were preached and accepted in a crude and material form; purification meant the observance of weird taboos and external ceremonies; the future life a paradise of sensual enjoyment—in Plato's scornful phrase—" eternal drunkenness." [1] Yet the ideas which lay at the root of Orphic teaching were capable of a higher interpretation. Poets like Pindar and Æschylus made use of them in their effort to accommodate religious authority to the claims of the more elevated moral consciousness of their day.[2] Of the response which they could evoke from philosophy the *Phaedo* of Plato is an imperishable monument. In this, and in other of his writings, the same thinker who poured the vials of his anger upon the pardon-mongers and stewards of superstitious mysteries, transformed the Orphic doctrines of the soul's imprisonment in the body, of its pre-existence and immortality, and of its judgement in another world, into an instrument of the loftiest metaphysical and religious teaching.[3] Herein Plato was treading in Pythagorean steps.[4] The scientific researches of this school were intimately bound up with their religious tenets and ascetic rule of life.

---

with God; only by becoming God can immortality be attained. In Orphic teaching the soul is conceived as a fallen god which can be released by purifications and sacraments from the prison of the body (ecstasy, Greek *ecstasis*, means " stepping out " of the body) and regain its divinity (see Burnet, *Early Greek Philosophy*, c. ii, pp. 80–4). For the Homeric (Olympian) religion, gods and men are different orders of being; no man can become a god, and therefore there is no human immortality. Only a favoured few were carried by the gods to Olympus *during their life*, none after death. Hesiod holds that heroes might go at death to Elysium instead of Hades. It was far otherwise in the primitive religion and in its sixth-century revival. It should be observed that the Greek belief in immortality utilised materials drawn from primitive religion, while that of the Hebrews arose in complete independence of it; see above, c. iii. § 15, p. 74 *note*. Consequently the Greek conception, unlike the Hebrew, implied pre-existence, i.e. immortality *ex parte ante* as well as *ex parte post*. On the whole subject, see Guthrie, *Orphism*.

[1] See the whole passage in condemnation of the mysteries and of Orphic teaching, *Rep.*, ii. 363 ff.

[2] See Pindar, *Olymp.*, ii. 62 ff. and *Fragments*, 129–33; Æschylus, *Eum.*, 269 f. (judgement after death); and (of special interest for the problems it raises) the *Bacchae* of Euripides, one of his latest plays.

[3] Especially in the eschatological myths in the *Gorgias*, *Phaedo*, *Republic*, *Phaedrus*. See Stewart, *The Myths of Plato*, and Adam, *Religious Thought in Greece*.

[4] The *Phaedo* is dedicated to a Pythagorean coterie in European Greece. Socrates had been closely associated with several Pythagoreans who took refuge in Greece after their expulsion from Italy during the last half of the fifth century.

Pythagoras himself had set the example of this fusion, teaching that science was the true purification of the soul, and that salvation was to be attained through initiation into its mysteries. From that time onwards, philosophy meant for the Greek thinker a " way of life." [1] The philosopher, in the eyes of the Pythagoreans and of Plato, was the saint of rationalism. In the *Symposium*, the Orphic faith in the ecstatic union of the devotee with his god is moulded into an intellectual intuition of absolute beauty, the crown of a laborious pilgrimage up the mountain-chain of scientific reasoning.[2] We shall see further fruits of this conception when the time comes to speak of Neo-Platonism in the early centuries of the Christian era. From the same Pythagorean source flowed the distinction, derived by analogy from the Hellenic games, of the three types of human life. Some, like those who came to these festivals to sell their wares, choose the path of material satisfaction, of gain and pleasure; others, like the competing athletes, aspire after honour in the field of action, in politics or war; while there are those who, like the lookers-on at the games, prefer the life of the spectator, contemplating, with a mind untrammelled by the cravings of its bodily prison-house, the vision of perfect truth. This conception of intellectual contemplation (*theoria*) as the highest human activity, akin to the divine, realised first by the Pythagoreans and developed by Plato and Aristotle, carries us into the very heart of the Hellenic genius.

VI. Conclusion (§ 19).

§ 19. The process of expansion recorded in this chapter illustrates the intellectual quality of Hellenism. There is a logic inherent in all the creations of the Greeks. A glance at their architecture, with its mastery of form and function, and its mathematical symmetry, suffices to show how the scientific spirit informed imaginative art. The belief that " God ever geometrises " dominated both their theory of nature and their æsthetic production. Art for the Greeks is regarded always as a form of wisdom (*sophia*). Not only the Greek thinker, but the Greek artist, possessed the sense of truth, that led them to distinguish clearly between the ideal and the actual, giving both their due. They felt, too, the inspiration of that power, to which the one among modern poets who has entered most fully into the

[1] Cf. Plato, *Rep.*, x. 600.   [2] Plato, *Symp.*, 210.

spirit of ancient Greece dedicated his life, the vision of intellectual beauty.[1] Severity and truth are marks of Greek art.
When, for instance, Homer says "Helen," he means "Helen";
when Virgil says "Dido," he means "Cleopatra," or "Carthage."
A like logic is discernible in the process of their development.
We have seen above how the records of political history, of poetic
literature, and of scientific thought, reveal an ordered sequence
of forms.[2] What the Ionian philosophers remarked in nature is
true also of the mind of Greece; everywhere there is variety
and change, nothing is at rest. But the changes, though ceaseless
and pervasive, were guided throughout by rational law. Type
succeeds type, school follows upon school in logical sequence,
till the range of possible forms has been exhausted, and the cycle
of development is complete. The cardinal service of Greece
to civilization was to create in action and to define in thought
the essential characters of human experience. The terms in
use to-day to express the distinctions and groupings that form
the basis of our understanding of the world; in politics—monarchy,
aristocracy, democracy; in literature—epic, lyric, dramatic,
tragedy and comedy; in knowledge—the names of the arts and
sciences, poetry, physics, astronomy, mathematics, history,
philosophy itself—are all terms invented by the Greeks. The
forms which they thus distinguished and named were evolved
by them in the process of their own life-history. No race has
ever grasped with so clear an insight, and defined with such
precision, the truths of life and knowledge.[3] It is because of this
marvellous gift of intellectual judgement, enabling them in
thought and deed to realise the objects for which these terms
stand, that all succeeding generations have been content, and in
fact obliged, to build on the foundations which they laid.

[1] See Shelley, *Hymn to Intellectual Beauty.*
[2] See especially the study of defective forms of political government
in Plato, *Republic*, books VIII and IX, where the logical order in which
Plato treats of them presents many analogies to the actual course of
development in Greek history.
[3] The Hippocratean clinical records, for example, are concise statements of facts, unencumbered by any superfluity of language. Even the
Greek orators show a wonderful economy in their speeches.

CHAPTER V

THE GREATNESS OF ATHENS

I. THE ATHENIAN STATE (§§ 1–6).

§ 1. IT was at Athens in the fifth century that Greek civilization reached its zenith. Athens was then the chief political and commercial city of the Hellenic world, whither flowed all the currents of literature, art and knowledge. In the famous phrase of her statesman Pericles, she became " the school of Hellas." History affords no parallel to the wealth and variety of creative genius that Athens in this century produced or gathered to herself from all quarters of Greece. In a single city, whose free population was not greater than that of a moderate-sized English town, there dwelt, within three generations of human lifetime, statesmen such as Themistocles and Pericles; the three tragic poets Æschylus, Sophocles and Euripides, and the comic poet Aristophanes; Phidias and his marvellous school of sculptors; the historians Herodotus and Thucydides; the philosopher Anaxagoras; Socrates, the greatest of all human teachers; and Socrates' immortal disciple Plato. There were numberless others, statesmen and poets and thinkers, many of them little more than names for after time, who yet, in a less brilliant epoch, would have been among the famous men of history. It seems as though the individuality of Greek civilization strove for the brief period of its maturity to surpass the bounds of possible achievement.

§ 2. Though Athens developed into a great commercial city, the basis of her civic life was agricultural. By the seventh century the population of Attica had been united in a single commonwealth, monarchy had given place to the rule of a landed aristocracy, class distinctions of nobles, farmers and craftsmen had become definite, and the evils of debt and personal bondage were already acutely manifest. The smaller landholders had become hopelessly indebted to the larger, and were allowed to pledge their personal freedom to their creditors. The close of that century saw the publication of a code of laws, an event of moment in the history of all early communities, and especially so in the case of Athens, where " equal law " (*isonomia*) was the pride of her citizens, and the science of jurisprudence attained a level of perfection unequalled in the Hellenic world.[1] Thanks to her proximity to the sea and her harbour of Piræus, Athens was enabled to take her full share in the expansion of trade; here, as elsewhere, the influx of wealth and the rise of a plutocracy of merchants intensified the prevalent unrest. The root of the trouble was that political privileges had been confined to land-holders. Solon first allowed men with mercantile capital to purchase land from impecunious landowners and so to qualify for active citizenship and public office. Early in the sixth century, called to power in order to solve the economic crisis, he succeeded, by reform of the criminal law, and, above all, by the institution of popular tribunals to which the magistrates were accountable, in laying the foundations of democracy. In ancient society the law court rather than the assembly was the home of political liberty, where the people won control over the executive. Constitutional changes followed in rapid succession throughout the sixth century. Pisistratus' tyranny, resting probably on the support of his employees in the mines of southern Attica, was remarkable in its respect for law and constitutional procedure, its encouragement of agriculture and trade, and the stimulus it gave to art and culture. He also encouraged the small reclaimer of waste land in Attica. Athens now extended her commercial and diplomatic relations over both shores of the Ægean.[2] The tyranny of the Pisistratids was short-lived; for the thirst for political equality, once aroused in the Athenian citizen-body, was uncompromising and unquenchable. Pisistratus' family were expelled by a popular revolution backed by Spartan force, but their real enemies were the Alcmaeonidæ, a rival noble family; and in the closing years of the century Clisthenes dealt a death-blow to the territorial influence of the

[1] On *isonomia*, see Herod., iii. 80 f.; cf. v. 78, where the term employed is *isêgoriê*, "equality of speech."
[2] See Prof. P. N. Ure, *The Greek Renaissance*, c. vii., on the connexion of tyranny in general and that of Pisistratus in particular with capitalism and employment of labour. The argument is developed more fully in his later work, *The Origin of Tyranny*. Pisistratus' rule was of epoch-making importance for Athens in art, literature and religion. Athens then became the centre of Homeric influence in Greece. On this, see Murray, *Five Stages of Greek Religion*, p. 61. As her population grew, Athens drew her food supply from Eubœa and the Euxine; hence the extension of her maritime power to the east and north-east was essential to her existence. It was with her as with Holland in the later sixteenth and seventeenth centuries. This explains why the Athenian democracy consistently advocated imperial expansion.

aristocracy and reorganized the government on a frankly democratic basis. He not only admitted alien residents to full citizenship, but broke up political groupings based on local land ties, replacing them by new tribes, whose members were drawn from various parts of Attica. Thus, when the tide of invasion burst upon Greece at the dawn of the fifth century, Athens was able to confront the crisis with an outfit of political institutions worthy alike of the temper of her citizens and of her new-won status in the commonwealth of Hellenic city-states. Alike in capacity for political development and in freedom of intercourse with other cities, Athens presented, at this time and henceforward, a notable contrast to the state then dominant on the Greek mainland Sparta.[1] From their home in the secluded valley of the Eurotas, the Spartan aristocracy held the southern Peloponnesus in absolute subjection, and, thanks to their unquestioned courage and skill in arms, were recognized as the leading military power in Greece. But Sparta was a barrack rather than a state : the training and life of her citizens were governed by the one aim of efficiency in war; she retained her primitive institutions for centuries almost unchanged; and, scorning trade, guarded her borders rigorously from the intrusion of strangers. She contributed little or nothing of lasting value to the structure of Hellenic civilization. Her strength lay in her support of the *ancien régime* everywhere in Greece, in her *Herrenvolk* policy, and the separatism that ensured her supremacy. She produced brave soldiers, but few statesmen of distinction; her more gifted citizens were objects of suspicion at home, and, when freed from the atmosphere of Spartan tradition, became easy victims of corruption. We wonder at the fame that Sparta won in the eyes of contemporary Greece, and at the moral authority that she wielded over many of the best Hellenic minds. When Plato despaired of the political salvation of Athens, it was towards Sparta that he looked for a remedy. The reason lay in this : that, narrow and unfruitful and oppressive as was the Spartan aristocracy, its stability, unity of principle and loyalty to the state seemed to furnish the needed complement to the restless and emotional democracy of Athens.[2]

[1] Thucydides gives expression to this contrast in the speech of the Corinthian envoys at Sparta in 432, i. 70, and also in the Funeral Oration of Pericles, ii. 35–46, extracts from which are quoted in § 5 of this chapter.
[2] Plato's picture of the timocratic state in *Rep.*, viii. 547–8 is admittedly analogous to the Spartan. Its guiding principles are ' honour ' (*timê*) and ' victory.' It is the least corrupt of the types of ' unjust ' states.

§ 3. The war with Persia afforded Athens her supreme opportunity. We have already told the story of the rapid rise of
the Persian empire, and of the subjection of the Asiatic Greeks
to its yoke. Its navy, recruited from the merchant cities of
Phœnicia, threatened to convert the Ægean into a Persian sea.
The autonomy of the Greek city-states clashed with Persian
imperialism, while democratic movements, threatening the
political and economic *status quo*, threw its conservative defenders
into the arms of Persia. Greek nationalists stigmatised this way
of escape as " Medism," for it dates from before the rise of Persia.
The sea-power of Polycrates of Samos had endangered Persian
control of the coasts of Asia Minor. Darius' Thracian conquests
opened the eyes of Miletus which at first had ' medised.' The
revolt of the Ionian Greeks in the first years of the fifth century
impressed upon the government at Susa the need for consolidating
their western frontier, and in 490 a punitive expedition was
despatched by sea against the Athenians, who had aided the
abortive rising of their Ionian kinsmen with an armed contingent. The Persian force was faced and beaten on the plain
of Marathon, on the north-eastern coast of Attica. It is difficult,
in view of subsequent events of greater magnitude, to realise
what this victory meant to Greece. For the first time, the Persian
Colossus had been countered in the open field. For Athens,
Marathon furnished an imperishable memory; long afterwards,
when her greatest orator told how his fellow-citizens rallied to
the death-struggle against Macedon, his thought reverted to
those who fell gloriously at Marathon.[1] To the Persians, doubtless, it meant little more than an awkward set-back to their forward
frontier policy. It rendered necessary operations on a large scale ;
but the imperial levy took time to muster, and a revolt of Egypt
and the death of king Darius involved several years' delay. It
was not till 481 that the host assembled under Xerxes at Sardis,
with the fleet in the Ægean hard by, for the definite conquest
of Greece. The critical moment for Hellenic civilization had
come at last ; as the Persians advanced, half of the Greek cities
gave in their submission, and the oracle at Delphi played traitor
to the Hellenic cause. Sparta, the backbone of defence on land,

---

Later, in the *Laws*, Plato is much less tolerant towards Spartan institutions. Aristotle criticises Sparta severely in the *Politics*, ii. 9, vii. 14,
15. Polybius (vi. 48–50), in his examination of Spartan institutions,
pronounces them unequalled for preserving independence and self-
sufficiency at home, but most inadequate for the conduct of external
relations and empire.   [1] Demosthenes, *de Coronâ*, § 208.

thought, as ever, chiefly of the Peloponnese. It was now that Athens stood forth as the champion of Hellenic freedom. Twice her citizens witnessed undismayed from their island refuge at Salamis the ravaging of their lands and the destruction of their city. Her navy secured the decisive victory of Salamis (480); and in the year following her soldiers fought side by side with the Spartan infantry at the " crowning mercy " of Platæa. Athens found a leader of commanding ability, both in war and statesmanship, in the person of Themistocles. Greece was saved, and her salvation was due primarily to the patriotism of Athens.[1] Never again was Hellenic liberty menaced from the East. The danger had been twofold. In the West also Carthage had attacked the Greeks of Sicily in the year of Xerxes' invasion, to meet with a crushing defeat on the Himera at the hands of Gelo, the tyrant of Syracuse. Gelo's triumph inaugurated a brilliant epoch of Syracusan sovereignty. Indeed, Syracuse henceforward stands second only to Athens as a centre of Hellenic art and culture.[2]

§ 4. The Greek victory was magnificent, but in no wise miraculous; it affords the first clear illustration in history of the secular triumph of quality over quantity. The Greeks had done at Salamis and Platæa what Alexander did afterwards at Issus and Gaugamela, and Clive in modern times at Plassey.[3] Human history belies at every point the foolish epigram that " God is on the side of the big battalions "; if Napoleon ever said this, it must have been with the implicit reservation, " quality being equal." The true marvel lies in the use the Athenians made of their victory. In the hour of triumph, they displayed the same insight into facts and breadth of vision as in that of overwhelming danger. When Sparta and other Greek states were content to rest upon their laurels, Athens resolved to prolong the struggle till every Greek city in the Ægean area had been freed from the Persian yoke. Policy as well as patriotism

[1] See Herod., viii. 143 f., on Athenian patriotism at this crisis. The expedition of 490 is related by him in vi. 94–120; that of Xerxes in vii–ix. Æschylus dramatised the defeat of Xerxes in his *Persians*.

[2] Pindar addressed several of his finest odes to Sicilian princes, including Gelo's successor Hiero; Æschylus visited Sicily more than once, and died at Gela; Gorgias of Leontini was a famous sophist and master of rhetoric; in the fourth century Plato visited Syracuse on two, if not three, occasions. Gelo was Captain-general of an exclusive Capitalist oligarchy. The Ionian cities in W. Sicily had in despair called in Carthage. Syracuse offers a striking contrast to democratic Athens.

[3] The Athenians themselves saw clearly that the victory was due to the strength and skill of their navy, the sagacity of Themistocles, and their spirit of unwavering patriotism (see Thuc., i. 73, 74, 144).

doubtless pointed in this direction, but it is to the eternal honour
of Athens that at this moment she identified the call of civic
interest with that of Hellenic independence. She reaped her
reward a thousandfold; in political greatness, alike in her
internal civic life and in her commerce and empire upon the
seas; and also, as we shall see, in the noblest fruits of intellectual
culture that have ever fallen to human kind. The war of
liberation (478–470) left her the unquestioned mistress of Ægean
waters. The fortification of the city and of its port, the Piræus,
secured her from Spartan rivalry on the land. Her fleets policed
the Ægean, henceforward closed, as were the coast-lands of
western Asia, to the Persians. These facts formed the basis
of the understanding which terminated in 448 the long conflict
of more than forty years. Athens was left in possession of a
monopoly of eastern trade. The liberated cities were still
organised in a league under her presidency, with a common
treasury at the sacred island of Delos, to which each city contributed an appointed quota for the maintenance of the pro-
tecting navy. So brilliantly had Athens made good her avowed
intention. But, as the century wore on, her policy underwent a
change. The presiding state of the Delian confederacy developed
into the sovereign city of a subject-empire. Her former allies
became tributaries, their claim to secede from the league was
sternly trampled down, the treasury was removed to Athens,
and their internal institutions were remodelled in the interest
of Athenian sovereignty. Since Athens was a democracy, the
subject cities must also be democracies. It is characteristic of
Greek political history that friendships and enmities between
states depended largely on the political complexion of the party
in power. Democratic governments allied themselves with
Athens, aristocratic governments with Sparta. In the time of
Pericles (460 to 430) the Athenian empire comprised the islands
of the Ægean, the coast-cities of Thrace and Asia Minor, the
Hellespont and the sea-passage to the Euxine, though Naxos
revolted in 465 and Samos in 440. Athens further displayed
her activity in vain attempts to master central Greece, and in a
military expedition to Egypt, which ended in disaster. The city
grew in wealth and population, as the natural result of her extensive and varied trade. Bitterly as her empire was resented
by its subjects, there is no evidence that it was unjustly governed.
Our verdict must be guided by two considerations. By the
centralisation in the Athenian courts of commercial suits involving

different cities and of the most serious criminal causes, the most
highly developed system of judicial administration then existing
in the world was thrown open to the whole of eastern Greece.
Moreover, Athens fully recognised the obligation imposed on
her by sovereignty. Her citizens, so at least her foremost states-
ment felt, were bound to live worthily of their empire. The
efforts of Pericles to realise this ideal won the confidence of a
democratic people. The dream of a pan-Hellenic union under
the leadership of a single city never came so near to fulfilment
as in the Athenian empire in the Periclean age.

§ 5. When we turn from the external power of Athens to
consider her inner public life, we find that, from the time of
Clisthenes the government was controlled by the will of the free
citizen-body.[1] We have seen how to the Greek the true life of
the citizen was the service of the state in peace and war. At
Sparta this conception was realised by the governing aristocracy ;
endowed with estates worked by the subject population, they
had leisure to devote their whole lives to military service. Pericles
and his successors in the fifth century strove to make such a life
possible for the democracy of Athens. The introduction of pay
for attendance in the assembly and the law courts, which were
occupied largely with political causes, was the means employed
to effect this end. Over and above the business of local government, it was open to every citizen to attend in person, to vote
and to speak, at the weekly meetings of the sovereign assembly
(Ecclesia), where questions of foreign and imperial policy and of
finance were determined, magistrates elected, and their reports
discussed and scrutinised. The Boulé was charged with the
preparation of legislation for the Ecclesia ; and a tenth of the
number (the *prytany*) sat as a permanent executive in the town
hall during each month of the year. Panels of several hundred
jurors, chosen by lot from the citizen body, adjudged on political
and religious impeachments ; the conservative poet Aristophanes
pours bitter scorn on the litigious excesses of these Athenian
" wasps." [2] The spirit of faction ran high ; the aristocratic

[1] The free population of Attica in the Periclean age may have numbered about 250,000.   Thuc., ii. 31 asserts that *c.* 430 the Athenian citizen
force numbered 30,200.   To these must be added some 20,000 of the
lowest property class, making 50,000 adult male citizens ; women, children
and the aged, would be more than double this number, making up perhaps
200,000 free persons, *plus* 50,000 *metics* or resident aliens.   The census
of 309 B.C. shows a decrease of adult male citizens to 21,000, *plus* 10,000
metics.

[2] Aristophanes, *Wasps, passim.*

party advocating peace and friendship with Sparta, the democratic party, with its strength in the maritime population, championing the extension of the empire over sea and land. But when all allowance has been made for excesses of party spirit and individual ambition, the Athenian democracy was not unworthy of the ideals of the great statesman who established its supremacy. Pericles gave expression to that ideal in his speech in praise of the soldiers who fell in battle in the campaign of 431. The speech is recorded by the historian Thucydides, and the following passages may be quoted in illustration of Pericles' conception of Athenian democracy :

" Our form of government does not enter into rivalry with the institutions of others. We do not copy our neighbours, but are an example to them. It is true that we are called a democracy, for the administration is in the hands of the many and not of the few. But while the law secures equal justice to all alike in their private disputes, the claim of excellence is also recognised ; and when a citizen is in any way distinguished, he is preferred to the public service, not as a matter of privilege, but as the reward of merit. Neither is poverty a bar, but a man may benefit his country whatever be the obscurity of his condition. There is no exclusiveness in our public life. . . . While we are unconstrained in our private intercourse, a spirit of reverence pervades our public acts ; we are prevented from doing wrong by respect for authority and for the laws, having an especial regard for those which are ordained for the protection of the injured, as well as to those unwritten laws which bring upon the transgressor of them the reprobation of the general sentiment. . . . We are lovers of the beautiful, yet simple in our tastes, and we cultivate the mind without loss of manliness. Wealth we employ, not for talk and ostentation, but when there is a real use for it. To avow poverty with us is no disgrace ; the true disgrace is in doing nothing to avoid it. An Athenian citizen does not neglect the state because he takes care of his own household ; and even those of us who are engaged in business have a very fair idea of politics. We alone regard a man who takes no interest in public affairs, not as a harmless, but as a useless, character ; and if few of us are originators, we are all sound judges of a policy. The great impediment to action is, in our opinion, not discussion, but the want of that knowledge which is gained by discussion preparatory to action. For we have a peculiar power of thinking before we act, and of acting

too, whereas other men are courageous from ignorance but
hesitate upon reflection. . . . To sum up, I say that Athens is
the school of Hellas, and that the individual Athenian in his
own person seems to have the power of adapting himself to the
most varied forms of action with the utmost versatility and
grace. This is no passing and idle word, but truth and fact;
and the assertion is verified by the position to which these qualities
have raised the state. . . . For we have compelled every land
and every sea to open a path for our valour, and have everywhere planted eternal memorials of our friendship and of our
enmity. Such is the city for which these men nobly fought and
died; they could not bear the thought that she might be taken
from them; and every one of us who survives should gladly toil
on her behalf." [1]

§ 6. Both the empire of Athens and the rule of the democracy
which created and fostered it were short-lived. Athenian
history in the fifth century falls into three periods; the first
marked by the rise of her power in the Persian war, the second
by its consummation under Pericles, the third by its decline
and fall. Greek public life is everywhere a record of kaleidoscopic
change, and the halcyon days of Pericles' leadership were clouded
even before the great statesman's death (427). The rivals of
Athens were waiting an opportunity to combine in an attack
upon her supremacy. The impulse came from the Isthmus
states and especially from Corinth, whose commercial interests
in western Greece were menaced by the growing ambition of
Athens. While the Corinthians stirred into activity the powerful
though sluggish forces of Sparta, the subject-cities of the Athenian
empire watched eagerly for a favourable occasion for revolt.
In 431 broke out the conflict known to history as the Peloponnesian war.[2] In reality all Greece was involved in the struggle;
the maritime power of Athens on the one side was ranged against
a coalition of her enemies under Spartan leadership. It lasted
with intermissions till 404, when the destruction of the Athenian
navy was followed by the fall of the imperial city. The story
of the war has been told by Thucydides, himself an actor in its
earlier scenes, in a work which remains for all time a magnificent
creation of reflective history. To him the conflict was a drama,
centering round the growing *hubris* of the Athenian democracy
and culminating in the retribution (*nemesis*) that ensued when, in

[1] Thuc., ii. 37–41 (*tr.* Jowett).
[2] It had been anticipated by an earlier war (460 to 445).

the effort to conquer Sicily, they overstepped the mark. As his predecessor Herodotus had traced the hand of a jealous providence in the *nemesis* that overtook the Persian empire, when in pride of power she hurled her hosts against free Greece; so Thucydides, in the spirit of a riper philosophy, saw in the catastrophe that befell his native city, at the instant when her thirst for universal empire seemed to have achieved its goal, the inexorable operation of the laws that determine the destiny of nations. The dialogue in which he narrates the ultimatum of Athens to the islanders of Melos, with its uncompromising assertion that necessity knows no law, that political expediency overrides all claims of moral obligations, and that the tyranny of the strong over the weak is the natural right of gods and men, is followed without a break by the story of the sailing of the Armada against Syracuse, its initial successes, its subsequent disasters and its annihilation.[1] Athens never recovered from the blow. Alcibiades, the friend of Socrates and the most versatile and brilliant political personality of the age, finding himself discredited by the disaster, joined her enemies, and counselled the alliance with Persia, which furnished them with unlimited resources for the creation of a naval power. Athens could be conquered only on the sea. Her people fought on with marvellous tenacity and courage against overwhelming odds; but their life-blood had been drained, and eventual ruin was inevitable.[2] When the end came, a garrison of the hated Spartans was lodged in the Acropolis, and the subject-cities, who had risen against Athens in hope of regaining their independence, lay helpless in the victor's grip. Though Athens was able to shake off the Spartan yoke, though the democracy was restored, and trade again flowed into the Piræus, her empire was no more; the genius of the city, after a brief period of political and military splendour, found its true and enduring home in the fields of literature and of thought.

[1] See Thuc., v. 89 ff. for the Melian dialogue. The sentiments remind us forcibly of the German defence for their violation of Belgian neutrality in 1914. Thucydides writes as a clinical observer of political disease.

[2] The aristocratic and pro-Spartan party worked within the city for the enemy. They had been active from 415 (the revolution of the Four Hundred); their political battle-cry was "Back to 460," i.e. before Pericles.

II. Art and Literature in Fifth Century Athens (§§ 7–12).

§ 7. We remarked above that all forms of creative activity in which the Greek genius found expression were gathered at Athens in the great days of the fifth century. This is true, in the first place, of the allied arts of architecture, painting and sculpture. The motive of all three was religious, the erection and adornment of temples for worship of the gods. Both the Doric and the Ionic styles of temple-architecture, the one massive and severe, the other more elegant and ornamental, had developed in the preceding epoch out of primitive forms of building in wood.[1] Sculpture too had its origin in wood-carving; wooden temple-figures gave place, in the age of commercial expansion and under the patronage of wealthy despots, to statues of stone. In the sixth century, the schools of Argos, Sicyon, Ægina and Athens rapidly advanced in mastery of technique, in knowledge of anatomical structure and in freedom of treatment, and the art of sculpture was freed from exclusive association with religious subjects. Statues of athletes illustrate the growing interest in types of masculine beauty. The climax of these earlier developments was attained in the Athenian school in the Periclean age, under the leadership of Phidias. To Athens came also Polygnotus of Thasos, the foremost painter of the time, famous for his large monumental compositions, e.g. the sack of Troy and Odysseus in Hades, and commended by Aristotle for his skill in the representation of human character.[2] The buildings of Athens had been destroyed by the Persian invaders, and in the two succeeding generations her statesmen set themselves to make the new city worthy of her imperial position. Pericles in particular strove to train the citizens to a love of the beautiful through his buildings and the sculptures that adorned them. For an age when books were comparatively inaccessible, it is impossible to overestimate the value in education of noble buildings. The Acropolis of Athens, with its entrance portal, its temples, and its statues, rendered the same service to the Athenians of that day as the richly carved cathedrals to the towns of mediæval Europe. In a passage of the *Republic*, Plato concludes his argument that the young rulers of the ideal city shall be sur-

[1] Of the Athenian temples of the Periclean age, the Theseum and the Parthenon (see § 8) were the chief examples of the Doric, the Erectheum and the Temple of Wingless Victory (*Niké Apteros*) of the Ionic, style.

[2] Aristotle, *Poet.*, c. 2, c. 6; *Pol.*, viii. 5.

rounded with an environment of grace and beauty with these words :—

" Ought we to confine ourselves to superintending our poets, and compelling them to impress on their productions the likeness of a good moral character, on pain of not composing among us ; or ought we to extend our superintendence to the professors of every other craft as well, and forbid them to impress those signs of an evil nature, of dissoluteness, of meanness and of ungracefulness, either on the likenesses of living creatures, or on buildings, or any other work of their hands ; altogether interdicting such as cannot do otherwise from working in our city, that our guardians may not be reared amongst images of vice, as upon unwholesome pastures, culling much every day by little and little from many places, and feeding upon it, until they insensibly accumulate a large mass of evil in their inmost souls ? Ought we not, on the contrary, to seek out artists of another stamp, who by the power of genius can trace out the nature of the fair and the graceful, that our young men, dwelling as it were in a healthful region, may drink in good from every quarter, whence any emanation from noble works may strike upon their eye or their ear, like a gale wafting health from salubrious lands, and win them imperceptibly, from their earliest childhood, into resemblance, love and harmony with the true beauty of reason ? " [1] No one who has passed his youth under the shadow of some noble cathedral or within the walls of one of our ancient colleges will dispute this judgement on the subtle and unconscious influence of the arts on the character and mind of man.

§ 8. The chief of the buildings raised by Pericles on the Acropolis was the temple of the maiden Athene, the Parthenon. The sculptures that adorned the temple, the work of Phidias and his fellow-craftsmen, have never been equalled in any age. Early in the nineteenth century most of those that remained were brought to England by Lord Elgin and are now in the British Museum. In the pediments were represented the birth of the goddess Athene from the head of Zeus, and the struggle between Athene and the sea-god Poseidon for the possession of the soil of Attica. On the metopes that adorned the outer band of stone, surrounding the temple above the line of Doric columns, were sculptured scenes of conflict from the heroic legend of the contest of Centaurs and Lapiths. In contrast to the scenes

---

[1] Plato, *Rep.*, iii, 401 (*tr.* Davies and Vaughan). Note Plato's recognition of the significance of the sub-conscious.

F

depicted on the outside of the temple, the frieze that girt the
outer wall of the *cella* (nave) presented in low relief the civic life
of contemporary Athens, the religious procession of the Pan-
Athenaic festival, men in chariots and on horseback, sheep and
cattle led to sacrifice, the magistrates of the city, musicians and
the maidens who bore the sacred woven robe, as an offering to
Athene seated among the Olympian deities. The central figure of
the whole, the colossal statue of Athene, wrought in gold and ivory
by Phidias, has perished. But the marbles in our national museum,
more than any other monuments of antiquity, reveal to the Englishman of to-day the qualities of energy and repose, lofty idealism
and serene beauty, that marked the art of the age of Pericles.[1]

§ 9. In the domain of literature, fifth-century Athens is
memorable for the creation of two new forms of expression, the
drama in poetry and history in prose. The impulse to dramatic
impersonation is common indeed to all mankind, for, as Aristotle
has observed in his *Poetics*, both the habit of imitation and
delight in its products are rooted in human nature.[2] But there
is a wide gulf between the rude improvisations of the early Greeks
and other races, and such finished masterpieces of dramatic art
as the tragedies and comedies of Periclean Athens. To survey
and interpret this rich treasure of dramatic literature lies beyond
the scope of this volume. It will suffice to indicate certain distinctive characteristics, a knowledge of which is prerequisite for
the intelligent study of the plays themselves.[3] The modern
reader, when he thinks of the drama, inevitably thinks of Shakespeare; but a Greek play differed strikingly, both in atmosphere
and structure, from the Shakespearian type, and the difference
is partly due to the historical conditions under which the Attic
drama came into existence.[4] Thus, for example, tragedy and

---

[1] It must be remembered that both the exterior of temples and the
sculptures were coloured.

[2] Aristotle, *Poet.*, c. 4. This treatise illustrates how in poetry as
in other fields, the Greeks not merely produced works, but thought out
the theory of their production. The extant portion of the *Poetics* treats
mainly of tragedy. The second book, dealing with comedy, is lost. Aristotle
notes (1449a 10) that both tragedy and comedy originated in improvisation.

[3] For suggestions as to English translations see the Bibliographical
Appendix.

[4] The difference between the Shakespearian and the Hellenic drama
was due mainly to the sense of order and rule characteristic of the Greek
mind. This tradition was canonised later by the French in the doctrine of
the dramatic unities, which, however, was never formulated by the Greeks,
and which won little hold in this country where Shakespeare had done his
work without it. "The unities were effective in France because the
French drama had proved itself, in practice, not very effective without

comedy were composed by different poets and performed at different festivals; the one treated of ideal subjects, the other portrayed human nature on a lower plane than the normal, and excited laughter by ridiculing human imperfections.[1] They differed in the circumstances of their origin; tragedy (tragos, a goat) arose out of hymns sung by a chorus clad in goat-skins among the Dorians in the northern Peloponnese, while comedy was of Sicilian growth, and had its birth in the untutored jests of rustic revellers (kômos, a band of revellers) who enlivened their processions at the vintage and harvest seasons by flinging personalities at their fellow-yokels in the surrounding throng. Three further characteristics, arising out of the history of the Attic drama, call for special notice. (i) In the dramatic " episodes " or acts, and in the choric odes sung in the intervals of the action, we see conjoined in a higher unity the two main streams of earlier Hellenic poetry, the epic and the lyric. It is the presence of the latter element, with its accompaniments of music and dancing, so that the three arts form a single æsthetic product in which the words of the song are the determining factor, that strikes us on first acquaintance as unfamiliar.[2] Now the choric hymn or

them. Shakespeare, without them, had made wonderful theatrical patterns of his own, perfect, some of them, in form and symmetry " (W. P. Ker, on The Humanist Ideal, Essays and Studies by members of the English Association, vol. vi.).

[1] See Aristotle, Poet., c. 2 and c. 5 init. Aristotle, be it noted, ignores a strictly realistic drama. At the close of Plato's Symposium (223) Socrates is pictured as arguing that the tragic poet must also be a comic poet. Milton, in the preface to Samson Agonistes, speaks of " the poet's error of intermixing comic stuff with tragic sadness and gravity." Shelley, in his defence of poetry, says, on the other hand, that " the modern practice of blending comedy and tragedy, though liable to great abuse in point of practice, is undoubtedly an extension of the dramatic circle," and instances King Lear. Aristotle's famous definition of tragedy, in Poet., c. 6, 1449b, 24 f. is as follows : " A tragedy is the imitation of an action that is serious and also, as having magnitude, complete in itself : in language with pleasurable accessories, each kind brought in separately in the parts of the work; in a dramatic, not in a narrative form; with incidents arousing pity and fear, wherewith to accomplish the catharsis of such emotions " (tr. Bywater). The second clause refers to the admixture of choric song with music and dancing; the word " serious " and the reference to " pity and fear " distinguish tragedy from comedy; catharsis is a medical term signifying " purgation." Bywater discusses the various interpretations of the term in the notes on the passage in his edition of the Poetics. The emotions are expelled as by a purge, through their very excitement in the drama; the spectator in Milton's words, " With peace and consolation is dismiss'd, And calm of mind, all passion spent " (closing lines of Samson Agonistes).

[2] See Plato, Rep., iii. 398. The arts of music and dancing developed in Greece in strict relationship to lyric poetry, which was always meant to be sung to an accompaniment and danced.

dithyramb was the original nucleus of the drama; the element
of narration was gradually detached and transformed, first, in
the form of interludes spoken by the chorus-leader between the
parts of the hymn, then by the introduction of one answerer
(*hypocritês*) or actor speaking from a stage (here we have the
beginning of dialogue and action), then by the addition of a
second, and finally of a third, actor.   Thus the dramatic factor
developed at the expense of the lyrical, until the part of the
chorus, originally dominant, became thoroughly subordinate to
the dialogue and the action.[1]   In this, and in the almost universal
selection of plots from the heroic sagas, we see the influence of
epic poetry.   Aristotle, who was fond of tracing the early anticipations of later forms, noted that " all the parts of an epic are
included in tragedy; but those of tragedy are not all of them
to be found in the epic." [2]   Both the earlier types of epic and
lyric poetry, as well as music and dancing, were thus blended
under the form of dramatic representation in this sovereign
creation of the Greek poetic genius.[3]   (ii) The external conditions
under which the plays were produced also had an influence on
their character.   For one thing, they were performed in the open
air, in a theatre hewn out of the slope of the Acropolis, hard by
the temple of Dionysus, and were witnessed by a vast concourse
of spectators, perhaps as many as 30,000, seated in concentric
curves rising above the orchestra and stage, which were situated
at the base.[4]   This rendered necessary the use of artificial devices
to aid sight and hearing, the buskin to raise the actor's height,

[1] The *Suppliant Maidens* of Æschylus, probably the earliest extant
Greek drama, shows the chorus as still predominant.   The decisive in-
novation was that of the second actor; it is associated with Æschylus,
who later employed a third.   There were never more than three actors
with speaking parts employed in the course of a Greek tragedy, though
a single actor might appear in different parts in different scenes.   The
messenger-speeches frequent in Greek tragedies are reminiscent of the
earlier narrative interludes.

[2] *Poet.*, cc. 5, 26; cf. cc. 4, 23, 24.

[3] The whole play was in verse, lyric metres being employed in the
choric songs, and the unaccompanied iambic metre ($\smile - = $ ♪ ♩ is the
iambic foot) of six feet (" the most speakable of metres," says Aristotle)
in the dialogue and speeches.   Coleridge illustrates the iambic measure
by the line, " Iambics march from short to long."   Mr. Vernon Rendall
suggests : " English quantities are seldom clear, but might be more so
in foreign words anglicised, e.g.

' A rose, acanthus, asphodel, chrysanthemum.' "

Euripides was fond of introducing solos from the stage in lyric verse.

[4] The plays were thus visible, and (thanks to the devices referred to
in the text) audible, to a concourse as large as that which assembles to-day
to witness a test match or an international football contest.

padding and masks symbolic of the part enacted, fitted with speaking tubes to enable the voice to carry its full distance. These instruments necessarily intensified the conventional character of the Greek drama, which represented types in the persons of individuals. Yet the Greek dramatists and actors succeeded through mastery of technique in largely overcoming these limitations, and we can trace the growth of individual characterization as we pass from Æschylus to Sophocles and from Sophocles to Euripides. But, even in its latest development, the Greek drama was far more simple in plot and structure than that of modern Europe.[1] (iii) The dramatic poets, like the athletes at the games, contended one against the other for a prize. When we remember that each competitor presented four new plays at a single festival, and that the contests were many and frequent, we can appreciate the wealth of dramatic creation in fifth-century Athens. The extant plays, seven tragedies of Æschylus, seven of Sophocles, eighteen of Euripides, and eleven comedies of Aristophanes, form but a small fragment of the body of dramatic works produced by these and many other poets of the age. The constant attendance at these festivals, and the practice there acquired of judging the awards, furnished, in a time when books were rare, an educative influence of extraordinary value to the Athenian public. We know from Plato's insistence on the moral significance of right standards of dramatic composition for the training of youth how deeply the teaching of the poets impressed itself upon the minds of the audience.[2] As in politics, so in literature, the Athenian citizen must have been, if not " an initiator," at all events " a sound judge " of æsthetic merit.

§ 10. The poet Shelley, in an essay from which we have already quoted, remarks of the Athenian drama that " it is indisputable that the art itself never was understood or practised according to the true philosophy of it, as at Athens." Stressing thus what we called above the intellectual quality in Hellenic art, he continues : " For the Athenians employed language, action, music, painting, the dance and religious institutions, to produce a common effect in the representation of the highest idealism of passion and of power; each division in the art was made perfect in its kind by artists of the most consummate skill, and was disciplined into a beautiful proportion and unity one

[1] E.g. there was far less scope for underplot than in modern drama.
[2] Plato, *Rep.*, ii, iii.

towards the other. On the modern stage, a few only of the elements capable of expressing the image of the poet's conception are employed at once. We have tragedy without music and dancing; and music and dancing without the highest impersonations of which they are the fit accompaniment, and both without religion and solemnity. Religious institution has indeed been usually banished from the stage." [1] It is this intimate association with religious observance that constitutes the most striking peculiarity of the Attic drama. The dramatic festivals were held in honour of the nature-god Dionysus, under the presidency of Dionysus' priest, in the vicinity of his temple and with the accompaniment of religious ceremonial.[2] In the centre of the *orchêstra* or dancing-place stood the altar of the god. Attendance was a pious duty incumbent on every good citizen. As an integral part of the worship of the *Polis* the festivals were directly under the charge of the civic magistrates, and the plays themselves furnish frequent illustration of the poet's patriotic feeling. The plots, at least in the case of tragedy, were usually drawn from the traditional tales of gods and heroes; the range and variety of this material may be gathered from the fact that more than two hundred different themes are known to have been handled by the fifth-century dramatists. Thus Greek tragedy dealt with ideal situations, and with events which, despite the freedom allowed to the poet in the treatment of characters and detailed incident, were thoroughly familiar to the audience, who believed them to have actually happened in the heroic past. From all this there arose in the mind of the Athenian public a close association between dramatic poetry and the teaching of moral and religious truth. That this was so even in comedy is evidenced by Aristophanes' claim that the dramatic poet was the moral teacher of the adult citizen.[3] But it was the three great tragedians, Æschylus (525–456), Sophocles

[1] Shelley, *A Defence of Poetry.*
[2] Note that tragedy and comedy both belong originally to Dionysus, i.e. to the mystery-religion as distinct from the Olympian. In the fifth century, Apollo, the typical Olympian god, whose service is not mysticism but clear self-knowledge, comes by his own in the drama; Sophocles' religion centres round Apollo. See Wilamowitz-Moellendorff, Lecture on *Apollo* (Oxford, Clarendon Press, 1908).
[3] Aristophanes, *Frogs*, ll. 1009, 1055. Cf. 686 : "Well it befits the holy Chorus to counsel and teach the city what is good," and 1500 ff., where Æschylus is called upon by Pluto to save the Athenian *Polis* by good counsels. In the preceding Chorus (1482 ff.) his wisdom is explicitly contrasted with Socrates' idle prattle. The whole of the closing scene (1418 ff.) turns on the vocation of the tragic poet to preserve the state.

(496–406) and Euripides (480–406), who invested the religious traditions of the Greeks with a new spiritual meaning. Æschylus, in language that has often suggested an analogy with passages in Hebrew prophecy, sought to "justify the ways of God to men," to interpret the almighty sovereignty of Zeus so as to harmonise divine righteousness with the facts of suffering and sin, and to reconcile the inexorable laws of destiny with freedom of the human will.[1] In Sophocles, the divine decrees are represented as working through the subtle medium of human character ; the unwitting transgression, the rash act that springs from blindness and ignorance, brings down unsuspected doom on an otherwise noble nature.[2] The poet's religion is that of Apollo, the god of purity and light, with its watchword, " know thyself." His ethical ideal is that of *sôphrosynê* in opposition to self-assertion and pride of life (*hubris*). With equal moral earnestness, though voicing a religious scepticism that contrasts with the conservative piety of his predecessors, Euripides rent asunder the veil of reverence which had concealed from critical analysis the acts and characters of the gods, and with relentless realism showed them for what they actually were. You demand fact, he seems to say, and here I give it you ; if, as you believe, these things really happened, the gods who did them were not good, but evil, not ideal divinities, but cruel and vindictive, with the worst passions of human kind. It was a disturbing picture that he drew, reflecting the changed temper of a rationalist age. Euripides was profoundly serious alike in this merciless analysis of the orthodox faith, in his unflinching resolve to see the truth and face the facts of life, and, above all, in his pity for the weak and suffering, for women, children, captives and slaves, for all the numberless victims of human injustice and natural law.[3] The

[1] See, especially, the *Prometheus Bound*. Probably the sequel, *Prometheus Freed*, showed Zeus as schooled to humanity by suffering.

[2] Such was the fate of Œdipus in the *Œdipus King*; see Arist., *Poet.*, c. 13. Analogous tragedies following on error of judgement and blind impulses form the theme of *Othello* and *King Lear*. For subtlety of character, see the *Philoctetes*. The fate of Deianira in the *Trachiniae* well illustrates how hope and fear unite to blind the judgement of a weak woman and to lure her to destruction. See above, c. vi. § 12.

[3] The *Hippolytus* illustrates these points. On the other hand, the *Bacchae* shows that Euripides could enter into the spirit of Dionysiac religion. As the fifth century wore on, the stories of the gods were taken less seriously and the cultured Athenian public, while conforming to the worships of the *Polis*, was frankly sceptical. In the vase-painting of the time we can trace the transference of interest from religious subjects to matters of technique in grouping of figures and execution. So in the art of the Renaissance epoch the devotional motive yields place to purely æsthetic motives in the treatment of the Madonna.

time had come when the supernatural powers of earlier belief
were yielding place in thinking minds to the forces of nature.
But when once this was evident, the vocation of the poet as a
teacher of knowledge was doomed; men looked to science, not
to poetry, for guidance in the search for truth.

§ 11. Tragedy had established itself at Athens already before
the Persian wars. But it was that crisis and the consequent
expansion of Athenian public life that gave the impulse to its
development. Each of the three great tragedians represents
one of the three epochs into which the history of fifth-century
Athens naturally divides. Æschylus had fought at Marathon,
and in his *Persians* dramatised the naval victory at Salamis.
Sophocles' art is the perfect expression of the idealism of the
Periclean age. Euripides, as we have noted, voices the intellectual unrest which gathered over Athens in the years of the
Peloponnesian war. But it is in Attic comedy that we find the
most direct relation between the drama and Athenian civil life.
Aristophanes, like most of the comic poets, was a conservative,
who idealised the tempered democracy of the time of the Persian
wars; in his plays, personal and Rabelaisian to a degree inconceivable under the conditions of modern life, he satirised the new
currents in poetry, philosophy and politics which were stirring
in the last third of the century.[1]   In the *Knights* (424) he held up
to ridicule the democratic statesman Cleon; in the *Wasps* (422)
the jurors in the popular law courts; in the *Birds* (414) the wild
dreams of empire that led to the Sicilian catastrophe; in the
Frogs (406) the modernist art of Euripides, the representative
in tragedy of the new culture; in the *Clouds* (425) the speculations
and teaching of Socrates; in the *Lysistrata* (411) and the *Ladies
in Parliament* (392) the claims of women to share in the public
life of the city, claims advocated by the Cynic followers of Socrates
and, later, by Plato in his *Republic*.[2]   The lyric songs interspersed
in his plays are of an extraordinary beauty. A feature of this
Old Comedy, which furnished the poet with a peculiar opportunity
for personal satire, was the *Parabasis*, a survival from the early
village-revels, when the chorus turned round in the middle of
the play to address the audience in a song reflecting on persons
and topics of the day. The fall of Athens and the ruin of her

---

[1] The coarseness of the Old Comedy had a ritual significance; here
as everywhere in the drama it is necessary to remember its intimate connexion with religious cults.

[2] See *Rep.*, v. The Greek title of Aristophanes' play is *Ecclesiazousai*,
lit., " female members of the *ecclesia* or popular assembly."

democratic policy dealt the death-blow to such outspoken political criticism. It is with peoples as with individuals; they can enjoy ridicule only so long as their consciousness of security remains unshaken. In the hour of strength, the Athenians cherished the right of every citizen to speak his mind unfettered by laws of libel, and this characteristic freedom of speech found its frankest expression in the Old Comedy. With the fourth century, on the other hand, comedy ceased to be personal or to concern itself with politics; the New Comedy was a comedy of manners, depicting types of social life, on lines followed by the Romans, Plautus and Terence, and in modern times by Molière, and by the English dramatists of the Restoration. The same epoch witnessed the decline of tragedy. But the works of the fifth-century dramatists abide with the Phidian sculptures among the highest achievements of the Hellenic genius in the field of æsthetic creation. In the words of a modern poet, thinking at once of the colossal statue of Zeus wrought in gold and ivory by Phidias for the temple at Olympia and of the tragedy in which Æschylus pictured the mighty Titan, giver of fire and the arts to men, enchained on " the frosty Caucasus " by the restless tyranny of the self-same God :

" Dead the great chryselephantine god, as dew last evening shed :
Dust of earth or foam of ocean is the symbol of his head :
Earth and ocean shall be shadows when Prometheus shall be dead." [1]

§ 12. Greek prose literature had its home in Ionia, where it developed two forms, philosophy and history.[2] Of the early Ionian philosophers we have already spoken; Anaximander was the first who is known to have composed a book. The literature of western Greece was poetic until well on in the fifth century, when the rhetorical studies of the Sicilian Gorgias led to important developments in prose writing; though both

[1] Swinburne, *Athens*. The drama referred to is, of course, the *Prometheus Bound*. The reader will be aware of the influence exercised over European dramatic literature in the seventeenth and eighteenth centuries by the models and canons of composition furnished by the Greek dramatists, and by Aristotle in his *Poetics*, an influence issuing in many respects in artificial formalism. The dramas of Calderon, Corneille, Racine and Voltaire illustrate this influence at varying levels of excellence. Milton's *Samson Agonistes* and Goethe's *Iphigenie* may also be referred to in this connexion. But the spirit of the Greek drama is far more adequately represented by Shelley's *Prometheus Unbound*.

[2] So also the speech-verse of the drama, the iambic metre, was of Ionian origin.

Parmenides and Empedocles had expressed their philosophy in verse. The earliest critical historian, Hecatæus, was a native of Miletus and figured prominently in the Ionian revolt against Persia. The opening words of his book, preserved in a fragment, show that he struck a new and scientific note, in comparison with the municipal chronicles of an earlier generation. "Hecatæus of Miletus thus speaks. I write as I deem true, for the traditions of the Greeks seem to me manifold and laughable." [1] The Greeks created history, as they created the drama; for they were the first to grasp its two essentials, the distinction, never clearly realised by Oriental annalists, between fact and fiction, and the necessity of a reasoned interpretation of recorded fact.[2] To say that they threw their personality into their writing and recorded their individual impressions and judgements, is only another way of stating the same claim. Hebrew history was anonymous, the product of a group; even the prophets preface their message, not with "Thus saith Isaiah, the son of Amoz," but with "Thus saith the Lord." The Greek historian, like the Greek philosopher, spoke in his own name; "this is the exposition of the enquiry of Herodotus of Halicarnassus," and "Thucydides the Athenian wrote of the war of the Peloponnesians and the Athenians." They did so with right; for history and philosophy alike express the reflective criticism of the individual thinker on the facts of life. Two great historical compositions of the fifth century have come down to us, and both are closely associated with Periclean Athens. Herodotus took up his abode there for some years before joining Pericles' colony at Thurii in southern Italy; Thucydides was Athenian born, and absorbed in youth the great traditions of Periclean statesmanship. Herodotus was a keen traveller and visited Egypt, Phœnicia, Babylon and the Euxine coasts as well as all quarters of the Hellenic world; his eager curiosity and desire to understand what he heard and saw, "the wonderful works of Greek and barbarian, and especially that the causes may be remembered for which these waged war

[1] Murray, *Ancient Greek Literature*, p. 125.

[2] Thus the Semites, for all their sense of the religious significance of historical events, left no history that deserves the name. The historical books of the Old Testament (e.g.) are mere chronicle, the expression of corporate rather than of individual judgement. The Greeks were the first to exercise a reasoned judgement on the past. Their word *historiê* was originally of wide comprehension; it meant "inquiry" and covered all research into matters of fact, natural history, geography and anthropology, as well as political history. We are told that a Greek historian of the fourth century (Ephorus) explicitly censured the introduction of legend (*mythos*) into *historiê*.

on one another," make him perhaps the most charactcristically Greek of all Greek writers.[1] In Hellenic politics his sympathies are strong for Athens and for democratic government; again and again he defends equality of laws and liberty of speech against the claims of tyranny.[2] In temper of mind hc is typical of a generation that wavcred on the border line between credulity and scepticism. It is constantly on his lips to tell us that the religious traditions of his people are old wives' tales, but he never can quite bring himself to say so; and behind all nature and human history he sees the hand of a mysterious " divinity that shapes our ends, rough-hew them how we will." With justice he has won the name of " the father of history," not merely because his is the first cxtant history that discriminates truth from fiction and seeks to know the causes of things that happen, but also because he first sought to co-ordinate his story under a single purpose, namely, to exhibit the rise of Persia and the judgement that overtook her *hubris* through the agency of Greece.[3] Thucydides' theme was more concentrated and his outlook on affairs more scientific. His purpose was to record the Peloponnesian war to the fall of Athens in 404.[4] While Herodotus tells the tale of Persian *hubris* with all the geniality and diffuseness of a literary artist exulting in the glamour of splendid triumph, Thucydides records that of Athens with austere and sombre gravity, moved by the single desire to unfold the truth in its bitter reality. Between the two writers lay not only

---

[1] Herodotus was born *c.* 484 at Halicarnassus in B.W. Asia Minor; visited Athens *c.* 450, settled at Thurii 443. He was Carian in stock, Ionian in culture, Athenian in sympathies. The latest reference in his book (vii. *c.* 233) is to events in 431–430 at the commencement of the Peloponnesian war. The words quoted are from the opening sentence of Book I.

[2] See c. iv. § 5, *note* 1 above; cf. with the passages there referred to, v. 78 and 92 f. (on tyranny at Corinth as illustrative of its evils), and on Athenian democratic patriotism vii. 138 f., viii. 143 f.

[3] On Xerxes' *hubris*, see vii. 7 ff., on the jealousy of Providence and the instability of human prosperity, i. c. 5, c. 30 ff. Books I–V bring the history up to the Ionian revolt, Book VI to the victory of Marathon, while Books VII–IX tell the story of Xerxes' invasion. Herodotus intended to cover the war of Liberation (see VII, 213), but left his work unfinished. Thucydides embodied a summary of the years 478–432 in Book I, cc. 89–117 of his history.

[4] Thucydides was an exile from Athens for twenty years, in consequence of his failure as commander of the fleet to save Amphipolis in 423. He was no friend to the post-Periclean democrats (e.g. Cleon) and stood for the moderate Periclean liberalism. He survived the fall of Athens (iv. 104–7, v. 26), but carried his history only as far as the year 411. Xenophon in his *Hellenica*, an inferior work to Thucydides', continued the narrative from this point up to the battle of Mantinea (362).

the downfall of Athens, but the age of intellectual enlightenment. In language, and still more in thought, Thucydides is of
the lineage of the Sophists. Writing as a statesman for the
instruction of statesmen, he analyses minutely the causes and
effects of moral and political phenomena.[1] We have referred
already to his narrative of the Sicilian expedition, recorded with
a dramatic intensity unequalled in historical literature. For
Thucydides, as for Euripides, the course of human life is determined, not by supernatural agents, but by natural law; he
exhibits a thoroughly sceptical reluctance to accept the plea
of disinterested motive for human action, and he has all the
intellectualist's faith in reason as the key to unlock the secrets
of men's characters and conduct. Finally, in the speeches
which abound in his work, we can trace the influence of the
new art of rhetoric, which had its home in Sicily, but was quickly
acclimatised at Athens.[2] In the last quarter of the fifth century
it began to exercise a decisive influence upon Attic prose. Oratory,
forensic and political, took a recognised place as a form of literary
art. In the fourth century we find not only the high-water
mark of Greek oratory in the speeches of Demosthenes; but,
in the philosophical dialogues of Plato, the most perfect achievement in prose that Greece, and possibly the world, has ever
known.

III. THE SOPHISTS AND SOCRATES (§§ 13–18).

§ 13. We have noted that the history of Thucydides, the
tragedies of Euripides and the comedies of Aristophanes alike

[1] See especially the Prologue (i. 1–22), the account of the plague at
Athens and its moral effect (ii. 47–54), the analytic study of political
revolutions (iii. 82–4), the exposition of Athenian *hubris* and imperial
tyranny (i. 73–8, iii. 37 ff., vi. 83 ff., and, above all, the Melian dialogue,
v. 84 ff.), and the contrast of Athenian and Spartan character and policy
(i. 70, ii. 35–46); also Cornford, *Thucydides Mythistoricus*.

[2] On Thucydides' speeches see his *Prologue* (i. 22) and Jebb's essay
in *Hellenica*. The Funeral Oration, quoted above (§ 5), can hardly be
other than an accurate report of Pericles' argument and phrases, probably
heard by Thucydides himself.

In reading the works of Greek (and Roman) historians, the close
affinity to poetry and especially to dramatic poetry, is noticeable, alike
in form, context and purpose. They understood by history something
very different from our twentieth-century conception. It was an art
rather than a science, and was never taught, like the sciences, in universities. Further, it was written for the edification of men of affairs.
Quintilian observes (*Inst. Orat.*, x. i. §§ 31, 34): "history is closely allied
to poetry and may be likened to a poem in prose; its aim is narration
rather than proof . . . its chief value is in furnishing examples for our
instruction."

in their various ways bear the mark of the new speculative movements that were stirring in the Periclean age. The growing tendency of thought was towards questions of moral theory and conduct. This was due in part to a sense of disillusionment with the physical enquiries of the preceding epoch; the various lines of speculation had been worked out to a finish and men were faced with a maze of conflicting conclusions which seemed to defy reconciliation. They despaired of attaining certainty in such matters, and turned to seek a knowledge more immediately related to practical life. Physical science too was becoming more departmental, and the specialists were inclined to resent the intrusion of the philosopher into their preserves. In any case, the moral problem was clamouring for treatment on rational methods of enquiry. We saw in the last chapter how a criticism of moral standards and institutions was the logical outcome of the effort to find a permanent substance beneath the changes of physical nature. This newly awakened interest in ethical questions was fostered by the special conditions of public life in democratic Athens, and by the general aspiration after a higher standard in religion and morality which the poets strove to satisfy. The time from 450 onwards was one of extraordinary fertility, both of criticism and of construction, in ethical and political thought, and preluded a momentous revolution in the intellectual life of Greece, and, through Greece, of mankind. For the first time in history the clear light of reason was directed upon the problem of human conduct. It was an epoch of enlightenment, like that named as such in the Europe of the eighteenth century, of which Voltaire was the central figure; and just as the modern enlightenment led forward to the great constructive philosophy of Kant, so the earlier prepared the way for that of Plato. The saying of Protagoras, " Man is the measure of all things," may be taken as its watchword.[1] A widespread conviction arose in the Hellenic world that, alike in the special professions and arts and in the art of living in general, an outfit of reasoned knowledge

[1] Protagoras of Abdêra in Thrace, born c. 500, died c. 430, legislated for Pericles' colony of Thurii. The best brains of Greece were enlisted in this undertaking; Hippodamus of Miletus, the greatest living architect, designed the city, and Herodotus, as has been noted above, was one of the colonists. Protagoras' saying, quoted in the text, meant that the judgement of each individual was the measure of what it was desirable to do or not to do in any practical situation. Later, the doctrine was applied by others to support a theory of the relativity of knowledge, viz. that what each man perceives is true for him when perceiving it, and that this is the only truth attainable. See Plato's *Theaetetus* for this development and a criticism of it as conclusive as anything in philosophy.

was an indispensable condition of success. Virtue (*aretê*), depended not merely on natural talent or on gifts of fortune, as
men had commonly supposed, but on an equipment of acquired
theory. A demand arose for a new type of education, and it was
met and fostered by a body of eminent teachers. The professors
of the new culture brought their knowledge to bear on the practice
of war, music and agriculture, as well as on more specialised
training in horsemanship, stagecraft and cookery. Manuals of
instruction, called *technai* (arts), were composed on a multitude
of such subjects. Above all, they taught rhetoric, the art of
public speech, indispensable to the aristocrat who found himself
constantly threatened with impeachments before the popular
tribunals, and to the young aspirant after political honours in
the law court and the assembly. The rise of rhetoric affected,
not merely the character of Greek public life, but the development of Greek literature through the kindred arts of grammar
and style. But its chief importance lay in the training it afforded
in the general conduct of public and private life. When Protagoras, in the dialogue of Plato which bears his name, was asked
by Socrates what benefits his young pupil would receive, he
answered that he would teach him to speak, and thereby make him
day by day a better citizen, more competent to handle the affairs
whether of the *Polis* or of his domestic household.[1] In fact, the
founders of rhetoric inaugurated a new era in ethical enquiry.
Words are the symbols of thoughts, and the study of the expression of moral ideas involves analysis of the ideas themselves.

§ 14. The teachers of the new learning were called Sophists.
The term meant simply " professors of wisdom (*sophia*) "; it
had not yet received from Plato the implication that the wisdom
professed was illusory.[2] They hailed from all quarters of the

---

[1] Plato, *Protag.*, 318–19; cf. 328 and *Rep.*, 600. The whole dialogue
should be studied as illustrative of the teaching of the Sophists. Isocrates
in the next century said that the Sophists claimed that those who learnt
from them would " know what ought to be done and through this knowledge achieve happiness."

[2] The primary suggestion of the term is that of professional teaching,
though it is also used in a wider sense of any wise man, e.g. of a poet.
Herodotus calls Solon a Sophist. The Sophists frequently taught for
pay; Protagoras is said to have allowed his pupils at the end of the course
to give what they thought his instruction was worth. Plato (*Protag.*,
317) says that Protagoras was the first to call himself a Sophist. Plato
sharply distinguished the true philosopher from the Sophist, applying his
favourite contrast of " real " and " seeming "; see *Gorg.*, 463, cf. *Soph.*,
221, " the practiser of an art of deception, who without real knowledge of
what is good can give himself the appearance of that knowledge." So
Aristotle, e.g. *Rhet.*, I, i. 4, " an impostor who pretends to knowledge,

Hellenic world, travelling from city to city and giving lectures and informal instruction in all branches of knowledge.[1] Hippias, one of the company of Sophists introduced in the *Protagoras*, claimed to be a master of every art; in addition to researches of real value in mathematical and astronomical science, he taught chronology, mnemonics, phonetics and the study of rhythms, the theory of sculpture, painting and music, and industrial crafts—the story runs that he appeared at the Olympic games dressed in clothes entirely of his own making. He was also a moralist and a poet, and served his native state as an ambassador. It would be an error to suppose that the Sophists' learning was superficial, for in those days it was easier to be a polymath than now, when the vast mass of material entails specialization; beneath Plato's hostility to the type we can detect his real respect for great thinkers like Gorgias and Protagoras. "Culture," said the latter, "does not flourish in the soul unless one reaches a great depth." The Sophists were not a sect, bound to a uniform doctrine; if we seek a modern parallel, we should find it in the journalists of to-day, or in the influence on intelligent public opinion of writers like Huxley, Ruskin and Matthew Arnold in the last half of the nineteenth century.[2] Plato might scorn the Sophist as "a wholesale exporter of spiritual goods manufactured by others," and in certain cases the scorn was doubtless justified; but there were not a few who united in their persons the gifts of the intellectual middleman with those of the original thinker.

§ 15. The ethical discussions, provoked by the teaching of the Sophists, were focussed round the terms nature (*physis*) and convention (*nomos*).[3] Individual Sophists differed widely

---

employing what he knows to be false for the purpose of deceit and monetary gain." It was George Grote (*Hist. of Greece*, viii. c. 67) who rescued the reputation of the Sophists from the stigma inherited from Plato and Aristotle. In this he had been in some measure anticipated by Hegel.

[1] E.g. Gorgias from Leontini in Sicily, Hippias from Elis, Prodicus from the Ægean island of Ceos, Thrasymachus (cf. Plato, *Rep.*, i.) from Chalcedon.

[2] Or again, Herbert Spencer. Among living writers, Mr. Bernard Shaw and Mr. H. G. Wells might be compared to the Greek Sophists. We may also think of the rapid extension in our universities of the application of theory to practice, in agriculture, engineering, commerce, domestic science, and especially welfare work and social service. The problem of present-day education is to do for the many what the Sophists claimed to do for the few.

[3] *Nomos* = "convention" and also "law," i.e. what is posited by human will, can be made and unmade, and varies in different times and places. It is used often in the sense of "law *and custom*," as when

in their conclusions; some, like Hippias, based moral duty
upon unwritten natural law, eternal and divine; others held,
like Thrasymachus, that by law of nature Might is Right, or,
again, that social justice was an artificial compromise imposed
by the weak in self-defence against the strong. Others, again,
like Protagoras, denied the existence of any unchanging natural
principle, and taught that the conventions of the city should
be accepted and observed by the citizen.[1] The tone of these
discussions affords a striking parallel to those of the later
eighteenth-century enlightenment, embodied in the writings of
Rousseau, Tom Paine and William Godwin; in the preamble
to the American Declaration of Independence, and in the mani-
festoes of the French Revolution; as also to those evoked in our
own day by the advocates of the claims of the superman and
of the super-state against the restrictions of conventional moral
valuations.[2] They exemplify the genius of the Greeks for grasping the essential and enduring problems of human conduct.
The same topic of nature and convention was threshed out in
its various applications to the origin of society and language,
the social position of women and slaves, the institution of private
property and the validity of religious tradition.[3] The outcome
of the controversy was to elicit a truer conception of nature
and of the natural, as meaning, not an imaginary primitive
condition devoid of all social acquisitions, but rather the full
realisation of the capacities of man's social nature. To unfold
this ideal of a developed human personality, and thereby to
heal the crude divorce between the interest or good of the individual and that of society, was the aim of Plato's *Republic*.

Aristotle (*Ethics*, v. c. ii. § 1) lays down that what *nomos* does not enjoin
it forbids.

[1] On Hippias' views, see Xenophon, *Mem.*, iv. 4; cf. Sophocles,
Antigone, 449–57, for a similar doctrine. For Thrasymachus, see Plato,
Rep., i, and cf. Glaucon's speech at the opening of Book II. Plato's
final verdict on the historic controversy between *physis* and *nomos* is
given in *Laws*, 889.

[2] The superman was a common theme in Greece in the last half of the
fifth century. He was typified by the hero Heracles; see Euripides'
play, *The Mad Heracles*. For the super-state, see the Melian dialogue in
Thucydides, v. 84 ff.

[3] On the origin of society, Plato, *Protag.*, 320 ff., *Rep.*, ii. (Glaucon's
speech). In regard to slavery, see Additional Note to this chapter. It
must be borne in mind that while Greek culture undeniably rested on a
slave basis, the Greeks were the first people to question its justifiability.
On communism, see Plato, *Rep.*, iv. 416–17 and v. Arist., *Pol.*, ii. criticises
these views and Phaleas of Chalcedon's schemes for equalising real property and state ownership of slaves, involving state control of industry.
On the position of women, see Additional Note, p. 161.

We shall return later to his solution of the problem, which was rendered possible by the critical enquiries of the Sophists. Though their teaching made for scepticism, and, as such, aroused the bitter antagonism of conservatives like Aristophanes, yet its issues proved essentially constructive. A thorough analysis of the traditional beliefs was necessary, if moral values were to be remoulded on rational principles. The trenchant criticism of the Sophists bore fruit in the speculative systems of Plato and of Aristotle.

§ 16. Incomparably the most notable thinker of the age was Socrates of Athens (469–399), the greatest human teacher who ever lived.[1] Amid the wealth of genius that adorned Athens in the last half of the fifth century, his personality was the most unique and impressive. Grotesque in gait and features—the stout figure, with bald head, snub nose, thick lips and protruding eyes, reminded Plato of the images of the satyr Silenus—he strutted barefoot and ill-clad through the streets of Athens, " like a water-fowl," says Aristophanes. His habits and bearing were strangely disconcerting, when he broke in upon a company of Sophists or revellers at a banquet, or of young nobles in the *palaestra*, or when he stood stark and silent for long stretches of time in the thoroughfare or the portico, wrapped in a mystic trance.[2] The inward voice, too—the *daimonion* (divine thing) he called it—which counselled him audibly against peril at critical moments of his life, forbidding him for instance to enter politics, singled him out from other teachers of his day.[3] He lived in comparative poverty, scorning to take pay for the fulfilment of what he regarded as a divine mission; and held aloof from the recognised avenues of civic distinction, save on two occasions, towards the close of his life, when he was forced into

[1] The three main sources of knowledge about Socrates are Xenophon's *Memorabilia*, the *Clouds* of Aristophanes, Plato's dialogues. The account in the text is based primarily on the last-mentioned source. It is not possible in this work to discuss the grounds for refusing to regard Plato's Socrates as a dramatic fiction; the reader is referred to the writings of Professors Burnet and Taylor (whose views have largely influenced the account here given) with the caution that their conclusions are by no means universally admitted. The author is, however, convinced that, unless Plato is accepted as the main authority on Socrates, it is impossible to give an intelligible explanation either of Plato's philosophy, or of Socrates' influence, or of the satire of Aristophanes. See Burnet, *Thales to Plato*; Taylor, *Varia Socratica*; and the Introduction to Burnet's edition of Plato's *Phaedo*.

[2] Plato, *Symposium*, 215–22; on the trances, *Symp.*, 174–5; cf. Arist., *Clouds*, 150.

[3] On the *daimonion*, see *Apol.*, 31, 40; *Rep.*, vi.

political prominence, and showed his wonted independence in resisting the mandates alike of democracy and of despotism.[1] On the other hand, he served on several occasions with conspicuous valour in the field, and his personal courage was proverbial throughout Greece.[2] Socrates was no recluse, nor was there in his nature anything of the rigidity of the intellectual aristocrat or the puritan ascetic; like another, he came eating and drinking, and his geniality was as characteristic as the self-control which provoked the wonder and the envy of his contemporaries. The secret of his influence lay in his force of personality and in the magic of his talk. In this, as also in his weird appearance and demeanour, his breadth of human interest, his passion for argument and his love for the city whose walls he never quitted save under protest—" I am a lover of knowledge, and the men who dwell in the city are my teachers, and not the trees or the country "[3]—he reminds us at times of Doctor Johnson. He left no written word, but lived for seventy years in the public eye, spending his days in conversations with all sorts and conditions of his fellow-men, rich and poor, statesmen and generals, poets and thinkers, humble craftsmen and women of the world, conversations which Plato describes as " ridiculous at first hearing; his talk is of packmen and smiths and cobblers, and he is always repeating the same things in the same words, so that any ignorant or inexperienced person might feel disposed to laugh at him; but words which in their heart are the only words that have a meaning in them, and also the most divine, abounding in fair images of virtue, and of the widest comprehension, or rather extending to the whole duty of a good and honourable man."[4]

§ 17. When Aristotle summarises Socrates' contribution to the history of thought in the words " induction and general definitions," we are apt to feel a shock of disillusionment.[5] His life-work must surely have meant more than that. Aristotle, of course, is concerned with Socrates' service to philosophic method, and every student knows how reform of method heralds each decisive advance in the history of science. Moreover, the Socratic induction implied the recognition of the real natures of things embodied in their sensible appearances; while definition, for him as for Aristotle, was no matter of mere words, but the

[1] The two occasions were in 406 and 403; see Plato, *Apol.*, 32.
[2] See *Symp.*, *loc. cit.*   [3] Plato, *Phaedr.*, 230.
[4] In the mouth of Alcibiades, praising Socrates, *Symp.*, 221–2.
[5] Ar., *Met.*, i. 6, xiii. 4.

precise expression of the essence of the things defined. In youth, as we learn from the *Clouds* and from the biographical passage in Plato's *Phaedo*, Socrates had been a keen student of the physical systems which then held the field. But they failed to satisfy him, for they spoke only of the " how " of things, and his desire was to know the " why "; and he " came out by the same door wherein he went." [1] The Pythagoreans alone, who had been led by mathematical enquiries to the thought of an intelligible reality behind the show of sensible phenomena, seemed to point the way to the goal of his endeavour, the reasoned knowledge of ideal good. Socrates was at once a scientific thinker and a religious mystic. His faith in reason was unquenchable; he was a true child of Greece in his conviction that only by intellectual labour can man's soul attain to the vision of perfect truth. Hence the discipline of philosophy was at the same time the fulfilment of a religious vocation. The tale is preserved how, when he was between thirty and forty years of age, the Delphic oracle declared Socrates to be the wisest of men, and thereby summoned him to the mission to which he devoted the remainder of his life. [2] How could this be, he asked himself, since God alone is wise, and he, Socrates, knew no wisdom ? We have here the key to the Socratic conception of Erôs or Love, child of Plenty and of Want, round which he played in his conversations, now in jest, now with deep seriousness— the thought of man as a creature of two worlds, midway between ignorance and knowledge, whose salvation lies in the passionate thirst for wisdom (*philosophia*) that guides the soul upwards from the love of the transitory things of sense to the intuition of an intellectual beauty, whose " light alone gives grace and truth to life's unquiet dream." [3] Socrates justified the oracle by saying that, though he knew nought else, he knew one thing— his own ignorance; while others thought themselves wise when they were not so. This is the " irony " of Socrates, which aroused such astonishment and irritation in his questioners. [4] How could he save their souls by revealing a knowledge for which he was still a seeker, or otherwise than by convincing them of

[1] See *Phaedo*, 96 ff. In his early manhood, Socrates met Parmenides and Zeno, and also Protagoras : Plato, *Parm.*, 130, 135; *Protag.*, 361.
[2] *Apol.*, 21 ff.
[3] Shelley, *Hymn to Intellectual Beauty*; see *Symposium*, 210 f.
[4] *Symp.*, 216. *Eirôn* = " sly " (Burnet, who compares the Scotch word " canny "). There was a great common sense in Socrates. It follows from the irony that he refused to be called a teacher, *Apol.*, 33.

their own ignorance, and thus wakening in them the desire to know ? This indeed was the mission to which he set his hand with unwearying loyalty; to examine into men's standards of conduct, the ends they loved and lived for, and to test them by a fierce annihilating logic, till the hearer was shaken out of his complacency and confessed himself paralysed and impotent. " An unexamined life," said Socrates, " is not worth living." [1] He compared himself to a gadfly sent by God to sting a noble horse, the Athenian *demos*, out of indolent slumber; and again to a spiritual midwife, who brings to birth true thoughts in the souls of men.[2] So we may fancy him asking the modern Englishman what precisely he meant by such terms as " honour " or a " gentleman " or a " Christian," why he aspired to enter Parliament, and why he sent his son to the university or to a public school. He would show relentlessly the vagueness of men's notions about such matters, and that they had never thought them out or envisaged the alternatives; above all, that their views and their practice were but a pale reflexion of the average opinion of the world around them. And this, moreover, in the one concern of surpassing moment, the pearl of great price, the chief good and end of life ! Socrates' teaching thus assumed a negative form which belies its real significance. He disclaimed the title of teacher; for he knew that the saving wisdom must be won by each man for himself, and that his own task lay solely in tearing aside the veil of ignorance which hid men from themselves. Self-knowledge, the Delphic watchword, was the one thing needful in life, and constituted virtue; vice, he said, was ignorance, or, to quote his seeming paradox, " no one errs of his free will." [3] He knew that prosperity without self-knowledge lay at the root of half the misery and evil in human life. He knew also, only too well, how men will pardon anything rather than being shown their folly, and how bitterly they resent the shattering of the self-satisfaction with which they have entrenched their souls. " I was not unconscious," he told his judges, " of the enmity which I provoked, and I lamented and feared this; but necessity was laid upon me—the word of God, I thought, ought to be considered first." [4] His central prescript to his

---

[1] *Apol.*, 38.

[2] *Apol.*, 30, 31; *Theaet.*, 150, 151; see also *Meno*, 79, 80, for the effect on his hearer.

[3] Self-knowledge, *Phaedr.*, 229; Xen., *Mem.*, iv. 2, 24 ff. Goodness is knowledge; *Laches*, 194, *Protag.*, 345, *Apol.*, 25; see Xen., *Mem.*, iii. 9, 4, and Arist., *Ethics*, vii. 3, 1145b, 21.   [4] *Apol.* 21e.

fellow-citizens, that they should "take care of their souls," carried with it an implication that marks an epoch not merely in Greek philosophy, but in all human thought about the soul. For the ordinary Greek of the fifth century, the soul (*psyché*) meant what it had meant for Homer and, as we have seen,[1] for the Hebrews, viz.: the life-principle that quits the body at death and passes to the under-world, where it exists as an inanimate ghost in a state of unconsciousness. To bid men "care" for such a soul as this was to use words that carried no meaning. On the other hand, Orphic and Pythagorian teachers had sharply distinguished the soul as divine and therefore immortal, from the body in which it was imprisoned as a penalty for ante-natal sin, slumbering, save in prophetic dreams; and had taught a way of release by purification from the necessity of reincarnation. Such a way of purification could certainly be described as "taking care for the soul." But Socrates taught something different from either of these views. He identified the soul with our conscious personality, the self possessed of the capacity for rational activity, both speculative and practical, which, if duly tended, found expression both in scientific knowledge and in moral character. This was a wholly new and revolutionary doctrine, and we can easily understand the significance it had for Socrates and the hostility it aroused in those of his hearers who were startled by its implications out of their complacency.[2]

§ 18. The end came in 399, when Socrates had reached the age of seventy. He was accused on the charges of impiety and of corrupting the young, and condemned to death. The wonder indeed is that it was deferred so long. The Athenians, like other people, were prone to suspect intellectuals, and Socrates had never shown himself friendly to democracy. He held that political government, like every other matter of practice, should rest in the hands of those who know. Above all—and here lay the nerve of the impeachment—among Socrates' intimates had been numbered the two men who of all others bore the odium of Athens' downfall, the oligarch Critias, one of the thirty tyrants set in power by the Spartans after their capture of the city, and Alcibiades, whose unbridled ambition had led him, first, to urge the ill-omened expedition to Sicily, and afterwards to counsel

---

[1] See above, ch. III, § 15, *note* 1.
[2] See Burnet on *The Socratic Doctrine of the Soul* (Proc. Brit. Acad., 1915–16), reprinted in *Essays and Addresses* (London, 1929), pp. 126–162.

the enemies of Athens to the policy that achieved her ruin. This, then, so the restored democrats must have reasoned, was the fruit of the new learning; and they turned upon Socrates as the true author of their misfortunes. In any case, their hostility was political rather than religious, for Socrates had been meticulously scrupulous in his observance of the worships of the city. As it was, he narrowly escaped a verdict of acquittal; had he but consented to withdraw into exile, or had his defence not taken the form of an uncompromising and almost disdainful vindication of his mission, his life would doubtless have been spared. But Socrates' nature was inaccessible to any thought of compromise; he had been posted by God as a sentinel and must be faithful to his watch. He repelled the offer of escape from prison, as an act involving disloyalty to the laws of Athens under which, as his parents, he had been born and bred, and died by drinking hemlock, a martyr to reason and the love of truth.[1] Alike by his refusal to renounce what he regarded as a divine mission, even to save his life, and by his refusal to impair the authority of the law by evading the penalty imposed by the courts, Socrates offers an ideal example of the " conscientious objector."

IV. PLATO (§§ 19–24).

§ 19. Among the younger companions of Socrates was Plato (427–347), a rich Athenian of good family, who devoted the years of voluntary exile, that followed his master's condemnation, to those writings which have best preserved the memory of Socrates' mind and personality. It lies beyond our scope to track the golden stream of thought that flows through the Platonic dialogues.[2] These are consummate masterpieces both

---

[1] See the *Apology*, *Crito* and *Phaedo* of Plato. The *Phaedo*, inscribed to Socrates' Pythagorean associates, is of special importance, (*a*) as illustrating the influence on Socrates and Plato of Orphic and Pythagorean ideas about the soul, of philosophy as a way of life, and of the Forms (or Ideas) as the true objects of knowledge; (*b*) for the biographical interlude, pp. 96 ff., where Socrates recounts his early intellectual history;' and (*c*) for the closing scene, describing Socrates' death, perhaps the greatest passage in all prose literature. Hegel observes (*Philosophy of History*, 281) that though Socrates did his duty loyally to the *Polis*, it was the world of thought, not Athens, that was his true home.

[2] All Plato's writings have come down to us. The grounds on which their chronological order has been determined with a high degree of probability cannot be mentioned here. The results may be stated as follows for the reader's guidance in a first acquaintance with Plato. The order within each period is more doubtful.

Period I (between 399 and *c.* 387): the *Euthyphro*, *Apology*, *Crito*,

of scientific reasoning and of dramatic art; we can well appreciate
how Plato in youth had been drawn to write poetry. The dialogue
form not only gave free play to the imagination of the artist,
but reflected naturally the living movement of the Socratic
conversations, and Plato's own conception of philosophic method
as the upward endeavour of kindred spirits, by challenge of mind
to mind, in the search for absolute truth.[1] Of these writings the
Republic, composed after his return to Athens and in the full
maturity of his genius, affords the best approach to the study
of Plato's philosophy.[2] It is the most comprehensive in range of
all the dialogues. Opening with the question " What is justice ? ",
it portrays the ideal society and the progress of the soul to philosophic wisdom, and closes with a picture of the life beyond the
grave. The problems of ethics and politics, psychology and
education, literature and art, religion and science, are handled
in a living unity, as factors in the single problem of the universe,
by a thinker whose proud boast it was to be " the spectator of
all time and all existence." [3] But Plato was inspired, not only
by the impulse of philosophy to know the truth, but also by an
ardent passion for practical reform. From his youth, when he
looked to enter the public life of his native Athens, up to his last
vain journey in old age to Sicily, he was possessed with a burning
desire to save the souls of men, and to build, as far as earthly
conditions allowed, the city of God on Hellenic soil. For him,
as for his master Socrates, philosophy was always a " way of

---

*Charmides, Laches, Lysis, Cratylus, Euthydemus, Protagoras, Gorgias,
Meno* (the last three being towards the close of the period).

Period II (*c.* 387 to *c.* 375) : *Symposium* and *Phaedo* (early); *Republic,
Phaedrus.*

Period III (*c.* 367 to *c.* 360) : *Theaetetus, Parmenides, Sophist, Politicus*
(or Statesman).

Period IV (*c.* 360 to 347) : *Philebus, Timaeus, Critias, Laws.*

The *Republic* marks the turning-point when Plato's thought, which
was always on the move, began to travel beyond the lines of Socrates'
philosophy. In the later dialogues, Socrates is (except in the *Philebus*)
no longer the chief speaker. On the whole question, see Burnet, *Thales
to Plato*, and *note* 1 to § 16. The *Epistles* of Plato are either genuine or at
any rate contemporary documents of high value.

[1] Plato's term for philosophy, both as science and as method, is
dialectic : it is derived from the verb *dialegesthai* (= to converse) and is
allied with " dialogue." Plato says that, even when a man is engaged
in solitary thought, the soul carries on a dialogue with itself (*Soph.*, 263;
Theaet., 189). Plato himself preferred oral teaching to the written word,
see *Phaedr.*, 275 f.

[2] The *Republic* was probably completed at the time when Plato was
engaged in founding the Academy, between *c.* 387 and *c.* 378. He was
then 40 to 50 years old.

[3] *Rep.*, vi. 486,

life." From Socrates too he had learnt that goodness was knowledge, and that the only sure basis of practical conduct was a reasoned apprehension of the principle of good. Thus both problems, the speculative and the practical, found for Plato their common solution in philosophy, in a knowledge that should reveal the inner truth of the world as ideal goodness, and form the goal of individual and social action. What is this knowledge ? And how can man attain to it ? These are the cardinal questions of Plato's philosophy.

§ 20. That knowledge must be knowledge of what *is*, that its object must have true being, was never questioned by Plato; for him not merely must reality be knowable, but knowledge can be only of the real. Where, then, is true being to be found ? Heraclitus had held that all in the sense-world was in ceaseless change, ever coming to be and ceasing to be, never abiding in being. The followers of Protagoras had applied this doctrine to show how, at least in the field of sense, each passing appearance was true to the individual percipient in the instant of his perception. Such views robbed truth of all its meaning, and Plato could not rest content with them. He was driven, therefore, like Socrates before him, to seek for being elsewhere than in the world of sense. Reflection on our actual thinking shows it to involve objects of a very different order from sense-data; for these can be known only by aid of general concepts, apprehended not by the senses but by thought. This is especially evident in mathematical judgements, and in those that express moral and æsthetic values. No sensible lines or circles are perfectly equal, and to call an action good or a picture beautiful implies a single standard of goodness or of beauty, to which the particular instances are imperfect approximations.[1] Thus Plato was led to the belief in an intelligible world, wherein there existed in unchanging being, as substantial realities, the Forms or Ideas, the perfect archetypes, " shared in " or " imitated by " their manifold and changing copies in the world of sense. These Forms alone were the proper objects of scientific " knowledge "; the particular instances of them in the sense-world, on the other hand, were objects of fallible and fluctuating " opinion," the source alike of speculative error and of moral delusion. He who thinks and lives in bondage to the body and to things of sense, for all his

---

[1] See the *Phaedo*, which shows how Plato (Socrates ?) was led to the doctrine of Forms (or Ideas) by the study of mathematical, moral and æsthetic judgements.

keen insight into the particular circumstances around him, is as one walking amid dream-phantoms in his sleep; the philosopher, with his mind's eye fixed on the intelligible realities, alone has waking vision.[1] Plato proclaimed the doctrine of two worlds and, perhaps for the first time in the history of western thought, ascribed true being to immaterial substances. Moreover, the Forms are not isolated spiritual atoms but constitute an intelligible economy or order, which it is the philosopher's main task to trace. Supreme in this super-sensible hierarchy is the Form of Good, the source both of knowability and of being in all the other Forms, itself " transcending knowledge and being." [2] In the *Republic* Plato evinces reluctance to expound directly this " highest object of knowledge," nor does he supply the deficiency anywhere in his writings; indeed, in a letter he states explicitly that " There is no writing of mine on the subject nor ever shall be. It is not capable of expression like other branches of study; but, as the result of long intercourse and a common life spent upon the thing, a light is suddenly kindled as from a leaping spark, and when it has reached the soul, it thenceforward finds nutriment for itself." [3] We know, however, that the Good formed the goal of all Plato's intellectual endeavour, and that he lectured on the subject in the Academy to the close of his life.[4] It gave unity and system to the intelligible world, harmonising the Forms in one sovereign and universal purpose. As in the sense-world the sun is the source of light and life to all created things, so in the thought-world the Forms derive their rationality and being from the Form of Good.[5] Such in outline was Plato's answer to the two questions, What is knowledge? and What is being? which form the burden of metaphysics in all ages. His solution is liable to misinterpretation, and in three directions. (i) The Forms, though apprehended by the mind through general concepts, are no thought-abstractions, but substances, existing independently of the mind of any thinker in an objective spiritual

[1] See *Rep.*, v. 471 ff. vi, vii. It is very possible that the doctrine of Forms or Ideas (Plato employs both words, *Eidos* (Form) and *Idea*— the latter is ambiguous in English) had been held by Socrates and derived by him from Pythagorean speculation. Plato subjected the theory, as presented in the *Phaedo* and the *Republic*, to criticism and radical modification in later dialogues (especially the *Parmenides*).
[2] *Rep.*, vi. 509. This expression formed the text from which, later, the Neo-Platonists drew the thought of the super-essential One = the Good, which is the highest member in Plotinus' spiritual triad (see later, c. ix, § 12). [3] *Epp.*, vii. 341 (*tr.* Burnet).
[4] Aristotle published his notes on Plato's lectures on the Good, but these unfortunately have not been preserved. [5] *Rep.*, vi. 504 ff.

world.[1] (ii) The Form of Good is not identified by Plato with God. God is not a Form, but a living and active soul, the self-moving source of the motion of the heavens and, as Plato relates in semi-mythical language in the *Timaeus*, the creator of the sensible universe, after the pattern of the Forms and in accordance with mathematical law. The doctrines that God is himself the supreme good, and that the Forms are his eternal thoughts, having their being in the divine intellect, were not Plato's, but modifications of Plato's theory which naturally suggested themselves to Neo-Platonic and mediæval thinkers.[2] Finally (iii) it must not be supposed that in denying scientific knowledge of things of sense, Plato rejected them as illusory or worthless. It is not because the sense-world has no truth, but because its partial truth is visible only to the mind that grasps its dependence on the Forms, that Plato insists that the latter are the true objects of scientific study. Plato, in fact, conceived the sense-world as fashioned by God in space out of geometrical figures, a theory not so far removed from Descartes' reduction of physical body to terms of figured extension. Plato was a deep student of the mathematical sciences, which he held to be the proper approach to philosophy; and there is a tradition that over the portals of the Academy were inscribed the words, " Let no one who is not a geometrician enter here." In his view, mathematics furnished the key to physical nature; his later theory of Forms was in all likelihood a doctrine of mathematical relations, akin to that of modern physics, save only that, for Plato, the mathematical interpretation, far from precluding explanation in terms of purpose, required for its foundation the essential Form of Good.[3]

[1] In the *Parmenides*, 132, the suggestion that the Forms are concepts in the mind is brusquely rejected.

[2] God endowed the sensible world with a world-soul, so that it might, as far as may be, resemble his own goodness. This conception was influential in later speculation. Philo (first century A.D.), the Jewish Hellenist of Alexandria, was the first to treat the Forms as thoughts of God. Burnet, *Thales to Plato*, c. xvii, holds that Plato was the first philosopher to base theism on a scientific foundation.

[3] On the mathematical sciences, see *Rep.*, vii. 522 ff. Plato's philosophy, like that of Socrates, was through and through teleological; the being or reality of each fragment of the universe lay in its function, i.e. in its realisation of a purpose or good. The Form of Good is best thought of as a single supreme purpose which gathers up all fragmentary and individual purposes into a systematic unity. All the laws of the being of special parts of the world can be deduced from this single supreme purpose. Thus Plato's doctrine is far removed from that of mechanical determinism; wherever he finds law, and he finds it everywhere, he finds rationality and the Good.

§ 21. In the nature of man, the distinction between the intelligible order and the sensible appears as that between the soul and the body. For Plato, as for Aristotle after him, soul (*psyché*) is the principle of life and motion, so that, wherever these are present, there is soul; and the human soul, far from being the only or the chief expression of soul, is but one form of its manifestation. Greek philosophy stands in sharp contrast to the modern tendency to regard the human mind as the pivotal fact of experience. Beside human and infra-human souls, there is in Plato's universe the soul of God, the world-soul, and the divine souls that move the stars. With a passionate intensity of conviction, Plato believed all souls to be inherently immortal; his final proof, stated in the *Phaedrus* and again in his latest dialogue, the *Laws*, argues from the fact of motion to the necessity of a cause of motion which is self-moved, and therefore can never begin or cease to move.[1] Consequently, human, like all other souls, existed before incarnation in the body, and will survive the body's death. Thus Plato explains how the imperfect copies of the Forms in the world of sense " remind " the soul of the perfect archetypes which it had known before its embodiment, and solves the difficulty how man comes by a knowledge that trascends the limits of sense-experience.[2] It enables him also to account for present suffering as expiation for evil done in a previous incarnation and to develop the genuinely ethical doctrines of rewards and punishments after death, and of progressive purification in a series of lives.[3] Here Plato is building on the soil of Orphic teaching, which came to him through the Pythagoreans and Socrates. The body is the prison-house and tomb of the soul; its death is the soul's liberation; the life of philosophy, which fixes the mind's thought on the super-sensible Forms, is the prelude to this liberation and, in literal truth, the study of death.[4] In temporal union with the body, the human soul appears, not in its native purity, but like the sea-god Glaucus in the tale, " encrusted with shells and seaweed," so that its essential nature, reason, is concealed from outward view.[5] In our actual experience, the soul forms a composite unity of three

[1] *Phaedrus*, 245 C, *Laws*, 893 b ff. The earlier arguments in the *Phaedo* and *Republic* were dropped in later dialogues; they were possibly Socrates' own as distinct from Plato's proofs.
[2] See the *Meno*, 81 ff., on this doctrine of recollection (*anamnêsis*).
[3] See the myths in the *Gorgias, Phaedo, Republic*, x, and *Phaedrus,* and Stewart's *Myths of Plato*.
[4] See the *Phaedo*, 64 f.   [5] *Rep.* x. 611.

powers : reason, the philosophic faculty, the rightful authority in the soul's economy, whose rule ensures harmony within, and also with the kindred reason in other souls and in the universe; the " spirited " or passionate faculty, impulsive and pugnacious, a willing servant of reason but liable, if undirected, to lead the soul astray on the path of self-assertion; and the appetites, associated with bodily pleasures, some lawful, others unlawful, but all alike insatiable in their thirst for satisfaction, and, unless sternly disciplined by reason, ever plunging the soul into a riot of anarchy and disunion.   Under the outward semblance of a man, we can picture a creature compounded of three natures, those of a man (reason), a lion (passion), and a many-headed hydra (appetites).[1]   The ethical and educational scheme of the *Republic* is largely based on this threefold psychological distinction; for example, the picture of three types of life, inspired respectively by love of pleasure, love of honour and love of wisdom; the analysis of moral virtue into the specific forms of wisdom, courage and temperance, which have their common root in justice, the principle enabling each part of the soul to do its proper work in the economy of the whole, and ensuring a harmony or " music " through the entire soul; the division of education into music and gymnastic, the disciplines of the appetites and of " spirit," forming the requisite moral basis for the use of reason in maturer years; and, finally, the conception of philosophy as a conversion of the soul from the darkness of the sense-world to the light of the world of Forms, and as a lifelong preparation for the unfettered exercise of reason in the world beyond the grave.[2]

§ 22. Against those who maintained that morality was mere convention and that the individual finds his true happiness in a life of self-assertion, Plato showed how man in the very core of his being was marked out for social co-operation. He formulated two positions in intimate conjunction, namely, that each individual has by nature a unique capacity which determines his particular function in society, and that this function can only be efficiently discharged, so as to bring happiness to the agent,

---

[1] *Rep.*, ix. 588–9; cf. the simile of the chariot of the soul, *Phaedrus*, 246 f.

[2] For Plato's psychology in application to ethics and the education of the young, see *Rep.*, ii–iv; for the higher training of reason, *Rep.*, vii (especially the allegory of the prisoners in the cave); also Nettleship's essay on *The Theory of Education in Plato's Republic* in the volume entitled *Hellenica*.

when it is regulated by the general good.[1] The economy of the
state is dependent on the psychology of the citizens, and this
analogy between the *Polis* and the individual governs the picture
of their good and evil types throughout the whole of the *Republic*.
Social functions will be apportioned on the basis of the individual
characters of the citizens; those in whose souls appetite is
dominant will perform physical labour, supplying the material
needs of the community as artisans or farmers; the " spirited "
souls will constitute the military class; the philosophic souls,
which have proved in repeated trials their capacity for the life
of reason, will be intrusted with the highest task of government.
Thus Plato is brought by logical steps to his famous paradox,
that " until philosophers are kings and kings philosophers there
will be no salvation for states or for the souls of men." [2] There
will be none for the state, since reason is the power in the soul
that makes for unity, and the realisation of reason in the philosophic life is the only safeguard against social anarchy. Nor will
there be for the individual soul; for, unless reason be sovereign
in the community, no private person can resist the corrupting
influence of public opinion and the allurements of the world.[3]
Believing that it was possible for the philosopher to attain in
the course of his earthly life to the culmination of speculative
knowledge in the vision of absolute Good, he drew the natural
corollary that failure to conform in conduct to that vision was
inconceivable. Knowledge on this exalted plane entailed conformity of conduct. It was impossible to sin against the light.
Christianity at once endorsed and modified the Platonic doctrine.
On the one hand, it held for the redeemed in Paradise who enjoyed the direct vision of God, the absolute Good (*non posse
peccare*); on the other, that direct vision was unattainable by
men in this life, even on the highest level of mystic contemplation. The saint, for all his saintliness, remains a sinner; he
sees God only " through a glass darkly " (*per speciem in aenigmate*),
never " face to face." Plato's Form of Good was not identified
by him with God (who was a " soul," not a " form "), but it
was knowable by the philosopher " face to face." Thus, inspired
partly by the conviction that in a perfect society all things must
be in common, and each member feel joy and sorrow in the joy
and sorrow of every other, partly by a sense of the danger even

[1] See *Rep.*, ii. 369 ff. The claims of individual self-assertion are voiced
by Thrasymachus in Book I, by Glaucon and Adimantus at the beginning
of Book II, and by Callicles in the *Gorgias*.
[2] *Rep.*, v. 473.   [3] *Rep.*, vi. 492.

to the chosen few of the curse of private interests, Plato denied
to the ruling classes the possession of private property and
replaced the private household by a single state-family, regulated
with uncompromising rigour by the philosopher-kings. In these
provisions we see at once Plato's passionate longing for unity,
and his clear grasp of the forces of evil that are ever ready to
assert their claims in the life of the individual and of the community. His austere idealism and unrelenting logic combined
to lead him, in the temper of a monastic founder, to banish all
temptations, such as private possessions and the dramatic art,
that might possibly provoke to moral licence. The world of
his day, and especially the political and ethical tone of fourth-
century Athens, is, in the *Republic*, unreservedly condemned.
The individual Athenian seemed to him to have been swept off
his bearings on a tide of emotional debauchery, the Athenian
state to have been rent asunder by party faction and the self-
aggrandisement of its leaders. If the souls of men or human
societies were to win salvation, it must be through a radical
change of heart, carrying with it the institution of severe self-
discipline and a revolution in the principles of life and government. Plato's keen insight into the evil of human nature and his
bitter sense of the hopelessness of actual society reminds us frequently of Tolstoi. But he differed from Tolstoi in that he was
always also a philosopher. His remedy for the evils of the world
was to place power in the hands of those who know. They alone,
who, as the fruit of long moral and intellectual training, have
attained to knowledge and love of the sovereign good, are qualified
to mould the citizen's character and direct the policy of the state.
In contrast to the ideal of Periclean democracy, Plato preaches
professorial socialism. In a famous simile in the sixth book of
the *Republic* he likens the Athenian people to the captain of a
ship, good-natured but sluggish, and easily influenced by the
flattery of artful mariners who vie with one another in cajoling
him to entrust the helm to one of themselves. None of them
has ever learnt the pilot's art or has the true knowledge that alone
avails to guide the ship aright. All the while, the true pilot who
is master of his craft remains neglected and alone. Thus in
Plato's view the Athenian *demos* had fallen into the hands of
unscrupulous and incompetent adventurers, while the philosopher,
by right of nature the true-born ruler, was condemned to the
inactivity of private life.[1]

[1] *Rep.*, vi. 488, 496.

§ 23. Needless to say, Plato failed to convince his fellow-citizens, and Athens pursued her course until the advent of the Macedonian conqueror.   Unwearying in his efforts after practical reform, he thrice visited Sicilian Syracuse, in the hope that as a despot's counsellor he might succeed in instituting the philosophic state.   But already in the *Republic* he had come to see that the ideal city was " a pattern set up in heaven," incapable of perfect realisation upon earth.[1]   In two of the later dialogues, the *Statesman* and the *Laws*, he evinced a more tolerant temper towards existing forms of government and, in the last-named writing, sketched a second-best polity as an accommodation of the ideal to the facts of life.   But his true vocation, during the last forty years of life, lay in the Academy, the college for scientific and philosophical research which he founded and endowed.   The Academy can justly claim to be regarded as the earliest university in history.   Students flocked thither from all quarters of the Hellenic world, notably Eudoxus,[2] a mathematician and astronomer from Cyzicus, and the young Aristotle from Stagira on the Macedonian coast.   The members of the school shared a common life, residing in the Academy, and engaging not only in strictly philosophical studies but in enquiries into mathematics, biology and problems of morals and jurisprudence.   Amongst its achievements was the development of solid geometry, and Plato, in sketching his programme of higher studies in the *Republic*, advocated state support for this new science.[3]   The subsequent course of educational thought and practice, alike in Graeco-Roman and in mediæval times, is grounded on Plato's institution of the Academy.   It became a custom to seek for legislative reformers in the ranks of the school.   Plato's latest writing, the *Laws*, is an example of this branch of its enquiries.[4]   The Academy had a long and memorable history; it served as the model for subsequent foundations, such as Aristotle's college in the Lyceum, and those of the Stoics and the Epicureans, and continued in being as the central home of Platonic teaching for a thousand years, until the pagan schools were finally disendowed and disestablished by the Christian emperor Justinian (A.D. 529).

[1] *Rep.*, ix. 592.
[2] On Eudoxus, see Heath in *The Legacy of Greece*, pp. 117 ff.   He discovered the theory of proportion expounded in Euclid, Book V ; and also the method of exhaustion for measuring curvilinear areas and solids, developed later by Archimedes.   [3] *Rep.*, vii. 528.
[4] His codification of Greek, especially of Athenian, law, as developed subsequently, exercised a great influence on Hellenistic and, through Hellenistic, on Roman, law.   See below, c. vii, § 6, *n.* 2.

§ 24. The philosophy of Plato, because of its other-worldliness and uncompromising idealism, has seemed to many minds more akin to the spirit of Christianity than to that of Greece, which looked to this life and its opportunities for the satisfaction of man's intellectual and moral aspirations. There is truth in this assertion, though the differences are more vital than the likeness. Plato's doctrines of the soul's salvation through laborious intellectual discipline, and of the spiritual direction of society by a scientific aristocracy, carry us a long way from the ideal of a spiritual kingdom to be entered, not by the wise and prudent, but in the spirit of a little child. Moreover, the root-conceptions of Plato's thought proved fruitful beyond expectation in moulding the Hellenic ideal of life. The conviction, expressed in the *Republic*, that the highest life is that not of pleasure or power, but of philosophical contemplation, remained the governing ideal of ancient thought. When the city-state lost its independence and the career of free public activity was closed to the Greek citizen, the best minds busied themselves more and more with the pursuit of knowledge. Aristotle, who, though often contrasted with Plato, yet builds at every point on his master's foundations and is rather to be regarded as the first great Platonist, shared his belief that the life of philosophy is that in which the soul finds fullest satisfaction and approaches most nearly to the divine. In the centuries that followed, the same conviction was held alike by Platonists and Aristotelians, by Stoics and Epicureans.[1] Nor was it confined to the Pagan world. Stripped of its peculiarly intellectual interpretation as the life of philosophy, the ideal of contemplative activity dominated mediæval Christianity.[2] The Mary and Martha of the Gospels became the types of the theoretic and active life; and the former had chosen the better part. The institution of monasticism, the writings of Dante, and the sculptures that adorn the cathedrals of the Middle Ages, are evidence of the hold which this thought, the product conjointly of the Christian and the Hellenic genius, had won over the spiritual aspirations of mankind. Plato, like all the greatest of the Greeks, whether in literature or philosophy, stands for something of universal value. Whenever the spirit of man turns from the world of sense and change towards that which is eternal, unchanging, and one, whether it be in intellectual or religious contemplation, it has claimed kinship with the spirit of Plato.

[1] And especially by the Neo-Platonists : See below, c. ix, §§ 10–14.
[2] See below, c. xi.

ADDITIONAL NOTE TO CHAPTER V

Among the ethical questions which the thinkers of the fifth-century enlightenment in Greece asked themselves, were two that possess a special interest for the modern reader. These are (i) the question of the status of women in the community, (ii) the question of slavery.

I. *The Status of Women.*[1]

In the Funeral Oration as reported by Thucydides, Pericles addressed the female mourners in well-known words : " If I am to speak of womanly virtues to those of you who will henceforth be widows, let me sum them up in one short admonition : to a woman not to show more weakness than is natural to her sex is a great glory, and not to be talked about for good or for evil among men." [2] This sentiment, inconceivable on the lips of a modern statesman offering public condolence to the bereaved in war, must have seemed entirely becoming to the majority of Pericles' hearers of both sexes. A century before, Theognis had written : " I hate a woman who is a gad-about "; a century later, Menander declared that " the house-door is the bound for a free woman." Women played no part in the recorded public life of Athens. Yet in art and poetry, as in religion, they are present everywhere; objects now of pity, now of terror, idealised in awe or analysed with subtle discernment, they are never ignored. The Homeric heroines enjoyed a dignity and freedom which contrast with their subjection and seclusion in after times; though it may be that Achæan, like mediæval, chivalry invested the wives and daughters of chieftains with a halo of romance denied to women of ignoble birth.[3] No dramatic literature is so rich in portraits of women as the Greek, which left no aspect of feminine humanity, save (until Hellenistic days) the love of

[1] See, in addition to other references given below, Xenophon, *Œconomicus* (*tr.* Dakyns); Benecke, *Women in Greek Poetry*; Zimmern, Part III, c. 12.

[2] Thuc., ii. 45; *tr.* Jowett.

[3] Possibly, too, as Professor Murray suggests (*Rise of the Greek Epic*, p. 75), the tradition of the matriarchal system once prevalent in the Ægean world survived the Achæan conquest. The same writer (p. 124) points out how in the *Iliad*, as an epic of warfare, we hear little of women (save in two great passages, *Iliad*, iii and vi. 237 to end) in Troy. On a military expedition, he thinks, women may have been taboo. Samuel Butler maintained the interesting paradox that the *Odyssey* was written by a woman, perhaps by Nausicaa (see his *Authoress of the Odyssey*).

G

youth and maiden, unexplored.[1] Clytæmnestra, Antigone,
Medea, Phædra and Alcestis stand on a plane with the great
heroines of Shakespeare's tragedies. In actual Greek life we
detect little that answers to this interest. The only woman of
note in Athenian history, Aspasia, was an alien and bound to
Pericles in a left-handed union.[2] At Athens the sphere of woman
was the home. The man's sphere, on the other hand, was the
Polis; the home counted for little in his life. At Sparta, for
military reasons, women were allowed greater freedom; they were
trained in public exercises that they might grow up to be strong
mothers of soldiers. The result, we are told, was that, though
handsome, they were hoydens, prone to luxury, avarice and
rebellion, and apt to engage in political intrigue.[3] The exclusion
of women from Greek public life evoked many protests in the
fifth and fourth centuries. That projects of reform were in the
air is witnessed by the two comedies, the *Lysistrata* (411) and the
Ecclesiazousae (392 or 389), in which Aristophanes lashed their
claims to emancipation. Women missionaries were to be found
among the Cynics. Euripides was stirred to pity and indignation
by the lot of women, who in childbirth were called upon to endure
worse sufferings than men in battle.[4] Plato was impressed by
the waste of good material for the service of the state. He held
that the difference between the sexes was one not of kind but of
degree; women were indeed weaker than men, but none the less
capable of sharing their civic functions, including that of philosophic sovereignty. Women might be found in each of the three
classes in his ideal city. As they shared in the vocations, so they
shared also in the education of men. There is no thought here
of " women's rights "; they were to be trained on masculine
lines and for the advantage, not of their sex, but of the community. The whole passage, in the fifth book of the *Republic*,
is strongly utilitarian. Moreover, Plato proposes to abolish the

[1] The sole exception in an extant play of the classical age is the love
of Hæmon and Antigone in Sophocles' *Antigone*. It is in the New Comedy
of the fourth century that the love of youth and maiden, culminating in
marriage, becomes a prevalent theme.

[2] After the law of 451, which laid down that both parents must be
citizens, if the children were to be legitimate, these second marriages
with non-citizen women were frequent. No obloquy attached to them.

[3] Later, they owned a large part of the Spartan lands. On the Spartan
women, see Aristotle, *Politics*, ii. 9; also Plato, *Laws*, 780 ff., Protag.,
342; and Euripides, *Andromache*, 595 ff.

[4] Eur. *Medea*, 248 ff. The soliloquy of *Alestis*, in the play that bears
her name, is very instructive. On her death, her boy-child will get his
chance; but what about the girl?

private household and embody all the citizens of both sexes in a single state-family. Marriage unions, the rearing (or exposure) of infants, and nurture in early childhood are to be controlled exclusively by the government.[1] His avowed motives were (a) eugenic, to preserve the quality of the ruling class, (b) fear of disunion and civic faction (stasis), the source of which lay in private interests and possessions, and (c) an ideal aspiration after a society which should know no divorce of " mine " and " thine," but throb with a single pulse of all its members.[2] Finally, Aristotle set himself to confine the projects of radical reformers within the bounds of common sense. Women, he held as against Plato, differed from men in kind; they were defective, though not entirely lacking, in intellectual and moral capacity; hence, while debarred from full citizenship, they must be ruled by men constitutionally, not despotically like slaves. They would enjoy a limited freedom and receive an education adapted to their subordinate vocation in the *Polis*. What seems to have impressed him was their lack of scientific intelligence and of the quality of mind that carries authority.[3] We can hear him echo the voice of male superiority in every age : " Be good, sweet maid, and let who can "—the men—" be clever." He kept in close touch with current Greek opinion, leavening it with a spice of liberalism; but in his handling alike of ideal values and of the facts of human nature he fell far short of Plato.

II. *Slavery*.[4]

Among the Greeks, as generally thoughout antiquity, slavery formed part of the traditional order, and, as such, was accepted without question. We read in Homer, and especially in the *Odyssey*, of slaves in relatively small numbers, captured in piracy or war. It was a fate that might befall any man : Eumæus and Eurycleia were of noble lineage; though it reft the victim of " half his manhood," it entailed no disgrace. Eumæus enjoyed " a good life " as an honourable retainer, who spoke to his master's family as man to man; lines of social cleavage were less rigorous

[1] Infanticide, sanctioned possibly by Plato in certain cases, was prevalent in many ancient societies, though probably not at Athens. The speeches of Isaeus furnish evidence to the contrary. It was generally the female infants who suffered this fate.

[2] See *Rep.*, v. to p. 467.

[3] See especially *Politics*, i. cc. 12, 13, and the criticisms on the *Republic* in ii, cc. 2–4.

[4] See, on the subject, Zimmern, c. xv, and Smith's *Dictionary of Antiquities*, art. *servus*.

in those simpler times.[1] In the next age, with the Dorian invasion, a new type of slavery appears; the slaves are a conquered population, bound to the soil, like the Spartan Helots and the *Penestae* in Thessaly.   Later still, the spread of industry and commerce brought in its train the slave-trade over the Ægean world; the chief recruiting areas were among the barbarians of Asia Minor, Thrace and the lands around the Euxine; the chief markets, in maritime states which controlled the carrying trade, like Chios and, subsequently, Athens.   At Athens, slaves were employed (*a*) in the household for domestic work rather than, as later at Rome, for luxury; (*b*) in large industries, especially in the silver mines at Laurion; (*c*) as state-slaves, e.g. as rowers on ships of war.[2]   The census return for the year 309 gave 400,000 slaves in Attica.   The great majority were barbarians; Greek captives were always open to ransom.   The lot of the ordinary Athenian slave had its alleviations and compares favourably with that of a later age at Rome or in the plantations of Christian slave-owners in modern times.   The slave was protected by Attic law; his life was not in his master's hands, and slave torture was restricted within precise limits. There was no distinction of dress between slaves and free men; though excluded from the temples, gymnasia and the public assembly, they were often allowed wide liberty of speech and action. Xenophon calls the slave the "fellow-worker" of the citizen, who should be ruled by persuasion rather than by force, and induced to work willingly by hope of emancipation.   He comments on the leniency shown towards slaves at Athens, a verdict confirmed by the pictures drawn in the New Comedy and by Plato's scornful censure of the licence characteristic of slaves in the democratic state.[3]   It was a common practice for a master to give domestic slaves their freedom, either in his lifetime or by will on his death.   Doubtless the slave's lot varied greatly according as he was a family servant or an apprentice in trade or, again, for his misfortune, an employee in the mines.   The ugly fact was present throughout Greek history.   But the assertion that Greek civilization rested on slavery as its basis is true

---

[1] For Eumæus, see *Odyssey*, xv. 380 ff.

[2] A poor man would have only one domestic slave, a rich man as many as fifty.   The abuses of slavery were most evident in the mines; Nicias owned 1,000 slaves at Laurion.   Cf. Thuc., vii. 87, on the sufferings of the Athenian captives in the Syracusan quarries.   The tale that certain of these won their freedom by reciting Euripides has been woven into Browning's poem, *Balaustion's Adventure*.

[3] Xen., *Mem.*, ii. 3, 3; *Rep. Ath.*, i. 10–12; Plato, *Rep.*, ix. 563.

only under reservations. The two things do not vary proportionately to one another. Slavery on an extended scale was subsequent to the rise of Hellenic art and science, and increased as that art and science passed into decline. Other nations, such as Egypt and Assyria, who employed slaves in far greater numbers, failed to achieve a culture comparable to that of Greece. The unique quality of Greek civilization cannot therefore be explained as due to slavery. Above all, the Greeks were the first to question its moral justification.[1] Even if their culture were due to slavery, so also was the thought of those who, like the Sophists, struck at the roots of the evil. That slavery was grounded not on nature but on convention was a common topic among the poets and philosophers of the fifth and fourth centuries. The Cynics declared boldly for emancipation. The Sophist Alcidamas preached throughout Greece that " the deity has made all men free; nature has enslaved no man." [2] Plato condemned the enslavement of Greek by Greek.[3] So likewise did Aristotle, who in his *Politics* handled the subject, after his wont, in the spirit of a conservative reformer.[4] Only those, he held, were slaves by nature who, like most barbarians, were disqualified by lack of reason and moral capacity for participation in the life of the *Polis*. Such " natural " slaves were doomed to servitude, as necessary instruments to the " good life " of the free Hellenic citizen. They were means to another's ends, not ends in themselves; in the language of a later day, they were " things," not " persons." The slave should be governed despotically, for his master's interest, not (save accidentally) for his own. True, he should be treated with humanity; and Aristotle went so far as to admit that though, *quâ* slave, he is incapable of rational life, and cannot stand in any relation of friendship (*philia* = bond of social union) with his master, such association may be possible for him *quâ* man. His attitude offers an obvious contrast to the Christian ideal of humanity. For Aristotle, the individual human being as such has no intrinsic worth. The view that inferior races may be trained to capacity

[1] See Murray, *Rise of the Greek Epic*, pp. 16 ff.
[2] So Euripides, *Ion*, 854–6.

> " The name alone is shameful to the slave;
> In all things else an honest man enslaved
> Falls not below the nature of the free."

[3] *Rep.*, v. 469. There appear to be no slaves in the *Republic*. In the *Laws*, where slavery is recognised, provision is made for mitigation of its evils. [4] See especially *Politics*, i, cc. 3–7, 13.

for fuller and relatively self-determined life never crossed his
mind. Their highest function was to minister to the material
wants of the Hellenic citizen. These limitations lie open on the
surface. They led, among the Greeks as elsewhere, to moral
abuses, the gravity of which no one will desire to palliate. The
fact that the Greek thinkers realised the existence of the problem
and attempted to offer a solution implies an immense advance
upon anything hitherto achieved in history. In restricting
slavery to those who were incapable of free life, they formulated
a principle which could be indefinitely extended in its application,
e.g. by the Stoics. Analogous problems exist for the modern
world, though the status and style of slavery have passed away,
e.g. how to achieve a high level of culture without sacrifice of the
many to the leisured few, and how to spread knowledge among
the masses without peril to the stability of society.[1] The practice
of the present day, as is evidenced alike in the treatment of lower
races and in the monotony and squalor of industrial conditions
in civilized lands, stands in glaring contrast with the avowed
ideal. It ill becomes the critic to cast a stone at the ancient
Greeks because their actual performance fell short of the precepts
of their greatest thinkers.

[1] The readers of the novels of the late Henry James may well wonder
how the cultured and charming world there portrayed could subsist apart
from the virtual, though not actual, slavery of the uncultured purveyors
to its comfort.

CHAPTER VI

GRÆCO-MACEDONIAN CULTURE

I. ALEXANDER (§§ 1–7).

§ 1. WITH the dawn of the fourth century we enter a changed world. Political power is no longer focused in Athens and Sparta, but shifts to new centres in the north; dreams of world-dominion on a scale unprecedented in Greek history are stirring the ambition of statesmen and military leaders. The brief sovereignty of Sparta that followed the downfall of the Athenian empire has little or no interest for civilization; the maritime cities quickly realised the hollowness of the victor's claim to be their liberator from the Athenian yoke, and that the little finger of her tyranny was thicker than the loins of Athens had ever been. The Greek world burned with shame and indignation when by the peace of Antalcidas (387) she handed back the Asiatic cities to the Persian king. Of far greater significance was the north-ward trend of political gravity, first, to Bœotian Thebes, whose serried phalanx shattered the once formidable Spartan infantry at Leuctra (371); then, by way of Thessaly, to Macedonia. The rise of the Macedonian kingdom is the central fact in the history of fourth-century Greece.[1] The Macedonians were akin to the Greeks in race and language; hardy mountaineers, born fighters, full of turbulent energy and devoted to their clan-chieftains, they had preserved the primitive habits of the early invaders of the Ægean world, despite the veneer of culture surrounding a court which had welcomed the tragedians Euripides and Agathon. A strong and politic sovereign, able to win and hold the devotion of the wild nobles and their retainers, had in this people a splendid instrument for a policy of military aggrandisement. Such a king, in fact, was Philip, who ascended the Macedonian throne in 356 at the age of twenty-two. In youth he had been trained at Thebes to appreciate Hellenic culture and, what was more to his purpose, to master the tactics of the phalanx. Like Peter the Great of Russia, who utilised western civilization for the consolidation of a semi-barbarous empire, Philip moved his capital from the interior to a site of vantage near the coast, reorganised his kingdom, and trained his warrior subjects in the

[1] Macedonians, who had fought with the Greeks against Persia, were admitted to the Olympic games in 476.

science of war. With the weapon thus forged, he conquered Thrace to the east, profited by the everlasting disunion of Greek states to subjugate the cities of the northern Ægean, and, partly by force, partly by the acts of diplomacy, of which he was a consummate master, won control of Thessaly and central Greece. A crowning victory at Chæronea (338) over the combined armies of Thebes and Athens laid all Greece at his feet. Chæronea meant more than the failure of the heroic efforts of Demosthenes, the patriot-orator of Athens, to save the cause of Hellenic liberty. On that fatal field was sounded the death-knell of the independent *Polis*. Henceforward the political history of Greece is that of her Macedonian conquerors.

§ 2. The subjugation of Greece was for Philip merely the initial step to the realisation of a project of empire which had been working in the minds of the statesmen and thinkers of Greece for more than half a century. The defeat of the Persian invaders of 480 had made manifest the superiority in war of a trained citizen army, animated by loyalty to the free city-state, over the vast but ill-disciplined levies whose sole bond of union was their common subjection to an Oriental despot. Persia learnt to recognise this superiority, and before the close of the fifth century had welcomed Greek condottieri into her service, while by her diplomacy and her gold she kept Greece disunited at home. The retreat of ten thousand Greek mercenaries from the heart of the Persian empire to the Euxine, through a difficult country, amid a hostile population, and harassed by a host of enemies, had shown that it was not merely on Hellenic soil that Greece was unconquerable; from that moment (401–400) the thought of a war of revenge, of a Greek invasion of Persia, loomed in the minds of Greek captains.[1] Philosophers and political idealists, like Plato and Isocrates, saw in a national crusade against the barbarian the opportunity for Hellenic union and the remedy for domestic strife.[2] But the city-states of Greece cherished their independence too dearly to tolerate political solidarity. The union was imposed from without by the Macedonian sovereign. Philip, supreme after Chæronea by force of arms, declared for the long-projected enterprise; his army was already marshalled for war, when he died at the hand of an assassin (336). The task of realisation fell to his son Alexander.

[1] E.g. King Agesilaus of Sparta and Jason of Pheræ, the powerful Thessalian chieftain.
[2] This seems to be the implication of Plato, *Rep.*, v. 470–1.

§ 3. Alexander stands at the close of an old, and at the beginning of a fresh, chapter in world-history. The invasion of Greece by Xerxes had opened a new phase in the secular contest between East and West. The conquest of the Persian empire by Alexander terminates this episode in the historic drama. The catastrophe was blinding in its swiftness. In the spring of 334 Alexander crossed the Hellespont, routed the advanced guard of the Persians on the Granicus, conquered the coast-lands of Asia Minor, and secured the control of the great highway leading through the mountains of the interior to the Cilician gates. In the following year he won his first great victory over king Darius in person at Issus, at the north-east corner of the Levant. The beaten king offered him the western half of his empire to the Euphrates; the compromise was haughtily refused. The capture of Tyre in 332, after a resistance that forecasts that of Carthage or of Jerusalem—the Semites were terrible when besieged—gave Alexander the sea-power in the eastern Mediterranean, and was followed by the conquest of Canaan and Egypt. In 331 he advanced to the heart of the Persian empire, and won his crowning triumph over Darius at Gaugamela in the valley of the Tigris. The death of the fugitive king in the succeeding summer made manifest Alexander's true purpose to the world. Hitherto the king of Macedon and captain-general of the Greeks, he now stood forward as the inheritor of the Persian kingdom, as the "King of Kings" in Darius' stead. The next five years witnessed a series of marvellous campaigns and marches, in which Alexander subdued the eastern satrapies to the Oxus and Jaxartes and beyond the Hindu-Kush, pierced the Khyber Pass, conquered the Punjâb and traversed the valley of the Indus to its mouth. On the refusal of his army to march eastwards to the Ganges, the fleet returned by the Persian Gulf, the land forces through the terrible desert of the Mekran. Alexander was back at Susa, the old Persian capital, in the spring of 324. A few months were devoted to the organisation of the vast empire. By June 323 he had gathered at Babylon a great army for the conquest of Arabia. There, stricken suddenly by fever, he died after a ten days' illness, at the age of thirty-two.

§ 4. The campaigns of Alexander opened a new world to Greece and by extending the range of knowledge had important results on scientific thought. But his great achievement was the diffusion of Hellenism over the eastern world. The political genius of Alexander is most evident in his deliberate purpose to fuse into one the Hellenic and the Oriental spirit. On the one hand he adopted Persian state, Persian dress, Persian customs; he practised and encouraged intermarriage, recognised the religions of the conquered peoples, and became in all things an Eastern to the Easterns. On the other hand, he incorporated Persians into the phalanx, trained their youth in Hellenic culture, and promoted their nobility in his service. Recognising clearly that this policy of fusion must rest on an economic basis, he strove to create a system of world-commerce, linking the Nile, the Tigris and the Indus with the Mediterranean.[1] Few of his Macedonian followers were able to share these great ideas; we read of periodic resentment and mutiny in the years following 330, provoking Alexander to the rare acts of severity that present a striking contrast to the habitual generosity and humanity of his nature. His chief instrument in welding together East and West was the foundation of cities on the Hellenic model. The cities of the Persian empire were few in number, a fact that explains the decisive finality of his victories in the field. Alexander planted cities everywhere on his marches, Alexandria, the most famous of them all, in Egypt, in the Euphrates valley, in the far north-east in Turkestan, on the Indus banks and on the shores of the Persian Gulf. These cities, with their colonies of Macedonian and Hellenic settlers, formed abiding centres of Greek culture. As the outcome of this policy, which was followed out by his successors, the life of the vast region from the Ægean to the Indus, from the Caspian to Ethiopia, was transformed in a greater or less degree by the Hellenic spirit. Greek science took root in Babylon; the art, religion and political government of India received the impress of the Greek mind. When we reflect that this achievement represents a mere fragment of Alexander's policy, accomplished in the few spare months between his campaigns, we realise that it has hardly a parallel in human history.

§ 5. The royal family of Macedonia claimed Greek descent, and Alexander was in all the essentials of character a Greek. At moments wild passions would break the bounds of his natural humanity and self-discipline, though for his few recorded acts of

---

[1] Everywhere Alexander presented himself as the champion of native religions and customs. He showed special favours, e.g. to the Jews. It is probable that the Jews, who were spread in large numbers over the Persian empire and kept up channels of intercommunication (especially with Jerusalem), rendered him great service as guides in his marches into what must have been practically unknown lands. Mahaffy, *The Empire of the Ptolemies*, p. 85, speaks of them as his " natural intelligence department."

violence he showed an equally passionate remorse. Greek culture was not with him, as with many of his officers, a thin veneer that veiled the barbarian; its poetry and thought had stirred deeply his ardent and enthusiastic nature. For three years of his youth, between the ages of thirteen and sixteen, he had been the pupil of Aristotle, the greatest thinker of the age; his imagination was nourished on the poems of Homer; his court and camp were the scene of athletic and dramatic festivals; in the hour of vengeance on Thebes he spared the house of Pindar from the flames. When he sat as " king of kings " on the throne of the great Darius, or assumed in Egypt the divine honours that marked the Pharaoh, he was never the victim of his own glory, but remained in heart and mind a Greek. He possessed great physical strength and courage, risking his life with apparent recklessness in the field; on one occasion in India he leapt with three companions into a besieged city and was wounded nearly to death. The king of the rude and warlike Macedonians had to hold their loyalty by personal prowess. Few great historical personalities are so free from meanness of spirit as Alexander. Open-hearted, truthful, ardent in personal friendship, chivalrous alike to friends and enemies, possessed of a noble pride and love of honour, he bound both generals and soldiers to his service by a strong tie of personal magnetism. The purity of his moral character was a proverb and a marvel to the age. With these qualities of mind and person were combined a clearness of insight, a capacity of adjusting means to ends, a supreme mastery of the art of war and the rare union of political imagination and con-summate statecraft. His hero of romance was the Achilles of the *Iliad*; but in Alexander we see grafted upon the ardour, courage and love of glory of the Homeric hero, the rich heritage of moral and intellectual culture evolved by the Hellenic race in the long course of its history.

§ 6. Tradition tells that the dying Alexander, when asked by his marshals to whom he bequeathed his empire, made answer, " To the strongest." For twenty years they plotted and fought for the inheritance, till the battle of Ipsus in Phrygia (301) determined the broad lines of partition for the succeeding age. The Balkan peninsula fell to Lysimachus, forming a separate Macedonian kingdom with suzerainty over European Greece. Ptolemy had occupied Egypt immediately upon the great con-queror's death, and his dynasty continued to rule that country till its incorporation within the Roman empire. The bulk of

Alexander's dominions, the Asiatic provinces from the Ægean to the Indus, passed to Seleucus, henceforward king of Asia. We cannot trace the detailed history of the conflicts among these dynasts through the two following centuries of storm and change. The politics of the eastern Mediterranean world were in the hands of Hellenic autocrats, often competent leaders in war and statesmanship, often romantic in their personality and fortunes, often, on the other hand, mere mediocrities, the puppets of chance and circumstance, selfish adventurers or shallow dilettanti or the slaves of debauchery and vindictive passion.[1] In an age which afforded unbounded opportunity to individual genius we find no leader of men of the front rank, save when for a moment, at the dawn of the second century, the heroic figure of the great Carthaginian passes to his doom across the panorama of the eastern world, cherishing to the bitter end undying hatred against Rome. But Hannibal was a Semite and an exile in alien lands, whose rulers, the Antigonids, Ptolemies and Seleucids, were cast in a very different mould. Their interest for history lies almost solely in their furtherance of Alexander's policy of Hellenising the East. Otherwise they pursued a path of personal aggrandisement, or followed in their methods of administration the models established by the former rulers of Macedon, Egypt and the Persian empire. Greeks in race, speech and manners, they ruled in Hellenic courts by the aid of Hellenic soldiery and Hellenic ministers, and with deliberate intention diffused and preserved Hellenic civilization, anticipating in their generation the historic mission of the Rome of a later day. The influence of this policy alike in East and West was incalculable. Its success was largely independent of the personality of the monarch, who, as we have noted, was often a *fainéant* or a ruffian ; Polybius expressly brands the Ptolemies as persons of no importance.[2]

[1] The first Seleucus, the first Ptolemy and the Attalid rulers of Pergamos are examples of able sovereigns ; Demetrius the Besieger of cities (*Poliorcetes*) and Pyrrhus of Epirus of romantic condottieri ; Antiochus *Epiphanes* (the God-manifest) of the dilettanti. The " tigress-princesses " of Macedonian blood add materially to the personal interest of the epoch (see Bevan, *House of Seleucus*).

[2] He contrasts their " nothingness " (*oudemeia*) with the superior capacity of the Seleucids, xxxiv. 14. Though Alexandria was an important centre of Hellenic culture (see the next section), the Ptolemies governed Egypt on the lines of the old Pharaohs, treating the country as a lucrative personal estate, with an exclusive eye to their own sovereignty and profit. Of the ministers of the Seleucids we hear little ; but the government appears to have been efficiently carried on, even under indolent dynasts. Bureaucracy had by this time established itself in the Mediterranean world.

Yet it was these very Ptolemies in whose case the habit of deifying the ruler became habitual. The old Egyptian kings had been worshipped as incarnations of Ammon (= Re). Even Alexander had been worshipped as a god during his life. The practice quickly spread, e.g. among the Seleucids. In origin it was Hellenic rather than Oriental. The Olympian religion as we have seen conceived the gods anthropomorphically, in a manner alien to the religions of the East; their difference from men was one not of kind but of degree, save in the fact of their immortality. In the Hellenistic age, the need of salvation was urgently felt, and the philosophic gospels (of which we shall speak presently) were too abstruse to appeal to popular imagination. Why, then, should not a living saviour be regarded as a god ? Moreover, the centralised monarchies established in the generation after Alexander needed a visible symbol of unity and of personal loyalty to the ruler. The practice of deification met these new requirements in the period of Macedonian overlordship as later in that of the Roman Empire. To Jews and Christians, nurtured in the pure monotheistic tradition, it seems a blasphemous abomination, but the Greek and the Roman viewed it with very different eyes. To them it meant very little more than canonisation means for Catholic Christianity to-day. It was a natural way of expressing gratitude for saving benefits. Were our records more ample than they are, we should probably find that the task of Hellenisation was in the hands of a competent bureaucracy, and that, as subsequently under the Roman empire, the administrative machine preserved its efficiency despite the vagaries of individual rulers. A noteworthy illustration of this efficiency is the systematic development of Egyptian agriculture under the Ptolemies, a task which had been neglected by the Persian rulers. As a result, Egypt became the chief granary of the Roman empire. Moreover, the Hellenic city, the great instrument of the policy, tended when once founded, to flourish by its own organic vitality. Of the nature of the culture thus developed at Alexandria at the Nile mouth, at Antioch on the Orontes, at Seleucia on the Tigris and at a hundred other cities which owed their existence to Alexander and his successors, we shall speak in a later section of this chapter. Of the three Græco-Macedonian dynasties, it was the Seleucid kings of Asia who bore the heaviest burden and yet carried forward the work of Hellenisation most effectively. Macedon and Egypt were compact states, homogeneous and comparatively easy of defence, while the Asiatic empire was hampered by the same lack of internal unity and cohesion as that of Persia in days gone by. Its monarchs proved unequal to contend at once against their rivals in the West and in the East, the Ptolemies and Macedonians on the one side, and on the other the Parthian power which arose in the third century in Irân.[1] The Punjâb soon recovered its independence,[2] the satrapies east of the Tigris fell to the Parthians, and early in the second century the descendants of Seleucus found themselves restricted to the lands between the Euphrates and the Levant, cooped up between Parthia and Rome. A hundred years more and their rule vanished even from Syria, and the Roman legions confronted the Parthians on the Euphrates. Yet in the course of these few generations the house of Seleucus achieved great things for civilization. By founding a multitude of cities in Syria and Babylonia, in Asia Minor and the lands around the Caspian, they planted Hellenism in the middle East and prepared a meeting-ground for Greek and Oriental thought.[3] The debt was not merely one-sided; if Hellenic culture took root in Asia, the religions of the East also began to win a hold over the Mediterranean world. The fusion was pregnant with momentous issues. It was at Antioch, the Syrian capital of the Seleucids, that the disciples of the faith which the East gave to the West were first called by the Greek name of Christians.[4]

§ 7. We remarked above that the advent of the Macedonian power meant the downfall of the Hellenic *Polis* as an independent political unit. This was the price paid by Greece for the opportunity of extending Hellenism over the East. That achievement was possible only for a large state, and throughout all antiquity a large state meant despotism. We shall see how Rome, too,

---

[1] The Parthian kings were a Scythian dynasty who established themselves on the Iranian plateau.

[2] It must be remembered that Greek cities with Greek colonists were planted in the Punjâb, and that Greek influence in that part of India did not cease with the recovery of independence. A native prince wrote to Antiochus I, asking him to send a Greek sophist to the Punjâb; Antiochus replied that sophists were not for sale (Bevan, i. 297).

[3] Seleucia on the Tigris replaced Babylon, which henceforward was merely a religious centre; Seleucia continued as a Greek city under the Parthians (Tac., *Ann.*, vi. 42). Strabo (xi. 509), who lived in Augustus's time, attributed the lack of development of the resources of Hyrcania and the Caspian district in his day to the fact that it had never been ruled by Greeks. The Græco-Macedonian government, like our Egyptian and Indian civil service, eagerly fostered material and economic improvements, roads, irrigation, drainage, etc. On the above, see Bevan, i. 281, and, generally, chapters xi to xiv of his work.

[4] Acts xi. 26. Mithraism began to spread in western Asia under the successors of Alexander; see c. ix. § 8.

ceased to be a republic when she had acquired a world-empire. The devices employed by modern nations in order to reconcile an extended territory with the maintenance of political freedom, the printing-press, steam transit, communication by electricity and, above all, representative government, were unknown to the ancients. But our assertion, though true in the main, must be accepted with certain reservations. For one thing, the free city-state died hard. The Græco-Macedonian period witnessed repeated struggles between the forces of republicanism and of autocracy, and in not a few cases the republics were able to hold their own. This was so, beyond the limits of Alexander's empire, in the West, where communities like Syracuse, Tarentum and Massilia remained independent till they were absorbed under the sway of Rome. Elsewhere we find that individual cities preserve or recover independence, in accordance with varying circumstances of time and place. In European Greece, Athens, Sparta and the Ætolian and Achæan leagues, secured a transitory autonomy; the like is true of Byzantium, Heraclea on the Euxine, Chios and certain Ægean towns. The island-city of Rhodes, especially, enjoyed a brilliant epoch of commercial prosperity under a republican government, which suppressed piracy, protected weaker states without exaction of tribute, founded a remarkable code of maritime law, and fostered both religion and culture, preserving its freedom from international complications until the middle of the second century.[1] Pergamos, again, flourished as a home of art and culture under dynasts of its own, the house of Attalus, rich merchant princes who valiantly defended Hellenism against the inroads into Asia of barbarian Gauls. But the majority of Hellenic cities were subject politically to one of the three Macedonian kingdoms. These cities, for the most part, were allowed entire liberty of local government, and many, like Smyrna, or the chief cities of Cilicia, Phœnicia and the Orontes valley, were recognised as " sacred and inviolate," standing outside of the ordinary system of administration. Their position under Macedonian rulers, as later under Rome, was analogous to that of the free Hanseatic towns in the days of the Holy Roman empire. The dynasts were careful to observe the forms of courtesy due to the high traditions of the Hellenic *Polis*, to speak not of " subjects " but of " allies," of " voluntary contributions " in place of " tribute," to foster

[1] Rhodes was founded in 408, and was the middleman between Alexandria, Syria, the Euxine and European ports.

their material welfare by generous largesses, especially to the civic temples, and generally to veil under a guise of acknowledged liberty the hard reality of subjugation. The cities in their turn were ready to flatter the despots with divine honours, a clear sign of degeneration from the temper of the fifth-century *Polis*.[1] The Seleucids at all events were sincerely phil-Hellene and knew well that Hellenisation could be accomplished only through the civic organism. Yet, when all allowance has been made for the independence of individual cities, for the multiplication of new municipalities in the Seleucid kingdom, and for the indulgent policy of its rulers towards old and new alike, the truth remains that the sovereignty of the Greek *Polis*, and with it the fountain head of the spirit of political liberty, had passed away. We can therefore appreciate the passionate resistance offered to Philip by Athens under Demosthenes, and the refusal of the Greek states to be blinded, by the dazzling splendour of Alexander's victories, to the real sacrifice which those victories entailed. They felt instinctively that a blow had been struck at the roots whence Hellenism had sprung. So in fact it was; slowly but surely the Greek race lost its ancient energy during the Græco-Macedonian and Græco-Roman epochs. The Greeks " were like the freeholder of an ancient family, who has mortgaged and lost his inheritance, but is still allowed to live on in the old home. The essential charm of ownership was gone for them, and with it all the joy and intensity of social life; and though this very calamity might widen their mental horizon, and find them new interests and fresh work to do, the stream of their intellectual effort would never again run so clear and strong as in the days of the perfect freedom of the individual city-state." [2] Doubtless at the same time new possibilities were opened out for Hellenism. The transformation of economic conditions carried with it far-reaching social and political consequences. With the eastern trade largely in the hands of Greece, business enterprises developed on a new and expanded scale, the old methods of banking were superseded, and the cleavage between the capitalist and the industrial worker was widened, with the inevitable results that the security of the leading commercial cities was menaced by the fear of revolution. Prices everywhere rose out of all proportion to the increase of wages; between the fourth and

---

[1] The restored democracy of Miletus conferred divine honours on the degenerate Antiochus II (*Theos*). On the apotheosis of princes, see Murray, *Five Stages*, pp. 133 ff.

[2] Warde Fowler, *City-state*, pp. 301–2.

third centuries the drachma lost half its value; the masses were in constant danger of starvation; nor did there exist an extensive middle class to bridge the gulf that parted the very prosperous from the miserably poor. Hence the cries for the stock revolutionary panaceas, cancellation of debts, equal division of land, confiscation of personal property and liberation of slaves, which drew theoretical support from Stoic ideas, now rapidly spreading among the *intelligentsia*.[1] Moreover, the conquests of Alexander brought a larger world within the field of man's vision than was compatible with the maintenance of a merely civic patriotism. The despotism of Macedon and Rome, breaking down the barriers that severed Greek from barbarian, Western from Oriental, paved the way for the ideal of cosmopolitanism which found expression in the Stoic philosophy, in Roman jurisprudence and, ultimately, in the religion of Christianity. There was that in the creations and in the spirit of the Greek genius which transcended the limitations of the race that gave them birth. Hellenism was a light, not only for the Hellene but for mankind, and the hour wherein it set in its native skies saw its dawn among the non-Hellenic peoples.

II. HELLENISTIC CULTURE (§§ 8–10).

§ 8. The decay of Hellenism was very gradual; for Greek culture preserved its freshness and distinction through the long period of decline. The well springs had been sapped; but the stream still flowed, though with scantier and more sluggish volume; and the waters were those of Greece. Our purpose here is to outline the general character of that culture in the so-called " Hellenistic " period, between the dominion of Alexander and that of Rome (330 to 30 B.C.).[2] In a later chapter we shall speak of Hellenism under the Roman empire. Two governing facts must be stated at the outset. First, the loss of civic independence meant that the serious business of government was no longer a concern of the individual citizen; literature and thought henceforward move in an atmosphere of personal interests, and

[1] See Tarn, *The Hellenistic Age*, pp. 108–40, on " The Social Question," with detailed illustration from revolutionary movements at Sparta during the fourth and third centuries (Agis, Cleomenes and Nabis).

[2] The term " Hellenistic " is inadequate, but in current use. " Græco-Macedonian " is a better term. " Alexandrian," which is often employed, is very misleading. The import of the term " Hellenistic " is much narrower than that of " Hellenism."

of social, as distinct from public, life. Secondly, Greece is more
and more conscious of her accomplished past; hitherto creative
of the present and the future, she now becomes historical and
reflective. It is when the impulse to creation is decaying and
energy begins to flag that a race turns towards its past achievements to analyse and to record. " The owl of Minerva does
not start upon its flight till the evening shadows begin to fall." [1]

§ 9. Hellenistic literature and Hellenistic art are the product
of these changed conditions of life and thought. Broadly speaking, the literature is marked by scholarship and learning, by
criticism and reflection, by imitation of old models, the pouring
of new wine into old bottles, or, again, by the desire to furnish
social entertainment for a cultured public, in close dependence
on the patronage of the great. In this field, as in that of action,
it was an age of clever second-rate men; the really eminent
scientist, Eratosthenes, was nicknamed *Beta* (i.e., in Class II),
though this was probably the expression of the jealousy felt by
specialists for a colleague of wider intellectual outlook than their
own. If we except Rhodes and Athens, the chief centres of literary
and scientific activity were the courts of despots. Poetry of
course was freshest where life was most free, as in Sicily, beyond
the range of the Macedonian empire, or at Athens, the home of
great traditions, where at least the show of political independence
was zealously preserved. The idylls of the Syracusan Theocritus
(*c.* 270) were the last achievements of the Greek poetic genius
deserving of mention in the same breath with Homer and the Attic
dramatists.[2] Theocritus created a new form of literature and
was the source of inspiration to the pastoral poetry of all succeeding times, including the *Eclogues* of Virgil, Milton's *Lycidas*
and Shelley's *Adonais*. At Athens flourished the New Comedy
of manners (330 to 250), that portrayed typical characters and
situations of Greek social life. In place of the living personages
lampooned by Aristophanes; Menander and his fellow-dramatists
brought upon the stage the querulous father, the spendthrift son,
the parasite, the confidante and the courtesan, the miser and the
braggadocio adventurer, the *Harpagons* and *Dugald Dalgettys*
of the age. In comedy, epigram and epic, the love interest
between man and woman, conspicuously absent from earlier
Greek poetry, became a dominant motive; [3] the Rhodian poet,

---

[1] Hegel, Preface to the *Philosophy of Right*.
[2] Though Theocritus lived at Alexandria under the second Ptolemy,
the spirit of his poetry is Sicilian.
[3] Euripides was the first of the Greek dramatists to make the love of

Apollonius, for example, imitating the earlier epic form, wrote in hexameter verse the story of the Argonauts and the passion of Medea for Jason. The spirit of romance found beautiful expression in elegies that had their home in Alexandria. The same city, under the patronage of the Ptolemies, was the centre of Hellenic erudition. Two great libraries, one of which contained 700,000 manuscripts, testified to the ardour with which princes and scholars collected the classics of the past. Schools of critics and commentators laboured at the tasks of editing and interpretation. By the side of the scholar arose his parasite, the pedant. It was an age at once of general culture and of specialist research. Thanks to the papyrus, there came into being a cultured reading public. Philological and æsthetic criticism flourished at Alexandria; the departmental sciences were pushed forward by the aid of new data and appliances; and among the learned men who had their home in the Museum were the geometer Euclid; Archimedes, who discovered the principle of the lever; the geographer Eratosthenes of Cyrene, who first measured a degree of latitude on the earth's surface; and the Homeric scholar, Aristarchus of Samothrace. Eratosthenes' estimate of 28,000 miles for the earth's circumference was a truly astonishing approximation to the truth. It was Eratosthenes, too, who embodied in his map the fruits of the famous voyage of Pytheas of Marseilles (late fourth century) along the Atlantic coast of Europe to Britain and by the shores of the North Sea to the mouth of the Elbe. In fact, the Greeks of the fourth and third centuries may be regarded as the creators of geographical science. In the middle of the third century the great mathematician and astronomer, Aristarchus of Samos (c. 310–230), formulated the heliocentric hypothesis, following the tracks of Pythagorean and Platonic science.[1] It was at Alexandria too that anatomy first became the basis of medical science (Herophilus, c. 300 B.C.). In the Jewish colony at Alexandria, which enjoyed peculiar privileges, the contact of eastern and western culture bore fruit in the production of the

---

the sexes a central theme. Love, however, in the ideal modern sense is rare in Greek literature. (See *Antimachus of Colophon and the Position of Women in Greek Poetry*, by E. F. M. Benecke.)

[1] See Burnet, *E. Gk. Ph.*, p. 299, and Heath, *Aristarchus of Samos*. Burnet remarks that Copernicus, in a letter to Pope Paul III, admitted that his studies of Pythagorean science had given the impulse to his rediscovery of the heliocentric theory. Euclid lived in the reign of Ptolemy I; Archimedes and Eratosthenes belong to the third century, Aristarchus of Samothrace to the first half of the second century.

Septuagint, the Greek version of the Old Testament scriptures.[1] The period is noteworthy also for its historical works, of which the best-known is that of Polybius (second century), a Greek republican statesman, who was carried as a hostage to Rome at the time of the conquest of Macedonia, and enjoyed the friendship of the celebrated Scipionic circle. He recorded in his own tongue the expansion of the Roman power, inspired by the conviction—a rare tribute from a Greek author—of the fitness of the Roman race to rule the world. Significant of the success of the policy of Hellenisation were the histories of Egypt by a native priest Manetho, and of Babylon, also by a native priest, Berosus. It was a Babylonian scientist, bearing the Greek name of Seleucus, who championed the new heliocentric theory of the heavens in the second century. The freer political atmosphere of Athens and Rhodes gave a stimulus to famous schools of rhetoric. Of the philosophy of the age we shall speak in a later section. The period was also one of the organisation of knowledge in schools and libraries. University centres, on the model of Athens, arose over the Hellenic world, as at Rhodes, Pergamos and Tarsus in Cilicia. At the close of its history, Greek culture perished of inanition in learned academies; but it was in learned academies that it rose again to life in the Italy of the Renaissance. One more feature of Hellenistic literature deserves remark. Authors wrote no longer, as the Athenian dramatists had written, for their fellow-citizens; but, in conformity with the new world outlook, for a public that was at once cosmopolitan and trained in the culture of the past.

§ 10. The art of the period likewise, from the beginning of the fourth century onwards, reflects the altered outlook upon life. If the architecture and sculptures of the age of Philip and Alexander lack the repose and grandeur of the earlier style, there is gain to compensate the loss in an increased mastery of technique, a freer rendering of human emotion, and a wonderful power of individual characterisation. As time went on signs of degeneration become visible in the love of florid elegance and the conscious effort after archaism. Among the noblest monuments of fourth-century sculpture two may be studied in the British Museum, the *Mausoleum*, the tomb erected at Halicarnassus to king Maussollus of Caria (*c.* 350), a work in which Scopas of Paros

---

[1] The Septuagint (LXX), so called because it was supposed to have been the work of seventy translators, was produced in the third and second centuries. The early Christian church knew the Old Testament chiefly through this version.

bore a part, and the *Nereid shrine* from Xanthus in Lycia. Both are evidence of the hold that Greek culture had won among the non-Hellenic races of Asia Minor. At Olympia may still be seen the *Hermes* of Praxiteles, a sculptor of the Athenian school, whose statues of the goddess Aphrodite created a new type of female beauty in art. Perhaps the most characteristic artistic development of the time was the rise of portraiture. Alexander sat frequently to the sculptor Lysippus and to the great Greek painter, Apelles of Colophon. No paintings of this age have come down to us; but the features of the leading dynasts are preserved on a large number of gems and coins. In architecture, the fourth century saw the adoption of the florid Corinthian capital (e.g. in the *Chorēgic monument of Lysicrates* at Athens, c. 335), and the supersession, in Greece proper, of the severe Doric by the richer Ionic style. When we pass on to the third century we find the best art, like the best poetry, flourishing where life was most free. At Alexandria there was little worthy of record save an artificial revival of native Egyptian art under the patronage of the Ptolemies. Town-planning, a favourite interest of the Greeks since Pericles employed Hippodamus of Miletus to lay out Thurii in squares, and Dionysius I remodelled Syracuse, naturally flourished under the Macedonian dynasts; Alexandria and Antioch were built on systematic and elaborate designs. The most beautiful of all cities, in site and structure, was Pergamos, the creation of the princes of the house of Attalus. Both Pergamos and Rhodes were centres of living art in the third and second centuries. The former grew around a hill-fortress into the capital of cultured princes, who, like the Medici of the Renaissance, gathered about them philosophers and artists. The Pergamene sculptures, commemorating the victories of Attalus I (241–197) and Eumenes II (197–159) over the Gauls, were the finest of the age.[1] Rhodes at an earlier date had crowned its heroic resistance to the forces of despotism by the erection of the Colossus, a statue of the sun-god over 100 feet in height, the work of a pupil of Lysippus. The famous Laocoon group was modelled in the Rhodian school, and the Rhodian Protogenes was one of the great painters of the day. Subsequent developments of sculpture are represented by such well-known works as the *Apollo Belvedere* and the *Venus (Aphroditē)* of Melos. Genre-

---

[1] E.g. the *Dying Gaul* of the Capitoline Museum (often erroneously called the *Dying Gladiator*). The art of Pergamos was remarkable for its dramatic realism and mastery of technique; it was more truly alive than any other art of the age.

painting, pictures of interiors like those of the great Dutch
artists of the seventeenth century, had also a vogue, and furnishes
an analogy to the scenes from social life in the New Comedy.
Under the Seleucids, Greek art spread eastwards over the Asiatic
continent; modern scholars assure us that it was from the Greeks
who ruled for a brief span in the Punjâb that the Indians learnt
to build and carve in stone. We must remember, too, how the
literature and art of the Hellenistic age directly set its mark on
those of Rome, and thus, through Rome, influenced later civilization even more deeply than the great master-works of the age of
Pericles.

III. ARISTOTLE (§§ 11–15).

§ 11. When Israel lost her national independence she sought
a refuge in religion. The decline of the Hellenic city-state left
the Greeks without that source of consolation. We have seen
that the popular faiths of Greece had ceased to influence the
more thoughtful and earnest of the race; these—the aristocracy
of culture—turned to philosophy for guidance and support. It
is the philosophy of this age that has most profoundly influenced
later generations of mankind. The greatest of Plato's pupils,
Aristotle, had for three years been Alexander's tutor—perhaps the
most impressive conjunction of personalities in human history.
Aristotle, like Alexander, stands at the parting of the ways.
His philosophy is rooted in that of Plato; there is hardly one
of his leading ideas of which the germ is not to be found in the
Platonic dialogues.[1] Even more than Plato, whose attitude to
the life of his age was one of remorseless condemnation, he is
a representative of Greek life as embodied in the city-state.
That the knell of the free city had sounded at Chæronea, Aristotle
seems scarcely to be aware. It is his strong grasp of the actual
in nature and human life, and his interest in the social and physical
phenomena of the Hellenic world, that make his philosophy such
an illuminating commentary on Greek culture. Plato saw deeper
into the springs of human action. but Aristotle was the more
typical Hellene. His political ideal was the Hellenic city-state
reformed rather than revolutionised; his ideal for the individual

[1] Aristotle was, in fact, the first Platonist. To interpret his philosophy
as an original development of Plato's is far more accurate than to stress
the contrast, as has too frequently been done in later times. Aristotle
was, of course, anxious to make clear to his own generation the points
wherein he diverged from the dominant system. This has given a handle
to misinterpretation.

was the life of reason, informing, as a principle of proportion
and measure, the rich and varied field of citizen duty presented
in the life of the Greek state. It is this sense of the value of
attained fact, of the necessity of realising the ideal form amid the
material of actual conditions, that distinguishes Aristotle from
Plato. Like Plato, he held the contemplative life to be the highest;
like Plato, he held that to be most real which is most knowable,
and sought this reality in the eternal truths which are objects,
not of sense, but of thought. But these eternal forms were not
in his view denizens of a world remote from that of actual experience; they were the governing principles of the world in
which he lived.[1]

§ 12. To indicate the scope and value of Aristotle's philosophy
in a brief compass is an impracticable task; especially as there is
no single writing of his which, like Plato's *Republic*, furnishes
a comprehensive groundwork of study. His works were specialised
treatises, frequently preserved in the form of lecture notes by
himself or his pupils, addressed to minds versed in the several
subjects and presupposing a knowledge of other parts of the
system. Science, as we have noted, was already in process of
differentiation into departments, and Aristotle's writings abound
in technical terms and formulas divorced by a wide gulf from the
language of common converse. It is not that Aristotle is really
harder to understand than Plato. Plato soars on strong wings
towards the sun, and few there are that can attend him on his
flight. "The thyrsus-bearers are many, but the inspired are
few."[2] Yet his genius draws the reader irresistibly into the
upper air, dazzled and confounded though he be by the unwonted
splendour. Aristotle wields no such magical attraction. To
study his philosophy there is need from the first of patient effort
and of the full strength of that " desire to know " which he tells
us is natural to man.[3] The range of his learning was unequalled
in that or any other age. The extant treatises alone comprise
works on logic or scientific method, on *first philosophy* or *metaphysics*,[4] on physical nature and on moral science, on psychology,

[1] In Raphael's cartoon of *The School of Athens*, Plato is portrayed as
pointing upwards to the heavens, Aristotle as pointing downwards to
earth. Jaeger's *Aristotle* makes clear the development of his thoughts
away from Platonic otherworldliness towards concentration on positive
science.   [2] *Phaedo*, 69.

[3] *Met.*, i. 1; the opening words.

[4] The name *metaphysics* (i.e. after the *physics*) was assigned to this
treatise by later editors in antiquity, for the purely accidental reason
that it followed next after the *Physics* in the published order of Aristotle's

on rhetoric and on poetry, together with a large number of remarkable writings on biological science. Aristotle may be reckoned the founder of zoology, and his pupil, Theophrastus, the founder of botany. It is these last that Charles Darwin had in mind when he wrote, " Linnæus and Cuvier have been my two gods, though in very different ways, but they were mere schoolboys to old Aristotle." [1] In one sphere alone was he out-shone by others of his age, in mathematics, where his deficiencies, because of his immense authority over succeeding times, long proved a hindrance to progress in those sciences, such as astronomy, which rest on mathematical foundations. In view of the impossibility of surveying this vast body of speculative enquiries, we shall select two problems, which will serve to illustrate both the cardinal tenets of Aristotle's philosophy and its divergence from that of Plato, and to introduce the reader to conceptions which deeply influenced the subsequent course of Hellenic and mediæval thought. These are his doctrine of Being and his ideal of the chief Good for man. [2]

§ 13. (I) *The Doctrine of Being*. It was the fact of change, manifested alike in physical motion, in the growth of living organisms, and in man's intellectual and moral development, that constituted for Aristotle the main problem of speculative science. Change implies that which changes, i.e. permanent subjects of change, concrete things and persons which become now hot, now cold, now good, now bad, taking on the forms of heat and cold, virtue and vice. Cold does not become heat, nor virtue vice; it is not the form which changes, but the in-dividual recipient of the forms. These concrete individuals, this stone or this tree or Socrates, are compounds of matter (*hylê*) and form (*eidos*); they are not reducible to mere form, for, as we have said, form cannot change; nor are they reducible to matter, for nothing exists save as a definite somewhat, endowed with a character or form, as stone or tree or man. Mere matter, wholly indeterminate and void of form, is no actual existent, but a limiting conception, necessary to explain becoming and change; how indeed could anything come to be out of that which was not already something definite ? The forms, again,

---

works. Hence the general use of the term metaphysics to signify the science of being, which is the matter of this treatise. Aristotle himself called the science *first philosophy* or *theology*.

[1] Darwin, *Life and Letters*, iii. 252.

[2] For the sections that follow, the reader is referred to the works on Aristotle mentioned in the Bibliographical Appendix.

do not exist, as Plato had supposed, in a super-sensible heaven, cut adrift from the actual world of our experience; for what could such separate forms contribute either to the being of our world of change or to our knowledge of it ? Thus for Aristotle it is the concrete individual, not the mere universal, that has substantial being. When asked, What is *substance* (*ousia*), he answered, " this stone," " this tree," " you " and " I." [1] All other modes of being are qualities, affections or relations of this fundamental mode, and can exist only in dependence on substantial being; " black " or " equal " can be only if there be a black thing or equal things. Now philosophy has for its business to discover the *causes* of these individual substances and thus to explain the changes which they undergo, and Aristotle shows how such explanation demands the co-operation of four kinds of cause. In order that anything may come to be, say, a statue, there are required (*a*) the matter (*hylê*) out of which it arises, e.g. the marble block; (*b*) an external principle of motion that starts the process of change, e.g. the mind, hand and tool of the sculptor; (*c*) the form (*eidos*) realised in and through the process, e.g. the form of the Phidian *Zeus* or the *Hermes* of Praxiteles; (*d*) the aim and end of the process, e.g. the completed statue as the goal of the sculptor's work. Thus we must posit a material, an efficient, a formal and a final cause. It is obvious that the three last-mentioned causes tend to coalesce. It is the form (*c*) of the statue which is the sculptor's aim (*d*), and the thought of this aim in his mind is the motive impulse (*b*) that initiates and guides the process of his work. The conception of form as the end or purpose of development, in contrast to undeveloped matter, is the fundamental thought of all Aristotle's philosophy. Alike in biology, in psychology, in ethics and in the theory of art, his explanation, like Plato's, is teleological. The cosmic process, through all its detail, is interpreted as the progressive actualisation of the capacity to receive form, and in each case the process attains its end in the realisation of the appropriate form. The undeveloped must thus be explained in the light of the developed, not vice versâ ; the man is prior to the child, the oak to the acorn, and to begin at the beginning is simply to begin at the wrong end.[2] Thus Aristotle expresses the distinction of matter

[1] In fact, Aristotle gave divergent answers to this question : but the text states the main drift of his solution of the problem.

[2] This shows how different, despite his insistence on the idea of development and his genius as a biologist, was Aristotle's interpretation of organic nature from that of modern evolutionary science. Nor did he

and form more fruitfully in dynamic terms as that of potency (*dynamis*) and actuality (*energeia*). The child is the potency of the man, the acorn of the oak; when the forms of man and oak are actualised in the respective individuals, the process is complete, the end achieved. But, be it observed, for the process to start at all, form and actuality are presupposed, though in another individual of the species; the child can come to be only through the agency of an actually existing human father. By this line of thought, Aristotle is led to the eternal being of *God* as pure form. Since only in the strength of an already existing actuality (form) can an individual's potency move towards actualisation, since " man only can beget man " and the production of the statue demands the prior existence of the form in the sculptor's thought, so is it also with the primal fact of change, the motion of the universe. If we are to escape from an infinite regress of causes, there must be an eternal first mover, to account for the eternal and primary motion of the heavens; and since the cause is ever other than the effect, the mover than the moved, the first mover cannot, as Plato held, be self-moved, but must be himself unmoved.[1] This unmoved first mover is pure form, eternally actual and divine. In Aristotle's theism there is no place for a Creator, because the universe has no beginning in time, and the act of creation would imply movement and change and potency in God; nor for a Providence, for God is beyond and apart from nature, and his life is not one of practical activity but of simple contemplation (*theoria*). He does not even know the universe, but is pure self-conscious intelligence, at once the subject and the object of his own most perfect thought. Alone in this absolute transcendence, God draws the world towards himself

---

apply the idea of development to species, which he regarded as separate and fixed. His teleology led him to reject with contempt the hints at an evolutionary process by natural selection and the survival of the fittest, which had been thrown out by Empedocles. " We may suppose that all things have fallen out accidentally just as they would have done if they had been produced for some end. Certain things have been preserved because they had spontaneously acquired a fitting structure, while those which were not so put together have perished and are perishing, as Empedocles says of the oxen with human heads." This, in Aristotle's opinion, would be to explain nature as due to chance, whereas nature does not work in vain and achieves the goal normally (" for the most part "). See *Phys.*, ii. 8, and Burnet, *E. Gk. Ph.*, p. 243 (on Empedocles), whose translation of the passage I have here given. Cf. also (on Anaximander), *E. Gk. Ph.*, p. 71.

[1] The influence of Aristotle's argument to God as Pure Act and as unmoved mover of the universe on medieval Christian philosophy was profound, as any reader of Dante knows.

as the goal of its desire. "The final cause produces motion as does an object of love, and through that which it moves (the outer sphere of the fixed stars) moves all things else." "On such a principle, then, depend the heavens and the world of nature. And its life is such as the best which we enjoy and enjoy but for a short time. For it is ever in this state (which we cannot be), since its actuality is also pleasure. . . . If thus God is always in that good state in which we sometimes are, this compels our wonder; and if in a better, this compels it yet more. And God *is* in a better state. And life also belongs to God; for the actuality of thought is life, and God is that actuality; and God's essential actuality is life most good and eternal. We say therefore that God is a living being, eternal, most good, and that life and duration continuous and eternal belong to God; for this *is* God." [1]

§ 14. (II) *The chief Good for man.* Aristotle's argument to God's existence from the fact of motion furnishes the philosophical groundwork to the theology of the Middle Ages. It held the chief place among the proofs formulated by Aquinas, and will be recognised as the source whence Dante drew his conception of "the Love that moves the sun and the other stars." [2] The passage from the *Metaphysics*, quoted above, suggests Aristotle's answer to the second of our problems, that of the *summum bonum*, or chief good for man. Whereas Plato had insisted uncompromisingly that knowledge of absolute good was essential to true virtue and felicity, and that the goal of man's nature was realisable only in a life of devotion to philosophy, Aristotle turns from the search for the Absolute to that for the specific form of human goodness, an end attainable by the good citizen of the Hellenic *Polis* within the compass of his earthly life. It is to be found here or nowhere; for the individual soul, as the form of the organic body, lives in union with the body, its matter, and can have no separate claim to immortality. To determine the form of the good life, wherein consists human felicity (*eudaimonia*), is the problem of political science, which treats of the development of man's natural capacities towards the realisation of this end. It is handled by Aristotle in two treatises, the (*Nicomachean*) *Ethics* and the *Politics*. [3] For Plato, political

---

[1] *Met.*, xii. 7 (*tr.* Ross).

[2] Aquinas, *Summa Theol.*, i. q. 2, art. 3, *Summa contra Gentiles*, i. c. 13; Dante, *Paradiso*, xxxiii. 145.

[3] The reader, if unfamiliar with Aristotle's works, is advised to commence his study of them with the *Ethics*; for English translations, see Bibliographical Appendix.

science was inseparable from metaphysics, the philosopher must be king and the king a philosopher; Aristotle, on the other hand, distinguishes sharply between knowing and doing, and between theoretical and practical science. He approached the problems of morals in an empirical and inductive spirit. Both works were designed as manuals for the legislator in his practical task of educating the citizen to the complete form of social virtue.[1] He defined felicity (*eudaimonia*), the chief good for man, as " activity of the soul in accordance with virtue (*aretê*)," and virtue as " a settled disposition of will, being in the relative mean, determined by rational principle, and as the man of practical wisdom would determine it." [2] By the " relative mean " must be understood not a standard of mediocrity or compromise with evil, but the observance of the due proportion, as against excess and deficiency of feeling and purpose, in each of the varying situations that call for action. The nerve of the definition lies in the appeal to a reasonable principle (*logos*), by which is meant, not an abstract formula of conduct, but a " right judgement in all things," constituting in the soul of the citizen the sovereign excellence of practical wisdom (*phronêsis*). Aristotle discusses a host of problems arising out of this conception of human goodness, such as the formation of moral principle by habituation in right conduct, the nature of voluntary action and responsibility for wrong done, the specific forms of virtue and their corresponding vices, the standard of justice in reference to its application by the law, the relation of felicity and pleasure, and the ideal of human friendship.[3] He devotes particular attention, in view of Socrates' and Plato's identification of virtue and knowledge, to the intellectual requirements of goodness and the good life. Though he does not question the need of intellectual excellence as essential to moral goodness, the fact of the man of weak will, who knows what is right yet does what is wrong, precludes their identification; the wisdom, moreover, that is requisite is not the theoretic wisdom (*sophia*) of the philosopher, but the practical

[1] Hence the interest of the *Ethics* as reflecting current Greek ideals and types of conduct. "Aristotle's system," writes Eucken, "is wholly rooted in the classical world; its fundamental views, its valuations, work on uninterrupted in him. . . . Aristotle's system brings the substance of the classic world of Greece to marvellously perfect scientific expression, and so hands it down to future humanity " (*The Problem of Human Life*, p. 45.)

[2] *Ethics*, i. 7, ii. 6.

[3] Habituation, *Ethics*, ii; responsibility, *Ethics*, iii. i; the specific forms of virtue and vice, *Ethics*, iii. 6 ff. and iv; justice, *Ethics*, v; pleasure, *Ethics*, vii. 6 ff., x. 1–5; friendship, *Ethics*, viii and ix.

wisdom (*phronêsis*) of the statesman.[1] It would be hard to exaggerate the influence of Aristotle's discussion of these questions on the thought of later times. The ethical doctrines of the Stoics, the Neo-Platonists, and even the Epicureans, are in large measure developments of those of Aristotle. His treatment of responsibility for crime affected Roman jurisprudence; the ethical sections of Aquinas' *Summae*, and the structure and content of Dante's *Divina Commedia*, show the impress of the *Ethics* at every turn.[2] If Christian speculation on man's ultimate felicity followed naturally in the track of Plato's other-worldliness, it drew freely on Aristotle's ethical teaching in the application of that ideal to man's life on earth. Aristotle himself, despite his emphasis on the points where he diverged from his master, strikes, at the close of the *Ethics*, a strong Platonic note. Since felicity consists in the exercise of the soul's highest activity, and since in the human soul reason is by nature supreme, it must needs be that the form and end of man's development attains its most complete expression in the life of philosophic contemplation. In that life, he can enjoy, if only intermittently, a fragment of the satisfaction which God, as pure reason, enjoys eternally. When Aristotle speaks of man's obligation to direct his life by that in him which is most like to God, and of the wonderful felicity that such whole-hearted devotion brings with it, and identifies this free service with the life of philosophic study, we cannot fail to recognise in his language the direct reflexion of a personal experience. "A man should not, in accordance with those who so advise, think human thoughts, because he is a man, or mortal thoughts because he is mortal, but as far as in him lies he should put on immortality, and do all to live in accordance with the highest there is in him; for though this be small in bulk, yet in power and worth it rises above all else."[3]

§ 15. Aristotle was not merely the disciple of Plato but the herald of a new era in the history of thought. The material available for knowledge had been immeasurably enriched through the campaigns of Alexander, and vast collections, gathered by the scientists who accompanied those expeditions, lay at Aristotle's disposal. He utilised them freely both for his biological researches and to assist a reconstruction of philosophy which should cor-

[1] On weakness of will, *Ethics*, vii. 1–5; on the intellectual excellences (especially *sophia* and *phronêsis*), *Ethics*, vi.
[2] See below, c. xi. §§ 10, 11, 14.   [3] *Ethics*, x. 7.

relate the special sciences in a comprehensive system. Two
achievements were his especially; he determined the method of
scientific enquiry, and mapped out the provinces of human
knowledge. Aristotle was the real founder of logic, not in the
sense of John Locke's celebrated epigram that "God has not
been so sparing to men, to make them barely two-legged animals,
and left it to Aristotle to make them rational," [1] but in that,
building always on Plato's foundations, he analysed the processes of scientific reasoning, and formulated the method by which
demonstrative, as distinct from merely probable, truth could be
attained. The formalism and artificiality of the pseudo-Aris-
totelian logic of the later schoolmen provoked a natural reaction
among the great pioneers of science in the sixteenth and seventeenth
centuries, which still cumbers the minds of many who are
ignorant of the history of thought. In fact, Aristotle, who was
never the slave of formulæ, would have recognised in Galileo and
in Descartes the true fulfilment of his own principles of scientific
method. Every fresh epoch in the progress of speculative
science has been inaugurated by a reform in logic. So it was,
not only with the *Organon* or logical "instrument" of Aristotle,
but with the *Discours de la Méthode* of Descartes, the *Novum
Organum* of Bacon, the Critical Method of Kant, and the Dialectic
Method of Hegel. Philosophy and science differ from popular
thinking, not so much in being busied with different objects as
in their handling of the same objects in a different way. The
plants and animals which form the object-matter of botany
and zoology had been already grouped and distinguished and
vaguely understood before these sciences arose; the task of
science was to correct and systematise these popular classifications,
and to fix with precision the essential characters of things and
their laws of growth. Aristotle, in his generation, realised that
the problem of method was of decisive moment, and set himself
to analyse the logic of science with unrivalled insight into the
nature of the processes of human thought. Secondly, he defined
the various provinces of the sciences as parts of a single whole.
No philosopher has so justly balanced the proportion of whole
and part in knowledge, or has kept so firm a grasp on the real
distinctions of things, while comprehending them in a unified
system. It was his genius for systematisation combined with the
universal range of his enquiries, his appreciation of the variety
of ruling principles in the world of our experience, his unerring eye

[1] Locke, *Essay on the Human Understanding*, IV. xvii.

for the differences and affinities of type throughout the universe, and his precision in the formulation of philosphic method, that justify Dante in styling Aristotle "the master of those who know." [1] They explain why the philosophy of the western world moved for two thousand years largely on the lines that he laid down. His authority in all matters of secular knowledge was sovereign throughout the later Middle Ages.[2] Even when the spirit of the new learning proclaimed the supersession of authority by free enquiry and abjured the Aristotle of the schools, it followed unwittingly in his steps. As the great organiser of knowledge, he holds in things of the mind a place analogous to that of the Roman empire in the field of government and law.

IV. STOICS AND EPICUREANS (§§ 16–18).

§ 16. To Plato and Aristotle philosophy was a "way of life," by which alone man could attain knowledge of the highest good and therein find salvation. But its appeal was to the few who felt the call to intellectual contemplation; and even for these, philosophy tended to degenerate into sceptical indifference or arid formalism. The cultured layman needed something less abstruse and more directly practical than was offered him in the Academy and the Lyceum. The old landmark, the city-state with its religious worships and moral obligations, was fast vanishing from sight; cut adrift from his moorings, he sought a creed which should save his soul from shipwreck and pilot him to a haven of refuge from the ills of life.[3] In satisfaction of this demand there appeared, in the generation succeeding that of Aristotle and Alexander, the Stoic and Epicurean systems. Both were predominantly ethical in aim and doctrine; theory of knowledge (logic) and of nature (physics) served rather as the scaffolding than as an integral portion of their philosophic structure, while metaphysics, the kernel of Platonic and Aristotelian speculation, receded altogether into the background. Within the field of ethics, again, both claimed to furnish guidance for

[1] *Inferno*, iv. 131.
[2] See, on the authority of Aristotle, Dante, *Convivio*, iv. 6. This influence was not without its hindrances to progress, especially in the field of physics; e.g. the Aristotelian distinction between the upper heavens and the sublunary world lay like a burden on astronomers and physicists till the sixteenth and seventeenth centuries.
[3] Of course, the traditional religious conceptions and worship persisted among the masses, but they were no longer effective to direct men's lives, as did the *Torah* of the Hebrews.

the soul of the individual, to show him how to live wisely and attain peace from the turbulent world without and the storms of passion within. Both portrayed the character of the wise man as a model for imitation, and taught how this ideal was to be attained. But here the resemblance ceases. When we ask as to the nature of the philosophic life, the two schools give widely different answers. To the Stoic, it consists in following virtue, in obedience to an authoritative law of nature or reason; the sage, by subjugating emotion, and by detachment from the restless world of circumstance, disciplines his soul to self-sufficiency and inward independence. To the Epicurean, the good life is that of rational enjoyment of all the satisfactions which the world affords; the sage masters circumstances by using them as means to his convenience; the good is pleasure, i.e. not the momentary gratifications of the senses, but the fruits of " cool self-love," above all, the delights of intellectual study and of social intercourse. Taken at their best, Stoicism was the more exalted, Epicureanism the more genial and human, of the two ideals. The Stoic was a moral aristocrat, somewhat prone to pride himself on his ascetic fortitude and to despise his weaker brethren; while the Epicurean creed, especially in its recognition of the equality of the sexes and its insistence on the pleasures of friendship, was less exclusive and more democratic. On a lower plane, Stoicism degenerated into puritanic formalism and casuistical compromises with the world that squared ill with its lofty professions; Epicureanism into a complacent acquiescence in the coarser satisfactions of life. But both were alike indifferent to the course of society and government. That rested in the hands of the despot, his army and his civil service; the business of the individual lay elsewhere, in ordering aright the city of his own soul.

§ 17. Both schools had a long history, extending well into the Christian era. Of the two, Stoicism exercised by far the greater influence, alike in antiquity and over the modern world. Its doctrines appealed naturally to men of affairs, and were patronised and sometimes even practised, by the dynasts and statesmen of the Graeco-Macedonian age. It became popular, as we shall see later, with the republican nobility of Rome; there was something in the practical Roman temperament that was repelled by other philosophies but responded readily to the Stoic creed. It left its mark both on Roman jurisprudence and on Hellenic Neo-Platonism, wherein Stoic teaching is blended with that derived from Plato and Aristotle. Christian thinkers were attracted by its moral elevation and uncompromising idealism. In modern times, it stirred the admiration of such different philosophers as Descartes, Bishop Butler and Immanuel Kant.[1] What, then, was the secret of the hold which Stoicism won and kept so long over the hearts of men? The answer lies in its appeal to man's power of will, and in its resolute assertion both of human freedom and of divine providence. The Stoic taught that, impotent as man seemed to be in the face of hostile circumstance, of slavery, torture, disease and death, in reality he was absolute master of his will, and that on this mastery of will alone depended all the value and good of life. "Nothing is good without qualification but the good will"; this dictum, uttered more than twenty centuries later by the philosopher of Königsberg, would have been recognised by the Stoic as his own.[2] For the Stoic, as for Kant, the good will is unconditionally good. There are no degrees of goodness; if you are right you are absolutely right, if wrong, absolutely wrong. Whether you are right or wrong depends solely on the inner character of your volition. Further, the will is good when it wills the good, and the good is—what is. The order of the universe, the truth of all its happenings, the nature (*physis*) which is its creative energy, is perfect, is law, reason, God.[3] Therefore the wise man, the Stoic saint, recognises willingly in whatever suffering may befall him the fulfilment of the providential purpose, and asserts his unconditional freedom in the face of it by willing it to be what it is. His reason gladly goes forth to meet the kindred reason of the world. Thus, by strength of inward self-determination, he conquers passion and wins tranquility of soul: "*e la sua voluntate è nostra pace.*"[4] Hence the Stoic precepts, Follow nature, Follow reason, Follow virtue are merely different ways of saying the same thing. The Stoic said also, Follow God; for, despite the somewhat crude materialism of his physical theories, he held that the law which governs the course of nature

[1] Descartes, who wrote no work on ethics, when asked in 1645 by the Princess Elizabeth for his views on the subject, replied by recommending the Stoic treatise of Seneca *de vita beata* as sufficient for the purpose. See Descartes, *Œuvres*, ed. Adam and Tannery, vol. iv, pp. 251 ff., 263 ff.

[2] Kant, *Grundlegung zur Metaphysik der Sitten*, Sect. I. *init.* (*tr. Abbott*, p. 9).

[3] Professor Gilbert Murray, in his lecture on *Stoicism*, compares the *physis* of the Stoics to M. Bergson's *élan vital*. Stoicism, alone of Greek philosophical systems, approached near to Pantheism.

[4] "And his will is our peace"; Dante, *Par.* iii. 85.

H

was no blind mechanism, but the rational working-out of a divine purpose which was essentially good. In its thoroughgoing teleology, Stoicism fell into line with the traditions of Plato and Aristotle.[1] Its originality as an ethical creed lay partly in its appeal to the will, partly in its entire independence of the historic traditions of the *Polis*. From first to last, its message is addressed to the individual, bidding him stand, free from all conventional ties of human ordinance, foursquare in his own strength against all the winds that blow. In this personal appeal, as also in the trenchant dogmatism with which it was delivered, we catch the spirit of the first founder of the school. Zeno was a Semite of Citium in Cyprus, who settled while still young at Athens (*c.* 320) and taught there for more than half a century in the Painted Porch (*Stoa Poikilê*). Many of the most famous among his followers were natives of the islands and coastlands of the Levant, and the impress of the Semitic mind is clearly visible beneath the Hellenic setting of the system.[2] Stoicism, in fact, was the intellectual first-fruits of Alexander's policy of fusion. There was not a little about Zeno that recalls the Hebrew prophet; the latter's " thus spake Yahweh " seems to be echoed in the form " thus spake Reason." [3] The voice must needs be that of reason, for Zeno preached his gospel to Greeks, the one people of history from whom it was idle to expect a hearing unless you addressed yourself to their intelligence. But, this step once taken, the appeal was bound to embrace more than the private judgement of the individual hearer. Reason, as Plato had shown, is common ground; and a teaching that was in accord with it could be no gospel of purely personal salvation. Thus with the same breath the Stoic proclaimed a cosmopolitan ideal; the city that claimed the wise man's loyalty was that of nature, of reason, of God. This conception of a

[1] For Stoicism, all is determined, yet determined as the working-out of a rational purpose. The doctrine of correspondences in nature, which fitted in with this conception, afforded a basis for the accommodation of Stoic philosophy to the belief in divination and other features in the popular religion. Plutarch (see c. ix. § 7) illustrates this tendency. The Stoics made free use of allegory and myth; their allegorical method of interpretation was taken over by Christianity. The Stoics were, in fact, experts in accommodation.

[2] Chrysippus, the second founder of Stoicism (*d.* 206) was a native of Soli in Cilicia; he gave the doctrines of the school the systematic form which persisted for centuries. Cleanthes (third century) came from Assos in the Troad, Panætius (second century) was a native of Rhodes, Posidonius (early first century) of Syria. Tarsus, the chief city of Cilicia, with a university, was a flourishing centre of Stoic teaching.

[3] See Bevan, *Stoics and Sceptics*, Lect. I.

community comprising all mankind tallied with the wider outlook of the age and with the actual establishment of world-states, first under Macedonian rule, and, later, under Rome. It helped to shape the doctrine of a law of nature (*jus naturae*), underlying the positive enactments of particular communities, which was assimilated by Roman jurists, and through them wielded far-reaching influence on the ethics and jurisprudence of mediæval and modern times. St. Paul, a native of Tarsus, one of the chosen seats of Stoicism, used the language of that school to express the spiritual community of which all Christians are members. The thought of a heavenly citizenship recurs constantly in his letters; in his sermon at Athens he quoted from the Stoic Cleanthes' hymn to Zeus and declared, in words that echo cardinal tenets of the Stoic system, that God " dwelleth not in temples made with hands," and that he had " made of one blood all nations of men for to dwell on all the face of the earth." [1]

§ 18. Stoicism, it has been said, " ended in moral fervour and logical bankruptcy." [2] The doctrines of the Epicureans were from the first of less speculative interest, and their influence on the world was less widespread than those of the Stoics. Epicurus was a pure Hellene, probably a native of Samos, who came to Athens a little later than Zeno, and founded there a small community of personal disciples. The history of the sect is marked throughout by devoted adherence to the memory and the teaching of its founder. [3] Epicurus' theory of nature was not original; having an ethical gospel to preach, he took over, as a speculative foundation, the atomic philosophy of Democritus, the most logical and complete materialist system in existence. Democritus taught that the universe, and all that therein is, is reducible to terms of homogeneous atoms, in eternal motion in empty space. [4] Mechanical necessity determines alike the course of nature and that of human action; every

[1] The quotation from Cleanthes (Acts xvii. 28) is " For we are also his offspring." Cf., for Stoic ideas, Phil. iii. 20, Eph. ii. 19, etc.; and for the parallel between the Christian and the Stoic sage, 1 Cor. iv. 8, 2 Cor. vi. 10, Phil. iv. 12, 13.

[2] Brett, *History of Psychology*, p. 176.

[3] See Lucretius' poem *de rerum natura*, opening lines of Books III, V, VI for praise of Epicurus.

[4] See above, c. iv. § 15. Though Epicureanism had but little influence in later times, it may be noted that in the seventeenth century Father Gassendi, a friend of Descartes, published a system of philosophy which comprised a physical atomic theory and an ethical hedonism, analogous to Epicurus' doctrines.

trace of freedom and of purpose is rigorously excluded. Such doctrines were admirably adapted to serve as a basis for the ethical message which constitutes Epicurus' true claim to originality. His aim, pursued with a passionate fervour of sincerity, was to destroy the last stronghold which the traditional religion still retained in the popular mind. The terrors of a future life, of the bogey-land beyond, where so-called gods wreaked their inhuman will on impotent shades, were, in his view, the source of all disquietude and suffering to men in life. "It was fear that first made the gods." If, on the other hand, it be true that man's soul is but a transitory concourse of atoms, dissolved at death to form part of new aggregates, with total discontinuity of personal life and consciousness, fear is dispelled, and man may possess his soul in peace.[1] Pleasure, for Epicurus, is really to be interpreted as freedom from passion and disquiet (*ataraxia*), and this negative rendering of the term brings his ideal, despite many points of difference, into line with that of the Stoics.[2] It is entirely misleading to treat the saying "let us eat and drink for to-morrow we die" as anything but a parody of Epicurean doctrine. Epicurus and his companions lived a life of charming simplicity, marked by strong mutual affection; and his followers in later generations copied their example. Their rule and habits won a warm encomium from the satirist Lucian in the second century A.D. There can be no question that Epicureanism brought peace to many a troubled spirit in the stormy times that followed the partition of Alexander's empire. That it, as well as Stoicism, could inspire and exalt is shown by the magnificent poem in which the Roman noble, Lucretius,[3] embodied the physical tenets and the religious gospel of its founder.

V. Conclusion (§ 19).

§ 19. We shall return to the Stoic philosophy when the time comes to speak of the conflict between the spirit of Hellenism, as reflected in the teaching of the schools, and the new spirit of

---

[1] See the great passage, Lucretius, iii. 830—end. The popular idea of God and immortality were the bugbears of Epicureanism. But the Epicureans were not atheists. They believed, on the evidence of abnormal psychical experiences, that gods existed in a remote region of the universe, heedless of mankind, enjoying a life of blessedness and perfect self-sufficiency. See also the aphorisms translated in Wallace, *Epicureanism*, p. 110.

[2] See Lucretius, ii. 22 ff., iii. 59 ff., 995 ff., iv. 1037 ff., v. 1152 ff.; on the ideal of the wise man, iii. 322 ff.   [3] Lucretius died in 55 B.C.

Christianity. Here we need only remark that both ideals of life, the Stoic and the Christian, had their birth in the new world opened out by Alexander and his successors. This in itself is sufficient to belie the view that the force of Hellenism was extinguished with the downfall of the independence of the city-state. But it is equally the case that Hellenism had by that time well-nigh finished its work on purely Hellenic soil, and that its constructive energy was henceforward conditioned by fusion with the civilization of other lands. By the close of the fourth century, the structure of Hellenic civilization was already organic and complete. We have endeavoured to convey some idea of its character and history in this and the two preceding chapters. Its importance for human progress, both intrinsically and in its issues, is obvious and incalculable. The epoch which witnessed its creation, from the eighth to the third centuries before Christ, is among the most memorable in the history of mankind. For within it falls, not only the creation of Hellenism, but the transformation of primitive Hebrew religion into a faith of universal value. The first of the higher prophets, Amos and Hosea, were contemporaries of the pioneers of Greek colonisation in the Mediterranean. The Babylonian exile and the writings of the second Isaiah synchronise with the birth of philosophy in Ionia and the development of the Athenian state under Solon and Pisistratus.[1] The Psalmists were writing at Jerusalem during the Persian wars and the age of Pericles. Nor were Hellas and Israel alone in thus laying the foundations of the civilization of the coming time. More than once in these chapters we have carried forward our story to the point when Mediterranean culture was gathered into a single state under Roman rule. " Rome was not built in a day." Long before Alexander set forth to win the East for Greece, and to inaugurate the policy of which Stoicism and Christianity were alike the fruits, nameless statesmen and soldiers had been fashioning the weapons of war and government, and the fabric of institutions and of law, that enabled a small Italian township to acquire a Mediterranean sovereignty, and establish the world-empire of Rome.

[1] Murray, *Five Stages*, p. 57, cites Bevan to the effect that in Greece, nearer Asia (e.g. Palestine), China and India, the sixth-fifth centuries saw the rise of a new age.

CHAPTER VII

THE ROMAN REPUBLIC

I. THE FOUNDATIONS OF THE ROMAN STATE (§§ 1-4).

§ 1. ON a ring of hills by the banks of the Tiber, fourteen miles from its mouth, there stood in the early centuries of the first millennium groups of rude huts surrounded by a stockade, where shepherds took refuge with their flocks when raiders descended on them from the Sabine hills. As time went on, several of these hamlets were united within a single ring-wall, and a town came into being.[1] It occupied a favoured spot as the natural market of the plain of Latium, where the river still was navigable, and beyond the reach of the Etruscan pirates that harried the coast.[2] At the dawn of its history, this settlement formed one of the members of a league sanctioned by religious ceremonial under the presidency of Alba, in which the inhabitants of the plain united for mutual trade and defence against the highland tribes. The league was called the Latin league; the city on the Tiber banks was Rome.

We can trace in broad outline the beginnings of the growth of Rome. The first clear landmark in her story is the expulsion of the kings and the establishment of an aristocratic republic at the close of the sixth century (509). Already before that date she had risen to the chief place in the Latin confederacy, had secured the Tiber bank to the port of Ostia at its mouth, and had developed political institutions and an organized citizen-army. It appears that some time in the sixth century Rome became the capital of princes of alien stock who bore sway over southern Etruria and the whole plain of Latium.[3] The expulsion of the kings meant the overthrow of this foreign dominion. Yet the

[1] There are clear traces of the early fusion of two settlements, one of Latins on the Palatine hill and one of Sabines on the Quirinal; the Sabines appear to have won the mastery and to have been the forefathers of the patrician families. The citizens of Rome in the regal period were called *Quirites*, a name probably of Sabine origin.

[2] Rome was most favourably situated; the site, in Livy's phrase, was " uniquely marked out for the expansion of the city " (*ad incrementum urbis natum unice locum*): v. 54, 4. Rome held a central position in Italy, the central peninsula of the Mediterranean, equi-distant from Cadiz and Alexandria, fronting Africa, at once linked to and protected from central, western and southern Europe. The port of Brindisi connected Italy with the East.

[3] The Tarquins, possibly Greek colonists of Etruria, who acquired wealth and power in the pottery industry and trade. They are analogous to the Hellenic tyrants of the same epoch. See Professor P. N. Ure's *Origin of Tyranny*, c. viii.

Etruscan occupation had permanently changed the position of Rome in relation to her Latin neighbours. She never relapsed into her former position as one of many confederate Latin towns, but retained an effective suzerainty. Had it not been for the Etruscan domination, her constitution might well have taken a different form, with a Latin as one of the Consuls. In fact, rather than yield to this demand on the part of the Latins, Rome eventually wiped out the League. The Etruscan over-lords had laid the foundations of the future splendour of Rome; fragments of their architecture, such as the stone wall ascribed to Servius Tullius, remain to this day as witness of their skill; in the words of Montesquieu, " Already they had begun the building of the Eternal City." [1]

§ 2. How Rome rose from these humble origins through centuries of growth to the lordship of the Mediterranean world is one of the most memorable episodes in human history. Her empire was no brilliant creation of individual genius, but the slow and measured outcome of the national energy of a people of mixed origin, but united in purpose. It is because of this that it endured; its foundations were so surely laid in the character of the Roman people. " *Tantae molis erat Romanam condere gentem,*" wrote Virgil; he knew well that the " mighty work " was not the conquering of the Roman empire but the " building of the Roman race." [2] The record of their early history is for the most part legendary, for such rude annals as were committed to writing were destroyed when the Gauls burnt the city in 390; but the national character is clearly reflected in the legends that won belief. They were a race of iron-hearted warriors; it was the Roman people, not the fabulous Romulus and Remus, that were true nurslings of the she-wolf, sprung of the lineage of Mars. Tradition told, too, how the first Romans lived the life of freebooters, and how the state and the family alike had their origin in force. [3] The first of their kings gave them political union; the second, Numa, instituted the religious worships which throughout Roman history played the part of instruments of public policy. One legend may be quoted as peculiarly significant, the tale how three Horatii championed Rome in combat against

---

[1] *Grandeur et décadence des Romains*, c. 1.
[2] Virgil, *Æneid*, i. 37. " So mighty a work was it to build the Roman race."
[3] E.g. the legend of the rape of the Sabine women. See Hegel, *Philosophy of History*, Part III, Sect. I, c. i. Polybius, i. 37, remarks how the Romans employed force in all their undertakings.

three Curiatii of Alba. Two of the former were slain; the un-
wounded Horatius held the field alone against his three antagonists.
Feigning flight, he vanquished them singly, crippled as they
were by wounds. As he returned to Rome bearing the spoils,
his sister, betrothed to one of the slain Curiatii, broke out in
lamentation; her brother slew her on the spot. He was condemned for murder, but acquitted of guilt by the voice of the
people, in that he had wrought justice on one who mourned
the enemy of Rome. Thus, as after-ages believed, arose the
time-honoured right of the Roman citizen to appeal on a capital
charge to the popular assembly (*provocatio*). Let us mark the
significance of the story. The fortune of the Roman people,
as Montesquieu observed, throughout their history brought
their enemies upon them one by one.[1] Their wars open almost
always with disaster, but invariably close in victory. Above
all, the Roman never questioned that the claims of personal
interest must be subjected to those of civic loyalty. The instinct
of subordination and the habit of reverence for public authority
were ingrained deeply in his nature. To think and act as a
typical Roman citizen and soldier, to " do at Rome as Rome
does," was virtue (*virtus*) and fame.[2] To live and die for Rome
was his loftiest ambition. This spirit of sacrifice for the good
of the commonwealth is what ennobles Roman republican
history. The average Roman understood the meaning of public
responsibility and civic obligation. After-ages seized upon and
magnified this quality of Roman character. Late in her story,
when she was on the eve of disruption at the hands of barbarian
invaders, Augustine saw in it the justification of Rome's world-
empire. The Roman devotion to an earthly state was an example
to the citizens of the celestial city. Her fall from splendour
was equally the just penalty for the lapse from her ancient virtue.
Augustine's eulogy was echoed nine centuries after by Dante.
In the *de Monarchia* he claims that " the Roman people were
ordained by nature for empire," in that, " contemning greed,
and loving peace with liberty, they had foregone their own
advantage to secure the public safety of mankind." He points
to the sacrifice of the individual Roman citizen, who endured
" toil, poverty, exile, bereavement, loss of limbs and life, in the
effort to enrich the public good." [3] Both the saint and the poet

---

[1] *Gr. et déc*, c. 4.   [2] *Virtus* = valour, manliness, from *vir* = a man.
[3] Augustine, *de Civitate Dei*, Book V (see Figgis, *Political Aspects of
St. Augustine's City of God*, p. 11); Dante, *de Mon.*, ii. 5.

saw the facts idealised through the haze of intervening time; nor did their vision pierce beyond the bounds of Mediterranean history; but when all deductions have been made, their verdict rests on a foundation of truth. In "love of the fatherland and an unmeasured thirst for renown" lay, as Virgil knew, the secret of Rome's sovereignty among the nations.[1]

§ 3. Such a people was destined to excel in the tasks of law and government. Already in the regal period the foundation-stones of the Roman state had been well and truly laid. Thanks to the innate conservatism of the Roman character, it preserved through all developments the principles which had been silently evolved in prehistoric days as the unwritten customs of the race. The same forms and methods of procedure that regulated the life of the civic community in the seventh century before Christ survive, though modified and rationalised by Greek jurisprudence and Christian ethics in the *Digest* compiled twelve hundred years later by Justinian. We are thus enabled to reconstruct, not the acts of individuals or the detailed incidents of political history, but the general features of Roman society in the days of the monarchy. The Roman state was the family writ large. The Romans understood the meaning and the value of home-life and gave expression to it in their literature. The home-pieties (*Lares and Penates*) provided a religious sanction. Plato had proposed in his *Republic* to abolish the private household, on this ground, among others, that it divided the citizens' loyalty with the state.[2] But the Roman family was at once the mirror and the training-ground of civic patriotism. The same word "piety" (*pietas*) denoted the conscientious devotion of son to parent, of citizen to magistrate, of man to the gods. The civil personality of the Roman comprised three essential factors, freedom, citizenship and membership of a family. The Roman type of family is unique, when compared not only with the modern family but with that in other ancient societies, in its extreme assertion of patriarchal authority.[3] Its root-ideas of unity and power were realised exclusively in the person of its head. The father (*paterfamilias*) possessed throughout his life absolute authority (*patria potestas*) over the persons and goods of wife, sons, unmarried daughters, clients and slaves.

[1] *Æneid*, vi. 823. "*Vincet amor patriae laudumque immensa cupido.*"
[2] *Rep.*, Book V.
[3] The Romans were fully conscious of this; "the right of authority which we exercise over our children," we read in Justinian's *Institutes*, I. ix, "is the peculiar prerogative of Roman citizens."

Within the family he was sole owner of property, sole priest and guardian of the family *sacra*, and sole judge. He had the right to put to death his wife or child. In his hand alone it lay to rear or expose his new-born offspring. Family relationships were reckoned through the male line; a son was not regarded in law as a kinsman of his mother's relatives, and his relation even to his mother lay through the father.[1] Roman law took no cognisance of natural, as distinct from legitimate, paternity; the legally adopted son was reckoned as fully a son, one born out of lawful wedlock as not a son at all. On the death of the *paterfamilias* the sons became straightway heads of families, while the wife and unmarried daughters passed—" because of the inconstancy of a woman's disposition," says Gaius—into the guardianship of the sons. Thus a Roman woman of free citizen birth was either in the power (*potestas*) of her father, or (after marriage) of her husband, or (in widowhood) under guardianship of a male kinsman. In the well-known phrase of the Digest, " a woman is both the beginning and end of her own family "; for her motherhood was unrecognised by law and she could exercise no power over her children.[2] The father and the father alone represented the family; his relationship to the other members was unilateral, all the rights being on his side, all the duties on theirs. In the eye of the law, the *patria potestas* was as absolute in the family as was the *imperium* of the magistrate in the state.[3] But we should entirely misconceive the order of

[1] The *patria potestas* was, of course, restricted to citizens. The son, on his father's death, became a *paterfamilias* even though unmarried, but acquired *patria potestas* only on marriage. The wife, if married under strict form of law, passed into her husband's " hand " (*manus*) and became subject to his *potestas*, ranking as a daughter (*loco filiae*). A daughter was under her father's *potestas* (or, if he were dead, under that of a male kinsman) till marriage, when she passed into her husband's family. A striking peculiarity of the Roman family was the restriction of legally recognised kin to the *agnati*, i.e. those who would have been in the *potestas* of a single male ancestor, had he survived. For example, A's son was an " agnate " of A's brother or brother's son, not of his mother's father or brother. Later law gave increasing recognition to *cognati*, i.e. blood-relations whether through the male or female. On the whole subject, see Maine, *Ancient Law*, c. v. The chief capital offences on the wife's part were adultery and drunkenness; we hear of a Roman matron being put to death for stealing the key of the wine-cellar.

[2] The reference to Gaius is i. 144, to the *Digest*, 1. 16, 195, 5. " *mulier familiae suae et caput et finis est.*" A woman's family began with herself, for on her father's death she became *sui juris* (" on her own right "); it ended with herself, for directly she tried to continue it by marriage, she passed into her husband's *jus* and family. She could, of course, be *sui juris*, and yet under guardianship, e.g. of son or brother.

[3] A son, though in his father's power, could act as a citizen as if he

Roman society if we imagined that its conduct was determined solely, or even mainly, by considerations of theoretical right. In the case of the father as in that of the magistrate, legal theory was in practice modified at almost every point by ancestral custom. Chief among the restrictions on the *patria potestas* was the customary tradition that, in cases of serious disciplinary action within the family, the father must call the adult male members into counsel. When the wife was accused, her male kinsfolk also were summoned. Quite early in republican times we find the censor degrading a senator for divorcing his wife without taking advice from the domestic council.[1] The exercise of the power to expose an infant was severely limited, and that of the power to sell a wife absolutely prohibited, by religious custom. Sons and even slaves were allowed by custom to amass under the name of *peculium* what in time became virtually, though not in the eyes of the law, equivalent to private property. In actual fact, the father normally administered the family wealth in the spirit, not of a private owner, but of a trustee. So again the moral obligations of the father towards wife and child were fully recognised in practice. Cato the censor, an unbending champion of conservative tradition, felt it his duty every morning to see his baby properly bathed. The Roman matron enjoyed a position of dignity denied to mothers at Athens and in most other lands, a position all the firmer in that it rested on inviolable custom. As time went on, the advance of public opinion, the gradual disuse of the old forms of marriage which placed the bride in her husband's " hand " (*manus*), and the introduction of new methods of evading the law of tutelage, combined to secure for Roman women a freedom and independence hardly paralleled in ancient or modern society.[2] In one respect, indeed, the *patria potestas* remained unchanged; whether unrestricted, as in theory, or limited, as in practice, it endured throughout the lifetime of its holder. But even in early days its exercise,

---

were a *paterfamilias*, e.g. he could hold magisterial office and in that capacity exercise public authority over his father. The *patria potestas* did not extend to the *jus publicum*.

[1] The father was not legally bound to follow the advice of the domestic council, any more than the magistrate was legally bound to follow that of the senate; but the authority (*auctoritas*) in both cases carried great weight.

[2] The recognition of marriages whereby the wife did not, as under the old forms, pass into the husband's *manus*, constituted the first serious breach in the *patria potestas*; it dates from before the close of the third century B.C.

though rigorous, was rarely tyrannical, and gross cruelty was the exception, not the rule. Moreover, it must be remembered that the standards of domestic purity and of fidelity to family obligations, thus sternly inculcated, were long maintained in the Roman household and proved of incalculable service to the moral stability of the Roman state.[1]

§ 4. Rome was a city-state, and her early institutions, the king, the council, the assembly of the people, were those common to other branches of the Indo-European family. Already at the dawn of their recorded history the Romans had developed these germs of social organisation into a body of clearly defined organs and principles of civic government. The king (*rex*) as supreme magistrate possessed by right an absolute executive authority (*imperium*). Throughout Roman history the *imperium* of the executive magistrate persists as the pivot of constitutional development. Conferred by a formal vote of the community on one of their members nominated in their presence by the king (or, if there were no king, by an *interrex* appointed by the senate), and ratified by the authority of the senate, the *imperium* was legally absolute both in peace and war, and formed the source whence all other executive power was derived by delegation.[2] The king was at once leader in war, supreme judge and

[1] This finds expression in Virgil's lines (*Æn.*, ix. 448–9):

> *Dum domus Æneae Capitoli immobile saxum*
> *Accolet, imperiumque pater Romanus habebit.*

" While the house of Æneas shall dwell by the Capitol's immovable rock and the Roman father bear his sovereignty " (*tr.* Mackail).

[2] The *imperium*, in the regal period, was conferred by the following procedure, which illustrates admirably the formalism of Roman constitutional procedure. On the death of the king (*rex*), the senate (fathers of clans, entrusted with the charge of the religious observances of the community) appointed an *interrex*, who in turn appointed a second, for the *imperium* could be transferred to the new king only by nomination of one who already possessed it (sometimes a third or even a fourth *interrex* was appointed, to veil the breach of continuity by a plausible fiction). The last *interrex* of the series selected a king in consultation with the senate; the king-designate was then nominated by the *interrex* to the assembly for acceptance, and, if accepted, his appointment was finally ratified by the senate. Thus personal nomination, the senate's co-operation, and popular election were all combined in the process. The same procedure was followed under the republic in the case of magistracies carrying with them the *imperium*, e.g. the consulship and prætorship; only (*a*) the need for an *interrex* was normally absent, since magistrates with *imperium* were already in being to nominate the new candidate, and (*b*) after 336 the consent of the senate had to be given prior to the popular election, and thus became as purely formal as is the royal assent to an act of the legislature in Britain at the present day. It was as if the royal assent were given to every Bill introduced into Parliament prior to its acceptance or rejection by the two Houses.

head of the state-religion. Criminal jurisdiction was concentrated in his hands. The close analogy with the position of the father in the family is obvious at a glance. But in the state, as in the family, custom provided a limit to the exercise of absolute authority. It was a fundamental maxim of the Romans that the holder of power must fortify himself by counsel. The senate of heads of families, in theory a consultative body, meeting only at the magistrate's summons to discuss what the magistrate willed to lay before it, became in practice an august council of state, whose opinion could be ignored only by an act of virtual revolution. The *imperium* of the king was balanced by the *auctoritas* or moral authority of the senate.[1] Lastly, when any situation arose in the life of the community which necessitated a departure from established precedent, such as a declaration of war, the adoption into a new family of the last male survivor of an old one, or the election of a successor to the throne, it was obligatory to obtain the assent of the sovereign people.[2] They assembled for this purpose by " curies " or wardships, to vote on what was laid before them by the presiding magistrate, without amendment or debate. Self-government was thus the exception rather than the rule in early Rome, and the monarchical and aristocratic elements in the constitution far outweighed the popular. But, despite all contrary appearances, one conviction, rooted in the primordial tradition of the community, never wholly passed into oblivion; the citizen-body was the ultimate and sovereign source of all rightful power.

II. THE ESTABLISHMENT OF THE REPUBLIC (§§ 5–7).

§ 5. The opening of the fifth century saw Rome a republic. The last Etruscan kings had exceeded the bounds which custom prescribed to the exercise of the *imperium* and had been expelled by their Latin subjects (*c.* 509 B.C.). This revolution, if such it

---

[1] *Auctoritas* means " moral influence "; the English word " authority " in the sense of executive power would be expressed in Latin by *imperium* or *potestas*.

[2] Adoption was frequently practised at Rome, for it was of primary concern to the Roman to leave male posterity behind him and thus maintain his family in being. Failing a son of his body, he could adopt a son, who became in all respects the equal of one born in lawful wedlock. But if the adopted son was himself a father of a family, his transference to the family of his new father involved the extinction of a family and of its *sacra,* a matter of grave religious moment, requiring the special sanction of the community.

may be called, involved no change in the governing principles of the constitution; the *imperium*, hitherto vested in the king alone for life, was now conferred on two equal and supreme magistrates, elected annually by the people with the sanction of the senate.[1] The dual magistracy served as an effective check on the *imperium*; for, though each consul possessed it in its full scope, this very fact enabled one to veto the act of the other, and at Rome, as between two equal magistrates, the negative voice always prevailed. Moreover, a consul was hardly likely to override the will of the senate which had ratified his election, and into whose ranks he would pass, on the expiration of his year of office, for the remainder of his life. Thus the transition to the republic meant that the government of Rome fell into the hands of an oligarchy of patrician families. The hated title of king vanished, though provision was made for the temporary restoration of regal power in time of crisis in the person of a *dictator*. During the two following centuries (509–287) the small republic was beset by foes without, and torn inwardly by political conflicts. Chief among the latter was the long struggle of the plebeian citizens for equality of social, political and religious rights with the patricians, which closed by the end of the fourth century with the victory of the former all along the line. The distinction of the two orders may well have arisen out of racial differences, like that of Norman nobility and Saxon commons in English history.[2] Early landmarks in the struggle were (*a*) the law that no magistrate might execute a capital sentence on any citizen without its ratification by the assembly; (*b*) the establishment, as a result of a general strike of the plebeian body against the state (494), of ten plebeian officers (*tribunes*), for protection against patrician magistrates, and of a plebeian assembly; and (*c*) the publication in the middle of the fifth century (451–450) of the Twelve Tables, the earliest code of Roman civil law. The tribunate was an institution which had far-reaching results on later constitutional history. The tribunes were not magistrates, but plebeian officers, whose persons were declared sacrosanct (taboo, inviolable in religion), with the power of inter-

[1] The two magistrates were originally called " prætors," later " consuls," the prætorship becoming a distinct office.

[2] We cannot discuss here the vexed question of the origin of this distinction. Both patricians and plebeians were members of the citizen-body; but owing to the fact that the former were sole masters in religion, the latter were in practice excluded from privileges depending on religious ceremonial, e.g. marriage with equal status, membership of the senate, tenure of office that carried with it the *imperium*.

posing a veto (*intercessio*) on any act of magisterial oppression within the city boundary.[1] In course of time their powers widened; they became, first, the recognised popular political leaders, and, later, virtual masters by their right of veto of the whole machinery of the state. The gradual extension of magistracies as the duties of administration grew more numerous and complex involved a customary partition of spheres of authority (*provinciae*), and, by consequence, mutual checks of colleagues one upon another. The Canuleian law (445) removed social inequality between the orders by legalising the marriages of plebeian and patrician; the next century (367) saw the termination of the long contest for admission to the supreme magistracy by the law that one consul henceforward must be a plebeian. The other offices were opened in rapid succession, the victory of the plebeians culminating in their capture of the religious colleges (300). In 336, a plebeian dictator reduced the senate's control over the popular elections to a barren formality (*lex Publilia*); another in 287 (*lex Hortensia*) did likewise in regard to the laws passed in the plebeian assembly, which henceforward were *ipso facto* binding on the whole community.[2] The distinction of plebeian and patrician was thus deprived of any practical significance. Moreover, these same reforms implied, to all appearance, that the Roman state had passed from the form of oligarchy to that of democracy. That the event proved otherwise was due to causes which had their source in the external life of the community and will be considered in a later section. But the political struggle above outlined was far from being the only motive of internal ferment in the early republican period. We read also of the constant demand on the part of the poorer plebeians for allotments on the lands of conquered enemies, and for relief from the ever-present pressure of debt. The Roman of early times was at once citizen, soldier and farmer, and both his political and his social status rested on tenure of property in land. The military and political strength of the state was rooted in the soil,

---

[1] Neither the veto of the tribune nor the right of appeal to the people on a capital charge availed against the military exercise of the *imperium*. When a dictator was appointed all restrictions vanished; the appointment was equivalent to a declaration of martial law.

[2] We have purposely omitted details as to the different assemblies in the Roman state; suffice it to say that the oldest assembly of the " curies " ceases to be important after the regal period, that the assembly of the centuries (originally a military assembly in which the propertied classes had preponderating influence) elected the consuls and magistrates with *imperium*, while the democratically organised assembly of the tribes became in the period under review the chief legislative body.

and the agrarian problem is of the first importance throughout the course of Roman history. It was the growing tendency of the wealthier citizens, patrician and plebeian alike, to acquire large tracts of conquered territory, to the detriment of the wise policy of allotting such land in free holdings to the poorer population, that stirred the repeated agitation of the commons. Nor did the Licinio-Sextian law of 367, which limited the acreage of any such " occupied " lands in a single owner's family, do more than afford partial and temporary relief from evils which we shall find recurring, in a far more acute form, at a later stage of republican history. As for the problem of debt, the Roman law was terribly severe, entailing the enslavement of the debtor's person in the creditor's prison cells. Here, too, the legislation of 367 afforded some redress; in course of time the rigours of the law were modified so as to satisfy the demand for more humane treatment, while the growing commercial prosperity of the state rendered the citizen less liable to insolvency.

§ 6. Among these measures, one stands out as fraught with peculiar significance for Roman civilization. The code of the Twelve Tables, compiled by the decemvirs in 451 and 450, was the earliest written law of Rome. As such, it was regarded throughout the history of the republic and of the empire as the basis of the civil law (*jus civile*), i.e. of the law regulating the relations of Roman citizens (*cives*).[1] When Cicero was a lad, schoolboys still learnt its rhythmic sentences by heart, much as English children used to learn their catechism ; though a generation later it was already yielding place to the prætorian formulas. Nowhere was the aptitude of the Romans for right judgement in practical affairs more conspicuously displayed than in the field of law, their most enduring contribution to world-civilization.[2] Elsewhere their functions were those of the policeman and the middleman, to preserve order in the Mediterranean area

[1] The *jus civile*, being the local law of the city-state (*jus proprium civitatis*, Gaius), applied to none but citizens. Full citizenship carried with it the public rights (*publica jura*) of service in the army, voting in the assembly, and eligibility to public office, and the private rights (*privata jura*) of intermarriage and trade with Roman citizens. Under the republic there were grades of partial citizenship involving certain of these rights apart from others (see below, §§ 10, 17). " Latin " rights, again, enabled the possessor to share in the civil law. The same is true when the right, e.g. of trading with Roman citizens was granted to members of another community by special treaty. On the *jus gentium*, see below, § 20.

[2] Tradition records that the decemvirs studied Greek models. This may be so, though the influence is not obvious in the Twelve Tables. We shall see presently how Hellenism set its mark on later Roman jurisprudence.

and to hand on the culture of other peoples to after-time; their philosophy, such as it was, and their poetry, though instinct with the spirit of Roman manners and national history, were stimulated and inspired by Hellenic models. But their law was largely their own creation; the framework of Greek juris-prudence being implemented by praetorian *formulae* and Roman case-law. Thus early were laid the foundations of the majestic structure that arose, stone upon stone, in unbroken continuity during a thousand years of workmanship, till its final completion in the *Corpus juris* of the emperor Justinian in the sixth century A.D. There had been indeed a rich development of earlier customary law solidified into definite form in the period of the kings. Custom was always held by the Romans to be an authori-tative source of law, and the Twelve Tables themselves represent a selection from recognised custom, concentrating on points which were specially liable to abuse or had given rise to dispute. Though Livy could still regard the Twelve Tables as " the fount of all public and private law," Roman law, like our own, was not so much the product of legislative statutes as of unenacted custom, interpreted and formulated by the steady tradition of a learned class of practising lawyers (*prudentes*), as well as by the praetorian edicts. Though Greek influence is present from the outset and increases during the Republican period, the legal method (*prudentia*) is the expression of the distinctively Roman genius.[1] In many particulars, for example, plebeian customary law was preferred to patrician, with the aim of healing class-strife in the civic community. Thus the enactments of the code presuppose an organised state-law as already in being. Many of the primitive customs familiar to early Hellenic, Germanic and Scandinavian law had long vanished at Rome; hardly a trace survives of blood-vengeance or wife-purchase, or of the conflict between the jurisdiction of the clan and the state. Moreover, the Romans had early drawn the distinction between *fas*, the religious law regulating men's relation to the gods, and *jus*, the secular law of the human community; close as was the union between the religious and the political machinery of the city, infractions of *fas* were but rarely punished by the secular arm. With equal precision, they distinguished (i) public law, determin-ing the constitution of the state and the organisation of public power, from private law, determining the mutual relations among

[1] See de Zulueta in *The Legacy of Rome*, pp. 186 ff. and Cicero, *De Oretore*, i. 44, 197, there quoted (p. 187).

individual citizens; and consequently (ii), among offences, between injuries to the public interest, including the crime of murder, where action lay with the executive magistrate, and injuries to private individuals, where the law intervened only on the complaint of the aggrieved party. In the former case, the state needed not to employ legal process, but redressed instantly its own wrongs; e.g. the quæstor could distrain on goods owed to the state without a judicial warrant. Public vengeance was thus self-executed; against the community the individual had no rights, and could bring no action at law. The law relating to private offences, as disclosed by the Twelve Tables, illustrates the gradual advance from (a) the primitive custom of personal vengeance, through the stages of (b) voluntary compensation by monetary payment dependent on the wills of both parties, and (c) obligatory compensation determined by law, to (d) entire prohibition of personal redress and the inclusion of all private injuries in the category of public injuries, under cognisance of the law of the state. In the Twelve Tables, murder alone comes under the last-mentioned head. Elsewhere, private redress is tolerated where not expressly forbidden. Voluntary compensation is allowed for flagrant theft and grave injuries to the person; for minor offences the payment is fixed by law. Certain crimes, e.g. the ill-treatment of parents by children, the removal of boundary stones and the destruction of standing corn, were dealt with by religious law. But except in a few special cases there were no regular courts of criminal justice; the wrongdoer must be haled in person before the magistrate, who referred the case to a private citizen (*judex*) for his decision on the issue of fact.[1] Here again we have an illustration of the Roman sense for clear distinction; they entrusted the ruling in law to the magistrate, as the depositary of state-*jus*, and the hearing of the facts to the *judex*.[2] This procedure applied

---

[1] It was not till the dictatorship of Sulla (80 B.C.) that standing criminal courts (*quaestiones perpetuae*) were systematically established. In the case of public crimes, where the penalty was capital or a fine exceeding a certain sum, the right of appeal to the people (*provocatio*) was allowed. Most crimes were treated as private wrongs, the state intervening only on the instance of the individual sufferer, and simulating in its procedure the methods of private redress.

[2] The magistrate could not pronounce a judgement (*sententia*) in a disputed case; he could only refer the case to a *judex* and, in referring it, determine the nature of the claim. This constituted the hearing *in jure*. There followed the hearing of the facts *in judicio* before the *judex*, who gave his verdict. Only when the defendant admitted or acquiesced in the plaintiff's claim was reference to the *judex* dispensed with and the case decided straightway by the magistrate (*in jure cessio*).

equally to civil causes, with which the Twelve Tables were primarily concerned. The civil law regulated the whole mass of relationships between citizens, marriage and the family, guardianship, emancipation of son or slave, testamentary succession, property and contracts, with a narrow formalism indeed, yet with a precision and freedom from mysticism peculiar to Rome among all early societies known to history. Though all property was regarded as derived by implicit transference from the community and could therefore be held only by citizens, private ownership had long been an established fact, and the citizen, once secure in his title, was left in almost entire liberty of using it and disposing of it at will. The Roman law of inheritance was already far in advance of other early Indo-European codes, in that provision for intestacy was subordinated to the recognition of testamentary bequest, the Roman being at liberty to select his heir, to determine legacies, and to appoint guardians for his surviving children.[1] Within carefully defined limits the life and property of the citizen were protected by the law, which was as studious to provide a *tutor* for the infant and a *curator* for the lunatic as it was inexorable in its enforcement of the creditor's full claim against the person of the insolvent debtor.[2] The Twelve Tables penalised usury and fixed a legal rate of interest. They determined also the machinery of judicial procedure in a spirit that was straightforward and sternly practical; respect

[1] Before 450 intestate succession was the rule, and a testament required the assent of the people by a special law and was subject to control by the priestly college (the *pontifices*); after 450 this control becomes a mere form. Collective ownership doubtless once prevailed at Rome, private ownership being restricted to a small plot on which stood the citizen's house; but collective ownership had disappeared long before the Twelve Tables. The only restrictions on the citizen's liberty of using and disposing of his property were certain minor safeguards of the rights of neighbours and the interest of the community. Gibbon (c. 45) remarks that among the Romans "the insolent prerogative of primogeniture was unknown."

[2] Women were allowed to hold property under the Twelve Tables. The law of debt was extremely rigorous. The only legal form of contract in early Rome was the *nexum* or loan (lit., binding tie). If the debtor failed to repay within thirty days of the time stated in the contract, the creditor could enforce his claim without further legal proceedings by arresting the debtor and haling him off to his private prison. The Twelve Tables provided that he must be detained there for a further period of sixty days; then, unless an agreement had been reached, he was brought thrice before the magistrate, and (unless a third party came forward as champion at his own risk) might be killed or sold into slavery by the creditor. At any prior moment, payment of the debt meant the debtor's liberation. The rigour of this law was gradually abated in the early centuries of the republic.

for legal forms went hand in hand with freedom from needless delay and cumbersome ceremonial. Legal torture of citizens was unknown then and throughout the history of Roman law. The details of procedure rested as yet in the hands of the priestly colleges; the public might read the code, but were debarred from knowledge of its interpretation. It stands to reason that this first body of published law was characterised by a rigidity and narrowness expressive of the traditions of a small and simple community. The centuries that followed saw its progressive modification and expansion, till by the close of the republican epoch not a clause retained its original significance. But the Twelve Tables were never abrogated. While the Roman people held to their traditions as to a rock, their practical sagacity devised innumerable expedients for adjusting ancient law to the complex needs of a rapidly growing society, and for harmonising radical changes of detail with a tenacious conservatism in regard to the legal inheritance of the past.[1]

§ 7. We know little or nothing of the men who thus fashioned the institutions and law of Rome. The work was wrought, not by individuals of exceptional genius, but by the people. The names that occur in the pages of early Roman history are those of average Romans, of citizen-soldiers whose lives are barely distinguishable one from the other, and form a monotonous sequence, save only when an Appius Claudius, decemvir or censor, appears upon the stage. Early Roman history is the record of laws and civic policy, the planting of colonies and the making of military roads. It is not Canuleius or Licinius that signify, but the measures that bear their names. Moreover, the character of these measures was determined not so much by deliberate forethought as by the pressure of present fact. The Romans never planned their constitution, which, like their law, grew up as occasion required, and presents in consequence a singularly unsystematic picture.[2] This absence

---

[1] The free use of legal fictions was a means of adjustment common both to Roman and English law. Adoption was an early and conspicuous instance. So was the tacit acceptance, to be noted later, of the modifications introduced into the law by the answers of jurisconsults, which claimed all the time to be strict interpretations of the traditional code. See Maine, *Ancient Law*, c. ii. A legal fiction is a natural device for combining conservatism and continuity in legal development with the requisite adaptation to new experience.

[2] Polybius (vi. 11) observes how the Romans shaped their constitution, "not on a theory, but through frequent conflicts and practical crises," choosing the prudent course in each situation as it arose; and (vi. 43) contrasts the greatness of Rome with that of Athens, in that the

of logical design is illustrated by the institution which formed the keystone of the structure. In the very heart of the republican government we find the absolute and indivisible *imperium* in the possession of two consuls, as equal and supreme executive officers. To the political theorist, such duplication of supreme authority would be a sure presage of disaster. Yet the device, inconceivable as it appears on paper, worked admirably in practice; for it was the outgrowth of experience and founded on the bedrock of fact. So overpowering was the burden of the magisterial *imperium* in the Roman commonwealth, that it was a more urgent need to impose limits on its abuse than to provide for its unfettered exercise. Dual control was the one expedient open for averting despotism. Inaugurated with the republic, it endured for five centuries; when in the event it proved powerless in the face of military autocrats, it was restored in altered form as the theory of the early empire.[1] In this, as in much else in the character of the Roman state, we are reminded of the temper and practice of our own people. The constitutional history of Rome and that of England present the same broad features of gradual development on a basis of racial tradition, of unbounded respect for form and precedent, of elasticity in practical application, and of restriction of theoretical powers by use and custom. Both endured for centuries with unbroken continuity, thanks to their adaptability to changing circumstances. Both form a tissue of illogical contrivances, quaint fictions and effete survivals, the easy price paid for institutions that are not the work of a single lawgiver, but the congenial expression of national experience. The analogy holds good also of their conduct in war. War generally found the Romans unprepared, a sure sign that their policy was not militant but pacific. They almost invariably suffered heavy reverses in the early stages of the struggle, but always emerged victorious at the close. They learnt their lesson in the midst of conflict, and never acquiesced in defeat. We shall remark later on the similarity between the methods by which Rome and Britain adjusted their maxims of government to meet the varying requirements of a vast empire. The function of both has been to police the world within their range of influence. Both were

---

former was chiefly due to the type of constitution, the latter to individual genius.

[1] See c. viii, § 7 below, on the dual control of *princeps* and senate in Augustus' scheme of reorganisation.

guided, alike in bestowing privileges and in preserving peace, by motives of interest rather than of imagination. But, despite these striking analogies, there remains one great difference in the constitutional life of the two peoples. Whereas in England the centre of political gravity lies in Parliament, that of Rome lay not in the legislature but in the executive. " The great contests for freedom in this country," said Edmund Burke, " were from the earliest times chiefly upon the question of taxing. Most of the contests in the ancient commonwealths turned primarily on the right of election of magistrates or on the balance of the several orders of the state. The question of money was not with them so immediate." [1] English political history is full of such issues as the right of the Crown to levy ship-money, of Parliament to tax America, of the House of Lords to reject the Budget. In early Rome the question of taxation was non-existent. There the whole struggle for liberty had for its goal the limitation of the *imperium* of the chief magistrate.

III. The Expansion of Rome (§§ 8–13).

§ 8. The process of the expansion of the Roman state falls into three epochs: (a) the conquest of the Italian peninsula; (b) the struggle with Carthage for the sovereignty of the western Mediterranean; and (c) the acquisition of a like supremacy over the Hellenic East.

(a) *The Expansion of Rome in Italy.*[2]

The period (450–270) which saw the rise of Rome to be mistress of Italy coincided with the political conflicts which closed with the passing of the Hortensian law (287). For a century and a half after the expulsion of the kings she had fought uninterruptedly with her immediate neighbours; in the first fifty years of the struggle her very existence as an independent city-state was almost annually at stake. After 450 Rome began to

---

[1] Speech on *Conciliation with America*. At Rome there was no direct, and little indirect, taxation. Later, the provinces paid a fixed tribute (*stipendium*) into the Roman exchequer; the quotas being either paid to the provincial quæstors, or (as in Sicily and the East) being farmed out on a system that brought much profit to Roman capitalists.

[2] For the Romans of the republic Italy was bounded on the north, not by the Alps, but by the Apennines; the district between the Apennines and the Alps was called Cisalpine Gaul, i.e. Gaul on this side of the Alps. It was peopled by Celtic kinsmen of the tribes that inhabited Transalpine Gaul, i.e. Gaul on the further side of the Alps, the modern France and Belgium.

forge ahead; by 350 she was supreme over southern Etruria
and the plain of Latium. Even the victorious onset of the
Gauls and their sack of the city in 390 only interrupted for a few
years the even tenor of her advance. When once she was secure
in Latium, the old Latin league ceased to exist, save in religious
ceremonial. Rome was helped in these early days by the lack
of any strong sentiment of unity among her Italian foes. We
find little trace of a common Italian consciousness comparable
to that which in early Greece found expression in leagues of cities
and in the Olympic games. It arose doubtless at a later date,
but only after Italy had been absorbed politically into the Roman
state. The conquest of Latium brought Rome into direct
relations with the Greek cities on the Campanian coast, and therewith into conflict with the powerful hill-tribes of central Italy.
Rome stood forth already as the champion of order, commerce
and Hellenic culture against the marauders who found a happy
hunting ground among the rich but unwarlike Greeks. There
followed the long and arduous struggle with the Samnites (343–
290), which left Rome the sole power northwards to the ridge of
the Apennines and eastwards to the shores of the Adriatic.
Finally, early in the third century, Pyrrhus, king of Epirus, the
first captain of his age, brought his highland warriors and
elephants across the sea, on the pretext of defending the Greeks
of Tarentum against the southward advance of Rome. A professional soldier of the school of Alexander, he nourished wild
dreams of achieving in the West triumphs like those of Alexander
in the East; but he lacked Alexander's statesmanship; and Rome,
a free and consolidated state, proved an antagonist of a quality
far different from Persia. On Pyrrhus' failure the Greeks of the
south fell an easy prey to the Roman legions, and Rome ruled
unchallenged from the plain of Lombardy to the straits of Messina.

§ 9. That " Rome was not built in a day " is true not only
of the character and institutions of the sovereign city, but also
of her world-empire; and these early struggles for supremacy
in Italy covered a period twice as long as that which sufficed
for her conquest of the whole Mediterranean area. We can
trace in them the lines on which she afterwards mastered and
ruled the world. We remark, first, the efficiency of her military
organisation. The legion, observed one of the Latin writers,
was the inspiration of a god.[1] It combined the weight of the

[1] Vegetius, quoted by Montesquieu, c. 2. In actual fact, it was
modelled, but with improvements, on the military organisation of the

Macedonian phalanx with superior mobility, as was proved in the war against Pyrrhus. In armament and methods of warfare the Romans were always ready to learn from their enemies; defeat was the signal for reforms which enabled them to emerge from the war triumphant. Thus they borrowed the heavy javelin from the Samnites, as later they learnt the construction of large warships from the Carthaginians, and at the close of the second Punic war defeated Hannibal with the cavalry which had been the instrument of his early victories. Like the English, they " muddled through " their wars, a slang phrase which signifies the triumph of racial persistence and the capacity of using defeat as a means to victory. They too were modest as to the reason of their successes; they ascribed them to the " Fortune of the Roman people." What is most impressive is their unflinching self-confidence; Rome never made peace while a single enemy remained on Roman soil. It is a profound error to suppose that the Romans were an aggressive people, bent on subduing, first Italy, and then the world. It is far truer to say that their wars came upon them inevitably, in the order of things. At each stage in their history they were faced with the alternative, to go forward or to go back. Rome never went back. Beset by turbulent neighbours, the task of policing her own borders involved her in constant war; and war meant in the long run extension of empire. She was compelled to intervene in order to allay the conflagration, and intervention entailed eventual occupation. There was cynicism in Rome's policy, and her diplomacy was always guided by the maxim of self-interest; but she never thirsted for conquest, and the story of her empire is that of the identification of self-interest with the cause of law, order and civilization.

§ 10. The history of Rome's expansion over Italy illustrates, in a yet more striking manner, her native genius for administration. At each stage she riveted her conquests with the iron bolts of military roads and colonies. That " all roads lead to Rome " is true, not only in metaphor of the highways of civilization, but literally of the great thoroughfares which radiated from Rome, first, through Latium and southern Etruria, then over Italy, and finally over the countries of the Mediterranean area.[1] The Roman colony was not, like that of the Greeks,

---

Greeks. On the organisation of the legion and its superiority to the phalanx, see Polybius xviii. 11–15.

[1] The earliest of these roads in Italy was the *Via Appia*, begun in 312 by Appius Claudius, the censor. It ran across Latium in a straight

an independent city-state, but a military settlement of farmer-soldiers in the midst of conquered enemies. So long as these colonies remained faithful, the Roman legions might be beaten in the field, but the Roman state stood firm. In her treatment of the vanquished, the Roman maxim was " divide and rule " (*divide et impera*). No bond of association, in early days not even the rights of trade and intermarriage, was tolerated among her subject-communities. The old local federations were everywhere dissolved. Rome maintained this cardinal principle unimpaired throughout her history. The same mistrust of subordinate associations which led her to abolish the Latin league, served under the empire as the motive for her prohibition of a local fire brigade at Nicomedia, and for her persecution of the Christian church as an unauthorised corporation.[1] On the other hand, all the Italian communities alike were bound by links of varying stringency to Rome. Italy formed henceforward a single state under Roman suzerainty. War and peace, foreign relations and the coinage, were the exclusive concern of the ruling city. For the rest, a distinction was drawn between territory directly administered by Rome and that of her Italian " friends and allies," analogous to that in the India of to-day between the native states and the districts governed by the British civil service. The former comprised about one-third of Italy, including Rome, the colonies of full Roman citizens, and other towns with full or partial citizen-privileges (*municipia*). These colonies and *municipia* enjoyed a liberal measure of self-government, though Rome retained the right of intervention, and prefects were annually sent from the capital to administer justice. Among the Italian " allies," on the other hand, the " Latin " colonies occupied a privileged position, with full rights of trade and intermarriage with Roman citizens. Up to the middle of the third century, the colonists retained the right of recovering their Roman citizenship in the event of their return to the capital. But the mass of the " allies " had their

line to the coast, and was continued later through Samnium by Bene-ventum to Venusia (in Apulia) and Brundisium (the modern Brindisi). The *Via Latina* ran further inland from Rome to Capua; the *Via Flaminia* northwards across the Appennines to Ariminum (Rimini) on the Adriatic, and was extended in 187 to Placentia (Piacenza) on the Po under the name of the *Via Æmilia*. In the second century the *Via Domitia* was constructed along the *Golfe du Lion* to link Rome with Spain, and the *Via Egnatia* across the Balkan peninsula from Dyrrachium (Durazzo) to Thessalonica (Salonika) and the Hellespont.

[1] See Pliny's letters to the emperor Trajan (early second century A.D.). Bk. X, letters 33, 34 (the fire brigade); 96, 97 (the Christians).

status determined by special treaty. In the case of Hellenic cities, the terms were generally liberal, while other communities, in less civilized regions, were reduced to virtual bondage. All were liable to service with the Roman army in the field.[1] No clearer example can be furnished of the elasticity of the Roman administrative system and its capacity for adjustment to varying local conditions than the picture presented by their rule in Italy in the period between the Gallic invasion (390) and the outbreak of the first Punic war (264).

§ 11. (b) The wars with Carthage.

The story is told how Pyrrhus, on leaving the Greek cities of southern Italy to their fate, exclaimed, " What a battlefield we are bequeathing to the Romans and the Carthaginians ! " For centuries the Sicilian Greeks had struggled against Carthage for their island ; now only the narrow straits parted Sicily from Rome. The Carthaginian predominance in the western seas was yet unchallenged, though Rome had already begun to police the coast of Italy with her fleet. Since the sixth century she had carried on trade with Sicily, Sardinia and Carthage, and had become thoroughly familiar with Hellenic and Phoenician custom. The conflict between the two great western powers was the most terrible in ancient history. It opened in 264, and lasted, with a twenty years' break for the combatants to recover strength (241–219), till the crowning victory of Scipio over Hannibal at Zama in 202. To dwell on its history lies beyond our scope. The first Punic (Phoenician) war (264–241) gave Rome her first provinces of Sicily and Sardinia and Corsica, and the sea power over the western Mediterranean. In the interval that followed, she subdued the Gauls between the northern Apennines and the Alps. The second war (219–201), ever memorable for the invasion of Italy by the great Hannibal, closed with the conquest of Spain and the reduction of Carthage to the position of a vassal-state. Never in her long history was the heroic patriotism of the Romans more conspicuous

---

[1] The division into citizens (full or partial) and allies dates from the fourth century. Partial citizenship meant the possession of private without public rights. The private rights in question were those of trade and intermarriage, the public those of the franchise and eligibility to magisterial office. " Latin " rights were granted to communities outside Latium, both in Italy and (later) in the provinces ; these are not to be confounded with the members of the old Latin league. The allies were autonomous as regards local government and lay outside the sphere of Roman legislation and executive government.

than in the dark hours when the relics of her shattered legions hung desperately round the invader. When the consul Varro drew near the city after the terrible disaster of Cannæ (216), the senate—his political foes—went forth to meet him with their thanks that he had not despaired of the republic. A few years later, when Hannibal approached the gates of Rome, the land on which his camp was pitched was sold in the city at its full market-value in time of peace. The moral of the issue of this historic conflict is clear as day. A commercial oligarchy—like Venice at a later day, jealous of its greatest citizens and dependent on mercenary soldiers—could not prevail in arms against a free republic.[1] Nor could the genius of the greatest of military leaders avail to undermine the solid fabric of the Roman colonies. The issue once determined, Rome hunted her foe to death with merciless severity. She extorted, first the exile, and then the murder of Hannibal, the one individual she had ever deigned to fear. Finally, when half a century later Carthage rose from her death-agony in a supreme effort to regain her freedom, after an heroic resistance she was levelled with the ground (147).

§ 12. (c) The conquest of the East.

Rome emerged from this titanic conflict the unquestioned sovereign of the West. Henceforward the problem that confronted her in this quarter was that of consolidation and government. We shall return in the next chapter to the manner in which she discharged her mission as a civilizing agent in Spain, Africa and southern Gaul. But before she could set her hand to this new task, she found herself perforce embroiled in the politics of the Hellenic East. It was no temper of *hubris* that impelled her to intervention, but the hard logic of facts. Exhausted by the Hannibalic war and staggering under the burden of her western provinces, she was in no mood for embarking on fresh adventures, the issues of which could not be foreseen. The militarist ambitions of the Greek kings of Macedon and Asia forced her hand. The dominant power in Italy could not then, any more than now, view with indifference the course of events

---

[1] Polybius (vi. 52) recognises that the military superiority of the Romans to the Carthaginians was that of patriotic citizen-soldiers over mercenaries. He remarks also (iii. 118) that the Romans were saved after Cannæ by "the distinctive character of their polity and their excellence in counsel," and attributes the rapid expansion of their empire to the same causes.

in the Balkan peninsula. As a great commercial power, Rome had to keep the peace in the surrounding seas. Macedonian troops had fought for Hannibal, and the Seleucid Antiochus III (the " Great ") was menacing the independence of Rome's allies, Athens, Rhodes and Pergamos. The issue was swift and overwhelming. Macedon was crushed in 197, Antiochus of Asia in 190. The Seleucid empire dismembered by Rome in the West and by the rising power of Parthia in the East, sank, after the battle of Magnesia (192), into the petty principality of Syria. Thus almost in one day had the sovereignty of the eastern Mediterranean fallen into the hands of Rome. Montesquieu has observed that " after the fall of the Carthaginians Rome fought only little wars and won great victories, whereas before she had won small victories and fought great wars."[1] In the brilliant story of her eastern expansion we note three salient facts. First, Rome appears at every point as the champion of order, the one effective police amid the sorely troubled Hellenic world. Hence she was allied constantly with peaceful commercial states, such as Egypt, Rhodes and Pergamos. Secondly, her policy was inspired by a sincere enthusiasm for Hellenism. We shall speak later of the pervasive influence of Greek culture in this age on the life and temper of the leading Roman citizens. Their idealism found expression in the dramatic scene that followed the victory over Macedon, when Flamininus proclaimed to the Greeks assembled at the isthmus of Corinth that they were henceforth free. A less ardent champion of Hellenism might have forecast the issue; anarchy raged throughout the peninsula for half a century, till Rome was driven to annexation. Thirdly, the reluctance of the Roman government to enlarge the bounds of their empire is most evident throughout this epoch. Their policy in Macedon will provide an illustration. After their first victory (197), they confirmed the vanquished sovereign as a dependent-prince under Roman suzerainty; when his successor twenty years later provoked a second war, he was deposed, and

[1] *Gr. et déc.*, c. 5. The swiftness with which Rome acquired world sovereignty deeply impressed contemporaries, e.g. the Greek historian Polybius, the aim of whose work was to show " by what steps and under what type of constitution the whole world fell under the single rule of Rome within three and fifty years " (i. 1); i.e. between the outbreak of the second Punic war (219) and the partition of Macedonia (167). He further points out (i. 3) how in this half-century the detached currents of events in East and West met in a single stream in the Roman empire, the history of the Mediterranean area acquiring for the first time an organic unity.

his dominions were partitioned among four local authorities; only when this experiment failed was the country constituted a Roman province (146). In Asia, Rome took nothing for herself; the provinces wrested from Antiochus were entrusted to client-princes and to her Hellenic allies. We may compare the successive expedients devised by the British government in India to postpone time after time the annexation of the Punjâb.

§ 13. If our purpose had been to write a history of Rome, it would have been necessary to trace, point by point, the detailed incidents of these conflicts, and to mark, at each successive phase, their continuous influence upon the structure of her internal government. It was, for instance, the pressure of war at her gates that gave leverage to the plebeians, who formed the backbone of the army, in their struggle with the patrician aristocracy. So, again, the incorporation of the Italian and Mediterranean peoples within the sphere of Roman suzerainty had, as we shall see later, far-reaching issues upon her legal and administrative system. But our present interest in the story of the making of the Roman empire is not so much with the process as with the results.[1] These may be summed up in a word; by the middle of the second century Roman rule was established, in its broad essentials, over the Mediterranean world. In the west she ruled directly the provinces of Sicily, Sardinia and Corsica, Gaul south of the Alps, Hither and Farther Spain, and Africa. In 121, the coast-lands between the Alps and the Pyrenees were incorporated into the province of Narbonese Gaul, the " Provence " of a later day. In the East there were only two provinces, Macedonia with Achaia (Greece), and Asia—i.e. the western region of Asia Minor, bequeathed to the Roman state in 133 by the last Greek prince of Pergamos. Beyond the frontiers of these provinces lay a ring of principalities, such as Numidia in Africa, Egypt, Syria (the relic of the Seleucid monarchy) and innumerable minor states, ruled internally by their own governments, but controlled in respect of all foreign relations by Rome. The establishment of these client-states under Roman suzerainty was a cardinal feature of Roman policy under the later republic

---

[1] It is not the personality or the feats of Scipio Africanus that count in history, but the use that Rome made of his conquest of Spain. Hannibal overthrew Flaminius and his legions by the Trasimene lake, but the name of his victim still lives as the maker of the highway by which the Roman armies crossed the Apennines to the Po valley and the foothills of the Alps.

and the early empire. They served as buffer-states between Rome and powers like Parthia, saved the burden of military occupation and government, and fostered the spread of civilization outside the bounds of the provinces. The succeeding century saw the rounding-off of this imperial system in the formation of new provinces and dependent states, the reform of internal administration, and the determination of the permanent frontiers of the empire. At the time we have reached, the function of Rome in world-history was already marked out. That function was twofold; in accordance with the difference of conditions confronting her in West and East. In the West, her mission was to implant law and civilization among barbaric or semi-barbaric peoples. In the East, on the other hand, she found in being a civilization far superior to her own. There her task was not to create, but to conserve; to save from anarchy and ruin the fabric of Hellenic culture, and to carry on the work of Alexander and his successors by leavening with that culture the peoples of the nearer and the middle East.

IV. ROME IN THE SECOND CENTURY (§§ 14–20).

A. Rome and Hellenism (§§ 14–16).

§ 14. The ability of Rome to rise to the height of her responsibilities rested primarily on the character of her citizen-body. The influx of wealth and the spread of Hellenic culture during the period of the great wars had combined to effect a profound revolution in the moral and economic life of the Roman community. Up to the time of the Punic wars Rome was comparatively poor, and a measure of real equality prevailed among the citizens. Now, almost suddenly, she found herself rich, the centre of Mediterranean commerce, with the markets of east and west at the feet of her merchants and financiers. The results were obvious in the rise of a plutocratic class whose wealth gave them influence at Rome and in the provinces; in the growth of luxury among the senatorial aristocracy which conservative magistrates like Cato the censor vainly strove to check; in the habit of financial speculation; in the appearance of huge landed estates; the decay of the yeoman-farmer; and the wholesale importation of slave labour from the East. Agriculture in Italy could not compete with imported corn from overseas. The moral and political results were of equal gravity. In the early days of Mediterranean expansion the Roman administrators and merchants astounded, by their simplicity of life and severe integrity, a world habituated to Punic and Hellenic corruption. But already in the first half of the second century Cato could complain that " he who steals from a burgess ends his days in chains, but he who steals from the community ends them in gold and purple." [1] The ancient code of morals yielded swiftly to the changed conditions; indolence and incapacity spread among the governing class; while the nobles lived in splendour on the spoils of the provinces, and the tax-farmers and contractors utilised their riches to found a new and rival power in politics, the impoverished masses, crowded in the capital, degenerated into an idle and pleasure-loving proletariate. These changes in social life and manners, consequent on Rome's swift rise to sovereign power, were fraught with baneful issues, not only on her imperial policy, but on the internal stability of the state. Even more pervasive and far-reaching were the results of her assimilation of Hellenism.

§ 15. It was in Campania in the fourth century that Rome was first brought into constant relationship with Greek civilization. The fact that she started on her history as a city-state with institutions analogous to those of the city-states of Greece formed a link which Romans and Greeks alike were quick to recognise. When in 229 the Romans appeared for the first time on the eastern shores of the Adriatic, they were straightway admitted to membership in the Hellenic games. The Greeks never looked upon them as "barbarians." In return, the Roman government and individual Romans like Flamininus adopted eagerly a phil-Hellenic attitude in foreign policy. The fruits of this closer intimacy were seen during the third century in the impulse given by Greece to Latin literature. The native poetry of Rome, hymns, ballads and rustic comedy, was rude in form and matter. Poets were held in low esteem, and there is no sound basis for Macaulay's conjecture that the early political struggles inspired a rich ballad literature. Roman poetry had

[1] See Mommsen, Book III, c. ii. Cato (consul 195, censor 184), a veteran of the Hannibalic war and an able administrator of Spain, led the conservative opposition to the new influences. Polybius (vi. 56), himself a Greek patriot, contrasts the honesty of the Roman official in the first half of the second century with the corruptibility of the Greek : " Those who handle public funds among the Hellenes, even though the sum be merely a talent, take ten account-checkers and ten seals and twice as many witnesses, yet cannot be faithful to their trust; while among the Romans, men who handle vast sums as magistrates or ambassadors, observe their obligations on the security of a simple oath."

its beginnings in translations and imitations of Greek classics, and employed metrical forms of Greek origin, especially the epic hexameter.[1] But it would be an error to suppose that the Roman poets, in following Greek models, were slavish imitators of their masters. They infused into their works the spirit of Rome. Ennius, who was contemporary with the second Punic war and took that historic conflict for the theme of his epic, gave expression to the qualities of gravity and virile energy, of imperial pride and political sagacity, that were distinctive of Roman character. The same is true of the Latin comedy of manners in the second century; Greek models were adapted to reflect the interests and social life of Rome. One peculiar style of poetry was native to Roman literature, the " satire " or medley (*satura*), first composed by Lucilius in the middle of the second century, which portrayed in hexameter verse scenes of social life, interspersed with literary and political criticism, autobiography and personal adventure, and the intercourse of friends. The Roman writers displayed a peculiar felicity and charm in this vein of poetry; in the words of a modern critic, " Not Horace only, nor all the satirists after Horace, but Montaigne and Pepys also, belong to the school of Lucilius." [2] Latin prose literature had its birth in this same epoch; the practical interests of the Romans led them early to break ground in the fields of forensic oratory and history. Here again we feel their ever-present sense of the greatness of Rome, her genius for law and order, her imperial destiny. But there is yet another characteristic distinguishing Latin literature from that of Greece. The greatest Roman poets show a true understanding and love of nature. The Greeks had written of nature in imperishable verse; but with all their sense of her beauty and grandeur, she remained to them an alien power, able indeed to rouse their wonder, but one with which they never really felt themselves at home. Nature to the Greek was always something outside himself, something to be known about or conquered, not something to be loved.[3] The Roman poets loved nature as akin to themselves. The Greek lived in and for the city, and, if he travelled abroad, it was to

---

[1] The earliest Roman verse was in the so-called " Saturnian " metre, exemplified in the English line,

" The Queen was in her parlour | eating bread and honey."

[2] Mackail, *Latin Literature*, p. 35. *Satura*, as the text implies, includes more than the English term " satire "; Quintilian (*Inst. Orat.* x. c. 1, § 93) observes that it is purely Roman (*satura quidem tota nostra est*).

[3] Hesiod and Alcman, however, must be excepted.

see the cities of men; his estates were a source of revenue, not a chosen retreat. The Roman gladly fled the city for the country; he was the first to appreciate a country home and to create a resort for time of leisure among the mountains or by the sea. So Catullus quitted Rome for his villa on the lake of Garda, Horace for his Sabine farm, Virgil for the bay of Naples. It was the same with the man of business and the lawyer, when, as in Horace's famous simile, he shook off the burden of public affairs and retired to " the fields of Venafrum or Lacedæmonian Tarentum." [1] The Romans carried into their converse with nature something of the warmth of intimacy that marked their personal relationships, and that draws the reader of their literature into sympathy with the poet's daily life. First of all races, they knew and expressed in their verse a sense of delight in natural beauty akin to that of Chaucer or of Shakespeare.

§ 16. With the spread of contemporary Hellenism of the Hellenistic, Alexandrian type, Roman society became at once more luxurious and more refined. Too often Greek culture meant but a thin veneer that hardly veiled the natural coarseness and brutality of Roman manners. On the mass of the people its influence was scarcely felt at all, except, perhaps, in the gradual effects on popular religion of the identification by the poets of Roman with Hellenic deities. The highly abstract gods of early Rome became somewhat more personal and concrete. The aristocracy, on the other hand, learnt from the Greeks to value literature and the arts.[2] The masterpieces of Greek sculpture were carried to Rome to adorn the houses of victorious generals. There is a saying of George Meredith to the effect that the one abstract idea which the military mind

[1] Horace, *Odes*, iii. 5, ll. 55–6.
[2] The distinguished circle that gathered round Scipio Æmilianus (conqueror of Carthage in the third Punic war) included, besides noble Romans, the comic dramatist Terence, the satirist Lucilius, and the deported Greek statesman Polybius. Polybius (born c. 206, died c. 124) was restored to Greece from exile in 150; attended Scipio on campaigns in Africa and elsewhere, and acted as Roman commissioner in Greece from 145. His history comprised 40 Books, of which the first five only are extant in their entirety; extracts from the others have been preserved by Byzantine compilers. They cover the years between 219 and 145. Polybius' work is marked by impartiality of judgement and fidelity to ascertainable fact; the author, though consistently loyal to his native Greece, is inspired throughout by a sense of the invincible strength of the Roman power, and the nobility and greatness of Roman character and institutions. Chance largely rules human affairs (i. 4); but there was nothing fortuitous, in Polybius' eyes, in the acquisition of a world-empire by Rome (i. 63). The philosophical reflexions, which are obtrusively lavished on the reader, are, in general, somewhat banal and verbose.

I

is able to grasp is that of booty, and doubtless the vulgar thirst for plunder had much to do with this spoliation of Hellenic treasures.[1]   But when once the works of art were displayed in Rome, they exercised a subtle influence on the public taste. The Romans became interested not merely in preserving the monuments of the past, but in encouraging such new creations in art and literature as the Greek genius was still able to produce. Creative art implies a public, and this public was now furnished by Rome.   The Romans never became artists; indeed, their patronage dealt Greek art its final blow.   Greek philosophy, too, began to trickle into Rome during the second century, though the Romans had little capacity for disinterested specula- tion, and long resisted the intrusion.   The doctrines of the Stoics and Epicureans, which centred round the problems of practical life, were the earliest to take root in Roman society. They helped to modify and eventually to undermine the old Roman standards of piety and virtue.   Signs of sceptical thought are already present in the poems of Ennius.   The elder statesmen of the second century, such as Cato, were suspicious of Greek influence; in the middle of that century the senate passed a decree that all philosophers should quit the city.   But resistance to ideas was as impracticable as resistance to wealth and luxury; slowly, but surely, for good and for evil, the spirit of Greece, in Horace's phrase, " took captive her rude conqueror." [2]

B. *The Roman State in the Second Century* (§§ 17–20).

§ 17. It was one thing to create an empire; another, and a far harder, to govern it.   The problem that confronted Rome was not merely that of devising new machinery of administra- tion for her provinces, but also that of readjusting the central government at home.   The methods that sufficed for an Italian municipality were bound to prove inadequate for the metropolis of the Mediterranean world.   Already in the epoch of the wars with Carthage the character of the Roman state had undergone radical transformation, not by deliberate design but under pressure from the facts.   Power was concentrated not, as might have been expected after the Hortensian law of 287, in the hands of the citizen democracy, but in those of an exclusive ring of

[1] Polybius (ix. 10) laments the Roman practice of robbing conquered cities of their art treasures, contrasting with it their earlier self-restraint and simplicity of life.
[2] Horace, *Epp.* ii. 1, 156.

noble families, with the senate as their organ.[1] Recruited
from magistrates and ex-magistrates, and comprising among its
members tried soldiers and statesmen at a time when consuls
and citizens were serving in the field, the senate was the only
constitutional body qualified to direct affairs of state. The
increase in the number of executive officers entailed by the
enlargement of public responsibilities, until there were no less
than twenty annual magistrates in possession of the authority
to convene the people, and the fact that there were three popular
assemblies competent to pass binding acts, called imperatively
for the regulative control of a standing council.[2] Moreover,
in days when the nation was fighting for life the senate proved
itself worthy of power ; it was, so Pyrrhus' envoy told his master,
a council of kings. Thus it came about that the *imperium* of
the magistrates and the legislative sovereignty of the people
bowed before the moral authority of the senate. At the close of
the third century, the senate, in addition to its historic power of
giving advice to the magistrates, wielded almost exclusive control
over foreign affairs, provincial organisation, finance, religion
and all vital matters of public policy. A little later, it claimed
the rights, foreign to constitutional tradition and disputed by
the popular opposition, of suspending magistrates from their
functions, and of endowing the consuls with virtually dictatorial
powers by the decree " that the magistrates should see that
the state took no harm." [3] We find in fact at Rome a situation
analogous to that which prevailed in eighteenth-century England,
when the forms of parliamentary government were manipulated,

[1] Polybius, writing of the Roman constitution at this epoch, describes
it (vi. 10) as a blend of monarchy (the magistrates with *imperium*), aristocracy (the office-bearing families) and democracy (the *comitia*, or popular
assembly). See also Mommsen, Book I, c. ii.

[2] The magistrates possessed of *imperium* at the beginning of the
second century were (i) the two consuls, (ii) six prætors, of whom two
administered justice at Rome and four governed provinces, (iii) proconsuls and proprætors in increasing number, i.e. former consuls and
prætors whose *imperium* was prolonged for military functions after the
expiration of their year of office. In theory, the *imperium* knew no
limits ; but in practice distinctions were drawn between the " greater "
and " less " *imperium* of the consuls and prætors respectively, and between
the exercise of *imperium* in the civil area of Rome (*domi*) and in the
military (*militiae*). The *imperium* of the pro-magistrate was restricted
to the latter field. Except in the case of the dictator, whose *imperium*
was *sine fine* (without limit), the *imperium* was restricted to a specific
provincia (see n. 2 to p. 228). The watch-dog was thus provided with a
leash.

[3] In the first century B.C., the resolutions of the senate (*senatus consulta*) began to acquire legal force through a virtual usurpation of authority
alien to the spirit of the constitution.

in an era of commercial and imperial expansion, by a coterie of great Whig houses. At Rome also the senate and the higher magistracy became the monopoly of noble, i.e. office-bearing, families.[1] This growing exclusiveness, combined with the spread of wealth and luxury among the ruling aristocracy, issued inevitably in the outbreak of the disease chronic in the ancient city-state, i.e., party faction; from 134 onwards, civil conflict between senate and democracy raged with an intensity hitherto unknown in Roman history. A like narrowness was reflected in the dealings of the Roman government with the peoples of Italy. The line between Roman citizens and the non-citizen population became far more rigid. Those Italian communities which had joined Hannibal were reduced to practical serfdom. Even the loyal cities, e.g. those with Latin rights, found that they were left with burdens in lieu of privileges. When we consider that the Italians were akin in stock to the Romans, that in energy and character they were at least their equals, and that they were compelled to bear the brunt of military service in remote quarters of the empire, we can appreciate the ruinous issues that were bound to flow from this short-sighted and autocratic policy. In effect, all the symptoms that herald an epoch of internal disruption were rife in Rome and Italy before the close of the second century.

§ 18. The same period saw the foundation by Rome of her system of provincial government.[2] The organisation of a new province was determined by a law, based on the report of a senatorial commission, which laid down the principles of administration and finance. As regards taxation, the practice was to maintain, as far as possible, the system previously in existence.[3] The law of Rome was introduced, save in the case of privileged cities, " allied " and " free," which had the right,

[1] This new nobility was entirely unconnected with the old distinction of patricians and plebeians, which had ceased to have practical significance. Rank was now measured by the number of forefathers who had held the highest offices. It became increasingly difficult for a " new man " to enter the ring of noble families.

[2] The word *provincia* meant originally the special function of the magistrate. When in 241 the first extra-Italian territory, Sicily, was acquired, it was entrusted to a magistrate as his special sphere; and the like was done in the case of subsequent territorial extensions. The word thus came to mean a territorial region under the government of a magistrate with *imperium*.

[3] So the old system of tithes was preserved in Sicily and in Asia. It led to the un-economic and oppressive practice of farming out the collection of the tithes in kind to *publicani*, who sold the produce and paid over a fixed sum to the state, keeping the profits on the sales.

if they chose, to their own law, and were exempt from interference by the governor. Even beyond these limits local law
and custom were widely tolerated. Roman colonies and *municipia*, again, formed self-governing communities within the
province. Hellenic cities, especially in Sicily and the East,
enjoyed a large measure of autonomy; the Romans, with their
keen eye for adjustment of methods to local requirements,
realised from the first that civilized Greeks needed very different
handling from the barbaric tribes of Africa or Spain. Yet
even in these western provinces privileged urban communities
were fostered as centres for the diffusion of Roman culture.
In the provinces, as in Italy, old local confederations were everywhere broken up. Beyond the limits of the privileged towns,
the authority of the governor was absolute, save only for the
terms of the original constitution. Each province was assigned
to a prætor, the number of these magistrates being increased
to six after the second Punic war; or, later, to an ex-consul or
ex-prætor, continued in power for the purpose during a second
year. He was assisted by a quæstor as financial administrator,
and by a military and civil staff. Since a governor held office
only for a year, and brought out his staff with him from Rome,
the difficulty of securing continuity in provincial administration
was very great. It was met, partly by the standing constitution
of the province, partly by the fact that each successive governor,
like the prætors at Rome, published an edict on entering his office,
normally inclusive of the contents of the edicts of his predecessors.
While in office, he was sole commander of the forces, sole head
of the executive, and supreme judge. In a province where
military operations were not called for, the judicial circuits
constituted his chief duty.[1] As no Roman magistrate holding
the *imperium* could be called to account during the tenure of
his office, while charges lodged subsequently were heard at
Rome and before a biassed tribunal, the temptations to rapacity
were almost irresistible. In early days, governors prided themselves on their integrity; but, as Mommsen observes, " It is

[1] The governor would judge cases normally by native law, which
the Romans were careful to sanction. In criminal cases, a *consilium* of
Romans, drawn from residents in the province and from the governor's
staff, would be summoned for consultation. The two duties that no
governor could neglect were war and judicial sessions. In other matters,
a lax administrator might let a peaceful province govern itself, often with
disastrous results. Cicero, when proconsul in Cilicia, enquired into the
methods of the local magistrates and found that they had been plundering
the local exchequer for years.

not practicable for any length of time to be at once republican and king." [1] The spread of luxury in the Roman aristocracy intensified the evils of provincial absolutism. Even a just governor found it increasingly difficult to control the host of tax-farmers and financial agents that swarmed over the more wealthy provinces. As time went on, just governors were few and far between. The system was doomed to eventual disaster for lack of effective control over the provincial autocrat. The central government was far away, and there was no trained bureaucracy to ensure permanent supervision on the spot. The signs of coming disruption that we have noted in Rome and Italy were evident also, and in an aggravated form, throughout the provincial empire.

§ 19. The transformation of a simple agricultural community into a populous and wealthy centre of world-commerce and world-dominion involved corresponding changes in the tenor and processes of the law. The period between the legislation of the Twelve Tables and the close of the second century was a great constructive period in legal history, in which the rigidity of the early code was broken down, new machinery devised and a systematic body of jurisprudence brought into being by means of interpretation, revision and enlargement. To the two recognised sources of (i) historic custom, which was constantly creative of new law, and (ii) positive statutes, in which this age was prolific, there had been added in the fourth century (iii) the prætorian edict.[2] The higher magistrates had always possessed the right of issuing, orally or in writing, notifications to the public (edicta); and when in 367 the judicial functions of the consuls were transferred to a special magistrate, the prætor of the city (praetor urbanus), it became customary for him to affix in court, for the information of litigants, tablets containing the formulæ of his procedure and the rules in accordance with which he proposed to apply the law. This edict,

[1] Mommsen, Book III, c. ii.

[2] The prætorian edict was the source of most later Roman law. It represents the work, not of professed lawyers, but of generations of practical administrators, who adjusted the civil law to the requirements of Italy and the provinces. It is called in the *Digest* " the living voice of the civil law." The ground of the development of prætorian equity lies in the practice of the prætors to grant a " formula " (i.e. a decree appointing a *judex* and instructing him on the law of the case), whenever they considered that an action, even if not covered by the narrow civil law, was reasonable and just. The edict indicated the sort of cases for which the prætor was prepared to grant a formula (i.e. to allow an action) and the nature of the instructions which he would issue to the *judex*.

called the " standing edict " (*edictum perpetuum*), to distinguish
it from incidental orders relative to particular occasions, was
in theory valid only during the prætor's year of office; but
it became the practice for each successive prætor to embody
in his edict the main provisions of that of his predecessor, with
such modifications and additions as were deemed necessary.
Thus arose a body of judge-made law which soon took rank
beside the customary and statute law of Rome. The prætor,
be it noted, had no power to legislate or to adjudge a suit; he
could only grant or refuse an action at law by means of a written
" formula " addressed to the *judex*, the private citizen whom
he appointed to decide the facts of the case. But this restricted
function was extended by the *lex Æbutia* (*c.* 150), which em-
powered the prætor in giving instructions to the *judex* to modify
or virtually to nullify, the literal provisions of the civil law in
the light of equity and reason.[1] A single example will make
clear the nature of this development. By the strict terms of
the law, an engagement entered into in due form was binding,
even when secured by the fraud of one of the parties. The
prætor, though bound to grant an action, would notify that
in granting it he would instruct the *judex* to penalise the defendant only if he found that no fraud had been committed.
Such procedure was capable of almost indefinite extension,
and furnished an effective means for securing the victory of
the spirit over the letter of the law. Moreover, this same period
saw the birth of scientific jurisprudence. Up to the close of
the fourth century, the principles of legal interpretation remained
a closed secret in the hands of the priestly college. In 304 a
freedman of Appius Claudius the censor published certain of
the pontifical rules, and half a century later the first plebeian
pontifex maximus started the practice of giving legal advice to
the citizens in public. Henceforward a knowledge of the law
was open to all Rome. As a natural consequence, a legal literature came into being. Practical law books were followed by
methodical expositions of the principles of the civil law. In
the last century of the republic, the foundations were laid of the

---

[1] The Æbutian law placed the prætorian *formula* on a level with
actions under the civil law. Since the procedure by *formula* was simpler
and more elastic, the older methods, though never abrogated, fell largely
into disuse. Moreover, the specific instructions on points of law embodied
in the *formulae* rendered the *judex* to whom the case was referred more
dependent than heretofore on the prætor's ruling. Henceforward prætorian
equity dominates the history of Roman law.

system of legal science which was elaborated by the great jurists of the early empire.[1]

§ 20. By far the most important legal development in this epoch was that of the law of nations (*jus gentium*).[2] The civil law was confined to Roman citizens or to members of a non-Roman community to whom legal capacity had been guaranteed by special treaty. When Rome became a great commercial power, there was obvious need for a law which should be applicable to foreigners, both in their dealings with citizens and among themselves. It was to meet this need that a second prætor was appointed in 242, with the special function of dispensing justice in suits where non-citizens were involved. His annual edict, embodying the necessary adjustments of the civil law to alien peoples, formed the basis of the law of nations.[3] It may be described as that part of the *jus civile*, which accorded with the local law of other peoples, modified to suit varying conditions, and enlarged by the assimilation of Hellenic and other foreign elements into a body of equitable principles suitable for application throughout the Roman world. This was no sudden creation; it grew by slow gradations in the course of centuries, and represented the accumulated experience of a race which possessed in a singular degree the power of adapting legal means to the ends of a political society. It reacted in turn on the civil law, chiefly through the equity law (*jus honorarium*) of the urban prætor.[4] Eventually, and by virtue of

[1] The answers to legal questions given by celebrated jurisconsults (the *responsa prudentium*) depended for their authority on the fame of the individual who gave them. Professedly interpretations of the Twelve Tables, they involved in fact modification, expansion and reconstruction. Principles were developed which the framers of the early code had never dreamed of. Maine (*Ancient Law*, c. ii) points out that this kind of law was the work, not of the Bench (for at Rome there was nothing analogous to the Bench of judges in modern England), but of the Bar, though *prudentes* did not plead in court. Cicero was not a *prudens*. The opportunity thus afforded to the lawyer to consider hypothetical cases, as well as actual matters of fact, facilitated generalisation and the formulation of broad principles. It must be remembered that almost every Roman who aspired to public office in republican times was trained to a knowledge of the law. It was the one serious profession, beside that of arms : and most of the governing class practised both.

[2] On the *jus gentium*, see de Zulueta in *The Legacy of Rome*, pp. 199 ff.

[3] The second prætor was called the *praetor peregrinus*, because he adjudicated among non-citizens (*peregrini*). The origins of the *jus gentium* lay in a time prior to the institution of this office. It must be understood that *jus gentium* does not mean " international law," but the law applicable to individuals belonging to non-Roman peoples. It was mainly concerned with contracts and was based on the custom prevalent among Mediterranean communities. See Maine, *Ancient Law*, c. iii.

[4] The law of the prætorian edicts received this title, as issuing from the *imperium* of the magistrate (*honos* = magisterial office).

its inherent reasonableness, it replaced the narrow provisions of the *jus civile* as the law of Roman citizens. Thus it came to be regarded as a universal code, valid for all mankind and based on the sense of equity natural to man as man. From the court of the *praetor peregrinus* it spread to the provinces, where existing local law was supplemented by the law of nations and the edicts of the governors. The governors brought back to Rome their experience of foreign law, and helped to build on broad foundations the fabric of Roman jurisprudence. Thus, in the fullness of time, the local law of a single Italian city-state, enriched by accretions from alien sources and transmuted by the adaptive genius of the Roman people, was fashioned into a juristic system for the whole Mediterranean world.[1]

V. CONCLUSION (§ 21).

§ 21. Before the world could reap the fruits of Roman jurisprudence, the republic was doomed to endure the throes of revolution. The second century had brought Rome face to face with the problem : Could a city-state with republican institutions rule an empire? Was it credible that, where Periclean Athens had failed, Rome, with her meagre experience of self-government, would succeed? Despite her ability to conquer and to police, she had never proved equal to the task of creating an organic public life. Her conception of authority remained to the end external and disciplinary. The Roman state rested upon force, and the weapon, as is its wont, recoiled upon the user. How deep-seated was the malady that preyed upon the social organism will be manifest if we recall the symptoms noted in the preceding pages. Economic stability was sapped by the wealth that flowed into the capital from all quarters of the Mediterranean, by the simultaneous rise of plutocracy and pauperism, by the decline of agriculture and the substitution of slave labourers for the free cultivators of the soil. Politically, power tended to be concentrated in the

[1] The development of Roman law in the epoch between the Twelve Tables and the fall of the republic may be best studied in connexion with the history of contracts. See Maine, *Ancient Law*, c. ix : " the positive duty resulting from one man's reliance on the word of another is among the slowest conquests of advancing civilization." In early societies, where rights and duties are not voluntarily created by the individual, but are either (*a*) inherent in the station to which he is born, or (*b*) commands issued by the head of the family or tribe, there is no room for contract. The civilized world owes both contracts and wills to the legal genius of ancient Rome.

hands of a short-sighted and unimaginative oligarchy, enriched by the plunder of the provinces, who traded on the achievements of their forefathers and knew no public obligation save that of their own maintenance in office. Equally self-interested were the two centres of opposition to the senate, the order of knights (*equites*), comprising the rich bankers· and merchants, and the indolent city proletariate, who thronged the assembly to barter the suffrages of the sovereign people for a corn dole or for payment in hard cash. The agricultural middle class that had saved Rome from Hannibal either had vanished or lived too far from the capital to play an effective part in public life. The cleavage between the Roman and the Italian grew ever wider; the grant of the franchise was denied, and the " allies " of Rome, who bore the brunt of her military service, were treated as alien dependents. Morally, the old standards of piety and civic virtue had fallen into decay; the rectitude and conscientiousness which were once the distinctive glory of the Roman, were his no more. The Roman had learnt to rule by learning to obey; now, even in the legions, a mutiny of citizen-soldiers was frequent. Touched by the spirit of Greece, the habit of solidarity and loyalty to the republic was yielding to the claims of personal ambition. Was it possible that a community, torn by internal faction, who had alienated their Italian kinsmen, should maintain control of a vast provincial empire ? The armies were massed upon the frontiers under the command of proconsuls to whom, and not to the republic, they had sworn allegiance.[1] Here was the point of danger for the coming time. How long would a victorious general, with unlimited authority over his soldiers and the resources of his province, be content to exhibit the self-restraint and civic loyalty that had been a second nature to the Roman of early days ? It was the conjunction of these conditions—the inherent inability of a city to govern the world, the demoralisation of the Roman senate and people, and the new-born power of the provincial governor—that led in the course of the succeeding century to the fall of the republic and the creation of the Roman empire.

---

[1] The *sacramentum* or oath of military allegiance was (probably) in early days the oath sworn under penalty to the gods by both parties to a private transaction, each asseverating that his assertion of claim was true. See Mommsen, Book I, c. ii, and *Encycl. Britannica*, art. *Roman Law* (11th edn.), vol. xxiii, pp. 548 ff. The use of this word to signify the Christian " sacraments " and the Mithraic and Greek " mysteries " is found in Tertullian. See Hastings' *Encyclop. of Religion and Ethics*, art. *Sacraments (Christian Western)*.

CHAPTER VIII

THE ROMAN EMPIRE

I. The Institution of the Empire (§§ 1–8).

A. *The Fall of the Republic* (§§ 1–3).

§ 1. The story of the fall of the republic is of extraordinary interest, both for the sake of the events and personalities, and because we have so full a knowledge of the period. It opens with the tribunate of Tiberius Gracchus in 133, and closes with the definitive establishment of the empire by Augustus in 27 B.C. We saw in the last chapter how the seeds of revolution were germinating in the Roman state from the moment when it became the sovereign of the Mediterranean world. The problem confronting it was that which beset ancient civilization throughout its history, of uniting civic liberty with the expansion of empire. The Romans, with their capacity for adjusting principles of government to varying situations, might have discovered a solution, had they been able to realise the meaning of self-government within the bounds of their own civic community. The cause of their failure lay in the degeneration of public life. The Roman republic was divided against itself, and therefore could not stand. Of the three organs of the state, the magistracy, the senate and the popular assembly, the two last were already evincing signs of atrophy. The *imperium* of the magistrate alone retained its force, and, when all checks had been removed, asserted itself in a new form and with overwhelming power. Victorious generals, seeing that the state lay at their mercy, seized the sovereignty thus placed within their grasp. Amid all the changes and chances of its destiny, the root-idea of the Roman commonwealth persisted in unbroken continuity. "Arms and the man" was the watchword alike of the Rome of Aeneas and of the historic empire. The *imperium* was the bed-rock of the world-despotism that arose out of the ruins of the republic. It stood forth, naked and unashamed, as the sole source of authority and law. And in the shadow of the throne, where senate and assembly once had stood, loomed ominously the dark presences of the legionary and the bureaucrat.

§ 2. We will summarise briefly the successive phases of the crisis :

(i) The attack on the governing aristocracy was opened in

133, when Tiberius Gracchus, as leader of the democratic opposition, carried a law to allot farms in Italy to free cultivators at the expense of rich occupiers of state lands. What is significant is that he developed the latent powers of the tribunate as a weapon against both the magistrates and the senate, and that he found himself forced to use those powers unconstitutionally. On his attempting to hold office for a second year, he was murdered in a riot fomented by his political enemies. Ten years later (123–122) his brother Caius, also as tribune, took the field on wider ground, and, securing the support of the financial order (the *equites*) by granting them privileges as tax-farmers and as *judices* in the courts, and that of the populace by a corn dole and the promise of colonies overseas, challenged the senate's control of provincial administration and of finance. The senate retaliated by open violence, and the party struggle was brought to the verge of civil war.

(ii) Thus far the conflict was confined to the political arena, though unconstitutional weapons had been employed by both the contending parties. The tribunate had suddenly been revealed as the most formidable power in the state. The senate emerged from the conflict victorious but shaken, and henceforward the reformers looked more and more to military support. They found their opportunity, when in the closing years of the second century Rome was roused by a menace that threatened her very existence from without. Germanic tribes had invaded Gaul, crushed the Roman armies in the southern province, overrun Spain, and were about to move on Italy. An able soldier, Caius Marius, summoned year after year to the consulship by popular acclamation, remodelled the army, and by two decisive victories (102, 101) saved the state. His military reforms, the abolition of distinctions of rank and wealth in the legion, and the substitution of voluntary enlistment for the citizen-levy, by creating a professional army, severed the tie that bound the soldier to the civil community. Henceforward the successful general was the arbiter of internal politics. Early in the first century the government was faced by a second crisis even nearer home. When Caius Gracchus had proposed in a spirit of true statesmanship to redress the grievances of the Italians by granting them the franchise, he had been deserted by the city democracy.[1]

---

[1] The Italians represented the best stock in the Roman state; that they had to bear the heavier military burdens without corresponding privileges is the most serious proof of the incompetence of the government to handle problems of state. Many attempts were made, from 125 onwards, to redress their grievances, but in vain.

In 90 and 89 the Italians won the franchise by force of arms. This conflict passed without a break into a civil war (89, 88) between two rival generals, Marius, the champion of the popular party, and Lucius Cornelius Sulla, the champion of the senate. Sulla's triumph made him master of the state, and as dictator he used the power of the sword to restore the senate to almost uncontrolled supremacy (81). The Sullan restoration was itself a revolution, in that it was effected by arms. After a ruthless extermination of his political opponents, he reigned as an absolute sovereign; and though he acted in the interest of the old order and resigned his despotism when his work was done, it was inevitable that others should follow where he had shown the way, and use military power for less impersonal ends.[1]

§ 3. (iii) The twenty years that followed the Sullan restoration revealed the incapacity of the senate to maintain the position he had won for it. Foreign war, this time in the East against king Mithradates of Pontus in Asia Minor (88–64), brought to the front a new general in the person of Pompey (Cnæus Pompeius). In 67 and 66 he was entrusted with extraordinary powers that clearly foreshadow the later autocracy of the emperors. By the Gabinian and Manilian laws he received the *imperium* with preeminence over all provincial governors in the East for three years, a staff of twenty-five *legati*, and unlimited resources of men, ships and money. After carrying out the reorganisation of the East, he returned to the capital in 61, the commanding personality in the Roman state.[2]

[1] Mommsen's brilliant sketch of Sulla's work and personality (Book IV, c. 10) should be read, but with extreme caution. Sulla unquestionably possessed great ability, alike as soldier, diplomatist and politician; he showed also considerable literary taste, introduced Aristotle's works at Rome, wrote his own memoirs, etc., and had a gift of ironical humour. An aristocrat to the backbone, his *hauteur* made him indifferent to personal power. He was entirely without moral scruple, and effected little that was constructive. His most enduring work was the organisation of criminal law. Anyone who wished to argue that political expediency is a futile guide when divorced from ideal ends would find in the swift collapse of Sulla's restoration of the senate a striking confirmation of his case.

[2] Mithradates was a most formidable antagonist. His death, after defeat, in 63, was followed by the reconstruction of western Asia by Pompey, referred to in the text. It occupied the best part of two years and was of permanent importance. To the old provinces of Asia and Cilicia were added three new provinces, Bithynia, Syria and Crete. In Palestine, Pompey restricted the temporal power of the Jewish high priest, removing from his jurisdiction the Hellenic cities which had arisen in numbers under the Seleucids. Pompey showed great wisdom in recognising vassal princes, free cities, tribal cantons, as instruments of government under Rome. He left western Asia, in a position analogous to that of British India at the present day, part administered directly by Roman

(iv) The history of the next twelve years (61–48) centres round three persons, of whom two owed their position to the support of the legions. On the one hand, Pompey, athirst for power yet too timid to clutch the prize within his grasp, drifted eventually into the rôle of a defender of the senate and the republic. On the other hand, the democratic leader, Caius Julius Cæsar, the nephew of Marius, who in youth had narrowly escaped death at the hands of Sulla, secured, by a temporary coalition with Pompey and the rich financier Crassus, a military command in Gaul, analogous to that previously conferred on Pompey in the East.[1] During his nine years' tenure of this command (58–49) he not only forged the weapon with which he dealt the death-blow to the republic, but by his conquest of Gaul and the extension of the Roman frontiers to the Rhine staved off for centuries to come the tide of barbarian invasion. In this, as in so many incidents in his career, Cæsar displayed in an extraordinary degree the distinctive capacity of so many great men in history, of blending personal ambition with vital national interests. Between these two rivals, eyeing one another with mutual suspicion and sharpening their swords for the combat, stood the figure of the great orator, Marcus Tullius Cicero, a liberal conservative, who strove hard to save the republican constitution from falling a prey to military despotism. Like Demosthenes at Athens in the fourth century, he filled the rôle of the last champion of a free city-state. His policy was one of twofold reform : to unite the senate and the financial interest (the *equites*) in support of law and order against anarchy, and to broaden the basis of the state by associating the middle classes in the Italian municipalities with the government of the Roman state.[2] But the narrow rigidity of the senatorial nobility, who, having learnt nothing and forgotten nothing during the turmoil

---

officials, part in the form of protected states. See Duckworth in Jackson and Lake's *Acts* (*Prolegomena*, vol. i, pp. 177 ff.), who compares the king of Cappadocia to the Nizam of Hyderabad, and the extra-Roman kingdom of Armenia to that of Afghanistan. Rome was studious to tolerate all varieties of religious belief and local custom. Vassal princedoms *within* the empire disappear in the first century A.D.

[1] Cæsar (born probably in 102) was late in rising to the front rank in Roman politics. Until his consulship in 59, he was a dark horse, though he had shown independence in opposition to Sulla in youth and conspicuous ability as a soldier and administrator when prætor in Spain in 61. On Roman Gaul, see below, § 15. It is impossible to judge to what extent Cæsar planned his despotism in the years prior to 49.

[2] This twofold policy was summarised in the watchwords, *concordia ordinum* ("harmony of the orders") and *consensus Italiae* ("the united opinion of Italy").

of over fifty years, still clung desperately to the last shreds of
their monopoly of power, and the personal ambition of the two
great military captains, rendered futile all Cicero's efforts to
combine senators and *equites*, Romans and Italians, in defence
of the historic principles of the constitution. Even he, born
Whig though he was, was driven at the close to advocate the
institution of a single " moderator of the republic," who, he
vainly hoped, might rule in loyal co-operation with the senate,
by law and not by the sword. Had the republic been capable
of salvation, it would have been saved by Cicero. It is equally
true that if Cicero had been capable of saving it, he would have
recognised that the task was impossible. That in the event he
died rather than renounce the republican ideal goes far to explain
the hold he won on the respect of after-times. For the rest,
vanity and lack of courage blinded him to the realities of the
situation he endeavoured to control.[1]

(v) We are thus brought to the final act of the drama, when
in the spring of 49 Cæsar at the head of his army crossed the
Rubicon, the little stream that formed the boundary between
his military command and Italy. To the amazement of all,
who looked trembling for retaliation at his hand for Sulla's
massacre of the democrats, his victorious advance was marked
by a moderation and clemency that won him general support
in Rome and Italy. The next year (48) saw Pompey crushed
at Pharsalia. It was the triumph of genius over talent. The
republicans held out in the west for three years longer; but
in 46 Cato, the uncompromising idealist of the party, fell on
his sword at Utica in Africa, and in 45 the crowning victory
of Munda in Spain left Cæsar the unchallenged sovereign of the
Roman world.[2]

[1] Cicero's letters (a selection, translated admirably by Jeans, has been
published by Macmillan) are an invaluable commentary on this period.
See also the historical introductions in Tyrrell's edition of Cicero's correspondence. On Cicero as man of letters, see below, § 19.

[2] Cato was a rigid Tory, who modelled his policy on that of his ancestor,
the censor of the early second century; his uncompromising advocacy
of a narrow senatorial policy, backed by his personal integrity, proved
a serious hindrance to Cicero's liberal policy. Cato's high moral character,
his republican idealism, and the fact of his self-inflicted death on realising
the hopelessness of further struggle, made him an object of reverence to
after time. So Lucan, under the early empire, wrote the famous line :

" *Victrix causa diis placuit, sed victa Catoni* " (i. 158).

(" The victorious cause won the favour of the gods, but the vanquished
that of Cato.")

Dante's selection of Cato, as the type of antique pagan virtue, to be the
guardian of the shore beneath the mount of Purgatory (*Purg.*, canto i),

B. Julius Cæsar (§§ 4–6).

§ 4. Cæsar invested his sovereignty with a show of legal
sanction by concentrating in his person a number of republican
offices, such as the consulship and the tribunate. It was definitely
established in 45 by the bestowal of the dictatorship for life.
This revival of an office which, save in Sulla's case, had long
passed into desuetude, as well as his adoption of the style *Imperator*, shows how once again, as in the old days of the monarchy,
the *imperium* was the sole fountain of authority in the state.
Just as the monarchy had been transformed into a republic by
the dual limitation of collegiality (two consular colleagues in
place of a single king) and of time (election for one year), so now
the abolition of these restrictions brought about the change from
a republic to a monarchy. A real revolution had been effected,
in true Roman fashion, without an absolute suppression of constitutional forms. In virtue of these and other powers, Cæsar
appointed magistrates and provincial governors, enlarged the
number of executive offices, and wielded exclusive control over
questions of war and peace, foreign affairs, and the administration
of the empire. Popular election became a mere form for ratifying
the nominations of the dictator. The senate was increased in
numbers to nine hundred, of whom many were provincials; for
Cæsar initiated the imperial policy of levelling up the provincials
to equality with Romans. High offices in communities overseas
were thrown open to freedmen. In effect, the senate became an
instrument for registering his edicts. In legislation he instituted
a vast body of measures, many of them of far-reaching scope,
including economic and agrarian reforms, the uniform regulation
of municipal constitutions, the extension of the franchise, e.g.
to Gades (Cadiz) in Spain, first of provincial cities to receive the
grant, and the reorganisation of the fiscal system.[1] Great

---

was based on Virgil's picture of Cato dispensing justice to the virtuous
dead (*Æn.*, viii, 670, " *his dantem jura Catonem* ").

[1] A large part of the *lex Julia municipalis*, dealing with the Italian
municipalities, and fragments of the *lex Rubria*, dealing with the urban
organisation of Cisalpine Gaul, are extant. These laws distinguish between the jurisdiction of the Roman prætor and that of the local magistracy, and regulate the form of municipal government by magistrates,
senate and assemblies, which had grown up in preceding times. Cisalpine
Gaul was admitted to full citizenship by Cæsar, and incorporated into
Italy by Augustus (then Octavian) in 42. Cæsar abolished the bad
system of taxation by tithes in Sicily and Asia; and handled with great
ability the economic situation caused by the civil wars. In Rome he
restricted the corn doles and abolished the corrupt popular clubs. He
intended, but did not carry out, a codification of the law.

public works were planned and carried out in Italy and the
provinces; transmarine colonies were founded, e.g. at Corinth
and on the site of Carthage. Cæsar's reformed calendar is still
accepted, with slight modifications, by the civilized world. The
swiftness and energy with which he designed and effected a
great historic reconstruction were as amazing as his movements
in the field. Hegel justly discerned in Cæsar " the paragon of
the Roman adaptation of means to ends." [1] In the last five
years of his life he spent but eighteen months in Rome, and his
achievements represent merely the initial stages of a comprehensive scheme of imperial government. Nevertheless they
determined the lines on which the Roman world was governed
for centuries—the personal rule of a monarch through his personally appointed staff of officers, the effective control of the
legions and the provincial administration, the extension of citizen-
privileges throughout the empire, the maintenance of internal
peace and equal law, the delimitation of the frontiers and their
defence against non-civilized invaders. In all these respects,
Augustus, his successor, built on the foundations laid so swiftly,
yet with so sure an insight, by Julius Cæsar.

§ 5. The last-mentioned problem, that of frontier defence,
had been perforce neglected during the epoch of civil revolution.
We have spoken of the danger that threatened Italy at the
close of the second century through the westward movement
of barbarian hordes from their homes in the north and east
across the Rhine and the Danube. Then Marius with his reformed army had saved Rome. Half a century later Cæsar's
conquest of Gaul permanently secured her northern frontier.[2]
In Africa, Cyrene (74) and Numidia (46) were added to the roll
of provinces. The immediately pressing danger was from the
East. Pompey (67–62) had reorganised the political system of
western Asia at the close of the Mithradatic War.[3] The Seleucid

[1] *Philos. of History*, Part III, Sect. II.
[2] Cæsar was only just in time. In his first campaign in Gaul (58)
he had to face two invasions, that of the Helvetii along the Rhone and
that of the Germans under Ariovistus through the Burgundy gap between
the Vosges and the Jura. Ariovistus was on the point of establishing
a powerful Teutonic state in Gaul. Had Cæsar not been victorious, the
Teutonic tribes must have overwhelmed the empire and therewith the
entire structure of Græco-Roman civilization. Cæsar's conquest post-
poned the catastrophe until that civilization, and, with it, the Christian
faith, had taken root among the invading peoples. The new territory
was at first attached to the old province of Narbonese Gaul; Augustus
established three new Gallic provinces.
[3] See above, § 3. In addition to the provinces there mentioned, Crete
was attached by Augustus to the province of Africa; Cyprus (incorporated

dynasty ceased to be; their western dominions passed to Rome, while the new province of Syria marched with the Parthian empire in the valley of the Euphrates. In 54 the Parthians annihilated a Roman army at Carrhæ; honour and safety alike called for the military action that had already been too long delayed. Here, as in Gaul, the problem was real and urgent. Cæsar did not manufacture wars for wars' sake; in east, as in west, the existence of the Roman state was in jeopardy. Cæsar lost no time in grappling with the issue; in the spring of 44 the eastern legions awaited their commander; but on the Ides of March (March 15th), the eve of his departure from Rome, he was attacked by conspirators in the senate-house and perished at the foot of Pompey's statue.

§ 6. The murder of Cæsar has been justly described as the greatest blunder in history, for it accomplished nothing save the removal from the scene of the greatest Roman; after thirteen years of civil war—the death agony of the republic—the empire was reconstituted by his adopted heir. The circumstances of the problem did not admit of any alternative. In the view of after-ages, nurtured in the traditions of the Roman empire, for whom that empire was sacred, not only as the fount of law and civilization, but as the divinely predestined instrument for the spread of the Christian faith, the deed appeared as the blackest of crimes. In the lowest depths of Dante's *Inferno* were placed the three arch-malefactors of history, Judas Iscariot, the traitor to the founder of the catholic church, Brutus and Cassius, the traitors to the founder of the catholic empire. Crime it was not, but a blunder; for, like the passionate resistance of Demosthenes to Philip of Macedon, it was the outcome of an intelligible idealism. We have observed again and again in these pages how profound was the value to Greek and Roman civilization of the city-state, with its atmosphere of free discussion and civic equality. Small wonder if the descendants of the men who under the ægis of the city-state had fashioned the Roman empire, with its majestic structure of law and government, were jealous for the institutions that had made Rome and Romans great. No ties of personal gratitude, no experience of Cæsar's clemency or admiration for his genius, could destroy that intense devotion for the republic to which he had dealt the death-blow.[1] We cannot expect the

in 58) was attached at first to Cilicia but constituted as a separate province by Augustus.
[1] Cæsar's clemency to his fellow-countrymen was notorious; he refrained from proscriptions and confiscation, and in assigning lands to his

last republicans of Rome to have understood, what Cicero failed to understand, that the doom of the city-state was sealed. They avenged the blow by means which the moral code alike of Greece and Rome sanctioned as honourable, when employed against a despot, and slew Cæsar, not for motives of personal vengeance or ambition, but for civic liberty and in the name of Rome.

C. Augustus (§§ 7, 8).

§ 7. In 31, by the victory of Actium over Antony, the young Octavian, Cæsar's great-nephew and adopted heir, became, in Shakespeare's phrase, " sole sir o' the world." [1] It was Octavian, better known to history by his title of Augustus, who perfected in detail the imperial system under which the world was governed for well-nigh three hundred years. The decree is still extant, inscribed on stone, which proclaimed the motive and character of this achievement.[2] It opens with a sentence that rings strangely in our ears when we think of the real nature of his work : " I transferred the republic from my own authority to the control of the Roman senate and people."

What was the intention of those words ? They meant that Augustus, to quote a modern writer, had " learnt his lesson at the foot of Pompey's statue." The haughty spirit of Julius— we may recall Dante's picture of him among the great of ancient days, " Cæsar with the falcon eyes "—would not brook to conciliate republican sentiment by a show of citizen equality. Augustus, the dispassionate master of statecraft, veiled an

veterans carefully respected the rights of existing owners. His answer to Cicero's expression of gratitude for his clemency towards the political adversaries who had fallen into his power at the surrender of Corfinium impressed Macaulay as " the finest sentence ever written." It is as follows : " I triumph and rejoice that my action should have obtained your approval. Nor am I disturbed when I hear it said that those whom I have sent off alive and free will again bear arms against me; for there is nothing which I so much covet as that I should be like myself, and they like themselves " (see Trevelyan, Life and Letters of Macaulay, c. xvi). But Cæsar's was not a lovable character and, as far as our knowledge goes, he made no real friends. Cicero, who disliked and distrusted him, testifies to the force of his personality. In both these respects, we are reminded of Marlborough and Napoleon rather than of Alexander.

[1] Antony and Cleopatra, Act V, Scene 2. Octavian's father, Caius Octavius, was an Italian bourgeois who became governor of Macedonia and married the daughter of Cæsar's sister. His son was born in 63, the year of Cicero's consulship, and was therefore nineteen at the time of Cæsar's murder, and thirty-one when he won the Battle of Actium.

[2] The Ancyran monument from Angora in Asia Minor. Copies were set up in various centres in the Roman world. Augustus defined his position as head of the state in 27, and again in 23. Both groups of measures are treated together in this section.

absolute autocracy under the guise of constitutionalism. A thorough child of Rome in his respect for outward forms and established precedent, he was resolved to preserve in being the cherished institutions of the past. Julius had been styled *dictator*, a term which offended republican sentiment by its association with military command, and *imperator*, the title by which soldiers hailed their victorious general; Augustus would be simply *princeps*, i.e. the first man among his fellow-senators.[1] In his bearing towards the Roman nobility, the dispossessed lords of the world, he acted the part superbly. His life was simple and severe, without a trace of the etiquette and ceremonial of a court. He saw to it that his powers were conferred in the old republican fashion by the vote of the senate or the assembly. His autocracy rested on the combination in his single person of two republican offices, the tribunate, the highest in rank, which formed the basis of his authority in Rome, and the consular *imperium*, with primacy over all other holders, which secured to him the control of the army and the provinces. These were precisely the two powers whose enlargement had brought about the dissolution of the republic in the preceding age. Henceforth the army took the oath of allegiance to the *princeps* alone. As chief pontiff, he was master of the machinery of the state religion, which was still an important factor in law and politics. The same spirit of conservatism, which Augustus displayed in determining his personal status, was visible in his readjustment of the system of government. The city proletariate, it is true, was shorn of its legislative powers, and the assemblies of the people quickly degenerated into a farce.[2] On the other hand, the senate was treated with studied consideration. It conferred the *imperium* on the sovereign, voted from among his list of nominees for candidates for office, and passed decrees which had the force of law. The *princeps* and the senate ranked on an equality as supreme tribunals; each controlled a separate treasury, and the government of the empire was partitioned between the two authorities. But it was significant that the provinces entrusted to the senate were the peaceful districts of the interior; those on the frontiers, where the legions were concentrated, were kept by the emperor in his own hands. Egypt, in particular, because of its importance strategically and as the chief granary of Rome, was administered by him through

[1] Until the time of Diocletian, *princeps* is the proper title of the emperor, and *principate* of the empire.
[2] There are only two recorded examples of popular legislation after Tiberius.

a prefect of equestrian rank inferior in status to the governors of the regular imperial provinces. These last were styled *legates* or military lieutenants, while the senatorial governors retained the republican title of *proconsuls*.[1] It is obvious that this shadow of dual control was an artificial experiment designed to conciliate the old Roman aristocracy. For the time it served its purpose; but already under Augustus' successor the servility of the senate showed that, in spite of outward forms, the real power rested with the emperor and with him alone.[2]

§ 8. Such, in principle, was the *régime* established by Augustus in Rome; if we look farther afield, there are three features of the work carried out by him during his long reign (31 B.C.–A.D. 14) that are deserving of special notice. First, as regards the administration of Italy and the provinces. Augustus strove earnestly to realise the hope that Cicero had vainly cherished of an incorporation of the Italians on equal terms in the fabric of the Roman state. They were encouraged to look upon the great past of Rome as their own and to join with patriotic pride in the task of imperial reconstruction. Among the burghers and country folk of Italy, Augustus found, not only the fresh blood which should reinvigorate the public service, but men of literary genius, Virgil, Horace, Livy and Ovid, who could celebrate the glory of Rome and of Cæsar in enduring monuments of verse and prose. He fostered the development of municipalities, agriculture and public works throughout the peninsula. The first steps were taken in the process of breaking down the barriers that parted Rome from Italy, Italy from the provinces. A comprehensive survey, an imperial " Domesday Inquest," was compiled for the whole empire; and the registers, stored in municipal archives, served as the basis for an equitable system of taxation. " There went out a decree from Cæsar Augustus that all the world should be enrolled." [3] The provinces were for

[1] *Legates* held office for three years, and often for longer; *proconsuls*, who had no military command, for only one. Moreover, the emperor influenced the appointment of proconsuls through his control of consular elections and of admission to the senate.

[2] Augustus saw this clearly, as is shown by his last recorded words : " What think you of the comedy, my friends ? Have I played my part well in it ? " Through a reign of more than forty years his infinite patience, profound reserve and keen insight into men and things never failed him. All his acts were the outcome of conscious forethought. The story goes that he never discussed affairs of state, even with the empress Livia, without making notes beforehand. He is perhaps the greatest of the *politiques* of history.

[3] Luke ii. 1 (R.V.). Julius had already laid down the lines of the *census* and provincial survey. The whole undertaking took fifty years to complete. Its results were summarised in the " Breviary of the

the first time administered as departments of a single state. The authority of the governors was controlled and oppression of the provincials checked by the withdrawal of the dangerous privilege of requisitioning supplies at will, by the appointment of an independent financial administrator personally accountable to the *princeps*, and by the provision of effective machinery for petition and appeal to Rome. Though taxation was lightened, the revenue was increased. Trade restrictions within the empire were everywhere abolished. Local government was extended and reorganised on a uniform basis, and provincial councils were instituted with wide powers. When the populace of Ephesus broke into riot on the occasion of St. Paul's visit, the town clerk bade them remember that there were *Asiarchs*, i.e. provincial councillors of Asia, to whom they might refer their grievances.[1] If Augustus was less generous than Julius in granting the citizenship, it was the desire to foster civic patriotism in Rome and Italy that made him chary of extending the franchise to provincials.[2] Further, he laid the foundations of a permanent imperial civil service, recruited at first from the order of knights (*equites*) and from the Italians, later in increasing measure from the ranks of freedmen (enfranchised slaves). The administration of the empire passed gradually from the hands of the Roman aristocracy into those, not merely of Italians, but of provincials of intelligence and education, especially men of Greek and Græco-Oriental origin. Thus a career with brilliant prospects lay open to all, and the creation of an expert bureaucracy ensured continuity in provincial government. Secondly, Augustus endeavoured, by personal example and public legislation, to stem the tide of decay in Roman religion and morals. Poets were encouraged to uphold the ancient standards of austere simplicity and to celebrate the worthies whose piety and civic virtue had been the glory of the early republic. Temples were erected and historic rites restored. Stern penalties were imposed for moral offences, and laws were passed to discourage celibacy. The emperor's efforts proved futile; for morals cannot be reformed by law, and the degeneration of the wealthier classes and the spread of Hellenism pre-

---

empire," a register of the resources of the state and its budget, bequeathed by Augustus to Tiberius (see Tacitus, *Ann.*, i. 11). The work was carried on and kept up to date by the emperors of the second century and by Diocletian.

[1] Acts xix. 18.

[2] The number of Roman citizens in B.C. 70 was 450,000, in B.C. 28 (Augustus' first *census*) 4,000,000, in A.D. 13 (the second *census*) 5,000,000.

cluded the return to the simple standards of a bygone age.[1]
The one exception to the general failure of this policy was the
worship of the emperor himself. Augustus had no illusions
about the matter, and, while sanctioning the payment of divine
honours to Julius, prohibited his own worship in Italy. But it
spread like wildfire in the provinces, and developed before long
into the official religion of the world-state. There was nothing
to outrage Roman feeling in the practice, for religion at Rome
had always been largely political, and a statesman might be
canonised without a violent breach of self-respect. As regards
a living emperor, worship was addressed to his *genius* or guardian-
deity; as applied after his death, it was but a natural expression
of pious gratitude. The provincial councils, referred to above,
were closely associated with this religious service of " the *genius*
of Rome and Augustus," which became in the course of the first
century of our era the outward symbol of the political unity of
the empire.[2] Lastly Augustus completed the work begun by
Julius of fixing the boundaries of the empire. They had been
marked out by nature; in the east, the Euphrates; in the west,
the Atlantic; in the south, the deserts of Africa and Arabia;
in the north, the Rhine and the Danube from the Channel to the
Black Sea. War and diplomacy had combined to secure Syria
against the Parthians, and the standards lost at Carrhæ had
returned to Rome in triumph. The gravest menace was on the
northern frontier. Here the Teutonic tribes surged ceaselessly
against the newly fortified entrenchments on the Danube and the
Rhine. In campaign after campaign, Augustus' generals strove
to master the Germans who dwelt between the last-named river
and the Elbe. The defeat of Varus in A.D. 9 finally determined
the emperor to renounce the forward policy. Along the natural
frontiers were massed the legions, eight on the Rhine, eight on
the Danube, eight in Syria, while the Roman navy policed the
waters of the Mediterranean.[3] Thus was preserved the *pax
Romana*, the Roman peace. It endured for four centuries,
broken only now and again, when, on an emperor's death, the

[1] On Augustus' social and religious legislation, see Pelham, *Essays
in Roman History*, " The domestic policy of Augustus."
[2] The worship of the emperor implied no theological belief. Virgil
and Horace readily accepted the deification of Julius. The emperors
themselves were under no misconceptions; when the dying Vespasian
was asked by his friends how he was, he replied, " I fear I am becoming
a god (*Vae, puto deus fio*)."
[3] This represents the distribution under Tiberius. The total force
was about 320,000, in twenty-five legions.

generals of the frontier armies moved Romewards and fought for the imperial throne.

II. The Empire in the First Three Centuries (§§ 9–16).[1]

§ 9. The Roman world was governed on the maxims of Augustus until the accession of Diocletian in 284. For the first and only time in history, civilized mankind was incorporated into a single state, and that state a military despotism. It is not our task to trace the gradual disappearance of the disguises in which its founder had shrouded the hard fact of his autocracy; how first the popular assembly, then the civic magistracies, and finally the senate either fell into disuse or, where they survived, retained merely a local and honorific value.[2] The state, for instance, was still officially known as the " republic " till the close of the third century. Of the basis of the emperor's power we have already spoken. The most disturbing factor in the system was the problem of the succession. In practice, the reigning prince often designated a son or a male kinsman as his successor by securing the conferment upon him of the *imperium* and the tribunitian power. Frequently, and above all in the second century, the Roman usage of adoption was called into play. These precautions did not avail to prevent periodic conflicts, as on Nero's death in 66, and with increasing frequency in the third century, when a successful general, backed by one of the frontier armies or by the prætorian body-guard, claimed the vacant throne. The empire, like the ancient kingship, was not hereditary, but elective; and the theory that any Roman citizen was eligible was preserved throughout its history. This explains why, as will be seen in a later chapter, on its restoration in the West in the ninth century, a Frankish chieftain could be regarded as the legitimate successor of Augustus. Nor need we dwell, for all their personal interest, on the lives of individual emperors.[3] For many readers, the story of the empire is that

[1] From this point onwards all dates refer to the Christian era, unless otherwise specified.

[2] The senate survived longest in effective being; of its powers, that of appellate jurisdiction lasted until the third century.

[3] We may distinguish the following groups of emperors in chronological sequence :

    (i) emperors of the Julio–Claudian line : Augustus (to 14), Tiberius (to 37), Caligula (to 41), Claudius (to 54), Nero (to 68).

    (ii) emperors of the Flavian line : Vespasian (to 79), Titus (to 81), Domitian (to 96).

of its rulers; while the system they controlled, affecting the destiny of millions, remains virtually unknown.[1] Even in the case of those princes whose ability is most conspicuous, the literary records are largely occupied with the trivial details of court-gossip. It is only by gathering up the tale told by inscriptions scattered over the provinces that we learn to gauge the imperial system in its true proportions. We then discover that the wild vagaries of a Caligula or a Nero, which loom so large in the pages of Tacitus and Suetonius, served only to rouse a transitory agitation in the capital. The huge machine performed its appointed revolutions, heedless of the caprices of its master. When St. Paul appealed to the imperial tribunal, it was from Cæsar, not from Nero, that he expected and received justice. How great, on the other hand, was the influence which a capable and energetic ruler could exert in the fields of military defence, internal administration and law, will be manifest from a single illustration.

§ 10. If autocracy ever merits praise, the emperor Hadrian (117–138) might claim to be regarded as a heaven-sent autocrat. Born at Rome in 76—his father, a native of Spain, but of Italian lineage, was Trajan's cousin—he was early trained to office; at fifteen he was serving in the army, at seventeen acting as judge in private suits; he held in succession commands in Britain, Mœsia and on the Rhine, and followed his great kinsman through his victorious campaigns in Dacia and in the East. Thus, when on Trajan's death he succeeded to the throne at the age of forty-one, his natural powers of judgement and imagination and his tireless ardour for work had been matured by wide experience both in peace and war. Hadrian was a statesman rather than a soldier, and used to boast that he had won more by the weapons of policy than by those of arms. In his reign of one and twenty years, he set his mark, in principle and in detail, on the entire structure of Roman administration and law. He organised the imperial council of state, the imperial secretariat and the system

---

(iii) Adoptive emperors : Nerva (to 98), Trajan (to 117), Hadrian (to 138), Antoninus Pius (to 161), Marcus Aurelius (to 180).

(iv) Barrack emperors (nominees of the army) : from 192 to 284. The ablest of these were Septimius Severus (193–211), Aurelian (270–275) and Probus (275–282).

[1] The Misses Maria and Julia Bertram, in Jane Austen's *Mansfield Park* (c. ii), aged 13 and 12 respectively, could repeat " in chronological order, with the dates of their accession . . . the Roman emperors as low as Severus."

of imperial postal communications.[1] Public works and charitable institutions sprang into being at his initiative; agriculture was fostered, universities were endowed, Roman citizenship and Latin rights liberally bestowed. " He had as all-embracing a knowledge of the public finances," wrote his biographer, " as any careful householder of his private affairs." No detail was too minute to engage his attention; a tablet discovered in S. Portugal shows him regulating the life of a mining village, laying down rules for the local shoemaker and barber, arranging for the monthly cleaning of the boilers in the public bath, and (merciful provision !) exempting schoolmasters from the payment of rates.[2] The emperor's labours were most evident and enduring in the fields of law and provincial government. He inaugurated the classic age of Roman jurisprudence. To his personal stimulus were due the practice of issuing imperial rescripts binding upon the courts, the compilation of the Perpetual Edict,[3] and the recognition of the opinions of the great jurists as possessing the force of law. The emperor now became the supreme judge of all criminal appeals. He mitigated the rigours of the *patria potestas*, granted to women the right of making wills, abolished human sacrifices and severely restricted the torture of slaves. Humanity was the leading note of Hadrian's character and actions.[4] A favourite symbol on his coins was that of a weeping woman raised by the emperor from the ground. More than half his reign was spent in rapid progresses through the provinces. He is said to have marched twenty thousand miles, on foot and clad in full military accoutrements.[5] In 121–6 he visited every quarter of the empire, from Spain to Syria, from Britain to Africa, reforming the military administration, fortifying the frontiers, visiting sick soldiers in hospital, living when in camp on the rations of the legionaries, inspecting industries and, above all, instituting public works and rebuilding cities. After little more than a year in Rome, he set forth on a second journey, and passed six

[1] The average rate of travel in the postal service was five miles an hour : thirty to fifty miles was an ordinary day's journey, but 100 could be covered, if necessary.

[2] See H. S. Jones in *The Legacy of Rome*, p. 129.

[3] On the Perpetual Edict, see below, § 17.

[4] He refused to sanction charges of high treason (*majestas*), or to accept legacies save from personal friends, and from those only if they died childless; thus removing two of the worst abuses incidental to the empire.

[5] Hadrian was a great hunter as well as a great walker; he had extraordinary powers of physical endurance, led habitually a simple life, and was a stern disciplinarian.

years (128–34) in the East, to whose compelling call his temper of mind was singularly responsive. What makes Hadrian so interesting is the insatiable curiosity and intellectual enthusiasm that cast a glamour of romance over his unwearied discharge of official duty. " Restless in everything all his life " is the verdict of his biographer Spartianus. He was an inveterate sightseer, climbed mounts Casius to see the sunrise and Etna to see the sunset, reinterred the bones of Ajax at Troy, visited the potters' sheds in Britain, the tombs of Pompey in Egypt and of Epaminondas at Mantinea, was initiated into the mysteries of Eleusis, and carved his name on Memnon's statue. At Athens, where he rebuilt on a lavish scale, he presided as archon at the festival of the Great Dionysia. He was phil-Hellene to the core— as a lad he had been nicknamed *Graeculus* (the little Greek)— cultivated the society of men of letters, and prided himself not a little on a knowledge of music and the plastic arts, and on his own efforts in prose and verse.[1] His taste, like that of Hellas in its decline, was far from pure; he loved the exotic and ex- travagant, preferred Antimachus to Homer, Ennius to Virgil, and designed temples—one, in honour of Venus and Rome, was on the site of Golgotha—in which, as mocking critics remarked, the goddesses could not stand erect. His favourite, Antinous, an Asiatic Greek, set the type of sensuous male beauty for the sculptors of the day. The second century was an age of religious revivals, and the stranger and more alien the worship, the stronger was its fascination for the Roman world. Hadrian, too, was fond of consulting dreams and oracles, forecast his life for each suc- cessive year, deified Antinous and named a star in his honour after his death. The tales recorded in the Talmud of his talks with the rabbis, though legendary, are significant of the im- pression he left on the Jewish mind. His endeavour to abolish the rite of circumcision, and to plant a Græco-Roman colony (*Ælia Capitolina*) on the ruined site of the holy city, provoked the Jews to their last and most terrible revolt (134–6). To the Christians the emperor displayed a scornful tolerance. In all this he was the type of second-century culture, with its cosmo- politanism, its archaism, its preciosity and its decadence. " *L'Orient surtout l'attirait,*" writes Renan; " *il en voyait les impostures, le charlatanisme, et s'en amusait.*" But Hadrian was no mere dilettante; he remained at heart a son of pagan Rome.

---

[1] He was on friendly terms with the Stoic slave Epictetus, and the Greek historian of Marseilles, Favorinus.

" He was most assiduous," says Spartianus, " in the observance of Roman worships and despised those of other lands." He had no illusions; his caprices never disturbed the even tenor of his judgement. In his person, the ideal civil servant had donned the imperial purple; to illustrate by modern analogies, Hadrian had more affinity with Lord Milner or Sir Robert Morant than with Oscar Wilde. Fame, we are told, he sought ardently, but by other paths than these. He knew well that it was the Britannic and the Germanic *limes*,[1] the cities he built and the laws he made, that gave him his claim to rank as one of the greatest administrators that ever lived. His last recorded acts, as he lay dying in Rome, reflect his many-sided personality; the jibe at the court physicians, " too many doctors are death to a prince "; the lines addressed to his departing soul, which mirror in Latin the lingering beauty of the last age of Hellenism;[2] and, what concerned him more than all the rest, the designation in the person of Antoninus Pius of a worthy successor to the imperial throne.

§ 11. Turning from the emperor to the empire, we find that the government of the world in the second century lies in the hands of a vast bureaucracy. The heads of its departments at Rome were originally members of the emperor's household, and were still regarded as his personal assistants, analogous to the secretaries and estate managers of a private noble. The chief of these were the four *procurators*, viz. the controller of finance, the legal adviser, the receiver of petitions and the imperial secretary.[3] In conformity with the historic maxim that the magistrate should fortify himself by advice, important business was habitually debated in the imperial council of state.

---

[1] On the *limes*, see below, § 13, *note* 2.

[2]

> *Animula, vagula, blandula,*
> *Hospes comesque corporis ;*
> *Quae nunc abibis in loca ?*
> *Pallidula, rigida, nudula,*
> *Nec ut soles dabis iocos.*

Rendered by Marcus S. Dimsdale (*Latin Literature*, p. 526):

> " Soul of me, vague, debonnair,
> Guest of this body and friend,
> Say whither now thou wilt fare,
> Pallid and rigid and bare,
> Little soul,
> All thy jests at an end ? "

[3] Styled respectively, *a rationibus, a cognitionibus, a libellis, ab epistulis.* From Hadrian's time onwards these offices were filled, no longer by freedmen, but by citizens of equestrian rank.

The administration of Rome and Italy was entrusted to four prefects, of the city, of the prætorian guard, of the corn supply and of the watch, all of whom also discharged high judicial functions.[1] In the imperial courts, which had gradually effaced the senatorial, appeals were heard from all quarters of the Roman world. Of the provinces, which had increased in the second century to over thirty, the imperial were twice as numerous as the senatorial.[2] Firm and effective control was maintained by the central government; the provincial governors were selected for their integrity and talents, paid by the state, and assisted by independent financial officers and a permanent staff of trained administrators.[3] Under the Flavian and Antonine emperors, knights increasingly replace freedmen in the imperial service. Free-born Romans were no longer unwilling to hold posts in " Cæsar's household." Substantial justice was obtainable in the imperial courts throughout the empire. Taxation, if burdensome, was levied on an equitable and uniform basis, furnished by the census-registers which were periodically brought up to date.

[1] Styled respectively, *urbi*, *prætorio*, *annonae*, *vigilum*. The prætorian prefect presided, from Hadrian's time, over the council of state and the supreme criminal tribunal.

[2] On the matter of this section, see W. T. Arnold, *Roman Provincial Administration*, esp. cc. iv, vi, vii; a list of provinces is given, with explanatory notes, in *Appendix* I. The following is the list under Augustus :

Sicily (senatorial), Sardinia and Corsica, Gaul (4 : one senatorial), Spain (3 : one senatorial), Africa (senatorial), Cyrene and Crete (senatorial), Syria, Galatia, Bithynia (senatorial), Pontus (senatorial), Asia (senatorial), Macedonia (senatorial), Achaia (senatorial), Mœsia, Noricum, Rhætia, Illyricum, the Alpine districts. Egypt was administered on special lines, by a prefect of equestrian rank.

The following were added after Augustus' death :

Germany (2; in A.D. 17); Mauretania (2), Britain and Thrace (these between 40 and 46); Arabia, Dacia, Armenia, Mesopotamia and Assyria (these between 105 and 141, under Trajan).

From time to time provinces were redistributed between the emperor and the senate. The senatorial provinces disappear at the close of the second century.

In addition, certain areas were administered by procurators under the supervision of a neighbouring provincial governor; when the process of Romanisation had advanced, these were frequently constituted as provinces. Judæa was under a procurator, supervised by the imperial legate of Syria (see Luke ii. 1). Vitellius, the future emperor, when legate of Syria, secured the deposition of the procurator Pontius Pilate.

[3] The tenth book of the letters of the younger Pliny (*tr.* in vol. ii of the *Loeb* edition) consists of the despatches that passed between Pliny and the emperor Trajan during the former's governorship of Bithynia in 111. Bithynia had been constituted an imperial province by Trajan. The correspondence furnishes an admirable illustration of provincial administration under the early empire.

The chief source of direct revenue was the land tax, supplemented by a tax in kind for the maintenance of the army in certain provinces, an income-tax on special professions and trades, a five-per-cent. legacy duty levied on the wealthier classes, and the income from state domains, mines and the emperor's private lands (*patrimonium Caesaris*). Of indirect taxes, the chief were the customs duties which varied in different provinces. We shall see in a subsequent chapter how the burden of taxation increased during the third century until it became well-nigh intolerable, with ruinous results on the economic prosperity of the empire. But, before that date, the government displayed a singular liberality in the employment of the revenue. Relief was readily granted in cases of plague, famine and other extraordinary calamity; restrictions on trade were everywhere abolished; public works, such as harbours, roads, bridges, irrigation and the reclamation of waste lands, were vigorously carried out in all quarters of the empire. Especially noteworthy is the policy, initiated by Nerva and extended by his second-century successors, of establishing, in Italy and elsewhere, institutions for the relief of widows and orphans, professorships and other educational endowments, and land banks for the encouragement of agriculture, the profits from which were devoted to the maintenance and education of poor children.

§ 12. The city, as of old, was the chief instrument of civilization utilised by the imperial government for the maintenance of Hellenic culture in the East and the implanting of Roman culture in the North and West.[1] Under the early empire, the towns of a province comprised (i) the allied and the free cities, owing their independence in the one case to formal treaty, in the other to gift from Rome; (ii) Roman colonies and *municipia*, which differed rather in dignity than in privileges; and (iii) the mass of tributary unprivileged towns, which preserved their old local institutions under the control of the provincial governor. These last were in course of time converted for the most part into *municipia*, by the bestowal of citizen or Latin rights. From the third century, the allied and the free cities diminished in number and were restricted in their privileges. Pliny gives

[1] At first, the Roman policy was to make every possible use of the existing machinery; e.g. they recognised tribal chieftains and councils as instruments of local government. When this system proved inadequate, they established city communities, recruited from Italy, among the native population. Where they found cities in being, as was the case in the East, they utilised them.

a list of 175 towns in the Spanish province of Bætica towards the close of the first century; there are three allied and six free towns, nine colonies, eight *municipia*, twenty-nine towns with Latin rights and 120 tributary. Municipal government was almost everywhere aristocratic and modelled on the historic form of Rome; colonies and *municipia* were controlled by annual magistrates elected by the popular assembly from citizens possessed of a high property qualification, and by a senate consisting mainly of magistrates and ex-magistrates. In process of time, there was a marked tendency in the direction of interference by imperial officials; popular election fell into disuse, and it became increasingly difficult to induce candidates to face the heavy expenses attendant on the tenure of municipal office. The early centuries of our era saw the rise of a vast number of cities, many of which long survived the fall of the empire, and flourish even at the present day. The military stations of the frontier legions furnished the nucleus of new towns, and we can trace the fort growing into a village, the village into a town. The names of Leon in Spain, Caerleon upon Usk in Britain, preserve the record of such an origin (*legionis, castra legionis*). Each municipality administered a considerable tract of surrounding country; sometimes a large city would control a number of dependent townships, giving rise to a municipal hierarchy. So in Gaul under Augustus, Lugudunum (Lyon) was the administrative centre for sixty-four communities, each of which had its own chief town (Amiens and Nantes were two of these), while Marseilles and Nîmes had authority over other towns in the vicinity. The provincial towns also elected deputies to attend the provincial councils, whose meetings, associated with the worship of the emperor, played an important part in local administration and furnished the closest approximation in antiquity to the institution of representative government.

§ 13. The most pressing responsibility, throughout the first three centuries, was the guardianship of the frontiers. Augustus' counsel, to keep within the bounds he had set, was faithfully observed by his successors. The chief exceptions were the inclusion of Britain under Claudius (41–54), and of Dacia (= Hungary prior to 1914–18), Armenia, and the Euphrates-Tigris provinces under Trajan (98–117). Trajan's victorious campaigns in the East crowned the energetic policy of the first-century emperors; Parthia ceased to be formidable, and the Euphrates frontier remained undisturbed till the rise of the Persian kingdom in the middle of the third century. In the North and West, on the other hand, the tide of barbarian migration swelled in ever-growing volume. The Teutonic tribes, a menace to Italy since the days of Marius, who had been thrust back from Gaul by Cæsar, and had foiled the effort of Augustus to extend Roman sovereignty to the Elbe, now fought unceasingly against the fortress-barrier along the Rhine and the Danube.[1] The line had been strengthened by the stockade built by Hadrian from above Coblenz to near Regensburg on the Danube, enclosing the Black Forest within the empire.[2] It held out for two centuries; but fighting was incessant all along the frontier, and any laxity in the Roman grip brought instant retribution. Dissensions within the empire and movements of the tribes beyond its pale provoked periodic crises of exceptional severity, followed by intervals of comparative calm. Thus, after the terrible wars waged by Marcus Aurelius against the Marcomanni and the Quadi on the upper Danube, quiet prevailed for two generations, till the storm-centre shifted to the lower reaches of the river, where Goths from the Euxine threatened the Balkan provinces in the middle of the second century (250–270). Their defeat by Claudius secured the line of the Danube for another hundred years. Coincidently with the Gothic war, the Rhine barrier was broken by the Alemanni and the Franks (c. 258).[3] After a desperate struggle, that lasted, with varying fortunes, from the reign of Gallienus to that of Diocletian, peace was once more restored in the north-west. In the course of these conflicts, the practice, inaugurated by Cæsar, of granting lands to Teuton settlers within the empire, became part of the general policy of the government. The enemies of one generation furnished recruits for the defending legions of the next. The Roman armies were enlisted for long service, and almost wholly from the population of the provinces. Soldiers

[1] The original home of the Teutons was in the west—Baltic lands, i.e. southern Sweden, Jutland and Pomerania. Thence, between 600 and 200 B.C., they moved west and south-west, expelling the Celtic tribes from the lands east of the Rhine. At the same time they absorbed much of the superior Celtic culture with which they were in contact. In the second century B.C., Teutons first crossed the Rhine and invaded Gaul.

[2] Within the palisade ran the *limes* or military road. At a later date the palisade was partially replaced by a stone wall. Forts were erected at intervals of from two and a half to nine miles along the *limes*. The great bulwark stretched for several hundred miles.

[3] The Alemanni, as their name (= all men) implies, were a con-federation of tribes, as also were the Franks (= free men). The name of the former survives in the French *Allemagne*, that of the latter in *France* (also *Franconia*, *Franche-Comté*, *Frankfurt*). The Alemanni were in contact with Rome from 213, the Franks from 253.

from Commagene in Asia Minor would be quartered in Germany or Britain, and established, on their discharge, with a bounty and a plot of land, in the countries where they had served. Many famous towns, such as Cologne (*Colonia Agrippinensis*) and Colchester (*Camulodunum*) owed their origin to these settlements of time-expired veterans. The cosmopolitanism of the army was but one symptom of the cosmopolitanism of the imperial system. The civil service also was recruited from provincials. The old lines of cleavage between Roman and Italian, Italian and provincial, had ceased to exist. When in 212, by the *Constitutio Antonina*, the emperor Caracalla bestowed Roman citizenship on all free-born citizens of the empire, his immediate motive may have been to increase the revenue, but the act was the logical completion of the policy of the two preceding centuries.[1] Thanks to the paternal government of the empire, the ideas and institutions for which Rome stands in history had taken firm root throughout the Mediterranean world.

§ 14. The significance of this fact and its bearings on the future will be made clear if we illustrate the manner in which Rome discharged her mission of government in the provinces of western Europe, Spain, Gaul and Britain.

(I) *Spain* was one of the earliest of the Roman provinces. Conquered and organised in the third century B.C. by the great Carthaginian, Hamilcar Barca, it passed at the close of the second Punic war to Rome. To master the tribes of the interior was a long and difficult task that taxed to the full the energies of successive Roman governors, among whom Cato the censor and Tiberius Sempronius Gracchus, the father of the agrarian reformer, were conspicuous for their ability. Natural conditions aided the guerrilla warfare in which Spaniards have always excelled, and the labours of war and organisation continued uninterruptedly through the second century. Cato developed the mines, which the Phœnicians had worked many centuries before, and cultivated the vine and the olive. Between 80 and 72 B.C. the democratic leader, Sertorius, finding in Spain a refuge from the Sullan restoration, trained the native tribes in the arts

---

[1] The immediate motive of Caracalla's edict was to extend the range of application of the five-per-cent. tax on citizen's inheritances. The grant of citizenship was limited to the actual free inhabitants of the empire in 212; freedmen, persons with Latin rights, and those settled on lands within the empire, who acquired their position at a subsequent date, did not *ipso facto* become citizens. Justinian extended the citizenship to include these.

K

of war and peace and founded military colleges for the education of their noble youth. The policy of Romanisation was actively fostered by Julius and Augustus. Fifty Spanish towns received the full citizenship; Gades and Tarraco were the centres respectively of commerce and of government; Saragossa and Astorga still preserve Augustus' name.[1] The great military and commercial highway that led from Italy round the Gulf of Lions was continued beyond the Pyrenees along the eastern coast of Spain, whence it struck through the interior to the Guadalquivir and the port of Gades (Cadiz). By the time of Augustus' death, Roman language, dress and customs prevailed over a great part of the peninsula. Spain was divided into three provinces; of the three legions stationed there by Augustus two could be safely withdrawn by the close of the first century. Pacification and Romanisation went hand in hand. Julius Cæsar's secretary and Augustus' librarian were native Spaniards. Already in the first century Spain had given to Roman literature, the moralist Seneca, the republican poet Lucan, the geographer Mela, the agricultural writer Columella, Rome's best epigrammatist, Martial, and the greatest of her literary critics, Quintilian.[2] Early in the following century she gave Rome one of the noblest emperors in the person of Trajan. When at length the barbarian invasions broke upon the West, they found Spain so thoroughly Romanised that the continuity of her culture was not seriously imperilled. The Christian faith was securely rooted in a country that had possibly been the scene of St. Paul's later missionary labours, and had since played a prominent part in the life of the western church. Thirty-seven separate churches were represented at the council of Elvira in the third century. Hosius, bishop of Cordova, was the chosen counsellor of Constantine at the council of Nicæa. The Visigoths, unlike the Vandals, had taken kindly to Roman culture before they established their power in Spain. Isidore of Seville was one of the few scholars in the degenerate days of the seventh century who was able to pass on fragments of ancient learning and legal lore to the thinkers of the early middle age. Even the Saracen conquest of the eighth century did not avail to efface all traces of the past; Gothic chieftains

[1] In 1861 fragments of the laws of Malaca (Malaga) and Salpensa, and in 1870 fragments of those of Osuna, were discovered, throwing much light on municipal government in Spain under the early empire.
[2] On Seneca and Quintilian, see below, §§ 21, 22. It has been remarked as illustrating the civilizing work of Rome that Roman soldiers and officials taught foreigners like Seneca and Quintilian to write real Latin.

kept the light of Roman and Christian tradition still flickering in the mountain fastnesses, and the stream of Roman influence can be traced unbroken from the days of Scipio to the rise of the modern kingdoms of Portugal and Spain.[1]

§ 15. (II) " All *Gaul* is divided into three parts "; so run, as every schoolboy knows, the opening words of Cæsar's *Commentaries*. Augustus, in apportioning the land into provinces, reorganised the three regions as *Belgica* (N.E.), *Lugudunensis* (N.W. and C.), *Aquitania* (W. and S.W.), names which survive as Belgium, Lyon and Aquitaine. In the south along the Mediterranean coast lay the older province of Narbonesc Gaul, through which ran the great road from Rome to Spain. Its centre in republican times was the ancient Greek colony of Massilia (Marseilles), an allied city of Rome, governed by an oligarchical constitution which excited the admiration of Cicero. After its fall before Cæsar's army in the civil war,[2] it was outstripped by newer foundations such as Forum Julii (Fréjus, the station of the fleet, as is Toulon to-day) and Arelate (Arles) at the Rhone mouth, the great port for inland trade. This southern province, the " Provence " of after times, was naturally Romanised long before the newly conquered interior; and the difference persisted at a later day, in the field of language, as that between the *Langue d'Oc* of Provence and the *Langue d'Oil* of the rest of France. The three new Augustan provinces were organised in tribal cantons under Celtic magistrates with a native militia. The chief seat of government and commerce was Lugudunum (Lyon), a colony founded in 43 and peopled by Roman citizens, at the point where the road up the Rhone valley diverged into branches leading to the various camps on the German frontier. There met the council of the Gallic provinces, which co-operated with the Roman government in taxation and in gathering the Celtic tribes around the worship of Rome and Augustus.[3] Urban life developed rapidly in the cantons; among the earliest towns to rise into importance were Rheims and Treves in the province of Belgica, the latter of which became the capital of Gaul and of the West at the opening of the third century. The east of

---

[1] In Africa the Saracens obliterated all traces of Roman influence. The Saracen emirs of Cordova, on the other hand, were enlightened rulers, who preserved many relics of the past.

[2] Dante, *Purg.*, xviii. 102. " Cæsar, to subdue Ilerda, stabbed Marseilles and then raced to Spain."

[3] The population of Gaul was not exclusively Celtic, but included Iberian and Germanic tribes. The Roman government settled conquered Germans on Gallic soil.

Gaul was Romanised more quickly than the west. As urban communities arose, Roman rights were extended; Cæsar had admitted Gauls into the senate, and a speech of Claudius has come down to us in which he granted the right of holding office to enfranchised Gauls.[1] " Every community," wrote Cæsar of this people, " is split into two parties," and the Roman authorities made full use of these divisions to secure their rule against revolt. The Druidic religion was suppressed by law; it offered no long resistance, and had almost vanished when Christianity spread over the northern provinces. The country was rich in material resources; " in Gaul," wrote Josephus, " the sources of wealth have their home and flood the earth with their abundance." Agriculture was the basis of its prosperity; while in the north-east sheep-breeding gave birth to the cloth industry which early brought to Arras and Tournai a foretaste of their mediæval and modern fame. The Celts were great huntsmen and supplied large contingents to the cavalry of the Roman armies. They possessed a rare aptitude for learning; Autun (Augustodunum) and Bordeaux (Burdigala) were seats of famous universities and schools; the ready wit and gifts of speech of the Celts made them renowned as early as the first century for oratory and teaching.[2] Plastic art, especially of scenes from daily life, foreshadowing the reliefs that adorn the Gothic cathedrals of mediæval France, developed round Treves; and in the fourth century Ausonius of Bordeaux, one of the most graceful of later Latin poets, sang in hexameter verse the praises of the charming scenery of the Moselle. The churches of Gaul, from the second century onwards, furnished many of the leaders of western Christendom. Bishops from Britain travelled to Arles to attend its councils. In a word, by the time that the Visigoths, Burgundians and Franks poured over her plains and river-valleys, Gaul was fairly equipped for the task of Romanising and Christianising her conquerors. Later still, in the ninth century, her schools were the chosen home of mediæval learning.[3]

[1] Tacitus, *Annals*, xi, cc. 23–5, summarises the speech. Early in the sixteenth century portions of it were found at Lyon. See Arnold pp. 145 ff. for details.

[2] The school at Autun for the noble youth of Gaul was already in existence under Tiberius.

[3] It must be remembered that between the Gallic provinces and the frontier stretched the two German provinces (Upper and Lower), consisting of a narrow strip of country guarded by military outposts, with the great camps of the Rhine legions. Upper Germany was the broader of the two, since it comprised a large tract of debatable waste land, including the Black Forest. It was enclosed by Vespasian and settled with

§ 16. (III) *Britain* lay on the remote outskirts of the Roman world; its occupation under Claudius constituted the only permanent exception to the principle that the empire should not spread beyond the limits determined by Augustus. It was governed as part of the empire for almost four hundred years. Three legions (more than 15,000 soldiers), recruited largely from the Romanised natives, were continuously stationed in the island. The influence of Roman civilization was restricted, save for a brief interval, to the regions south of the wall that Severus built from Wallsend, east of Newcastle, to Carlisle, of which much is still standing.[1] Within this area Cornwall alone remained wholly untouched by Rome. In the north there were extensive military settlements massed chiefly along the wall, and in the town of York. But it was in the south, especially in Gloucestershire, the east of Somerset, Hampshire and Northamptonshire, that there was, as is shown by the numerous remains of isolated Roman houses, a considerable population of Romanised civilians, and it was here mainly that Rome set her mark on the Celtic population. As in all parts of the empire, the rule of Rome meant colonies and military roads. Colchester, Lincoln, York and Gloucester were Roman colonies; Verulamium (St. Albans) enjoyed the dignity of a *municipium*. York was the scene of the coronation of the emperor Constantine and of the burial of the emperor Severus. Of the great roads, Watling Street ran north-west from London to Wroxeter; Ermine Street from Colchester by Huntingdon and Lincoln to York; the road from London by Staines forked at Silchester into branches towards Southampton, Salisbury and the south-west, and Gloucester; the Fosse Way ran diagonally from Lincoln by Leicester to Cirencester and Bath. Forest land was cleared for agriculture; Britain supplied corn to the Rhine legions; British builders were known over western Europe, British cloth was exported, Kentish oysters were in great request at Rome, and the south-eastern ports became thriving centres of trade. The influence of Rome was not always beneficial; on articles of common use, e.g. pots, fashions of stereotyped ornament destroyed the native Celtic freedom of design. The

---

coloni Caesaris, cultivators tied to the soil. Roman culture spread here among the Germanic tribes to a greater extent than in Lower Germany above Coblenz.

[1] Hadrian had already made a road (the *limes*) along this line. A ditch, earthwork and road were erected farther north, from the Firth of Forth to the Firth of Clyde, by Antoninus Pius, and completed at the end of the second century by Severus.

Roman language spread first among Celtic nobles, then among
the main body of the native population in the south and east;
Roman law and methods of government were potent instruments
of civilization. Plutarch tells of his conversation with a Greek
teacher returning from Britain to his home on the shores of the
Levant. With the extension of Christianity, Britain came within
the pale of the Church—the foundations of a Christian church
have been disclosed at Silchester; and the new faith spread to
Wales and beyond the bounds of the empire to Ireland. At the
beginning of the fifth century, pressure on the continental frontier
of the empire led to the abandonment of Britain by the imperial
government.[1] Upon the collapse of Roman rule the Celtic
element in the province reasserted itself. Arthur, a Celtic leader
who bore a Roman name, is the half-historical, half-legendary,
impersonation of the Celtic resistance to the Saxons. With the
Saxon occupation, most of the traces of Rome's influence perished :
Anglo-Saxon law owed nothing of its contents to that of Rome;
Christianity gave way to heathenism, save in Ireland and the
unconquered fastnesses of Wales; and the Roman towns were
laid waste by the invaders. So far as traces of the old provincial
life survived in Saxon Britain, they were Celtic and not specifically Roman.[2] In London, the greatest of Roman towns,
there is not a single existing street that can be proved to run
along a Roman line.[3] A remnant of the Celtic population under
Saxon masters can indeed be traced in Kent and Wessex; the
clearings of corn-land and the great roads preserved the record
of Roman policy; and among the rich variety of designs which
appear on the earliest Old English coins many can be traced back
to Roman origins. More than thirty towns and villages still
bear names derived from those (whether Celtic or Latin) in use
during the Roman occupation.[4] But with these few exceptions
Rome left no enduring mark on the life-history of Britain.[5]

[1] When the British appealed for protection to the emperor Honorius,
he bade their cities defend themselves as best they could.
[2] All over England the river names, which are *at latest* Celtic, were
handed on unchanged to the Saxon conquerors.
[3] E.g. the foundations of Roman buildings lie across the line of Cheap-
side. Many Roman roads come within a short distance of the city; e.g.
Clapham High Street (Stane Street), Mile End Road (the London–
Colchester road), Kingsland Road (Ermine Street), Oxford Street (the
road to Silchester, with Watling Street branching off northwards at the
Marble Arch).
[4] E.g. Lichfield (*Lētocētum*), Manchester (*prob. Mammium*), Rich-
borough (*Rutupiae, Repta Caestir*), Winchester (*Venta*) and the village of
Mancetter in Warwickshire.
[5] On Roman Britain, see Tacitus' life of his father-in-law Agricola,
who commanded in Britain under Titus and Domitan. In this section

III. LAW AND LITERATURE (§§ 17–24).

a. Law (§§ 17–18).

§ 17. The period from Augustus to Diocletian was the golden age of Roman jurisprudence, which was enriched and perfected at the hands of illustrious jurists acting as the ministers of the sovereign *princeps*. The old civil law was shorn of formal excrescences and effete survivals; the *patria potestas*, for example, lost much of its traditional rigidity. The extension by Caracalla of Roman citizenship to all free provincials paved the way for the incorporation of the law of nations (*jus gentium*) into the civil law (*jus civile*) of Rome. The chief features of legal history in the three centuries under review were (i) the completion of prætorian law by the Perpetual Edict, (ii) the rise of imperial legislation, (iii) the development of a scientific jurisprudence.

(i) Prætorian activity in the field of law-making was at its height in the last century of the republic. Under the early emperors it became the practice for prætors to adopt the edict of their predecessors with scarcely any modification. This practice was recognised by Hadrian when he entrusted an eminent lawyer, Salvius Julianus, with the task of revising the edicts of the urban and peregrin prætors, and of issuing the codified result as a permanently binding edict (*edictum perpetuum*). Henceforward no additions or alterations could be introduced. The like was done also for the magisterial edicts in the provinces. The edict of Julianus thus completed and closed the body of prætorian equity, and thereby marked the final assertion of imperial sovereignty over the republican magistracy in the domain of law.

(ii) The legislative authority under the republic was the assembly (*comitia*) of the Roman people. Augustus still referred important measures, dealing with moral reforms, manumission of slaves, the status of freedmen, and judicial procedure, to the assembly for formal approval, but from Tiberius' reign onwards its legislative functions passed to the senate. Among the members of this body were many eminent lawyers, and its decrees (*senatus consulta*) play a large part in the legal development of the first two centuries. The emperors, while exercising an increasing control over the deliberations of the senate, hesitated as yet to legislate purely by their own authority. But already

I have been specially indebted to the help of my former colleague, Professor F. M. Stenton.

prior to the third century the imperial " constitutions " obtained
the force of law, and after that date became the sole instrument
of legislation. They comprised (*a*) *edicts* or public ordinances,
interpreting the law, which the emperor, by virtue of his *imperium*,
posted up as the prætors had done in time past, (*b*) *rescripts* or
written judgements on petitions addressed to him by private
persons and by magistrates, (*c*) *decrees*, or rulings on judicial
appeals, and (*d*) *mandates*, i.e. instructions, mostly of an administrative character, despatched to the governors of provinces.[1] A word must be added on the machinery of criminal
law, which had been first effectively organised in the last age
of the republic, when Sulla extended the system of standing
commissions (*quaestiones perpetuae*) with prætorian presidents
and equestrian *judices*. These disappear at the close of the
second century, as does also the criminal jurisdiction of the
senate, conferred upon that body by Augustus. Here, again,
the emperor, acting through his delegates, especially the prætorian
prefect, absorbed all judicial authority; so that both in civil
and criminal causes his tribunal became the supreme court of
appeal for the Roman world.

(iii) Roman law had been fashioned, not on a preconceived
system, but inductively, on the basis of practical experience;
and consisted of a huge aggregate of rules and practices, resting
on ancient custom, or designed to meet particular requirements.
Its principles were implicit in its structure rather than explicitly
formulated. The first jurist who endeavoured to disengage
these principles, and to arrange the vast body of private law
in accordance with the nature of its contents, was Quintus
Mucius Scævola the younger, *pontifex maximus* about 100 B.C.
Scævola may fairly claim to be regarded as the founder of Roman
jurisprudence. From his time onwards the scientific study of
the law made rapid progress. Augustus granted official recognition to the work of the jurists, by ordaining that certain of them,
selected for their eminence, should possess the right of giving
opinions with imperial authority (*jus respondendi ex auctoritate
principis*). Their written answers to questions of law submitted

[1] Theoretically, the *edicts* lost their validity on the death of the *princeps*,
though they were often renewed by his successor. *Rescripts* were binding
instructions to the judge on the special matter of the case at issue, whereas
edicts were rules of general import. *Mandates*, when concerned with
points of law, had the force of *rescripts*; in many cases they dealt with
matters of temporary policy. Strictly, they do not come under the head
of *constitutions*.

to them, delivered to the court under seal, were henceforth binding on the magistrates and on the private citizens, often unlearned in the law, who served as *judices*. From Augustus' reign onwards the schools of jurisprudence, organised as corporate societies, wielded increasing influence on the development of jurisprudence.[1] They not only moulded the law into a system but leavened it with speculative ideas of an order undreamed of in republican times. The first-fruits of their labours were seen in the above-mentioned edict of Julianus and in systematic treatises composed by lawyers of the age of Hadrian and the Antonines, such as Celsus, Cæcilius Africanus and Gaius. These were followed between 170 and 230 by Quintus Cervidius Scævola and his pupil Papinian, the greatest of all the Roman jurists. Both were of Hellenic race; it was characteristic of this age of cosmopolitanism that the mind of Greece impressed its stamp on Roman law. Under Severus Alexander (222–235) flourished Ulpian and Paul, the former of whom, a Tyrian by descent, furnished material for one-half of Justinian's *Digest*.[2] The line of great jurists closes in the middle of the third century with Ulpian's pupil, the Greek Herennius Modestinus. Not long afterwards imperial rescripts take the place of the *responsa prudentium*, and, in interpretation as in legislation, the emperor remains the sole fount of law.

§ 18. These great masters of jurisprudence infused a new spirit into the law of Rome. Their intellectual energy is manifest in the effort to trace the underlying intention of dealings between parties, and to formulate it as a regulative principle for all cases that might conceivably arise. In their treatment of the law of obligations, for example, they devoted much thought to contracts where the *bona fides* or unexpressed intention had to be taken into account. " The law of obligations," says a modern authority, " and it alone, constitutes what is, in the truest and strictest sense, the imperishable portion of Roman law. It cannot be abolished. The intention of the purchaser and hirer, etc., is the same in all ages, and it is this intention that Roman law has made clear. . . . It is this wonderful discrimination, this clear-

---

[1] In the first and early second century there were two great schools at Rome, founded respectively by Labeo and Atteius Capito, Augustan jurists, and called, after followers of the two founders, the Proculian and Sabinian schools. See Sohm, *Institutes of Roman Law*, § 15.

[2] Scævola was a member of Marcus Aurelius' council of state; Papinian was prætorian prefect under Severus, his old fellow-pupil, and was killed by order of Caracalla (212). Ulpian and Paul held the prætorian prefecture under Severus Alexander, an emperor of Hellenic race.

sightedness in the adjustment of conflicting principles, guided
by a never-failing power of discerning the common elements;
this unique faculty for giving outward expression to the law
inherent in the concrete circumstances, which law, when found,
supplies the rule—with many practical variations, of course—
for all other circumstances of the same kind; these are the
features to which the writings of the Roman jurists owe their
incomparable charm, and the work they achieved its indestructible
force." [1]   At the same time these thinkers inspired Roman
jurisprudence with ideas derived from Greek philosophy, which
were destined, in this new medium, to influence the ethical and
juristic thought of later times.   The most striking instance is
the concept of law of nature (*jus naturale* or *naturae*).   Its source
lay in Stoicism, the one Hellenic system which evoked a wide
response from the practical Roman mind, and still, in the second
century, the foremost philosophical school of Greece.   Ulpian
was mainly responsible for incorporating this concept in the structure of Roman jurisprudence.   It comprised the universal rules
of conduct which flow from the nature of man as a rational being,
irrespective of race or time; such as those enjoining recognition
of the tie of kindred, respect for engagements, equitable ap-
portionment of gain or loss, supremacy of the intention over the
words in which it found imperfect expression.   Thus a slave has,
under the law of nature, rights denied to him by the civil law and
the *jus gentium*.   We shall return to this concept of *jus naturae*
in a later chapter.[2]   It had a long and memorable history, and
furnished a governing principle for the moral and political thought
of western Europe through more than fifteen hundred years.

---

[1] Sohm, § 15, pp. 73–4.
[2] See c. xi, §§ 15 ff.   The dividing line between law of nature (*jus
naturae*) and law of nations (*jus gentium*) was hard to draw.   Ulpian
solved the problem by defining the former as common to all animate
beings, while the latter was common to all mankind.   No other jurist
of the epoch took this view, though it appears in Justinian's *Digest* and
in mediæval writings.   Gaius, a pure Roman and of earlier date than
the great Greek and Græco-Oriental jurists, alone identifies *jus naturae*
and *jus gentium*, defining the latter as "the law which natural reason
appoints for all mankind."   Justinian followed him in this.   The case
of the slave, referred to in the text, points the difference.   War and
slavery are both contrary to law of nature, under which all men are born
free; they, and contracts, arise out of *jus gentium* : cf. *Institutes*, lib. i.
Tit. iii. 2. *Servitus autem est constitutio juris gentium, qua quis domino
alieno contra naturam subiicitur* ("Slavery is an institution of the law of
nations, by which a man is made subject to a foreign lord contrary to
nature").   *Jus gentium* included *jus inter gentes*, the nearest approach
reached by antiquity to "international" law.   See Encyc. Brit., 11th
ed., art. *Roman Law*, pp. 561, 562.

b. Literature (§§ 19–24).

§ 19. The literature of the epoch stands in close relation to the changing public life of the Roman state.

(i) The last generation of the republic produced two great poets : Lucretius, who expressed in hexameter verse the philosophic doctrines of Epicurus, and Catullus, whose lyrics rival those of Burns or Heine, while his range and personality recall Byron.[1] Among prose writers two names stand pre-eminent. Cæsar's genius in literature was second only to his genius in war and statesmanship. His speeches and letters were famous as masterpieces of style ; his record of the Gallic war is incomparable as a great historical narrative, and the very self-suppression of the author conveys a unique impression of his magnificent achievement.[2] But the truest representative of the age was the orator and republican statesman Cicero, whose prose writings —speeches, letters, treatises on oratory and philosophy—were recognised as the supreme models of the Latin language in his own and all after-time. Classical Latin means Latin as Cicero wrote it. Cicero used it to embody two great orders of ideas— the greatness of Rome and the ideal of humane culture. As to the one, we may quote the words of Newman : " Cicero vividly realised the status of a Roman senator and statesman, and the ' pride of place ' of Rome, in all the grace and grandeur which attached to her ; and he imbibed, and became, what he admired. As the exploits of Scipio or Pompey are the expression of this greatness in deed, so the language of Cicero is the expression of it in word. And, as the acts of the Roman ruler or soldier represent to us, in a manner special to themselves, the characteristic magnanimity of the lords of the earth, so do the speeches or treatises of her accomplished orator bring it home to our imagination as no other writing could do. Neither Livy, nor Tacitus, nor Terence, nor Seneca, nor Pliny, nor Quintilian, is an adequate spokesman for the Eternal City.

---

[1] On Lucretius' Epicureanism, see above, c. vi, § 18. He was little appreciated in antiquity, save by Virgil, whose thought and verse alike reveal his influence. Quintilian couples him with a third-rate Augustan poet, and writes him off as elegant in his own line but difficult to comprehend (*Inst. Orat.*, x, c. 1, § 87). It was left to the nineteenth century to recognise his poetic genius.

[2] In Quintilian's judgement, had he possessed the leisure, Cæsar's oratory would have equalled that of Cicero ; it was marked by the energy, directness and fire that he showed in the conduct of war (*Inst. Orat.*, x. 1, § 114).

They write Latin, Cicero writes Roman." [1] Oratory had been
from the first the art most respected and practised by the Romans;
from Cicero's day onwards, it became the central subject of
literature and of education. Poetry, history, philosophy, even
science, were valued as instruments of rhetoric; to be an orator
was the ambition of the able youth of Italy and the provinces,
and all their studies, at school and at the university, were organised
as a discipline to this end. Cicero's influence, thus immediately
operative on his own and the succeeding generations, continued
uninterruptedly through mediæval into modern times. While
Cicero the republican was destined to inspire the French Revolution, Cicero the humanist deeply influenced the culture of the
Renaissance. The matter of his philosophic writings may be
lacking in originality and speculative power; but Cicero's fame
as the greatest man of letters that ever lived rests rather on the
union in his person of the thinker and the man of affairs, and,
above all, on the fact that he embodied and expressed the urbanity
and humanism which mark the Græco-Roman age of civilization.
Thanks to the preservation of his letters, we know him better
than any other historic figure of antiquity.

§ 20. (ii) As the war with Carthage furnished a theme to
Ennius, and the conquest of Gaul to Cæsar, so the consolidation
of the civilized world under Augustus was the central fountain
of inspiration to the writers of the Augustan age. Prolific in
almost every field both of poetry and prose, it was, as the name
suggests, an age of direct literary patronage on the part of the
emperor and his ministers of state. We still speak, somewhat
superficially, of periods such as those of Louis XIV or Anne
as " Augustan " ages in French and English literature. The
favour of Augustus was free and generous, and doubtless served
as a stimulus to men of letters to celebrate the empire and its
ruler. But the chief source of inspiration was the empire itself—
the golden age of law and peace, that seemed to embrace all
civilized mankind, and to have closed for ever the disorder and
tumult of the civil wars. Filled with a sense of this achievement,
Livy compiled the history of Rome from its legendary beginnings
to the crowning of the structure by Augustus; even the ex-

---

[1] *Idea of a University* (Lecture on *Literature*), pp. 281, 282. The
last words mean, of course, not that Cicero's style was that of the typical
Roman, but that it reflects supremely the pride and majesty of the
imperial state. Some contemporaries accused him of being " unduly
turgid and Asiatic and redundant " (the *Orator* of Cicero, ed. Sandys,
Introduction, p. lx).

republican Horace turned from the placid delights of his Sabine farm to glorify the work of the emperor and the duty of patriotism in a noble group of odes.[1] But the poem which stands for ever as the supreme embodiment of the splendour and majesty of Rome is the *Æneid* of Virgil. Almost every line is inspired by a sense of the divine destiny of the imperial city, *nunc maxima rerum*, " now sovereign of the world." It was by decree of fate that Æneas was driven a wanderer over land and sea after the fall of Troy, till the providence of heaven established him on Latin soil as the forefather of the founders of Rome.[2] Piety— filial loyalty to the gods—was the motive of all his actions; of his desertion of Dido, the foundress of Carthage, Rome's historic enemy; of his journey to the underworld, where he beheld the forms of the great Romans that were to be; of his alliance with a Latin prince, and his foundation of a Latin city.[3] From first to last we are conscious of the poet's purpose, to tell how great was the labour to found the race of Rome.[4]

§ 21. The literature of the post-Augustan age is very different in tone. It was but for a moment that the stream of creative imagination could find satisfaction in the fact of empire. It could not permanently coalesce with what was after all a military despotism. We see signs of the change already in Ovid, the last poet of the Augustan era. A careless and irresponsible man of pleasure, a lover of society and the gay world of the capital, he possessed a marvellous skill in versification and poetic craftsmanship, and, what is more significant, for romantic narration. Ovid was not a poet of the highest rank, but one of the best second-rate poets in literature.[5] He deserves special

[1] The *Odes* referred to are Book III, *Odes* 1–6; *Odes* I, 12, 21, 35, 37; III, 14; IV, 2, 4–5, 14, 15, and the *Carmen Seculare*, bear on the same theme. The reader unversed in the classics is advised not to burden himself with reading Livy, even in a translation. He is inferior as a historian, both to the Greeks, and to Cæsar and Tacitus among the Romans.

[2] *Æn.*, i. 32 (*acti fatis*); cf. i. 208–10.

[3] *Æn.*, xii. 838–9. The pride of the Romans is as distinctive as their piety (*Æn.*, vi. 781, 823). Virgil realised that the Roman temper was pacific rather than militarist (*Æn.*, i. 286, *Romanos rerum dominos gentemque togatam*, " the Romans, lords of the world, the race clad in the gown of peace ").

[4] *Æn.*, i. 37; cf. i. 1–300; vi. 679–end; vii. 1–285; viii. 608–end; xii. 791–842; passages embodying the idea of imperial Rome. Virgil had been moved to write his (earlier) *Georgics* primarily by his love of country-life, but also because of Augustus' express desire to commend the care of agriculture to the Roman aristocracy.

[5] He was " a poet utterly in love with poetry," to quote Professor Gilbert Murray's appreciation of Ovid in his *Essays and Addresses*.

mention in this place, because his best work, the *Metamorphôses*, where the figures of Greek mythology are reflected through a strange romantic atmosphere, exercised a deep influence both on the Middle Ages and on the Renaissance. Dante drew on it for his knowledge of Greek legend, and it was the favourite classic of the great humanist, Montaigne. Still more extensive is the debt of later ages to Seneca of Cordova, Nero's chief minister and victim, and the foremost man of letters in his day. Seneca wrote voluminously, and in the flamboyant style; his work on physics, though destitute of scientific value, was received as authoritative by the Middle Ages, and his tragedies, full of wearisome rhodomontade, were ranked by Ben Jonson with those of the Attic dramatists.[1] The ethical treatises, on the other hand, are more deserving, both in style and contents, of their former great reputation. They developed the tenets of Stoicism in an elegant and attractive form, and were marked by sincerity of conviction, insight into human nature and a clear grasp of philosophical principles. To the humanists of the sixteenth century, and even to Descartes in the seventeenth, they appeared to be the last word in ethics. This is only one of many instances of the disproportionate value that attached, in the Middle Ages and in the Renaissance, to the post-Augustan writers who transmitted the noble inheritance of classical antiquity. In fact, Seneca was neither a great statesman nor a great thinker; his importance as a middleman of culture far outweighed his real merits.[2] In his sympathy for human weakness and sorrow, he struck a note which was alien to the traditions of orthodox Stoicism, and heralded the benevolent projects of the emperors of the second century. It was the presence of this new spirit in Seneca's writings that gave rise to the Christian legend of his personal friendship with St. Paul. Nor must we ignore the part he played in the process by which

[1] Mackail, *Lat. Lit.*, p. 175. In the lines prefixed by Ben Jonson to the first folio Shakespeare, we read :

" And though thou hadst small Latin and less Greek,
From thence to honour thee I would not seek
For names ; but call forth thund'ring Æschylus,
Euripides, and Sophocles to us,
Pacuvius, Attius, *him of Cordova dead*,
To life again, to hear thy buskin tread
And shake a stage."

[2] Quintilian, who appreciated his merits, while deprecating the baneful effects of his faults on contemporary taste, concludes his *critique* with the words : " He achieved the goal he set before him ; yet his nature fitted him for higher aims " (*Inst. Orat.*, x. 1, § 131).

the diction of classical Latin changed into that of the Middle Ages.[1]   An analogous significance attaches to two others of his contemporaries, both of whom shared his fate at Nero's hands; Lucan, Seneca's nephew, who sang the civil wars in epic verse and with republican sympathies; and Petronius Arbiter, whose novel, descriptive of the adventures of a Greek freedman in Italy, has preserved not only a brilliant picture of social manners but the sole remnants of popular speech under the early empire.[2]

§ 22. The period from Vespasian to Hadrian is known as the silver age in Latin literature.   Among a host of writers, three stand in relief because of their hold on after-times, Statius and Quintilian, who flourished under Domitian, and Tacitus, under Nerva and Trajan.   Statius is familiar to all readers of the *Divina Commedia* as the poet whose spirit joined the pilgrims in Purgatory and, after Virgil's departure, mounted with Dante and Beatrice into Paradise.   He won this tribute partly as an epic poet who followed, though at a far distance, in Virgil's footsteps, but chiefly for the strange legend that recorded his conversion to the Christian faith.   Quintilian's writings were of greater intrinsic merit and wielded an even more extensive influence.   Like Seneca, of Spanish birth, he practised in Rome

---

[1] Seneca's dramas are stiff and pompous, but in his Dialogues and Letters he is really important as exhibiting Latin at a stage when it is acquiring the flexibility of the modern Romance languages.   He shows a new freedom in using infinitives and adjectives as nouns, and in the enlarged use of prepositions which can carry in a concise way as much meaning as in French.   He was an innovator in inventing words, or at any rate in introducing many of them to respectable writing.   Such, for instance, are the Latin originals of the words " inspector," " favourable," " vulnerable," and " temporary."   How far the speech of common or cultivated persons differed from the style of Latin imposed on the world by the pre-eminence of Cicero it is difficult to estimate; but it is clear that Seneca introduced many useful words hitherto regarded as colloquial into good prose.   The gain he shows in flexibility of language is remarkable, and, though too anxious to make points, he writes at his best with a freedom and naturalness which are quite modern.   Quite modern, too, is his mastery of the short sentence, his betrayal of his own little weaknesses, his confidential air that the reader is interested in trifles concerning himself.   The neglect of his writings dates from the nineteenth century and is undeserved.   Montaigne, the father of the modern essay, learnt much from him.   (For this note I am indebted to the kindness of Mr. Vernon Rendall.)

[2] The novel had come to stay.   It originated among the Greeks of the Hellenistic period, but the Roman *satura* contributed a new element. In the middle of the second century, the chief Latin writer of prose romances was Apuleius; the best-known of his works is the tale of *Cupid and Psyché* in Books IV–VI of the *Metamorphôses* (or *the Golden Ass*). The tale has been translated by Walter Pater in *Marius the Epicurean,* and also in the *Loeb* translation of Apuleius, and in Andrew Lang's edition of Adlington's version.   See Mackail, *Lat. Lit.*, pp. 238 ff.

as a teacher and an advocate, and sharing to the full the Roman enthusiasm for oratory, published in 93 his chief work, the *Institutio Oratoria*. Its rediscovery in the sixteenth century marked an epoch in the history of humanism. In its twelve books, along with much other matter relevant to the study of rhetoric, were comprised a review of the entire field of Greek and Latin literature, unequalled in antiquity for breadth of view and appreciative judgement, and two discussions on the education of young children and of those of riper years. It was these last that specially stirred the minds of sixteenth-century scholars, who devoted earnest thought to projects of educational reform. Treatises on education in all times have for the most part borne the mark of mediocrity; but Quintilian's is an honourable exception. In a style dignified, polished and free alike from verbosity and affectation, he sketched the training proper to a Roman of the empire on principles that hold good for every age.[1] Moreover, following closely the example of Cicero, Quintilian fixed, for good or for evil, the conception of rhetoric that loomed so large in later Roman and mediæval

[1] Quintilian has been translated in the *Loeb* series by Butler. The review of classical literature is in Book X, c. 1, the treatment of education in Books I and XII. Quintilian held that the moral vices of the age were due to defective training, and insisted, among much else, on the value of literature in education, on the necessity of studying in youth the best authors, on the harm done by cramming and inferior text-books, on the need of the best teachers for beginners, the injuriousness of corporal punishment and the value of eurhythmics and physical exercises. On education under the early empire, see Hatch, *Hibbert Lectures* (1888) on *The influence of Greek ideas and usages upon the Christian Church*, lect. ii. There were grammar schools in the towns, and universities in the chief cities throughout the Roman world. Professors were highly paid, by state endowments and by grant of immunity from municipal burdens, a privilege of increasing value. University teachers were licensed, and selected either by the Emperor (compare our Regius Professors), or by local councils, or by special boards of electors; academic dress was worn by teachers and students; the terms "professor," "faculty," date from this period. In fact, the Roman system forms a stage in the development of the university, transitional between the Platonic Academy and its Greek successors, on the one hand, and the mediæval (and modern) universities, on the other. The main branches of education under the empire were (*a*) *Grammar*, i.e. the study of diction and *belles lettres*, (*b*) *Rhetoric*, i.e. the study and practice of literary expression and argument, including original composition and also logic, which led on to (*c*) *Philosophy*. Dio Chrysostom tells how he found, in a Greek colony north of the Euxine, that nearly every resident knew the *Iliad* by heart. Public lecturing had an enormous vogue, contributing (as also did state patronage) to the decline of intellectual life by fostering a thirst for popular display in the lecturers and a superficial curiosity in their audiences. That there was also a genuine desire for knowledge is illustrated by Eunapius' tale of two college students, who could afford only one gown between them, so that the one had to stay in bed while the other attended lectures.

education. The third name that calls for mention, not so much for his unquestioned greatness as a writer, as for his influence on the judgement of posterity, is that of Tacitus. Amid the equable and halcyon atmosphere of the reign of Trajan, " a time when men may think what they will, and say what they think," he looked back upon the days when Roman society trembled beneath the sinister suspicions of Tiberius and the wild caprice of Nero, and when the Roman world, on Nero's death, was devastated by the contending armies of the claimants to the throne. In the *Annals* and the *Histories* he stamped the rulers of the first century with the indelible brand of his irony and indignation. Tacitus, if not the greatest of Roman historians, was the greatest Roman writer of history; by the power of his style, his mastery of epigram and innuendo and his subtlety in the analysis of motive, he determined for fifteen centuries the verdict of the civilized world upon the early empire. It is one of the triumphs of modern historical research to have reversed, or at least to have profoundly modified, that judgement. Neither Tacitus, nor the satires of Juvenal, his contemporary, suffice any longer to guide our estimate of imperial Rome; but their terrible indictment of the degradation of Roman life and morals, and their sense of bitter disillusionment, stand in dramatic contrast to the hopes with which, a century earlier, Virgil had hailed in the founder of the empire the herald of a golden age.

§ 23. Between Tacitus and Augustine there is no first-rank figure in Latin literature. A considerable body of writings have come down to us from the three intervening centuries, largely by Christian authors and of varying interest; the philologist, for example, can trace the change, referred to above, from classical towards mediæval Latin. The beautiful *Pervigilium Veneris*, in its use of the stanza and the refrain, heralds the Provençal poetry of the early Middle Ages.[1] At the beginning of the fifth century, Jerome, in his cell in Palestine, composed the Vulgate, or Latin version of the Scriptures, which influenced the future of the language almost as deeply as Luther's translation influenced the German, or the Authorised Version of 1611 the English, tongue. Jerome's contemporary in the West, Augustine, was the last Latin author of original genius. Standing on the border-line between antiquity and the Middle Ages, he

[1] See Mackail, pp. 243–6. The authorship of the poem is unknown, and its date uncertain, though it indisputably belongs to this intervening period.

represents the fusion of Græco-Roman culture, now in the throes
of dissolution, and the victorious spirit of Christianity.   Of his
work as thinker and theologian, and of his incalculable influence
as an authority in western Christendom, we shall speak in a
later chapter.   We note here merely his reverence for Rome
and Roman law, and the enthusiasm with which he absorbed
the thought and literature of the past.   Though he read the judgement of heaven in Alaric's sack of Rome, he vindicated the
rightful claim of the empire to world dominion as the prize due
to Roman virtue.   The arguments of the second book of Dante's
de Monarchiâ were drawn from Augustine's book, *The City of
God (Civitas Dei)*.   The intimate association of Latin literature
with the life of the imperial state was preserved in this last great
utterance of ancient Rome.   With Boethius, the minister of
Theodoric the Ostrogoth in the sixth century, a writer noteworthy rather for his influence on mediæval learning than for
originality of mind, Latin literature reaches its close.[1]

§ 24. Meanwhile, in the eastern provinces, the Greek language
and literature held its own.   The spread of Hellenism in the
West had created for Greek works a wider public; every cultured
Roman was able to read them in the original.   Innumerable
books on history, biography, the physical and mathematical
sciences, literary criticism, and philosophy, were composed by
Greek authors in the century before and after the birth of Christ.
Galen's epoch-making work in medicine dates from the latter
half of the second century.   Of the course of philosophic thought
and the rise of Christian theology we shall treat in the ensuing
chapter.   One name must be mentioned here, that of Plutarch of
Chæronea, who, both as a citizen and as a writer, revived something of the best spirit of the great days of Greece.   He wrote
much and on many subjects, including ethics and religion.[2]   But
his fame with posterity rested chiefly on his incomparable bio-
graphies of the famous Greeks and Romans of the past.   Plutarch
was not a great historian, and wrote, partly for edification,
partly from an ardent sympathy with noble character and noble
action.   His *Lives* have probably influenced literature and history
more widely than any other single work of classical antiquity.
They furnished Shakespeare with material for his dramas; they
went far to inspire the republican idealism of the French Revolutionary leaders.   For young and old they still form the best

[1] On Augustine, see below, c. ix, § 22; and on Boethius, c. x, § 8 and
c. xi, § 8.   [2] On Plutarch's philosophy of religion, see below, c. ix, § 7.

introduction to Greek and Roman history. To all lovers of historic personalities they give as keen a delight to-day as eighteen hundred years ago.

IV. Conclusion (§§ 25-7).

§ 25. The change from republic to empire was symptomatic of the deeper and more gradual change that was passing over the thought and life of the Græco-Roman world. Hellenic civilization arose and flourished in intimate association with the city-state; its supersession by a world-despotism carried with it a revolution in men's intellectual and spiritual outlook. Ideals of life were henceforward dissevered from political activity. Men sought for consolation and support either in philosophic speculation or in supernatural religion. We saw, when speaking of the Hellenic world under the successors of Alexander, how both the dominant philosophic schools, the Stoic and the Epicurean, claimed to satisfy this demand of the individual soul, in detachment from the public life of the state. In religion, the conservative efforts of Augustus to restore the old national worships proved fruitless; they could not prevail against the new and strange faiths that spread in this age from the eastern world to Rome. The religions of Isis, Cybele and Mithra found a multitude of adherents, in the imperial city and throughout the provinces, among those who had not the capacity or the inclination to pursue the austere paths of metaphysics. Those paths were for the wise and strong, and of such there were few; others, in equal need of spiritual satisfaction, turned elsewhere, and above all towards the East. The East, too, was turning towards them. Of the nature and issues of this contact we shall speak in the ensuing chapter; alike as a creative stimulus and as provocative of reaction, it proved the most momentous crisis in human history.

§ 26. Side by side with this demand for spiritual satisfaction on the part of the individual we remark a growing consciousness of the common humanity of mankind. We have seen its expression in the jurists' conception of a law of nature, in the reflexion within the sphere of law of Stoic cosmopolitanism, and in the measures of public philanthropy enacted by the paternal care of the great emperors of the second century, Trajan, Hadrian and the two Antonines. Yet more striking is the presence of this sense of universal brotherhood in the epic poem of Virgil.

We have spoken of the *Æneid* as the noblest and most enduring monument of the majesty of the Roman empire. This is the thought to which Tennyson gave utterance in his lines on Virgil :—

> " Now thy Forum roars no longer,
>   fallen every purple Cæsar's dome—
> Tho' thine ocean roll of rhythm
>   sound for ever of Imperial Rome."

Other Latin poets had voiced, if in less splendid verse, their sense of Rome's imperial greatness. But there is a further quality in Virgil's poetry that has no parallel in earlier literature. He looks out upon life with a breadth of sympathy, a deep and universal tenderness, that is in strange contrast with the pride of intellect and exclusiveness of culture which mark the literature and philosophy of his predecessors. In his catholicity of feeling Virgil is the herald of a new era in the spiritual history of mankind. Later generations, bred in the Christian faith, singled him out among pre-Christian writers as an *anima naturaliter Christiana*, a spirit by nature Christian—by nature, i.e. without the aid of revelation. Doubtless the famous fourth Eclogue, in which the poet foretold the return of the golden age in language strikingly suggestive of the Messianic prophecies of Isaiah, gave the stimulus to this reverence for Virgil to the uncritical spirit of the early Middle Ages.[1] Doubtless, too, the imperial poet shared in their eyes the peculiar sanctity which attached to the institution of the Roman empire. But the feeling sprang from something deeper than these more conscious motives. Virgil, alone among pre-Christian poets, was touched by the " still sad music of humanity " to a breadth of human tenderness that heralds the democratic message of Christianity. In the sixth book of the *Æneid*, the father of Rome beholds in the underworld the dead thronging the banks by " the deep pools of Cocytus and the Stygian marsh." " Hither all crowded and rushed streaming to the bank, matrons and men and high-hearted heroes dead and done with life, boys and unwedded girls, and children laid young on the bier before their parents' eyes, multitudinous as leaves fall dropping in the forests at autumn's earliest frost, or birds swarm landward from the deep gulf, when the chill of the year routs them overseas and drives them to sunny lands. They stood pleading for the first passage

---

[1] See above, p. 58, *note* 1. The sixth book of the *Æneid* caused Virgil to be regarded also as an authority on the world beyond the grave.

across, and stretched forth passionate hands to the farther shore." [1] We can trace in Virgil a desire for the life beyond the grave, which comes nearer to the spirit of Christian hope than any utterance of the Greek philosophers. It was no mere æsthetic devotion of poet to poet, nor a mere echo of popular tradition, that led Dante to seek Virgil's guidance through Hell and Purgatory to the threshold of the Christian Paradise.

§ 27. The Middle Ages, strong in the conviction of revealed truth, made bold to interpret the history of the Roman empire in the light of the divine plan of government for the world. They saw in the work of Julius and Augustus, as in the story of the chosen people of Israel, a *praeparatio evangelica*. Modern historians, on the other hand, have been content to limit their inquiry and their judgement to its actual effects upon the happiness and civilization of mankind. If in this spirit we ask what the establishment of the imperial system meant for the Roman world, we must rest our conclusions not so much on literary histories that express the natural hostility of republican idealists, as on the evidence for the effects of the system on the silent millions, whose welfare was the chief concern of the imperial government. It is in the equitable adjustment of taxation, in the impartial administration of law, in the founding of cities and public works, in the unimpeded development of commerce, in the extension of citizen privileges and local self-government, which for the first time opened up wide prospects of advancement for all freemen, and, above all, in the effective defence of the frontiers and the maintenance of universal peace, that the true nature of the imperial system is disclosed. The two great historians who have interpreted Rome to the modern world manifest a striking agreement in their verdict. Gibbon, writing in the last half of the eighteenth century, summed up his survey of the state of the Roman world in the second century A.D. in these well-known words :—

" If a man were called to fix the period in the history of the world during which the condition of the human race was most happy and prosperous, he would, without hesitation, name that which elapsed from the death of Domitian to the accession of Commodus.[2] The vast extent of the Roman empire was governed by absolute power, under the guidance of virtue and wisdom. The armies were restrained by the firm and gentle hand of four successive emperors, whose characters and authority

[1] *Æn.* vi. 305–14 : *tr.* Mackail.   [2] A.D. 96–180.

commanded involuntary respect. The forms of the civil administration were carefully preserved by Nerva, Trajan, Hadrian and the Antonines, who delighted in the image of liberty, and were pleased with considering themselves as the accountable ministers of the laws." [1]

Gibbon's work was compiled in the main from literary records; since he wrote, the progress of historical inquiry has laid bare a vast and varied mass of contemporary inscriptions.[2] A century after the publication of the *Decline and Fall*, Theodor Mommsen embodied a comprehensive survey of this new material in his volume on the Roman provinces under the empire. His judgement, if more cautious in expression, is to the same effect at that of Gibbon.

" Even now there are various regions of the East, as of the West, as regards which the imperial period marks a climax of good government, very modest in itself, but never withal attained before or since; and, if an angel of the Lord were to strike the balance whether the domain ruled by Severus Antoninus was governed with the greater intelligence and the greater humanity at that time or in the present day, whether civilization and national prosperity generally have since that time advanced or retrograded, it is very doubtful whether the decision would prove in favour of the present." [3]

How far is this judgement true ? The question must be faced, if we are to measure the value either of Rome's work in history, or of the new forces that broke in upon her sovereignty and possessed themselves of her inheritance. We must not suffer our vision to be blinded by the magnitude and the duration of her power, or forget that the verdict of history is always passed on the quality rather than on the quantity of the achievement. If we fix our minds on this, we shall hardly accept the statements of Gibbon and Mommsen without reserve. Their judgement is true, if by happiness we mean material comfort, and if we take economic welfare and the maintenance of social order as our standards of civilization. It is easy to understand how, after generations of public strife and private suffering, the advent of a world-peace under the ægis of the Cæsars seemed to the poets of Augustan Rome like the dawn of a golden age.[4]

[1] *Decline and Fall*, c. 3.
[2] Gibbon also made use of the records collected by the French *Académie des Inscriptions*.
[3] *Provinces of the Roman Empire*, Introduction.
[4] E.g. *Æn.*, i. 295, vi. 791-2.

The Roman empire realised the ideal of paternal government in a degree to which history affords no parallel, save in the rule of Britain over India and Egypt until recent times. And, if paternal government is the last word in civilization, the downfall of that empire in the centuries that followed was the most melancholy event in the annals of mankind. The poets dreamed that Rome would stand for ever, and even the stern reality of the decline and fall hardly availed to dispel the illusion. Yet already in the hour of its inauguration there was that within the empire which foreshadowed its dissolution. A bureaucratic despotism, for all its integrity and its enlightenment, could evoke no living response from the subject-peoples who reaped its benefits. The spirit of man craves not comfort, but liberty, not economic stability or equitable administration, but the right, at the cost of infinite toil and tribulation, to work out its own salvation. Its desire in all ages is not for happiness, but for life. In the colossal structure of Roman government men were conscious only of the crushing burden, and awaited in dumb passivity the hour of their deliverance. They were pawns in the hand of the Fate, transcendent and inexorable, that brooded over the fortunes of the world.[1] Rome was impotent, for all her majesty of power, to reinvigorate the peoples beneath her sway. She offered them no " causes " that could stir men's hearts to effort on their behalf with a good hope of triumphant realisation, such as Christianity (or Communism) offers to the modern world.[2] The founts of life were elsewhere, in the wild hordes of Teutons that even now were beating against the frontiers, and in the new faith, born under Augustus' principate among a despised people of the East, and destined ere long to shake to its foundations the fabric of Græco-Roman civilization

[1] Cf. Napoleon's saying : " *la politique est la fatalité*." On the impossibility of an active sentiment of loyalty to the empire, see Davis, *Mediaeval Europe*, pp. 19, 20.

[2] See Bevan, in *The Hellenistic Age* (pp. 98 ff.), on absence of " causes " in this age, and how Christianity furnished a " cause."

CHAPTER IX

CHRISTIANITY

I. The Expansion of Christianity over the Roman World
(§§ 1–6).

§ 1. A GENERATION had not passed since the establishment of the
Roman empire by Augustus when the founder of Christianity
was born into the world. *Imperante Augusto natus est.* The
significance of this fact in world-history cannot be measured
solely by the influence wielded by the Christian church on the
religious and social life of Christendom. The church, like all
other institutions, was but the outward embodiment of the living
faith from which it drew its energy. The foundation of that
faith was the personality of Jesus. The spirit of his life passed
into the lives of his immediate followers and through them
into the world around, transforming men's hearts and minds
with a suddenness and swiftness without parallel in history.
A new power was at work, which revolutionised the entire
fabric of Mediterranean civilization.[1] At the moment when Jesus
died on the cross by sentence of a Roman procurator, his mission
had to all appearance ended in failure; only a handful of unlettered rustics, mostly women, remained faithful to the last.
Three centuries later, Constantine, in establishing Christianity
as the uniform religion of the empire, was simply acknowledging
an accomplished fact. It was not merely that the old cults
were supplanted by a new, but rather that the entire substructure of Græco-Roman society, from which those cults had
sprung, was undermined, and that in its place there was arising
a new order, permeated by the spirit of Christianity, which
was reflected, not only in the field of religious faith and worship,
but in morals and law, in art and literature, in the treatment
of slaves and women, in men's whole outlook upon life. When
we ask, as the student of history needs must ask, for the grounds

---

[1] This assertion is perfectly compatible with the recognition of the
historic continuity between Christianity and pre-Christian Jewish and
Hellenic thought. A fair mind can hardly fail to be impressed by the
disparity between the Christian faith, as we find it working in the world
in the early centuries, and any other philosophical or religious creed
known to history. Affinities in points of detail would not be so arresting,
were not the differences of spirit and influence so profound. Effects
demand adequate causes. No combination of causes is adequate that
excludes, as a predominant factor, the personality of Jesus.

of this transformation, they are to be found in the unique quality of the faith that Jesus inspired in his disciples. The question is not one of the speculative value of Christian dogma. Christianity was not a new philosophy, but a new religion. Jesus bade men believe, not in an idea, but in a person, who had lived and died as a man amongst men. He claimed that in this person the Son of God from love of man had taken human form, and been born on earth, at a definite moment of history, to found the kingdom of heaven and bring salvation to mankind. Idea and actuality, fact and value, were indissolubly conjoined in the person of Jesus. It was only after Christianity had won its empire over the Græco-Roman world, that its speculative implications were disengaged from this core of concrete religious faith, and formulated, under the influence of Hellenic thought, in a system of theological doctrine. It was the overpowering impression of Christ's personality and sacrifice that gave life to the instruments of church and dogma, and won for the Christian gospel the allegiance of the Mediterranean world.

§ 2. Christianity arose and spread in relation to a historical context. In its origin, it was rooted in the soil of Judaism; its advance was conditioned by the culture of the Græco-Roman world. Born a Jew, observant in all points of Jewish ceremonial, circumcised on the eighth day in accordance with Mosaic prescript, Jesus declared that he came not to destroy the law, but to fulfil. His first mission was " to the lost sheep of the house of Israel." His teaching is reminiscent at every turn of the Jewish scriptures and of the religious tradition and practice of the Jewish race. Preaching in the synagogue at Nazareth, He took for His theme a passage from the Servant-songs of the Second Isaiah.[1] The kingdom which he proclaimed to be at hand was the natural fulfilment of the vision of the prophets. When those who, like the Pharisees, looked for the coming of the kingdom and the resurrection from the dead, failed to recognise in him the promised deliverer, it was not he that rejected Judaism, but Judaism that rejected him.[2] In their very refusal they were treading in the

[1] Is. lxi. 1; See Luke iv. 16 ff. and above c. iii, § 15 ad fin.
[2] The Pharisees (= " separated ") combined devotion to the law with its interpretation in the light of later tradition, which was often of a liberalising tendency. They were strongly nationalist and had a large popular following; they looked for a restored kingdom under a secular prince of Davidic line, and opposed the priestly ideal of the Sadducees. The Sadducees were aristocratic and sacerdotal, and very conservative in their adherence to the law as opposed to later tradition; e.g. they denied the resurrection (Acts xxiii. 6–8; Matt. xxii. 23–33). Christianity

steps of their forefathers who had killed the prophets and stoned those who had been sent unto them. For Christ's doctrine of the kingdom, founded on the larger hope of Hebrew prophecy, stood in sharp contrast to the patriotic aspirations of his contemporaries. While they expected a Messiah who should achieve a secular liberation from the hated yoke of Rome, and establish in Zion a nationalist theocracy over the princes and peoples of the earth, he broke for ever with these particularist ambitions, and, resisting the temptation to institute an earthly sovereignty, declared that his kingdom was not of this world. Herein lay the incompatibility between the old faith and the new. Henceforward their severance could only be a question of time. The rapid spread of Christianity in Jerusalem in the years following Christ's death provoked the bitter hostility of the Jewish ecclesiastical authorities, to whom the Roman government allowed a wide measure of autonomy.[1] The propagation of the gospel among the Gentiles brought the issue to a crisis. Already before the conversion of Saul of Tarsus it had won adherents among the non-Jewish population in Syria and Cyprus.[2] Were these Gentile converts to be subjected to the rite of circumcision and the manifold rigours of the Mosaic law ? Was it not possible to be a Christian without also being a Jew ? It was on the morrow of his first missionary journey that St. Paul, despite strong opposition within the Christian community and his own strong Jewish attachments, carried the day with his policy of emancipation.[3] He proclaimed the watchword of his mission in his letter to the Galatian churches : " For in Christ Jesus neither circumcision availeth anything, nor uncircumcision, but faith working through

---

made many converts among the Pharisees; the Sadducees were bitterly hostile (Acts v. 17). The future of Judaism rested with the Pharisees, whose view of the law as supplemented by tradition lay at the root of the Rabbinical teaching in the early centuries of our era.

[1] See the Additional Note to c. iii. above, on the Roman administration of Judæa. For the Jewish persecutions of the Christians, see Acts viii. 1–4 (before 42); xii. 1–2 (in 43–4); they were directed against the tendency to liberalism and Hellenism among Christian Jews of the dispersion (e.g. Stephen), rather than against Christianity as such.

[2] Acts xi. 19–21; especially among Gentile proselytes to Judaism, who were very numerous in the eastern provinces of the empire; there were many who accepted Judaism in everything except circumcision and certain other ceremonial practices.

[3] Acts x, xv. 1–31 (decision of the church at Jerusalem); xxi. 17 ff.; Gal. ii. In the Epistles to the Galatians and the Romans, St. Paul, in face of opposition from Judaising Christians in Asia, defines his attitude towards the Jewish law. The result was the rising at Jerusalem after his return from his second journey in 58, fomented by Jews from Asia (Acts xxi. 17 ff.).

love." [1] The die was cast.   From this time onwards Christianity,
though still confounded with Judaism by the outside world,
developed as a free and independent faith.   The dispersion of
the Jews after the destruction of Jerusalem by Titus (70) and the
still more terrible subjugation under Hadrian (136) struck a
fatal blow both at Jewish nationalism and at the Judaising
party within the church.   Jerusalem ceased to be regarded as
the religious centre of Christianity, and the Judaising Christians,
who survived for many generations under the name of Ebionites
or Nazoræans in the region east of the Jordan, had no influence
on its subsequent history.   By the reign of Trajan the distinction
of Jew from Christian was recognised throughout the Roman
world.[2]   In that larger world, and not within the narrow pale of
Judaism, lay the future of the new religion.   But, long before
the process of emancipation was complete, Christianity had been
impregnated with the spirit, and, to a certain extent, the letter,
of the parent faith.   From Israel it inherited the belief in one
God, the creator and ruler of the universe, the father of mankind,
who, as a spiritual person, demanded from his children the
personal service of a righteous life.[3]   It inherited also the Old
Testament scriptures, which were accepted as a divine revelation,
while they were divested of their particularist implications and
interpreted in the light of the conviction of Jesus' Messiahship.
Therewith was received into Christian practice a code of moral
precepts, unique in purity, and applicable to the homeliest
concerns of daily life.   Moreover, the worship of the early church
was largely modelled on the simple service of the Jewish synagogue

[1] Gal. v. 6.
[2] The Ebionites (= " poor ") were separated from the church by the
end of the second century, but survived, especially in Egypt and Arabia,
till the fourth.   The Jews found it to their interest to make the distinction clear to the Roman authorities, for, while Judaism was officially
tolerated, Christianity was not.   In the second century the Jews ceased
to proselytise actively, and Judaism has remained a separate religion
ever since.   As Judaism recoiled from the West, so Christianity has never
struck root on Semitic soil.
[3] This belief stood in striking contrast to the Græco-Roman cults,
which were never predominantly ethical, and often definitely immoral.
Judaism and Christianity stood alone in grounding morality on religion,
yet without reducing religion to terms of an ethical rule.   These two
religions realised that worship is more than discipline, though involving
discipline as an inherent factor.   Mithraism, which never took root on
Hellenic soil, is an exception to the general rule (see below, § 8).   Greek
philosophers attained to a spiritual monotheism; but its groundwork was
scientific rather than ethical, and they failed to establish a society on
its basis.   It remained the belief of individual thinkers or, at most, of a
philosophic school.

with its prayers, its hymns, its reading and exposition of the scriptures. Christian spiritual experience found expression in prophetic vision, like that of the seers and prophets of ancient Israel. The vivid expectation of Christ's second coming (the *parousia*), and the whole circle of beliefs and hopes associated therewith—in the resurrection, the divine judgement and the age to come—took shape in imagery and language that present a close analogy to Jewish apocalyptic literature.[1] The conceptions of Satan, of angels and evil demons, of an earthly millennium, of the condemnation of the wicked to physical torment, were but a few of these Jewish survivals which left an abiding impress on Christian eschatology. Finally, the record of God's dealings with the Jewish people was regarded from the first as a preparation for the gospel. Yahweh was the one true God, who " spake by the prophets " to the Christian as aforetime to the Jew. The ever-widening gulf between the society of Christ's followers and orthodox Judaism served but to enhance this consciousness of the spiritual obligation that the Christian faith owed to the religion of Israel.[2]

§ 3. The Roman empire furnished the field for the expansion of the Christian faith. Of progress beyond its borders little is known, and that little is of slight moment. St. Paul, the apostle of the Gentiles, and himself a Roman citizen, headed straight for the Hellenic provinces, founding churches in the chief centres of trade and culture, such as Ephesus, Thessalonica, Philippi, Corinth and Athens. His first appeal was to his co-religionists in the synagogues. Among his auditors were many

[1] See Charles, *Eschatology*, cc. ix–xi. There were numerous early Christian apocalypses, of which that ascribed to St. John alone found admission into the New Testament canon. Hatch (*Hibbert Lectures* for 1888, Lect. viii), points out how, while Greek ethics reflected the civic life and government of the *Polis*, Jewish ethics reflected the rule of the eastern sheikh, the paymaster and judge of his dependants. The ideas of wages for work done and of retributive justice, of atonement for sin and of remission of the debt owed by man to God, figure prominently in early Christian literature. Further, it should be noted that the belief in the resurrection of the body connects with Jewish antecedents, that in the immortality of the soul with Hellenic; Christianity taught both.

[2] Both Christian monotheism and Christian ethics developed under Hellenic influences in ways for which Judaism afforded no precedent. The belief in the person of Jesus took shape in language and ideas akin to those current in the Græco-Oriental mystery-religions. Much is being done by scholars at the present day to throw light on this difficult and extremely interesting question. While Jewish Christians accepted Jesus in the light of apocalyptic Messianism, Greek Christians accepted him in the light of the mystery-cults, with their sacramental teaching. See Kennedy, *St. Paul and the Mystery-Religions*.

who, though not professing Jews, were conversant with the Jewish faith and well disposed towards it; the hostility of the orthodox and the ready adhesion of these Gentiles led swiftly to the preaching of the gospel beyond the Jewish pale. Carried a prisoner to Rome in 61, St. Paul found a Christian community already in being; three years before, he had written to them a letter, commending their faith as known throughout the world.[1] On his acquittal by the imperial tribunal two years later, he resumed his missionary labours, returning to Rome to perish, with St. Peter, in the persecution under Nero in 64. In less than twenty years since St. Paul first set sail from Antioch, Christianity had taken firm root throughout the empire, alike in east and west, in congregations organised under chosen elders (*presbyters*) or bishops.[2] Of its history in the half-century between Nero

[1] St. Paul's chief missionary activity in Asia Minor, Macedonia and Greece, dates from his second journey (52–8); see Acts xv. 36 to xxi. 16. The epistles to the Thessalonians, Corinthians, Galatians and Romans date, probably in this order, from the same period. The epistles to the Ephesians, Philippians and Colossians were written during his captivity at Rome (61–63). On the church at Rome, see Acts xviii. 2, Rom. xv. 24, where St. Paul speaks of it as having been in existence for some time before the date of his letter (58). On the faith of the Roman church, see Rom. i. 8.

[2] In the apostolic age, the general supervision of the churches was in the hands of the Apostles, who travelled from church to church, exercising the higher functions (e.g. ordination and confirmation) which afterwards devolved on the bishops. The local ministry had but a limited and subordinate scope. The two features, of local self-government of each church and general supervision of all the churches, were thus present in germ from the outset. The former received definite shape earlier than the latter. Government of each church by a single bishop, presbyters and deacons was the rule at Antioch in the time of Ignatius (early second century), and was general throughout Christendom in the third century. At first, the terms "presbyter" and "overseer" (Greek, *episcopos*) or "bishop" were identical in usage; gradually the bishop's office was separated from that of the presbyters. In the early third century, the bishop was still elected by the laity, with whom he stood in close personal relations as the shepherd of his particular flock; but in the chief towns there grew up during that century a large body of presbyters and deacons, between the bishop and the laity. The presbyters became the spiritual, the deacons the administrative, intermediaries of the bishop. In the fourth and fifth centuries the gulf between the bishop and the laity widened, the clergy (with many new grades of offices) were alone in close touch with the bishop, and the election of the bishop passed from the people into their hands. In place of popular election followed by approval by the clergy, clerical election was followed by popular confirmation. The same two centuries saw also (*a*) the vindication by the presbyters of the right to celebrate the eucharist and to preach, i.e. the rise of a sacerdotal conception of the priesthood, and (*b*) the parochial system, with a presbyter in charge of each parochial church. All these changes came about slowly and naturally; they were not the result of any deliberate policy, though maintained by deliberate policy when once established.

and Trajan there is scanty record; but the results show that the period was one of unbroken and vigorous activity. The two chief centres of Christian life were the churches of Rome and Antioch, which worked in close co-operation. The story of the persecutions in the second century reveals the presence of Christian communities, not only in Italy, Greece and Asia, but in Africa and Gaul, in Britain, and in the wilds of Dalmatia. The converts, though drawn in the main from the proletariate, included men and women of wealth and station.[1] Christians had risen to high rank in the army and the civil service; some were appointed even to provincial governorships. "We are of yesterday," wrote Tertullian as the century drew to its close, "but we have filled your whole world, cities, islands, country towns and settlements, even the camps, the tribes, the decuries of judges, the palace, the senate, the bar. We have left you only your temples. We can count your armies: the Christians of a single province exceed them in number."[2] Christianity had become a force to be reckoned with in society and in the world. Philosophers and men of letters took note of its existence. The government was alarmed at the rapid spread of an unlicensed confraternity, and issued stern decrees for its suppression. The Christians felt the necessity of championing their faith in the face of popular calumny and official persecution; and the abler minds among them composed apologetic writings in its defence. Meanwhile, disruptive tendencies were at work within the church. The prophets and prophetesses of Montanism, voicing the revolt of personal inspiration against eccesiastical discipline, spread the menace of anarchy from Phrygia to Africa and the west; while, in the eastern provinces, Gnostic teachers threatened to dissolve the faith in an historical Christ into a phantasmagoria of speculative

---

See C. H. Turner, on "The organisation of the church," *Camb. Mediaeval History*, vol. i. c. 6. The institution of a priesthood, entered voluntarily, open to all, and independent of civic and political institutions, was peculiar to Christianity; the first two features distinguish it from Judaism, the last from Græco-Roman cults.

[1] Christianity first took root among the workers in industrial and commercial centres; e.g. the oldest church at Alexandria was beside the wharves; and, even at the height of its worldly sovereignty, it never lost the democratic impress stamped upon it by its founder and his disciples. Through its influence, the poor acquired a status denied to them by the best thought and practice of Greece and Rome. Prior to Christianity, the Greek word employed in the New Testament for "poor" (*ptóchos*) was used always in a depreciatory sense, to mean one who cringes and begs. See Bosanquet, *Theory of the State*, p. 297, and Liddell and Scott's *Lexicon* (*s.v. πτωχός*).

[2] *Apol.*, 37, tr. Bigg, *Origins*, p. 258.

abstractions. On the one hand lay the danger of antinomianism, on the other, that of absorption into Hellenic metaphysics. The nucleus of dogmatic theology, of which we shall speak presently, is discernible in these second-century controversies. They called into play the intellectual weapons that had been forged by the genius of Greek philosophers. Side by side with the intellectual legacy of Hellenism, Christianity began also to absorb the political legacy of Rome. Need was felt for a regulating authority, alike in faith and practice. Though each church as yet preserved its local independence, there prevailed throughout Christendom a strong consciousness of unity, which was bound to issue in the establishment of a central regulative organ. The world had long been habituated to look to Rome as to the fountain of law and justice. Her secular vocation and authority had been recognised by St. Paul, who taught with no uncertain voice the duty of obedience to the civil government.[1] To " render unto Cæsar the things that are Cæsar's " was an accepted part of the Christian rule of life. It was inevitable that the imperial system should set its mark deep on the structure of the Christian community. As in the secular economy of the empire all roads led to Rome, so the Roman church and its bishop formed the natural centre of ecclesiastical intercommunication for the other churches of Christendom. Not that there was yet any question of the formal recognition of the primacy of the Roman see. The Roman bishops claimed no right to override the autonomy of local churches. Such authority as they possessed was *de facto* rather than *de jure*.[2] But Rome felt from early days an instinctive consciousness of œcumenical responsibility. The first

[1] See Rom. iii. 1–7, and compare 1 Peter ii. 13–17. These passages define the Christian position in opposition both to Jewish nationalism and to anarchical tendencies among early Christians. The duty of obedience to the " powers that be," as " ordained of God," is insisted on uniformly by the Fathers of the first six centuries.

[2] In theory, all bishops were equal; each stood for the unity of his particular church. But, in practice, a hierarchy arose naturally within the episcopate. The provincial system of the empire gave the metropolitan an authority superior to the other bishops of the province. The greater the see, the greater the *prima facie* claim of its bishop to a commanding dignity. Rome, Alexandria, Antioch and (after Constantine) Constantinople were rivals for eminence in the fourth century. The same period saw the definite assertion of papal claims to appellate jurisdiction and to legislative authority, especially by the worldly and able pope Damasus (366–84). The council of Sardica (343) had recognised the pope as judge of appeals, under reservations. Pope Liberius (352 to 366) had been the first to issue decretals. Papal authority was largely extended by the greatest of the early popes, Leo I (440–61). See C. H. Turner, *loc. cit.*, and Davis, *Mediaeval Europe* (Home University Library), p. 125.

epistle of Clement, written at the close of the first century, expresses the active interest of the Roman church in the spiritual welfare of other Christian communities. These in turn viewed the Roman church with natural veneration. Her illustrious apostolic tradition, gathered round the martyrdoms of St. Peter and St. Paul, the numbers and influence of her members, the bounty which their wealth enabled them to dispense to less favoured congregations, and, above all, her unquestioned orthodoxy and sobriety of judgement—these combined with her central position and the prestige of the imperial metropolis to strengthen her growing authority as the leader of Christendom. Irenæus, a Gallic bishop of Asiatic birth, and the foremost champion of orthodoxy in the closing years of the second century, spoke of her " superior sovereignty " (*potentior principatus*) as the exponent of apostolical faith.[1] In all the most important developments in the life of the church, such as the organisation of the episcopal hierarchy, the fixing of the New Testament canon, the formulation of the baptismal confession as the apostolic rule which served as the nucleus of a creed, and the regulation of internal discipline, Rome played a leading part. "*Dans la pratique*," writes a modern scholar, "*on s'inspire partout des idées romains.*" Especially in the handling of such delicate questions as moral offences among Christians, the treatment of apostates in times of persecution, and the growth of ascetic practices, her sound judgement and instinct for ecclesiastical statesmanship were of incalculable service to Christianity.[2] Nor was the Roman church merely a disciplinary and legislative power. Her constancy amid persecution gave evidence that her zeal for orthodoxy and order was inspired by

---

[1] Irenæus, iii. 3, 1; see Harnack, *History of Dogma*, ii. p. 157, *note* 3.

[2] Duchesne, i. 519. Marriage in particular was strictly regulated; religious marriage with episcopal sanction was usual by the end of the second century, though the church recognised civil marriages. Slavery was viewed in a new spirit of humanity; Christian masters were expected to instruct their slaves, slave-marriages were encouraged, and, at the close of the second century, a slave, Callistus, became bishop of Rome. The term slave is never found in Christian epitaphs. Christian thought readily assimilated the teaching of the Roman jurists, that all men were by nature free and equal; the existence of slavery was explained as due to sin, and its legality was justified as a form of remedial punishment. But the influence of the church was strong in favour of manumission. Christianity set itself from the first against infanticide, abortion and the sexual aberrations characteristic of Hellenic practice. Moral discipline extended to minor details, e.g. manners at table, women's dress, mixed bathing, the wearing of cut flowers and jewellery, attendance at theatres, etc. Rome was careful to control ascetic practices; the home of monasticism and of the anchorites (third century onwards) was Egypt.

a grasp of the spiritual essentials of the faith. In matters of doctrine, Rome stood consistently for the apostolic tradition.[1] She held to Christianity as a religion, resisting firmly all tendencies to reduce it to a speculative theory of the schools. To Rome it was chiefly due, that the impulse towards the unity of Christendom crystallised into definite shape as the conception of a single visible church, catholic (i.e. universal) and apostolic, the earthly embodiment of the invisible kingdom of God, and the necessary instrument of man's salvation. Thus many of the salient phenomena in the church's history—the multitude of its adherents, its growth in wealth and secular influence, its organisation through episcopal synods, the severance of clergy from laity and the rise of sacerdotalism, the multiplication of heresies, the concentration of interest on doctrinal problems, and the progressive assimilation of the heritage of Græco-Roman philosophy and law—appear as the progressive unfolding of germs that were already alive in the early Christianity of the second century.[2] There is no break in continuity from the apostolic age to that of Constantine.

§ 4. The general policy of the empire towards the religions of its subjects was one of mingled toleration and uniformity. Throughout antiquity religions were national, the citizen being under obligation to the gods of his community. As the peoples of the Mediterranean world were absorbed politically into the Roman state, their local cults continued to be recognised side by side with that of Rome. No inconsistency was felt when a Roman pontiff worshipped Cybele or Mithra, or when an Egyptian devotee of Isis offered incense at the altar of Augustus. Only in rare cases and on grounds of morality rather than of religion were particular rites prohibited by the Roman govern-

[1] E.g. the apostolic writings, the apostolic succession to the episcopate, the apostolic rule of faith. In the second century, the Roman baptismal confession had expanded into the rule of faith virtually identical with what is known as the Apostles' creed (see later, § 17). Rome was the sole arbiter of tradition in the West; in the East, Antioch, Jerusalem and Alexandria all claimed to be authoritative depositaries. On the respect for oral tradition and its causes, see Davis, *Mediaeval Europe*, pp. 120 ff. Literary records could be allegorised in very various ways; tradition was employed to test the text. Distrust of literary skill and reluctance to publish the highest truths to the profane also tended to strengthen the influence of oral tradition.

[2] Provincial synods were common, especially in Africa and Asia, in the third century. We find sixty Italian, and ninety African, bishops in attendance at their respective synods. The chief instrument of intercommunication was by letter from one bishop or group of bishops to another. There was no œcumenical council before that of Nicæa in 325. The church councils became the organ through which federated Christendom developed both its creeds and its canon law.

L

ment, such as those of the Druids in Gaul with their accompaniment of human sacrifice, or the casting of children into the
flames before Moloch among the Semites of Africa.[1] On the
other hand, all alike were expected to pay honour to the *genius*
of Rome and of Augustus, the religious symbol of the political
unity of the empire. This tribute involved no renunciation of
other divinities and no profession of religious faith; it was but
a formal act of allegiance to Cæsar on the part of Cæsar's subjects.
That anyone should boggle at it on religious grounds was incom-
prehensible to the Roman mind. In fact, associated as it was
by skilful policy with the autonomy of the provincial councils,
it was accepted everywhere, not merely without a murmur,
but even with ardour, save by Jews and Christians. Their refusal
to bow in homage to any god save one, perfectly intelligible to
us to-day, excited in the Roman only irritation and contempt.
In the case of the Jews, whose faith was national, the authorities
were prepared to compromise, sanctioning their worship as a
religio licita, though they forbade under heavy penalties the conversion of Roman citizens to Judaism.[2] So long as Christianity
was undistinguished from Judaism, it shared in this official
toleration; Gallio, in the *Acts*, viewed the outcry of the Jews
against St. Paul as a petty internal squabble, and, with the
indifference of a modern civil servant, confronted with a sectarian
dispute among the natives of India, " cared for none of these
things." It was not his business to wrangle over technicalities
of the Mosaic code, but to repress crime and keep the peace.[3]
The persecutions at Rome in the first century under Nero (64)
and Domitian (96) were not due to an official policy of suppression, but arose out of local and temporary circumstances, in
connexion with allegations of specific crime. The historian

[1] In 186 B.C. the *Bacchanalia* were prohibited at Rome on moral
grounds. The account, given by Livy, 39, 8–17, is the chief precedent
for the later Roman policy towards Christianity. It must be borne in
mind that religion, which to us means a direct contact between the soul
and God, and is consequently a matter of conscience, was for the Roman
primarily an affair of the individual in his relation to the state (the gods
of the city). Conscience had little to do with it; the all-important thing
was worship (*cultus*). Neglect of due observance was a political crime.
There was no place for the conscientious objector. See Hatch (*Hibbert
Lectures*, 1888, p. 21). On the worship of the emperors, see above, p. 247.

[2] Hadrian prohibited circumcision and instituted Græco-Roman
worship at Jerusalem. Despite the terrible vengeance enacted for the
revolt that ensued, the Jews retained their rites and worship. Early in
the third century, Severus penalised conversion to Judaism, but by this
time the Jews had ceased to proselytise.

[3] Acts xviii. 12–17.

Tacitus thus describes Nero's attempt to divert from himself the odium caused by the great fire of 64. "Consequently, to get rid of the report (that Nero had ordered the fire), Nero fastened the guilt and inflicted the most exquisite tortures on a class hated for their abominations, called Christians by the populace. Christus, from whom the name had its origin, suffered the extreme penalty during the reign of Tiberius at the hands of one of our procurators, Pontius Pilatus; and a most mischievous superstition, thus checked for the moment, again broke out, not only in Judæa, the first source of the evil, but even in Rome, where all things hideous and shameful from every part of the world find their centre and become popular. Accordingly, an arrest was first made of all who pleaded guilty; then, upon their information, an immense multitude was convicted, not so much of the crime of firing the city, as of hatred against mankind. Mockery of every sort was added to their deaths. Covered with the skins of beasts, they were torn by dogs and perished, or were nailed to crosses, or were doomed to the flames and burnt, to serve as a nightly illumination, when daylight had expired. Nero offered his gardens for the spectacle, and was exhibiting a show in the circus, while he mingled with the people in the dress of a charioteer or stood aloft on a car. Hence, even for criminals who deserved extreme and exemplary punishment, there arose a feeling of compassion; for it was not as it seemed, for the public good, but to glut one man's cruelty, that they were being destroyed." [1] It was in the reign of Trajan that Christianity was first proclaimed an illicit religion, the existence of which contravened the law of the empire. When in 112 Pliny as Governor of Bithynia reported to the emperor for instructions, the answer was in strict conformity with imperial tradition. There was no desire to persecute, and Trajan showed evident reluctance to take proceedings; but the law must be obeyed. Every inducement was offered for recantation; and, above all, charges must rest on definite and responsible information. The rescript approving Pliny's action was brief and incisive. "You have adopted, my Secundus, quite the right course in examining the cases of those who were denounced to you as Christians. For indeed no general rule can be laid down which might afford what may be called a fixed form of procedure. They must not be sought out : if they are denounced and convicted, they must be punished, yet with this limitation, that any one

---

[1] Tacitus, *Annals*, xv. 44; *tr.* Church and Brodribb.

who denies that he is a Christian and proves his denial by deed, that is to say by adoring our gods, however suspicious his first conduct may have been, shall earn pardon by repentance. But anonymous placards ought not to be regarded in the case of any crime; for that would be a very bad example, unworthy of our time." [1]   The hostility of the crowd, such as St. Paul had faced in earlier days at Ephesus, vented itself frequently in charges of immorality, to which a confraternity that holds secret meetings is always liable.[2]   The Roman administration was studiously careful not to take action on such irresponsible evidence.   Christians, if proved to be such, were condemned as Christians, for the " name."   But Trajan's successors were not invariably so indifferent to the public clamour.   The martyrdom of Polycarp at Smyrna under Antoninus Pius (155) and the Lyon persecution under Marcus Aurelius (177) were fomented by the mob. In the course of the second century the churches of Asia, Greece, Gaul and Africa all suffered under the strong arm of the Roman state.   Its policy alternated between active repression and tacit tolerance.   The most conscientious emperors were the most rigorous to enforce the law.   Commodus indeed might be wheedled into indulgence by the entreaties of his Christian mistress, and Hadrian's sceptical indifference might incline him to discount the political danger of an illicit confraternity, but the very loyalty of Marcus Aurelius to his Stoic creed served but to blind him to the faith which led the slave girl Blandina to face with joy the beasts in the Lyon arena, or the aged Pothinus to answer the legate's question, " Who is the god of the Christians ? " with the proud words, " If thou art worthy, thou shalt know."   " Sheer obstinacy "—such was the Stoic emperor's reflexion in the *Meditations*; and for all his Hellenic wisdom he bade the terrors of the arena to be added to those of death.[3]

§ 5. The persecutions of the second century brought thousands

---

[1] Pliny, *Letters*, x. 97 (*tr.* Bigg. *Origins*, p. 95). Pliny applied three tests; the accused must repeat a prayer to the official Roman deities, burn incense at the emperor's statue, and disavow Christ. The second was the most serious in Roman eyes; to refuse it was treason (*ib.* p. 93).

[2] The fact of secrecy rendered Christianity a natural object of suspicion and misconstruction not only to the vulgar but to the government.

[3] Marcus Aurelius, *Meditations*, xi. 3. On the Lyon martyrs, see the letter from the churches of Lyon and Vienne to those of Asia in Eusebius, *H.E.* v. i. and Bigg, *Origins*, pp. 175 ff. For the martyrdom of Polycarp, Bigg, *Origins*, p. 155. The wonderful story of the *Acts of Saints Perpetua and Felicitas*, martyred at Carthage in 203, has been edited by Armitage Robinson, and is sketched by Bigg, pp. 293 ff.

of adherents to the gospel. "The blood of the martyrs was the seed of the church." The spectacle of their constancy stirred even the bureaucrats and the legionaries to pity. Epictetus showed a truer insight than Marcus Aurelius when he observed how the Galileans were disciplined to despise tyrants, and that the demonstrations of the schools were impotent to generate such a faith.[1] Doubtless the Christians were often provocative in speech and action, and courted death by their contumely towards heathen worships. Such displays were hardly calculated to move their enemies to admiration. It was their devotion to their Master that was compelling and conclusive. When Polycarp was bidden to curse Christ, he answered : " Eighty and six years have I served him and he never did me wrong; how then can I curse the King my Saviour ? " Their love one towards another and their simple purity of life refuted more effectively than all the literary efforts of the Apologists the current allegations of debauchery and treason. But it was inevitable that as the faith grew in influence and favour, the resolve of the government to enforce the law should become more pronounced. Its attitude was that of the practical man in all ages; appealing to commonsense and reasons of state, it pursued a vacillating policy of kicks and kindness, and called it justice. The more capable among the third-century emperors saw instinctively that Christianity was a dissolvent agency, alien in spirit to the culture of which the empire was the guardian. The political unity of the state required expression in a uniform worship, and the hour had not yet come when that function could be fulfilled by the new religion. Above all, the eyes of the rulers were fixed on the need of defending the frontiers against the tide of Teutonic barbarism, and the spread of Christianity in the army seemed a menace to military discipline. For this reason they favoured Mithraism, a soldier's creed, and in no wise irreconcilable with the official worship of Augustus. Hence we find that two deliberate attempts were made, one by Decius in the middle years of the third century, one by Diocletian and his colleague Galerius at the opening of the fourth, to exterminate the Christian faith. The last-mentioned was the most terrible that the church was ever called upon to endure. For two years it raged with full blast throughout the empire. It formed the crowning struggle between paganism and Christianity. In the West, the rigour of the persecution abated on Diocletian's abdica-

[1] Epictetus, iv. 7, 6.

tion in 305, but in the East, the ancient nursery of Christianity, it continued with increasing ferocity till the eve of Galerius' death in 311. Its failure carried with it the final triumph of the new religion. The event came swiftly. In 312, Constantine, master of the West by the victory at the Mulvian bridge, entered Rome under the Christian banner. In the following year, conjointly with his eastern colleague Licinius, he proclaimed liberty of conscience and restored to the church its confiscated buildings and lands. In 324 the overthrow of Licinius laid the Roman world at the feet of Constantine; and, the year after, the Christian bishops who had gathered at his summons passed into the council chamber at Nicæa amid the salutes of the imperial soldiery. Christianity was officially established as the religion of the Roman empire.[1]

§ 6. The efforts of the Roman government to crush Christianity claim notice for two reasons. In the first place, the nature and methods of its religious policy reflect the deep cleavage that parted the old order of society from the new. It is quite true that the persecutions, save those of Decius and of Diocletian, were neither persistent nor universal, and that in the intervals the church enjoyed comparative tranquility and was recognised in practice, though not in theory, as a property-holding and autonomous corporation.[2] But in principle the empire could

[1] Constantine's motives in recognising Christianity as the religion of the empire were doubtless in part political. But his family were pro-Christian, and there is no reason to question the sincerity of his preference. The emperors of this age, whether pro-Christian or anti-Christian, and despite moral shortcomings, were often sincerely devout. This is equally true of Diocletian, Galerius and Constantine. It was an age of soldier-princes, and soldiers are not wont to be freethinkers. Rationalist scepticism was out of keeping with the times. Constantine was not baptised till just before his death in 337; but there was nothing unusual in this. In considering his recognition of Christianity, we must banish entirely the modern ideas associated with an "established" church. Decius and Diocletian tried to exterminate Christianity because, not being a state-religion, it had no right to exist. Constantine solved the difficulty by declaring it to be the state-religion. His action was doubtless advantageous to the imperial government, but it was a disaster of the first magnitude for Christianity. For (a) secularism invaded its domain, and (b) in Duchesne's words (iii. 1), the church "épousait un malade, qui devient bientôt un moribond." The baneful results which Dante attributed to the unhistorical "Donation" of Constantine had their real source in the establishment of Christianity as the state-religion (see Dante, de Monarchia, iii. 10 and 13; cf. Inf., xix. 115 f., Par., xx. 55 ff.). (The Donation was a forgery, purporting to be the grant by Constantine to Pope Sylvester of temporal authority over Rome.)

[2] Thus Severus Alexander decided that certain ground belonged not to the Roman innkeepers but to the Christian community, while Gallienus restored sacred buildings and property to the churches after the Decian

only be hostile, seeing that its roots were planted in the soil of a Hellenism to which the Christian gospel appeared as foolishness. Secondly, the story of the persecutions throws into relief the spirit that was the driving-power of early Christianity. The annals of ecclesiastical institutions and doctrinal controversies are apt to blind our eyes to the presence of this essential force. Christianity, as a faith working in the world for its redemption, had of necessity to objectify itself in a visible framework of institutions, documents and creeds. These outward embodiments must needs appear inadequate when measured by the living experience which they struggled to express. The hierarchical church of Irenæus and Cyprian, with its liturgy and canons, its authorised title-deeds and rule of faith, its property and buildings, its severance of clergy from laity, its growing secularisation, and, above all, its claim that membership of a visible society is a prerequisite of salvation (*extra ecclesiam nulla salus*), might easily be thought a derogation, when compared with the life of the primitive confraternity of the apostolic age. The atmosphere seems more clouded than that in which moved the first disciples, united in brotherly love as members of an invisible kingdom, and awaiting in hourly expectation the second coming of their Lord. The record of the martyrs serves to remind us of our error. Behind the visible institution the living faith endured. But, side by side with its message of hope and salvation to the individual, it had taken shape as an organised community, bearing witness to the conviction that Christ, though ascended into heaven, was still present among his followers on earth. There was no inherent contradiction between the faith and its visible embodiment. Christianity was never merely an institutional religion.[1] Neither was it the religion of a book. Even

persecution, and Aurelian adjudicated at Antioch in an internal dispute among Christians, and ordered that the cathedral should be placed in the hands of the bishop nominated by the bishops of Rome and Italy. In all these instances, drawn from the third century, the existence of the Christian church as a corporate body was implicitly recognised.

[1] This statement must not be taken to imply that Christianity, as a missionary faith working for the redemption of the world, could dispense with embodiment in a visible church. It means merely that the visible institution, which was a necessary instrument of this mission, was the outward symbol of the spiritual body of Christ and, as such, was a means and not an end in itself. Moreover, no rigid line of demarcation can be drawn between the earthly institution (the Church militant), which derives its origin and authority from Christ Himself, and the heavenly community, the " mystical body of Christ, of which His faithful followers are ' very members incorporate.' " The visible church is not, like the State, a merely earthly society.

the New Testament scriptures were a means and not an end. Nor, finally, was it the religion of a creed. Dogmas, like documents and institutions, were but instruments of its mission. The Greek word for creed is *symbolon*, a " symbol." Not these alone, but the faith that gave them life, enabled Christianity to emerge victorious from its warfare with the Roman state and with Hellenic culture. It was the love of Christ, informing the lives of his followers, that overcame the world.

II. PAGAN RELIGIONS AND GREEK PHILOSOPHY (§§ 7–14).

§ 7. Christianity in the third century was confronted, not only by official persecution, but by the conflicting claims of a variety of philosophic and religious faiths. The times were favourable to a revival of religious enthusiasm. The empire presented a melancholy spectacle. Without, there was the barbarian menace; within, financial exhaustion and civil discord; and in men's hearts, mingled apathy, world-weariness and fear. To pagan and Christian alike the wrath of heaven seemed to have fallen upon the world. In their distress they sought salvation, not from the emperor, the great Leviathan or mortal god, but from supernatural powers. The crying need was for direct communion between the soul of the individual and the gods. To satisfy this need was the common profession of the hosts of faiths, Hellenic and Oriental, that jostled together in the disordered panorama of the third century. They appealed to both sexes and to every rank in society, with the voice now of reason, now of sensuous emotion. Neo-Platonism had its gospel for the philosopher, Mithraism for the legionary, the cults of ancient Egypt for the jaded *femme du monde* of the capital. On the one side, the crudest superstitions, the practice of magic, black and white, the belief in dæmons, oracles and omens, in mysteries and purifying ceremonial, in astrology and occult probing of the future, spread mushroom-like over the empire from the imperial palace to the frontier camps in Britain and Mesopotamia. Early in the century, the empress Julia Domna, wife of Severus, had striven to blend the traditions of Pythagoras with Christian accretions in a new cult, which gathered round the memory of Apollonius of Tyana, a first-century Pythagorean.[1] At the opposite pole stands the specu-

[1] See the *Life of Apollonius*, written by Philostratus at the empress's request. It is accessible with a translation in the *Loeb* series. On the Egyptian cult of Isis, see Apuleius' description in the *Metamorphoses*

lative system of Plotinus, the supreme effort of the Hellenic genius to realise philosophy as religion. Between these two extremes, on varying planes of spiritual endeavour, a diversity of creeds flourished in an atmosphere of mutual toleration. The prevailing temper of the public mind was towards syncretism, the conscious effort to force all varieties of thought and worship into harmony. An admirable example of this tendency is furnished by the amiable and learned Plutarch, who lived at Chæronea in Bœotia under the early empire (48–120). A man of sincere piety and warm affections, he varied his tranquil literary labours with the punctilious discharge of official duty as mayor and priest of his native borough. Plutarch was the foremost man of letters of his day, and a thorough conservative, whose mind lingered, as we have already seen, on the history, thought and religion of the past. Convinced of the value of religion to the maintenance of social order, and of the necessity of satisfying the claims both of the vulgar and of the educated, he set himself to show how the polytheistic cults of Greece, Egypt and the East were all alike symbolic accommodations of a reasonable faith in God to the popular intelligence. The method of allegory furnished him with a facile instrument. Greek philosophy in this age showed itself more tolerant of magic and superstition than did Christianity with its insistent championship of truth. Plutarch was not a powerful thinker, and his adaptation of Platonism hardly supports the doctrines which he erected on its basis. But he was representative of the temper of his age, in his Platonism, in his endeavour after a *rapprochement* between reason and faith, and above all in his insistence on the problem of evil, and his belief that philosophy can lead the soul to union in ecstasy with God.[1] There were many of lesser

(xi. 5): he wrote as a convert. From Asia Minor came the worship of Cybele, from Syria that of the Dea Syra. All these religions taught a gospel of salvation for the soul from bondage to the material world, a " way of return " to God by immediate contact with him in trance or ecstasy. Cybele, Isis, etc., were regarded, when worshipped in the Hellenic atmosphere, as diverse manifestations of one supreme divinity. The mystery-cults of Oriental origin differed from the Hellenic in their tendency towards pantheism and in the plasticity of their deities, whose characters and acts could easily be adapted to suit the needs of different races. They were also distinguished by the proselytising zeal of their adherents.

[1] Of Plutarch's fame as a biographer we have spoken in the preceding chapter, § 24. There is an excellent account of his speculative and religious views in Bigg, *Neo-Platonism*, c. v. His treatises *On Isis and Osiris* and *On the Failing of the Oracles* (a circumstance which caused him much anxiety) should be consulted. An unbridled freedom in the

note in the ensuing age who strove, as he had done, to mediate a compromise between religion and philosophy. Where all came to the same thing in the end, it was easy for anyone to believe anything; the Stoic or the Platonist could solace his soul by initiation at Eleusis, and an emperor could reconcile devotion to Mithra with the respect due to the ancient gods of Rome. Atheism alone found no favour, and the followers of Epicurus, who denied providence and immortality, had fallen into general discredit. Lucian, *railleur* and rationalist, the Voltaire of an un-Voltairean age, who let his irony play freely with all forms of sophistry and superstition, has left on record his appreciation of the simplicity and geniality of the Epicurean rule of life. For the rest, it was an affair of live and let live, save always for the Christian, in whose eyes all pagan faiths alike were false and idolatrous.[1]

§ 8. Of the third-century religions other than Christianity the most widespread was Mithraism. Its ancient home was among the primitive Aryans of Iran, who worshipped Mithra, as did also their kinsmen in India, as the deity of light and truth, warring against the powers of darkness. In the teaching of Zoroaster, Mithra held a subordinate place among the gods, but his worship, fostered by the Persian kings and modified by Semitic influences from Babylon, took root in the east of Asia Minor under the successors of Alexander, and had the Romans not conquered Mithradates of Pontus, its expansion westwards might have preceded the foundation of Christianity. Actually, its hold on the West dates from the close of the first century A.D. The chief instrument of its dissemination was the army, which was recruited in large numbers from the eastern

use of allegory and a recognition of the value of myth (cf. Plato) prevailed in Hellenic thought from the early days of Stoicism (see Murray, *Five Stages*, pp. 146 ff.). Christianity made free use of the allegorical method. On the problem of evil Plutarch is loyal to Hellenic thought in rejecting the Oriental solution that evil is due to matter, the creation of an evil god. He follows Plato in holding that it is due to the evil soul, and that, while positive, it is not ultimately real; the way is open, by aid of the gods, for moral struggle and victory. He misinterprets Plato when he identifies the evil soul with the soul of the world and asserts that God created the world in time. Bœotia, it may be noted, was an ancient home of oracles and divination.

[1] On religion in the third century see Inge, *The Philosophy of Plotinus*, vol. i, Lect. ii, iii; Cumont, *Oriental Religions in Ancient Paganism*; Kennedy, *Saint Paul and the Mystery-Religions*. The Christians were popularly classed with atheists even late in the second century; compare the proclamation at the mysteries in Lucian's parody : " If any atheist or Christian or Epicurean has come as a spy upon the festival, let him flee " (Luc., *Alex.*, 38).

Asiatic provinces and spread the cult in the second and third centuries to the remotest frontiers of the empire. A bas-relief, with the familiar image of Mithra plunging his dagger into a bull, dedicated in London by a discharged veteran of the Britannic army, may be seen to-day in our national museum. Sixty chapels to Mithra are known to have existed in Rome. The chief centres of the faith were the camps along the Germanic and Danubian frontiers. In the Hellenic provinces, the chosen field of Christianity, it took no root. Its virile moral code, the quasi-military organisation of its churches with their strong *esprit de corps*, its doctrines of resurrection, immortality, and final justice were well calculated to stir the devotion of soldiers.[1] But it failed to appeal to the intelligence and developed no theology or sacred literature. The nerve of its teaching was the belief in Mithra as the mediator between the supreme deity and man, and the redeemer of the human race from the powers of evil. He was the unconquered warrior, identified often with the sun-god, eternally young, under whose banner men could fight victoriously against evil passions within and evil dæmons without. Mithraism was a purely practical creed, in which the life of contemplation (*theôria*) found no place. It had many points in common with Christianity; beside the faith in a divine mediator and the hope of resurrection, it taught the efficacy of prayer, sacramental union with God, and his providential presence in all the events of daily life. Certain of its rites were analogous to the baptism, confirmation and eucharist of the Christians.[2] Many of these affinities, e.g. baptism, were due to a common Oriental tradition, others, such as the adoration of Mithra by shepherds, and his ascension, were probably borrowed from Christianity; in a few cases, chiefly of ritual, Mithraic usages may have passed into the practice of the church. But the divergencies cut deeper than the likeness. The fact, noted above, that Mithraism failed to take root on Hellenic soil, is sufficient of itself to mark the difference. A religion that appealed to the heart to the exclusion of the head could not conquer the world. Above all,

[1] The neophyte's oath was analogous to that of a conscript; the rite of full initiation, admitting to the grade of *miles* in the Mithraic church was called by the military (and old legal) term *sacramentum*. Women had a very subordinate place in Mithraic worship, which was always masculine and military.

[2] Sunday was observed as a holy day and December 25th as the festival of the rebirth of Mithra. Mithra, too, had his ascetics. Mithraic architecture and art certainly influenced the Christian.

the Mithraic redeemer had no historical foundation. The worshipper of Mithra felt no contradiction between his belief and
that of the other faiths surrounding him.[1] To the Christian
the two were irreconcilable. The one absorbed polytheism,
the other uncompromisingly rejected it. Hence while Christianity flourished amid persecution, Mithraism died peacefully
of inanition. The patronage of the third-century emperors
who, valuing its influence on the tone of the army, adopted
the Mithraic style " *pius, felix, invictus*," and dreamt thus of
sanctioning their authority by divine right, and of an alliance
between throne and altar, did not avail to save it from extinction. The successes of the barbarians hastened its decay, and in
the fourth century it had yielded to Christianity even in the
ranks of the legions. Its last surviving adherents seem to have
been absorbed in Manichæism.[2]

§ 9. Mithraism, for all its vogue, was not a formidable rival
of Christianity. The real issue lay between the religion of the
gospel and the " way of life " of the Hellenic schools. At the
moment the church thought otherwise, and, recking little of
the speculations of the cultured, marshalled her forces against
the polytheism of the multitude. But she had evinced from the
first a capacity to enlist the intelligence in the service of the
faith. The time was not far distant when she would have
to meet the philosophers on their own ground. We shall see
presently how already in the third century the Christian
Platonists of Alexandria were absorbing the intellectual inheritance of Hellas into the structure of catholic theology.
But though Greek philosophy had value for Christianity,
Christianity had none for Greek philosophy. To minds trained
in the atmosphere of the schools, its historic revelation and its
democratic message of salvation were alike contemptible; what
to the Jews had proved a stumbling-block was foolishness to
the Greek.[3] The bitterest opponents of the new religion were

[1] Mithraism as practised in the Roman empire shows many signs of
syncretism, e.g. with the cults of Cybele in Phrygia (this gave women
a place) and of the Celts in Gaul. Certain attempts were made at a
synthesis with science and philosophy on a crude plane, especially in
astrology. But Mithraism never showed any real capacity of fusion with
western speculation. The attempt, for instance, to identify the sun
with the supreme intelligence of the universe, does not imply a serious
philosophy.

[2] On this section, see Cumont, *La réligion de Mithraisme*. Our knowledge of Mithraism is derived almost entirely from archæological sources :
no Mithraic liturgies or other writings have survived. On Manichæism,
see below, § 22, p. 332, *note* 2.

[3] 1 Cor. i. 23. The early Christians instinctively felt the danger of

to be found among those who, like the emperor Marcus Aurelius, were most eminent in wisdom and virtue and most deeply permeated with the thought and ideals of Greece. It was because such men realised so fully the worth of Hellenic culture that they were the least willing to renounce it for a faith whose spirit was alien to all that they prized most dearly. Happiness, or the chief good for man, lay for them, not as for the Christian, in a heavenly fruition, to be attained by renunciation of the world and self, but in the perfection of man's natural powers in a life of specifically human activity. Nor was it a goal to which the way was open wide to all mankind; the good life was only for those endowed with the Hellenic character and qualified in the wisdom of the schools. Sacrifice was indeed requisite for its achievement; but the sacrifice was that of the lower passions in the service of philosophic reason. " *Sei vornehm* "—ensue distinction "—was the animating principle of Græco-Roman culture, and the distinction it enjoined was that of the philosopher realising a rich personality in a life of human interests which to the Christian wore branded with the stamp of sin. This divergence of spiritual outlook is most evident when we set the teaching of Christianity beside that of the philosophic school which, as we have seen in an earlier chapter, appealed most forcibly to the cultivated Roman in the first two centuries of our era. The Stoic and the Christian codes of ethics had much in common—the recognition of the unconditional command of duty and of the intrinsic worth of virtue, austerity of moral discipline and the ideal of a spiritual commonwealth embracing all mankind. But the differences are more radical than the resemblance. For the Stoic, human nature was all sufficient for salvation. His faith was only for the wise and strong, who could attain by effort of their own wills the mastery of their souls. It offered a gospel, not of confident hope, but of resignation and detachment. The Stoic sage was an intellectual and moral aristocrat, self-centred even in the discharge of obligation towards his friends. " So far as words go," wrote Epictetus explaining the right attitude towards one oppressed with grief, " be not slow to fit thyself to his mood and even if so it be to lament with him. But have a care that thou lament not also from within." [1] There was no

---

alien ideas *within* the church; see especially St. Paul's epistle to the Colossians. The fact that the church did not regard Greek philosophy as a serious opponent in the third century is quite compatible with the view taken in the text that it was a most formidable antagonist.

[1] Enchir., 16.

room in the system for forgiveness; every man had to take the irremediable consequences of his acts. Stoicism, indeed, taught men to face the storms and disillusionment of life with the unruffled calm of self-respect, and at the close to meet death, if need be by their own hand, with a melancholy fortitude. It was the creed of those who had little to learn or to unlearn, and who did their duty with their gaze fixed on the great things of the past. Its strength lay in its realisation of the meaning of suffering; its weakness in its ignorance of the meaning of love. This is why it failed to hold its ground on the rise of Neo-Platonism.[1] Its last great teacher was the emperor Marcus Aurelius. His *Meditations*, penned in camp upon the Danube, are a strange comment on Plato's dream, now visibly realised, of a philosopher who should be king. They reveal a noble spirit, tirelessly busied with the duties of his office in peace and war, bearing the burden with a practised cheerfulness, uncomplaining and unresentful, friends with his own soul, but without hope and without joy. He knew nothing higher than himself save the abstract order of the universe, whose inexorable law he studied to follow with loyal resignation. We bow in admiration before this high embodiment of pagan culture, yet with a sense that it was powerless to inspire the world or to recreate its youth. The *Meditations* stand for ever, in the phrase of Renan, as the gospel of those who are without religion.

§ 10. The third century saw the rise of Neo-Platonism, the final utterance of the speculative genius of Greece. Though

---

[1] The Neo-Platonists, as we shall see, absorbed much of Stoic doctrine into their system. Stoicism was a dying creed when Christianity, in the course of its development, came to settle its account with Greek philosophy. "Stoicism throve, because, like Christianity, it is a philosophy of suffering; it fell because, unlike Christianity, it is a philosophy of despair" (Bigg, *Christian Platonists*, p. 288). The Cynics, on the other hand, who were imbued with the missionary spirit and appealed to simple folk, were still numerous in the days of Augustine. Cynic ethics influenced Christian practice; the word "anchorite" is derived from their term (*anachôrein*) meaning "to go into retreat." Stoicism, too, left its mark both on Christian theology (e.g. the doctrine of the *logos*) and on Christian ethics. The conception of life as warfare, the practice of self-examination, and the recognition of man's dependence upon God, are familiar to the Stoics. "Can any one," asks Seneca (*Ep.* 41, 2), "rise superior to fortune save with the help of God?" St. Ambrose (late third century), by education a Roman official, popularised in his sermons Cicero's paraphrases of Stoic ethics (in the *de Officiis*). There was much in Stoicism, despite its Hellenic dress, that tallied with the lofty moral code of Judaism. The early Fathers adopted also the theories of natural law and of a state of nature, prior to the institution of civil government, which had passed from Stoicism into Roman law.

rooted in Platonic soil, fertilised and enriched by the inheritance of Aristotle and the Stoics, Neo-Platonism was no mere republication of traditional doctrines, but a union of old and new. For more than three centuries the Hellenic mind, reflecting the temper of the world in which it moved, had been thinking its way towards a closer fusion of philosophy with religion.[1] This led naturally to a revival of Pythagorean and Platonic teaching, in which stress was laid on the hope of salvation from the ills of earthly life by means of intellectual love of, and mystic union with, the divine principle. The supersensible world, where Plato of old had sought and found true being, was conceived in more concrete form as the dwelling place of a God who stood in intimate relationship to the souls of men. Herein lies the intrinsic interest, the distinctive appeal, of Neo-Platonism. The time is past when its doctrines could be dismissed by critics as a fantastic thaumaturgy, or as a hybrid of Hellenic metaphysics and Oriental superstition. The loyal child of Greek philosophy, its mysticism, like that of Plato or of Spinoza, was grounded on reason. It aimed at a synthesis of experience by the method of scientific logic. Plotinus, the first and greatest of its masters (204–70), came indeed from Alexandria, the historic meeting-place of East and West; but he taught and wrote his *Enneads* at Rome, and his mind was the mind of Greece. Other thinkers followed in his steps, but the *Enneads* form the best approach to the study of Neo-Platonism.[2] They claim our attention here, both for the reasons we have just indicated, and also for their lasting influence on the structure of Christian theology.

§ 11. Plotinus' philosophy, like that of Plato, appears to start from the contrast of two worlds, the sensible and the spiritual. In fact, its whole purport is to overcome the dualism. The spiritual alone has true being; the sensible is no alien reality, but an image begotten by the spiritual in its likeness, in accordance with a universal law.[3] " It is necessary that

[1] On the precursors of Neo-Platonism from the first century B.C. onwards, see Bigg's *Neo-Platonism* and *Christian Platonists*, and Inge's *Philosophy of Plotinus*, vol. i, Lect. 4 and 5. Numenius of Apamea (flor. 160–80) was perhaps the most important, but little is known of his teaching.

[2] The *Enneads* are in six books, each containing nine (Greek *ennea* = nine) treatises. They were thus arranged by Plotinus' pupil Porphyry, whose life of his master should be read. For works on Neo-Platonism and translations, see the *Bibliographical Appendix*.

[3] Reality or true being (*ousia*) belongs to soul and that which is above soul; such defective being as is possessed by things of sense is derived from the supersensible. Soul creates the sense-world after the pattern

each principle should give of itself to another; the Good would
not be Good, nor Spirit (*Nous*) Spirit, nor Soul Soul, if nothing
lived dependent on the first life." [1] This law, with its implications, especially for the human soul and its salvation, is the
keystone of Plotinus' system. The universe, from its highest
principle, the One or the Good, to its lowest limit in indeterminate, non-existent matter, presents a continuous scale of
being and perfection.[2] The whole is a harmony; only the
fragments, in their isolation, sound a discordant note. The
world of sense is real, after its kind; it may be called a world
of appearance, if by appearance we mean, not an illusion that
is actual only in the mind of the thinker, but a partial manifestation of reality. Its being, like that of all else, is neither
mental nor non-mental; just as, in the spiritual world, mind
and its object form inseparable moments in a single reality.
Here, as elsewhere, Plotinus set his face firmly against dualism.[3]
Mind both makes and finds its object. Complete thought and
complete reality are one and the same. On the lower planes,
e.g. in perception of sensible things, imperfect apprehension is
in strict correspondence with the imperfect being of the object.
The sense-world is real, not because it is known by mind, but
by grace of the creative soul informing it. It is the mirror

---

which it contemplates in Spirit (*Nous*). I follow Dean Inge (ii. 37, 38)
in translating *Nous*, the second person of the Plotinian trinity, as " Spirit,"
rather than as " mind," or " thought," or " reason," not because *Nous*
does not mean these, but to avoid confusion between *Nous* and the lower
faculty of discursive, logical intelligence (*dianoia*). *Nous* is intuitive
vision, i.e. reason at its highest grade; there is no opposition between
Nous and reason, no short cut to the Absolute, which can be reached
only by way of speculative thought. I have, however, used the phrase
" spiritual world " (in contrast with the world of sense) of the *whole* supersensible world, including Soul universal, which is below, and the One,
which is above, *Nous*.

[1] *Enn.*, ii. 9, 3, *tr.* Inge i. 195.
[2] On the One, see below, § 13. Matter (as for Aristotle) is bare
possibility of being, a limiting point, devoid of all quality, at which the
creative activity, that flows forth through all things, is finally exhausted.
Plotinus' " matter " must not be understood in the current sense of the
word; it is prior to space and to body, and there is also supersensible
matter. That it is somehow positive, and a cause of defect and evil,
is a difficulty which Plotinus' concept of matter shares with that of
Aristotle. For Plotinus, the scale of existence is one with the scale of
value; hence positive disvalues, such as evil, give a positive character
to matter, which, on the scale of being, is merely negative (non-existent).
See Inge, i. 131 ff.; 162; ii. 77 ff.
[3] There is hardly a trace in Greek philosophy of the familiar modern
doctrine, known as subjective idealism, that things have no reality independent of the percipient or thinking subject, that they exist only as
ideas in the mind, that, in Berkeley's phrase, their *esse* is *percipi*.

that reflects, though " in a glass darkly," the world of spirit.
" All things that are *here* "—we are reminded of the *di là* and
the *di quà* of Dante—" are also *there*." For, " whence else,"
asks Plotinus, " could they have come ? " And, if we include
soul among things of earth, " all that is *there* is also *here*." [1]
Thus our experience of the sense-world points us to its source
in the supersensible. It bears upon it the marks, not only of
imperfection (plurality and change), but of its ideal archetype.
Here Plotinus' thought is in line with the high tradition of
Greek philosophy. Grades of perfection and imperfection imply
the existence of a perfect standard ; plurality and change the
existence of an unchanging One. Grades of reality are discernible also within the supersensible world, which contains
diversity, though it transcends time and change. Thus all
things are linked together in an unbroken chain of being. In
this conception, Plotinus finds at once the cause of their existence
and their hope of restitution. For everything that is is active,
in proportion to its grade of being ; to be is to act and to produce.
The higher its place in the scale, the richer and the more pervasive is its causal efficacy. The One, the supreme source of
being, overflows of its plentitude, generating in a timeless act
an offspring, inferior to, yet like, itself, which in its turn gives
forth of its being to another, that is likewise creative, until,
in the series of successive emanations, the stream of energy is
wholly spent. This conception of the causal process contrasts
sharply with that of modern evolutionary science.[2] For Plotinus,
creation, as the act of spirit or soul, is not in time, though the
timeless causality is mirrored in the sense-world under the form
of a temporal history. The cause, again, is of necessity more
perfect than the effect ; the relation is one-sided, and the agent
suffers no degradation through any reaction from the effect.
The complement of this downward process is the return of all
things towards their primal source. Since every product bears
the impress of its cause, there is that in its nature which has
its true home above. Like is known by like, and draws like to

[1] *Enn.*, iii. 2, 4 ; v. 9, 13 ; Inge, i. 197–9.
[2] The Neo-Platonists were of course aware that *historically* the more
imperfect is prior to the more perfect, and Proclus in particular stressed
this repeatedly (see Whitaker, *The Neo-Platonists*, on the *Commentaries*
of Proclus). But this recognition of obvious facts was always subject
to the cardinal principle that the temporal process is dependent on the
timeless reality of the perfect archetype, apart from which the whole
upward development is inconceivable. Here lies the difference between
their doctrine and that of evolutionary science.

itself. The creative source is also the final goal. The One is the beginning and the end, the Alpha and the Omega, of the universe. The whole creation "groaneth and travaileth together" in a desire which rest in the One alone can satisfy.

§ 12. Plotinus shared to the full the craving of the age for release from bondage, and dwelt at length on the upward pilgrimage by which the soul may regain its true fatherland. In essence, the soul is immaterial, and abides, without loss of individuality, but free from the trammels of the body, in the supersensible world. "There," united with all other souls in the tranquil life of Soul universal, it has its eternal home.[1] "Here," in the world of time and change, it is coupled with a material body. But its essential nature, though obscured thereby, is not obliterated; even when most deeply sunk in the slough of material accretions, it hungers for its source. "He who has learnt to know himself will know also whence he is." The soul is a "wanderer from God," leading an "amphibious" life, an immortal nature clad in the garment of mortality.[2] Its impulse to mount leads, first, to habituation in political or social virtue, then to purification by means of ascetic discipline, the moral preparation for the theoretic "way of life." The ensuing stages represent a progressive illumination. The exercise of the discursive intellect, in scientific and philosophical studies, enables the soul at length to rise to the consummation of the life of contemplation, in the immediate vision, transcending the bounds of knowledge, in which it attains union with the supreme unity.[3]

[1] *Enn.* vi. 4, 14; iv. 3, 12. The statement in the text refers to the higher soul within each individual soul; it is not the whole soul that thus has its abiding-place above. On the universal soul, see below, § 13; it must be conceived, not as a collection or society of souls, but as the individual source of all soul; particular souls, e.g. of men and women are not its parts, but its offspring. Plotinus is quite definite in asserting that individuality is preserved in the supersensible world (*Enn.*, iv. 3, 5); the timeless element in the soul is the man's true self. More than any other Greek philosopher, he recognises the importance of personality; but it was left to Christian thought to give full expression to its claims. "Soul" (*psyché*) includes all "life," animal and plant life as well as human; all nature is informed with "soul" in varying measure.

[2] See *Enn.*, iv. 7 for Plotinus' masterly argument to prove the immateriality and immortality of the soul. He realises, of course, that the immortality is timeless. The whole doctrine may be profitably compared with that of Spinoza's *Ethics*, Part V. The soul is "of the same essence" (*homo-ousios*) with the divine (*Enn.*, iv. 7, 10).

[3] There is comparatively little in the *Enneads* about this "ecstasy." Porphyry (*Life of Plotinus*, c. 23) tells us that Plotinus experienced it only four times during the years of their association. It came suddenly, and was attended by complete suspension of self-consciousness; the soul did not even know whether it was in the body or no (cf. St. Paul's vision,

The process is one of detachment, first, from the body and all things of sense, then from every object of thought that claims independence of our consciousness, till the seer and the seen are one. " Strip thyself of everything," is Plotinus' bidding.[1] " In this state, the seer does not see or distinguish or imagine two things; he becomes another, he ceases to be himself and to belong to himself. . . . We ought not even to say that he will *see*, but he will *be* that which he sees. . . . If then a man sees himself become one with the One, he has in himself a likeness of the One, and if he passes out of himself, as an image to its archetype, he has reached the end of his journey. And when he comes down from his vision he can again awaken tho virtue that is in him, and seeing himself fitly adorned in every part, he can again mount upward through virtue to Spirit (*Nous*) and through wisdom to the One. Such is the life of gods and of godlike and blessed men; a liberation from all earthly bonds, a life that takes no pleasure in earthly things, a flight of the alone to the Alone." [2]

§ 13. The supersensible world is no blank unity, but an ordered diversity of structure, continuous with its offspring, the world of time and change. It consists of a triad of *Hypostases*,[3] or substantial realities, graded in an ascending scale of unity and perfection. At the lower limit is Soul universal, the world-soul of Plato and the Stoics, where abide in union the formative principles (*logoi*) that are the generative causes of sensible nature.[4] But the universal Soul points upwards to a higher grade of unity For it generates the world of sense in the light of the Forms, the intelligible archetypes of things of

---

2 Cor. xii). It was an experience of unspeakable joy. Self-consciousness, involving the distinction of subject-self and object-self, is transcended in this immediate vision; see Inge, i. 236 ff. : and ii. 125 62 (where the whole question of mystic union with God is reviewed).

[1] *Enn.*, v. 3, 17.

[2] *Enn.*, vi. 9, 10 and 11, *tr.* Inge. (I have substituted "the One " for " God " in the rendering of the last sentence but one; Plotinus says " to itself," meaning the One). The whole passage, *Enn.*, vi. 9, 7–11 should be read (Inge, ii. 135–42). Cf. *Enn.*, i. 6, 7; v. 5, 3 and 8.

[3] *Hypostasis* was a Stoic term; the implications are self-dependence, individuality, concreteness. On the use of the term in Christian theology, see Bigg, *Christian Platonists*, pp. 203–4, 299 *note*, and below, § 19.

[4] Individual souls have their home (as we have pointed out) in Soul universal; but they abide *also* in Spirit (*Nous*) and in the One. Compare Dante's conception of the souls of the redeemed in Paradise, who, pending the Day of Judgement, are at once operative in different spheres and have their true abode with God in the non-spatial empyrean. The entire supersensible world in Plotinus is, of course, non-spatial; there is diversity, but no local separation.

sense. Where have these Forms their being? At this point, Plotinus deviates from his master's teaching. Whereas for Plato the Forms were substances, independent of the mind that thinks them, Plotinus, insisting that " the objects of Spirit (*Nous*) do not exist apart from Spirit," held that they had their being in indissoluble union with *Nous*. *Nous*, the divine mind of spirit, is the second *hypostasis*, which thinks in one timeless act of thought the eternal truths, that constitute its own being, and are thus one with, not other than, itself.[1] But even on this high plane of unity, difference is still discernible, both in the objects of Spirit and in its relation to them. The distinction of thinker and thought implies, even in perfect self-consciousness, a difference of aspect, and points to a yet higher principle of absolute simplicity, called by Plotinus the One, the Father, the Good. As the One, it is the source of unity throughout the supersensible and sensible worlds; as the Father, it is the primal cause of all existence, outpoured from its plenitude of being; as the Good, it is the supreme object of desire, the goal at which all things aim. In Plato's phrase, it " is beyond all existence (*ousia*) and all knowledge." [2] Plotinus is no pantheist; the absolute One transcends being and all that is. It also transcends knowledge, and can be characterised only by negation; it is " *not* this," " *not* that." Yet it is truer to affirm of the One, than to deny; for though excelling all assignable perfections, it includes them in the richness of its super-being, and is not less than they, but more. Only by *being* it, in the vision of communion, can we experience the One as it is. For the rest, attempts after description must be couched in analogies drawn from the imperfect imprint visible in its effects. The image, of which Plotinus never wearies, is that of light, which streams in parted rays from the sun, illuminating and giving life to the utmost verge of creation, where it is lost in the darkness that is mere privation. The simile was Plato's; through Plotinus and

[1] Spirit (*Nous*), the objects apprehended by Spirit (the spiritual realities), and the act of spiritual apprehension, are one and the same; Spirit apprehends itself as the world of Spirit in a single intuition. *Nous*, as Inge points out, is really the " God " of Plotinus' system.

[2] *Rep.*, vi. 509 (see above, c. v, § 20). The One is thus the source of all existence and of all value; a transcendent Absolute. Plotinus, true to the main Greek tradition, keeps well clear of Stoic pantheism. The conception of the One as above being and above knowledge deeply influenced Christian speculation, especially through the pseudo-Dionysius (see § 14, *note* 4). The " way of negation " (*via remotionis*), viz. the view that, in strict truth, positive predicates can only be denied, never affirmed, of God by the human mind, has its origin in Neo-Platonism.

his Christian followers it has furnished an unfailing inspiration to the theology, the metaphysics, and the poetry of the western world.[1]

§ 14. The three *hypostases* that form the Plotinian trinity illustrate how this great thinker gathered up into an original synthesis the rich deposit of earlier philosophy. In the Soul universal we trace the divine world-soul of the Stoics, in Spirit (*Nous*) the self-thinking God of Aristotle's *Metaphysics*, in the One the Platonic Form of the Good.[2] Plotinus came nearer than any of his precursors both to the fusion of religion and metaphysics, and to the reconciliation of the claims of the one and of the many to a place in the system of reality. He was the first to give coherent form to a philosophy of emanation. The school he founded flourished for more than two centuries and was still in being when Justinian closed the pagan academies in 529.[3] From that time onwards the history of Neo-Platonism falls almost wholly within the pale of Christian thought. It was in fact the gate through which Hellenic philosophy went forth to permeate Christian theology and the mediæval schools. It influenced the western church through Augustine, the eastern through the Greek fathers of the fourth and fifth centuries and, later, through the writings of the pseudo-Dionysius.[4] Thus

[1] Light was conceived by Plotinus as an incorporeal energy, issuing forth from the luminous body. This simile is found at every point in Dante's *Paradiso*. The following stanza (liv) from Shelley's *Adonais* is in the spirit of Plotinus :

"That Light whose smile kindles the Universe,
    That Beauty in which all things work and move,
    That Benediction which the eclipsing Curse
Of birth can quench not, that sustaining Love
Which through the web of being blindly wove
    By man and beast and earth and air and sea,
Burns bright or dim, as each are mirrors of
    The fire for which all thirst; now beams on me,
Consuming the last clouds of cold mortality."

[2] From the first century B.C., or even earlier, the materials for the concept of a supersensible trinity were shaping themselves in Hellenic and Jewish-Hellenic thought (e.g. in Philo). The distinctive teaching of Christianity fitted naturally into the triadic mould; and early Christian speculation, nursed at Alexandria in the atmosphere of later Platonism, developed on lines parallel to Neo-Platonism. There is no one-sided dependence of Christian on Neo-Platonic thought.

[3] The last great name is that of Proclus, who taught at Athens in the fifth century. He was the main channel through which Neo-Platonism influenced mediæval thought.

[4] These writings of a Christian Neo-Platonist of the sixth century were ascribed to Dionysius the Areopagite, one of St. Paul's auditors at Athens (Acts xvii. 34).

we find ourselves at one of the critical moments in the history of civilization, when the religious development that culminated in Christianity was brought into direct contact with the speculative system that had gathered in the full harvest of Hellenic philosophy. We are impelled to ask why it was that, instead of Neo-Platonism absorbing Christianity, Christianity assimilated Neo-Platonism. To answer this question, we must indicate the differences that underlay their manifold affinities. (1) Neo-Platonism, like Christianity, opened a way of salvation through knowledge of God; but the knowledge was the fruit of scientific study, and the way could be traversed only by an intellectual and moral aristocracy. Its message, like that of the Stoics, was for the wise; the ignorant and the vicious were objects of a compassion that scarcely concealed contempt.[1] While the Christian held that man was by nature sinful, and his redemption possible only by grace of God, Plotinus, faithful to the Greek tradition, taught the inherent perfectibility of the human soul. The ideal of the self-sufficiency (*autarkeia*) of the wise man haunted Hellenism to its close. It is most conspicuous in the Plotinian rule of detachment. The nearer the individual approached to God, the more absolute was his isolation from his fellows. The law of vicarious suffering, with its implication of the mutual responsibility of each for all, had no place in Neo-Platonism. An individualist creed could not hope to prevail against a society, bound together by a common ideal of self-sacrifice, and inspired with a democratic fervour to save the souls of men.[2] (2) The appeal of Christianity was strengthened by the belief in a historic revelation. Neo-Platonism, though not avowedly hostile to revelation, treated it as mythical and symbolic, and relegated it to a subordinate place in its economy.[3] Its heart was set on the realm of ideal

---

[1] *Enn.*, ii. 9, 9. " The wise man . . . knows that there are two sorts of life, that of virtuous people, who can rise to the highest degree of life, that of the spiritual world; and that of vulgar and earthly persons, which is itself double; for sometimes they dream of virtue and participate in it to some small extent, and sometimes they form only a vile crowd, and are only machines, destined to minister to the first needs of virtuous men " (*tr.* Inge, ii. 188).

[2] We can see here the principle that underlies " institutional " religion and missionary effort. The slight significance attached by Plotinus to political institutions and the structure of society is a striking difference between his system and those of Plato and of Aristotle.

[3] Certain Catholic modernists furnish a parallel: to say that only values matter, not facts, is an easy way out of scientific and historical difficulties. For Neo-Platonism, temporal events were not illusory, but on a low plane of reality, and therefore unimportant. A curious but

values, not on that of temporal events. Metaphysics counted for more than history, and in metaphysics there is no room for revelation. The tenacity with which Christian theology strove to weld together these two aspects of fact and value will come before us in a later section. The issue was not merely one of speculative theory, but involved questions that vitally affected the religious life, such as the value of human personality, the nature of the body, the belief in particular providences, moral responsibility, and the origin of evil.[1] (3) The last-mentioned problem weighed heavily on the mind of the third century. Plotinus discussed it frequently, and his statements were not always consistent; but his prevailing view was that matter is the source of evil. This doctrine, if pressed to its logical conclusion, would lead to the condemnation of physical nature and the human body as intrinsically corrupt. Moreover, it lands the mind in a hopeless dilemma; for, if matter be real, we are confronted by a dualism of good and evil principles; while, if the reality of matter be denied, that of evil also vanishes There is, in fact, no solution to be found along this oft-trodden path. For Christianity, on the other hand, evil has its root in the soul of man, who in self-will abused his power of free choice.[2] (4) We pass, finally, to the nature of God and his relation to man. Of the difference between the graded *hypostases* of the Plotinian trinity and the Catholic doctrine that the three persons are consubstantial and co-equal, we shall speak presently, in connexion with the theological con

---

logical result was that Neo-Platonism was more tolerant to magic and popular superstitions than was Christianity; these things did not matter much either way. It is only fair to Plotinus to observe that he managed the worldly estates of his wards with remarkable sagacity (see Porphyry's *Life*, c. 9).

[1] The belief, derived from Judaism, in the resurrection of the body, saved Christianity from many aberrations. If the body is " the temple of the Holy Spirit," it cannot be regarded merely as an encumbrance to the spiritual life. Neo-Platonism, denied particular providences (*Enn.*, iii. 2, 1), and it is difficult to follow Plotinus in his vindication of freedom of the will; both those convictions were cardinal in Christianity, which saw in the course of history the working-out of a divine purpose (see below, § 23).

[2] Plotinus at times has recourse to a similar explanation (see *Enn.*, iv. 8), where, after experiencing the ecstatic vision, he marvels why the soul is imprisoned in the body. Three suggestions are offered : the soul is not fully actual till it has found creative expression in the world of sense; it is impelled thither by necessity of spiritual law, in order to reproduce the spiritual order (iv. 7, 13); it chooses to fall by an act of self-will (*tolma*, pride), or is forgetful (v. 1, 1) and bewitched (iv. 3, 12). But the last suggestion is inconsistent with Plotinus' main doctrine (i. 8), that matter is primal evil (see Inge, i. 254 ff.).

troversies of the fourth century.[1] The crucial divergence of
the two faiths lies not here, so much as in the scheme of redemption by which man achieves union with God. Neo-Platonism
claimed to furnish a mediation between God and man on a
principle of one-sided dependence. Man, the effect, could rise
in knowledge and love to his divine original. But God could
not stoop down to man. The cause abides, in bleak aloofness,
unconscious and heedless of what transpires beneath. The
student of Plotinus can hardly fail to be troubled by the difficulty
of understanding this fundamental principle of his philosophy.
How can the One pour forth of its fullness to beget a world
of which it has no consciousness and for which it has no desire?
Plotinus' answer that "all things, so far as they are perfect,
beget," that it is a primal law of being thus to give itself, and
that "the One could not be alone," is intelligible only on an
interpretation which he would have indignantly repelled, that
the One is moved to show forth its glory in a creation with which
it can be bound in love.[2] The Christian doctrine of the Incarnation, that God gave himself to the world in love, would have been
anathema to a thinker, impregnated, as was Plotinus, with the
spirit of Hellenic culture. To ascribe to God an act of voluntary
humiliation that would have shattered the cherished self-respect
of a Greek philosopher must have seemed impiety. The view
that evil had its source in matter made such a belief still more
inconceivable. We can no longer feel surprise at the deep
antipathy with which the Neo-Platonists viewed the progress of
the new religion. Other of its doctrines were acceptable and
familiar; that God was one and a moral personality was taught
by Judaism; that man could rise to union with him was taught,
in their several ways, by the mystery-cults and by philosophy.
But that "the Word (*Logos*) was made flesh and dwelt among
us," that God for man's salvation became man, was original to
Christianity, and marks the point of irreconcilable cleavage

[1] See below, § 20.
[2] *Enn.*, iv. 8, 6. The generation of the effect is not of the *essence* of
the One, but is necessary to its *manifestation*. This law, that being overflows in creation of what is other than, and inferior to, itself, is accepted
by Plotinus apparently without any misgiving; but, as stated by him,
it remains brute fact, admitting of no rational explanation. No philosophy can be expected to demonstrate its ultimate grounds; we can
claim only that they should be such as can account for facts. But the
Christian belief that "God so loved the world," though far from solving
all speculative difficulties, goes a long way further towards an intelligible
solution. It enables us to build on the analogy of our own experience of
creative love, instead of falling back on a blind impulse of emanation.

between the faith of the gospel and the religion and philosophy of Hellenism.[1]

III. THE CATHOLIC FAITH (§§ 15–23).

§ 15. The faith of the first Christians cannot be expressed in formal propositions. The difficulty is not primarily due to the critical problems, of authorship and interpretation, arising out of the study of the four gospels and other early Christian literature.[2] It lies in the fact that Christian theology was gradually elicited, and attained definite form only in the fourth and fifth centuries. Yet it was implicit in Christianity from the first; for Christ imparted to his disciples no ecstatic vision, but communicable knowledge and truth. His revelation and rule of life appealed to the reason as well as to the heart and

[1] See St. Augustine's statement of the difference between Christian and Neo-Platonic teaching. "In the books of the Platonists, which I read in a Latin translation, I found, not indeed in so many words, but in substance and fortified by many arguments, that 'In the beginning was the *Logos*, and the *Logos* was with God, and the *Logos* was God; and the same was in the beginning with God, and that all things were made by him, and without him was nothing made that was made; in him was life, and the life was the light of men; and the light shineth in darkness and the darkness comprehended it not.' Further, that the soul of man, though it bears witness to the light, is not itself that light, but God, the *Logos* of God, is the true light that lighteth every man that cometh into the world. And that 'he was in the world, and the world was made by him, and the world knew him not.' . . . Also I found there that God the *Logos* was born not of flesh, nor of blood, nor of the will of a husband, nor of the will of the flesh, but of God. But that 'the *Logos* was made flesh and dwelt among us,' this I found not there." *Conf.*, vii. 9, *tr.* Inge, ii. 206, 207.

[2] We cannot here enter upon the mass of problems connected with the critical study of the New Testament. During the past half-century a vast literature has accumulated on this subject, and the results of scholarly research have constantly been published in a form accessible to the general reader. It must be carefully borne in mind that the prevalent opinion of the learned on these matters is apt to swing now to the left, now to the right, and that latterly the dominant tendency has been in a more conservative direction than was the case a generation or so ago. The once familiar antitheses, for example, between the Christ of the Synoptics and the Christ of the Fourth Gospels, or, again, between the Pauline and Johannine interpretations of Christianity, must be considered with reserve; as also that between ideas of Palestinian and those of Hellenistic derivation. Our concern is rather with the essentials of the faith that inspired the Apostles and their immediate followers in the first generations of missionary activity. On this the reader is referred to Professor C. H. Dodd's concise and masterly summary in his book, *The Apostolic Preaching*, where he shows how the teaching of the Apostles as recorded in St. Paul's Epistles (the earliest documents of the Apostolic age), in the Synoptic and the Fourth Gospels, and in the earlier chapters of the Acts, displays a remarkable consistency in the fundamentals, outlined in this and the following section. He adds at the close some very instructive comments on the development of the views of the first Christians on the *Parousia*.

will.[1] The object of this knowledge was no idea, or abstract dogma, but a person. " I am the way, the truth and the life." Christ and Christ crucified was the nerve of the apostolic preaching. Ignatius answered the Docetists of Philadelphia, when they objected : " If I find it not in the archives, I believe it not in the gospel," with the words " My archives are Jesus Christ." [2] This faith had its source not merely in Christ's assertion of his divine sonship; his whole life, lived in unity with the Father, was the compelling revelation that took shape in the simple confession of the church of the first century, " Jesus Christ, the Son of God, the Saviour." [3] Jesus was, first, the Christ, the Messiah of Jewish expectation, who had come to found, and would return to accomplish, the kingdom of God. He was also the Son of God, who had come forth from and ascended to the Father; the divine mediator who by his incarnation, death and resurrection had " broken down the middle wall of partition " between God and man.[4] To all minds familiar with the Hellenic tradition, this assertion of Christ's sonship implied essential unity with the Father as divine. Thus the thought of God's fatherhood, heralded by Jewish monotheism, acquired a wholly new significance; God was the Father, no longer of the Jewish nation in its exclusive collectivity, but of Jesus Christ, and, through him, of each and all among mankind.[5] Thirdly, Jesus Christ was the Saviour, who by the sufferings of the cross had redeemed the world, and reconciled fallen humanity to God. " God so loved the world, that he gave his only-begotten Son, that whosoever believeth on him should not perish, but have eternal life." Henceforth all members of the human race,

[1] The goal of spiritual experience is declared to be knowledge both in the Pauline and in the Johannine writings, e.g. John xiv and xvii. 3, Col. ii. 2, 3, and *passim* (*epignôsis*). " I will pray with the Spirit," writes St. Paul, " and I will pray with the understanding also " (1 Cor. xiv. 15). Widely different as are the knowledge of the Christian religion and that of the Platonic philosophy, they are at one in that for both (*a*) the supreme good is the supreme reality, (*b*) this supreme good is knowable, (*c*) this knowledge is indissolubly bound up with love.

[2] Ign. *Phil.*, 8; see Bigg, *Origins*, p. 110, who explains that by " archives " were probably meant the Old Testament and the evangelic records. The Docetists held that Christ's human form, sufferings and death were only a semblance; in other words, that God did not *really* become man in Christ.

[3] In Greek, Ιησοῦς Χριστὸς Θεοῦ Υἱὸς Σῶτηρ, forming the anagram ΙΧΘΥΣ, meaning " fish," a common symbol among the early Christians (Duchesne, i. 44).

[4] Eph. ii. 14 ff. Here is the point of contact between the new faith and the Græco-Oriental mystery-cults. St. Paul already uses language analogous to theirs.   [5] See Harnack, *History of Dogma*, i. 64, 65.

liberated from bondage, were entitled to share, as adopted children, in Christ's inheritance of the glory of God.[1]

§ 16. We saw in an earlier chapter how the hopes both of the individual and of the community found utterance in the religious life of Israel, and how Judaism failed to effect their reconciliation. In Christianity, they stood in inseparable union as moments of a single process. On the one hand, the new faith recognised the infinite worth of each human individual in the sight of God. It declared the redemption through Christ of his entire personality, both soul and body; as God had been made flesh, so man's body would share in the resurrection unto life. Thus decisively did the Christian gospel part company with the thought, persistent among eastern races, and issuing in extravagant asceticism, that matter is evil and the body by nature corrupt.[2] On the other hand, only through membership of Christ's kingdom could the individual find salvation. In foregoing his private selfhood, and identifying his will, after Christ's example, with that of the Father, he won peace and joy as a member of Christ and of his kingdom. Here again we remark the divergence between the teaching of Christianity and that of many religions of the East. Self-discipline is not the means to an absorption of the individual in the Absolute; the Christian does not gain his soul in order that he may lose it, but loses it that he may gain it, in union with Christ and with his brethren. The antitheses of individual and society, egoism and altruism, self-expression and self-sacrifice, cease to bear a meaning on the plane of this inner, interpenetrative union of minds and wills in the love of Christ. At the same time, the scope of the kingdom is inevitably broadened to include the whole human race. Membership of the kingdom and eternal life are one and the same.

[1] John iii. 16; Rom. viii. St. Paul was well aware that in Roman law the adopted son was in every respect the equal of the son born of the father's body. In Rom. viii. 19–22, he conceives the redemption as embracing the whole created universe.

[2] See, especially, 1 Cor. xv. St. Paul would say " body, soul and spirit." (On this tripartite psychology see Charles, *Eschatology*, pp. 467–472.) Early Christianity had to struggle hard against the Oriental dualism referred to in the text. It appeared in Docetism, Gnosticism and (later) Manichæism. Marcion, a very important second-century figure, cut the knot of the problem of evil by positing a second divine power, the creator, subordinate to and derived from the supreme God, yet his rival. Our knowledge of this, as of other early heresies, is defective, for it is mainly based on the statements of orthodox opponents; in Hatch's (*Hibbert Lectures*, p. 10) phrase : " when catholic Christianity had routed the enemy, it burnt the camp." The orthodox solution of the problem of evil was in terms of free will (Irenæus, Origen).

Moreover, the kingdom, being eternal, is conceived as both present and future, as both in heaven and on earth. Though not, like Cæsar's empire, of the world, it yet works in the world for the world's redemption. This temporal process is likened by Christ to the grain of mustard-seed growing into a tree whose branches overspread the earth, and to the leaven that leavens the whole lump.[1] The church is a spiritual society, whose members, whether living or dead, form one communion of saints under Christ's kingship. It is the living body of which he is the head.[2] In it, and in the hearts of its individual members, dwells the Holy Spirit, continuing the earthly mission of Christ until the full accomplishment of his kingdom. Finally, the conditions of salvation are spiritual; repentance, entailing through Christ immediate forgiveness, the hunger and thirst after righteousness, faith in Christ's saving power, and love. Only against the unloving and the self-satisfied are the doors of the kingdom closed. Even for such, there is the hope of forgiveness; for their sin is ignorance of the truth, they "know not what they do." [3] Thus the early faith of the first century, rooted in the person of Christ, the Son of God and Saviour of the world, harmonised implicitly the manifold claims of man's nature. Historic fact and ideal values, the temporal and the eternal, nature and spirit, reason and revelation, *gnôsis* and *praxis*, the individual and the community, human responsibility and divine grace—all these seeming contradictions in religious experience found their synthesis in a faith, which meant for the Christian the reasonable service of Christ as God and man.

§ 17. Christian dogma, like the institution of the visible church, was a necessary and natural development of the primitive faith. Doubtless it is a far cry from the sermon on the mount to the creeds of the fourth-century councils. Hellenism, with all that this term stands for in religion and science, had come in between. But the appropriation of Hellenism was the

---

[1] The temporal form of the kingdom was doubtless dominant in the minds of the first Christians; but even when thus conceived, it was never, despite the vivid expectation of Christ's second coming, *merely* future. Christian thought soon realised that the temporal form was inadequate to express the eternity of the kingdom (e.g. Origen saw this clearly). But it held firmly to the reality of temporal happenings, handling thus with rare judgement one of the most difficult of speculative problems, the relationship of eternal truths to events in time.

[2] Rom. xii. 4, 5; 1 Cor. xii; Eph. i. 22, 23; ii. 11 ff.; iv and v.

[3] For the gist of the apostolic preaching, see Matt. xxviii. 19, 20; Luke xxiv. 47; Acts ii. 38, x. 34–43, xvii. 30, 31, xx. 21, 25, xxvi. 16–23, xxviii. 31.

logical outcome of the impulse towards universalism that Christianity received from the teaching of its founder. The knowledge imparted by Christ was a living growth, the significance of which was destined to evolve in the minds of successive generations of his followers. " When he, the Spirit of truth, is come, he shall guide you into all the truth." [1] In the words of a great modern philosopher, " It was not till the feast of Pentecost that the Apostles were filled with the Holy Ghost. To the Apostles, Christ as living was not that which he was to them subsequently as the Spirit of the church, in which he became to them for the first time an object for their truly spiritual consciousness." Thus the articles of belief, which set forth in explicit form the essential implications of the Christian revelation, were rightly regarded as the deposit of apostolical tradition. The rule of faith, formulated in the Roman church and accepted throughout Christendom in the course of the third century, was couched as follows : " I believe in God, the Father Almighty; and in Jesus Christ, his only Son our Lord, born of the Holy Spirit and of the Virgin Mary, crucified under Pontius Pilate and buried, raised from the dead the third day, ascended into heaven, seated on the right hand of the Father, from whence he shall come to judge the living and the dead; and in the Holy Spirit, in the Holy Church, in the remission of sins, in the resurrection of the flesh." [2] This simple creed, comprising three articles which answer to the three terms of the primitive baptismal confession " in the name of the Father, the Son and the Holy Spirit," together with a brief summary of the gospel history, represented the faith of the Christian church at the dawn of the epoch of doctrinal controversy. It formed the basis for the edifice of speculative theology that arose in the fourth and fifth centuries. The product of Palestinian Christianity, it as yet bore little, if any, impress of Greek philosophical influence. It was not long, however, before that influence inevitably made itself felt. The church found itself confronted with the task of interpreting its faith in terms of reason. If Christianity were to justify

[1] John xvi. 13. The quotation that follows is from Hegel's *Philosophy of History*, Part III, Sec. 3, c. ii.
[2] Duchesne, i. 504, 505, who points out that this formula, known certainly to Tertullian, dates probably from the first years of the second century. The points embodied are all to be found, though not in formal shape, in the letters of Ignatius (c. 110 A.D.). C. H. Turner, *Camb. Mediaeval History*, vol. i, c. 5, suggests that the origin of the primitive creed may be found in the teaching handed over by St. Paul to his converts at Corinth, 1 Cor. xv. 3 ff.

its claim to redeem the whole nature of man, the demand of the intellect to think out its teaching could not be denied. From the earliest times four motives combined to foster the growth of a reasoned theology. There was, first, the necessity of presenting, especially to Hellenic converts, an intelligible account of the new religion. The Greek asked questions, and wanted to know how and why. Signs and wonders, even the personal magnetism of the preacher, were not of themselves sufficient to satisfy his mind. He required to know the logic of the gospel, and to have it explained in terms of the inheritance of Hellenic thought. Secondly, the objections raised on grounds of reason by writers hostile to the faith had to be met with intellectual weapons. The Christian apologists of the second century did much in this way to lay the foundations of speculative theology. Thirdly, as has been already noted, conflict of opinion made itself heard within the Church as to the meaning and relative value of different tenets of the faith. Already St. Paul, in the epistles to the Galatians and the Romans, had been forced to combat Judaism and to define the Christian conception of justification and the relation of the gospel to the Mosaic law. In his epistle to the Colossians, he had expounded the theory of Christian *gnôsis* (= knowledge) against the precursors of second-century Gnosticism.[1] Lastly, though not till later in the day, the voice of reason itself stimulated the more speculative minds in the church to think out the articles of the revealed faith as a coherent system of theological knowledge. The outcome of these processes was the appropriation by Christian thought of the intellectual legacy of Hellenism.[2] A scientific theology required an equipment of philosophical ideas and a medium of philosophical language such as Greece, and Greece alone, could furnish. At every stage in the speculative discussions of the fourth and fifth centuries we can trace the influence of Hellenic thought working its way with pervasive subtlety into the structure of the Christian faith. Everywhere it brought light, clarity of thought and diction, the sane voice of reason.

---

[1] Since the dogmas of catholic Christianity were formulated in view of prevalent heresies, they are often more significant in what they deny than in what they affirm. The doctrine, e.g. that the world was created *ex nihilo* by a free act of the divine will was intended to ward off (a) the dualistic theory of a pre-existent matter, (b) the Neo-Platonic theory of necessary emanation (see Pringle-Pattison, *The Idea of God*, Lect. XVI).

[2] The synthesis with Greek philosophy began in the apostolic age at Ephesus (see above, § 3), and was continued later at Alexandria (see the next section).

Informed by the Hellenic spirit, Christianity stood firm against the wild fantasies of Oriental mysticism. But it remained faithful to its apostolic credentials. It never degenerated from a religion into a theory of the schools. The rejection by catholic Christianity of the Gnostic theosophies of the second century meant the decisive refusal to be absorbed in Hellenism.[1]

§ 18. The catechetical school of Alexandria formed the nursery of Christian theology, and the greatest name was that of its master, Origen.[2] Alexandria, with its museum and university, was the crucible in which the thought of the East fused, in manifold combinations, with the philosophy of Greece. There had studied the Jewish Platonist Philo, the chief Gnostic teachers, and Plotinus. Late in the second century the catechetical school was presided over by Clement, the first of the Christian Platonists of Alexandria, a Greek convert with an enthusiasm for *belles lettres*, who found in Christianity the coping-stone of Hellenic philosophy. When Clement, who had little zest for martyrdom, fled before Severus' persecution in 203, Origen, at the age of eighteen, took his place as leader in the school. His nature was cast in a very different mould. To a

[1] The centre of Gnosticism was Alexandria. It was the religion of a philosophic school, and had its origin before Christianity. (On pre-Christian *Gnôsis*, see Murray, *Five Stages*, p. 143.) There were many varieties of Gnostic opinion. The chief teachers, Valentinus and Carpocrates, were men of remarkable speculative ability, and are at one (*a*) in rejecting the creator-God of the Old Testament and referring the creation of the material world to an inferior divine power (dualism, condemnation of the sense-world as evil), (*b*) in asserting the unknowableness of the supreme God, (*c*) in interposing a multitude of abstract powers, organised in a hierarchy of mediators, between God and the created world, (*d*) in denying the reality of Christ's life in the body, his passion and resurrection, (*e*) in grouping men in rigid castes, of which the highest, the "pneumatics" (spiritual *illuminati*) possessing *gnôsis*, were alone capable of full salvation. Free will and the worth of the practical life (*praxis*) were discountenanced. The tendency to interpose a plurality of mediating powers between God and man reacted on Christianity, practically in the worship of saints, theoretically in the belief in an angelic hierarchy, developed later by the pseudo-Dionysius (see Webb, *History of Philosophy*, Home University Library, pp. 96, 97). The serious issue between Gnosticism and Christianity was this : Is the gospel a record of historic fact or an edifying myth ?

[2] On this section, see Bigg's Bampton Lectures on *The Christian Platonists of Alexandria*, and the shorter and more popular account by the same author, in his *Neo-Platonism*, c. x. The Alexandrian Church in the second century enjoyed great prosperity, and had escaped persecution : the catechetical school stood in close relation to the university —the curriculum embraced the sciences, philosophy (especially ethics) and Christian theology. Porphyry said of Origen that, though a Christian in his manner of life, in his views on God he was a Greek; but this statement (quoted by Eusebius) ignores the fact that the conception of God as love is the centre of Origen's theology.

fiery zeal for the faith he united depth of learning and a genius
for daring speculation unique in the annals of the early church.
In ascetic practices, which he carried to immoderate lengths, he
was the forerunner of St. Anthony and the Egyptian anchorites
of a later generation. The son of a martyr, he thirsted passionately for martyrdom. But it was his erudition and the
ardour with which he probed the problems of religion to their
first principles that determined his pre-eminence in the germinating epoch of Christian theology. His literary activity was
enormous. Aided by a workshop of stenographers, he produced,
we are told, six thousand rolls of manuscript. Following in
the steps of the Alexandrian editors of Homer under the Ptolemies,
he applied himself to the text of the scriptures, collated manuscripts, and in his *Hexapla*, published in parallel columns six
versions of the Old Testament, including the Hebrew and the
Septuagint. On the basis of this textual criticism, Origen
composed commentaries on every book of both Testaments,
appending to each passage a threefold interpretation, in its
literal, ethical and spiritual significance. The method of allegorism, though carried to extremes, enabled him to present a
harmony of the Scriptures and, above all, to develop from them
a coherent speculative theory of God, man and the universe.
In these commentaries, together with the earlier treatise on first
principles (*peri archôn*) and the refutation of Celsus' attack on
Christianity, Origen raised and discussed, with uncompromising
audacity, the burning issues of later theological controversy.
God, the supreme and transcendent good, communicates through
his Son, the Word (*logos*), of the plenitude of his being to the
universe, which, as the effect of his creative activity is—here
Origen is at one with Neo-Platonism—of necessity inferior to
its cause. All nature, informed by his presence, furnishes a
symbolism of the divine purpose, a " divine visual language,"
in Berkeley's phrase, which whoso runs may read. Man, like
the evil angels, fell by misuse of the gift of freedom ; Christ, the
logos, is the means to his recovery and eventual restitution.[1]

---

[1] The history of the term *logos* is very instructive. It means " word "
and also " argument," " reason." (1) Aristotle used it to mean the
formula of definition, which expresses the essential " form " of each of
the various kinds of beings (e.g. triangle, horse, man). (2) The Stoics
used it to signify the active force inherent in physical nature, as a whole
and in its different parts. (3) Philo of Alexandria gave it a theological
application, to mean " the whole mind of God as travelling outside itself
and expressing itself in act," and also the mediator through whom man
attains knowledge of the Father. (It is disputed whether the use in the

In the divine economy, Father, Son and Spirit form a perfect and timeless harmony of three distinct *hypostases* or individual subjects, coeternal, and, though Origen mistrusts the term, as one current in Gnostic writers, consubstantial. But they are not coequal; though Origen fights hard against subordinationism, he gave a handle to those of a later generation who, after the manner of the Neo-Platonists, affirmed the inferiority of the second and third persons of the Trinity to the first.[1] The entire history of the universe is interpreted by Origen as a progressive process of redemption, from the law of nature to that of Moses, from Judaism to the Christian gospel, from the gospel of apostolic tradition to the eternal gospel, when the veil of symbolism shall be wholly done away, and men shall share in a purely spiritual communion with God.[2] Origen ever presses behind the letter to the spirit. As the temporal gospel is the shadow of the eternal, so is the temporal church of the eternal; it is not the act of ordination that makes the priest, but the spirit of Christ; Christ's presence in the bread and wine of the eucharist is not corporeal but spiritual.[3] Heaven is no place, but a spiritual condition, for God's being knows no temporal or spatial limitations; the creation of the world and the generation of the Son are alike timeless operations of his activity. Following in Plato's steps, Origen reconciled divine justice with the reality of evil by the

Fourth Gospel is derived from Philo or from Palestinian Judaism, where it was also current.) (4) Plotinus employed the term with a meaning analogous to the Stoic. The *logoi* are spermatic powers, breathed into the sensible world by the universal soul. (5) In the fourth gospel, esp. John i. 1–14, and in Origen, it is applied to a historical person and means Christ, the Son of God, being associated for the first time with the belief in the Incarnation. Origen conceives it as immaterial power stretching forth into the material world.

[1] Subordinationism, as the name implies, means the inferiority of the Son and the Spirit to the Father. Origen must not be regarded as heralding Arianism; had he lived in the fourth century, he would probably have joined hands with Athanasius. He was broaching a new question that was not yet ripe for settlement. The danger in his day was in the other direction, viz. of Sabellianism, which blurred the distinction of the three members of the Trinity into mere modes or aspects. Origen was consequently insistent on the reality of the distinction.

[2] The Scriptural basis for the "eternal gospel" is Rev. xiv. 6. The idea constantly recurs, especially in Joachim of Flora, a Calabrian abbot of the twelfth century. Origen grasped clearly that eternity transcends time.

[3] See Bigg, *Origins*, c. xxiii, where he refers to the partiality of the Reformation theologians for Origen. Origen held that a pious layman was a true priest, while absolution pronounced by a bad priest was invalid. Erasmus, too, said that he learnt more Christian philosophy from a single page of Origen than from ten pages of Augustine. It was the tribute of one great scholar to another.

M

doctrine of the soul's pre-existence; while, after the death of
the body, it will pass to a state of purification, and in the end all
souls, cleansed by fire, will share in the universal restitution.[1]
Thus all nature is a revelation; what men deem miraculous is but
the working of a spiritual law to which the whole creation is
subordinate.[2] Origen's Platonism found expression also in the
ascription of a higher grade of goodness to those who had achieved
intellectual enlightenment. His faith, it must be owned, was
that of a school rather than of the church. Of his system, part
was absorbed in the body of catholic theology, part explicitly
rejected as erroneous. Even during his lifetime a suspicion of
unorthodoxy gathered round him. He died at Tyre in 254
from sufferings endured in Decius' persecution, in communion
with the church. The impression which the grandeur and
tenderness of his character and his incomparable learning made
on his contemporaries lingered long after his death. Origen
was one of those who belong less to their own age than to the
future, whose thought, through its high originality, foreshadows
the ruling ideas of after times.

§ 19. It would carry us too far to attempt a survey of the
doctrinal controversies that raged throughout Christendom
from the fourth to the seventh century. We shall select for
illustration that which gathered round the teaching of Arius
and received its definitive solution in the catholic doctrine of
the Trinity. It was not a mere question of words nor even of
philosophical conceptions, but one that concerned the very
being of the Christian faith. The gospel declared that Christ
was both God and man; the fact had been accepted without
question from apostolic times; but how—this was the disturbing
problem—was this fact to be conceived? [3] The difficulty was
twofold. In the first place (a), in what relation did Christ, the
Son, stand to the Father? Is the Godhead that was manifested

---

[1] Origen grounded this belief, partly on the divine love, partly on the
presence of a spiritual element in human nature (Platonism). Immortality implied pre-existence to the Greek mind. Origen criticised tren-
chantly the current materialistic view of the resurrection and the expectation of temporal rewards for virtue in the life to come. His vindication
of the purely spiritual nature of God was decisive in the struggle against
Christian materialism.

[2] Origen was critical on the question of miracles. The crowning
miracle of Christianity, in his judgement, was its acceptance by a multitude
of believers. Here he anticipates the noble argument of Aquinas, *Summa
contra gentiles*, i. 6. He attached more weight to the evidence of prophecy.

[3] The triple name (Father, Son and Holy Spirit) was used in the
formulæ of baptism and of benediction from the earliest times, though its
meaning and implications were diversely conceived until the fourth century.

in human form identical with the creator of the universe? If
so, how were their unity and their distinction to be held together
in thought? On the one hand, unless there be a real unity,
either Christ is not divine, or two gods must be affirmed, at the
cost of a relapse into pagan polytheism.[1] If, on the other hand,
the reality of the distinction be questioned, Christ's mediation
becomes chimerical, the divine and the human fall asunder as
in Judaism, and the hope of union with God through Christ
must be renounced. Hesitation on any of these points imperilled
the gospel of redemption. Each party to the controversies felt
that he was contending for an essential truth. The full bearings
of the issue were not evident at the outset; and a great variety
of opinions, both extreme and moderate, were put forward on
either side. There were those who, like the Sabellians of the
third century, in their anxiety to safeguard monotheism, blurred
the distinction of Father, Son and Spirit into one of attributes
or aspects of the one God. Others, like Arius, whose intellect
rebelled against the admission of real distinctions within the
divine unity, denied that the Son was consubstantial, coeternal
or coequal with the Father.[2] Arius maintained that the *logos*
was created in time, that " there was a time when he was not,"
and that Jesus, having as man by his free will chosen the good,
was adopted by God as his Son and endowed with the divine,
though created, *logos*. Here arises (*b*) the second aspect of the
difficulty. How were the divine and human natures in Christ
united in a single personality? Did God enter into a real union
with human nature, thus raising that nature to the plane of the
divine? Otherwise, redemption is chimerical and the hope of
the Christian vain. Yet the distinction of the two natures
must equally be recognised; for, if Christ were merely divine,
his human manifestation and bodily sufferings were phantasmal
(Docetism, Gnosticism); if he were merely human, the gulf
between man and God remained unbridged. In the event,
both problems found their solution in the doctrines of the Trinity
and of the Incarnation. Of the latter, which was not defined

[1] The latter alternative, if the problem be extended to the Holy
Spirit as well as to the Son, is tritheism—the assertion of three gods.
[2] Sabellianism (early third century) was thus the earlier danger.
Arius, an Alexandrian priest, was not a thinker of great ability, though
he gave his name to the controversy. His position was based on that
of two far more remarkable theologians, Paul of Samosata and Lucian
the Martyr, who taught at Antioch " adoptionism," i.e. the view that
the man Jesus was adopted (at the incarnation, or at the baptism, or
after his death) by the Father as Son of God, and endowed with the *logos*.

till after the theological disputes of the fifth century, we shall
speak in the ensuing chapter.[1] The trinitarian dogma that
emerged as the fruit of the Arian controversy suffered doubtless
from the inherent defects of language and the inadequacy of
speculative thought to express the convictions of spiritual faith.
Western Christendom, guided by the practical Roman mind,
early reached a definition—one substance and three persons—
and would have been well content to evade the metaphysical
problem of what it really meant. The serious discussions centred
in the Hellenic East. The Greek did not cease to be a Greek
when he became a Christian; he went on asking questions until
he found an answer. It was the great triad of Cappadocian
Fathers—Basil of Cæsarea, and the two Gregories, of Nazianzus
and of Nyssa—who probed the heart of the problem, and furnished
the speculative ground-work for its solution. The concepts
round which the controversy gathered, of *ousia* (essence) and
hypostasis (individual substance) had long been familiar to Greek
philosophy.[2] Was the Son (and the Spirit) of the same essence
(*homo-ousios*), or of like essence (*homoi-ousios*), or of different
and unlike essence (*an-omoios*), with the Father ? These and a
multitude of alternative formulæ were put forward by various
parties in the course of the long debate. In the event, the victory
lay with those who affirmed one *ousia* and three *hypostases*. The
Greek theologians, with much hesitation, admitted the Latin
formula, " one substance, three persons " (*una substantia, tres
personae*) as the equivalent of this doctrine.[3] Arianism was

---

[1] See c. x, § 19.
[2] *Ousia* goes back to Plato and, especially, Aristotle (see above, c. vi,
§ 13); it means both individual substance and the essential nature of a
thing. On *hypostasis*, see above, § 13. The two terms were used as
equivalents as late as the fourth century, e.g. by Athanasius. When
they were distinguished, *ousia* was taken to express the essential nature,
hypostasis to express individual personality.
[3] The Greek bishops complained (with some reason) of the poverty
of the Latin tongue to express philosophical ideas. *Ousia* and *hypostasis*
were both rendered by *substantia*; the term *essentia*, the natural equivalent of the former, not being yet in current use. Seneca (Ep. 58, 6) tells
us that Cicero used to render ουσία by *essentia*; but this equivalent did
not establish itself. Augustine, at a later date, translates the Greek
formula as " *una essentia, tres substantiae*." *Substantia* was the natural
equivalent of *hypostasis*; but since it was used to translate *ousia* at the
time of the controversy, another word had to be found. The Latins put
forward *persona*; this, however, suggested to the Greeks the taint of
Sabellianism, for Sabellius had spoken of *tres personae*, using *persona* in
its familiar meaning of " status." In the end, they accepted *persona* as
the equivalent of *hypostasis*. So Augustine (*de Trin.*, v. 9) observes that
as *essentia* normally = *substantia*, it is best to say " *una essentia* or *substantia ; tres personae*." See also p. 329, note 2, and Aquinas, *S. Th.*, i. q. 29,
art. 1.

condemned as heretical, and the term *homo-ousios*, carrying with it the assertion of equality of the Son to the Father, was incorporated into the creed of the catholic church.[1]

§ 20. The dogma of the Trinity, if we consider its metaphysical bearings, is the point where the Christian revelation comes into closest contact with the problems of Greek philosophy. The Hellenic schools, before the days of Plato, had set their minds to work out the question of the One and the Many, with the result that an abstract monism (reality is ultimately One, not Many) and an abstract pluralism (reality is ultimately Many, not One) were alike discredited. Philosophy pointed, for the Greek thinkers, as for Hegel in modern times, to a synthesis of unity and plurality, in which each factor should be recognised as real. A unity that does not unify is no true unity, and to unify there is needed a manifold as real as the unifying principle. A plurality, again, must, if real, be a plurality of " somewhat," and the " somewhat " constitutes a common nature that serves as a real principle of unification. This reasonable conviction, that a bare unity of being is inconceivable, was embodied by Christian theologians in their interpretation of the divine nature as a Three in One. Such a conception might thus claim to be in closer accord with the demands of speculative reason than the unequal *hypostases* of Neo-Platonism.[2] The Arians, on the other

[1] The creed known as the Nicene (from the fifth century) asserts " being of one substance (Greek, *homo-ousios*) with the Father." This confession was adopted, not, as its familiar title suggests, at the council of Nicæa (325), but at that of Constantinople (381). The earlier creed adopted at Nicæa, before the Arian controversy reached its height, certainly implied the same doctrine. The title " Nicene " creed is, therefore, not entirely a misnomer. The actual creed of the council of Nicæa was the first expression of the faith that was stamped with the official sanction of the church : it was based on that in use in Palestinian Cæsarea. The creed of Constantinople (our " Nicene " creed) resembled it closely enough to pass muster as an expanded edition. It was adopted in the East from the fifth century, both in the liturgy and in the baptismal rite; in the West, it never superseded the primitive baptismal creed, but passed into liturgical use in the sixth century in Spain under the Visigoths, and thence in Rome (see C. H. Turner, *loc. cit.*). The full bearings of the doctrine of the Trinity are brought out in the so-called " Athanasian creed," which may be dated from the sixth century, or even earlier.

[2] The philosophic reader may bethink himself of an obvious solution of the problem of the One and the Many, irreconcilable with Christian theology, viz. the doctrine of an Absolute immanent in its diversity of manifestations, which in their unconditioned unity form the universe, as held, e.g. in modern times by Hegel. But no advocate of this solution will be blind to the philosophical difficulties that beset it. Christianity stood, indeed, for a transcendent God, the creator of the universe, a belief which it took over from the religion of Israel; but it affirmed, also, his immanence in the human soul. The problem of reconciling God's transcendence and his immanence is a living problem for modern philosophic thought.

hand, defined the relationship of the Son to the Father in terms
of the narrow, formal logic which has proved the bugbear of
serious metaphysics in every age.[1] Moreover, the synthesis of
unity and plurality within the divine nature is the natural complement of the Christian belief in man's redemption to unity
with God, conceived as involving no annihilation of human
personality, but as a real union in which the individual achieves
the full crown of his perfection.[2] It would, however, be a grave
error to suppose that the doctrine of the Trinity was developed
primarily as the solution of a speculative problem. Its motive
was religious rather than metaphysical. Like the belief in the
Incarnation, which carried with it the assertion of a real diversity
in the Godhead, its roots were planted in the ethical monotheism
inherited by Christianity from Israel. The reconciliation of
divine transcendence with divine immanence was asserted, not
as a metaphysical inference, but as a moral fact.[3] The primary
significance of the doctrine lay in its bearing on the Christian
gospel of salvation for all mankind. It was, for Athanasius and
later for Augustine, more than a credal formula; for it formed
the keystone of a speculative world-view, which enabled Christians
to face and to answer metaphysical problems to which Hellenic
philosophy offered no satisfactory solution. This was the reason
why the controversy was not confined to the doctors and political
leaders of the church, but evoked intense party-feeling in the
mass of the Christian community. Theological songs, composed
by Arius, were sung by Alexandrian dockers, and introduced on
the theatrical stage; if you ask a baker at Constantinople, says
Gregory of Nyssa, the price of a loaf, he will answer you that the
Father is greatest, the Son subordinate. One of the sects was
nicknamed the Pastrycooks, after the trade of their Syrian
chief.[4] Arianism spread like wildfire among the barbarian
immigrants; its profession by East Goths and West Goths,
Burgundians, Suebes, Vandals and Lombards, disturbed the unity

---

[1] Arianism affords an excellent illustration of the method of the
" abstract understanding," the relative value of which, and its limitations,
are emphasised by Hegel in his *Logic*. Its weapons were scholastic; its
logic appealed to, while it degraded, that of Aristotle; and its temper
was anti-Platonic.

[2] The highest human experiences, of intellectual insight, and, above
all, of love, point unmistakably to the conclusion that individual personality is realised, not in isolation from, but in union with, that of others
(see Shakespeare, *The Phoenix and the Turtle*).

[3] See W. R. Matthews, *Studies in Christian Theology*, pp. 54, 55.
The fathers maintained the unity of substance against Hellenic polytheism, the distinction of persons against the purely transcendent unity of
the God of Israel.   [4] The Bathyrians : Duchesne, ii. 578.

of Christendom for centuries. The storm of theological controversy among the peoples of the empire constituted an urgent political problem for the government. The emperors intervened, now in a hopeless endeavour to allay the agitation by artificial compromise, now to employ the secular arm in defence of Arianism or of orthodoxy. The baneful, if inevitable, results of the close alliance between church and state were exemplified at every turn of the struggle.[1] We have here something more than an illustration of the influence of speculative ideas on practical life. The heart of the public was touched by a sound instinct that the issue under debate was one that threatened the very existence of Christianity as a religion.

§ 21. The protagonist in this theological drama was Athanasius, bishop of Alexandria (c. 296–373). Born, like Origen, in Egypt, but a Greek in race and mind, he was present, though under thirty and a deacon, at the council of Nicæa (325), and three years afterwards succeeded to the episcopal throne. The Alexandrian bishop wielded an almost absolute sovereignty over the church in Egypt and enjoyed a prestige second only to that of Rome in Christendom. Without the erudition of Origen, or the *flair* for metaphysical speculation of the Cappadocian triad, Athanasius was enabled to dominate the church for half a century by his force of·personality, his clear and resolute grasp of the essentials of the faith, and his indomitable will. A vigorous and incisive style, the expression of a keen and lucid intellect, gave to his writings a compelling power; the pamphlets which poured from his pen at each stage of the theological crisis sounded a clarion call in defence of the catholic and apostolic faith. He stood firm as a rock amid the tempests that engulfed the world. Five times he was driven from his episcopal throne, once for as long as six years; condemned by successive councils and synods and by the imperial government, he fought single-handed—*Athanasius contra mundum*—for half a century against the combined ecclesiastical and political forces of the empire.[2] His own Egyptian church, the populace of

[1] Constantine imposed a premature settlement at the council of Nicæa (325); several of his fourth-century successors actively favoured Arianism; Theodosius (sole emperor from 395) finally determined the triumph of orthodoxy, under the guidance of St. Ambrose. The brief pagan reaction under Julian excited little more than amusement, being regarded by most sensible people as a Quixotic anachronism. For the eventual suppression of Arianism among the Lombards in the eighth century, see c. x, § 12.

[2] His episcopate lasted from 328 to 373; the five exiles were in 335–7, 339–46, 356–62, 362–4, 365–6.

Alexandria, and the anchorites of the desert, remained staunch
in his support through the darkest hours. The cells of St.
Anthony and his followers afforded a sure retreat from persecution.
In the event he triumphed, after weathering alike the Arian
policy of Constantius and the pagan reaction under Julian (361–3).
His victory was due to the fact that he stood unswervingly for
the apostolic tradition, to which, after transitory and devious
distractions, the mind of the church always returned. Athanasius
was far more than a partisan of orthodoxy; uncompromising in
essentials, he cared little for niceties of formulæ, and strove with
rare statesmanship to rally all shades of catholic opinion round
the standard of the faith. He battled for the gospel of salvation,
for the conviction that "God himself became man that we might
be made God." [1] Faith in the Incarnation was the single watchword of his life. The doctrine thus resolutely championed by
Athanasius against the Arians became in his hands the first
principle of a new metaphysical synthesis, in the strength of
which the Church could fearlessly confront the pagan classical
tradition on its own ground. Nothing was further from his mind
than to offer a refuge in irrationalism from the imbroglio in which
that tradition had found itself entangled. Rather he claimed
by the aid of a reasonable faith to save the intellect from the
menace of obscurantism and superstition that endangered it
on every side. It is significant that Athanasius applied to the
doctrine of the Trinity the term ἀρχή which Greek philosophers
from Thales onwards had used to denote the ultimate principle
of metaphysical explanation. While on the one hand that
doctrine affirmed God's infinite transcendence as Creator of all
existence save His own, and His consequent incomprehensibility
to the human mind; it proclaimed on the other hand His knowability for all men through His self-revelation in Christ. The
divine "economy," displayed in the creation of the world and
in its redemption from the evil wrought by man's self-will and
fulfilled in the person of the Incarnate Word, was henceforward
the presupposition of any intelligibility that reason could find
in man and nature. Thus the ghost of the two-world philosophy
that was the stumbling block of Platonism was finally laid,
when the invisible things of God were declared to be made

---

[1] *De Incarnatione verbi Dei*, § 54, and very frequently elsewhere. This
conviction was traditional at Alexandria : Clement (*Protrept.*, i. 8) had
written : "The word of God became Man, in order that thou also mayest
learn from Man, how man becomes God " (*tr.* Bigg). It is found also in
Irenæus.

manifest for faith in the visible processes of nature and history, and the spiritual order to be immanent in the temporal. We do not naturally look to Gibbon for a eulogy of even the most illustrious of the defenders of the Christian faith; and his tribute to "the immortal name of Athanasius" is a striking illustration of the standing judgement of history.[1]

§ 22. The thought of the West, in theology as in the problems of law and government, was always directed to the satisfaction of practical rather than of speculative interests. It left metaphysics to the East, and viewed with some impatience the persistent efforts of the Greek thinkers to express the doctrines of the Trinity and the Incarnation in terms of philosophical exactness. The Westerns did not understand that the history of the world, in the long run, is largely determined by ideas. As against any attempt to convert the Christian faith into a theory of the schools, they were entirely in the right, and, as the story of Athanasius makes clear, had the best minds of the East on their side. It is difficult to overestimate the service rendered by the Roman church in this particular during the centuries of doctrinal controversy. But when full allowance has been made for the practical insight and strong faith of the Western church, it remains true that it was prone to rest exclusively on the voice of apostolic tradition, and, if ever it did grapple with questions of speculative principle, to resolve them on the plane of juristic rather than of metaphysical thinking. Tertullian, whose fiery, intolerant and gloomy spirit clouded the dawn of the third century, was a conspicuous instance of this defect; his keen, legal intellect defined indeed the doctrine of the Trinity in words which forestalled the decision of a later generation, but which were drawn from the vocabulary, not of philosophy, but of jurisprudence.[2] All the more remarkable

[1] See Gibbon, c. xxi, where we read constantly of the "great" Athanasius, of his "intrepid" nature and "calm courage," of "the ascendancy of his genius," and how "in the various turns of his prosperous and adverse fortune, he never lost the confidence of his friends, or the esteem of his enemies." "Athanasius displayed a superiority of character and abilities which would have qualified him, far more than the degenerate sons of Constantine, for the government of a great monarchy." He was, in fact, free from many of the weaknesses that often tarnish the characters of great leaders of men. He disdained all exhibitions of vanity and took no pleasure in vulgar flattery. A born fighter, he struck hard at the living among his opponents, but spared the memory of the dead. He carried loyalty to his friends to the verge of rashness; and the austerity of his life was tempered by a saving grace of humour.

[2] It was Tertullian who introduced the formula "*una substantia, tres personae*" into Christian theology, borrowing both terms from Roman

is the fact that a century later there appeared in Africa a theologian with a genius for metaphysics. Augustine, bishop of Hippo (*b.* 354), deserves to rank in the annals of Christian theology beside and even above Origen and Athanasius. The story of his wild and passionate youth, his inner conflicts, his intellectual ardour, his early eminence as a rhetorician, his " spiritual *Aeneid* " among many schools and creeds, and his conversion through St. Ambrose, consummated by the experience in the garden at Cassiæum, is familiar from the pages of his *Confessions*. His own tumultuous and intense soul was ever his absorbing interest, colouring, and at times distorting, his vision of religious and philosophic truth. Self-consciousness was the dominant note of his philosophy and life. For him, as for Cardinal Newman, there were two and only two indubitable realities, himself and his Maker.[1] That he should have anticipated by twelve hundred years the *cogito, ergo sum* (" I think, therefore I am ") of Descartes is a startling but characteristic instance of the originality of his thought. He was the first philosopher to recognise the claim of human personality to a central place in the metaphysic of experience. Both Plato and Aristotle had found in reason the real man and had taught that to follow reason was the road that led to self-realisation; but both had failed to reach an adequate concept of personality. Plato left unsolved the problems of the integration of reason with the inferior powers of the soul and of the union of soul and body in the individual; Aristotle, in answering these problems, had been driven to separate the higher power of reason from the soul defined as the form of the organic body, and to posit an impersonal cosmic intellect with which the individual soul entered into a mysterious contact that baffled the comprehension alike of his Greek and mediæval interpreters. Augustine was the first to give the concept its full extension. He anticipated the researches of Freud and Jung. By his inclusion of instincts and unconscious impulses (*irrationabiles motus*); in his emphasis on the will in opposition

---

law, where *persona* meant an individual subject capable of holding property and *substantia* the property held (cf. our phrase " a man of substance "). He conceived God as analogous to a single property held by three persons, and the two natures in Christ as analogous to two properties in the possession of a single person. Such juristic fictions might pass muster in the West, but could not satisfy a serious philosopher. See Bigg, *Christian Platonists*, pp. 202 ff.; Harnack, iv. 131 f., 144 f., and above, p. 324, *note* 3.

[1] See Newman, *Apologia*, c. i. Augustine was fully conscious of his originality as a psychologist. " What I have found, I have found in my own mind and nowhere else " (*de immort. animae*, iv. 6).

to the classical traditions (*quid sumus nisi voluntates*), he may be regarded as the precursor of William James, who called him "the first modern man," and of many recent advocates of voluntarism. As a believer in the doctrine of the Word made flesh, he could not but question the Platonic view of the bodily organism as irrelevant to man's true selfhood. The same faith secured the objectivity of personality and disproves the charge of an exaggerated subjectivism to which Augustine's philosophy at times gives a certain plausibility. He is never weary of insisting on the soul of man as fashioned in the likeness of the Creator and of dwelling on the many analogies it presents to the Trinity, which, for him as for Athanasius, is the basic principle of the world-order. The constitution of the soul is in his view indissolubly bound up with the divine "economy." Of special note are his analyses of memory, of self-consciousness and of spiritual contemplation. As bishop of Hippo in his native province from the age of thirty-one (395), he played an active part in the affairs of the church, reconciling the Donatist schismatics to the orthodox faith, contesting heresy, prodigal of speech and writing, devoting his rare gifts of intellect and personal charm to the cause of union and internal peace. But it was his speculative genius that wielded so powerful an influence on the later religious thought of Latin Christendom. Both during the Middle Ages and at the epoch of the Reformation, Augustine's writings were the mine wherein theologians, both Catholic and Protestant, delved for gold. No other of the Fathers left so deep and enduring an impression on the fabric of Christian thought. This was due, not to the coherence of his speculations, which were diffuse and often inconsistent, but rather to his learning, his power of exposition, his wide range of intellectual interests, and, above all, to the distinctive impress of his many-sided personality. Augustine was at once a mystic, possessed by a longing for the infinite, and an ecclesiastical statesman, jealous for the maintenance of authority and of the unity of the catholic church.[1] That his mysticism implied no disparagement of reason is evident from his ascription to God of truth as an essential characteristic, and on his insistence on the argument to God's existence from the capacity of the finite intellect to apprehend eternal truth in the light that radiates from the splendour of the divine mind. *Deus illuminatio mea* is the

[1] On Augustine's mysticism see Dom Cuthbert Butler's *Western Mysticism*.

cardinal principle of his epistemology. Faith, so far from being opposed to reason, is its complement, being itself an act of intellectual apprehension and, as *fides quaerens intellectum*, provocative of intellectual effort after full clarification of its mysteries. Augustine was the resolute foe of the irrationalism and superstition, which, under the guise of fortune, chance or circumstance, had, throughout the classical tradition, been posited over against the power of human character as one of the two forces that co-operate to shape the destiny of the individual and the course of history. In his view, the sole source of the evils that condition and limit man's effort after the infinite lay in the sinfulness of his will, and the sole remedy in the gift of divine grace. By this gift he was enabled to rise to the higher plane of intellectual perception which Augustine distinguished as *sapientia* from that of *scientia* or philosophic knowledge, such as was attainable by the methods of discursive thinking canonised in the writings of Greek philosophers. Thus humanistic learning first found its due place in man's life, enjoying its full rights under the aegis of a Christocentric metaphysics. This is what Augustine meant when he spoke of Christ as "the foundation for a new physic, a new ethic and a new logic." [1] The ἀρχή and the categories of the gospel furnished at once the transformation and the justification of those of Aristotle. Every word he wrote is the outcome either of personal feeling or of the pressure of a practical crisis. Controversy with the Manichæans, the Donatists or Pelagius, is blended with the outpouring of Christian aspiration, and the love, which never deserted him, for the great teachers of the pagan world. Through the medium of his mind, the spirit of Plato passed into that of the western church. Under the influence of Victorinus, he had been led from Manichæism, which appealed early to him by its insistence on the reality of evil, to the doctrines of Plotinus; and when, like his teacher, he embraced Christianity, the new loyalty perfected rather than displaced the old. [2] His Christian faith was engrafted on

[1] Cochrane, *Christianity and Classical Culture*, p. 417.
[2] Manichæism was the religion of Manes of Ctesiphon (the capital of the Persian kingdom), in the middle of the second century. It taught a dualism of two eternal divine powers, of light and darkness, and ascetic renunciation of the body and of the material world as belonging to the realm of evil. Manes was probably unacquainted with orthodox Christianity, and his religion was not a heresy, but a rival. Despite persecution, it survived in the East till the Mongol invasion, and traces are found even in the West for several centuries. It had many adherents in Turkestan, India and China, and is one of the most important phenomena of religious history.

a Neo-Platonic stock. In his eyes, Plotinus was the halfway house to the true faith. We have quoted above the passage from the *Confessions* where he marks the point of divergence between Neo-Platonism and Christianity.[1] "That 'the Word (*Logos*) was made flesh and dwelt among us,' this I found not there." To Augustine, as to Athanasius, the Incarnation was the cardinal message of the gospel, God's free gift of suffering love to sinful man. This grasp of the divine love, as taught by St. John, and of divine grace, as taught by St. Paul, working on Augustine's vivid sense of personal sin, was the nerve of his polemic against Pelagianism. Pelagius, a British monk, who, after a long sojourn in Palestine, appeared at Rome early in the fifth century, taught that each man was solely responsible for his own virtue or vice, the maker, as a free agent, of his own spiritual destiny. He denied the inheritance of original sin, disparaged the efficacy of prayer, and relegated divine grace to the position of an external adjunct to human effort. The issue, raised clearly for the first time in the history of thought, was that of the relation of morality to religion. Pelagius voiced a popular and belated Stoicism, the doctrine that man can be saved by his own strength. To Augustine such a tenet was intolerable. If true, the need of Christ's redemption vanished. He searched the problem to its depths in the light of his own spiritual experience. Building on the epistle to the Romans (especially on Rom. v. 12), he affirmed that all men were born in Adam's sin and could be saved only by the free and irresistible grace of God, developing the doctrines of sin and grace to extremes in which catholic theology has declined to follow him. While endorsing his convictions of the necessity of prevenient grace, i.e. that the first aspiration of sinful men towards God must be divinely aided, and of God's foreknowledge of man's choice, the church refused assent to his abrogation of human freedom, and to the terrible doctrine that, out of a race doomed to eternal damnation, a few brands have been snatched from the burning by a *fiat* of the divine will.[2] God willed, so the church firmly maintained,

---

[1] *Conf.*, vii. 9. On what follows, see Bigg, *Neo-Platonism*, pp. 330 ff. The early *Confessions* should be studied in conjunction with the restatement of Augustine's position in the *Retractations*, written at the close of his life (430).

[2] The Gnostics also had held to the belief that the individual's character and destiny were determined independently of his freedom of choice and action. The problem was thus a standing one from the early centuries onwards. It arose out of the consciousness of sin. The Greeks never questioned human freedom; for Plato (see the myth of Er in *Rep.*, x) it is

that all mankind should be saved. Calvinism, in its extreme form, has its roots in certain passages of Augustine. The controversy with Pelagius formed but a fragment of Augustine's theological writings. These ranged over the whole field of Christian speculation. His treatise on the Trinity remained the classical authority for western Christendom. The East had its own doctors and owed but little to Augustine. But in the West. he was for centuries the fountain-head of Christian theology and metaphysics. In the "City of God" (de civitate Dei, 413–26), as in the historical work undertaken by Orosius at his instigation, the history of the world was interpreted as the unfolding of the issues of man's first sin and the accomplishment of God's purpose of redemption. The aim of this great treatise was to restore the shaken faith of Christendom in divine providence.[1] The hour was dark, for the barbarians were at the gates of Rome. In 410 the city was sacked by Alaric and his Visigoths. Twenty years later, as Augustine lay dying at Hippo, Genseric, with his hordes of Arian Vandals, was spreading fire and slaughter throughout Africa.

---

modified by destiny and inherited conditions, while Aristotle (Ethics, iii. c. 1) considers it absurd to question moral responsibility. If a man is responsible for his good acts, which no one doubts, he is responsible also for his bad acts (which alone he tries to evade). A man's acts are " in his power." The nearest approach to determinism is in Stoicism, which bears traces of Semitic origin. It was Augustine who first explicitly raised the speculative issue.

[1] The central thought of this treatise, which is unsystematic in structure and packed with lengthy digressions, is the contrast between the City of God (i.e. the invisible community of saints, symbolised imperfectly by the visible church), and the earthly City (i.e. the invisible community of the reprobate, symbolised imperfectly by the series of historic kingdoms). Civitas for Augustine means " society," not " the state." Augustine does not unreservedly condemn the state, which is grounded, not only on the fall of man, but on the intrinsic sociality of his nature. Rather, in the true classical spirit, he recognises its ethical function, and, particularly, the rightful authority of the Roman empire (see above, c. vii, § 2). The state of innocence would have been a social state, but without coercive authority, which is justified as a means for remedying the effects of sin. Thus the earthly City of the treatise is not organised society as such, but human society organising itself apart from God. The contrast is rooted in that of the two loves, love of self and love of God. Love of self is manifested in history as ambition for earthly power. The work exercised an immense influence on later thought, and gave a handle to very diverse interpretations in the Middle Ages. It is not to be regarded (as has often been alleged) as the first attempt to construct a " philosophy of history." It is rather a "theodicy," i.e., an interpretation of universal history as the drama of divine operation, enacted on the stage of human history, exemplifying the principle of the Incarnation (God manifest in the flesh) as displayed in the medium of temporal occurrences. See Figgis, The Political Aspects of St. Augustine's City of God, especially cc. iii and v.

§ 23. Our purpose in the foregoing sections has been to illustrate the influence of Hellenism on the process by which the primitive Christian faith was shaped into a body of theological doctrine. Before quitting this subject, we may pause to remark how Christianity, in gathering in the inheritance of Rome and Greece, achieved, in the sphere of religion, the union of two aspects, constitutive of all experience, those, namely, of historic fact and ideal value. We are wont to think of these two aspects as if they belonged to different worlds; on the one side, a world of particular occurrences, temporal events, historic situations, on the other, a world of ideal standards, absolute ends and eternal truths. When we review the course of ancient history, we realise that the Roman mind was almost wholly immersed in the world of fact, and that the source of its remarkable achievements lay in its capacity to adjust means to practical ends. Absorbed in the emergency of the hour, it ignored or even disdained the claims of speculative theory, which lives and works in the realm of ideal values. The Greek mind, on the contrary, viewed the world of fact, of practical situations, as a springing-board whence to leap by a *salto mortale* into the realm of ends and meanings, the world of absolute and timeless truths. Phenomena were but the occasion and the stimulus; reality had its abiding home in the essence of things, in the Forms of Plato, in the intellectual actuality which is Aristotle's God, in the spiritual world of Plotinus crowned by the simple and unchanging One. The difference appears, again, as that between law and morality, between the life of the politician and that of the philosopher.[1] We have said, echoing Bacon, that, to the Greek, philosophy was a religion; or rather, that his religion was philosophy. To the Roman, religion meant rising duly to the occasion, doing the fit thing at the fit time. In the discharge of its obligations, his main concern was to ensure formal correctness; absorbed in the means, he let spiritual ideals take care of themselves. The Greek found peace in intellectual detachment, the Roman in security against the transitory contingencies of the actual. Now Christianity stood, as a religion, for the union of historic fact, the great concern of Rome; and of ideal value, the great concern of Greece.[2] It affirmed this union as indissoluble,

[1] See, especially, Plato, *Theaetetus*, pp. 167 ff.

[2] We have seen in the third chapter how keenly sensitive were the Hebrews, throughout their religious history, to the pressure of historic fact. But whereas historic crises served the Roman merely as a stimulus to effective action, and the Greek as a stimulus to reflective thought, their

refusing to gauge the truth of fact save in the light of its meaning, or to accept values that were not the inner heart of fact.
The two worlds, the ideal and the actual, were for it not two,
but one. We see this in the pragmatic handling of world-
history, as, for example, in the " City of God " of St. Augustine,
and in the constant endeavour to read the sequence of temporal
occurrences as a theodicy, the revelation of a divine and eternal
purpose. The early church persistently resisted the endeavour
to relegate the faith to the realm of values, or to interpret it
merely as a philosophic theory, an abstract speculation of the
schools. It held firmly to the truth that the Divine Idea was
realised in the person of the historic Jesus.[1] " The Word was
made flesh and dwelt among us." In Him ideal and actuality,
value and fact, were one. But the church was far from restricting
the truth of Christ's actual existence to the series of historic
incidents comprised between his birth and crucifixion. It
taught that the life of the incarnate Christ is coextensive with
the entire spiritual experience, as yet unfulfilled, of humanity.
The Christian could not echo the Roman poet's faith in the destiny
of the eternal city—" to these I set nor bound nor period of
sovereignty; I have given them an empire without an end " [2]—
for he knew that all historical happenings were transitory and
that here he had no continuing city, but sought one to come.
For him, this earthly life and the whole course of human history
were but an episode in the unfolding, under conditions of time
and space, of the divine purpose, from which they drew alike
their significance and their reality. The credentials of the
Christian faith cannot be measured solely in terms of particular
incidents in its history. " Make of Christ," wrote Hegel, " what
you will, exegetically, critically, historically; demonstrate as
you please how the doctrines of the church were established by
councils, attained currency as the result of this or that episcopal
interest or passion, or originated in this or that quarter; let all
such circumstances have been what they might, the only relevant

---

significance to the Hebrew prophets and people was primarily ethical and
religious. Christianity learnt from Judaism the habit of associating moral
values with historic fact, and thus was enabled to mediate between the
one-sided interests of Roman statesmanship and Greek philosophy.
    [1] " The religion of the Incarnation cannot be mere theology—a system
of notions developed from certain metaphysical propositions—nor can it be
mere ethics, a code of laws on a theistic basis " (Figgis, op. cit., p. 34). This
is illustrated, not only by Augustine, but earlier by Athanasius, and also by
St. Paul (ibid., p. 35); see also Webb, God and Personality, pp. 81, 82, and
pp. 175–80.   [2] Virgil, Aen., i. 282–3.

question is : What is the Idea and Truth in and for itself ? " [1]
This does not mean that the Idea can possess truth apart from the
events of history. It means that the events of history cannot
possess truth apart from it. It means that there are not two
orders of truth, a truth of value distinct from the truth of fact;
but that the ghost of the two worlds, which haunted to the close
the mind of the Greeks and still haunts that of the East, was
finally laid by the declaration of the Christian faith that the
divine became human in order that the human might be made
divine.[2]

IV. CONCLUSION (§§ 24–5).

§ 24. The fourth century was a turning-point in the history
of Christianity. It witnessed the explicit acceptance of Hellenic
thought by the Christian faith, and of the Christian faith by the
Roman empire. The long struggle with Græco-Roman culture
and the imperial government was decided; *causa finita est :
Roma locuta est* ("the case is ended : Rome has spoken ").
Looking backwards, we can perceive how the conflict had been
attended throughout by the presages of an eventual reconciliation.
The influence of Hellenism upon Christianity was already apparent
in the apostolic age. The like is true of its relations with the
Roman empire. The empire from the first offered facilities as
well as obstacles to the propagation of the new faith. It secured
throughout the Mediterranean area not only an enduring peace,
but uniformity of speech and civilization, particularly in the
great cities, and communication swift and sure both by land and
sea.[3] Thus it furnished the material conditions for the expansion
of the gospel, and brought Christianity into immediate contact
with the civilization and thought of Greece. Roman jurisprudence, both in principles and in detail, was accepted, almost
without question, by the Fathers of the first six centuries. The

---

[1] *Philosophy of History*, Part III, Sect. 3, c. ii.

[2] The general question referred to in this section is further discussed at
the close of the concluding chapter.

[3] Greek was spoken in the commercial towns both in East and West.
The great roads could be traversed at all seasons, piracy had been suppressed in the Mediterranean, and lines of vessels plied at regular intervals
between the chief ports. There was a common coinage, common law and
common cosmopolitan culture throughout the empire. Teachers and
students travelled from university to university, from Bordeaux to Tarsus.
Missionaries of the Christian and other faiths did likewise. Irenæus (*adv.
haer.*, iv. 30–3) wrote: "The Romans have given the world peace, and we
travel without fear along the roads and across the sea wherever we will."

concept of a state of nature, anterior to the establishment of civil government; the doctrine that all men, as rational beings, were by nature free and equal; the distinction between natural and civil law; its application to the institutions of slavery, property and coercive jurisdiction—these ideas were confirmed and strengthened by the Christian beliefs in man's pristine innocence, and in the changed conditions which resulted from the Fall. The visible institution of the Christian church modelled itself instinctively on the majestic structure of the imperial government. The municipalities fostered by the Roman empire formed the chief centres of ecclesiastical activity. Ecclesiastical dioceses and provinces, especially in the period following on Diocletian's reconstruction, were shaped on the lines of the political divisions of the empire. The secular capitals, such as Antioch, Alexandria, Lyon, Carthage and, later, Milan and Constantinople, became the dominant sees in their respective quarters of the Roman world. We have seen how the rise of the papacy was due, not only to the recognised need for ecclesiastical unification, still less to the personal ambition of the Roman bishops, who were individually by no means the foremost leaders of Christendom, but, in large measure, to the compelling logic of facts, which rendered it inevitable that the bishop of the imperial metropolis should acquire a pre-eminent status in the ecclesiastical hierarchy. So it was, again, that the partition of the empire in the fourth century, of which we shall speak in the ensuing chapter, was reflected in the growing independence of the eastern and western churches. The racial differences of character, temperament and language between the Greek and Latin peoples proved a constant obstacle to unity; though in theory both empire and church remained one and undivided, the division in secular jurisdiction was bound to accentuate the divergences of ecclesiastical policy and theological opinion The official establishment of Christianity under Constantine and his successors was fraught with far-reaching issues upon the life of the church. Henceforward there was a close alliance between the secular government and the most powerful ecclesiastical corporation within the empire. We have remarked how conflicts within the church led to the repeated and often baneful intervention of the secular sovereign.[1] In the domain of law,

---

[1] See above, § 20, p. 327, *note* 1. The absence of a paramount ecclesiastical authority (for the influence of the Roman see was as yet moral rather than legal, especially in the East) necessitated imperial intervention in the affairs of the church. No Christian thought of disputing it. It was

the easy, simple and equitable tribunals of the Christian bishops won increasing favour with litigants and increasing sanction from the imperial authorities.[1] But the gravest peril springing from the triumph of Christianity was that of worldliness and intolerance. The church had become rich and powerful; and the temptation to use the influence of the state to further its secular ambitions was well-nigh irresistible. Hardly had the age of persecution ceased, when that of secularisation entered on its long and disastrous history. Even in the fourth century, it looked as if the victory of the church over the world meant rather the victory of the world over the church. We are apt to ignore the other side of the picture, and to forget that the dawn of secularisation coincided with the institution of monasticism, and that, side by side with proud and worldly prelates like the Alexandrian bishops of the fifth century, stand the figures of Basil and the Gregories, of Martin of Tours, of Athanasius, Ambrose and Augustine.[2] It was the employment of the secular arm as an instrument of religious persecution that forms the heaviest indictment against the church of the later empire. The toleration promised by the first Christian emperor to his pagan subjects soon yielded to a policy of repression, confined indeed to the towns, and therein to the prohibition of the external observances of the old religions. In the country districts, paganism long survived (*paganus* = villager) with little inter-

---

exercised chiefly in summoning councils, in sanctioning their decisions, and in choosing between rival candidates for bishoprics. The emperor, of course, claimed no power to decide doctrine or to appoint or depose a bishop; but in practice he frequently exercised a determining influence in such matters. But the clergy were not state functionaries, and the church remained a self-governing corporation.

[1] It had been the rule from apostolic times for Christians to settle their disputes before the church. Now the ecclesiastical tribunals were recognised by the Roman state, not merely in cases involving religion and morals, but in all matters of law (see below, c. x, § 18).

[2] Anchorites appear in Egypt about 270 (St. Anthony); the first Egyptian monastic settlement was fifty years later. Both practices spread rapidly in the East, and afterwards also in the West. St. Martin of Tours founded monasteries in Gaul in the second half of the fourth century. The authorities of the church (especially at Rome) were inclined to be suspicious of asceticism; the danger of Manichæism was always imminent, and the solitaries and monks often regarded themselves as a superior type of Christians and were apt to prove a source of disorder. Duchesne compares the danger to that of industrial strikes at the present day. The monks and anchorites were popular with the masses and did not hesitate to use their influence, if need be, against the ecclesiastical authorities. " *Monachi multa scelera faciunt* " (" the monks commit many crimes "), wrote the Emperor Theodosius to St. Ambrose. The fifth-century councils regulated monasticism and secured episcopal control of the monasteries.

ference from the government. In the end it died of inanition, or was absorbed into the practices of Christian worship.[1] Very different was the treatment meted out to heresy. Persecution of Arian by Catholic, Catholic by Arian, became the order of the day.[2] The reign of mutual toleration that had prevailed in pre-Christian antiquity had passed away. The terrible consequences of the new spirit of intolerance for the religious life of the Christian world are obvious enough and admit of no palliation. Yet a sober historian will reflect that, if paganism had been tolerant, it was because its religions felt no repugnance to recognising the existence of the gods of other peoples; and that a monotheistic faith, like the Jewish or the Christian, which refused such recognition, represented an immense spiritual advance on the polytheism that had hitherto universally prevailed. Humanity had entered on a new path, and centuries had to elapse before it could grasp the compatibility of a monotheistic worship with religious liberty. To seek for toleration among the Christians of the first centuries is like expecting to find a knowledge of the law of gravitation before Newton.[3]

§ 25. If the empire thus set its mark upon Christianity, it is no less true that Christianity set its mark upon the empire. In particular, it contributed, though unconsciously, to its imminent disintegration. The practices of asceticism and celibacy, the improvement of the status of women and slaves, an increased regard for human life, and, above all, the recognition of divine law as superior to human ordinance, and a temper of indifference towards earthly governments, sapped the groundwork on which the Roman political and social system had been based. The Christian was the member of a commonwealth that knew no distinction of Greek or barbarian, bond or free; and he looked for a city that had foundations, whose builder and maker was God. The need for a temporal embodiment of the *Civitas Dei*

[1] The fourth and fifth centuries were a time of the rapid growth of devotion to local saints and of the incorporation of pagan rites and festivals into Christian worship.

[2] " Give me the world free from heretics and I will give thee heaven," were the words of Nestorius to Theodosius II.

[3] The way was paved for toleration by the religious controversies of the Reformation epoch and the rise of modern nation-states with national churches. The presence of dissentient minorities in many countries was of crucial importance. The free-thinkers of the eighteenth century sounded the knell of persecution : e.g. Voltaire's exposure of the Calas tragedy, which constitutes one of the great events in the history of civilisation. See Mark Pattison *Essays* (*The Calas Tragedy*). But now, in face of Nazi intolerance alike towards Jews and Christians, the battle has to be fought over again.

was met, not by the state, but by the church. He had been taught indeed to render unto Cæsar the things that were Cæsar's, and the recognition by Cæsar of the Christian faith strengthened this secular allegiance to the empire. But it was not the crowning bulwark of his security; he could read, as Augustine read, the handwriting of God in the very catastrophe of its dismemberment. The fall of the empire was due primarily to causes other than the triumph of Christianity; but Christianity assisted rather than checked their operation. The function of the gospel was not to repair the breaches in an outworn civilization, but to infuse a new spirit into the life of the peoples and to bring peace and joy into the souls of men. The peace that the empire had conferred was an external peace and its prosperity an economic prosperity. We have seen how the majestic and all-embracing system proved an overpowering burden upon its subjects. But in the domain of the spirit they were free, and Christianity unlocked for them the secret of their freedom. In the strength of the new-won faith they went forth gladly to meet labour and suffering, and found in that very labour and suffering the inward tuition which they craved. They cared little about the issue on the institutions or the learning of the past. Their faith was unshaken by the ruin of Hellenic culture and of the stately fabric of empire to which that culture had given birth. It was the price they paid gladly for the hope of a new life, the revelation of which forms the true ground of the distinction between ancient and mediæval history.

CHAPTER X

THE DECLINE AND FALL

I. INTRODUCTORY (§§ 1–3).

§ 1. GIBBON dates the decline and fall of the Roman empire from the death of Marcus Aurelius in 180. If we look merely to the stability of the imperial system and its effective defence of the frontiers, we must accept a much later date for the beginning of the end. So securely had the foundations been laid by Augustus that the empire maintained its integrity even in the West until the great invasions of the fifth century, while in the East it presented as firm a front against its enemies under Heraclius in the seventh century as under Diocletian in the third. But if we take a wider and more imaginative view of history, the grounds for Gibbon's conclusion become apparent. Long before the barbarians burst the barriers on the Rhine and the Danube, the civilization which those barriers shielded was sinking into decay. Not enough Romans were left to carry on the work of Rome. The political liberty from which it drew life had vanished, and already in the second century the seeds of economic ruin were germinating with appalling swiftness throughout the Mediterranean lands. If we think not merely of the Roman state, but of what Rome stands for in history, we must confess that, from the moment when despotism and bureaucracy cast their blighting shadow over the world, the culture of Greece and Rome was doomed to perish. The future belonged to ideas of another order, with which that culture had little sympathy. Those who resisted the new impulse and remained loyal to the past were inspired by resignation, not by hope. A creative literature is the surest index of the vitality of a civilization, and the fountain-heads of classical poetry were dry. Claudian of Alexandria, the last Latin poet worthy of the name, wrote indeed in the fifth century, but was a belated and solitary survival. The destiny of the western world lay henceforward in the hands of alien powers, the Germanic invaders and the Christian church; and in their life-history the spirit of classical antiquity no longer played a dominant part. Yet, even thus, Gibbon's judgement requires modification. The creative energy of Graeco-Roman civilization was not yet exhausted at the close of the second century. The third century was the golden age of Roman jurisprudence. In the philosophy of Plotinus it witnessed, as we showed in the last chapter, the final blossoming of the speculative genius of Greece. The foundation of New Rome on the Bosporus by Constantine opened a fresh and memorable chapter of imperial history. Therewith the tale of original and constructive achievement is closed. Even the *Corpus juris* of Justinian was but the codification of a law, of which the principles and the content were an inheritance from the past. Thus, if we are to essay the impracticable and to fix an opening date for the decline and fall, it seems reasonable to point to the close of the third and the early years of the fourth century, to the epoch of Diocletian and of Constantine.

§ 2. In our introductory chapter, we indicated the threefold function of Rome in history. She gathered up into one world-state the civilizations of the Mediterranean, and, above all, that of ancient Greece, which she enriched through her own original contribution in the field of government and law. She kept the peace for centuries, and preserved from dissolution the inheritance thus treasured beneath her sway. And, lastly, she passed on this legacy to the younger races from the north, who, trained in the school of Rome, grew, in the ages that followed, into the civilized nations of modern history. In regard to the first of these functions, we have shown how, by the close of the third century, her work was done. As for the second, we have still to see how she availed to keep the frontiers in West and East, thereby saving the old civilization and the new Christianity from being swamped by Teutonic, Slav and Saracen invaders. But it is the third task, that of implanting at least a fragment of ancient culture among peoples as yet uncivilized, that most concerns us in the later history of the empire. The problem was no new one. Already in Spain under the republic, and in Gaul under the early empire, the educative mission of Rome had borne rapid and surprising fruit. The alliance with Christianity, and the barbarian settlements within her borders, greatly enlarged its scope and influence. The Germanic peoples, though still uncivilized when they first came within Rome's sphere of influence, were endowed with rich potentialities of development. Their youthful energy, their poetic imagination, their love of freedom and above all their capacity for self-government, provided the natural basis for the evolution of a new type of social order. All they needed was an example and a training such as Rome, and Rome alone, could give. That she gave it, even in the hour of her decline, was her crowning achievement in history.

§ 3. Our task in this chapter is thus mapped out. We have not to consider, even in outline, the whole story of the decline and fall, but to select those features of the period which best illustrate the transition from the ancient to the mediæval and the modern world. We shall, first, speak briefly of the reconstruction of the imperial system, and especially of the partition of the empire under Diocletian and Constantine. We shall, next, explain the general character of the process by which the Teutonic invaders of the West from the third to the sixth century were brought into contact with Græco-Roman civilization and with Christianity, and of the immediate impression left by that contact upon their history. Finally, we shall turn to the empire in the East, and, after a survey of its administrative system and the successive crises which confronted it from without, attempt to measure the character and influence of its culture in the long period of more than a millenium, during which the emperors at Constantinople kept the gate in the face of the Slavs, the Saracens and the Turks.

II. The Reconstruction of the Empire (§§ 4–6).

§ 4. A reorganisation of the imperial system was called for by the changes that had come about since its establishment by Augustus. The republican institutions, which he studied to preserve, perished rapidly from sheer senility and inanition. By the close of the second century, despotism, working through a vast bureaucracy at Rome and in the provinces, was revealed in its nakedness and accepted without a murmur throughout the Roman world. A second change had resulted logically from the substitution of the empire for the republic. Though Rome still occupied a unique position, because of the greatness of her past, and as the seat of government, she had become less and less the real centre of the empire. The thought and energy of its rulers were concentrated on the armies on the frontiers. Even Italy counts only as the premier region among the surrounding provinces. The history of the empire is no longer that of Rome or Italy, but of the Mediterranean world. It was high time that these facts should be explicitly recognised in the constitution. But the most urgent motive for reorganisation lay in the military situation. Since the reign of Marcus Aurelius, the onset of the Germanic tribes, checked in the last days of the republic by Marius and Julius Cæsar, had threatened to break the barriers on the Rhine and the Danube; while, from the third century onwards, the rise of a powerful native Persian kingdom in place of Parthia in the Middle East provoked constant wars on the Euphrates. Moreover, the defending legions themselves proved a constant danger to internal peace. Their concentration in remote provinces left Rome at the mercy of the prætorian guards, the sole military force near the capital. In 193, for instance, the guards murdered the emperor and put the throne up to auction to the highest bidder. The frontier armies followed suit, and a struggle ensued that ended with the triumph of the Danubian legions under Severus. The phenomenon was repeated more than once in the course of the third century. A strong emperor might control the armies; but it became increasingly evident that this task, as well as that of defending the frontiers, required a reorganisation of the administrative system. It was accomplished by a soldier, and in a soldier's spirit; the same motive that prompted the recognition of Mithraism and the persecution of the Christians, inspired the reconstruction of the empire by Diocletian.

§ 5. By birth an Illyrian slave, Diocletian had risen through military capacity to be governor of Moesia (the modern Serbia and Bulgaria) and chief of the palace guard, and was acclaimed emperor by the army in 284. His reforms of the system of administration, if measures which served but to enlarge the bureaucracy and impose burdens yet more crushing on the population deserve to be styled reforms, were governed by three principles. First, civil and military functions were entrusted to different hands: the prætorian prefects with their vicars, and, under these, the provincial governors, corresponding in the bureaucratic scale to the *magistri militum*, the *duces* (dukes) and *comites* (counts), who held command over the armies. In the second place, the old provinces were increased in number to about one hundred, grouped in twelve dioceses, which were, in turn, subordinated to the four great divisions of Gaul, Italy, Illyricum and the East. Thirdly, the chiefs alike of the civil government and of the army were organised in a regularised system of grades, distinguished by their respective titles, emoluments and privileges. Rank was still, as ever at Rome, determined by tenure of executive office. The old tradition by which public services were left to private enterprise gave way to management by State officials, whose numbers increased by leaps and bounds, and who took rank by hereditary status. Rome and Italy were henceforward governed and taxed on a par with every other province. The root-idea of the system was the centralisation of all authority in the hands of the emperor, the sovereign of the official hierarchy. His unique position as autocrat of the world was asserted without disguise. His person, even his house, were proclaimed divine; throned and crowned with the royal diadem, surrounded by a court with all the pomp and ceremony of an Oriental sultan, and approachable only by the high officers of state, and by them with abject prostration, he was severed by impenetrable barriers from contact with the mass of his subjects. Continuity can be traced between the court-etiquette instituted by Diocletian and that of the Sassanid monarchs of Persia, and, less directly, of the earlier Achæmenid Persian dynasty. Thus was inaugurated the regime that prevailed for many succeeding centuries as the habit of the Byzantine empire. But Diocletian did more than remodel the bureaucracy, and institute an autocratic monarchy in place of the semi-republican principate. He recognised that the burden of government was too heavy a load to be borne by a single ruler. He desired also to provide a remedy against those disputes over the succession which had so often disturbed the peace, and weakened the efficiency, of the empire. He therefore put the empire in commission among four partners, two with superior, two with subordinate authority, associating three other Illyrian commanders with himself in the sovereign power. The two senior princes, styled *Augusti*, ruled respectively in East and West, with their capitals at Nicomedia in north-west Asia Minor, and at Milan; the two junior princes, styled *Caesares*, were entrusted, the one with Spain and the Gauls, the other with the Balkan provinces, with their capitals at Trêves and Sirmium (near Belgrade). Diocletian himself reigned over the Asiatic provinces from Nicomedia. The seats of government were thus brought into convenient proximity to the frontiers. This system did not survive in the precise form instituted by Diocletian, nor did it save the empire from internal quarrels between its rulers. But the principle of partition endured. A generation after Diocletian, Constantine founded on the site of the ancient Greek colony of Byzantium, the " New Rome " which still perpetuates his name, to be the seat of government for the eastern half of the empire. Grounds, alike of strategy and of commerce, marked out the city on the Bosporus as a centre that commanded both the Balkan and Asiatic provinces,[1] which were menaced simultaneously by the Visigoths on the Danube and by the Persians from the East.

---

[1] Gibbon's description of Constantinople in his seventeenth chapter has never been surpassed.

Byzantium was a natural fortress, impregnable save by assault at once from the sea and by land. In the event, " New Rome " was thrice saved during the fifth century at the expense of the Old. Alaric's Visigoths, Attila's Huns, and Theodore's Ostrogoths, turned their arms westwards towards Italy at the moment when the city of Constantine seemed to lie at their mercy. We shall return to the memorable history of Constantinople in a later section of this chapter. Finally, on the death of Theodosius the Great (395), the last sole ruler of the empire, the sovereignty was shared for nearly a century by two emperors, governing respectively from Italy and from Constantinople. Historians have been accustomed to speak of this change as a division of the empire into two, an eastern and a western empire. Such expressions are misleading; though its government was henceforward partitioned between two emperors, the empire itself remained indivisible and one.

§ 6. The significance of these changes was very great.[1] They contributed to prolong the life of the imperial state in the West for nearly two centuries, in the East for over a thousand years. Again, they indicate that the old Rome, the Rome of the republic, which Augustus had striven to perpetuate, was gone for ever. The change of capitals, the substitution of new offices for the historic magistracies, the installation of the pomp and splendour of an Eastern court, and the frank avowal of despotism, implied a radical breach with the traditions and sentiment of the past. The extension of Roman citizenship, and of equal rights at law, to all provincials, the enrolment of barbarian immigrants in the legions and the establishment of the Christian faith as the religion of the empire, show that Rome now stood for an order of institutions and ideas very different from those of three centuries earlier. Rome was still Rome, but whereas of old she had been an Italian city, she was now a cosmopolitan state. It was this changed Rome that confronted the wild Teutons, when, breaking across the Rhine and the Danube into the frontier provinces, they passed under the overpowering influence of Roman government and law. They found too, at least in Italy and the West, that the majestic image of empire which dazzled their vision proved to more intimate experience but the veil that shrouded the agony of a dying world. For the statesmanship of Diocletian and Constantine was impotent to heal the sore that preyed on the vitals of Græco-Roman civiliza-

[1] Mommsen is reported to have said to Sir William Ramsay that, if he had a second lifetime, he would devote it to the period between Constantine and Justinian.

tion. Their failure was not merely due to their absorption in the urgent military problem, and their consequent neglect of the economic crisis. That crisis was grave indeed, but it was a secondary symptom; the economic evils had their root in moral apathy and paralysis of human will. How could a military autocracy stir into fresh life the flagging energy of its subject-peoples? Bankruptcy, war, plague and famine; wasted lands, decaying cities, ruined trade; a diminished population, no longer capable of furnishing an adequate quota of recruits for the legions; a listless aristocracy, a middle class impoverished by exaction and almost crushed out of being, an indolent proletariate, vast multitudes of serfs and slaves; over all, the huge machine of government, stifling local independence and individual enterprise; around all, the terrible barbarian menace, drawing nearer year by year to the gates of Italy; such was the gaunt reality that crouched in the shadow of the fourth-century empire.[1] Little wonder that the masses sought a refuge in the other-worldliness of Christianity, or that, when in the event the imperial government vanished from the western provinces, men seemed scarcely sensible of the change.[2]

III. THE ROMAN AND THE TEUTON (§§ 7–12).

§ 7. The policy of the empire towards the Teutonic peoples presents the two aspects of resistance and of attraction. We have seen how war against the German hordes who pressed ceaselessly against the Rhine and Danube fortifications was a standing feature of imperial history from the days of Julius and Augustus. But the last-named emperor had already inaugurated

---

[1] We have summed up in this sentence a mass of economic and social phenomena, to the study of which much labour has been devoted by modern scholars. The decay of agriculture is especially important. The third and fourth centuries saw the change in the position of *coloni*, from free rent-paying cultivators to hereditary tenants tied to the soil (see Pelham, *Essays in Roman History*, "The Imperial Domains and the Colonate"). In the fourth century arose a body of landowners with privileges and powers that foreshadowed the feudal aristocracy of the Middle Ages (see Vinogradoff in *Camb. Med. History*, vol. i, c. xix). On the history of ancient (Græco-Roman) agriculture generally see Heitland's *Agricola*.

[2] The Christianisation of the empire reacted beneficially on the condition of the people, e.g., in mitigation of the hardships of slavery, encouragement of emancipation, promotion of philanthropic measures and, above all, in the relief which episcopal jurisdiction, now recognised as an integral part of the legal system, furnished to the pressure of bureaucratic tyranny. Government and people turned more and more to the church, whose courts were speedy, cheap and just. They enjoyed the confidence of the public, who preferred episcopal arbitration to the lay tribunals.

the policy of granting lands to barbarian immigrants within the frontier provinces. Lampridius, in his life of Severus Alexander, remarks that early in the second century the Roman world was crowded with undesirable aliens.[1] This system, so perilous and yet so useful, and fraught with far-reaching consequences both for the empire and for the Teutonic settlers thus admitted within its pale, was pursued deliberately and on an extended scale in the age that followed, especially by the Illyrian emperors at the close of the third, and by the successors of Constantine in the fourth, century. The new colonists supplied a remedy for the increasing depopulation of the empire. Above all, they formed an easy recruiting-ground for the frontier legions; in the event, the defence of the frontiers fell almost entirely into the hands of these half-Romanised immigrants of Teutonic origin. Franks were enrolled in the palace guard of Constantine; Julian led Gothic troops to fight the Persians on the Euphrates. The word " barbarian " (*barbarus*) came to be used as a synonym for soldier.[2] Yet this policy of assimilation tended inevitably to the breakdown of the old political and social order. The line of partition between Roman and barbarian grew less rigid. We have noted above the influence of the Christian faith, now universal throughout the empire, in weakening the consciousness of this cleavage. By the fifth century a barbarian colonist might rise to the highest posts in the imperial service. Stilicho, the general of Honorius against Alaric, was a Vandal, Rufinus and Ricimer, the viziers of the Eastern emperors, were respectively a Goth and a Suebe. On the other hand, the Germanic settlers were a source of continual unrest, and not infrequently allied themselves with their kinsmen beyond the Roman border. The grants of land which they obtained within the provinces were, more often than not, grants only in name, being in fact seized by force of arms from a reluctant but impotent government. This was, for instance, the case in Moesia with the Visigoths, who slew the emperor Valens in battle at Adrianople (378), and with the Burgundians, a generation later (413), on the left bank of the Rhine in the region of Worms and Spires. The Roman territory, beyond the Rhine and the Danube (the Black Forest and Dacia), had long been yielded; and in the early years of the fifth century Honorius left Britain to its fate. The dykes were bursting, and the tempest had begun to sweep over the peaceful provinces of the west and north. The invading chieftains

---

[1] See Vinogradoff, *Roman Law in Mediaeval Europe*, p. 4.
[2] See Vinogradoff, *Roman Law in Mediaeval Europe*, p. 5.

were already laying the foundations of Germanic kingdoms in Gaul and Spain, owning indeed a nominal allegiance to the emperor, but in reality ruling in independent sovereignty alike over Roman and Teutonic subjects.

§ 8. A brief summary of the main streams of invasion will assist to an appreciation of the catastrophe which, in over-whelming the empire in the West, at the same time initiated the transition to the new political and social order of the Middle Ages. The scene of the drama is western Europe, the time the fifth and sixth centuries; and six peoples played the leading parts in the action.

(i) Farthest towards the north, the *Franks* on the lower Rhine occupied Holland and Flanders, expelled the Roman garrison from Cologne early in the fifth century and pushed westwards over the former territory of the Belgæ to the Somme.[1] For the moment Roman authority was extinguished and Christianity barely survived in the northern parts of Gaul. The fact of the presence of earlier Frankish colonists, who fused easily with the invaders, facilitated the establishment of a kingdom which, a generation or two later, expanded under Clovis (481–511) into a great power, comprising the northern half of ancient Gaul and the western half of modern Germany.[2] Clovis was converted to the catholic faith, an event pregnant, as we shall see presently, with great issues both for the church and the Frankish empire. We find the kings of the Merovingian dynasty to which he belonged admitting a sort of dependence on the emperors at Constantinople, addressing them as " father "; diplomatic relations were constant between the two powers, and the emperor's head was stamped on money coined in Frankish Gaul.[3]

[1] The emperors of the later third and early fourth centuries kept the Franks successfully at bay, punishing them heavily in campaign after campaign. The two chief branches were (*a*) the Salian Franks, between the Scheldt and the Rhine, (*b*) the Ripuarian Franks, between the Rhine and the Meuse. The Salian Franks came from the shores of the North sea; one of their early kings was called Merovech (whence the name Merovingian), which means " sea-born." Clovis was king of the Salian Franks. Both branches were enrolled as " allies " of Rome. The Salic law dates from the last years of Clovis, but embodies many usages of greater antiquity.

[2] Clovis conquered first the Roman Syagrius, then the Alemanni in Suabia, then (after his conversion) the Visigoths in southern Gaul. " It irks me," he remarked, after his conversion to the orthodox faith, " that these Arians should rule in Gaul " (see Davis, *Mediaeval Europe*, p. 41). Clovis rode into Tours clad in the purple robe of a Roman consul. His portrait and those of other Frankish kings are vividly portrayed by the sixth-century historian, Gregory of Tours, whose work stands out amid the general decadence of art and literature in Gaul.

[3] Bury, *Later Roman Empire*, vol. i, p. 17, points out that the Ostro-goths, Lombards and Vandals failed to maintain their kingdoms for long,

(ii) While northern Gaul fell to the Franks, Aquitaine, in the south-west, became the seat of a Visigothic kingdom. We found the *Visigoths* (West Goths) across the Danube, fighting the emperor Valens in 378; driven westwards by Theodosius, they turned on Italy, and under their king Alaric, captured and sacked the imperial city in 410.[1] The city of the Cæsars had fallen : the city of the Popes was yet to arise. It was shortly after this dramatic catastrophe that they ceased from their wanderings and settled down in Aquitaine. From their capital at Toulouse, the Visigothic princes ruled, as theoretical vicegerents of the emperor, from the Loire to the Pyrenees. Rome naturally impressed her culture more deeply on the Visigoths than on the Franks. In the middle of the fifth century they joined with the Romans to repel the invasion of the Huns. A generation later, under pressure from the growing power of the Franks, they changed the seat of their kingdom to northern Spain, which they governed, together with the relics of their Gallic territory, till the advent of the Saracens in the eighth century. Even after the fall of the Visigothic kingdom, a few chieftains held out in the mountain fastnesses, preserving the traces of Rome and Christianity throughout the Middle Ages.[2]

(iii) The *Vandals*, a Germanic tribe akin to the Goths, crossed the Rhine in 407, and, after a wandering struggle with Rome and their fellow-Teutons, entered Spain and conquered the southern portion of the peninsula. About the same time the Suebi settled

---

while the Franks and the Slavs (in the east) founded enduring states, and suggests that the explanation is to be found in the fact noted in the text, of the presence of earlier settlers of the two latter races within the provinces. Such settlers gave a basis of security and permanence to the later settle-ments of their kinsmen.

[1] The Goths migrated from their Scandinavian home, first, to the district south of the Baltic, round the estuary of the Vistula, then to the northern shores of the Euxine. They fought the Romans on the Danube from c. 250 (c. viii, § 13). It was the pressure of the Huns, who conquered the East Goths in the middle of the fourth century, that drove the Visigoths into the Danubian provinces. Ulfila, the Visigoth, about the same time sowed the seeds of (Arian) Christianity among his people and translated the Bible into their language.

[2] Rome soon lost her hold of the Gallic communities that lay between the Frankish and Visigothic kingdoms. She kept the Rhône valley longer, though with difficulty, against the Burgundians; the temporary success of the Roman general Ætius and the expulsion of the Burgundians to the east of the Rhine was celebrated in the legend of the Nibelungs. Eventually the Burgundians were conquered by the Franks. In Spain, culture was preserved under Visigothic rule, especially at Toledo and Seville, e.g. Isidore of Seville (c. 560–636), a compiler of encyclopædias of science, history, theology and the canon law, which were important as forming part of the educational equipment of the early Middle Ages. The fusion of Visigothic and Romano-Spanish civilization was effective and lasting. Visigothic laws were quoted in the Spanish courts till the nineteenth century; Visigothic customs persisted in the *Fueros* of the Middle Ages.

in the north-west and west. Under their king, Genseric, the Vandals crossed the straits into Africa, and overran the Roman provinces with fire and sword. They were besieging Hippo at the moment when St. Augustine lay dying within the walls (430). By 455, Roman rule had been extinguished throughout Africa. In the same year Genseric sailed to Italy, and Rome once again fell a victim to a Teutonic conqueror. The Vandals were Arians, and **their** kings set themselves with savage ferocity to extirpate the orthodox Church in Africa. In the sixth century, Justinian crushed the Vandal power and recovered the African provinces; but his restoration of civilization and of catholic Christianity proved short-lived and abortive. The Saracen conquest of the eighth century finally obliterated every trace of Roman and of Christian influence in the lands south of the Mediterranean sea.

(iv) In the middle years of the fifth century, the empire was threatened by a different and a far more dangerous foe. The Franks, the Goths and the Vandals were Teutons, men of kindred Aryan stock to the Romans, and endowed, in varying measure, with the capacity for settled life and orderly government. But the *Huns* were Tartars, wild horsemen from the steppe-lands north of the Caucasus and the Aral sea. Alone of the invading races they came as mere destroyers. Swarthy, dwarf-like in stature, with long, shaggy hair and little beady eyes, living, eating and even sleeping, on horseback, they swept under Attila their king over the West, ravaging Gaul and Spain and threatening at every moment to descend upon Italy.[1] Teuton as well as Roman

[1] They had all the characteristics of the nomads of the steppe, repeated in the Mongols and the Turks, and present still in their primitive form among the Kirghiz and other Altaic tribes (see Peisker's remarkable chapter in *Camb. Med. Hist.*, vol. i). Ammianus Marcellinus (xxxi. 2) gives the following picture of the Huns (translated by Hodgkin, *Italy and her Invaders*, vol. ii, pp. 32–4) : " The nation of the Huns surpasses all other barbarians in wildness of life. In the first days of infancy, deep incisions are made in the cheeks of their boys, in order that, when the time comes for whiskers to grow there, the sprouting hairs may be kept back by the furrowed scars : and hence they grow to maturity and to old age beardless as eunuchs. They all, however, have strong and well-knit limbs and fine necks. Yet they are of portentous ugliness and so crook-backed that you would take them for some sort of two-footed beasts, or for the roughly chipped stakes which one sees used for the railings of a bridge. And though they do just bear the likeness of men, . . . they are so little advanced in civilization that they make no use of fire, nor of any kind of relish, in the preparation of their food, but feed upon the roots which they find in the fields, and the half-raw flesh of any kind of animal. I say half-raw, because they give it a kind of cooking by placing it between their own thighs and the backs of their horses.* They never seek the shelter of houses, which

* This is a misunderstanding on the part of the author. What the Huns did do was to use strips of raw meat thus to heal the sores on their horses (see Peisker in *Camb. Med. Hist.*, i).

realised the urgency of the common peril. In 451 the combined forces of the Roman Ætius and Theodoric the Visigoth broke their onset in a great battle near Troyes. Attilia retired on Pannonia and died in the year following, while meditating an attack on Constantinople. Quarrels ensued as to the succession, and the Hunnish menace vanished as swiftly as it had come. Two issues of their devastating invasion were of permanent importance. Attila's grim figure left a lasting impression on the creative imagination of the Germans and the Northmen, and looms mysteriously alike in the Teutonic and the Scandinavian sagas. The flight of the panic-stricken populace of northern Italy from the Hunnish terror to the safety of the islands in the Adriatic lagoons was the seed from which sprang the city of Venice.[1]

---

they look upon as little better than tombs; . . . nor would one be able to find among them even a cottage of wattled rushes : but wandering at large over mountain and through forest, they are trained to bear from their infancy all the extremes of cold, of hunger and of thirst. They are clad in linen raiment, or in the skins of field-mice sown together, and the same suit serves them for indoors and out. . . . Their heads are covered with bent caps, their hairy legs with the skins of goats; their shoes . . . are so clumsy that they cannot walk comfortably. On this account they are not well adapted to pedestrian encounters; but then on the other hand they are almost welded to their horses. . . . On horseback every man of that nation lives night and day; on horseback he buys and sells; on horseback he takes his meat and drink, and when night comes he leans forward upon the narrow neck of his horse, and there falls into a deep sleep. . . . More often they fight in no regular order of battle, but being extremely swift and sudden in their movements, they disperse and then rapidly come together again in loose array, spread havoc over vast plains, and, flying over the rampart, they pillage the camp of their enemy almost before he has become aware of their approach. . . . They are the nimblest of warriors; the missile weapons which they use at a distance being pointed with sharpened bones admirably fastened to the shaft; when in close combat, they fight without regard to their own safety, and while their enemy is intent upon parrying the thrusts of their swords, they throw a net over him and so entangle his limbs that he loses all power of walking or riding. Not one among them cultivates the ground, or ever touches a plough-handle. All wander abroad without fixed abodes, without home, or law, or settled customs, like perpetual fugitives, with their waggons for their only habitations. . . . If you ask them, not one can tell you what is his place of origin. . . . They are great truce-breakers, fickle, always ready to be swayed by the first breath of a new desire. . . . Finally, like animals devoid of reason, they are utterly ignorant of what is seemly and what is not; they are tricksters with words and full of dark sayings; they are never moved by either religious or superstitious awe; they burn with unquenchable thirst for gold, and they are so changeable and so easily moved to wrath, that many times in the day they will quarrel with their comrades on no provocation, and be reconciled having received no satisfaction."

[1] The settlements on the lagoons were older than the town of Venice, which was founded in the eighth century. It was not till the thirteenth century that the name *Venetia* was applied to the city on the Rialto as distinct from the whole lagoon area. On the earlier seats of government and the rise of the city on the Rialto (the Venice of to-day) to authority and independence of the empire, see Bury, *Eastern Roman Empire*, c. x.

(v) Italy itself was still unconquered; the Visigothic and Vandal invasions were but transitory catastrophes. The Roman emperors continued to rule, not at Rome, but at Ravenna. At length the end came; in 476 a Danubian chieftain, Odoacer, deposed the reigning Cæsar, a boy-prince, who bore the significant name of Romulus Augustulus. Henceforward Rome and Italy were governed by barbarian overlords, in nominal allegiance to the emperor at Constantinople. The deposition of Romulus Augustulus did not bring the empire to an end, for the succession fell to the eastern Cæsar Zeno. But, as far as the West was concerned, the work of Diocletian was undone. From 476 to 800 there is but one emperor, who rules from Constantinople. Twelve years after Odoacer's assumption of authority, the *Ostrogoths* (East Goths) from Pannonia descended from the north-east by the Isonzo and, under their king Theodoric, mastered Rome and Italy (488–93). Theodoric, an able and intelligent sovereign, preserved as far as was possible the existing religious and social order, excluding Romans from the army, but leaving in their hands two-thirds of the land and the entire civil administration. His reign is memorable because of two men of culture and learning, who held high offices in the state, both of whom figure as important links in the transition from classical antiquity to the civilization of the Middle Ages. One of them, Cassiodorus, founded monastic settlements at his native Squillace, where he set the monks to copy manuscripts of classical authors, by which means much of ancient literature was preserved through the dark centuries that followed. The other, Boethius, a keen student of philosophy, composed a Latin version of Aristotle which proved the chief medium by which the philosopher's logic came to stimulate early mediæval thought. He was put to death, presumably for treason, and in prison wrote his *Consolation of Philosophy*, one of the favourite works in the Middle Ages, which was translated into Anglo-Saxon by king Alfred and into English by Geoffrey Chaucer. In the middle of the ensuing century, Justinian's generals overthrew the Ostrogothic rule and united Italy, Sicily and Africa once more under the imperial government. A part of this western reconquest was retained by the empire for several centuries. Byzantine culture influenced Sicily, Southern Italy and, above all, the region around Ravenna; the churches of that city survive as noble examples of Byzantine art. It seemed for a brief space as though the New Rome on the Bosporus would replace the Old Rome on the Tiber as the sovereign city of the Mediterranean world.

(vi) The rule of the empire in Italy remained unchallenged only for fifteen years (553–68). Justinian was hardly in his grave when the *Lombards*, the last stream of Teutonic invaders, poured down on northern Italy.[1] A race of fighters, who cared little for agricultural pursuits, and left the old cultivators in possession of the soil, the Lombards possessed a remarkable capacity for government, and a natural instinct for making law.[2] They adopted the Latin tongue and the Christian faith, intermarried with their Italian subjects, and gave them equal rights at law. The Lombard power, from its centre at Pavia, spread, not only over Venetia and the plain that still bears their name, but also to the centre and south of Italy, where they founded the duchies of Spoletum and Beneventum. This last invasion wrecked all hopes of a reconquest of the West from Constantinople. The eastern emperors had neglected, to their cost, the defence of the Danube frontier, the way by which Alaric, Theodoric and the Lombards passed in succession towards Italy. Henceforward the imperial authority was confined to Venice and the territories that formed the Papal states of a later day. Italy, in the seventh and eighth centuries, was partitioned between (*a*) the emperors, whose viceroys, styled *exarchs*, held Ravenna, Naples, a large part of the south, and Sicily; (*b*) the Lombards, supreme in the north, with the offshoots above-mentioned in the centre and south; and (*c*) the Roman bishops, who had acquired, as we shall see presently, a virtual sovereignty in and around the imperial city. The Lombard invasion thus closes the story of the appropriation of the western provinces of the empire by peoples of Germanic stock.

§ 9. This brief survey of the Teutonic invasions raises the question : what were the effects of contact with Roman civilization upon the new masters of the western world ? In the first place, we must note the deep impression which the majestic structure of the imperial system wrought on the imagination of the invaders. It would have been natural enough had the luxury, corruption and effeminate manners of the later empire inspired contempt in

[1] The Lombards, whose home was on the lower Elbe, had been settled in Pannonia; in conjunction with the Avars, a Hunnish tribe, they had wiped out the Gepidæ in the old province of Dacia (Hungary). By agreement the Avars occupied the lands of the Gepidæ and also Pannonia, while the Lombards moved westwards to Italy. The Avars, as will be pointed out later, were a source of much trouble to the empire in the East.

[2] Old Lombard law proved capable of development into a reasonable and living system. King Rotharis framed a compilation in the middle of the seventh century. The first mediæval school of jurisprudence arose at Pavia early in the eleventh century; its teachers knew Justinian's *Institutes*, but took the Lombard law as their basis.

its vigorous and warlike conquerors. How otherwise, we are inclined to ask, could Alaric the Visigoth have felt towards the feeble and degenerate Honorius? But it was not so; or, if contempt was felt, it was silenced by the overpowering spectacle of what Rome had achieved, and still stood for in the eyes of the world. It was the empire, not the person or the court of the emperor, that took captive the barbarian victors, as at an earlier day Greece had captivated Rome. The successor of Alaric avowed his pride at his recognition as a vassal-prince by the Roman emperor. " It was at first," he said, " my wish to destroy the Roman name, and erect in its place a Gothic empire, taking to myself the place and the powers of Cæsar Augustus. But when experience taught me that the untamable barbarism of the Goths would not suffer them to live beneath the sway of law, and that the abolition of the institutions on which the state rested would involve the ruin of the state itself, I chose the glory of renewing and maintaining by Gothic strength the fame of Rome, desiring to go down to posterity as the restorer of that Roman power which it was beyond my power to replace. Wherefore I avoid war and strive for peace." [1] Athanaric at Constantinople broke out with the cry, " Without doubt the emperor is a god upon earth, and he who attacks him is guilty of his own blood." [2]

§ 10. The establishment of the invaders within the empire was no instantaneous catastrophe, but a process spread over several successive generations. We have seen that it was part of the imperial policy to enlist earlier colonists of Teutonic stock for the defence of the frontiers against their kinsmen from without. Thus the Visigoths aided the empire to repel the Huns, as at a later date the Franks beat back the Saracens. The naïve admiration with which they viewed the law and institutions of the empire made them eager to assimilate, within the limits of their capacity and after their own fashion, the inheritance of civilization which persisted beneath its sway. The historical significance of this process of Romanisation cannot easily be overestimated. It meant that the language, law and religion of the empire left an enduring mark on successive groups of immigrants, who were thus educated to habits of settled life, and trained at least in the rudiments of culture and of Christianity, before they finally threw over their allegiance to the Roman state. In the words of a modern historian, " The Roman empire was never overthrown, but took the barbarians into itself, and so went on changing slowly till it

[1] Orosius, see Bryce, *Holy Roman Empire*, p. 19.   [2] Bryce, p. 17.

passed away," [1] Of the influence of Roman jurisprudence, direct
and indirect, on the law of the Teutonic peoples, and of the transmission of such fragments of ancient learning as they were able to
absorb, we shall speak more particularly in the ensuing chapter.
The fact that a dark age supervened on the fall of the empire, in
which western Europe seemed plunged in anarchy and ignorance,
until the emergence in the eleventh century of the political and
intellectual order of the Middle Ages, must not blind us to the
value of the influences or to the real continuity between ancient
and mediæval civilization. We have to remember that Græco-
Roman culture was in its decline when the young races of the
north first felt its contact. It was well that it was so; had they
been confronted, in the infancy of their intellectual development,
with the thought of antiquity in the fullness of its splendour, they
could hardly have profited by its instruction. The meat would
have been too strong for their childlike minds. Above all, we must
keep our eyes fixed on the living energy with which they absorbed
and utilised the elements which they were able to digest. For
nations as for individuals, it is the fulfilment of the promise in
years to come that attests the value of the groundwork of education.
The story of the rise of the Romance languages of western and
southern Europe furnishes a simple illustration. They had their
origin, not in the literary Latin of the days of Cicero or Tacitus,
but in popular Latin, the speech of the soldiers and colonists in the
provinces, which developed on its own lines, and reflected the new
and living experience of the common people under the later empire.
Thus they assumed various distinctive yet cognate forms in
different quarters of Europe, blending to a greater or less degree
with the old Germanic and other native tongues, to emerge as the
Roumanian, Italian, Provençal, French, Spanish and Portuguese
of mediæval and modern use.[2] Centuries elapsed before the rude
materials were shaped into instruments of expression worthy to
rank beside the speech of ancient Greece and Rome; and Latin
survived to the age of Dante and even beyond as the literary

---

[1] Creighton, *Rome*, p. 118.
[2] There are nine Romance languages : 1. Roumanian; 2. Dalmatian
(extinct in the nineteenth century); 3. Sardinian; 4. Italian; 5. Ræto-
Romanic; 6. French (*Langue d'Oïl*); 7. Provençal (*Langue d'Oc*); 8. Spanish;
9. Portuguese. Sardinian is the most archaic. The first three bear little
trace of Germanic admixture (see the article " Romance Languages " in
Encyc. Brit., vol. xxiii). These languages arose on a subsoil of vigorous,
national life. Punic was still spoken in Africa in Augustine's time; he
urges his clergy to learn it. In the Basque speech and the Breton we have
survivals of the pre-Roman native languages.

medium for the educated minority among the Latin races of Europe. But the fact that in the event the noblest thought and feeling of these races found utterance in the Romance languages only heightens our sense of the stimulus imparted by the speech which, in the childhood of their history, they learnt from Rome.

§ 11. The reverence felt by the Germanic tribes for Rome was strengthened by the fact of their conversion to Christianity. We have observed how the church was led to invest the empire with a peculiar sanctity as the divinely appointed instrument for the establishment of the faith. " When Rome, the head of the world, shall have fallen," wrote Lactantius in the third century, " who can doubt that the end is come of human things, aye, of the earth itself? She, she alone, is the state by which all things are upheld even until now." [1] Thus there grew up in the minds of the newly converted colonists the idea of the empire as a divinely sanctioned order, to which, in right if not in fact, all nations and governments under heaven owed allegiance. The Roman empire came to be regarded, not merely as sacred, but as eternal and universal. The deposition of the emperor at Ravenna by Odoacer in no way impaired its being. The Augustus who ruled in the West had fallen, but the empire remained. Two centuries later the documents cited by Bede are dated by the regnal years of the emperors at Constantinople. The survival of the imperial tradition in the West was due, in large measure, to the church, which bore on its structure and policy the impress of the Roman mind. It kept alive, consciously and of set purpose, the memory of the Roman name. Alone of Roman institutions it had weathered intact the storms of Teutonic invasion. Thus it was that, in the hour of its unchallenged sovereignty, it reaffirmed its loyalty to the principle of the Roman empire, as the sole rightful authority in the secular government of mankind. Just as the church, in the belief of mediæval Europe, was by right the one catholic (universal) church, despite the actual severance of the Latin Christians in the West from the Greek Christians in the East, so was it also with the empire. The outcome of this conviction was the magnificent conception of the divine scheme of government which found its loftiest expression in the works of Dante. In that conception God's government of the universe rests on the principle of unity, for government to be good must be government by one, and God is one. This principle of unity operates in relation to man's earthly discipline through two sovereign powers, vicegerents of God upon earth for

[1] Bryce, p. 21.

man's salvation, and supreme respectively in things spiritual and in things secular, the one catholic church under the pope, and the one catholic monarchy under the emperor.[1]

§ 12. A realisation of the force of this conviction, which was shaping itself gradually in the mind of western Christendom during the epoch of transition from antiquity to the Middle Ages, is essential to an understanding, not merely of the theory, but of the facts, of history.   The lack of an effective imperial authority in the West was felt as a derogation from the rightful order of social government.   This belief, working in close conjunction with the exigencies of the practical situation, led at length to one of the most memorable events in the history of western Christendom. On Christmas Day, 800, a German king was crowned in St. Peter's church at Rome by pope Leo III as emperor of the Holy Roman empire.   To appreciate the significance of this act, we must resume the history of the west from the point we reached when we spoke of the last Lombard invasion of Italy in the sixth century   We saw then that the peninsula was partitioned between three powers, the eastern emperor, the Lombards, and the papacy.   The temporal power of the popes had been firmly established in central Italy at the close of the sixth century by Gregory I, the Great (590–604). Trained in diplomacy and in the study of the civil law—he had been prefect of the city and papal envoy at Constantinople—he united the austerity of a monk with high gifts of statesmanship and an unbending strength of will.   Personal humility, with him as so often with the great holders of the papacy, went hand in hand with pride of office.   He reformed the western church, organising monastic discipline in accordance with the rule of St. Benedict, whose life he wrote, fixing authoritatively, in his manual on pastoral rule, the duties of the bishops, directing the conversion of the Anglo-Saxons in Britain through Augustine, enforcing the celibacy of the clergy and instituting a uniform type of worship and of the music in the church.   Gregory was a man of action rather than a thinker : we see in him an example of the Roman mind untouched by Hellenism.   He took his theology from

[1] See Dante, *de Monarchia*, iii. 16, and *Purgatorio*, cantos 32, 33.   To speak of the distinction as one between church and state is misleading; for the thought of church and state as different societies is modern, and arose first at the time of the Reformation conflict.   If any mediæval institution answers to the modern conception of the state as a self-sufficient society, it is the church, rather than the empire.   The Middle Ages regarded the human race as a single society, administered by two hierarchies of rulers, the ecclesiastical and the temporal.   The distinction is one of offices, functions and jurisdiction.

Augustine of Hippo, interpreting his teaching, e.g., on the atonement, in a narrow forensic spirit, and was frankly hostile to pagan literature and learning.[1]   But in the field of public affairs, his activity was untiring and brilliantly successful.   The papal court was now recognised as the supreme ecclesiastical tribunal for Latin Christendom.   The authority of Rome made itself felt throughout Gaul, Britain, Spain and Africa.   The pope constantly intervened at the Byzantine court.   His influence with queen Brunhilda laid the foundations of the alliance between the papacy and the orthodox Franks.   In Italy, he played the part which by right belonged to the imperial exarch; alike in policy and in war he figured as the defender of the Italian Catholics against the Arian Lombards.   Both the secular and the ecclesiastical history of the next two centuries moved on the lines thus laid down by Gregory. Henceforward the bishop of Rome was not merely the effective spiritual head of Latin Christendom, but a secular Italian potentate, who utilised the patrimony of St. Peter, i.e., the territorial possessions and the wealth of the Roman church, as the champion at once of Italian independence and of the orthodox faith.   " The independence of the popes was struck like a spark between the rival temporal powers that divided Italy." [2]   The real enemy was the Lombard, who menaced the papal provinces at once from the north and from the south.   The natural protector of Italy was the emperor, but the government at Constantinople had its hands full with the wars against the Saracens, and its policy of iconoclasm (suppression of images) accentuated the religious cleavage that had long parted the East from Rome.[3]   In 751 the exarchate in Italy fell before the Lombards.   The popes, unable to resist without support, turned for assistance to the Franks.   The Franks were orthodox, and masters of a mighty dominion north of the Alps. They had saved Christendom from the Saracens, who, after conquering Spain from the Visigoths (711–13), passed the Pyrenees

[1] See c. xi, § 3, note 2.   Gregory is of great importance in the history of the canon law.   He appropriated and defined the ecclesiastical theory of law, society and government, under the influence of the early Fathers and of the civil law of Rome.   He was the first to make fully explicit the doctrine of the divine right of the secular prince.   See Carlyle, Mediaeval Political Theory in the West, vol. i, Parts III and IV.

[2] Bury, Later Roman Empire, ii. 156.   The power of the papacy is to be explained, not primarily as due to the individual genius of the popes, who were for the most part men of ordinary ability, but to the practical sagacity of Roman Christianity.

[3] Gregory III, elected in 731, was the last pope whose appointment was referred for sanction to the emperor.   The long struggle culminated in the schism of 1055.   But it was continuous from the time of Gregory I.   On the Iconoclast schism, which broke out in 725, see below, § 19.

and overran southern Gaul, to be crushed by the Franks under Charles Martel at Poictiers in 732. All Gaul was now in Frankish hands. Charles Martel had indeed turned a deaf ear to the papal appeals for help; but his son Pepin, who had succeeded him in 740 as mayor of the palace to the *fainéant* Merovingian kings, was willing enough to listen, when, in the year after the Lombard conquest of Ravenna, the pope anointed him king of the Franks in place of Childeric, and proclaimed him patrician of Rome (751-2).[1] Four years later, Pepin crossed the Alps, overthrew the Lombards in northern Italy and conferred Ravenna and the surrounding territory on the papacy (756). The pope was now in the position of unquestioned head of the imperial legacy in Italy. In 773 Pepin's son, Charles the Great (Charlemagne) incorporated Lombardy in the Frankish kingdom.[2] In 781 pope Hadrian I formally severed the tie of allegiance to the emperor of Constantinople. It was but the natural, though unexpected, issue, when on Christmas Day, 800, Charles, who had once more entered Italy to protect pope Leo III from his rivals in the church, was crowned at Rome as the successor of Augustus. The act was technically unconstitutional; for, despite the pretence of election by the Roman senate, which did not exist, and by the Roman army and people, who were not consulted, the pope had no right to institute an emperor. Such justification as he might claim was purely practical, on the ground that for two centuries the imperial idea in Italy had been represented and preserved by the popes.[3] They,

[1] Charles Martel had reformed the Frankish church on Roman lines and had supported St. Boniface (Winfrid, born at Crediton, c. 680) in his devoted missionary labours in pagan Germany. It was Boniface who, with the full assent of pope Zacharias, crowned Pepin king of the Franks. The mayor (*major* = chief) of the palace was the chief minister; under the later Merovingians he exercised all the authority of the king. Pepin had asked the pope whether it were well that one man should have the name of king, while another had the power. The office of patrician of the Romans was equivalent to a protectorate. It was at this time, and probably to express a real compact between Pepin and the papacy, that the Donation of Constantine was forged.

[2] Charles the Great (born c. 742) reigned from 768 to 814. He also conquered the Saxons up to the Elbe (772-804), fought the Avars (788-96), and in 811 incorporated the north-east of Spain in his empire, which thus stretched from the Atlantic to the Elbe, Bohemia and the Adriatic, and from Barcelona to the North sea. He was allied with the Abbasid Caliphs of Baghdad against the Ummayyads in Spain and the Byzantine empire.

[3] The act furnished a historic basis for the papalist claim, put forward in the eleventh century, that the imperial jurisdiction was subject to that of the pope. In fact, Charles had no intention of playing a subordinate part to the papacy. Even in matters of doctrine he claimed to rule the western church. In his eyes, his empire was the City of God, and he himself the divinely appointed head of Christians upon earth. The theocratic idea is dominant; Alcuin speaks of him as ruling the kingdom of eternal peace

and not the exarchs sent from Constantinople, had really stood for Rome. That the new emperor was a Germanic chieftain, whose forefathers of the age of Augustus had barely heard the name of Rome, was no bar to his eligibility; the empire had never rested on a hereditary basis, nor was it, either in principle or in practice, restricted by any limit of nationality. Diocletian had been an Illyrian and born a slave; as early as the second century the Spanish provincial Trajan had been called to the imperial throne. The grave fact that had to be faced was the presence of an emperor at Constantinople. Charles's coronation stood in glaring contradiction to the doctrine, universally accepted, of the unity and indivisibility of the empire. This difficulty of principle was overcome by the claim that the sovereign at Constantinople at this date, Irene, was a woman and a usurper, and that the empire was therefore vacant of a ruler.[1] In fact, Charles and his successors left no stone unturned to secure from the emperors at Constantinople the recognition of their title. This was first granted in 812, though with considerable reluctance; and from this time onwards there is a justification for speaking of two empires, an eastern and a western.[2] Latin Christendom looked henceforward upon the Frankish ruler at Aachen, not upon the emperor at Constantinople, as the secular vicegerent of God on earth. The empire, thus established in the West in the person of Charles the Great, survived, through the long period of its struggle against the rival power of the papacy in the eleventh, twelfth and thirteenth centuries, through the storms of the Reformation conflict, and even of the French Revolution, till, long after it had ceased, in Voltaire's phrase, to be either Holy or Roman or an empire, it was finally extinguished by the strong hand of Napoleon in the first years of the nineteenth century.

founded by the blood of Christ. See *Camb. Med. Hist.*, vol. ii, c. xix. Charles, though not a scholar, knew both Greek and Latin, was a diligent student of Augustine, and had the *de Civitate Dei* read to him at meals. The act of coronation seems to have come to Charles as a surprise, and the annoyance he felt was probably sincere; he judged the act premature.

[1] On this section, see Bury, *Later Roman Empire*, vol. ii, c. xi. Charles was regarded as the successor, not of Romulus Augustulus, the last emperor in the West (deposed in 476), but of Constantine VI, who had been deposed by the empress Irene in 797. The former alternative would have implied that the popes, in recognising the emperors in the East, had for two centuries given allegiance to usurpers.

[2] Bury, *Later Roman Empire*, ii. 320 *note*, quotes the words " *orientale et occidentale imperium* " used first by Charles in a letter to the emperor Michael I.

IV. THE ROMAN, THE SLAV, AND THE SARACEN (§§ 13–16).

§ 13. The Roman empire endured in the East with unbroken continuity until the capture of Constantinople by the Turks in 1453. From its final partition on the death of Theodosius (395) until the last decline set in during the eleventh century, it was the foremost military and naval power in the Mediterranean, the medium of commercial intercourse between East and West, and the guardian of the speech and civilization of ancient Greece. Its capital, the " New Rome " of Constantine, was the greatest city of the world. "As in his daily prayers," wrote Gibbon, " the Mussulman of Fez or Delhi still turns his face towards the temple of Mecca, the historian's eye will always be fixed on the city of Constantinople." [1] Though its subjects belonged to many races, Hellenes and Egyptians, Syrians and Armenians, Slavs and Bulgars, parted one from the other by wide differences of speech, manners and national sympathies, and imperilling at every crisis its political and religious unity, the imperial government preserved throughout the tradition of its Roman origin. The sovereign of the empire was the Roman *Augustus*, and its peoples were called *Romaioi*.[2] Latin remained the official language until the sixth century, when it gave way to Greek. Justinian's *Corpus juris* was the last great utterance of the Latin tongue in the East.[3] To the end, the spirit of the government was entirely faithful to the model of ancient Rome; both in its conservatism, degenerating at times into a blind adherence to tradition, at times achieving a wise adjustment to the changing requirements of the hour and place, and in its concentration on the age-long mission of Rome to defend the frontiers against enemies from without, thus preserving a civilization whose contents it was powerless to enrich. Epochs of disintegration and paralysis alternated for centuries with epochs of recovery and vigour.[4] On the shores of the Bosporus, Rome was still Rome, in its impotence as in its strength; though we look in vain for creative energy of thought or action among her peoples,

---

[1] Gibbon, c. 48.

[2] See Bury, *Later Roman Empire*, vol. ii, pp. 170–4. A *Hellene* came to mean a non-Christian. The Latin word *paganus* (= villager), which had this meaning in the West, was used in the East in Greek form (*paganikos*) to mean " secular " as opposed to " sacred," e.g. of dress.

[3] The century from Justinian to Heraclius (550–650) saw the transition from a Roman to a Hellenised empire in the East.

[4] Disintegration, after Justinian (in the late sixth century), after Heraclius (in the late seventh and early eighth centuries), after Leo III, the Isaurian (from the close of the eighth century). These three emperors had successively restored the efficiency of the empire.

she toiled unceasingly at her historic labour; and a thousand years elapsed ere the last embers of the Roman spirit were quenched in the successors of Augustus.

§ 14. It was in the defence of Christianity and Hellenism against invasion that the efficiency of the empire was most conspicuous. The border forts were repaired and extended by Justinian in the sixth century, and the ensuing epoch saw the development, in face of the Saracen menace, of an army and navy, trained in the art of war to a pitch hitherto unequalled in history. By scientific mastery of the problem of defence the empire saved civilization. Its task was one of tremendous difficulty. If the eastern provinces were harder to conquer, and furnished a more populous and warlike recruiting-ground than those of the West, their assailants were more formidable. The struggle had to be carried on simultaneously on several fronts. We will consider briefly the historical significance, first, of the wars with the peoples of the north, who attacked the Danubian provinces, and, secondly, of those with the Persians and the Saracens in the east and the south.

(i) The sixth and seventh centuries were the era of expansion of the *Slavs*, who, at their close, were securely established over the huge tract of country east of the Elbe and the Adriatic, from the southern shore of the Baltic to the Peloponnese.[1] In the Danubian region their fortunes were closely associated with the *Avars*, a nomadic people from the steppe-land, akin to the Huns, in whose wake they spread like a blighting tempest over eastern Europe, and founded an imposing, though short-lived, Tartar kingdom from Hungary to the Crimea. The Avars conquered the Slavs, and transplanted them in vast numbers to guard their western borders. These Slav colonists formed a solid bulwark, not only for their Avar lords against the Teutons, but for the Teutons against the Avars.[2] It was the doom of the Slavs to be " slaves," to toil and fight at the bidding of Teutonic or Tartar conquerors. In temper passive and unwarlike, though excellent

[1] On the Slavs, see Peisker in *Camb. Med. History*, ii, c. xiv. Their home was in the marshes of Polesie, in the middle Dnieper basin, now inhabited by the White Russians. The Slavs were a branch of the Indo-European family, blue-eyed and fair. They spread, in pre-historic times, westwards to the Carpathians and the Vistula, where they marched with the Germans. The later formation of the northern Slav states was due to German overlordship, of the southern to that of the Avars. The native Slav had little capacity for political construction.

[2] " The misery of the Slavs was the salvation of the West. The energy of the Altaians " (i.e. the Tartars) " was exhausted in eastern Europe, and Germany and France behind the Slavic breakwater were able freely to develop their civilization " (Peisker, *loc. cit.*, p. 434).

in defensive fighting under good leadership, they made no conquests, and formed no states on their own initiative; but lent
themselves readily to organisation, political and military, at the
hands of alien powers. "As a people who for immemorial ages
were deprived of justice and politically broken, the Slavs longed
only for an ordered legal state. . . . The appeal to law and not to
the sword is the basis of Old Slavonic thought and aspiration." [1]
But the Slav avenged himself nobly on his oppressors.[2] Like the
Greeks, in the age of Roman domination, he gave them civilization.
Two characteristics of the Slavonic peoples were already manifest,
the inability to form a compact political union, save under foreign
impulse, and the capacity to impress their speech and customs on
the conquerors who enslaved them. They showed a genius for
peaceful penetration. Avars, Bulgars and Russians alike were
absorbed by Slavonic culture. The Avar kingdom indeed
vanished as swiftly as it arose. Weakened by the constant
struggle with the empire in the East, it received its final blow at
the hand of Charles the Great. But the Slavs remained, both
within and without the empire. During the sixth century they
swept in masses over the Balkan peninsula; then, or not long
afterwards, they penetrated as far south as the Peloponnese,
merging their civilization in the Hellenic. In the ninth century
these Hellenised Slavs became Christians; and bishops, at Lacedæmon (Sparta) and other places, were appointed for their
spiritual direction. Under Heraclius (610–41), Slavs formed the
majority of the population in the Balkan provinces; two centuries
later, a solid block of Slavonic communities stretched from the
mouth of the Elbe to the shores of the Adriatic. It looked for a
moment as though central and eastern Europe lay at their mercy.[3]
The eastward advance of Charles the Great and his successors on
the one side, and, on the other, the Magyar settlement of Hungary,
and the victories of the Eastern emperors over the Bulgars, determined the event otherwise. But the seeds of the Slavonic states,
Bohemian, Croatian, Slovene, Serb, which loom so large in the
politics of modern Europe, were already planted.[4] An analogous

[1] Peisker, *loc. cit.*, p. 457.
[2] Bury, *Later Roman Empire*, vol. ii, p. 335, compares the Slavs in this
respect with the Greeks (see, generally, vol. ii, book v, cc. vii and xi).
[3] Bury, *Eastern Roman Empire*, pp. 374, 375.
[4] " The Slav nations of to-day are therefore not original, but a gradual
crystallisation since the sixth century into linguistic units, out of the peoples
transplanted by the Avars—a process already completed by the tenth
century " (Peisker, *Camb. Med. Hist.*, ii. 437). Long after the fall of the
Avar kingdom, shepherd-lords of Avar stock formed the nobility in Slav
communities. They were gradually absorbed, as were the Bulgars, in the

process can be traced, farther east, in the early history of Bulgaria and Russia. The *Bulgars*, a non-Aryan Tartar tribe, akin to the Huns and the Finns, had their home in southern Russia. A branch, pressing southwestwards, appeared by the Danube mouth in the fifth century, and two hundred years later had established themselves to the south of the river in the province of Moesia. There they ruled over the earlier Slav settlers, and, as we have noted, absorbed their manners and their language. Through the ninth century they waged fierce wars with the eastern emperors, pressing up to the walls of Constantinople. Greek captives were the instrument of their conversion to Christianity; in 863–5 king Boris, despite popular opposition, renounced heathenism for the gospel. A century later, the Bulgarian kingdom fell before the imperial arms. Besides the Slavonic tribes, both within and without the frontiers, and the Bulgars, the imperial government was in constant contact, both commercial and diplomatic, with the dwellers in the lands north of the Euxine sea. Of these peoples, many in number, and often formidable—Christian *Goths* in the Crimea; "*Inner*" *Bulgarians* on the Sea of Azov; "*Outer*" *Bulgarians* on the Volga; the Turkish *Khazars*, a powerful tribe dwelling between the Caucasus and the Don, who perpetrated the strange anomaly of embracing Judaism some time about the ninth century; the *Magyars*, a Finnish tribe, akin to the Huns, the Avars and the Bulgars, who moved westwards at the same epoch and settled permanently in the plain of Hungary; and the *Roumanians*, probably Avars and Bulgars who had become Romanised—we must content ourselves with a bare mention. But more attention is due to the people who were destined to become the leading champions of Slavonic civilization. The Rûs or *Russians* were not Slavs by race, but Scandinavian invaders from Sweden, who founded Novgorod, the Holmgard of the Icelandic Saga, and subjugated the surrounding Slavs. They ruled as a military aristocracy, monopolising the trade, which they carried southwards down the Dneiper and the Volga. Already at the dawn of their history, the guiding-star of Russian policy was fixed, to secure commercial access to the sea. Prior to the ninth century, their relations with Constantinople were mainly commercial; by that date, the Russian kingdom had grown into a powerful state, and counted more and more in the political system of eastern Europe. Like the Bulgarians, the Scandinavian

---

Slav peasantry. The Bulgarian Slavs took over the name of their former masters.

Russians became completely Slavonised; while in the eleventh century they acquired Christianity and letters from the eastern empire. The Russian script is the old uncial (capital) script of Greece. Russian mercenaries were enlisted in the imperial guards, and the Russian sovereigns adopted the Roman style of *Cæsar* (Tsar).[1]

§ 15. (ii) The conflicts on the European frontier, prolonged until the ninth century, resulted in the implanting of Christianity and culture among peoples destined to become members of the comity of European nations. In Asia and Africa, on the other hand, the empire was faced by powers of alien religion and race, who, far from possessing either the ability or the desire to fuse with western civilization, were its bitterest and most uncompromising foes. From the third to the seventh centuries the empire had been engaged in constant warfare, broken by longer or shorter intervals of peace, with the *Persians*, whose kingdom had arisen in the Euphrates–Tigris valley on the ruins of that of Parthia, and who were finally crushed in a series of campaigns by the emperor Heraclius between 622 and 628. Hardly had Heraclius secured his triumph when a far more terrible antagonist appeared on the scene. The very next year saw the first brush between the Roman outposts and the Moslem Semites, by the shores of the Dead sea. In 632 Mahomet died at Mecca, having rescued the nomadic Arabs from religious indifference and social decline, and for the first time in history secured, on the foundation of a mono theistic faith, the political unity of Arabia.[2] We are not called

---

[1] The title of Tsar and the device of the double eagle were adopted by Ivan III, who married the Byzantine Sophia Palæologus in 1472.

[2] On Mahomet (*Muhammad*) see Bevan in *Camb. Med. Hist.*, vol. ii, c. x, and Margoliouth's *Life* in the *Heroes of the Nations* Series; on the expansion of Islam, see Becker in *Camb. Med. Hist.*, vol. ii, cc. xi, xii. *Islām* means "surrender"; *Muslim* (Moslem), from the same verb, means "one who surrenders himself," with reference, probably, to his acceptance of the faith. How an illiterate Arab, aided by a shrewd business head and a rich widow's fortune, was converted in mature life to the consciousness of a religious vocation, preached a faith that ethically was far in advance of the Arab code, became the political leader of Arabia, founded a world-religion, and inspired his followers with a fiery zeal that enabled them in the event to conquer half the Roman empire and many lands beyond it, is still an unsolved problem. Nöldeke, a great Oriental scholar, gave it up in despair. Circumstances, such as the prevalent unrest in Arabia and the presence of vague national aspirations, conditioned the process, forcing Mahomet to become a political ruler, outside his original purpose. In his teaching, again, he borrowed from Jewish and Christian sources, accepting the Old Testament and holding Christ to be a human prophet with a divine mission. But this hardly accounts for his ethical and religious doctrine. The personality of the man was the determining factor throughout. He had rare gifts of insight into human character and of skill in managing men;

upon to dwell on the character of the religion of Islam, for it has played no part in the shaping of our western civilization.[1] Its rôle throughout mediæval and modern times has been that of an alien culture, which has influenced western society only indirectly, by provoking combinations of European peoples to resist its aggression.[2] The century that followed the prophet's death was a critical epoch in the annals of civilisation. Alike in West and East, the forces of Islam came within an ace of mastering the Mediterranean world. Had they triumphed, the issue would have been, not compromise or fusion, but the extermination of the Christian order of society.[3] It is the eternal merit of the empire that it bore the brunt of the onset, and, though it emerged from the struggle maimed and exhausted, saved Christian civilization from submersion. When Mahomet died, Islam was still restricted to Arabia. Ten years later, the Saracen warriors had overrun Syria, Mesopotamia and Egypt. The Persian kingdom, weakened by Heraclius' victories, fell an easy victim to their onset. Asia Minor suffered its first invasion in 651, Constantinople its first siege from 674 to 677. The Saracens had created a navy, and fought the empire on both elements. All northern Africa had fallen to them by the end of the century, and the chequered history of Carthage (Punic, Roman, Christian and Vandal) reached its final close (698). From Africa the conquerors crossed to Spain, overthrew the Gothic kingdom, and established the rule of the emirs at Cordova.[4]   Pouring by the passes of the Pyrenees

his sincerity is beyond dispute; he was without fanaticism and without fraud. It must be remembered that what with us would be literary dishonesty passed among the Arabs as a perfectly legitimate device.

[1] On Arab learning in the Middle Ages, see below, c. xi, § 9. Philosophy was always an exotic among the Mohammedans.

[2] Thus, in later days, the Austro-Hungarian monarchy of the Hapsburgs, a strange and thoroughly artificial conjunction of peoples, came into being from the common need of union for defence against the Turks.

[3] It is an error to suppose that the Moslem used the sword primarily as an instrument for propagating their religion. It was rather a weapon of political sovereignty. The conversion of non-Arabian subjects was not fostered; they ceased to pay taxes on embracing Islam. Islam as a religion was not intolerant (as late as the seventeenth century we read of Quakeress preachers, expelled from the Puritan colony of Massachusetts, taking refuge at Constantinople under the very eye of the Grand Turk). Becker, *Camb. Med. Hist.*, loc. cit., writes : "hunger and avarice, not religion, are the impelling forces, but religion supplies the essential unity and central power." The East found in Islam the means of liberation from the yoke of western culture, dominant since the conquests of Alexander. On the other hand, the West now swung free of Oriental influence, and resumed her age-long hostility.

[4] The caliphs viewed the conquest of Spain with some mistrust; but the African Berbers had to be employed in war. The Arabs showed signal

into Gaul, they swept northwards over the fair lands of Languedoc and Aquitaine to the valley of the Loire. Here, between Poictiers and Tours, they met their match; Charles Martel, the mayor of the palace under the Merovingian kings, and his Franks, saved the West by a decisive victory (732). But in the East the struggle raged with fury for three centuries. The Saracen power was at its zenith when Leo III (the Isaurian), the contemporary of Charles Martel, opened his reign by repelling their second onslaught on Constantinople (717–18).[1] Despite the Bulgarian wars in Thrace and the internal conflicts stirred by the iconoclastic policy of the crown, Islam was kept at bay during the eighth and ninth centuries. Crete and Sicily were lost to the empire; but Greece and the Balkans, the waters of the Ægean and the greater part of Asia Minor were firmly held. The fall of the Ummayyad caliphs in 750, and their replacement at Baghdad by the Abbasids, led to a cleavage among the Saracen powers that weakened their attacks.[2] The emirs of Cordova kept Spain for the Ummayyads. But it was not till the tenth century that the Saracen power ceased to be a formidable menace to the eastern empire.

§ 16. If we pause for a moment to take stock of the Mediterranean world in the course of the ninth century, the picture that it presents is at once simple and instructive.[3] We find in existence four great powers, two in the West and two in the East. In the West were the Christian empire of the successors of Charles the Great, and the Mohammedan kingdom of the Ummayyad emirs of Cordova. The boundary line between them, in northern Spain, marks the southern limit of mediæval feudalism. In the East were the Christian empire, ruled from Constantinople, and the Abbasid caliphate of Baghdad. The force of political gravity tended to bring together in alliance the eastern empire and the Spanish Mohammedans on the one hand, the western empire and the Abbasids on the other. Beyond the confines of the two Christian powers lay two secondary and independent kingdoms, that of the Anglo-Saxons in Britain, in close contact with the western empire, and that of the Bulgarians in northern Thrace, in

---

capacity in enlisting this wild and warlike race on their side; the Romans had never wholly succeeded in taming the Berbers.

[1] This successful resistance was more decisive in world-history than the victory of Poictiers. Had Constantinople fallen, the whole future of the East would have been transformed.

[2] The triumph of the Abbasids meant that of Persian over Arab, of religion over political (Arabian) nationalism : it was one more step in the recovery of the old tradition by the East.

[3] See Bury, *Later Roman Empire*, Book VI, cc. iv, xii.

close contact with the empire of the East.   In the centre of the
Mediterranean area, southern Italy and Sicily formed, as in the
old days when Greek fought Carthaginian, the scene of constant
and uncertain conflict.   While northern and central Italy were,
in political and ecclesiastical sympathies, mainly Latin; southern
Italy and Sicily were still, as in classical antiquity, mainly Greek.
History was repeating itself; the eastern empire with its Greek
civilization was once more contending for Sicily against the
Semites.   We have seen that in the ninth century the Arabs
succeeded in accomplishing, what Carthage never quite achieved,
the conquest of the entire island (827–902).[1]   But ere long the
analogy vindicated its claim; as Rome had aforetime intervened
against Carthage, so in the eleventh century the Arab power was
flung back from Sicily by the Normans.   Meanwhile, a host of
refugees from the iconoclastic persecution had come to strengthen
Greek influence in southern Italy.   There and in Sicily the seeds
were sown of the strange blend of races—Greek, Latin, Lombard,
Saracen and Norman—which has made the dwellers in these
regions so distinctive in temperament and character among the
peoples of southern Europe at the present day.[2]

V. The Empire in the East (§§ 17–20).

§ 17. The imperial administration in the East followed the
lines laid down by Diocletian.   It was a military autocracy, nor
was the principle of despotism ever seriously challenged.   Political
liberty was an idea that had no meaning for the peoples of the
eastern provinces.   The conspiracies that constantly menaced the
Byzantine sovereigns were directed against their persons, and not
against the character of the government.   The official aristocracy
were often a serious danger to the emperor's life and throne.   In
theory he was elected by the senate, which at Constantinople
included the chief administrative officers and exercised far greater
power than its Roman counterpart, and afterwards acclaimed by
the people, in accordance with the historic maxim of the Roman
state.   At the head of the huge bureaucracy were a group of
prefects (prætorian, of the east, of the city, etc.), who were
immediately responsible to the emperor.   In the reign of Justinian

---

[1] They tried in vain to win a foothold in Italy : they took Bari in 841,
Ostia in 846, appearing for a moment, but only for a moment, before the
walls of Rome.   They were driven out of Sicily by the Normans (1061–91).

[2] It is interesting to note that southern Italy and Sicily have in these
last days given birth to a revival of metaphysics, of which the most illustrious representative is Signor Benedetto Croce.

(527–65), the empire comprised the Balkan Peninsula, Thrace, the islands, Asia Minor, Syria, Egypt, Italy and Sicily, Africa and some outlying possessions in Spain.   Justinian initiated a policy of reorganisation which resulted, in the seventh and eighth centuries, in the division of what then remained into military districts, entitled exarchates and *strategiai*.[1]   The weakness of the government lay in oppressive taxation and in the intolerable burden of bureaucracy.   Strictures on its defective economy must be modified by the reminder that the commerce and finance of the Mediterranean world was for centuries directed from Constantinople, the London of the time.   The coinage of the eastern emperors was current over all Europe throughout the Middle Ages.   The strength of the empire rested on its military efficiency, its diplomacy and its jurisprudence.   Of the first we have already spoken. In diplomacy, the art of handling the barbarians was brought to a high level of efficiency.[2]   Their mutual rivalries were utilised for the advantage of the empire, a policy of subsidies was regularised, and the missionary activities of the church were systematically

[1] Justinian (born *c* 482) was a Macedonian peasant of Latin race, whose uncle, Justin, was elevated to the purple : the nephew was virtual ruler during Justin's reign (518–27), and succeeded him for thirty-eight years.   He was a thorough autocrat, with astonishing energy for administrative work, a strong sense of his duty as guardian of law and order, known to his courtiers as " the emperor who never sleeps," though prone to irresolution, jealous and inordinately vain.   The empress Theodora, who was gifted with a strong intelligence and an imperious will, had unbounded influence ; after her death, Justinian's policy was vacillating and ineffective. He died leaving the empire to face the Eastern peril in a state of financial exhaustion.   His interest in theology was genuine ; he regarded himself as the representative, alike of the empire and of the Christian faith, and strove diligently to live up to the conception.   He knew that he was a symbol, and loved all symbols that were visible expressions of religion and of the imperial office ; e.g. his church of Santa Sophia, and the *Corpus* of Roman law.   He reconquered Africa and Italy with the aid of able generals and a mercenary army, which included Huns, Vandals, Slavs, Persians and Arabs, controlled the papacy with a firm hand, and reorganised the civil and military administration.   Devoid of genius, Justinian, like Louis XIV of France, is one of the most impressive of the second-rank rulers in history. Despite the pressing dangers from the Avars on the Danube and the Persians in the Middle East, Justinian's eyes were rather fixed upon the West, in his desire to conquer Italy and recover the sovereignty of ancient Rome in the Western Mediterranean, and in his projects for a religious concordat with the Papacy.   Theodora, with surer political insight, realised the urgency of the Eastern problem and, in the interests of national unity, favoured religious toleration for the Hellenic subjects of the empire, whose theological sympathies, then as later, were strongly anti-Roman. She fully merits the proud place assigned to her in the mosaic of the apse of S. Vitale at Ravenna, where she fronts Justinian as an equal in regal majesty.

[2] The system can be studied at its best under Justinian.   Converted native chiefs were ruled from Constantinople through the local episcopate.

organised as an instrument of political control. Native manners and customs were studied with remarkable intelligence, and the foreign policy of the imperial government was based on admirably directed bureaux of information. The reports of the Venetian ambassadors of a later age, so valuable alike to their own government at the time and as materials for the historian of to-day, were modelled on those of the agents of the eastern empire.

§ 18. The name of Justinian is ever memorable in the annals of Roman law. By his codification he shaped it into the final form, freed in Dante's phrase "from the excessive and the irrelevant," in which it passed to the nations of the modern world.[1] Gathering up the threads of its history from the point reached in an earlier chapter, we find that, from the time of Diocletian onwards, the right of creating new law was concentrated exclusively in the hands of the emperor. "Since at the present day," we read in Justinian's *Codex*, "the power of enacting laws is reserved to the emperor alone, his authority alone must be deemed fit to interpret the laws." [2] All authoritative *responsa* or opinions on points of law emanated from him, in consultation with his judicial advisers, and all additions to the law took the form of imperial "constitutions." These were styled "laws" (*leges*) in distinction from the older law and the works of earlier jurists, which were entitled *jus*. Under Constantine and his successors, the trend of the imperial constitutions was towards humanising the existing law in accordance with the principles of natural right, especially in regard to the family and to testamentary successions. In certain fields, such as the law of marriage, the voice of Christianity had made itself heard.[3] We must remember, too, that the ecclesiastical courts,

---

[1] "*d'entro le leggi trassi il troppo e il vano*," *Par.*, vi. 12. Justinian in this canto speaks as the type of the Roman empire, whose mission, not of war, but of law and peace, was crowned by his legislation.

[2] *Codex* i. 14, 12, § 3, "*si enim in praesenti leges condere soli imperatori concessum est, et leges interpretari solum dignum imperio esse oportet.*"

[3] The influence of Christianity on Roman law, however, was not so extensive as has been supposed. An example is furnished by Constantine's repeal of the Augustan *lex Papia-Poppaea* which imposed heavy penalties on celibacy. Divorce, so easy under Roman law, was naturally restricted under Christian influence. The Christian empire prohibited the exposure of infants, and gave facilities for the manumission of slaves in church, in presence of clergy. Again, "*il n'y a à Rome que des mères naturelles, il n'y a que des pères légitimes. La paternité naturelle n'existe pas.*" (Girard, *Manuel* II, 3, § 3.) Christian law altered this in both directions. Legitimatisation of children became much easier. Bloody laws against heretics already appear in the fifth-century Theodosian code. The claims of the clergy to exemption from secular jurisdiction, and to certain rights or intervention in secular matters, were recognised by the later empire, and especially by Justinian.

presided over by the bishop, exercised concurrent jurisdiction with the civil tribunals. The instrument of the *formula*, the method by which the prætors had practised what Gibbon describes as "the art of respecting the name, and eluding the efficacy, of the laws," had now vanished, and, with it, the reference to private *judices*, and the historic distinction of the hearing *in jure* and that *in judice*. On the other hand, the opinions of the jurists of the second and third centuries received imperial recognition as an authoritative body of legal tradition. The law of Citations of Valentinian III (426) had enacted that the opinions of the five great masters, Gaius, Ulpian, Paul, Papinian and Modestinus, and of the authorities cited by them, should, when unanimous, be unconditionally binding on the judge; while, in cases where they were at variance, the court should decide in accordance with the majority, the voice of Papinian to prevail when the number of opinions on either side was equal. Thus Roman jurisprudence entered upon an epoch of scholasticism. The dead hand of the past blighted the living growth of the law. Its utterance was determined by counting the silent votes of the classical authorities. All that remained to the jurists of the present was to round off and codify the inheritance of antiquity.[1] From the third century onwards appeared numerous compilations of the law, initiated by private scholars or under imperial direction, especially in the East, where a famous law school flourished at Beirut; the most celebrated of these, the code of Theodosius, formed one of the chief sources for Justinian's codification.[2] The code of Justinian, prepared by two commissions of lawyers under the direction of his minister, Tribonian, appointed by the emperor, was published at intervals between the years 529 and 534. To describe its contents here is impracticable, for it would involve a survey of the whole domain of Roman law; and the task has been accomplished, where all can read it, in the famous forty-fourth chapter of Gibbon's history. Its aim was to embody, in methodical arrangement, all

---

[1] Pollock and Maitland (*History of English Law*, vol. i) remark that before 300, Roman jurisprudence, like Roman art, had been stricken with sterility, and that Justinian was as far removed in time from the jurists whose opinions he collected, as we to-day are from Coke.

[2] Published by the Emperor Theodosius II in 438. The *Codex Gregorianus* (c. 300) and its supplement, the *Codex Hermogianus* (fourth century), were also used by Justinian's commissions. All these three were collections of imperial ordinances. Interesting attempts to correlate and contrast Roman and Semitic law were (a) the *Collatio legum Mosaicarum et Romanarum* (c. 400), and especially (b) the Syro-Roman law book, a manual of Roman law compiled in Greek in the East during the fifth or the sixth century, and much favoured in the ecclesiastical courts.

that was still relevant in the unwieldy mass that had accumulated
during a thousand years. The spirit that informed it was, as we
should expect, that of strict conservatism ; the framers aspired,
not to create, but to find, a system. " Instead of a statue cast in
a simple mould by the hand of an artist," writes Gibbon, " the
works of Justinian represent a tesselated pavement of antique
and costly, but too often of incoherent, fragments." The labours
of the commissioners produced three works : (1) the *Institutes*, an
introductory text-book for students of the law, (2) the *Digest* or
Pandects, a codification of jurist-made law (*jus*), including such
portions of the law of the republic and the early empire as were
embodied in the writings of the jurists, and (3) the *Codex*, comprising the *leges* or imperial constitutions. To these there were
added (4) the *Novels*, published at a later date, containing the
emperor's decisions on points found doubtful in the earlier code.[1]
The *Novels* and much of the *Code* were the work of Byzantine
jurists. On the other hand, the *Digest* was a collection of excerpts
from the classical period, modified to some extent by Justinian.
Care was taken to preserve the spirit of the classical text. It is to
the *Digest* that Justinian's *Corpus Juris* owes its chief value.
Justinian himself introduced many reforms, e.g., to ameliorate
the legal position of women, children and slaves. The wife's
status was virtually equalised with the husband's, the ancient
patria potestas, though preserved in principle, was practically
nullified in application, and the order of intestate succession
determined solely on the basis of blood-relationship. It is significant of the rooted conservatism of the age, in law as in all else, that
Justinian claimed finality for his code and forbade that it should
ever be modified or enlarged. We have observed that he was
himself forced to transgress his prohibition, and the succeeding
emperors continued in like manner to issue *Novels* to meet the
changing requirements of the times. Thus arose a demand for
new editions of the code, such as were issued by Leo the Isaurian
in the eighth, and by Basil the Macedonian in the tenth, century.
The *Basilika*, or royal laws of the last-named emperor, remained

---

[1] The distinction referred to in earlier chapters of this book between the
jus civile, the *jus honorarium* (of the prætors) and the *jus gentium*, no longer
bore any meaning, save as ancient history ; the whole code of Justinian, as
enacted by the emperor, was civil law. As a matter of fact, it represents
the triumph of the *jus gentium* all along the line. The *Digest* compressed
the substance of over 1,600 rolls, with more than three million lines, into
150,000 lines. More than 95 per cent. of the material dated from the golden
age of jurisprudence between Trajan and Alexander Severus. The term
Codex implies book-form as distinct from the earlier rolls.

the statutory authority for the empire until its fall in 1453, and
were adopted anew as the law of modern Greece, when it regained
its independence in 1822.   Of the influence of Justinian's code in
the West, we shall say something in the ensuing chapter.   When
the study of Roman law was revived by the teachers of Bologna
in the thirteenth century, they took Justinian as their basis.   His
boast of finality was therefore not wholly without justification.[1]
To this day, Roman law means primarily the contents of his code.
We have remarked that it was the last word uttered at Constantinople in the Latin tongue.   Henceforward the empire in the
East spoke Greek.   Yet, though Justinian thus closed the long
story of the constructive achievement of Rome, it was surely not
in order to inaugurate an epoch of new life for Greece.   For the
Christian autocrat crushed also the dying embers of free Hellenic
thought.   In the very year (529) of the publication of the first
edition of the *Codex*, he bade the doors be bolted on the schools of
Athens, and the last pagan followers of Plato fled beyond the
Euphrates, to seek a refuge—so strange are Time's revenges—at
the court of the successors of Darius.

§ 19.   The establishment of a separate imperial government at
Constantinople reflected inevitably on the fortunes of the Christian
church.   In the fourth century, Alexandria had been the centre
of ecclesiastical life in the East, and on great issues of theology
and church statesmanship the Alexandrian bishops had worked in
close accord with Rome.   In the fifth century, the patriarch of
Constantinople, the natural adviser of the emperor on matters of
religion, became the chief ecclesiastical authority in the East.
Whereas at Rome the transfer of the government to Ravenna,
and the rapid downfall of the empire, strengthened the independence of the papacy and its authority over Latin Christendom, the
tendency in the East lay in the reverse direction.   The sovereigns
were all-powerful despots, and the patriarch of Constantinople
sank into a subordinate instrument of their policy.   The church,
in fact, if not in theory, became a department of the state, and the
patriarch a state minister of religion.   After the council of
Chalcedon (451), constitutionalism yielded place to autocracy—
the judgement of councils to imperial edicts.   This growth of what
has been aptly termed " Cæsaropapism " reached its climax under
Justinian.   The machine had triumphed over the organism ; and

[1] Yet the mediæval lawyers added to the *Corpus Juris Civilis* of
Justinian ; e.g. the *Liber de Feudis* was inserted in all complete copies, thus
facilitating the application of Roman law to feudal conditions.   See Figgis,
From Gerson to Grotius, pp. 10, 130.

the eastern church entered upon a period of comparative stagnation. The baneful effects were visible, both in the field of dogmatic theology, and in that of religious practice. From the fifth century, theological debate, though raging with ever fiercer intensity, tended to degenerate into a barren strife of words. The decision of issues vital to the faith was infected by personal animosities and political opportunism. Such was the case with the Monophysite controversy which, in various forms, dominated the ecclesiastical arena from the fifth to the seventh century. After the doctrine of the Trinity had been defined, the mind of the church turned naturally to that of the Incarnation. That " the Word was made flesh and dwelt among us " had been from the first a cardinal belief of the Christian faith ; but how was the union of the divine and human natures in Christ to be conceived ? On the one side lay the danger of so confounding his humanity in his Godhead as to negate its distinctive reality, and thus to destroy the whole significance of the Incarnation ; on the other, that of stressing the difference of the two natures to the point of affirming a double personality.[1] The Monophysites, who championed a single nature, leaned towards the former, the followers of Nestorius, asserting a difference of two *hypostases*, towards the latter of these two extreme positions. The issue at stake was a grave one ; but in effect, when once the implications of the problem had been explicitly realised, it was swamped in a morass of verbal disputation.[2] This was already manifest at the council of Chalcedon, which condemned Nestorius as a heretic, while affirming his tenets, only in a different form of words. The judgement of Isidore of Pelusium, a saint of the church, that men were claiming to dispute on a matter which was divine and transcended reason, in a frenzy of personal ambition, is amply confirmed by the scandalous scenes enacted at the two councils of Ephesus in 431 and 449.[3] The issue

[1] The Monophysite controversy was an aftermath of the Arian. Arius had held that Christ united a divine soul with a human body, i.e., that his humanity was not complete humanity. The issue raised might be stated thus : Did the divine Christ really suffer on the cross, or, in the phrase round which the controversy actually raged, was the Virgin Mary the " mother of *God* " (*theotokos*) ?

[2] For the justification of this statement, the reader may be referred to an authority who is not disposed to undervalue the discussion of problems essential to the Christian faith, viz. to Duchesne, especially vol. iii, c. 10, pp. 317 ff. : " *au fond*," he says, " *tout le monde était d'accord* " : and again " *au V*ᵉ *siècle, des gens qui pensaient de même tout en parlant les uns d'une nature, les autres de deux, ne parvinrent pas à s'endurer et s'entre-malmenèrent.*"

[3] The protagonist of the conflict in the fifth century was Cyril, archbishop of Alexandria. The student must be on his guard lest the character

was decided by the sane insight of pope Leo I, the Great, supported by the empress Pulcheria, at the aforementioned council of Chalcedon; but the fires of controversy continued to ravage eastern Christendom long after the mind of the church had been authoritatively declared. The Monophysite contention degenerated in the seventh century into the Monothelete, which restated the problem of the single or dual nature as that of one or two energies or wills.[1] The chief interest had come to lie in anathematising your enemy, or rather the enemy of the ruling power at Constantinople. Rome had spoken by the mouth of pope and emperor, and it only remained to exterminate the irreconcileables. The Nestorians, excluded from the empire, went their way, and spread the doctrine of the two natures from Persia, over China and the Indies, where their adherents still survive on the coast of Malabar; the Monophysites, backed by strong sentiments of nationality, held their ground in Syria and Egypt, and, despite Saracen and Turk, the Armenian, Syrian, Coptic and Abyssinian Christians uphold to this day the belief in a single nature. It is not surprising to find that the seventh century was also an age of spiritual decadence, marked by the baser forms of credulity and superstition. The reform instituted in the eighth century, came, as in secular administration, from above. The emperor Leo III, who had saved Constantinople from the Saracens, inaugurated the religious policy of his dynasty by a vigorous attack on the use of images (*icons*), on the worship of the Virgin, on the intercession of saints, and on the monastic communities which formed the stronghold of these practices. Iconoclasm, as the policy was named, was an aftermath of Monophysitism, prompted in Leo and his successors rather by a cool rationalism than by Puritan zeal; the images and sacred pictures which they removed from the

---

and actions of this prelate create a prejudice against the cause of which he was the ablest and the most unscrupulous champion. The quotation from Isidore is given by Gibbon, c. 47, *note* 32.

[1] Monophysitism means the doctrine of a "single *nature*"; Monotheletism that of a "single *will*." The former was advocated by Apollinaris, bishop of Laodicea, late in the third century; Nestorius, patriarch of Constantinople in the early fourth century, insisted on the reality of both natures. His views, though put forward in an indiscreet manner, were not substantially different from those afterwards pronounced as orthodox. There was really no serious reason for the condemnation of Nestorius. The orthodox solution is clearly formulated in the later creed which received the name of Athanasian, especially in the words; "Who, although he be God and Man : yet he is not two, but one Christ; One, not by conversion of the Godhead into flesh : but by taking of the Manhood into God; One altogether; not by confusion of Substance : but by unity of Person. For as the reasonable soul and flesh is one man : so God and Man is one Christ."

churches were replaced by landscapes and other works of secular art. The iconoclastic controversy also gave occasion for the display of the deep-rooted divergence of national temperament and aspiration within the empire. As earlier, in the Monophysite controversy, the anti-Hellenic feeling of the Syrian and Egyptian Christians rendered hopeless any reasonable compromise; so now the nerve of the iconoclast movement lay in the religious predilections of the population of central and southern Asia Minor. These abhorred, while the Greeks favoured, the presence of images in Christian worship. Leo III (the Isaurian) was a native of Commagene, and his advent to the throne meant the enforcement of Asiatic Christianity. In the event, on the fall of the Isaurian dynasty, the Greeks emerged victorious from the conflict. Finally, racial differences lay at the root of the schism between the eastern and western churches. The superior dignity of the Roman see was indeed never challenged in the East, but unofficial prestige is a very different thing from avowed authority. The intervention of pope Leo at the council of Chalcedon was swiftly followed by a breach in the relations between Rome and the eastern churches; though six centuries were yet to run before the breach became definite and final. It was natural enough that the patriarch of Constantinople should wish to be master in the East; and his aspirations were fostered by the emperors. We have seen above, that after the empire was restored in the West, in the person of Charles the Frank, the two churches owed allegiance to rival powers. But the real cause of schism was the incompatibility of mind and temper that parted the Roman from the Greek. Their national self-consciousness persisted to modify the religious life of Christendom long after the fabric of ancient civilization had passed away.

§ 20. We are wont to speak of *Byzantine* art and *Byzantine* literature; the term, though a misnomer when applied to the empire, which was Roman, is less inappropriate to the culture that centred in the old Greek colony of Byzantium. That culture preserved to the end its unbroken continuity with Hellenism, though the Hellenism was coloured by the spirit of Christianity. The East offers little analogy to the passing away of the old order, and the slow birth of a new, among the Teutonic peoples of the West. It knew no Middle Ages; or, if we use the words, it must be in a very different sense from that connoted by them in the West. Of Byzantine culture we may say that the art is of higher value than the literature or the thought; and that, even in art, the

period of creative vitality closes with the seventh century. The
masterpieces of Byzantine architecture, the Christian basilicas
such as still adorn Ravenna, Thessalonica (Salonica) and Constantinople, with their paintings and mosaics, date from the epoch
before, and contemporary with, Justinian. His church of Santa
Sophia (the holy wisdom), designed by Anthemius of Tralles and
Isidorus of Miletus, was the noblest basilica in Christendom.
Byzantine art was destined, in the fullness of time, to bear fruit in
Italy, and to inspire Cimabue and his successors to inaugurate a
new era in European painting. St. Mark's at Venice, the city
which preserved for so long a nominal fealty and a real commercial link with the eastern empire, though a building of more
recent date, is a genuine offshoot of Byzantine architecture.
Even after the seventh century, the art of the East had moments of
revival, when much fine work was produced; but the prevalent
note is that of conservatism rather than originality. In literature
this conservatism was even more pronounced. Of poetry there is
little that claims attention, and that little took the form of
Christian hymns.[1] Theology and history were the favourite
fields of authorship; but, after the sixth century, the works
produced were of inferior quality.[2] The philosophical tradition of
Greece was maintained by John of Damascus in the eighth, and by
Michael Psellus, who revived the study of Plato and Aristotle, in
the eleventh century; if those can be said to have been faithful to
the tradition, who, with all their learning and acuteness of intellect,
added no new thought to the inheritance of the past. The spirit
of Hellenism had vanished, but the letter remained; and the letter
was studied with genuine ardour by generation after generation of
Byzantine scholars. A classical education was sought after, not
only by clerics, as in the West, but by the laity. That archaism
was the dominant note from the fifth century to the fifteenth, is
evident from the sole use of classical Greek as an instrument of
literary expression. The spoken idiom was banned as unworthy
of the written word; and each successive revival of literature took

[1] Especially the hymns of Romanos in the seventh century. See on the
whole subject of Byzantine literature the article *Greek Literature* (*Byzantine*), by Krumbacher in the *Encycl. Britannica*.
[2] In the fourth century, Eusebius, bishop of Cæsarea, wrote his
ecclesiastical history, and theological literature was enriched by the Cappadocian Fathers (Basil and the two Gregories). Fourth-century literature
had its home, not in the Hellenic provinces, but in the Asiatic. In literature, religion and military defence, Asia is the important portion of the
empire. Sacred poetry centred in Syria and Palestine. Byzantine art
shows traces of Oriental influence. Procopius' history of the age of
Justinian was not unworthy of its subject.

the form of an artificial return to the masterpieces of antiquity.
No poet of genius appeared to wake the popular speech into life,
as Dante woke into life the vulgar tongue of Italy.   How could a
Dante have been born into the arid atmosphere of Byzantine
culture !   A language is the reflection of a people's free thought
and feeling; where these are stirring, the word must needs come,
and the man.   The mind and heart of the Byzantine world were
impotent to generate a fresh and living stream of utterance.   Yet,
within the limits of their capacity, the Byzantines laboured for
civilization; preserving the treasure of the past for others, who,
in the fullness of time, would understand its message.   They
implanted the rudiments of learning in non-Hellenic peoples—
Syrians, Armenians, Copts, Slavs, Bulgars and Russians.   They
sent forth teachers to distant lands, such as Theodore of Tarsus in
the seventh century, who passed from the lecture-halls of Athens
to Britain, where, as archbishop of Canterbury, he organised the
English church, and founded schools, whence Greek learning and
culture spread over western Europe.   King Ina of Wessex sent to
Athens for scholars, who might teach St. Aldhelm Greek.   " There
live even to-day," wrote Bede in the following century, " pupils of
these men, who knew Latin and Greek as their native tongue." [1]
Seven hundred years later, we find the Byzantine teacher still
busy at his task, and, in the very hour of the empire's ruin,
handing on the torch of Hellenism to the peoples of the western
world.[2]

VI. Conclusion (§§ 21–23).

§ 21.   There has been no attempt in this chapter to trace in
detail the fortunes of the Byzantine empire during the long period
that elapsed between the foundation of " New Rome " by Constantine and its final collapse in the fifteenth century.   The story
is a chequered one, of repeated oscillation from triumph to
disaster and from disaster to triumph ; epochs of astonishing
vitality alternating, as though by a periodic law, with lapses into
atrophy and disintegration.   Apart from the constant pressure of
powerful enemies both in East and West, disruptive tendencies

[1] Bury, *Later Roman Empire*, ii. 392.   The church of St. Nicholas at
Constantinople was built by a Saxon, who fled thither for refuge from the
Norman conquerers of Britain.

[2] Gibbon, c. 66, " In their lowest depths of servitude and depression,
the subjects of the Byzantine throne were still possessed of a golden key
that could unlock the treasures of antiquity, of a musical and prolific
language that gives a soul to the objects of sense, and a body to the
abstractions of philosophy."

were actively at work beneath the surface, sapping the foundations of the imposing structure of imperial autocracy; tendencies to mutiny in the army; to strife between circus-factions in the capital; to religious dissensions that stirred popular passion to the verge of revolution; to separatist movements, ecclesiastical and political, in Syria and Egypt; to rebellion among turbulent feudal chieftains; and, above all, save under the Macedonian princes of the eleventh century, to economic disorders, due to oppressive taxation and exhaustion of the resources of the exchequer. Yet what is most impressive is the amazing recuperative power of the empire. Again and again, in the hour of its deepest degradation, there appears, as if by magic, a saviour, gifted with rare qualities for war and statesmanship, by whose genius it is restored to all, or almost all, its historic splendour. A brief chronological summary reveals a succession of five of these periodic oscillations.

(i) When, after Justinian's death (565), the Avars and the Persians were closing in on both fronts upon the empire he had established, there arose within half a century a great soldier, Heraclius (610–41) who won decisive victories over both these enemies.

(ii) When Heraclius failed to stem the rapid onset of Islam, and this new peril had brought the fortunes of the empire to their lowest ebb, the ablest of his successors, Constantine IV (668–85) stemmed the tide of invasion by his five-years' defence of the capital and, thanks to the newly invented " Greek fire," by a decisive victory over the Mohammedan fleet.

(iii) The fall of Heraclius' dynasty was followed by twenty years of anarchy (695–717), during which six emperors in succession seized the throne by violence. The saviour presented himself in Leo the Isaurian (717–40), who—and after him his son Constantine V (740–75)—broke the eastern onset of Islam both by sea and by land, and by their victories over the Bulgarians restored the imperial suzerainty over the Balkan peninsula.

(iv) Of the Iconoclastic policy of the Isaurian emperors we have already spoken. Once again, an epoch of brilliant success was followed by decadence and confusion; once again, the empire found salvation in the advent of the " Macedonian " dynasty, founded by an Armenian usurper, Basil I. Under Basil (867–86) and his successors—all of them usurpers and all rulers of exceptional capacity alike in peace and war—it enjoyed for 150 years an unexampled prosperity (867–1025). The emperors of the Macedonian line were stern military captains, disdainful of luxury and

the "solemn plausibilities" of the court, who restored the
Euphrates frontier against the Mohammedans and extended
Byzantine sovereignty in the West over Southern Italy. They
liberally encouraged art and Hellenic culture in the capital, and by
developing industry and maintaining a monopoly of Mediterranean commerce, made the empire the wealthiest as well as the
most powerful state of the age.   In the North, Russia (i.e. the
Kingdom of Kiev) was converted to Christianity and received the
first and lasting impress of Hellenic civilization.

(v) On the death of Basil II (976–1025), perhaps the ablest
prince of the Macedonian line, the glory once more departed from
Constantinople, never to return in full splendour.   The inevitable
decline was indeed checked by the dynasty founded in 1081 by an
able and powerful feudal noble, Alexius Comnenus.   The recovery
was partial and ephemeral; it was the last heroic effort of an
exhausted empire.   The peril lay, as always, in the East, in the
onset of a new enemy, the Turks.   Resistance might have been
effectively prolonged, but for the persistent tendency of the
emperors, which we have already noted in Justinian, to divert their
energy and resources westwards.   The memory of the world-
dominion of Old Rome dazzled their vision; they nursed vain
dreams of Italian conquest, of reunion with the Papacy, and, later,
under the Comneni and afterwards, of salvation by aid of Venice
and the Crusader.

§ 22. Thus the eastern empire preserved its integrity, in the
Balkan peninsula and in Asia Minor, until the eleventh century.
From that date, it entered upon a long drawn-out and irrecoverable
decline.   It fell stricken by mortal blows, alike from the East and
from the West.   In Asia, the Seljuk Turks wrested away the provinces that had furnished the backbone of the army, and formed
a kingdom, whose name, *Rûm*, echoed the memory of its former
masters.   In Europe, the eastward movement of peoples, which
began with the Norman migrations, received a twofold impetus,
from the religious zeal of the Crusaders and the commercial
ambitions of Venice and other western states.   Sicily had been
long lost to the Saracens; in the eleventh century the Normans
occupied southern Italy; and now, in 1204, the Franks and the
Venetians attacked and took Constantinople.   Their rule was
transitory; but the empire never rallied from the shock.   Its
death-agony was prolonged, not by any inherent vitality, but by
the force of circumstance.   The devastating onset of Timur
stayed the hand of the Seljuks, already outstretched to grasp the

prize. By the fourteenth century, the empire of Justinian had dwindled into a petty Greek state, clinging round the walls of the capital. The final stab came from the Ottoman Turks. In 1453 Mahomet II stormed Constantinople, the last of Constantine's successors, Constantine Palæologus, being slain while defending the last breach with a courage that showed him not unworthy of the name he bore, and the Roman empire in the East vanished from the scene of history.

§ 23. There is a sombre justice in the fate that overtook the empire, to fall enslaved beneath the blighting tyranny of the Turk. The leaden weights of autocracy and of conservatism had crushed the life out of Christian Hellenism. In things of the spirit, it had staked its all upon the past, and the past proved powerless to save it. Yet the doom, though merited, was not final. The darkness that fell upon the Hellenic world persisted for nearly four hundred years. The Ottoman empire became one of the great military powers, whose fleets were the terror of the Mediterranean, and whose armies swept the plain of Hungary and thundered at the gates of Vienna. The veil has hardly lifted at the present day. The nineteenth century has witnessed the long-deferred liberation of the Hellenic and Slavonic peoples, who, through ages of bondage, held faithfully to the religion and the culture which they had inherited from the Roman empire. It lies beyond our purpose to forecast the fruits that may spring in the future, from the seed thus sown in the forerunners of the Greeks, the Serbs, the Bulgars, the Roumanians and the Russians of to-day. Our uncertain vision serves but to show how impracticable is the attempt to circumscribe the influence wielded by the Roman empire upon after-time. We have spoken of the structure of the empire, and of the value of its work within the bounds of its duration. It grappled effectively for centuries with the herculean labour of defending the frontiers of civilization against barbarism. We have learnt also to appreciate, with a juster criticism than was current fifty years ago, both the merits and the limitations of its culture. Up to and indeed for long after the age of Justinian, that culture was not unworthy of its great traditions. Thenceforward it displayed at best a negative force of self-preservation. Yet there is something pathetic, and even magnificent, in the tenacity with which the Byzantines of the later empire guarded loyally, through a vigil of a thousand years, the legacy of their Hellenic forefathers.

CHAPTER XI

THE LEGACY IN THE MIDDLE AGES

I. INTRODUCTORY (§§ 1–4).

§ 1. THUS far our discussion has proceeded within the bounds of what is commonly known as ancient history. Those bounds cannot be fixed with rigorous precision, and we have been led more than once in the last two chapters to carry forward our survey into the epoch of transition that parts antiquity from the Middle Ages. It now remains to confirm and illustrate our judgement on the significance of ancient civilization by a reference to its reception into mediæval life and thought. We shall choose our examples from the legacy of Greece and Rome. We have touched already on the manner in which the spiritual inheritance of Israel was absorbed by the church of the first centuries.[1] To trace out its subsequent effects within the Christian pale would involve a review of the entire history not only of mediæval Christianity, but of the sixteenth-century Reformation. Even the story of the Græco-Roman tradition covers too wide a field. We must leave unnoticed much that is of importance, and content ourselves with showing how Greek philosophy and Roman law contributed to mould the mediæval view of life. In conclusion, we shall speak briefly of the changes wrought by the final revival of classical learning in the age of the Renaissance.

§ 2. While scholars are in substantial agreement as to the essential features of ancient and modern civilization, those of the Middle Ages are harder to define. The name merely serves to indicate the chronological relation to what goes before and after, and throws no light on its positive character. Yet the period saw the birth of a new type of culture, none the less distinctive, because it is hard to characterise, and has often been misunderstood.[2] The Middle Ages were a scene of turmoil and

[1] See above, c. iii, § 11; c. ix. § 2.
[2] We refer here to the views on the Middle Ages which prevailed in Europe from the sixteenth to the nineteenth century, not from any desire to flog a dead horse, but because one-sided prejudice, bred of an inevitable reaction against the mediæval view of life, still obscures the thought of many outside the ranks of historical students. Gibbon did more than anyone to fix this prejudice in the mind of the public, Carlyle more than anyone to correct it.

conflict, the soil in which ideas and institutions germinated into maturity, silently shaping men's thoughts and wills, long before their implications and consequences were consciously apprehended.   Its peculiar interest lies in the spectacle of a civilization struggling to its birth amidst a welter of barbarism ; of the gradual conquest of brute force by right, anarchy by law, instinct and passion by reflective intelligence and reasoned purpose ; above all, of an ardour of aspiration which, in face of facts that seemed at every point to give the lie to the ideal, kept its gaze firmly fixed on the spiritual goal of human life.   There is, indeed, much in the Middle Ages that recalls, as we read its story, Hobbes' picture of the state of nature before the institution of civil society by the social contract.   " In such condition there is no place for industry, because the fruit thereof is uncertain, and consequently no culture of the earth ; no navigation, nor use of the commodities that may be imported by sea ; no commodious building ; no instruments of moving and removing such things as require much force ; no knowledge of the face of the earth ; no account of time ; no arts ; no letters ; no society ; and, which is worst of all, continual fear and danger of violent death ; and the life of man, solitary, poor, nasty, brutish and short." [1]   The seventh century might well have seemed such to the eyes of the seventeenth.   The modern reader is often tempted to echo the sweeping verdict of rationalism, and to see in the Middle Ages only ignorance and credulity, crime and witchcraft, tyranny ecclesiastical and secular, anarchy, war, rapine and persecution.   These things are there, but there is much else.   The barbarism of the early Middle Ages was in reality but the raw material from which were moulded, by strength of human mind and will, new forms of civilization, eminent alike for originality and grandeur. The Middle Ages stand for an order of society and for an order of thought.   As an order of society, it means a specific group of processes in the history of western Europe ; processes creative of political and ecclesiastical institutions, law, language, social custom and personal character, which are ceaselessly changing, and reveal at any given moment a rich diversity of features, yet are continuous, alike with the culture of the Roman empire, and with that of the modern world.   We think of the feudal system, the papacy and the Holy Roman empire, monasticism, the Crusades, the structure of the village, the growth of the borough, the trade-gild, the Romance languages, Norman castles,

[1] *Leviathan*, Part I, c. 13.

O

Gothic cathedrals, the rise of the university and the emergence
of the nation-state. But the Middle Ages mean also—and it is
with this aspect that we are particularly concerned—a specific
group of processes in the history of the human mind; processes
of reasoned thought as to the meaning and conduct of life, the
right government of society, and the relations of man and the
world to God. These processes, too, were, as living acts of man's
spirit, in constant change, varied in content, and continuous
both with the thought of antiquity and with that of modern
times. We think here of the *Divina Commedia* of Dante and the
Summae of Aquinas, of the speculations of philosophers and
jurists on the law of nature and on the ideal relations of church
and empire, of the *Fioretti* of Saint Francis, and of the visions
of Christian mystics. In point of time, as was natural, the
mediæval order of society achieved stability earlier than did the
order of reflective thought. But both stand from the first—we
are often tempted to forget it—in organic connexion with each
other. Mediæval philosophy was, in no small measure, an
induction from the facts of experience. Nor must the inconsistency between the theory and the practice of the Middle
Ages blind us to the real potency of its ideal aspirations over the
conduct of mankind. Dante's poem alone suffices as a reminder,
how every detail, alike of his personal experience and of the
story of political faction in the republics of Italy, was illumined
by his vision of the divine scheme for the government of the world.

§ 3. The mediæval view of life, like the order of society from
which it sprang, was the product of three factors, which came
into fusion in western Europe in the centuries following the break-
up of the Roman empire. There was the stream of Germanic
and Scandinavian immigrants, who founded lordships and kingdoms in Britain, Gaul, Spain and Italy, between the fifth and the
eleventh centuries. Though these people brought with them
no inheritance of learning or reflective thought, they had evolved
a type of custom and belief, an unconscious " way of life," which
left an enduring impress on the ideas of the Middle Ages. The
convictions that monarchy was the rightful form of human
government, and that law or right (*recht*) was not derived from,
but superior to, the state, whose function was to realise and
maintain law, were deeply rooted in the Germanic and Scandinavian mind; and found expression, at a later day, among the
cardinal principles of political and legal theory. Above all,
these races leavened mediæval thought with their strong sense

of the worth of individual liberty. In this point their view of life harmonised with the teaching of Christianity, which had insisted on personal responsibility, and on the infinite value of the individual in the sight of God. But it conflicted with the tendency of Hellenic thought to deny independence to the individual, and to regard him as a fragment of the universe, as a part, rather than as a whole. The mediæval mind strove earnestly to reconcile the two positions, by defining the status of the individual, as at once a self-contained whole, and a part of the larger orders of the human species and of the world. It never entirely succeeded in effecting the desired harmony; and, in the event, the individualism, which had always coloured its outlook, triumphed decisively over the Græco-Roman tradition. The second formative factor was the Christian church, with its ideal of other-worldliness, and its equipment of theology, law and ecclesiastical institutions. We have seen how, prior to the dissolution of the empire in the West, the church had absorbed much of the ancient tradition, and had developed with its aid an ordered system of thought and discipline. Hence it was enabled to act as the chief instrument in mediating between Rome and her barbarian conquerors, and in transmitting to them Græco-Roman civilization, though in a form radically modified by Christian faith and practice. This deposit of Græco-Roman culture was the third agency which co-operated in the fashioning of the mediæval mind. The first Teutonic invaders came into immediate contact with the language, law and government of Rome, and passed on what they were able to assimilate to the generations that came after them.[1] The western church also, in its ecclesiastical system, in the canon law, and in its use of the Latin tongue as the medium of literature and public worship, maintained unbroken the continuity of the Roman tradition. Not all the avowed hostility of pope Gregory the Great towards ancient culture could hinder the church from disseminating fragments of pagan learning.[2] Nor must we forget that the culture

[1] It is easy to explain why the Middle Ages regarded the legacy of Rome with even greater reverence than that of Greece. Greek culture was transmitted through Rome, and the Greek and Roman contributions were not clearly distinguished. Above all, Rome was closely associated with Christianity as being divinely ordained for a religious mission.

[2] When Gregory learnt that a certain bishop taught grammar and read the Latin poets, he admonished him in the following words (quoted by Poole, *Illustrations*, p. 8): "A report has reached us which we cannot mention without a blush, that thou expoundest grammar to certain friends; whereat we are so offended and filled with scorn that our former opinion of thee is turned to mourning and sorrow. The same mouth singeth

of antiquity was kept alive in the empire of the East, and that there was constant intercourse between the West and Constantinople throughout the Middle Ages. It will be clear from this review of the channels of communication, that the thought and culture of antiquity reached the mediæval world neither in its purity, nor as a whole. Only fragments were preserved, and the residue had to be harvested by a long and arduous labour of rediscovery. Nor were the surviving fragments the choicest fruits of the classical genius. They were the relics cast up from its wrecks. Porphyry, not Plato, Boethius, not Aristotle, unnamed codifiers of the later empire, not Ulpian or Papinian, nourished the infant mind of the West during the eighth and the succeeding century.[1] Perhaps even this was as it should be. Had the students in the Frankish schools of the ninth century been confronted with the entire *Corpus* of Aristotle or of Justinian, they would have been paralysed, not stimulated, by the wealth of thought that lay before them. A time would surely come when they would be ripe to enter upon the full heritage of Greece and Rome. In the meantime, we must do justice to the impulse furnished by the mangled and meagre relics of that heritage, as also to the stern disciplinary authorities that piloted the first thinkers of the Middle Ages on their search for reasoned truth.[2]

§ 4. A word must be added as to the chronological limits of the Middle Ages. To a comprehensive survey, it spreads over a thousand years, from the fifth century to the sixteenth; while,

---

not the praises of Jove and the praises of Christ." Tertullian and St. Jerome had expressed similar sentiments. " Grammar " was practically equivalent to " pagan literature."

[1] See, further, below, § 8. The Irish monks of the seventh and eighth centuries form a notable exception by their knowledge of Greek. An Irishman of the seventh century edited the Psalms from the Hebrew text. The Irish were great missionaries; a seventh-century writer observes that to them travel was a second nature. St. Columban (born in 543) converted Burgundy and founded there, and at Bobbio in northern Italy, monasteries which became famous seats of learning. His companion, St. Gallus, founded the monastery of St. Gallen on the lake of Constance. The libraries both at Bobbio and at St. Gallen were enriched with MSS. of the chief Latin classical authors. Later, Irish teachers were welcomed at the court of Charles the Great; on John the Scot, in the ninth century, see § 8. Learning in Ireland received a deathblow with the coming of the Northmen at the end of the eighth century.

[2] It must be remembered that the names of famous authors were assigned freely in mediæval times to work which later criticism would not assign to them. Roger Bacon's chief authority throughout his life was the *Secretum Secretorum*, supposed to represent Aristotle's teaching to his most intimate disciples. See the edition of the *Secretum* with Bacon's own notes, brought out by R. Steele. Aristotle, according to this book, was half a saint, and quoted the Vulgate.

if we confine its range to the epoch when the mediæval order was dominant and stable, the term is particularly appropriate to the period from 1100 to 1400.[1] In any case, it is a grave error to restrict the rediscovery of ancient learning to the fifteenth and sixteenth-century Renaissance, when mediæval society and thought were crumbling into decay. To apply the name, the " dark ages " to the five preceding centuries was possible only for men blinded to their true character by prejudices, inherited from those who knew the Middle Ages in the hour of their decline. The ninth and the twelfth and thirteenth centuries witnessed a genuine revival of classical knowledge, anticipating in vitality and fruitfulness the Renaissance of a later day. The daring speculations of John the Scot, the learning of John of Salisbury, the critical energy of Abelard, the genius of Aquinas for systematic construction, were worthy of the most notable epochs in the history of civilization.[2] The age which these men adorned saw also the institution of the universities of Paris, Oxford and Bologna, the building of noble churches and their enrichment with sculptures and glass of unequalled beauty, and, as we shall see presently, the moulding of the law of western Europe on the principles of the code of Justinian. To sum up, we may say that, from the time of the barbarian invasions and the dissolution of the Roman empire in the West in the fifth century, Europe entered upon a transitional period of anarchy and confusion, amidst which the mediæval order wakened slowly into life; that, somewhere about the year 1100, this order emerged into view, endowed with definitely recognisable organs and relatively stable functions; and that, after flourishing for more than three centuries, it yielded place, again by slow gradations, to new forces, political, religious and intellectual, the appearance of which marks the dawn of modern history. The close of the eleventh and the early years of the twelfth century are critical moments in the Middle Ages; and the thirteenth century, for reasons which we shall make clear in the sequel, forms the high-water mark of their development.

[1] If we seek to date the Middle Ages from the time when their dominant beliefs had their origin, we must go back beyond the first century, and include the whole view of Christianity and Neo-Platonism within the scope of mediæval history. So M. Picavet (*Esquisse*, c. 2) makes the Middle Ages extend from Philo of Alexandria to Galileo and Descartes. This merely shows the impracticability of fixing a hard and fast limit of time to historical periods.

[2] John the Scot, c. 810 to c. 875; John of Salisbury, 1110–80; Abelard, d. 1142; Aquinas, 1227–74.

II. THE RECEPTION OF GREEK PHILOSOPHY (§§ 5–14).

§ 5. " It cannot be expected of anyone," wrote Hegel, " to know at first hand the philosophy of the Middle Ages, for it is as comprehensive and voluminous as it is barren and ill-expressed." [1] The sting of this verdict, and its falsity, lies in the charge of barrenness; we can only conclude that Hegel had absolved himself as well as his readers from the labour of studying mediæval philosophy at first hand. The days are past when a serious historian can treat the thought of the Middle Ages *de haut en bas*. Yet it is not so long ago that teachers were wont to pilot their classes through Greek philosophy as far as Aristotle, and then, after a cursory reference to the Stoics and Epicureans, stride with seven-league boots over some two thousand years of the life of the human spirit, to plunge with Descartes into the problems of modern metaphysics. The Neo-Platonists and the mediæval doctors alike were dismissed with a few contemptuous generalities about mysticism, credulity and superstition. The student left the university, itself a creation of the mediæval genius,[2] hardly aware of the bare names of Plotinus or Aquinas. Abelard was known only as the hero of Pope's version of the letters of Eloisa. The schoolmen were branded as sciolists who travestied Aristotle's logic and wrangled in futile syllogisms over the problem of universals.[3] Even in Roman Catholic academies the mediæval tradition had passed almost out of mind. When Newman visited Rome after his conversion, he was amazed to find that no one cared about St. Thomas.

---

[1] *History of Philosophy*, E. Tr., iii. 38.

[2] On the mediæval universities, see Rashdall, *Universities of Europe in the Middle Ages*. Over seventy were founded between 1150 and 1500. Salerno, the great medical school, dates from the middle of the eleventh century; Paris (theology and philosophy) and Bologna (law) from the beginning of the twelfth; Oxford (arts) and Montpellier (medicine) from the middle of the twelfth. Cambridge, Padua, Salamanca and Toulouse arose in the thirteenth century. We note how learning migrated from the monasteries to the universities; Anselm was the last of the great monastic, Abelard the first of the great university, teachers. The mediæval universities were not the result of definite foundation; they grew naturally out of colonies of students, who gathered to learn from famous masters.

[3] The controversy on universals was as to whether general concepts, such as man, horse, etc. (*genera* and *species*), were mere notions of the mind without any real counterpart in things (Nominalism and Conceptualism), or existed also in things (*in rebus*) as constituents of their real being (Realism). Realists also held that universals existed prior to individual things (*ante res*) as eternal thoughts of God. This latter doctrine had its source in Neo-Platonism and was transmitted to the Middle Ages through Augustine. The main stream of mediæval thought is realist. There were many subordinate varieties of Nominalism and Realism.

That was in the half-century prior to the restoration of the Thomistic philosophy by the most illustrious of modern popes, assisted by his chosen allies in the university of Louvain.[1] Ten years later, in 1888, the *École pratique des hautes études* at Paris embarked on a series of researches into the relations between religion and philosophy in the Middle Ages. Their labours and those of a host of scholars of all nations who have followed in their train have enabled students to gauge in its true proportions the value of Neo-Platonic and of mediæval speculation. We know now, for instance, that the line of thinkers, from John the Scot in the ninth century to William of Occam in the fourteenth, drew inspiration, not merely or even primarily from Aristotle, but from many other sources, and especially from Neo-Platonism; that the logical controversy as to universals was but a subordinate and transitory episode in an epoch of far-reaching metaphysical ferment; and that, far from uncritically accommodating a garbled and jaded Aristotelianism to the dogmas of the church, mediæval thinkers essayed a reasoned synthesis of theology and metaphysics, which can claim to stand among the most impressive yet achieved in the history of thought.

§ 6. The problem was common both to Hellenic and mediæval philosophy, though each approached it from a different angle. The distinction is that between the religion of science and the science of religion. The thinkers of Greece, starting from metaphysical assumptions and working on a metaphysical method, found in philosophy the satisfaction of spiritual desire and the secret of the religious life. Aristotle applied the term "theology," i.e., the reasoned doctrine of God, to what we should now call metaphysical science. In consequence, religion was rationalised, and became the monopoly of the philosopher, a tendency which we have observed even in Plotinus, in whose system the religious factor came into its own more fully than in any earlier Greek philosophy. The thinkers of the Middle Ages, on the other hand, started from the presuppositions of theology, and worked their way to metaphysics.[2] They aimed at a reconciliation of reason

---

[1] Leo XIII in the encyclical *Æterni Patris* (1878). "Of all my encyclicals," he wrote in 1900, "that which is nearest my heart and has given me most comfort, is the encyclical *Æterni Patris* on the restoration of the Scholastic and Thomist philosophy." The centre of the revival was the university of Louvain under the direction of Mgr. Mercier, later a cardinal and archbishop of Malines.

[2] This difference of orientation was intensified by the fact that throughout the Middle Ages learning, at least in western Christendom, was a monopoly of monks and clerics. But we must not forget that among the Arabs and the Jews, lay thinkers also approached the problem from the point of view of theology.

and revelation, science and faith, in a coherent theory of the relations of man and the world to God. From the days of the Apologists and of Origen in the second and third centuries, Christian thinkers had felt that the two interests could not be divorced. Religion and philosophy alike claim to give knowledge, and knowledge of a common truth; neither is restricted to a special field of human experience, but both, as " spectators of all time and all existence," take the universe as their province. Religion, again, falls short of its ideal as religion, unless it embraces within its scope the whole nature of man, and satisfies, not merely his practical and emotional aspirations, but those also of his intelligence. In other words, religion must come to an understanding with philosophy. For the mediæval philosophers, as for the earlier Christian theologians, this was possible only by use of the Hellenic method, the logical instrument that had been forged by the genius of Plato and Aristotle. They built, indeed, with originality and freedom, for, as we have said, their orientation was new. " *Aliud tempus fuit tunc et aliud nunc est*," said Roger Bacon, " it was one time then, and now it is another." The school of Chartres was as distinctive in its teaching from that of the Academy as was the architecture of its cathedral from that of the Doric Parthenon.[1]   But they built in the strength of the legacy of Hellenic thought. Nor was this inheritance restricted to the mind of Christendom. It was the common source of inspiration to the efforts after a synthesis of theology and metaphysics put forth by each of the three great world-religions of the Middle Ages. For Islam and Judaism were confronted by the same problem as Christianity. Despite their diversity and mutual antipathies, these three religions had much in common. All three were monotheistic, and taught the doctrines of a divine creation and providential government of the world, of a supernatural sphere peopled by supernatural powers, of heaven and hell, of the immortality of the soul, and the hope of personal salvation. All three appealed to a revelation embodied in sacred writings and to the authority of prophetic teachers—Moses, Jesus, Mahomet—who had delivered an inspired message to mankind. All three found themselves obliged to explain and

---

[1] On the school of Chartres ; see Poole, *Illustrations*, c. iv.   It became famous under Fulbert early in the eleventh century.   John of Salisbury (middle of the twelfth century), the best-known of its members, the most learned writer of his age, was acquainted with Cicero and the chief Latin poets : see also Sandys, *History of Classical Scholarship*, pp. 537–42, and Poole, c. vii.   He was secretary to archbishops Theobald and Becket of Canterbury.

defend their faith in the face of heretics and unbelievers, and had recourse to the allegorical method, first utilised by the Stoics, as the instrument of theological exegesis. In other words, all alike felt, though in varying measure, the need of a rational theology, which should harmonise science and revelation. We shall see presently how these currents of religious thought among Christians, Arabs and Jews arose independently, at the close of the eighth century, and converged in the speculative systems of the Christian doctors of the thirteenth. It is the community of aim and method among the three streams of thought that gives the philosophy of the Middle Ages its characteristic unity. For Christian, Arab and Jew, philosophy meant the rational interpretation of religious experience, a *praeparatio evangelica* for their respective gospels. The solutions proffered were divergent, but the interest was the same. Mediæval metaphysics centred in the problems of the being and operations of God, the freedom of the will, and the immortality of the human soul. Its story is that of the fusion of a common deposit of Greek philosophy with the theological tradition of three different, though analogous, religions.

§ 7. We must guard here against a natural and familiar misconception. The mediæval synthesis was no frigid republication of ancient theories, in artificial conjunction with a revelation that belied their truth. That the mediæval thinkers felt a profound respect for authority in thought and action, in things spiritual and things secular, is beyond question, and has exposed them to the charges of servility and obscurantism. The tradition of scripture and the Fathers, the injunctions of the canon and the civil law, and the judgements of Aristotle and his interpreters, assuredly wielded at times an almost overwhelming influence. It was inevitable, in an age when individual self-assertion and the unbridled thirst for liberty of action threatened at every point to dissolve into anarchy the new-born structures of social order and stable conviction, that the need of authoritative control should be urgently felt both by thinkers and by statesmen. For Anselm and Aquinas, as for Hildebrand and William the Norman, authority was the rock on which alone the fabric of truth and justice could be reared. The Middle Ages were deeply conscious of instability and ignorance; of how insecure were the foundations of its society, and how much of the inheritance of the past was yet unknown. Little wonder that it clutched eagerly, and often uncritically, at the fragmentary relics of ancient wisdom

394 THE LEGACY OF THE ANCIENT WORLD

that lay beneath its hand. But the appeal to authority was no bar to intellectual independence. From the time when Abelard wrote his *Sic et non* in the twelfth century to the publication of Aquinas' *Summae* in the thirteenth, we note a continuous energy of critical selection and comparison among the divergent voices of the recognised authorities. When Aristotle clashed with scripture, the mediæval mind was forced to think for itself. Above all, men were ready and able to offer rational grounds for allegiance to the authorities of their choice. The dominant note of the mediæval spirit was not reverence for authority, but other-worldliness. To call the Middle Ages an age of faith is a truism; all ages are ages of faith, and the only pertinent enquiry is into the nature and quality of the conviction. To its thinkers and men of action the supersensible world possessed a reality denied to the scene of man's temporal pilgrimage. This does not mean that they were indifferent to motives of gain and glory, to the claims of military or political ambition, or even to those of knowledge of physical nature.[1] But those who were most absorbed in mundane concerns never questioned, when they paused to think, that these were of secondary moment, that "this earth, our habitation" was but a transitory stage of discipline, or that the only knowledge of intrinsic worth was that of man's spiritual goal and of the instruments that led to its attainment. The mind of the Middle Ages held unswervingly to the convictions that society ought to be controlled by the moral law, that above all differences of status and nationality men were linked in human fellowship as members of an ideal commonwealth, and that reason and revelation alike pointed to the knowledge of an end which was the absolute and perfect good for man and for the universe. It sought a reasoned basis for these convictions. The conception which it framed of the divine order of the world was one of unique speculative grandeur.

[1] It must not be rashly supposed that the mediæval thinkers were heedless of the interest of physical science. Albertus Magnus, following in the steps of Michael Scot, revived biological science in his commentaries on Aristotle, esp. the *de Animalibus*. Roger Bacon's experiments in chemistry were neither unimportant nor unique. Dante furnishes abundant illustrations of interest in astronomy and cosmology. Aristotle's authority exercised a baneful influence in physics, especially through his distinction of the sublunary and the superlunary worlds. Yet even here the best minds of the Middle Ages were opened to new ideas; e.g. Aquinas' words (*de cœlo et mundo*, Book II, Lect. 17) on the theory of planetary motions : "Though the phenomena can be saved on these hypotheses, we do not assert that they are true, since perchance the phenomena of the heavenly bodies may be saved in some other way not yet grasped by men."

Let any who feel disposed to cavil at its reverence for theological authority as involving the imprisonment of the human
spirit, set, we will not say, the *Summae* of Aquinas, but the *Divina
Commedia*, inspired in almost every canto by Aquinas' teaching,
beside Milton's *Paradise Lost* and Goethe's *Faust*, and ask dis-
passionately, which of these great poets, the child of the Middle
Ages or the inheritors of modern humanism, have most effectively
achieved an imaginative synthesis of man's relation to the world
and God. The answer to this question will serve as a measure of
the claim of the mediæval mind to originality and freedom, and
of its response to the inspiration that it drew from the legacy
of the ancient world.

§ 8. It was in the thirteenth century that the effort of mediæval
thought after a synthesis of theology and metaphysics culminated
in a relatively stable solution. This achievement was chiefly
due to St. Thomas Aquinas (1227–74). Aquinas stood at the
meeting-point of the three currents of thought that had flowed
in separate channels for some four hundred years. These were,
first, the philosophy of western Christendom, that took its rise
in the Carolingian schools of the ninth century; secondly, the
Arab philosophy, which had its birth under the Baghdad caliphs
of the eighth century, and reached its zenith under the emirs
of Cordova in the twelfth; and, thirdly, the unbroken speculative tradition of the scholars and *litterati* of the Byzantine empire.
(i) The Christian schools had been founded, by Charles the Great
and his Frankish successors, in Gaul and on the Rhine, at the
close of the eighth and the opening of the ninth century. The
first teachers, many of whom, like Alcuin of York, were drawn
from the British Isles, built as best they could out of the rubble
of the shattered edifice of Græco-Roman culture.[1] The materials
to their hand were unpromising. The Latin versions of certain
of Aristotle's logical treatises compiled by Boethius, the philosophic minister of Theodoric the Ostrogoth, in the sixth century,
the same writer's *Consolation of Philosophy*, a few late and
imperfect commentaries, and some inferior manuals of the same
period, furnished garbled hints of the great tradition, and an
introduction to the more formal rules of logic. Augustine and
other Fathers of the church helped to an acquaintance with
Neo-Platonism. Plato himself was known only through a Latin
translation of the *Timæus*.[2] On this fragmentary basis they

---

[1] See R. L. Poole, *Illustrations*, Introduction.

[2] The treatises of Aristotle referred to did not include the most important, which were not discovered till the eleventh century in the Christian

founded the teaching of dialectic, comprising a discipline in logical method with a tincture of Neo-Platonic rather than Aristotelian metaphysics, and forming, with grammar and rhetoric, the *Trivium* of the mediæval schools.[1] The marvel is that they made such use of what they had. A century had not elapsed before there appeared, at the court of Charles the Bald, a thinker whose writings are perhaps the most astonishing phenomenon in the history of philosophy. John the Scot (Johannes Scotus Erigena, *flor. c.* 850), working with rare originality and freedom on the basis of the Neo-Platonic tradition handed down by Augustine and the pseudo-Dionysius, produced in his treatise *On the Division of Nature* a system of philosophy which, alike in logical coherence and in speculative content, anticipates that of Spinoza. He asserted boldly that true religion is identical with philosophy. All that is, in so far as it has being, is God, the beginning and the end, the Alpha and the Omega, of the universe, which is, therefore, immortal and wholly good. Nature, i.e., reality (we seem to hear the *Deus sive Natura* of Spinoza), is interpreted in the light of a four-fold division : (1) That which is uncreated and creative (God as universal cause); (2) that which is created and creative (the world of archetypal ideas); (3) that which is created and uncreative (the sensible image of the ideas); and (4) that which is uncreated and uncreative (the final rest of restored creation in God's undivided unity). Thus evil has no real existence, but is mere privation of good; and, having no being, cannot be caused or foreknown by God. It is small wonder that John's response, in his tract on *Predestination*, to the appeal of archbishop Hincmar of Rheims, to defend human freedom against the assertion of predestination to damnation, fluttered the ecclesiastical dovecote and seemed more perilous even than the heresy of his antagonist. John the Scot was an

---

west. For Boethius, see c. x, § 8, and for Augustine, see c. ix. § 22. The works attributed to Dionysius the Areopagite, on the *Divine Names* and the *Celestial Hierarchy*, and composed late in the sixth century, were also very influential throughout the Middle Ages (e.g. upon John the Scot, who translated them into Latin, and upon Dante, Par. x. 115–17, xxviii. 97 to end). The translation of the *Timæus* was that of Chalcidius. This dialogue appealed to the mediæval mind as natural science set in a theological context.

[1] The *Trivium* was followed by the *Quadrivium*, consisting of arithmetic, geometry, astronomy and music. The whole curriculum was subordinate to the study of Christian theology. The origin of the *Trivium* and the *Quadrivium*, like that of the university, is to be traced to Plato's Academy and to the programme of studies outlined in the seventh book of the *Republic*. It is not a mere accident of history that logic is taught to-day in the French *lycées*. English public schoolboys are less fortunate.

isolated figure, and founded no enduring school; though here and there, in the ages that followed, we find a few daring minds who, quarrying in his mine of treasure, braved the wrath of the ortho-dox authorities and the terrible charge of pantheism.[1] But the Platonic tradition continued to dominate the thought of the early Middle Ages. After two centuries of speculative poverty, it woke to fresh life with Anselm of Aosta (1033–1109, abbot of Bec and archbishop of Canterbury), and Peter Abelard (1079–1142); the latter of whom entitled Plato the greatest of philosophers, and endeavoured, by his identification of the Holy Spirit with the world-soul, to accommodate Platonic teach-ing to the Christian doctrine of the Trinity. It was Abelard, too, who, marshalling one against the other the judgements of divergent authorities, Christian and pagan, forged the charac-teristic instrument of expression for the succeeding age. His fame as a master of dialectic was largely due to the fact that the rediscovery of the chief logical works of Aristotle inspired him to breathe fresh life into that branch of knowledge. Abelard was the pioneer of the second phase in the mediæval revival of learning, which was marked by the recognition of Aristotle, side by side with Plato, as a regulative authority in western Christen-dom. The opening years of the thirteenth century saw the rediscovery of the *Physics*, *Metaphysics* and *de Animâ*. At the same time the doctors of the West gathered in the fruits of Arab, Jewish and Byzantine speculation.

§ 9. (ii) The Arab philosophy, which arose under the caliphs of Baghdad in the eighth century, differed in two respects from that of the Christian schools of the West. From the first it reaped a richer harvest from the legacy of Hellenic thought. The Arabs had access to the entire Aristotelian *Corpus* and to a large

---

[1] On John the Scot, see R. L. Poole, *Illustrations*, c. ii. " Scot " means that he came from Ireland; " Erigena " is a later substitute for " Ierugena," which probably means " of Irish birth." A good edition of his works is sorely needed. How near John came to pantheism is evident from the following passages :

" When we hear that God does everything, we should understand that God is in everything, i.e. that he subsists as the essence of everything " (i. 72).

" He (God) is the beginning, middle and end : the beginning, because from him are all things that have essence; the middle, because in and through him all things subsist; the end, because they move to him, seeking rest from their motion and fixity of their perfection " (i. 12).

But John can hardly be charged with pantheism for he combines this doctrine with the assertion, on Neo-Platonic lines, of God's transcendence. The belief in a purely immanent God was branded as atheism in the Middle Ages, as later in the case of Spinoza.

mass of both Platonic and Neo-Platonic writings, through Syriac translations from the Greek. Hence the rapid advance and the comparative maturity of their metaphysics. But philosophy failed to acclimatise itself to the religious atmosphere of Islam. As Renan has remarked, the Arab genius, fertile in poetry and art, has never taken kindly to metaphysics. Their philosophy was always an exotic, which enjoyed a transitory efflorescence, thanks to the patronage of enlightened princes, first in Mesopotamia, and afterwards in Spain. On the fall of the Ummayyad emirs of Cordova, it was crushed out of existence by the hostility of orthodox Mohammedanism. The last great name was that of Averroes of Cordova (Ibn Roschd : 1127–98). But before its brief and brilliant splendour faded, it had handed on the torch to the adherents of another faith. The Arabs taught the Jews to think, and the lesson, once learnt, was not forgotten. The most illustrious of Jewish mediæval thinkers, Maimonides (Moses ben Maimon : 1135–1204) was the forerunner of a long line of philosophers, culminating in the seventeenth century with Baruch de Spinoza, whose system on its religious side—and no philosophy is more profoundly religious—reflects the conception of union with God through intellectual love, which his Jewish predecessors had inherited through the Arabs from Plotinus and Plato. Not only in finance and trade, but in things of the mind, the mediæval Jew played the part of a middle man of civilization. But, both among the Arabs and the Jews, the Platonic tradition was more evenly balanced by the Aristotelian, than it was in the Christian West, until the twelfth and thirteenth centuries.[1] Lastly, (iii) a third speculative current flowed into western Europe in the early years of the thirteenth century from the Christian East. The Byzantine scholars had preserved the genuine classical tradition, and knew Plato, Aristotle and the Neo-Platonists at first hand. The ties of intellectual contact between West and East were drawn closer by the Crusades, and especially by the Latin occupation of Constantinople in 1204.[2] The study of ancient thought had been revived there in the eleventh century by the Comnenian dynasty.[3] In 1205, pope Innocent III

---

[1] The student who is interested should consult Renan, *Averroes et l'Averroisme*, and the English translation of Maimonides' *Moreh Nebuchim* or " Guide of the Perplexed."

[2] It had never been entirely broken, e.g. the writings of the Pseudo-Dionysius had come from the East to the West through Rome in the eighth century.

[3] Michael Psellus was the chief thinker in this revival, which had its precursors in the late seventh century (John of Damascus), and in the ninth

despatched western missionaries to the East, while king Philip Augustus of France opened at Paris a college for Byzantine students. Theological discussions were actively carried on between the Latin and Greek churches. Amongst other results of this association, the works of Aristotle, hitherto studied in Latin translations of Arabic translations of Syriac translations from the Greek, were read henceforward by western scholars in the original.[1]

§ 10. The convergence of these three currents in the thirteenth century had momentous results on the thought of western Christendom. The influence of Aristotle, whose works could now for the first time be studied in their entirety, became increasingly predominant over the earlier Platonic tradition. In making this distinction, we must bear in mind that Aristotle's philosophy was grounded on that of Plato, and that it reached the Middle Ages overlaid with Neo-Platonic commentaries and accretions.[2] Plato, again, was known chiefly through a Neo-Platonic medium, in which a large measure of Aristotelian doctrine had been already fused with the Platonic. Thus it was possible for Arab and later Christian thinkers, in possession of the Aristotelian *Corpus*, to embody the results of both traditions in a single speculative system. Broadly speaking, we may say that Aristotle's contribution to mediæval thought was twofold, in that (a) his logic, and especially his theory of the syllogism, set the type of scientific method; while (b) the contents of his physical, psychological, political and metaphysical treatises were accepted, with reservations as to the eternity of the world and the mortality of the soul, as a basis for construction in the natural and moral sciences.[3] Aristotle, in effect, supplied the theory of nature, which was needed to supplement the church's theory of grace. When, on the other hand, mediæval thought

---

(Photius). The Syriac Christians, through whom the Arabs came to know Greek philosophy, had learnt in their turn from the Byzantine Greeks.

[1] Aquinas, for instance, though ignorant himself of Greek, employed a Greek scholar, William of Moerbeke, as his collaborator on Aristotle.

[2] Among these accretions were two treatises assigned in the Middle Ages to Aristotle, that " *On causes* " (*De causis*) and the so-called " *Theology*." Both were translations from the Neo-Platonist Proclus. The *Fons vitae* of the Jew, Avicebron (Ibn-Gebirol), hailed also from the same source, and was probably influenced by John the Scot.

[3] The church hesitated long before sanctioning the study of the newly-discovered Aristotle. It was the labours of Albert of Cologne and, especially, of Aquinas that secured eventual recognition for the Aristotelian tradition as harmonised by them with the doctrine of the catholic church, especially as regards the points mentioned above.

was turned to the nature of God and the destiny of the human soul, it followed mainly in the tracks of Christian Neo-Platonism. The principles that grades of perfection within our experience imply the reality of an absolute standard ; that the higher the grade of being the more pervasive is its causal efficacy ; that the effect is inferior to, yet mirrors the likeness of, its cause ; that evil is nothing positive but privation of good; that the rational soul is a substantial entity independent of the body and immortal ; that the human intellect in this life can know God only by analogy, and by denying of Him all that we are able to conceive ; that universals (the Platonic Forms) exist timelessly as thoughts in the divine mind, and that, in God, essence and existence, intellect and will, thought and reality, are one and the same; these and many other tenets common to the main body of mediæval speculation are all of them, though blended in their presentation with the teaching of revealed religion, in their origin " fragments of the great banquet " of Plotinus. We may go further and say that in the spirit, if hardly in the letter, they carry the mind back beyond Plotinus to their fountain-head in Plato. There is, however, a remarkable exception to this general tendency to draw on the Platonic tradition for the theory of supersensible reality. In their endeavours to base the belief in the fact of God's existence on rational grounds, the great majority of mediæval thinkers refused to accept as valid the famous *a priori* argument of Anselm (the " ontological " argument), viz. that our thought of God involves his necessary being. They preferred to appeal to the Aristotelian proof (the " cosmological ") from the experienced fact of motion to the existence of an unmoved mover as its first cause.[1] Despite their sense of the worth of human personality, they shrank from exalting the mind of the finite individual into the basis of so ambitious a construction. Their instinct told them that the ontological argument was hard to reconcile with their firm conviction of God's transcendence. For more than five hundred years, Anselm's bold flight found no following, until, in an age that looked to human reason as the key to all the secrets of the universe, his proof was revived, as a chief cornerstone of metaphysics, by Descartes.

§ 11. But the reception of Aristotle was not the sole or the

[1] For the ontological proof see Anselm's *Proslogium*, Gaunilo's criticism (analogous to Kant's) and Anselm's reply; also Aquinas' criticism, *S. Th.*, I. q. 2. art. 1, and *S.c.G.*, I. 10. For the cosmological proof, see Aquinas, *S. Th.*, I. q. 2. art. 3, and *S.c.G.*, I. 13. The ontological argument is a development of hints in Augustine and the Neo-Platonists.

greatest intellectual achievement of the thirteenth century. The touch of the Greek spirit stirred the thinkers of the age to energy of creative thought. They would have learnt their lesson ill had it been otherwise. The mediæval mind had long laboured to effect a synthesis of reason and revelation, in the conviction that both alike had their source in God, and as such could not stand in mutual contradiction. The advocates of a double truth, i.e. that what is valid in philosophy is false in religion and *vice versâ*, won few adherents.[1] On the other hand, there were not many to echo the frank avowal of John the Scot, that "true philosophy is true religion, and conversely true religion is true philosophy."[2] The great majority steered a course between these two extremes. Anselm thanks God that "what by thy gift I first believed, I now by thy illumination understand, so that even though I refused to believe in thy existence, I could not fail to grasp it with my intelligence."[3] "God alone," wrote Abelard, "is the plenitude of all the sciences, whose gift all science is." And of revealed truth he said : "It is not to be believed because God spake it, but it is accepted because we are convinced that it is true."[4] But Aquinas (1227–74) was the first to define with the requisite lucidity and precision the nature at once of the relationship and of the distinction.[5] To do so was an urgent necessity; for the organised system of Christian theology was now at last confronted with an equally organised system of metaphysics in the Aristotelian *Corpus*, and there were points where the latter appeared to clash directly with the faith.

[1] This was maintained by Siger of Brabant, an Averroist contemporary and opponent of Aquinas at Paris. See Mandonnet, *Siger de Brabant*, on this, and on the whole matter of §§ 9–11.   [2] *De predestinatione*, i. 1.

[3] *Proslogium*, c. 4 ; cf. *Monologium*, c. 1. Anselm's " I do not seek to understand in order to believe, but I believe in order that I may understand" (*credo ut intelligam*, *Proslog.*, c. 1) is a far cry from Tertullian's " it is certain because it is impossible " (*certum est quia impossibile est*).

[4] *Introd. ad Theologiam*, ii. 2, 3.

[5] Aquinas wrote, besides a multitude of other works, two *Summae*, i.e. encyclopædic treatises, covering the whole fields of theology and metaphysics. They were entitled the *Summa Theologica* and the *Summa contra Gentiles* (against the heathen); the latter was designed for the use of missionaries to the Mohammedans and the Jews, who required a justification of the Christian faith on grounds of reason. The two *Summae* form the most systematic expression of thirteenth-century thought. They comprise also much discussion of psychological, ethical and political questions. References to the *S. Th.* are by parts (e.g. II. 1 = 1st division of Part II, II. 2 = 2nd division of Part II, etc.), questions and articles (into which each question is subdivided). Thus *S. Th.*, II. 1. q. 17 art. 1 = the 1st article of the 17th question of the 1st division of Part II. Only the Second Part (II) is further subdivided into parts (1 and 2). References to the *S.c.G.* are by parts and chapters. The *S. Th.* has been translated by the English Dominicans.

Averroes, the " Commentator " *par excellence*, had interpreted
Aristotle rightly as holding that the world was eternal and that
the human soul perished with the body of which it was the form.
Either it must be shown that the master taught otherwise—and
this was no easy task—or an endeavour must be made to reason
out the truth where his authority proved defective. Aquinas
set himself to meet the situation thus created. He set his course
midway between the Augustinian Neo-Platonism which held the
field in the orthodox schools and the literal Aristotelianism of the
disciples of Averroes. As against the former, who had dallied
dangerously with the principle that pagan philosophy and Christian dogma were both immediately inspired by God, he drew
with a firm hand, perhaps, as some would object, with too firm
a hand, the line of demarcation between reason and revelation,
nature and grace. His native genius for grasping the distinctions between things had been fortified by the study of Aristotle
and of Roman law. That " every thing is what it is and is
not another thing " was implanted as deeply in the typically
Italian mind of Thomas of Aquino as in the typically English
mind of bishop Butler. As against the Averroists, on the other
hand, he stood for independence of tradition and freedom of
enquiry. " The argument from authority," he declared, " is
of all arguments the weakest." " What was well said by the
ancients we will accept for our profit; what they said wrongly,
we will discard." " The aim of philosophy is not to know what
men have thought, but how the truth of the matter stands." [1]
It would carry us beyond our purpose to discuss the detail of
Aquinas' solution, or to dwell on the other speculative problems
which witness to the originality of thirteenth-century thought.
We have already indicated that the mediæval philosophers
devoted themselves to an analytic study of human personality—
a field in which ancient thought afforded them no sure guidance.
It is noteworthy that the three problems, of God, freedom, and
immortality, first came by their own at the hands of Aquinas
and the other great thinkers of the thirteenth century.[2] Greek

---

[1] *S. Th.*, I. q. 32. art. 1 ; cf. q. 1. art. 1–8, *sup. Boeth. de Trin.*, q. 11.
art. 3, and *de unitate intellectus contra Averroistas*, c. 27. In Dante's poem,
the vision in Paradise of the union of the divine and human natures in
Christ is declared by Justinian to be clear with the intuitive self-evidence
that attaches to the metaphysical principle of Contradiction (viz. that A
cannot both be and not be B in the same sense and at the same time),
Par., vi. 19–21.

[2] " Genuine theology is thus at the same time a real philosophy of
religion, as it was, we may add, in the Middle Ages."—Hegel, *Logic*, § 36
(E. Tr. by Wallace, p. 73).

philosophy had treated these questions with scant justice. They kept their place in the forefront of modern thought, long after the Middle Ages had passed away; constituting the central issue of metaphysics, at the close of the eighteenth century, for Immanuel Kant. The creative impulse to reasoned thought, which awoke at the first reception of the Hellenic legacy in the dawn of the Middle Ages, has operated with unbroken continuity from the ninth century to the present day.

§ 12. Aquinas' greatness as a philosopher rests chiefly on his achievement as a mediator, not only (as we have just seen) between the Platonic and Aristotelian traditions, but, more generally, between the Judaic–Christian religious legacy and that of Hellenic metaphysics. In this lies his originality as a thinker, that he thus provoked new speculative problems of which Plato and Aristotle had hardly dreamed and which went far to determine the subsequent course of philosophical enquiry. Three examples will serve to make this clear. (1) His distinction between faith and reason was endorsed in principle by the leading thinkers of the next six centuries, and still persists in the minds of philosophers at the present day. They are different and mutually exclusive modes of apprehending truth, for faith is *de absentibus* and implies defective insight, while reason, proceeding from self-evident principles by way of vigorous demonstration, attains to full comprehension of its objects. *Impossibile est quod de eodem sit fides et scientia.*[1] Impossible, that is to say, for a given mind at a given moment; for Aquinas is far from suggesting that a truth revealed to faith may not also be demonstrable by reason, so that it can be apprehended now in the one way, now in the other. This is the case with what he calls the " preambles of faith," e.g., God's existence and unity, which, though falling within the content of revelation, admit also of proof by natural reason. On the other hand, many revealed truths (e.g., the Trinity and the Incarnation) altogether transcend the grasp of reason and are accessible only by the way of faith.[2] Not that any contradiction is conceivable between faith and reason, both alike having their source in God; faith is *præter naturam*, not *contre naturam*. Its objects are intrinsically intelligible; for the redeemed in Paradise who enjoy the direct vision of God, they will be (as Dante says) as self-evident to the intellect as is for us the basic principle of Contradiction. Faith is relative to man's

[1] de Ver. xiv. g. *ad resp.*

[2] Though even here there is scope for the exercise of reason, in the refutation of sophism and error and in adducing probable arguments in support of truths that lie beyond its grasp.

present state *in viâ*. Reason therefore, as giving full insight, is the superior mode of apprehension, though faith, as resting on divine revelation, speaks with a higher authority and achieves a higher grade of certitude.[1] On this distinction between faith and reason is grounded that between theology on the one hand and, on the other, metaphysics and the sciences. The theologian, taking his start from principles of revelation, known by the light of grace infused by the Holy Spirit, works downwards from God to the world of His creation; the philosopher (and the scientist) starts from the creaturely, which is the proper object of human reason, and works upwards to God by principles of rational demonstration. From the distinctions thus drawn, two results follow, of cardinal importance for the thought of the succeeding age. The door is thrown open for the advance of the physical sciences, whose autonomy is secured against any intrusion from the theologian in the supposed interest of truths revealed to faith. Reason is established in all, and more than all, its ancient rights, so far, that is, as the interpretation of sensible phenomena is the subject of enquiry. As, in political theory, Aquinas heralds the advent of constitutional government, so, in theory of knowledge, he heralds that of modern science. The second noteworthy consequence concerns the status of religious faith. With the gradual restriction of reason, in the hands of Descartes and those who followed him, to the methods of mathematics and the sciences, and the realisation (e.g. by David Hume) of the narrow bounds of demonstrative reasoning, more and more of the (so-called) knowledge, religious, ethical, æsthetic and other, to which man attaches value and significance, was relegated away from the sphere of " cognitive " faculties to that of irrational belief and referred to the " sensitive " faculties of feeling and imagination.[2] The paradoxical result was that, in the heyday of the " Age of Rationalism," reason fell into general discredit. Not only poets, like Wordsworth and Shelley, but philosophers also, whose horizon stretched beyond the data and methods of the positive sciences, have turned to other activities than those of intellect in their search for truth, appealing, as did Bergson, to non-inferential intuition, or, as did William James, to a

[1] See *S.c.G.*, I. 3–7 and my *Towards a Religious Philosophy*, Additional Note to c. XI., pp. 215 ff, for Aquinas' argument to the need, in view of man's function and appointed goal, of a revelation transcending the scope of natural reason.

[2] See Hume, *Treatise* (Bk. III, Pt. I, Sec. I). Hume's use of the term " judgement " in this connexion is ambiguous and instructive. We may compare the views of the Logical Positivists to-day.

pragmatist criterion. For this trend towards anti-rationalism, Aquinas cannot be wholly acquitted of responsibility. He had drawn too rigid a line of demarcation between faith and reason. Though he allowed a restricted place to reason within the domain of faith, his analysis of the procedure of reason was defective. It never occurred to him to ask, whether faith (and other non-logical operations) was not integral to all rational processes, whether any exercise of rational activity was possible, even in metaphysics and the sciences, without an act of reasonable faith.

§ 13. Secondly (2), Aquinas conceived God, in accordance with the Jewish–Christian religious tradition and in a manner alien to that of Greek philosophy, as the supreme and sole existent, whose nature or essence is to be. In Him, essence and existence, which in all other beings fall asunder, are one and the same. He Himself is self-existent, the sole ground of His own being; "I am that I am" is the final answer to all further questioning. How then, if God is infinite and total being, can we ascribe real existence (as we needs must) to the finite world of our experience? Are we not impaled on the dilemma of Kant's fourth antinomy?[1] If God is, there can be no universe; if there be a universe, there is something outside God. Aquinas answers this problem by his doctrine of Creation. Being for him is no abstract concept, else it would indeed be what Hegel called it, "the poorest of all predicates"; it is pure activity, the power to be and to impart being. As Plotinus had said, "it is of the nature of being to beget," i.e. to go forth from itself in creative energy.[2] It is because of God's infinite wealth of being that he displays infinite power to create and conserve in being what owes all its being to Him and yet is other than Himself. The problem thus set by the Christian revelation, and the solution offered, alike constitute a new departure in the history of thought. Neither Plato, whose demiurge was but an architect, fashioning the sense-world in a given "receptacle" after the likeness of timeless Forms, nor Aristotle, the activity of whose God was confined within the bounds of His self-consciousness, had ever entertained the idea of creation. For them the problem which has eluded enquiry all down the ages, Why is there an existent world at all?, simply did not arise. The categorical assertion of God's being marks the difference between the theistic faith of Christianity and the conclusion of any inferential process. Whereas Greek

---

[1] *Critique of Pure Reason*, A. 452–460 = B 480–489.
[2] On Plotinus, see c. IX, pp. 303–6.

philosophy and modern science alike concentrate attention on the general characters of things, which, being expressible in concepted formulæ, are intelligible to human reason; Christianity grapples with the problem of their existence which, since it allows of no such formulation, presents a final inexplicability to the intellect. This is the *raison d'être* of the age-long controversies between religion and science, theology and metaphysics. Except for a Christian philosophy, like that of Aquinas, these controversies are without a remedy. For such a philosophy they are quarrels over unsubstantial shadows, which vanish in presence of an existential faith and " leave not a wrack behind." [1]

§ 14. My last illustration (3) shows how Aquinas utilised the Aristotelian legacy in the service of a purely Christian theology. I refer to the principle known as *analogia entis*. It is obvious from what we have just said that the being of the Creator and that of His creatures are very different modes of being, parted one from the other by an infinite gulf. The one is total being, self-existent, necessary and infinite; the other is partial being, dependent, contingent and finite. The one is wholly in act, exclusive of all potentiality, becoming and not-being; the other is through and through permeated by unrealised possibilities, change and not-being. How can man's finite mind, riddled by these deficiencies, bridge the gulf even in conception, so as to attain knowledge of the Creator? Man seems to be faced by an ineluctable dilemma, tossed helplessly between Scylla and Charybdis. Either the term " being " is applicable univocally (i.e., in the same meaning) to the Creator and the Creatures, in which case " being " is a generic character common to the two specific modes, and the door is open to all the wild vagaries of anthropomorphism, i.e., the interpretation of God's being in terms of the creaturely being of our human experience. Or the term " being " is equivocal (i.e., different in meaning); so that we have no warrant for regarding God's goodness, power or wisdom as having any affinity to our own. For all we can tell, God's goodness may be our badness. Our only resource is to follow the *via remotionis* and to refuse to ascribe to God any positive predicate drawn from the finite world of our experience. Any such determination of His character is to impress a limit on the un-

---

[1] Those contemporary theologians, especially on the Continent, who, paying scant heed to the main Catholic tradition, follow Kierkegaard, Karl Barth, and other champions of an "existential" Christianity, would find in Aquinas all, and more than all, they claim to have garnered from the Reformers of the sixteenth century.

limited. Everything that can be affirmed of God is, strictly, affirmed falsely; at best it has an ambiguous value as symbolism or metaphor. We escape from the Scylla of anthropomorphism only to be wrecked in the Charybdis of agnosticism. Aquinas evaded this dilemma by borrowing from Aristotle's doctrine of the Categories the theory of analogous predication. Being is asserted of God and of the creature neither univocally nor equivocally, but analogously. That is what Aristotle had asserted of being in the ten Categories (substance, quality, relation, and the rest); they were not ten species of a common genus, " being," nor were they wholly different from one another in their " being "; there was identity amid the difference and differences amid the identity. You could not single out or specify with clear precision the identical factor from that of difference, so inseparably were they integrated in the unity of each mode of being. In adapting to his purpose this logical doctrine, Aquinas gave it a new and far more profound application, alike in metaphysics and in theology. It was possible henceforward to predicate positively of God by transferring to Him such perfections as were discernible in human experience, in accordance with the following scheme of proportion. As the " being " of the Creator is to that of the creature; so are the Creator's goodness, intelligence, power, etc., to the goodness, intelligence, power, etc., of the creature. Thus the gulf was bridged; and theology was freed from the dangers both of anthropomorphism and of agnosticism. Another dilemma, which is a besetting menace to philosophy, was likewise shorn of its terrors. Neither the extremes of Monism nor Pluralism can hold their ground against the doctrine of *analogia entis*. In light of that doctrine, it is no longer possible to say : " Whatever it is, it is all one," or " If you analyse far enough, you will be faced with an absolute diversity." Pantheism was thus warned off the theological premises and a Christian philosophy saved, and Christianity saved, from one of the chief pitfalls of modern Idealist metaphysics. No more convincing refutation of pure immanentism (Spinoza's, Hegel's, or, in more recent times, Gentile's) can be found than in Aquinas' masterly tractate, *de unitate intellectus contra Averroistas*. It stands, side by side with the first part of Plato's *Theœtetus*, as one of the final achievements in the history of philosophy.

III. The Reception of Roman Law [1] (§§ 15–22).

§ 15. Roman law, like Greek philosophy, reached the Middle Ages in a debased and fragmentary form.[2] The code of Justinian was virtually unknown in the West until the eleventh century, save in those parts of Italy where the eastern emperors retained their jurisdiction. Elsewhere the chief source of legal tradition was the code of Theodosius II (438), a compilation framed by eastern lawyers, but promulgated coincidently in the West by Valentinian III. In the five succeeding centuries, the epoch of the barbarian invasions and the dark age that followed them, we can trace the influence of Roman law on the new kingdoms in four directions. (i) Barbarian chieftains began to write down, in imitation of the Roman practice, their native Germanic law. Thus did Euric the Visigoth (c. 470), Clovis the Salian Frank (486–511), the kings of the Burgundians and of the Ripuarian Franks (sixth century). Bede tells how Aethelberht of Kent (c. 600), after the coming of Augustine to Britain, collected the laws of his people " according to the pattern of the Romans." [3] Of these Germanic codes the most remarkable were those of the Lombard kings of northern Italy in the seventh and eighth centuries, whose work served as a basis for a scientific jurisprudence, and persisted in force long after the conquest of Lombardy by the Franks in 744. (ii) The Teutonic kings also compiled codes of Roman law for their Roman subjects, who retained their legal status as Romans under barbarian overlords. Under the Goths, Franks, and Lombards, law was personal rather than territorial. Bishop Agobard of Lyon (c. 850) tells how five men might meet together in a single room, each with a claim to be judged in accordance with his own racial law.[4] To borrow Maitland's analogy, it was as with the peoples of British India to-day; though we must suppose one of them to be possessed

---

[1] The term " Reception," generally used of the introduction of Roman law into Germany at the close of the fifteenth century, and later into the common law of Scotland, is used here to mean the influence of the Roman legal tradition on the law and thought of western Europe throughout the Middle Ages.

[2] On the matter of the following sections, the author is largely indebted to the early chapters in vol. i. of Pollock and Maitland's *History of the Laws of England*, Vinogradoff's *Roman Law in Mediaeval Europe*, and Gierke's *Political Theories of the Middle Age* (*tr.* Maitland).

[3] Bede, *Eccl. Hist.*, ii. 5, "*juxta exempla Romanorum.*" The example of Roman law acted as a stimulus not only to the written compilation of existing native law, but to its enrichment by means of royal statutes.

[4] Vinogradoff, p. 16.

of an old law-book, too good for them and for us, which becomes
in course of time a subject of scientific study and the basis of a
revival of jurisprudence.[1] Of these later Roman codes the
most important was the *lex Romana Visigothorum*, drawn up
by Alaric II, the son of Euric, in 506 for the use of his Roman
subjects in Gaul and Spain, and known commonly as the *Brev-
iarium Alaricianum*. Written in very tolerable Latin, it comprised a clear statement of those portions of Roman law which
were intelligible to the degenerate lawyers of that age and
relevant to the practical requirements of the Visigothic courts.
In its formal arrangement into institutes, common law (*jus*)
and statute law (*leges*), it anticipated the threefold division
adopted in the East a generation later by Justinian. Despite
the comparative poverty of its contents, it kept alive the law
of Rome, and remained for over five hundred years the chief
authority in the countries north of the Alps.   In its train there
appeared in western Europe a customary version of Roman
law, standing to the old law in much the same relation as the
Romance languages to the pure classical Latin. (iii) During
the same period Roman elements crept into native Germanic
law, and conversely, the inheritance of Roman law was gradually
coloured by elements of Germanic origin. The laws of Euric
derived from a Roman source such provisions as the prohibition
of legal actions after a lapse of thirty years, and the admission
of women to inheritance on equal terms with men. Among
Franks and Lombards, formulæ for contracts were adapted
from Roman models. The converse tendency may be illustrated by the incorporation of Germanic customs in the *lex
Romana Curiensis*, an eighth-century code compiled for the
Romance population of eastern Switzerland.   (iv) Finally, the
tradition of Roman law was preserved by the western church.
We have seen how problems of internal discipline had from
early times engaged the attention of synods and councils, and
how, when the empire became Christian, episcopal jurisdiction
received official recognition. Thus, from the fourth century
onwards, came into being the canon law. Its main sources
were the scriptures, the writings of the Fathers, the decrees of
general councils, certain letters of the Roman bishops, and
the custom of the church. From these materials were formed
collections of canons, which were enlarged by extracts from
Roman law-books, and by a mass of spurious papal letters,

[1] Pollock and Maitland, i. p. 15.

produced in France during the ninth century, and known as the *pseudo-Isidore*. In 774, the collection framed early in the sixth century by a Scythian monk, Dionysius the Small (*Exiguus*), was presented by pope Hadrian I to Charles the Great, and adopted as a standard canonical authority throughout the Frankish kingdom. In language, in form, and in many of its maxims, the canon law reflected the influence of the civil law of Rome. Pope Gregory the Great (590–604) had known and utilised Justinian's *Digest*. When the Frankish monarchy began to decay in the ninth century, the canon law alone continued to show signs of life. By preserving something of the tradition and spirit of Roman law, it contributed materially to the eleventh-century revival of jurisprudence in the schools of Pavia and Bologna.

§ 16. " The study of Roman law never dies. When it seems to be dying it always returns to the texts and is born anew." [1] So it was in Provence and in northern Italy in the eleventh century, as at a later day in France and Germany. In that century the mediæval order was shaping itself into definite outline on every side. Hildebrand (pope Gregory VII) thundered the claims of papal supremacy into the ears of all Christendom; Norman rulers, gifted with a rare capacity for law and government, reared with a strong hand the fabric of political order in their dominions; Bernard at Clairvaux disciplined the pious, for the service of God and his church, under the austere rule of Benedict; Anselm and Abelard woke the slumbering intellect of the schools to new vitality. The time was ripe for lawyers, in south-eastern France, at Pavia in Lombardy, at Ravenna, once the seat of Justinian's viceroys, and, above all, at Bologna, in the school founded by Hildebrand's champion, Matilda of Tuscany, to turn away from the *Breviary* of Alaric and the mangled sources that had sufficed a more ignorant generation, and to study the *Digest* at first hand. In 1038, the emperor Conrad II had restored Roman law as the territorial law of the Roman city. In 1076, the *Digest*, which had been a dead letter for more than four centuries, was cited in a Tuscan court. A line of great juristic teachers, from Irnerius (*c.* 1100) to Azo and Accursius (*c.* 1250), made the university of Bologna the legal training ground for all Europe. [2] They set themselves first to recover the

---

[1] Pollock and Maitland, i. p. 24.

[2] Accursius' *glossa ordinaria* summed up the work of the glossators (from Irnerius onward), who as theoretic jurists studied the *Corpus* as a system. Later, the post-glossators set themselves to apply the principles to practical needs : see de Zulueta in *Legacy of Rome*, pp. 378 f.

text of Justinian's *Corpus*, then to unfold its interpretation. The fruits of their labour and teaching are manifest in many treatises of the twelfth and thirteenth centuries, such as the Provençal *Codi* (*c.* 1150), a summary of Justinian's code for the use of judges, and the *Coutume de Beauvaisis* of Philippe de Beaumanoir (*c.* 1280), which shows how legal ideas of Roman origin had been already blended with the local custom of northern France. In England, Roman doctrines were introduced from Bologna towards the close of the twelfth century by Vacarius, who founded a school of law at Oxford. But the most striking example, both of the extent and of the limits of the Roman influence in this country, is furnished by Bracton's famous treatise on the laws of England (*de legibus Angliae, c.* 1250), where the teaching of Azo of Bologna is applied with a thoroughly characteristic independence. The legislation of Norman and early Plantagenet sovereigns had evolved a large measure of order and stability out of the chaos of local custom, and Englishmen, justly proud of their established tradition, viewed with natural suspicion any attempt to impose a cosmopolitan jurisprudence on the developed structure of native law. Hence the resistance offered alike by king and nobles to the importation of Roman ideas from the schools of Italy. The church also, in England and elsewhere, was inclined to be jealous of the civil law. The same age that saw the rise of the university of Bologna gave birth also to the codification of ecclesiastical law. Gratian's *Decretum* (1139–42) became the legal text-book of the church courts. A century later (1234), pope Gregory IX embodied subsequent enactments in a complete and authoritative code of canon law.[1] Inferior in legal quality as was the canon law to the civil, these efforts in codification are proof, both of the impulse towards a scientific jurisprudence that was stirring in the papal courts, and of the growing claims of the papacy to extend its legal jurisdiction. It was the epoch of the struggle over investitures, and the rivalry of church and empire. The story of this specifically mediæval conflict lies beyond our province. It is enough to indicate that it was fought out, not only in the political area, but also on the ground of legal argument, and that both parties to the

---

[1] Gratian's *Decretum* was the first attempt to present a *Corpus* of church law. Its title was *Concordia discordantium Canonum*. Canonists commented on its text, just as the civilians of Bologna commented on the *Corpus Juris Civilis*. The collection of Gregory IX was known as the *Decretals*; it became henceforward the chief law-book of the Church. Boniface VIII and Clement V added further decretals, known respectively as the *Sext* and the *Clementines*.

controversy appealed for support to the inheritance of Roman law.

§ 17. Great as was the influence of the law of Rome on that of the mediæval peoples, it left a yet deeper mark on their moral and political ideals. Morality and law alike claim to regulate man's action as a social being; and the line of distinction between them is by no means easy to define. For the Greeks, both in their theory and in their practice, the obligations to conform to the law of the *Polis* were also moral duties. That they were not unconscious of the distinction, is evident from the question raised by their philosophers, whether the dictates of morality were founded on nature (*physis*) or on mutable convention (*nomos*).[1] But the whole tendency of Hellenic thought, as we see it in Plato and Aristotle, was rather to moralise law than to reduce morality to legal terms. The standard of conduct was conceived as good rather than as duty; the *Polis* was looked upon as the fitting sphere for a life of civic virtue, and law as the means to its achievement. In the Middle Ages, on the other hand, the governing ethical concept was that of moral law. Several grounds combined to bring about this change of orientation. For one thing, Christianity took over the Old Testament scriptures, where the Mosaic legislation is presented as covering the whole field of moral and religious obligation. The terms "law," "commandments," "statutes," as interpreted by the developed spiritual consciousness of prophets and psalmists, refer, not merely or mainly to external actions, but to the inner disposition of the heart. They are sanctioned by the authority, not of a secular sovereign, but of God himself. Such precepts, claiming divine origin and absolute validity, while retaining the title and form of law, could hardly be compared, in view of their richer spiritual import, with the laws of the Hellenic *Polis* or the *jus civile* of Rome. Again, to the Christian, with his vivid consciousness of sin and his doctrine of man's fall, the moral life inevitably assumed the form of a discipline under the stern control of law, rather than of a harmonious realisation of natural human aspirations. Thus far, perhaps, there was little risk of falling into the confusion, which has constantly obscured ethical thinking, of resolving morality into legalism and its science into jurisprudence. It was otherwise when the influence of Roman law came into play. For the Roman, moral and religious practice had always been coloured by legal formalism. If the Latin word

[1] See above, c. iv, §§ 14–16; c. v, § 15.

virtus (manliness) suggested the excellence of the citizen-soldier, the term for " duties " (*officia*) pointed to the life of the punctilious bureaucrat, spent in a ceaseless round of official functions. If the Greek strove to moralise law, the Roman legalised morality. We have seen how the great jurists of the early empire accommodated Stoic doctrine to their science. They taught that behind the civil law of Rome, behind even the common law of nations, lay the law of nature, rooted in man's constitution as a rational and, therefore, a moral being. The acceptance of this juristic tradition went far to strengthen the mediæval tendency to interpret morality under the form of law.[1] The groundwork was laid for a reconciliation between the enacted law of the land and the principles of morality, as being two different but mutually consistent expressions of reason, which was the image of the divine original, stamped at the creation upon the soul of man.[2] This *rapprochement* was facilitated by the obvious facts, that the discharge of legal obligations fell within the scope of moral duty, and that justice was recognised by mediæval thinkers as one of the cardinal moral virtues. Side by side with the triad of the theological virtues, faith, hope and charity, revealed under the Christian dispensation, and attainable only by its believers, they set prudence, fortitude, temperance and justice, which, as pagan philosophy had witnessed, were the fruit of man's rational nature, independent of special revelation.[3] The distinction is familiar to all students of Dante and of the allegorical creations of mediæval art. It is in the interpretation of justice that the relationship of morality and law is most apparent. Aristotle, in treating of

[1] The Fathers of the church appropriated these ideas of the jurists. We find them, e.g. in Augustine. An example of the influence of Roman legalism in religious thought is afforded by the history of the doctrine of the atonement. Christ's sacrifice is presented as the payment of legal satisfaction, either to the devil (Augustine's theory that God buys man from the devil by Christ's death on the cross), or to God (Anselm's view, based on Tertullian, Cyprian and other western teachers), who has been defrauded and must be repaid; since the debt is too great for man to repay, Christ offers himself and thereby satisfies the claim, receiving forgiveness from God, and (since he needs it not himself) bestowing it on man.

[2] Law of nature is, however, sometimes understood to mean the principles (e.g. to nourish and rear their offspring) implicit in the nature of *all* animals. But the view stated in the text predominates in mediæval thought (see Aquinas, *S. Th.*, II. 1. q. 95. art. 4. ad. 1ᵃᵐ; II. 2. q. 57. art. 3).

[3] The statement in the text needs amplification, in that the theological virtues, when infused by grace into the soul of the Christian, raise the natural (Aristotelian) virtues to a higher plane, so that, thus enriched, they merit the title of " infused " virtues (see Wicksteed, *Reactions*, pp. 492–3, 516–22).

this virtue as a form of moral excellence, had chiefly in mind its application to the legal practice of the Greek city-state. The Roman jurists, approaching the question from the point of view of the law, recognised that justice rested on a moral basis. They defined *jus* as " the art of the good and the equitable " (*ars boni et aequi*); and justice as " the constant and perpetual volition to assign to each man his *jus*." The Christian Fathers accepted these definitions, which were adopted both in the civil and in the canon law. Aquinas followed closely on their path. No one can stir a step in the field of mediæval thought without realising how ethical and political problems were debated on the *terrain* of jurisprudence, and solved by the aid of concepts that had their source in Roman law.[1]

§ 18. It was Aquinas, who, in the light of the reception of Aristotle and of the *Digest*, fixed the main outlines of the theory of law for the later Middle Ages. He devoted to the subject a special section of the first division of the second part of his *Summa Theologica*. A summary of his doctrine will show how deeply the conception of a law of nature had set its mark on the mediæval mind. It will show also how reflection on the principles of law opened the door to larger problems of political government. For Aquinas, the ultimate source of all law is the eternal ordinance of God (*lex aeterna*), " the very principle (*ratio*) of the government of things, existing in God as the ruler of the universe," and, as such, not other than God himself.[2] This eternal law is the time-

---

[1] Aristotle, on justice; *Eth. Nic.*, v. The jurists' definitions; *jus, Dig.*, i. 1, 1, *justice, Dig.*, i. 1, 6. Aquinas discusses justice in *S. Th.*, II. 2. qq. 57 ff.; his definition of justice is given in q. 58. art. 1, of *jus* in q. 57. art. 1 and 2, of *lex* in q. 90. art. 4. By *justitia* mediæval thinkers meant both " justice " and " righteousness." Law (*lex*) is a species of right (*jus*), viz. its written and promulgated expression. The English language, with its one word " law," enhances the difficulty, already felt by mediæval writers, of distinguishing between *jus* and *lex*.

[2] The section referred to is *S. Th.*, II. 1. qq. 90–108, forming a treatise *de legibus*. The scheme is as follows :—

A. Introductory (qq. 90–2).
B. The several kinds of law :

lex æterna (q. 93)

lex divina	lex naturalis
(q. 91. art. 4, qq. 98–108)	(q. 91. art. 2, q. 94)

lex vetus (O.T.)	lex nova (N.T.)	lex humana
(qq. 98–105)	(qq. 106–8)	= (i) jus commune gentium (q. 95)
		(ii) jus civile (lex positiva)
		(q. 91. art. 3)
		(qq. 95–7)

less judgement of the divine reason, made binding by the divine will, known as it is by the blessed in paradise, and by us, through the reflections that flow from it.[1] These reflections are (i) God's revealed law as declared in the Old and the New Testaments (*lex divina*), and (ii) the law of nature (*lex naturalis*), "the participation of the rational creature in the eternal law," consisting of principles of action self-evident, infallible, universal and unalterable, promulgated by God, for "God instilled it into man's mind so as to be known by him naturally."[2] From natural law in turn is derived positive man-made law (*lex humana*), enacted by human will and resting for its basis on a social compact. "A thing is made just in two ways; in one way by the very nature of the thing, and this is called *jus naturale*; in another, by a certain compact (*condictum*) among men, and this is called *jus positivum*."[3] Human or positive law comprises (*a*) the *jus gentium*, closely akin to natural law and deriving therefrom a portion of its cogency, e.g., the prohibition of murder, which is deducible from the precept of nature to do no evil to any; and (*b*) the *jus civile*, which, though derived also from natural law, involves local and temporal determinations, and draws its cogency from human enactment, e.g., that a given crime should be punished in a particular way. The end of this positive law is " the temporal tranquillity of the state," and its validity depends on four conditions : It must trace its derivation to natural law, must be ordained for the common good of the state, must be framed by the person in whose hand is the government of the community, and must serve as a directive rule for human acts of justice, whereas divine and natural law are regulative of all human actions whatsoever.

§ 19. This distinction of natural and positive law carried with it corollaries of the utmost importance for political theory.

[1] *S. Th.*, II. 1. q. 91. art. 1, q. 93. art. 2.
[2] On the precepts, see q. 94. art. 2. In addition, Aquinas mentions secondary and variable dictates of natural law, such as observance of contracts and the institution of private property, added by human reason in conformity with the immutable primary precepts. The problem of property had been urgent since the days of the Roman jurists, and pressed heavily on the Christian Fathers. In the state of nature, all things were common ; yet private property was a fact, and seemed essential to social order. The jurists generally referred it to the *jus gentium* as distinct from *jus naturae* : the Fathers (e.g., Augustine) explained it as due to man's sin, but as a necessary remedy for the consequences of the Fall. But the doctrine of natural law, that all men had a right to the necessaries of life, was unimpaired ; Aquinas even held that it was lawful, in certain cases, to take a rich man's goods and give them to the poor. The canonists taught that a man possessed wealth only subject to the condition of right use. [3] *Positivum*, i.e., posited, enacted by human will.

The maxim of Augustine, that an unjust law was no law at all, was universally accepted in the Middle Ages. Positive law, though promulgated by pope or emperor, had no validity, if it were inconsistent with the law of nature. A tyrant's laws are no true laws; according to Aquinas, obedience to them is not obligatory " in the court of conscience," save in so far as transgression would give rise to scandal or disorder.[1] Obviously such views offered wide latitude for interpretation. A fortiori, a law that contradicts lex divina had no claim upon the subject under any circumstances. No one in the Middle Ages dreamed of questioning the doctrine that God must be obeyed rather than man. In the second place it followed that positive law was a mutable instrument of government, dependent for its original enactment, and for its interpretation, on the ruling authority.[2] The prince in a monarchical state was, like Aristotle's ideal ruler, a lex animata, a living fount of positive law; where, as in a republic, the people exercise sovereignty, the executive magistrate was subject to the popularly enacted law. Thus the texts of the Roman Digest : " the will of the prince has the force of law "; " the prince holds all law (jura) in his heart "; " the prince is free from the bonds of the laws," could be reconciled with the mediæval system of society, though always subject to the reservation that the laws in question were positive human law. Here, again, there was room for diversity of interpretation. Aquinas himself favoured a form of constitution which, like Aristotle's " polity," united the characteristics of monarchy, aristocracy and democracy. The prince should be elected by the people, and assisted by a nobility based on the possession of eminent virtue.[3] We can thus trace the lines on which the political thinkers of the Middle Ages solved the problem of the relation between law and the state. The conviction that the state derived its rightful authority from law, and that its mission was to realise the reign of law, was implanted deep in the Germanic mind. The doctrine diametrically opposed to this, and known both to

---

[1] See q. 93. art. 3, ad 2[am], q. 95. art. 1, 2, 4; II 2. q. 57, art. 2. ad 2[am]; de regimine principis, I. cc. 3–11; Dante, de Monarchia, ii. 5. It was open to reformers to appeal against the actual state to the ideal state in which these requirements would be satisfied; and the appeal was sanctioned, not only by morality, but by law.

[2] II. 2. q. 60. art. 6; II. 1. q. 90. art. 3.

[3] II. 1. q. 105. art. 1. The prince should be subject to the vis directiva (guiding force) and be entrusted with the vis coactiva (coercive force) of human law (q. 96. art. 5. ad 2[am]). That the executive ruler should take counsel, was a principle as firmly rooted in Teutonic, as in Roman republican, custom.

Hellenic and to modern thought, that might is right, and that the state is wholly independent of ethical restraint, found no adherents, even among the most ardent champions of monarchical power throughout the Middle Ages. The ever present danger of anarchy and private war invested law with a halo of ideal attributes. It was reverenced as the immediate utterance of God, speaking to the princes and peoples of the earth. When the theory that the state was above all controls of morality or natural law was asserted by Machiavelli in the sixteenth century, it seemed a monstrous subversion of ethical and religious principle. But a difficulty of another kind had arisen, three centuries earlier, when mediæval theory was first confronted with the political doctrines of the Greek philosophers. We have seen how Plato and Aristotle taught that the state, as existing by nature, was superior to law, which served as the instrument of its ethical function. Here lay the problem : how was the Germanic conviction that the state was subordinate to law, to be reconciled with the classical tradition that law was subordinate to the state ? A solution was reached by aid of the distinction between law of nature and positive law. While the state and its ruler derived their right from the higher authority of natural or, *a fortiori*, of divine, law and were consequently subject to ethical obligations ; positive law, representing the variable applications of natural law to particular circumstances of time and place, was the creation of, and dependent upon, the state. Thus the outcome of mediæval theory was to broaden the concept of law so as to include within its scope the moral foundations and ideal purpose of political society.

§ 20. The fusion of native Germanic ideas with the legacy of Greece and Rome is further exemplified in the mediæval doctrines of monarchy, and of the derivation of sovereignty from the public will.[1] The Teutonic peoples showed an instinctive preference for monarchical government. Their belief in its inherent rightfulness was strengthened, not merely by the fact that, throughout the Middle Ages, a strong ruler was the only

---

[1] The principles (a) that law, rooted in the custom of the community, is supreme, and (b) that recognition by the community was requisite for each successor to the kingship, were imbedded in the Teutonic tradition. Roman jurists had laid down that the *original source* of all political authority lay with the Roman people ; Teutonic societies regarded the consent of the people as an *actually existing* condition of all rightful rule. So, again, the law in Teutonic societies was regarded as that of the community, not as that of the king ; whereas, on the Roman doctrine, the emperor was the supreme legislative authority. See Carlyle, *Mediæval Political Theory in the West*, vol. iii. Introduction.

P

effective safeguard against anarchy and injustice, but also by political and legal theories. The character of these may best be studied in the first book of Dante's treatise on Monarchy (de Monarchia). He marshals both speculative and practical arguments in support of the claims of monarchical government, and, particularly, of the Holy Roman empire as a universal monarchy, embracing by right the entire human race.[1] The nerve of his metaphysical argument was the conception of the created universe as a whole composed of parts, such as the human species, subordinate forms of association (kingdoms, provinces, civic communities and households), and individual men; each of which parts was in its turn a whole, possessing a relative independence, and a specific end or good, in definite subordination to the end or good of the whole universe. Thus he reflected the effort of mediæval thought to do full justice, alike to the claims of the universal whole, emphasised by the Hellenic tradition, and to those of the individual, recognised as of intrinsic value both by the Germanic spirit and by the teaching of Christianity. The created universe in its entirety formed a commonwealth, ruled by God as king; and human society should, by right, mirror the constitution of the macrocosm of which it was a member. Aristotle, too, had taught that unity of end carried with it unity of direction (ordinatio ad unum). Again, scripture declared that man was created in God's image; and the human race could only realise this divine intention if it possessed unity, which it does most perfectly when united under the rule of one. That unity was the root of good, while evil consisted in forsaking unity for multiplicity, was a cardinal tenet of mediæval (as of Neo-Platonic) metaphysics; a concordant unity of human wills is, therefore, essential to a good disposition of human society, and this concord is best secured under a single governing will.[2]

[1] See, especially, de Mon., i. cc. 5–8, 15.

[2] It is noteworthy that neither Dante, the originator of this last argument, nor any other thinker attained to the conception of a real unification of the wills of individual members in a group-will, and that when the doctrine of corporate personality was introduced into juristic theory by the great master of canon law, pope Innocent IV (Sinibald Fieschi, pope 1243–54), it was regarded as a legal fiction (persona ficta). The mediæval conviction of the exclusive reality of individual personality was so deep-rooted that it proved an insuperable obstacle to the growth of an adequate legal theory of groups and corporations. The influence of Roman law, which furnished the concept of societas, i.e., an artificial partnership of individuals, tended in the same direction. It was not till well on in the eighteenth century that Rousseau, in his doctrine of the general will (volonté générale), lighted on the thought which was needed to overcome the individualist tradition of man's relation to society (see Maitland's Introduction to Gierke).

To these arguments Dante added others of an ethical character, e.g., that justice and liberty are best secured under a monarchical government, and that a universal monarchy alone can serve as an effective super-national tribunal.[1] Finally, he supports his conclusion by adducing the fact of history, that God sent his Son into the world at a moment when, for the first time since man's fall, it reposed in peace under the universal sovereignty of Augustus.[2] Thus we see how, for Dante, the political theory of Aristotle, the tradition of Roman history and law, and the world-outlook of the Christian religion, converged to strengthen and expand the native Germanic partiality for monarchical rule. It follows that all monarchy, whether ecclesiastical or temporal, is of divine right; for all lordship is from God (*omne dominium est a Deo*).[3] It follows also, and here reflective theory is in close harmony with Germanic tradition, that all monarchy, as a *ministerium a Deo commissum*, is " office," i.e., it involves duties as well as rights.[4] The monarch, says Aquinas, is " a public person " ruling " for the common good." His function is three-fold : to establish the good life in the community, to preserve it in being when established, and to promote its progress to a still higher plane.[5] Hence the monarch's power is necessarily limited by the duties of his office. Neither pope nor kaiser can for a moment claim that *L'église* or *l'état, c'est moi*. His private and his public personalities are manifestly distinct. Commands issued *ultra vires* are null and void. He is the representative of his people, bearing their person, as John of Salisbury puts it ; his dignity is inalienable, for he did not confer it on himself, and therefore cannot of himself dispose of it.[6] " The authority of the prince is his only for use, for no prince can create his own authority." [7] We are here confronted by the second of the

---

[1] *de Mon.*, i. cc. 10–14.   [2] *Ibid.*, i. c. 16.

[3] The doctrine that secular princes ruled by divine right commended itself to the early church, as supported both by the New Testament, and by the Jewish tradition of the king as the Lord's anointed. See Luke xx. 25, John xix. 11, Rom. xiii. 1–7, 1 Pet. ii. 13–17 ; and also 2 Sam. i. 16 and v. 3. In the later Middle Ages, it became the watchword of the imperialists, who maintained that the secular ruler held his authority directly from God, not indirectly through the pope (see *de Mon.*, iii).

[4] The phrase quoted is as old as the ninth century. Thus the doctrine of divine right implied that the monarch's power was conditional on its proper exercise.

[5] *de Mon.*, i. c. 15. See also the quotations from mediæval writers in Poole, *Illustrations*, pp. 232, 234–5.

[6] *Universitatis subiectorum personam gerit.* Cf. Aquinas, *S. Th.*, II. 1. q. 90. art. 3. ad 2[am] and Dante, Par. xii. 89–90 for the distinction between the pope's private personality and his papal office. Dante does not hesitate to place popes in hell.   [7] *de Mon.*, iii. c. 7.

afore-mentioned convictions of mediæval political theory, that
of the derivation of sovereignty from the popular will.

§ 21. Despite this bias towards monarchical government,
the theory of the sovereignty of the people was germinating in
the mediæval mind. It was also part of the tradition of the
Germanic races. Moreover, the Christian church had accepted
from Augustine, that in man's pristine state of nature there
prevailed freedom from coercive authority, and that lordship
and servitude were reciprocal consequences of the Fall. " God
willed not that the rational creature made in his image should
have lordship save over irrational creatures. . . . The condition of servitude is rightly understood as imposed on man
as sinner." [1] With the rediscovery of Aristotle, a new and a
very different theory was disclosed to the thinkers of the thirteenth century. Political society, with its forms of organisation and government was rooted, not in sin, but in the original
sociality of human nature. Aquinas had no hesitation in accepting the Hellenic tradition. Had man continued in the state of
innocence, he would have developed, not indeed *dominium
servile*, but *dominium politicum*. The garden of Eden, in short,
would have been administered by a constitutional monarchy.
Men would not have been equal, for there would have been
grades of virtue and of knowledge.[2] Lordship and social preference are creations of the law of nations (*jus gentium*), and
rest on reason; though the state, like the visible church, is
relative to a scene of probation, and has no significance in the
life beyond the grave. How then did the state come into being ?
The answer to this question, dating from the time of the quarrel
over investitures in the eleventh century, was, that it originated
in a contract, by which the people, the ultimate sovereign,
handed over their rights and powers to a ruler, and thereby
instituted a civil society (*societas*).[3] This term, whose individualist implication we have already noted, had been applied
to the organised community by Cicero. Roman law taught that

[1] Aug., *de Civ. Dei*, xix. c. 15. See Gierke, *note* 16. Gregory VII
(eleventh century) and John of Salisbury (twelfth century) voice this view.
It finds expression later in Milton's lines on Nimrod, *Paradise Lost*, xii., init.
Servitude and coercive jurisdiction were, however, justified like private
property, as remedial instruments, incidental to man's altered circumstances after the Fall. As such, they were regarded as sanctioned by the
divine will. Thus a door was left open for the reception of the Aristotelian
tradition.

[2] *S. Th.*, I. q. 96. art. 3 and 4.

[3] So John of Salisbury and Aquinas. Appeal was made to Augustine
and to 2 Sam. v. 3.

by the *jus gentium* a free people could institute a superior, and that in actual fact the powers of the Roman emperor had been thus conferred by a single statute.[1] It is obvious that this doctrine of a social contract, like others that we have mentioned, lent itself to a wide diversity of interpretation. The champions of autocracy could stretch the terms of the surrender in the interest of the monarch, while the advocates of popular rights could insist on the inherent sovereignty of the people, and erect a theory of republicanism on the maxim that "the people is greater than the prince" (*populus major principe*). This last was the direction followed by two notable political thinkers of the later Middle Ages, Marsilius of Padua (*Defensor Pacis*, 1324–26), and Cardinal Nicolas of Cues (1401–64).[2] Aquinas, as we have seen, preferred to steer a middle course. Here, as elsewhere, he displayed the rare sobriety of his judgement, and his consummate skill in blending the Græco-Roman legacy with the spirit of mediæval life. It is easy, but scarcely profitable, to criticise the theory of the social contract as abstract and unhistorical. It would, indeed, be difficult to find a more fitting formula to express the facts of feudal society. That society was characterised by the assimilation of public to private law. The king ruled over the "estates" of the realm, with a title analogous to that of any feudal proprietor. The feudal tie, as illustrated, for example, by the coronation oath, was contractual in its nature, and bound ruler and ruled by reciprocal obligations of protection and obedience.[3] Above all, the contract theory,

[1] The *lex regia*, of which we hear in the third century and in Justinian's *Corpus*. It was erroneously believed that Augustus had received his power in this way.

[2] Marsilius taught the absorption of church in state. A striking anticipation of his position, however, is found in the *Tractatus Eboracensis*, written by a canon of York under Henry II. Marsilius is a republican : the right of legislation is vested inalienably in the people, acting as a primary assembly, or through elected representatives. The ruler is appointed, and can be deposed, by the people, and his authority is always subordinate to the popular will. Nicolas of Cues, in his *de Concordantiâ Catholicâ*, written during the Conciliar movement, gave noble expression to the mediæval ideal of a perfect harmony between the order of the universe and that of human society; temporal and ecclesiastical authorities are independent, but harmonious, instruments; government rests on popular sovereignty, and the elective and representative principles are championed, both in church and in state. The new spirit of nationalism is clearly recognised. This great work best illustrates the attempt to unite old and new ideas, at the close of the mediæval period.

[3] See Figgis, *From Gerson to Grotius*, pp. 10 ff., 129 ff. The idea of civil society as based upon contract was distinctively mediæval, and originated probably out of the promises to obey the law and govern justly, made by the king on his accession.

resting, as it did, on that of natural law, kept alive, through the Middle Ages, the faith that government was founded on right, and not on violence, and that above and beyond the ruler lay the binding dictates of ideal justice. If the doctrine of divine right served to justify the secular state in its struggle against ecclesiastical domination, that of the social contract became the watchword of popular resistance to the growth of arbitrary despotism.

§ 22. Mediæval theory, as we have indicated, developed in close conjunction with mediæval practice; and its bearings can hardly be appreciated without a study of the historical movements of the time, such as the rivalry of papacy and empire, the effort to substitute conciliar government in the church for papal absolutism, and the rise, as the fruit of a growing national consciousness, of the independent kingdoms of modern Europe. But the work of the mediæval thinkers possessed significance not only for contemporaries, but for aftertime. They achieved a synthesis, and on a grand scale; in theoretical science, between metaphysics and theology; in practical science, between the claims of human personality and those of the larger systems within which man's life is lived. The solutions that they offered were not final; but they held their ground for generations, and when they fell, the theories that replaced them were their own offspring. The structure of modern ethical and political thought, from the seventeenth to the nineteenth century, was built, in the main, of stones hewn in the mediæval quarries. The doctrines of a state of nature, of natural law, of the social contract, and of the rights of man, are still alive in political theory.[1] They loom large not merely in the philosophy of the eighteenth-century enlightenment, but in the manifestos of political reformers, in the American Declaration of Independence, and in the debates of the French revolutionary assemblies. If Bentham and his disciples scorned these ideas as abstract jargon, and substituted the standard of utility for that of right, they still inherited the individualist implications of the rejected doctrine.[2] Lord Acton knew what

---

[1] As is evidenced by R. G. Collingwood's *New Leviathan*. On the application of the conception of law of nature by the founders of international law in the seventeenth century, and on their obligations to Roman law generally, see Maine, *Ancient Law*, c. iv.

[2] These implications still harass our political thinking, even when we are striving our hardest to be quit of them, thwarting the recognition of a true theory of group-personality in our reflections on government and law. They were fortified by the illegitimate intrusion, in the seventeenth century, of the concepts of mechanical physics into the domain of political and moral science.

he meant when he said, that not the devil, but St. Thomas Aquinas, was "the first Whig." Modern constitutionalism is the child of the Middle Ages. Its origin lies farther back than the times of Hobbes and Locke, in the days when Aquinas and his successors strove, with a broader speculative outlook, to base the institution of civil society on natural law, and to harmonise the ingrained individualism of the Teutonic peoples with the metaphysical legacy of Greece and the juristic legacy of Rome.

IV. THE RENAISSANCE (§§ 23–28).

§ 23. The power of ancient culture to leaven and shape civilization is seen vividly in the effects of the rediscovery of Greek learning in the age of the Renaissance.

If we pass in thought from the fourteenth century to the seventeenth, from the Europe of the Hundred Years' War to the Europe of Richelieu, and from the speculations of the later schoolmen to those of Galileo, Bacon and Descartes, we seem to be moving in a different world. The difference is that between mediæval and modern civilization. The velocity with which one phase of history succeeds another is not uniform, and, in these intervening centuries, change had followed change with astonishing swiftness. A new order was brought to birth, both of society and of thought. By 1600, the institutions—economic, political and religious—which symbolised the hard-won stability of mediæval society, were everywhere falling into decay. Feudalism lingered as an effete survival, or as a grotesque, or romantic, memory; the Catholic church was viewed with hatred and horror by millions in northern Christendom; while the Catholic empire had lost all relics of supernational sovereignty, and scarcely commanded even a titular respect. In their stead were arising commercial and industrial communities, with hands outstretched to grasp the prize of a world-trade; Protestant churches with diverse creeds and forms of government; national states, powerful, mutually suspicious and jealous of their independence.

The nation-state, the type of political organisation characteristic of modern Europe, arose in the sixteenth century in Spain, France and Tudor England, contemporaneously with the gradual break-down of mediæval universalism. Its watchword was "sovereignty," with its twofold implication of complete independence as against all states outside its borders, and internally of the institution of a clearly recognisable authority, normally an individual prince supreme alike over subordinate corporations and individual citizens, in whose hands lay the sole right of making and enforcing law. It arose as the original expression in the field of political government of the natural growth of self-consciousness in European peoples which was also reflected in the rise, heralded, e.g., by Dante, of national languages and literature in place of Latin, and in the revolt against the papal jurisdiction in the countries which embraced the Reformation. This new-born national consciousness could not rest satisfied with political structures that were at best imitations of historic models. Mediæval ideas of world-unity (e.g., the conception of the Holy Roman Empire) took shape, consciously or unconsciously, under the influence of the tradition of the world-empire of ancient Rome. So the city-states that arose in Italy and Flanders in the interest of economic freedom were but tame republications of the old Hellenic *Polis*. To-day, after more than three centuries, when we are reaping a hundred-fold this baneful harvest of national separatism, the glory has departed from the nation-states. The present generation is witnessing the evolution, under pressure of political, economic and moral forces, of a new type of social structure. By an impulse as natural as that which in the sixteenth century led to the establishment of nation-states, the peoples of the civilized world are groping their way towards the formation, on the one hand, of federal states (the British Commonwealth, the American Union, the union of Soviet republics, as well as smaller confederations like Switzerland), and, on the other, of a regulative super-national authority, such as would be represented by a fully effective league of nations.[1]

In the field of thought, the change was yet more startling. Moral and political obligations were grounded no longer on a universal scheme of divine providence, but on the needs and mutual relationships of human individuals. The authority of Aristotle and of the doctors of the church had yielded place to the claim of private judgement. Above all, intellectual interest was centred on the study of physical fact, and the discovery of laws of nature. The scientific spirit, dormant since the fall of Hellenism, had awoken to life in the mind of western Europe, which had grown to intellectual manhood during the long minority of the Middle Ages. Men were asking themselves new questions, to which the mediæval tradition gave no answer. Its ideals and

[1] See below, Appendix I, p. 469.

methods of knowledge were as alien to the intellectual temper
of the sixteenth century, as the ardour of knight-errantry to the
readers of *Don Quixote.* The children mocked at the aspirations which had stirred their fathers to heroic ventures. The
contrast between the mediæval spirit and that of the Renaissance lay in this, that the one was absorbed in the scheme of
divine providence and man's eternal destiny, the other, in his
life on an earth, recognised as a scene of intrinsic value, and
pronounced, as by God on the creation morning, a thing that
was very good. The other-worldliness of the Middle Ages had
yielded place to the desire to know man in his relation to nature,
and nature in its relation to man. It was a sign of the times
that, whereas mediæval learning had been the monopoly of
monks and clergy, and the voice of the layman found expression
only in poetry and art, the laity now claimed the right to think.[1]
Equally significant is the contrast in the subject-matter of
literature. We have only to turn from Dante to the great
humanists of the sixteenth century, Rabelais, Montaigne, Cer-
vantes and Shakespeare, to appreciate the magnitude of the
revolution. Shakespeare's interest is almost wholly absorbed
in human life, as enacted amid its actual surroundings; and,
in portraying men's intellectual perplexities and moral crises,
he gives scarcely a thought to God or to the life to come.[2] By
the sixteenth century, humanism was in the ascendant; and
the spirit of secularism was dominant, explicitly in men's thought,
and instinctively in their practice. The age of Reason had begun.

§ 24. It is customary to speak of this epoch as the Renaissance, marking thereby, as its distinctive feature, the rebirth of
classical culture in western Europe. We are told in all the
history books how, in the dark hour when the Turks were closing round Constantinople, the exodus of Greek teachers from
the East disclosed the secrets of the Hellenic genius to the
wondering gaze of the western world. Broadly, indeed, this is
the truth; the fifteenth century saw a wide extension of men's
knowledge of antiquity, and the rediscovery of treasures that

---

[1] See C. S. Lewis, *The Allegory of Love.*

[2] Such references, e.g., as are to be found in *Hamlet,* in his famous
soliloquy, or in the words

> " There's a divinity that shapes our ends,
>   Rough-hew them how we will,"

might in this respect at least have been uttered by a poet of antiquity. See
also Webb, *History of Philosophy* (Home University Library), p. 76, for
references to *Measure for Measure* and *Much Ado about Nothing.*

had lain buried for a thousand years. But we must not forget that classical culture had been already active and fruitful far back in the Middle Ages. From the late eighth century onwards, the story of Western civilization is a progressive anticipation of the Renaissance. Michelet, in a famous passage of his history, recalls how the Sibyl thrice offered her treasures to the Etruscan lord of early Rome.[1] The analogy is in one point misleading; for Tarquin twice rejected the proffered gift, whereas the mediæval thinkers from the first clutched eagerly at all they could get, and strained their youthful energy to the full in the use of it. The few mediæval scholars who knew Greek had before them but scattered fragments of the literature. They were neither able nor curious to determine the text; they were concerned exclusively with the interpretation, with what Aristotle's writings meant to them, rather than with what they meant to Aristotle.[2] The fifteenth and following centuries saw the rediscovery of manuscripts long consigned to oblivion, and the restoration on this basis of the original text of the Greek masters. Above all, there was a rapid spread of the study of the Greek language in the universities and schools. Thus the Renaissance drew its inspiration direct from classical antiquity.[3] Had this been all, however, it would hardly have figured as an epoch in the history of civilization. The rediscovery of Hellenic culture evoked a deeper response in the mind of western Europe. Its significance lay, not so much in the realisation of the positive achievement in science and philosophy, embodied in Greek literature, far as this achievement stretched beyond the horizon envisaged by the Middle Ages. Nor did it lie merely in the revelation of beauty in art and poetry, that fixed the gaze of painters and poets on the deathless masterpieces of the Hellenic genius. The source of inspiration was rather the spirit that informed the life and thought of ancient Greece, the habit of free enquiry, the confidence in reason, the untiring energy of thought and action,

[1] *Histoire de France*, Introduction to the volume on *The Renaissance* (1855).

[2] This statement must be read with reservations. Aquinas, for instance, had laboured, with the aid of William of Moerbeke, to get at the true text of Aristotle. But the obstacles were insuperable. Even if a sufficient number of manuscripts had been available, the critical faculty was lacking; and, in the days before printing, the permanence of a scholar's labours rested on the fate of a single copy of his work. There was not much inducement to spend time and energy on the production of a sound text.

[3] The home of the Renaissance was Italy, where the new spirit was alive in the first half of the fifteenth century. It spread north of the Alps after 1450, encountering more active resistance in the northern universities, the strongholds of mediæval philosophy in its great days.

and the delight in the actual world, present before man's eye as a field for practical experiment, æsthetic creation and reasoned knowledge. This was the key that unlocked to the peoples of the modern world the gate of their earthly paradise.

§ 25. They were swift to reap the fruits of their discovery. Familiar as we are at the present day with the advance of science, we read with amazement of the marvellous achievements that mark the golden age of the Renaissance. If we take the brief period of little more than seventy years, the span of a single human life, between the fall of Constantinople in 1453 and the sack of Rome by the Germans in 1527, we find that within it were laid the foundations of scientific knowledge for the five succeeding centuries. (a) The physical surface of the globe was first explored. Daring seamen, guided by scientific research and trained in the new learning at the school founded by Prince Henry of Portugal (" the Navigator " : 1394–1460), sailed along the Atlantic coast of Africa, rounded the Cape (1486–9) and laid open to the Portuguese the wealth of the Indies. As the fruit of the same scientific impulse, united with the desire of the Spanish sovereigns for commercial expansion, Columbus in 1492 reached the New World.[1] Thirty years later Magellan's expedition (1519–22) circumnavigated the globe. The issues of these great voyages and of numberless others in the same age were evident in the revolution that rapidly came about in the fields of commerce and of empire.[2] In a word, civilization, hitherto centred in the Mediterranean, became, in an ever-increasing degree, oceanic. (b) A vaster transformation of men's outlook upon nature was effected when the place of the earth in the solar system was determined by Copernicus in 1543. For more than a thousand years the learned as well as the vulgar had accepted the Ptolemaic hypothesis, with the

[1] The chief instrument of these discoveries was, of course, the mariner's compass, which had been in use in the Mediterranean since the thirteenth century. The art of cartography, which was rapidly perfected in this age, was an invaluable requisite.

[2] The influx of precious metals altered the value of money and the scale of prices; the imported products of the East led to changes in dress, food and the style of life among the well-to-do classes. It has been remarked (by Mr. C. S. Lewis) that the interest of the *Merchant of Venice* is focussed on the precious metals. The leading maritime nations eagerly competed for access to and control of the Asiatic markets; and the northern states, France, Holland and England, contended for sea-power, first against Portugal and Spain, then amongst themselves. The struggle lasted till the close of the Napoleonic war in 1815. The foundations both of British commerce with India and the Far East, and of British colonies in the New World, were laid within a century of the voyages of da Gama and Columbus.

428   THE LEGACY OF THE ANCIENT WORLD

earth as the centre of the universe. We still speak, in terms of
that hypothesis, of the rising and setting of the sun. The
Copernican theory of the daily rotation of the earth, and of
its revolution and that of the other planets round the sun, was
decisively confirmed by Galileo (1564–1642), with the aid of
the new invention of the telescope. It was no longer possible
to accept the Aristotelian distinction between the unchanging
heavens and a mutable sub-lunary world. Galileo and Descartes
(1596–1650) together called mathematical physics into being,
swinging free from the mediæval doctrine of spiritual forces, and
interpreting physical nature, organic and inorganic, animate
and inanimate, exclusively in terms of matter and motion. We
cannot wonder that conservative authority suffered a rude shock,
and fought stubbornly against the new ideas. In 1600, Giordano
Bruno, a fervent admirer of Copernicus, was burnt at Rome;
in 1633 Galileo was forced by the Inquisition to retract his views
on the motion of the earth.[1] The expansion of man's view
of the universe to include worlds beyond worlds in unbounded
space, the relegation of the earth, his habitation, to an insignificant and transitory position within one of these numberless
systems, and the explanation of nature in terms that seemed
to exclude any reference to purpose or freedom, struck at the
roots of long-cherished convictions as to his spiritual worth
and destiny. So indeed it must have appeared; though the
thinker who of all others in that age most vigorously vindicated physical science from metaphysical or theological intrusion, and who saw even in living organisms nothing but the
mechanism of matter in motion, was also the first of modern
philosophers to proclaim the independent sovereignty of mind,
and to base all knowledge of the external world on man's immediate consciousness of his existence as a thinking being.[2]
(c) The sixteenth century witnessed the rebirth, not only of
astronomy and physics, but also of the biological sciences.
The Renaissance, in Michelet's phrase, bore fruit alike in the
rediscovery of the world, and in the rediscovery of man. The

[1] The tale that he muttered the words " *e pur si muove* " (" all the same
it does move ") as he rose from his knees is legendary; yet the thought was
doubtless in his mind. In 1624 the *Parlement* of Paris decreed the death
penalty for anyone who advanced opinions contrary to those of Aristotle.

[2] Descartes, for whom the *cogito, ergo sum* (I think, therefore I am)
was the most certain of all truths. The dethronement of man's planet
from its central seat in the physical universe by the heliocentric theory was
accompanied by an extreme anthropocentric doctrine in metaphysics (see
the closing sentences of this section).

anatomical researches of Vesalius (1514–64) formed the groundwork that led, in the succeeding century, to Harvey's discovery
of the circulation of the blood.[1] Descartes built on Harvey's
work, when he strove to explain the facts of psychical life in
terms of physiological process, and to trace the links that con-
nect the physical stimulus, through the sense organs and the
nervous system, with the brain, and thus give rise to mental
feelings and sensations. For the first time the problem of the
relation of mind and body was formulated in scientific terms.
The revolution thus effected in men's view of physical nature
and organic life extended also (d) to the field of their moral,
intellectual and social interests. The new spirit was active in
reshaping the structure of religious belief, of philosophy and of
political government. The study of the ancient languages and
literature, the unfettered exercise of criticism on authorities
and documents, struck at the credentials of the existing ecclesiastical order. The scriptures were examined in the original
Hebrew and Greek. We have noted that, whereas in the Middle
Ages the study of the text had been subordinated to symbolic
and allegorical interpretation, interpretation was now grounded
upon knowledge of the text. The invention of printing (c. 1455)
was here of decisive importance. Early in the sixteenth century
the Spanish cardinal Ximenes directed the preparation of a
polyglot edition of the Bible in Hebrew, Greek and Latin (published 1522).[2] Above all, a reading public came into being outside the bounds of the university, the monastery and the church.
The appeal to the judgement of the individual layman substituted a new criterion for the disciplinary authorities which had
guided the thought of the Middle Ages. Everywhere, in the
closing years of the fifteenth and early years of the sixteenth
century, there arose a humanistic revival, resting on the classics
of Israel, Greece and Rome; and an individualist revolt, which
found utterance first in religion and later in philosophy. These

---

[1] Vesalius was a Fleming, who studied at Paris and migrated to Italy,
where anatomical researches were most freely practised. He was condemned, later, by the Spanish Inquisition for dissecting the body of a
grandee, and, despite Philip II's patronage, forced on a pilgrimage to
Jerusalem; he died on the return journey. Fabricius ab Aquapendente
(1537–1619) had founded modern embryology under inspiration from
Aristotle. Hervey (1578–1657), building on Fabricius' work, commented
on Aristotle's treatise on *The Generation of Animals* (1651). He rested
his enquiries on Herophilus (c. 300. B.C.), as did Vesalius on Galen and
Sydenham on Hippocrates. In 1532, Rabelais edited the first Greek text of
Hippocrates' *Aphorisms*. See Singer in *The Legacy of Greece*.
[2] See Allen, *Age of Erasmus*, pp. 259 ff.

movements co-operated with the spirit of German nationalism to bring about the Reformation. Moreover, political loyalties were still, as in the Middle Ages, inextricably interwoven with those of religion; cleavage and reconstruction in the one involved cleavage and reconstruction in the other. The cosmopolitan ideal that had hovered before the mind of mediæval Europe had broken down under the pressure of national aspirations. We have only to read the history of the Tudor monarchy to see how the ambition of strong sovereigns evoked a popular response. This new spirit of nationalism found expression in the demand for national churches, in the rise of national litera-tures and in political speculations, such as those of Machiavelli in Italy, and of Hobbes in the England of the Puritan revolu-tion. " Reason of state," to the exclusion of ethical control, was frankly proclaimed as the criterion of policy and govern-ment. German Lutheranism pinned itself to the maxim that the religion of the prince determined the religion of the people.[1] Finally, the appeal to private judgement, that had been the watchword of the Reformation, became in the following century the foundation-stone of metaphysics. Within the narrow circle of Protestant theology, the principle of rationalism found but negative and restricted expression.[2] It came by its own for the first time in the " I think, therefore I am " of Descartes. It reigned over the thought of western Europe till the close of the eighteenth century.[3]

[1] The Lutherans subordinated church to state; and the Tudor monarchs secured the same result in England. Henry VIII, in Stubbs' phrase, was determined to be " the pope, the whole pope, and something more than the pope "; Elizabeth, by Act of Parliament, was recognised as " over all causes, as well ecclesiastical as temporal, throughout her domin-ions supreme." The Calvinist churches, on the other hand, stood for the distinction of church and state as two societies, of which the former was wholly independent of the latter (save, of course, where the absorption of the state in the church, as a single theocratic society, was possible, as at Geneva and in certain New England colonies).

[2] The Reformation churches were by no means partial to intellectual liberty. Calvinism, the least tolerant form of Protestantism, gave rise to political freedom (as is illustrated by the history of Geneva, Scotland, New England), but indirectly; for within the congregation, social distinctions had no place. All alike were sinners in the sight of God, and those who were predestined to salvation owed it to God's free grace, and to no human merit. Democratic equality in religion was bound, sooner or later, to find applica-tion in politics.

[3] The appeal of Descartes and his successors was to the *reason* in the individual thinker. For reason, though part of the nature of the individual is not his private monopoly, but the source of a knowledge valid for all rational minds. Truth implies a common standard, independent of particular tastes or wants. " Private judgement " is strictly a con-tradiction in terms; if it be " judgement," it is not merely mine, but claims universal validity as truth.

§ 26. Such was the potency of thought to transform man's
outlook upon life, and, by generating knowledge, to inaugurate
a new era of civilization. The Renaissance was the rebirth of
science, and, in naming science, we name the modern world.[1]
We need not wonder, then, that the champions of the new
movement were keenly conscious of the breach with the past,
or that they condemned, over-hastily and often without a hearing, the entire structure of mediæval learning. These bold
fighters came to destroy as well as to create. John Wessel,
one of the pioneers of educational reform in the latter half of
the fifteenth century, having learnt in Greece itself to read
Aristotle in the original, stung the Dominicans into fury by
his abuse of Aquinas. "Was Thomas a doctor?" he asked;
"so am I." "Thomas scarcely knew Latin, and that was his
only tongue; I have a fair knowledge of the three languages.
Thomas saw Aristotle only as a phantom; I have read him
in Greece in his own words."[2] They were on stronger ground
who demanded a new discipline of method to replace the formal
logic of the schools. That instrument had indeed sunk into
decrepitude; the life had well-nigh vanished from the great
Aristotelian tradition, and the rattle of dry bones echoed throughout the land. Even had it preserved its vigour, the scholastic
logic could hardly have sufficed. The new science called for a
new method. Galileo and his compeers walked in untrodden
paths wherein the syllogism furnished little guidance. Bacon,
in his *Novum Organum* (1620), and, with a firmer hand and
deeper insight, Descartes, in his *Discours sur la Méthode* (1637),
endeavoured to construct a logic that aimed, not at the attainment of formal consistency, but at the discovery of scientific
truth. The triumphs of science were, in fact, won by the
method of experiment, and by the application of mathematics
to the study of physical nature. The former was a new-forged
weapon; the latter rested on the work of the mathematicians
of ancient Greece. Herein lies the chief significance of the
Renaissance for modern civilization. It was not merely the
classical scholars who drew inspiration from antiquity. Science
also owed its awakening to the legacy of Greece and Rome. The

[1] "Science" is, of course, used here in its proper and comprehensive
meaning, viz., methodical investigation by human reason of the facts of
human experience. Science thus comprises history, ethics and metaphysics, as well as psychology and the natural sciences. The essence of
scientific as distinct from unscientific thinking lies, not in the object
thought about, but in thinking about it on rational method. Here, too, as
elsewhere, "God cares a great deal more for adverbs than he does for
verbs." [2] Allen, *Age of Erasmus*, p. 12.

great discoverers, with all their contempt for the Aristotle of mediæval tradition, were eager to recognise the obligation. Copernicus told the pope that his hypothesis of the earth's rotation had been suggested to him by the records of Pythagorean astronomy. Columbus sailed on his western voyage believing not merely in the sphericity of the earth, but that eastern Asia was comparatively near to the coasts of Europe; and the source of both convictions, the true and the erroneous, lay in the tradition of Hellenic science.[1] If Aristotle suffered unmerited obloquy through the sins of his degenerate disciples, this was an added motive for a return to Plato, the mathematician *par excellence* among Greek philosophers. Mediæval thought, when it swung loose from orthodox bearings, had invariably drawn freely on Neo-Platonic sources. Now for the first time Plato's complete works could be read, and in the original. This revival of Platonism had its home towards the close of the fifteenth century in the Florentine Academy, established under the patronage of Lorenzo de Medici. Ficino (1433–99), one of the chief among its members, translated not only Plato, but Plotinus and Proclus into Latin. The Swiss reformer, Zwingle, carried Florentine Platonism into the field of Protestant theology. Meanwhile at Padua Aristotelian freethinkers defended Averroës' denial of divine providence and of human freedom against the orthodox scholastics. That even these last felt the humanist impulse is evident from the reaction towards a simpler method and a more critical interpretation in the Spanish university of Salamanca. The Jesuit Suarez (1548–1617) united a return to Aquinas with liberal views on politics, hardly to be looked for in a Spanish ecclesiastic, such as the sovereignty of the people and their right to depose princes.[2] The revival of learning thus coloured the speculation alike of philosophers and theologians, of scholars and men of science. In literature and art its influence was all-pervading. We need not pause to insist how the Elizabethan drama or Jacobean architecture were stamped with the classical tradition. It set its mark on all the arts in all civilized countries of Europe. But it is interesting to note that the earliest opera, the *Eurydice* of Jacopo Peri, per-

[1] See Payne, *History of the New World called America*, i. 102–5, for Toscanelli's letter formulating these arguments. M. Picavet (*Esquisse*, p. 193) points out that both beliefs are to be found in Albertus Magnus and Aquinas.

[2] Scholasticism spread even in the Protestant ranks; Melanchthon, who did the thinking for the Lutheran Reformation, worked with mediæval methods and on an Aristotelian basis.

formed at Florence in 1600, on the occasion of the marriage of Marie de Medici to Henry IV of France, claimed to be "founded on the declamation of the ancient Greeks." [1]

§ 27. The revival of learning had two widely divergent effects on European culture. On the one hand, it stimulated to original creation. We have seen above how magnificently true this was in the domain of science. It was the same in the arts. The architecture of the Italian Renaissance was no tame imitation of the ancient styles. If Shakespeare drew on antiquity for the plots of his drama, it was but to portray living Elizabethans in Greek and Roman guise. On the other hand, archaism was in the air, and archaism stifles originality; the glamour of the historic past blinds men's vision to the possibilities of the future. It had been thus in the latter days of Hellenism, when scholars were content, from sheer lack of constructive energy, to gild the shrines of their great progenitors. Thus was it also, in a certain measure, in the age of the Renaissance. This tendency to archaism was most apparent in theology, and in pure scholarship. Orthodox Catholicism and orthodox Protestantism alike recked little of the march of science or of the claim of the human intellect for liberty of thought. If the Inquisition burnt Bruno and forced Galileo to recant, Calvin sent Servetus to the stake in the market-place of Geneva. It was in the Protestant churches that the Christian religion was faced, for the first time in its history, with the temptation to degenerate into the religion of a book. The invention of printing, with all its inestimable advantages, had opened the door to the domination of the letter over the spirit. The new learning had its dangerous side. Humanist scholars, intent upon the text, were led often to stress the form rather than the substance, the manner of expression rather than the living thought. Too frequently logic was banished to make room for grammar. The passion for verbal correctness was but scholasticism masquerading in a

[1] We have spoken in the text exclusively of the influence of the Græco-Roman legacy. Israel, too, came by more than her own in the Reformation epoch. See above, c. iii, p. 67, *note*. The Old Testament tradition deepened its mark, at all events in Protestant countries, on language, theology, law (e.g., New England), political ideas (theocracy), literature and art, as is evidenced by its influence on Milton's *Paradise Lost* and *Samson Agonistes*, on Racine's *Esther* and *Athalie* (Racine was Jansenist in sympathies, i.e., a Catholic Calvinist), on Bunyan and Dryden (who could use an Old Testament story for the purpose of political satire in *Absalom and Achitophel*: and a satire must be intelligible to the general public), and also of the oratorio as a new form of musical art, in which Old Testament subjects replaced the Catholic mass as the theme of sacred music (Handel).

less honourable dress. The learning of the Middle Ages was contemptuously dismissed because its Latin was not Ciceronian. The ideal of " formal " education reigned in the reformed universities and schools. Ascham (1570) taught that to write Latin like Cicero was the high-water mark of scholarly ambition.[1] Book-learning, especially in the lore of classical antiquity, became not seldom the test of academic eminence. The light of Hellenism was obscured by an excessive veneration for Latin literature.[2] Erudition reaped the honours that were due by right to discovery. This, it must be understood, was but one aspect of the humanist revival, but its presence, fraught with baneful issues in the story of education, must not be ignored. Yet, even in the domain of classical learning, the gain more than compensated for the loss. The foremost minds of the new learning soared high above the clouds that dulled the vision of their disciples.

§ 28. The spirit of free enquiry that inspired the revival of classical learning found brilliant expression in the person of Erasmus of Rotterdam. Erasmus was, if not the greatest scholar, at all events the greatest man of letters, of the Renaissance. Born about the year 1466, thrust at an early age into the uncongenial atmosphere of a Flemish monastery, he discovered his vocation as a scholar by the aid of the monastic library. In Paris, he learnt and taught the Greek language, and laid the foundation of his fame as the leading humanist in Europe. From Italy the new learning had already spread northwards beyond the Alps, borne to Paris by the French invaders of Italy, and to Germany and Flanders along the commercial highway of the Rhine. It struck root in Britain, and when, in 1499, Erasmus's English friends brought him on his visit to this country, he was welcomed by a distinguished circle of kindred minds. In the reign of Henry VII, Grocyn, Linacre and Colet had journeyed to Italy to drink at the headwaters of humanism. The new spirit had taken root among the traders of London, the home of Colet and More, where Grocyn held a living, and classical studies were a fashionable pastime at the court. Movements of thought in England have generally been associated with the larger world of affairs rather than

---

[1] Though Erasmus and Bacon knew better. " *La Renaissance, qui compte un si grand nombre d'érudits, a produit beaucoup moins de penseurs* " (Hauréau, *Hist. de la phil. scolastique*, iii. 429).

[2] Scaliger compared Virgil with Homer, almost wholly to the disparagement of the latter.

with the cloistered life of the universities, and Erasmus noted how there was more Greek learning in the busy metropolis than in the academic seclusion of Oxford.[1] Favoured by Henry VIII and archbishop Warham, he renewed his visits to England, lectured at Cambridge, advised Dean Colet in his foundation of St. Paul's school, and wrote his brilliant satire on the ignorance and superstition of princes and clerics, the " Praise of Folly " (*Encomium Moriae*), at More's house in Chelsea. But Erasmus belonged strictly to no nation; his culture was cosmopolitan, and he made his home indifferently, wherever in that troubled age he could find a haven of refuge, in Paris or in London or in Basel. His editions of the New Testament and of the Greek Fathers show his enthusiasm for the Greek language. It had been so in the early days of poverty : " First I will buy some Greek books, and after that some clothes." His " Proverbs " (*Adagia*), " Colloquia " and " Letters " are rich in the learning of the ancient world.[2] Both in his thought and in his style we can see that the classical tongues were to him no dead languages, but a living source of inspiration His humanism was ever free from formalism. He had caught the free spirit of Greece; by nature a knight-errant of intellect, he displayed in his life and writings a power of wit and irony rivalled among the ancients by Lucian alone. In *Julius exclusus* (1517), he poured the vials of his satire on the most militarist and secular of the Renaissance popes. Julius II approaches the door of Paradise, and to his amazement is confronted by St. Peter with the catalogue of his crimes. The anonymous pamphlet roused Europe to wrath and laughter; Erasmus, with natural timidity, disclaimed the authorship. A fighter in things of the mind, he shrank from the conflicts that were darkening the field of action. The outbreak of the Reformation brought him only sorrow and anxiety. He had lavished his wealth of wit and learning on the abuses and ignorance of the monks and clergy, but he

---

[1] British philosophy, for example, has rarely been academic and its appeal has been directly to the cultured public outside the universities. This is true of Hobbes, Locke, Berkeley, Hume, Butler and the Utilitarians. On the other hand, German philosophy has been the work of professors writing for professors. Such exceptions to the rule as Schopenhauer and Nietzsche were voices crying in the wilderness, in revolt against the academic tradition. The result is that, while British philosophy has often lacked precision and depth, it has wielded considerable influence on the public mind and provided men of affairs with a training in the handling of ideas.

[2] They have been used with admirable skill by Charles Reade in his novel, *The Cloister and the Hearth*.

trembled before the prospect of confusion and anarchy opened
out by Luther's breach with Rome. "If Luther stands by the
Catholic church," he wrote in 1521, "I will gladly join him."
Religious strife and civil wars were little to the taste of the
scholar, whose *Complaint of Peace thrust forth from all lands*
(1517) had but just issued from the press. He viewed the
Reformation conflict with the natural conservatism of an intellectual. Yet his keen intelligence had served, no less than the
ruder weapons of Luther, to sap the authority of the church.
He, too, as well as Luther, had "hit the pope on the crown,
the monks on the belly"; "by his irony," wrote a contemporary, "he had injured the Roman pontiff more severely than
had Luther by his wrath." In truth, Erasmus was a champion
of liberty, and his mistrust of the Reformers was based not a
little on his fear of their intellectual obscurantism. Thus amid
the storms of religious and social revolution he went down to
the grave at Basel in 1536, distrusted alike by Catholic and by
Protestant. His fame for all ages is that of an apostle of light
and liberty. He was the forerunner of Montaigne and Voltaire,
one who, impregnated with the true Hellenic spirit, looked to
reason and knowledge to guide and renovate the world.

V. Conclusion (§ 29).

§ 29. We have traced in this chapter, briefly and through
representative selection, the story of the Græco-Roman legacy,
during the thousand years between the disruption of the Roman
empire, and the coming of age of the European peoples in the
sixteenth and seventeenth centuries. We have seen the fruits
of the reception in the impulse to classicism, and the impulse
to liberty of thought. In the event, these two currents ran in
divergent channels. The one sought models for imitation, either
in erudition and scholarship, within academic precincts, or,
beyond them, in literature, politics and the arts. Two of the
chief facts of modern civilization, the plays of Shakespeare and
the French Revolution, were influenced, in no small measure,
by the examples of Greek and Roman character depicted in the
pages of Plutarch's *Lives*. The Parliamentary debates in England during the seventeenth and eighteenth centuries are packed
with classical allusion, as when Sir John Eliot branded Bucking-
ham as a Sejanus, and Pitt cited Virgil in his appeal for the
abolition of the slave trade. Oratory was consciously modelled

on Demosthenes and Cicero. Artists were trained in the study
of the antique; architects turned aside from the Gothic style of
the later Middle Ages to the classic monuments of the south;
and there is scarcely a page of English poetry that does not bear
the impress of the literature or the mythology of Greece and
Rome. On the other hand, the spirit of Hellenism woke the
impulse to creative thought. It inspired new philosophy, new
science. The controversy, now of long standing, between the
claims of a classical and a scientific education, was but one
symptom of the divergence. We have shown how the very
knowledge of nature, that has striven to displace a formal
classicism, was fostered into life by the spirit of Hellenic thought.
It is to modern philosophy and modern science, rather than to
the archaism of the humanist revival, that we must look for the
true measure of the enduring worth of Hellenism. Not Casaubon,
nor Scaliger, nor Bentley, for all the wealth and purity of their
scholarship, but Galileo, Descartes, and Newton, were the true
inheritors of the kingdom. Theirs was the faith in reason, to
set and to solve the riddles of an experience which is ever changing and therefore ever new. Theirs was the desire, not to copy,
but to create; to win fresh realms for knowledge, to discover
fresh fields of truth. Above all, it was by their labours that
humanity was enabled to recover, hardly and after the travail
of generations, the title-deeds of its birthright of free thought.
The modern world needs, at times, a salutary reminder, that its
enjoyment of this liberty is due to those who had learnt their
secret from the first champions of reason, and had lit their torches
at the ever-burning hearth-fires of ancient Greece.[1]

[1] For further reference to the subsequent course of the humanist
movement, see below, Appendix III.

CHAPTER XII

CONCLUSION

ON PROGRESS; AND ON THE LIVING INTEREST OF ANCIENT CIVILIZATION

I. On Progress (§§ 1-5).

§ 1. THE civilizations of Israel, Greece and Rome are the basis of our world; and, since it is in relation to our world that we think and act, they are also the basis of ourselves. To justify and illustrate this claim has been the object of this book. But, over and above the historical appeal, the genius of these peoples still lives as an inspiration and an example. We shall speak presently of the living interest of ancient culture for the modern world, but reference must first be made to a yet more general problem, that arises out of the theme of the preceding chapters.

We have taken a wide sweep, from the early civilizations of Egypt, Babylonia and Crete, stretching back to the fourth millennium before Christ and even beyond, to the birth of modern science in the fifteenth to the seventeenth centuries of our era. It is natural and reasonable to ask: How far do the known facts support a belief in progress? Is the march of human history a forward movement, if not uniformly, at least on the whole? Or is it, as it seemed to Hesiod of old, a process of retrogression? Or are the currents intermingled, and the record one of advance chequered by failure, of victory by defeat? To some minds, history unfolds a series of cyclical revolutions; civilizations appear, flourish and decay, in obedience to a periodic law. To others, the whole sequence has seemed capricious and un-meaning, a medley of upward and downward motions, a madness without a method, yielding no sign of rational principle or inform-ing purpose.

These are large questions, ranging over the whole fields of philosophy and history; and we must content ourselves with a few general reflections. The last-mentioned alternative, at all events, can be excluded at the outset. The very search for a solution implies a faith in the possibility of a rational interpre-tation. To hold that historical facts can be recorded, but not explained, is a confession of intellectual bankruptcy, a negation of the claim of history to be a branch of scientific knowledge.

Man is, above all things, a metaphysical, that is, an ideal-forming, animal; he seeks for reason everywhere, in history as in nature, and his thirst will not be quenched until he find it.

§ 2. A little reflection will limit still further the range of alternatives. Neither an uncritical optimism nor an uncritical pessimism can stand for a moment in the light of the facts. History shows no unbroken advance or retrogression. The scene disclosed is a vast battlefield, where the forces that make for civilization contend with varying fortunes against those that make for anarchy and barbarism. In one quarter, they press forward with a persistent sweep, despite resistance and transitory repulse; in another, the line sways to and fro, hardly holding the ground; in yet another, it is broken and overwhelmed by the destroyers. Whole civilizations, as in Egypt or China, seem to have vanished, save only as their buried fragments are unearthed by the spade of the archæologist, to be enshrined, as data for the expert and a spectacle for the curious, in the galleries of our museums. Where progress is discernible, it is already pregnant with the seeds of dissolution, and yields, slowly but surely, to inward stagnation or the pressure of forces from without. The religion of Israel, at the very hour when the prophetic vision had pierced to the goal, congealed into a rigid formalism; the swift growth of Hellenism was followed by lingering decay; the might of the Eternal City fell before the barbarian invaders. Facts like these have suggested to reflective minds in all ages from Empedocles to Nietzsche, the idea of a cyclical revolution.[1] But a closer survey reveals a distinction fatal to this hypothesis. In the records of the East, indeed, phase seems to follow phase in interminable cycles, without discernible connexion or ordered sequence; as " Amurath an Amurath succeeds," each conquering race develops its own culture in comparative indifference to that which it supersedes, and gives way in turn to a successor equally

[1] The Orphic brotherhoods and the Stoics taught this doctrine. It is familiar to Indian thought. In Nietzsche, it takes an extreme form, as that of cyclical *recurrence*, the past being repeated in the future in precise detail. Faith in progress is distinctive of Christian thought. The Greeks, generally, regarded the course of history as a retrogression from a golden age in the remote past : so Hesiod, and Plato in the *Republic* (esp. Books VIII and IX, which illustrate the periodic law of deterioration in all earthly societies). Lucretius furnishes an exception, in his conception of evolution-ary progress : see Book V, lines 771 to end, especially lines 1454–7 : " Thus time by degrees brings each several thing forth before men's eyes and reason raises it up into the borders of light; for things must be brought to light one after the other and in due order in the different arts, until these have reached their highest point of development " (*tr.* Munro).

heedless of its achievements.[1] This is the monotony, often remarked in the story of the East, of cycles of civilization that rise and fall, but are bound together by no organic tie of progress. When, however, we turn our eyes westwards to the Mediterranean world, we behold a very different picture. Western civilization, from its beginnings in the city-states of Greece and Italy, to the time when the modern nations emerge slowly from the wreckage of the Roman empire, displays throughout the signs of an ordered evolution. This was due mainly to the intellectual quality of the Greek genius, which stamped on its creations the hall-mark of individuality and life. In the fields of political action, artistic production, and speculative thought, the diversity is that of variations on a common theme. The inner thread of continuity is never cut. Even the revolutions that appear to engulf the past are but the prelude to its restitution. The backward eddies serve rather to strengthen than to retard the current. We strike here on a law of human progress. Great ideas, it has been said, must die to live. So Judaism died to be reborn in the western mind as Christianity, Hellas to be reborn as Hellenism.[2] Epochs of so-called decadence are in truth epochs of transition from an old life to a new. It may even have been thus far back in the obscure period of northern immigration that intervened between the Minoan civilizations and the dawn of historic Greece. It was so, certainly, in the dark age of Teutonic invasion, which issued, as we know, in the birth of an intellectual and social order, the product of a new impulse in fusion with the legacy of the past.[3] In the introductory chapter we pointed out how Israel, Greece and Rome severally stood for one of the essential factors in a complete civilization. The vision of a spiritual kingdom, comprising all peoples as its members under God as king; the claim of reason to think, create and act with untrammelled freedom; the recognition of authority and law as necessary instruments to man's conquest over barbarism; these three conceptions, blended in the course of ages with one another and with ideas derived from the races of northern Europe, are acknowledged in their union as the ideal of the modern world.

[1] Of course, this statement is only true with reservations. The point is that an *inner* connexion, the growth of the later phase *out of* the earlier, seems to be lacking.

[2] Inge, *Outspoken Essays*, p. 223.

[3] Thus the title of *The Decline and Fall of the Roman Empire*, established by the authority of Gibbon, is, if taken absolutely, a misnomer; an equally just view, directed upon the future, would mark the period as that of *The Rise of Teuton, Saracen and Slav*.

It would be idle to deny that much has perished in the process, or that the advance, even in western lands, has been restricted to certain lines of development. We may question whether men's practice has kept pace with the progressive enlargement of their horizon. We know but too well that the profession of a religion of universal peace is compatible with the enactment of a world war. The naïve optimism of the middle and later years of the last century has been rudely shattered. There is all the more reason to insist that a survey of western civilization reveals, in its broad outlines, a picture of relatively coherent evolution.[1]

§ 3. The error of the Victorians may be ascribed, in part, to their lack of critical discernment; in part, to their failure amid an enthusiasm for construction to recognise the ugly facts that stared them in the face; in part, to the complacency that blinded them to the chasm between ideal aspiration and attainment.[2] Above all, it lay in their defective criterion of progress. They construed progress in terms of human happiness, and happiness in terms of economic welfare. They never dreamed that men could be comfortable and yet not happy, happy and yet not comfortable. We have seen how the paternal despotism of the Roman empire, while furnishing the Mediterranean peoples with security and material provision to a degree previously unknown, failed to give them the one thing necessary to their happiness, inward peace. They scorned the proffered comforts, and took refuge in a faith that hourly exposed them to penury, contempt and martyrdom. We may question whether all our mastery over physical nature and all the improvements that are the harvest of modern science have increased the sum of human

---

[1] We are surely justified in treating western civilisation, throughout the last three thousand years of its history, as a relatively closed system. The occasional incursions of the East into the West, such as the Hunnish, Saracen and Tartar invasions, contributed little that was constructive to its development. The single exception of moment was the permeation of the West by Jewish religion through Christianity, and the Jews dwelt within the Mediterranean area. Western culture preserved, and still preserves, a comparative homogeneity, for which intermarriage serves as a rough criterion.

[2] We must not fail to give due credit to the constructive energy of the Victorians, manifested not only in technical invention and in the expansion of industry and commerce, but in pure science, literature and political action. It was the age of Faraday and Darwin, of Thackeray and Dickens, of Carlyle, Tennyson and Browning, of the organisation of British India, the growth of the overseas Dominions, the extension of the franchise, and the institution of national education. The present generation is keenly critical of its immediate progenitors; this is always the case, and signifies that it has absorbed their achievement and, fortified by that inheritance, is turning to fresh efforts of its own.

happiness.[1] When we contemplate the conditions of life in modern cities, the hustle in which men spend their days, the blighting uniformity that has sprung from the growing specialisation of labour, the ugliness with which the industrial revolution has defiled the land, we realise that all the efforts of bureaucracy and benevolence to make life tolerable for the masses are but the palliative of a disease that is gnawing at the vitals of modern society.[2] The measure of happiness is not, as the Utilitarians fancied, material prosperity, but fullness of life. The old doctrine of Aristotle is still valid, that the end of man is not to live, but to live well; that felicity lies in the realisation of the highest promise of his nature; and that pleasure is not an external commodity, but the sense of living, the glow of consciousness, inherent in the free exercise of faculty.[3] Christianity, in endorsing this conception of felicity, transferred its realisation to another sphere. It assumed that the fruition, if confined within the compass of the present life, was attainable only by a select few, and very imperfectly even by these. It had no illusions about earthly progress, and it read in the pages of history a lesson of warning rather than of hope. But it was at one with Hellenism in gauging happiness by a spiritual, not an economic, standard. The moral, intellectual and æsthetic interests, satisfaction of which alone makes life worth living, find little justification on the economic level. Moral excellence is not, within our experience, proportioned to prosperity; if it were, the term " duty " would be shorn of all its meaning.[4] The joy that attends the creative effort of the lover, the discoverer or the artist, is something different in kind from pleasure.[5] The manifest fact that, every

[1] Of course, if we were transplanted back to the days prior to these discoveries, we should regret their absence; but the question is whether those who lived then were more unhappy than those who live now. We may remember, too, the words of the old French marquis in the play : " en mon temps on avait Dieu."

[2] Let the reader journey with his eyes open from Fenchurch Street to Poplar, or take his stand for half an hour on the platform at Stratford, or at Landore Junction in South Wales. It has been observed that the faces of the men and the women in East London contrast favourably, in point of happiness, with those to be seen in the West. Idleness has more to do with unhappiness than poverty; the cure, in the majority of cases, is to eat less and work more. The cry of the crowd, in Lewis Carroll's tale, for " less bread, more taxes " is not so irrational as it sounds.

[3] Eth. Nic., x, cc. 4, 5; and cf. above, c. vi, § 14.

[4] See Kant, Critique of Practical Reason (tr. Abbott, Bk. I, c. I). Moral experience implies the contrast between duty and inclination; if moral action were necessarily the most pleasurable, the motive of duty would disappear, and the action would lose its moral quality.

[5] See Bergson, " Life and Consciousness," in the volume entitled Mind Energy.

day and all day long, men and women sacrifice comfort, health and economic gain in the pursuit of truth, goodness, and beauty, welcoming any burden so long as it affords scope for high activity, shows the irrelevance of material welfare as a criterion of progress.

§ 4. It is when we pass to details, and endeavour to unravel the various threads of progress and to estimate their value, that the enquiry is beset with difficulties. The task lies beyond our scope, and we must be content with one obvious illustration, drawn from the history of knowledge. If signs of progress are to be found anywhere, we expect to find them here. The issue is not complicated, as it is in the records of moral and religious experience, by the severance of theory from practice.[1] The speculative advance of knowledge is at the same time its realised achievement. We have traced in the foregoing chapters the continuity of Hellenic thought from its birth in the sixth century B.C. to the logical fulfilment of its earlier efforts in the systems of Plato and Aristotle, and thence to its differentiation into the special sciences, and its diffusion among various philosophic schools. We have seen the revival of Greek metaphysic in close alliance with religion in Neo-Platonism, its absorption into Christian theology, its recovery after centuries of comparative oblivion by the thinkers of the Middle Ages, and its crowning triumph as the motive that inspired the creation of modern science in the sixteenth and seventeenth centuries. At each stage there was loss as well as gain; but even when the stream of intellectual energy ran thinnest, the event proved that the gain more than compensated for the loss. Hellenism was decaying from within, when the Teuton and the Saracen swept over the Mediterranean lands; and the Christian church, with its contempt for pagan learning, abetted rather than stemmed

[1] We must remember, (a) that, even in morals and religion, this distinction is not absolute : ideals are the outcome of conduct, and react upon conduct; (b) that, the higher the aim, the wider the gulf that separates profession from performance; and (c) that the practice of an age is to be judged by its highest expressions. We do not measure the intellectual plane of the late seventeenth century by the scientific attainments of Nell Gwynne or Titus Oates, but by those of Locke and Newton. Similarly, the spiritual achievement of the Middle Ages is to be judged in the light of men like Anselm, St. Bernard, and St. Francis of Assisi. Finally (d) the problems of conduct have been complicated by the recognition, distinctive of Christian ethics, of obligation towards all mankind. Our duty to our neighbour is tolerably clear, when (as was the case in the Hellenic *Polis*) our neighbour is, intellectually and morally, our equal; it is anything but obvious when we are called upon to practise it towards the criminal, the lunatic, and the savage.

the tide of barbarism. Yet the inheritance survived the storm, maimed, indeed, but potent to nourish the growing minds of Christian Franks and Moslem Arabs. We have seen, too, how the Middle Ages, despite their ignorance of the physical sciences, won a knowledge of their own. The three problems, of God, freedom and immortality, which had received but stepmotherly treatment at the hands of Greek philosophers, came by their own in the philosophy of the Middle Ages. In the hour of the rebirth of science they were not consigned to oblivion, but were borne onwards, in close contact with the new interest in physical nature, into the heart of modern thought. The effort after their solution, pursued by widely divergent methods and issuing in very different conclusions, as we pass from Descartes to Kant, from Kant to Hegel, from Hegel to the thinkers of to-day, bears witness to their dominant and enduring interest for metaphysics.[1] A like growth is traceable in the history of the positive sciences. The Middle Age, with its mind fixed on the spiritual purpose of the universe, found a key to every riddle in the teleology of Aristotle, construed in the light of the Christian revelation. The scientific thinkers of the Renaissance sought an explanation on wholly different lines. Rejecting final causes as irrelevant and beyond human ken, they set themselves to interpret physical nature as the product of mechanical laws, which could be formulated with perfect simplicity and precision in mathematical terms. The discoveries of science during the last three centuries have been mainly due to the instruments and methods of mathematical measurement. In the hands of Galileo and Descartes, Leibnitz and Newton, mathematical physics forged ahead with lightning rapidity, setting its stamp on the metaphysics, psychology, ethics and theology of the seventeenth and eighteenth centuries, and wielding, for the time, an almost unquestioned sovereignty over the realm of thought. Chemistry followed in its train, resting for its foundations on the mathematical measurement of weights and volumes.[2] The biological sciences, though of

[1] We have here an illustration of a law that governs intellectual progress. The enrichment of knowledge is never by mere accretion of new to old; the process is one of interpenetration, in which new and old alike are modified.

[2] Yet chemistry owes much to the mediæval alchemists. They had not, however, our simple and easy system of mathematical calculation. The adoption of the " zero " from the East, enabling *ten* to be written as 10, was a great advance. See *The Earliest Arithmetics in English*, ed. R. Steele, who points out that " in the thirteenth-century scientific treatises addressed to advanced students, contemplated the likelihood of their not being able to do simple division."

contemporary origin,[1] hardly entered upon their inheritance till
the nineteenth century was under way. Their exponents, too,
have sought to bring the phenomena of organic life under the laws
of chemistry and physics. The same aspiration has haunted
even those who, following out the natural order in the development of the sciences, turned, as psychologists and as historians,
to study the nature and operations of the human mind. The
endeavour to apply mechanical principles to the facts of life,
of consciousness, and of human society, has led inevitably to
the recognition of their limits. Science finds itself here in the
presence of individuality, which defies quantitative measurement
and is incapable of expression in mathematical formulæ. Hence,
we can observe in the scientific thought of the present day,
an effort towards a new line of interpretation, which gives their
due to the concepts of meaning and value, and affords a basis
for a common understanding between science and philosophy.
It seems as though the hour has come for a reconstitution of the
broken unity of knowledge. This endeavour, visible in the
attempts to reconcile once more the long severed claims of philosophy and religion, and to effect a *rapprochement* between metaphysics and the physical sciences, is not merely a deeply interesting feature of modern thought, but an evidence of the coherent
development exhibited in the intellectual life of the western
world.[2] To this mark of intellectual progress must be added
another, relative, not to the content of knowledge, but to its
diffusion. The last two generations have set their hands to a
task without precedent, that of opening the gates of knowledge
to the whole of civilized mankind. The intellectual inheritance
is to be no longer, as in antiquity and the Middle Ages, the
monopoly of a favoured few. The democratic spirit has invaded
the realms of art and learning. The nations that have shouldered

[1] Vesalius (1514–64) and Harvey (1578–1657) were respectively the
contemporaries of Copernicus and of Descartes.
[2] The *rapprochement* between philosophy and mathematical physics is
evident in the writings of Mr. Bertrand Russell, Professor Alexander,
Professor Whitehead, Lord Haldane, and, recently, of Sir Arthur
Eddington and Sir James Jeans. M. Bergson works in the same direction
from biological, physiological and psychological data. Psychology, which
has one foot in the domain of the physiologist, the other in that of the
philosopher, furnishes an obvious meeting-point between philosophy and
science. Even Signor Croce, who insists uncompromisingly on the severance between these two, affirms the identity of philosophy and history (i.e.,
of ideal value and temporal happenings). Yet the ghost of the distinction
between the "eternal truths" of mathematics and "matters of fact"
(i.e., between values and events) still haunts the sanctuaries (or, shall we
say, the graveyards?) of metaphysics.

the burden of universal education have hardly yet awoken to a sense of their audacity. Knowledge has its perils; as Plato saw, when he put the searching question, how could the state study philosophy without being ruined ? [1]   Ideas are forces, terrible in their power to sway multitudes for weal or bane. The speculations of a recluse, spread abroad by the press, may furnish leverage for a revolution. Rousseau's *Contrat Social* heralded the guillotine. Out of the mouth of science has come forth blessing and cursing, the cures for foul disease and the ghastly implements of human slaughter. But these dangers, and that of the degradation of literature and the arts through their prostitution to a meretricious popular demand, must not blind us to the magnitude or to the promise of the adventure. That the modern world has dared to face the risks is a fresh instance of the unconquerable faith in reason, that was born, five and twenty centuries ago, in ancient Greece.[2]

§ 5. The foregoing illustration carries us but a little way towards a solution of the general problem of human progress. It is confined to one aspect of western civilization during some five and twenty centuries. Even were it supported by a survey of other fields of experience, it would at best serve as fragmentary confirmation to those whose conviction that the world is purposive rests on evidence other than that of historical fact. History of itself offers no revelation of a theodicy.[3]   For such an enterprise we should require to broaden our survey so as to include not merely the whole story of human development, but the process of cosmic evolution. In a celebrated address Huxley maintained that the cosmic process stood in direct antagonism to man's effort to realise his ethical ideals.[4]   Man, as a moral agent, is engaged in a life-and-death struggle with physical nature, ever on the alert to reconquer the ground he has arduously won. Such a dualism belies the truth that man is part of the cosmos, and his moral endeavour itself a phase in the evolutionary process.

[1] Rep., vi. 497.   See *Appendix* III, below.

[2] Nothing has been said in the text on the all-important question of progress in literature and the arts. For reasons stated in the preface, the author has refrained as far as possible from drawing illustrations from this field. The discerning reader will apply the suggestions offered above with the needed reserves and modifications. Further, the question would arise whether one art can be ranked higher in the scale than any other. The development of music, side by side with the other arts, in forms that show obvious advance on ancient and mediæval models, is perhaps the most striking sign of progress in modern art.

[3] See Appendix I, below.

[4] See the Romanes Lecture on *Evolution and Ethics*, reprinted in the volume with that title in Huxley's collected works.

The study of infra-human species and of inorganic nature rather
indicates that this process is one from less to greater individuality,
and that, to this extent at least, it bears the mark of progress.
We may question, indeed, whether anything discoverable in
the universe is wholly bereft of individuality. Even the atom
may have a will of its own. But we are clearly justified in
saying that, below the level of organic life, within the preserves
of the physicist and the chemist, uniformity among individuals
of a given type is not the exception, but the rule. They can
be treated, for purposes of scientific study and its practical applications, as if they were all alike. It is otherwise in the case
of biological species. Classification here becomes increasingly
difficult and artificial. In the animal world, capacity for variation
and for learning by experience is manifested in a multitude of
different grades. " The ox knoweth his owner and the ass his
master's crib "; dogs and horses respond to the touch of human
love; the poet and the gardener tell us that the like is true
of plants.[1] When we turn to humankind, the field of anthropology and history, the record is through and through personal.
Whereas the physicist revels in the uniform, resolving the most
unique occurrences into the interplay of general laws, the historian
knows that his material cannot be handled in the lump, and
labours to pierce behind the broad features of a social order to
the concrete thoughts and acts of its individual members. He
explains events by deciphering a plan, not by subsuming particulars under uniformities. The higher the plane of civiliza
tion, the less scope there is for generalisation. Personality figures
less in the story of the Basuto or the Mongol than in that of
Periclean Athens or Dante's Florence. Thus far, the cosmic
process, and that of human history, reveal a consistent picture.
Both have their dark shadows; there is infinite waste in nature,
and, like history, she " paints her grey in grey." But a graver
difficulty awaits us, if we are moved by these analogies to draw
an inference to universal progress. Empirical science cannot
guarantee the future, any more than empirical history. Its
predictions are conditioned by the assumption, which no amount

[1] Cf. Shelley, *The Sensitive Plant*; and Wordsworth's
    " For 'tis my faith that every flower
      Enjoys the air it breathes."
"All life," said Plotinus, " is a kind of spiritual vision "; *Enn.*, III. 8. 8
(see Inge, i. 161). The psychology and sociology of plants is a relatively
unexplored field; there are sympathies in nature that call for study, as
well as mechanism. Plants form associations and secure their ground
against rivals. On the whole question, see Bergson's *Creative Evolution*.

of experience can justify, that the unknown is governed by the same laws as the known. It can give no assurance even of the permanence of organic life on our planet. For all that science can tell us, it may well be, as Cyprian thought in the third century, *senuisse jam mundum*, that our world is ageing to its death.[1] Yet man's belief in the purpose of the universe is undimmed by those forebodings. For it is grounded, not on historical experience, but on faith. There is no absolute anti-thesis between faith and reason. The mediæval thinkers ren-dered lasting service to philosophy by their insistence on the inability of unaided reason to satisfy its inherent claims.[2] We may not assent to their interpretation of the content of the faith that reason requires as its complement. But the principle that underlay their argument still holds the field. It was reaffirmed in the later eighteenth century by Immanuel Kant, when he declared that the ultimate problems arising out of man's experi-ence, the being of God, the freedom of the will, and the ethical order of the universe, indemonstrable for scientific knowledge, find their solution, not indeed in religious experience, but in moral faith. Practical reason thus gives the assurance which reason in its speculative exercise is impotent to confirm or to deny. We cannot here discuss the difficulties attendant on the doctrine of religious and moral faith. It is enough to indicate that the belief in a rational purpose governing the course of history must be justified, if at all, on this basis and on this alone. Intellectual research and moral action alike rest on the con-viction that the universe, the object of our knowledge and voli-

---

[1] It is at this point that I fail to follow Professor Alexander (*Space, Time and Deity*) in his view that the present stage of the evolutionary process is bound to be succeeded by one marked by the emergence of a new and higher quality than mind. His faith in " deity," as he calls this next higher, and yet unknown, quality, rests, I gather, on the law that each new quality is conditioned by a new and more complex configuration, arising within an older and simpler configuration, of spatio-temporal elements. But what empirical warrant (and his philosophy claims to be empirical) is there for supposing that the process in the future will be to a higher com-plexity ?   May not the process be reversed, and the qualities of mind, life, etc., successively disappear ?   Professor Alexander appears to me to make heavy drafts upon the future.

[2] While, on the one hand, the fact that we want a thing (e.g., personal immortality, or to understand the universe) is no guarantee that we shall get it, and the exercise of reason is throughout a discipline in repressing personal inclination in the service of truth; there is, on the other hand, justice in the claim of mediæval (and modern) thinkers that a desire, which is not personal to the individual, but deep-rooted in human nature, must, if the universe be not unmeaning, find somewhere and somehow its satisfaction. This assumption underlies all religion, all morality and all science.

tion, is an intelligible system. We cannot, with our finite capacity and finite experience, formulate its purpose, still less can we construe it in detail; we can but conjecture, here and there, the fragmentary signs of its operation. In face of the easy optimism, which brushes aside the palpable suffering and evil of life as accidental ingredients in the best possible of worlds, and of the warped temper of the pessimist, who measures the infinite whole in the light of his own experience of disillusionment, we do well to remind ourselves of Butler's *dictum*, " that we are not competent judges of this scheme from the small parts of it that come within our view in this present life." [1] It is well also to remember that the effort to understand the most trivial fragment of the universe is implicitly conditioned by a belief in the coherent order of the whole, and that not only religion and morality, but also science and history, rest on the foundations of a reasonable faith.[2]

II. ON THE LIVING INTEREST OF ANCIENT CIVILIZATION (§§ 6–12).

§ 6. If the past were no more than the historic groundwork of the present, its appeal would be less insistent. It is interesting to learn our origins; but, after all, they belong to a bygone age, and it is in the present that we are called upon to live. We have to create the future; and there is peril, as well as profit, in the study of the past as past. The richness of the inheritance may serve but to paralyse the energy and enslave the mind. History itself points a warning, when it tells how the Jews of the dispersion and the Greeks in the last days of Hellenism were stifled by the hot air of archaism. They had not the strength to let the dead bury their dead, but squandered their declining energies in building the sepulchres of their forefathers. We can read the same lesson in the lives of individuals. No one who has passed his youth under the shadow of buildings enriched by the learning and piety of many generations, would deny

[1] Cf. *Analogy*, Introduction; and *Sermon* XV. On optimism, cf. Voltaire, in *Candide*, c. iv : " *Les malheurs particuliers font le bien général ; de sorte que plus il y a de malheurs particuliers, et plus tout est bien.*"

[2] This is the true " free man's worship." Mr. Bertrand Russell's well-known essay with this title (reprinted in his *Mysticism and Logic*) errs, it seems to me, in that he builds on the distinction of fact from value. The world of fact revealed by science is for Mr. Russell purposeless, and man is driven for consolation to a world of values, that exists only in his imagination.

Q

their power to refine and ennoble the growing mind. Yet those whose years are spent amid such associations are too often crushed beneath their burden. We do not look instinctively to the cathedral cloister for the signal that heralds the coming day. We turn rather to the wharves and factories, the creations of yesterday, where thronging crowds are forging a new world, heedless of the traditions of the past. All down the ages, knowledge and the arts have arisen and fructified in close contact with industry and trade. Athens and Alexandria, Florence and Venice, Antwerp and Rotterdam were great commercial cities, where artists and thinkers drew life and gave it back, by just exchange, amid the seething tide of human energy.[1] If this be so, the study of antiquity must needs seem an irrelevant luxury, divorced, for the vast majority of mankind, from the serious business of life. The question arises, therefore : has it not a value for the present, quite apart from the light it throws on the background of our history ? We answer that it has ; that it is still a living source of inspiration, with power to stimulate and direct the thought and action of the modern world.

§ 7. The creations of Israel, Greece, and Rome cannot be measured by their antiquity, or even by their influence on after-time. Their worth is independent of chronology, and endures untouched by the lapse of centuries. The prophecies of Isaiah, the tragedies of Æschylus, the Parthenon marbles, Plato's dialogues, the *Aeneid* of Virgil, exist in their imperishable grandeur and beauty, now as in the hour of their first production. They have even gained in meaning, through the larger experience which is ours to-day. They are not ancient or modern, not merely Hebrew or Greek or Roman, but great visions, great thought, great poetry, with a meaning for all peoples and for all time. They reveal what is most permanent and universal in the life of the spirit. Man's nature, his relations to God and to the world, and the problems arising out of these relations, were interpreted with unequalled insight and power of expression by the great minds of antiquity ; and their creations have the lasting value of the ideas they represent. They have the value also of the spirit that informed them. We have learnt something

[1] The same is true in our own land. Erasmus found London a head-quarters of Greek studies ; Shakespeare and Milton came to London from the fields of Stratford and Buckinghamshire. Our hopes for the art and science of the future rest on cities like London, Manchester, and Glasgow. It is no unreasoning caprice that has planted our new universities in centres of industry and commerce.

of the nature of that spirit. It was the spirit, in the hearts of the prophets and psalmists of Israel, of longing for the vision of the living God. It was the spirit of freedom, in the artists and thinkers of Greece, the desire of their reason to know themselves and the world, and, in the power of that knowledge, to realise their ideal of human excellence. In the Roman, it was the spirit of reverence for public law, inspiring the citizen to willing sacrifice for the community, the statesman, the soldier and the jurist to erect a firm bulwark of authority against the tide of disorder, and the poet to sing with patriotic ardour the glory of the Latin race. Hence it is that not only the works, but the men who wrought them, are an abiding possession for all ages. " Their names are held in everlasting remembrance." Isaiah and St. Paul, Pericles and Alexander, Socrates and Augustine, were more than makers of history; they live, not merely as themes for the historian, but as ideal types of personality. The philosopher of to-day, wrestling with speculative problems of which the ancients hardly dreamed, can gather strength for his endeavour by seeing with the eyes and thinking with the mind of Plato or of Aristotle. Men of action can find, in the deeds of bygone leaders, inspiration to guide them in their task of shaping the future of the world. Alexander nourished his imagination on the *Iliad*, that his own acts might be informed by the temper of the heroic age. It was in a like spirit that Napoleon studied Cæsar. The secret of Plutarch's influence over later generations lay in the unique charm and moral insight with which he portrayed the characters of the famous men of old, for an example to those of after-time.

§ 8. We will consider, briefly, this living interest, first of Hebrew, and then of Græco-Roman civilization.

(i) Israel dwells in our midst; little skill is needed to discern its presence in our science, our art, our finance, our revolutions. The marvellous persistence of the Jewish type, both of physiognomy and of character, blinds us to the changes wrought by time and persecution. King Saul himself might have sat as a model for Rembrandt's great picture at the Hague.[1] Driven from his native land by the Roman conqueror, the Jew of the dispersion henceforth made the world his home. Sheltered now for a brief season by his Semitic kinsmen at Baghdad and Cordova, now branded as a pariah for long centuries throughout Catholic Christendom, he set himself, in prosperity and in tribulation,

---

[1] *David playing before Saul*, in the Mauritshuis.

to master the instruments of western culture. Banned from political office and social intercourse, he sought release from bondage by the path of philosophy, which could close to him, and by that of finance, which Christian scorn left open to the unbeliever. The Jew of the Old Testament showed little desire or capacity for metaphysics; it was at Alexandria under the Ptolemies, and, above all, from the Arabs of the Middle Ages, that he learnt the lesson of Greece, to think. The fruits of Jewish Hellenism are visible in a long line of philosophers from Philo to Maimonides, from Maimonides to Spinoza, and from Spinoza to Bergson and Einstein in our own day.[1] For the rest, the modern Jew is the old Jew writ large. His portrait reveals the same arresting contrasts. Now as then, intense pride of race goes hand in hand with an easy cosmopolitanism, a readiness to assimilate foreign culture, and an extraordinary plasticity in adjusting his life and habits to those of alien lands. Himself of no country, he belongs to all; the unity he cherishes rests, not on civic loyalties, but on a spiritual faith.[2] He despises place and title and all " the solemn plausibilities " of life; the seed of Abrahram can afford to smile with pity on others' puny claims to Norman ancestry.[3] He has probed the secret sources both of ethical and of economic power, and his grasp on the gold of the spirit and on that of the currency is firm and unrelenting. He combines a reverence for spiritual values with an almost uncanny sense of the bearings of historical situations; like Elijah on mount Carmel, he will descry the coming tempest in the cloud that is yet " small as a man's hand." Again, the craving for riches and material possessions is, as of old, blended with a deep conviction that the poor and the lowly are the chosen children of Jehovah. The benevolence of the wealthy Jew,

---

[1] The Jew has, in these latter days, shown his power also in the arts, especially in that of music; Mendelssohn was a Jew. The ancient Hebrews had little gift for art. What the Jew has never succeeded in acquiring is the nicety of critical discernment, for which western culture is indebted to Hellenism. This defect is apparent even in works of a high order of imaginative genius, such as Disraeli's novels.

[2] The Jews of the Old Testament were always merging with their neighbours. The statement in the text must not be taken as suggesting that the Jews of to-day lack loyalty towards the land of their adoption; such an assertion would be manifestly false.

[3] It is not merely because of legal disabilities that Jews have rarely been found in high public office. Disraeli is, of course, an obvious exception. But Jews seem naturally to prefer other avenues to power. It is worth remarking that no Jew is eminent in the annals of modern war, yet the ancient Jews were great fighters. The ideals and temper of modern Judaism are unsympathetic towards any form of militarism.

especially to his own people, is proverbial. Hence the Jew comes forward, now as the bulwark of capitalism, now as the champion of the proletariate; Rothschild and Karl Marx are but the modern representatives of an age-long cleavage within the ranks of Judaism.[1] The faith professed by Jews in all lands remains, in essence, the same ethical monotheism that inspired the prophets in the time of the captivity. Their daily life is still regulated in minute detail by the law, delivered by Ezra to the restored community twenty-five centuries ago.[2] Only the language of their fathers is dead, save to the expert in the university and in the synagogue. The very fact is suggestive of the living influence of the religion of Israel among men. The Bible, alone of the master-works of antiquity, has preserved its vitality in the distorting medium of translation.[3] We have seen how the faith and worship of the Hebrew set an enduring mark on Christianity, and how the Old Testament scriptures were incorporated by the early church in the canon of inspired writings. Their translation into the vulgar tongues by the Reformation scholars gave fresh stimulus to their influence. The temper of Protestant enthusiasm found congenial nourishment in the ideals, and also in the practice, of ancient Israel. The sword of the Lord was unsheathed against his foes in the religious wars of the seventeenth century with a vindictiveness as merciless as in the days of Joshua and Gideon.[4] Cromwell heartened his cavalry at Dunbar with the old Hebrew war-cry, " Arise, O Lord, and let thine enemies be scattered." Frederick's Prussians marched to victory at Leuthen to the chant of Hebrew

[1] Karl Marx, though a baptised Christian, was the son of a converted Jew; one of his first writings was an attack on Jewish capitalism in the interest of the Jewish proletariate. It is often said that the Bolshevist leaders are mostly Jews; but this is true also of leaders of other parties in the Russian revolution. The Russian *intelligentsia* is largely Jewish.

[2] The domestic life of the poorest and most ignorant Jews can furnish a model of moral purity to the most cultured Christian societies (see the sympathetic study in George Eliot's *Daniel Deronda*). The popular travesty of the Jewish character, in so far as it has any foundation in fact, is an exaggeration of defects which are the outcome of centuries of Christian persecution. Even in these defects we can trace the amazing persistency of the race, driven to pursue its ends along devious paths.

[3] This is true both of the English Authorised Version and of Luther's German translation. Of course, no modern rendering can perfectly reproduce the meaning and spirit of the original. But that meaning has been deepened, and its value enriched, by the spiritual experience that is embodied in the languages of modern peoples. We translate *Elohim* by " God," *nephesh* by " soul "; but " God " and " soul " mean far more to us than the Hebrew equivalents to those who used them.

[4] Cf. the types of Scottish Covenanters in Scott's *Old Mortality*, especially Ephraim Macbriar and Habakkuk Mucklewrath.

Psalms. Fathers named their children after the worthies, and even after the texts, of the Old Testament. Milton's *Paradise Lost* and *Samson Agonistes*, Racine's *Athalie* and *Esther*, and the vogue of the Scriptural oratorio in eighteenth-century music, show how the influence pervaded poetry and the arts. Its echo is audible even in Dryden's satire and in Byron's lyrics. The works of John Bunyan carried it into every homestead throughout the land. Recent years have witnessed a reaction. Theologians no longer seek with confidence for the evidences of Christianity in the miracles and prophecies of the Old Testament. The ten commandments are no longer interpreted as an epitome of Christian ethics. The young grow up to manhood unfamiliar with the narratives of Hebrew history.[1] It is the inevitable revolt against an age of bibliolatry, with its narrow conception of revelation, its strained interpretation of the text, its bondage to the letter, rather than to the spirit, of the scriptures. We may regret that, at the moment when critical enquiry has, for the first time, thrown clear light on the ordered evolution of spiritual life in ancient Israel, and rendered possible, as never before, an understanding of God's education of his chosen people, the records of this process should be losing their hold upon the world. Yet the sacrifice is worth making, if men's apprehension of Christ's teaching is liberated from its long association with a code in which the precepts of justice and mercy were obscured by traditions of ferocity and barbarism. The Psalms can never lose their power to express the spiritual aspirations common to every race and time; and there are surely many who, in these last years, have turned for relief from the tragic spectacle of a world at war to the prophetic vision of a day when " they shall not hurt nor destroy in all my holy mountain : for the earth shall be full of the knowledge of the Lord, as the waters cover the sea." [2]

§ 9. (ii) The place held by classical studies in our schools and universities bears witness to the living potency of Greece and Rome in modern life.[3] It is true that their inheritance

[1] There is matter here for regret, not only because of the religious and literary value of the Old Testament, but because many boys and girls miss what is perhaps the only opportunity in their lives of reading first-hand historical documents.

[2] Is. xi. 9 = Hab. ii. 14. The truth of the statement that the Psalms possess an ever-living spiritual value is not disproved by the reservations that must be made in regard to certain Psalms, such as the 58th, 69th and 109th, which contain passages in a vein directly contradictory to the express teaching of Christ.

[3] The term " classical," as applied to the languages and literatures of

has been subjected to misuse from its advocates and malignity from its foes. Popular opinion ranks Greek and Latin with Hebrew and Sanskrit as " dead " languages.¹ It opposes classical to modern studies, and a scientific to a humanistic ideal of education. This prejudice is mainly due to the facts that in the generations following on the Renaissance a training in Greek and Latin came to mean the study of philology rather than of literature, history, and thought, and that the ideal set by the great humanists was tarnished with pedantry and antiquarianism. The efforts of teachers were frequently confined to making their pupils compose slavish imitations of classical models. Thus arose a breach between a discipline that taught the pupil to fix his eyes exclusively on the past, and that which trained his mind to analyse the phenomena of the present, and predict those of the future. Yet, as we have seen, the modern sciences themselves had their roots in the impulse that sprang from Greece. It would be indeed strange if the spirit that could touch the mind to such fine issues should have lost its magic in the few centuries that have since elapsed. A classical education, again, in contrast with that in the applied sciences, is commonly disparaged as unpractical. The word " practical," in everyday thought and speech, is almost synonymous with " vocational." Men mean by it something that contributes directly to professional efficiency, to earning a material livelihood; they forget that without friendship, morality, religion, and art, life would not for a moment be worth living.² The Greeks of ancient days were wiser. They

---

Greece and Rome, is apt to carry misleading associations. It suggests opposition between the classical and the romantic. We think of the rigid and prosaic standards of the eighteenth century, when the *Poetics* of Aristotle had become a storehouse of dogmas for dramatic criticism, and the " unities " were all in all. The results of this doctrinal pedantry were laughable enough, and provoked the revolt of the " Romantics " in Germany against the " classicism " of France. Voltaire had written a *Philoctetes*, in which the plot of Sophocles' masterpiece was adapted to the taste of Parisian society by the insertion of a heroine and her chaperon. It was high time that Goethe led the revolt in the name of Shakespeare and of the living spirit of Greece herself. The great poets of Greece and Rome stand on a height far above the antithesis of classical and romantic; their works are " classics " in the sense in which all great art is " classical," as enrolled among the master-creations of the human mind. On the confusions implied in the antithesis, see Professor W. P. Ker on *The Humanist Ideal* (*Essays and Studies* by members of the English Association, vol. vi).

¹ Latin has remained to this day a spoken language in Roman Catholic colleges; and in recent years, on the initiative of Dr. Rouse, of the Perse school, Cambridge, the " direct " method has been applied with success to its teaching in many English schools.

² Mr. G. Sampson, in his *English for the English*, p. 10, remarks : " I am prepared to maintain, and, indeed, do maintain, without any reserva-

saw clearly that education, to be practical, must take account of these higher humanistic interests. Since man's end is not merely to live, but to live well, they distinguished between the knowledge that is a means to livelihood and that which is an integral factor in a good life. The one was "necessary," as a training for vocations which no man would follow of his own will, but are forced on him by the pressure of material wants; the other, as the satisfaction of spontaneous human desire, was "liberal" or free. Thus they escaped the confusion of thought that opposes theory to practice. They grasped what we are just beginning to understand, that even the economic life can only be conducted with efficiency, if it rests on a foundation of scientific knowledge. This conception of a liberal education, embracing in its scope literature and the arts, science and philosophy, morals and religion, is as valid now as it was then. The teacher of to-day has more to learn from the pages of the *Republic* than from all our modern text-books of pedagogy, English, German, American, put together.[1]

§ 10. But Greek culture means something more for the world to-day than an instrument of youthful education. The people who created science, who first grasped the meaning and worth of freedom in thought and action, and displayed in their activities such independence of character, energy of will and clearness of intellectual vision, cannot fail to stir a like response in all who study their works with understanding. The Greeks are, now as ever, the surest guides to lead mankind along the path of self-expression. They were the greatest masters of experiment in life that the world has known.[2] In life, as in science, the fruitfulness of the experimental method is not to be gauged by the success or failure of isolated adventures, but by the daring and skill with which men work out an idea to its issue, probing every

---

tions or perhapses, that it is the purpose of education, not to prepare children *for* their occupations, but to prepare them *against* their occupations." It should furnish a relief for the monotony, which, in this age of specialisation, weighs with a crushing burden on the spirits of millions, especially clerks and manual labourers in large towns.

[1] The literature of pedagogy, extending over more than 2,000 years, and multiplying to an appalling degree at the present day, contains some half-dozen or so of works that are worth reading. Of these, the *Republic* is by far the greatest. In recent times, Newman's *Idea of a University* forms an honourable exception. The array of educational manuals on the shelves of a college library affords as dismal a consolation to the misanthrope as the prospect from the platform at Landore Junction, referred to in an earlier note.

[2] Even in physical science, Greek thinkers used the experimental method, as far as their slender resources allowed. Their thought and action was always, in the wider and perfectly legitimate sense, experimental.

avenue that experience offers in the effort to bring theory to the test of fact. We find this energy of self-expression, not only in artists and philosophers, but in the ordinary Hellenic citizen, who was never weary, on his own lower plane, of seeing new sights, hearing new tidings, making new things. The Greek was a born craftsman, alike in special arts, such as pottery or shoe-making, and in the wider art of life. We may imagine what would rouse his interest, were he to appear in the England of to-day. Not our politics, for the cumbrous machinery of the modern state would bewilder his intelligence; not our warfare, which would strike him as horrible and barbaric; not our art, which would simply leave him cold.[1] The things that would stir him to enthusiasm would be our inventions, our aeroplanes and microscopes, our use of steam and electricity, the applications of scientific knowledge to the exploration of the ways of life. These would excite in him the wonder, not of a savage, but of a wise child, who recognises by unerring instinct the impress of the human mind forging the instruments of human life. The phrases "humanism," "humane learning," "the humanities," point to the distinctive quality that gives to Hellenism its abiding value. The theme of Greek thought and literature was humanity; man as he is amid his actual environment. But the Greek thinker never forgot, as the modern world is prone to forget, that man, with all his potency of thought and will, is part of a whole, a member of an ordered universe. Our passion, in the economic field, for production, heedless of leisure and the fitting enjoyment of the produce of our toil; our rejection, in the field of politics, of any institution or form of government that is not the creation of the popular will; the efforts of science, to remould nature after our heart's desire, and of philosophy, to interpret reality as relative, through and through, to human mind; would appear to his astonished vision as the wild audacity of *hubris*. Where, he would ask, in this seething whirlpool of motion, is there place for rest? Where lies the spiritual goal of all this striving, the unity of purpose that gives direction and meaning to man's hustling enterprise? He would point in answer, with calm assurance and a deep pity for our confusion, beyond the realm of becoming to that of being, beyond the temporal to the eternal, beyond the many to the one.[2] *Theoria*, as well as *praxis*, know-

[1] We can perhaps imagine the Athenian visitor touched to a thrill of recognition by *Deirdre of the Sorrows*.

[2] The contrast between the Greek and the modern view of life, here indicated, is admirably presented in Professor G. P. Adams' book, *Idealism and the Modern Age*.

ing as well as doing and making, is essential to enduring satisfaction. Human nature is two-sided; man's effort is both to
know things as they are and to discharge his moral obligations.
He cannot do the one without the other. If he is to keep clear
of fantasy and illusion, his knowledge must be closely related to
practical activity. If his practical achievement is to be fruitful,
it must rest on knowledge of what is. Man cannot act blindfold
or in the dark. He needs light, and light is what the Greeks
valued above all else. Further, if he is to know the world and
share its future, he must first know and shape himself. In the
power of self-knowledge he must be the architect of his own
character. Personality is an ideal rather than a *fait accompli*;
it is the finished form to be realised in the raw material of human
nature. So taught Socrates, Plato and Aristotle; and the lesson
is one that mankind, after more than two thousand years, has
still to learn from Greece.

§ 11. And what of Rome? Can the world still profit by her
example also? Or is the depreciatory judgement that we have
passed more than once in the course of the preceding pages,
our last word on Rome's work in history? It is true that, in
the higher things of the mind, the Roman lived on a lower plane
than the Greek, or even than the Jew. His world was one of
temporal events and historic situations, not one of enduring
values. Even within that world, he lacked imaginative vision.
He contributed little that was original to the art, the knowledge, the religion of after-times. Therefore the living interest
of Rome for the present day is proportionately less than that of
Israel or of Greece. The study of the Latin tongue and of Latin
literature cannot claim an equal place in a liberal education with
that of the Greek. But this does not mean that the work of
Rome was negligible, or its interest merely historical. The
masterpieces of Latin literature are worthy of their Hellenic
models. The study of Roman law is an integral part of a
modern juristic training. Moreover, the maxims and methods
of Roman public policy are still discernible in those of the
Roman church. We have seen how the influence of the empire
was already stamped upon its early history, notably in the
growth of papal prerogatives and in the severance of Greek
from Latin Christendom. In the Middle Ages, the papacy
fashioned after the likeness of the empire, claimed to inherit
its authority and its mission. Thomas Hobbes of Malmesbury,
writing in the days of the Puritan revolution, spoke of the

papacy as "no other than the ghost of the deceased Roman empire sitting crowned upon the grave thereof."[1] So at least it seemed to the Protestant philosopher and arch-enemy of ecclesiastical dominion. In an essay on von Ranke's *History of the Popes*, Macaulay insisted with his wonted energy of style on the historic significance of the Roman church. " The history of that church," he wrote, " joins together the two great ages of human civilization. No other institution is left standing which carries the mind back to the times when the smoke of sacrifice rose from the Pantheon, and when camelopards and tigers bounded in the Flavian amphitheatre." In its claims to temporal power, in the canon law, in its organisation, in its policy towards subordinate associations, as well as in its traditions and its seat of government, the papacy stands to-day as the inheritor of imperial Rome. It was while listening to the bare-footed friars chanting the office among the ruins of the Capitol, that Gibbon conceived the idea of narrating the " Decline and Fall." Now if Rome thus lives still in the literature, the law, and the religious life of the present day, it must be through some quality of lasting interest in the character of her people. We must do justice to her capacities as well as to her limitations. We find the clue if we think of the habit of mind that is stamped on the most characteristic achievements of the Romans, on their public policy and their jurisprudence, as also, at a later day, on the philosophy and the theology of the Roman church.[2] We see an intellect that revels in general rules, in clear-cut definitions and rigid distinctions, in subsuming cases under principles and in discerning the means appropriate to a given end. It is the legal cast of mind, with its formalism, its respect for precedent and the established order, its narrow horizon, its stereotyped doctrines, its abhorrence of vague conceptions and suspicion of all that savours of the visionary and the mystical.[3] Such an intelligence could not avail to unlock the secrets of the higher realms of knowledge. But its logic and precision furnished a

[1] *Leviathan*, c. 47. Sir Christopher Wren, thinking of Roman architecture wrote that : " Modern Rome subsists still by the ruins and imitation of the old."
[2] This Roman habit of mind is specially evident in Aquinas, for all his indebtedness to Aristotle and Neo-Platonism.
[3] The following quotation from Inge's *Outspoken Essays* (p. 246) affords an excellent example of the formalism of the Roman mind : " When the Romans repudiate their ' scrap of paper ' with the Samnites, they deliver up to the enemy the officers who signed it, though (with characteristic ' slimness ') not the army which the mountaineers had captured and liberated under the agreement."

discipline, which was, and still is, indispensable to intellectual progress. This quality of mind was the counterpart in the field of thought to the Roman instinct for government in the field of action. Rome realised more fully than any other race the value of authority. Authority is regarded with much suspicion by the present age. There is reason in the mistrust; for authority rests on force and fear, imposes an external discipline, and looks to the means, not to the end, of the moral life. But our suspicion is also fraught with danger; in their rebellion against external regulation, formal observances and the casuistry of the law, men may fall victims to antinomianism and anarchy. It is the spirit that giveth life, but the spirit can only win expression through the letter. Rome is there to put us in mind of the disabilities of our present state, that preclude man's attainment of his goal solely in his own strength, and necessitate the provision of outward controls as the conditions of inward progress. In the second book of the *de Monarchia*, Dante tells how he had once thought that the Roman race had won its sovereignty, not by right, but by force of arms alone; and how clearer insight had dispelled his error. The arguments by which he justifies its title to world-empire will hardly be convincing to the reader of to-day. But at the close of the treatise, he bases his theory of the functions of the empire and the church under the scheme of divine providence on grounds which, in principle, go to the root of the problem of authority and law. Man, as sharing alike in corruptibility and in incorruptibility, holds a middle place in the created universe. His twofold nature marks him as destined for the two ends of temporal and eternal felicity. The fitting means to these ends are the teachings of philosophy and of revelation. But, by reason of their sinful greed, men are unable to enjoy these fruits, and must, " like horses going astray in their brutishness, be held in the way by bit and rein," i.e., by the twofold directive power of the catholic empire and the catholic church. Thus alone, " upon this threshing-floor of mortality," can human life be lived in peace.[1] The enduring element of truth in Dante's theory of government is the recognition that, where there is no restraint of law, war and tyranny, the offspring of man's evil passions, must abound. If we owe

---

[1] *De Mon.*, iii. 16; cf. *Purg.*, xxvii. 140–2, where Dante, having passed through Purgatory, enters the earthly Paradise (the garden of Eden), the scene of pristine innocence, and is declared by Virgil free to follow his own pleasure, and is crowned and mitred by him as henceforth his own emperor and pope. He has passed beyond the stage of discipline, where external authority is needed, and is now a law to himself.

to Israel and to Greece the essential constituents of a good life, we owe to Rome its regulative instruments. She fell in the event because she confounded the scaffolding with the structure, the means with the end. The *pax Romana* imposed upon her subjects was no positive peace; it meant only repression of disorder. She knew not that behind Rome lay Jerusalem, behind the empire of this world the kingdom of God and Christ. One thing alone she saw clearly, that civilization must perish apart from government. Her history teaches, for all who have ears to hear, that, if liberty is to be more than an empty name, it must be founded on reverence for authority and law.[1]

§ 12. Thus it is that the civilized world can still learn its lesson at the feet of ancient Greece and Rome. In each succeeding age, artists, poets and thinkers have turned to this perennial spring of inspiration, to gather strength for their own efforts. History never repeats itself; and what the Greeks and the Romans did in their generation needs not to be done again. The art and the philosophy of the present and of the future will express the present and the future, not the past. They must be as original, in their form and in their content, as the life which they interpret. The creations of Greece and Rome mean little to the pedant and the dilettante, who are moved to study them by no impulse save that of idle curiosity. They mean much to those who labour with strength and courage to build the future, whether in art or science, thought or action; for such share most fully in the spirit that inspired them. When artists cease to draw life from the Phidian sculptures, when thinkers fail to find in Plato the living movement of the human spirit in its unwearied search for truth, when poets no longer turn, as Dante and Milton turned, to Homer and to Virgil as to the well-springs of poetic inspiration—then, and then only, will the Greek and Roman tongues be dead.

III. CONCLUDING REMARKS (§ 13).

§ 13. The speculative problems that we have touched upon in this closing chapter are not peculiar to the study of ancient

---

[1] The problem whether in an ideal society there is any room for authority, lies beyond our scope. The conception of the kingdom of heaven implies the sovereignty of God, " whose service is perfect freedom." Thus interpreted, authority is no longer an instrument, but an essential factor in the ideal life. Dante, of course, recognised such authority in Paradise. But this takes us far from the external authority of which Rome is the embodiment in history. On the question here indicated, see Webb's *Gifford Lectures, Second Course*, Lect. v.

civilization. They are common to all history, though presented by each succeeding age in a new and different form. They may be difficult to answer, but they must not be shelved. For they mark the points where history and philosophy meet on common ground.

The function of the historian is not merely to describe facts, but to explain them. In other words, he cannot cut off the ideal from the actual, and, reserving the actual for his own province, relegate the ideal to the philosopher. He must himself philosophise, or be unfaithful to his vocation as a historian. For ideals, though transcending the bounds of men's achievement, belong to the same world of reality; and the facts are not the facts without them.[1]

There is no such thing as a fact without a meaning. The meaning of a fact is not added to it from the outside, as if the fact could be complete without it. It is constitutive of the fact itself.[2] On the side of knowledge, it follows that the description of the fact includes the explanation of its meaning. Even in his initial selection of relevant data, the historian is guided by a hypothesis as to their significance; he is, from the outset, an interpreter, a judge. To assign a meaning is to value in the light of an ideal standard. Plato is more important than Aristippus, Cicero than Roscius, St. Paul than Silas, because, in the judgement of the historian, they contributed something of higher quality, of more enduring value, to the course of human civilization. In the long run, this judgement on what counts implies a philosophy—that is, a reasoned doctrine of the ideal ends of life. A given historian may not be conscious of this

---

[1] This implies criticism of the conception of a " philosophy of history," which means that history is one thing, philosophy another; that, after the historian has determined the facts, he hands them over to the philosopher for reflective valuation. It is no wonder that such a conception is anathema to the historian. He knows that he, too, has a mind and can judge. What he does not always see is that when he does so, he is *ipso facto* a philosopher. Herein lies the justification of Croce's doctrine of the identity of philosophy and history. Both alike, as implying the integration of values with facts, must, in ideal completion, form a single science. But, in the existing state of human knowledge, their methods and achievements are necessarily divergent.

[2] Doubtless, the meaning is unfolded by the context of other facts. This is but to say that the initial fact, and the other facts, are only so called by courtesy, that they are each a fragment of the total fact under investigation, as Picton's charge and Lord Anglesey's loss of a leg were partial factors in the fact of the battle of Waterloo. The same is true of the battle, which gets its meaning in the context of the Napoleonic struggle; and so on, until our search for a genuine fact expands into a philosophy of experience.

implication, but it is none the less involved in every step of his enquiry. Ideals cannot be dissevered from historic fact. They are the creations of actual minds in actual situations, and have their life and being in the acts and lives of actual men. Philosophy has often been tempted to dissociate the two realms, and to point men away from historical events to a timeless world of values. So did the Neo-Platonists; so, emphatically, did not Christianity, which, with a faith grounded in the historic personality of its founder, declared in one breath that the kingdom of God was life eternal, and that this kingdom existed here and now. The issue is even graver in the field of religion than in those of philosophy and history. Thinkers who, like Plotinus of old and certain Christian theologians, Protestants of the school of Ritschl, and Catholic modernists, in our own day, stress the reality of ideals to the point of scorning temporal facts, will always evoke a response from minds that revolt from bondage to historic events as from an irrelevant encumbrance to the spiritual life. They achieve by this means an easy escape from the difficulties raised in the path of religion by the advance of the historical and physical sciences; but it is at the cost of the very religion they desire to save. A Christianity cut adrift from the course of history is no longer a gospel of salvation to all mankind; it has become the preserve of an enlightened few. The world cannot be redeemed by an abstraction. The sternly practical Roman mind rejected the attempt to reduce religion to philosophy, bearing witness, by its instinctive sense that a living faith must find expression in the facts of history, to the truth of one of Christ's most pregnant sayings, that "the children of this world are in their generation wiser than the children of light." [1]

This conviction, that the events of history are not unmeaning but informed and sustained by an ideal purpose, is the basis of man's endeavour both in thought and action.[2] It is the motive

[1] In modern thought, the distinction of the two worlds of fact and of value has its source in Kant, whose tenets were applied to theology by Ritschl. It implies a dualism, which, if taken as ultimate, runs counter to the impulse of reason to find unity and system in experience. On Catholic modernism, see Giovanni Gentile's volume of essays, entitled *Il Modernismo*, and (from the Christian standpoint) Figgis, *The Gospel and Human Needs*, Lect. iii. "Complete severance," writes the latter (p. 124), "between the Christ of fact and the Christ of faith would, in the long run, be destructive of belief in either."

[2] This is obviously true of moral action, but the same faith lies at the root of all social intercourse. Commerce and industry rest upon credit, which is the analogue, in the economic sphere, of that which is "the sub-

force that inspires, not only the leaders among men, but the
humblest worker who labours faithfully to lead a worthy life,
and, so far as in him lies, to leave the world better than he found
it. It has proved an unfailing strength in troubled times, as
to Augustine and his fellow-Christians in the fourth century,
amid the wreckage of a historic civilization, and to ourselves
at the present day. For it gives assurance that time, in the
great words of Plato, is but " a moving image of eternity,"
and that the changes and chances of temporal history are a
revelation of the eternal gospel, bearing its age-long message :
" Behold, I make all things new."

---

stance of things hoped for, the evidence of things not seen." Faith is no
idiosyncrasy of the religious consciousness, but a primary condition of all
reasonable life.

CIVILIZATION AND HISTORY

§ 1. In the opening chapter of this book (Chap. I, § 1), we defined the field of history provisionally as identical with that of civilization. This definition provokes certain questions of a speculative character, the discussion of which would have been premature at the outset of our enquiry. Among these there are two, which concern respectively the philosopher and the historian. On both questions definite convictions have been repeatedly expressed in the course of the preceding survey, and particularly in the concluding chapter (XII). A fuller consideration of the grounds for these convictions can now no longer be deferred.

(1) The philosopher will ask, what is the status in reality of ideal value and how is it related to fact? Clearly in some sense the two realms fall apart; the pursuit of ideals implies that men are moved by desire for something that lies beyond their actual attainment. Even the drunkard at the door of the tavern displays this much of reason in his nature that he can want a thing before he gets it. The goods that men desire are infinitely various and of varying grades of perfection, but, however closely integrated they may be with what is present to the senses, they one and all as "goods" surpass the range of what is actually possessed. Moreover, ideals, when viewed in abstraction from their embodiment in facts, are seen to be, not temporal occurrences, but timeless entities; whereas the realm of actuality is constituted by events that occur in time. I cannot give a date in the time-series to my ideal of justice any more than to my conception of triangularity, as I can to the battle of Hastings or my own birth. If we try to think out the speculative problem thus presented, we find ourselves confronted by two alternatives. On the one hand, there are those, who, like the Platonists, ascribe to values a supersensible existence, whether in their own right, or as thoughts in the mind of God.[1] On the

---

[1] The alternatives are here stated in their extreme form. No mention is made of such intermediate theories as (e.g.) the Phenomenologist position that values (and universals) are "subsistent" entities, real though non-existent. See my Gifford lectures (*From Morality to Religion*, pp. 183–186). On the Platonist doctrine, see above, c. v, § 20, and c. ix, § 13, and for mediæval views on universals, c. xi, p. 390, *note* 3.

other hand, there are those who, like the advocates of scientific naturalism, deny the claim to objectivity, holding that values (and universals generally) are products of human thinking, "logical constructions" fashioned by actual individuals in the natural course of their mental development, and existing only in the minds of those who frame them. The nature of our answer to this metaphysical problem will already have become clear from the preceding chapters (esp. IX, XI and XII). A naturalist explanation of values is manifestly incompatible with faith in a theistic interpretation of the universe. Suffice it to say here that in naturalism there is at least this measure of truth, that ideals, whatever may be their ultimate status in reality, are closely integrated with facts. Actual institutions, laws and ways of conduct are what they are because individuals and societies have approved certain ends and devoted energy of thought and action to effect their realisation. Moreover, these ends have been shaped in men's minds under provocation from the facts of their inner and outer experience. Thus, as Christianity affirms, the two worlds, though widely different, are not, in the phrase of an early Greek philosopher, " cut off one from the other by a hatchet." [1]

§ 2. (2) Our second question is for the historian, since it concerns the scope of history, and therefore calls for more detailed consideration here. Were we right in treating history as though its field were coterminous with civilization ? For, if we take the term " history " in its widest sense, it seems to include much more. It can be stretched to cover the whole process of nature. Not merely human societies, but all living organisms, as well as the earth and the solar system, have a history ; and the business of the physical sciences lies largely in recording it. Some recent philosophers, following in the wake of evolutionary science, have posited " the historicity of things " as the basis of all that happens in the universe.[2] But before we commit ourselves to this wider view of history, a distinction must be borne in mind between mere *events* that occur without conscious agency and *actions* that have their source in man's purposive volition. To talk, as we habitually do, of the " action " of a bicycle or a chemical

[1] Anaxagoras (*fr.* 8). The point has been made with special reference to Christianity, in cc. x and xii, above.

[2] I have here in mind the philosophical doctrines of Alexander and Dr. Whitehead. See especially Alexander's essay on *The Historicity of Things* in the volume presented to Dr. E. Cassirer, and reprinted in the posthumous collection of Alexander's writings, *Philosophical and Literary Pieces*, edited by Prof. Laird.

substance is to close our eyes to this distinction. Now the proper field of history is the past acts of human beings. With events as such the historian is concerned only in so far as they condition men's purposive actions. This distinction between actions and events is grounded on the far-reaching assumption that man is free both to choose the end towards which his action is directed and to act in accordance with his preference. Otherwise man's so-called actions are mere events. This assumption is not the conclusion of an inferential process; rather it is "taken for granted" universally in the moment of action. It never enters into a man's mind, when acting, to question whether he is free to act or not. The question arises only for subsequent reflection, under provocation from scientific theories of mechanical causation. Man's freedom, as thus assumed, is not absolute, but relative, alike to his capacities of insight and strength of will, and to opportunity and circumstance, the former conditioning his act of volition, the latter his ability to achieve what he sets himself to do. The rejection of scientific determinism, i.e., the doctrine that all so-called "acts" are rigorously necessitated by their psychical and/or physical antecedents, does not mean that actions are wholly undetermined, or products of blind chance.[1] It simply implies that man is, in Aristotle's language, an ἀρχή, a causal agent capable of initiating a course of action. In reality there is no such an entity as "chance"; the use of the word is merely a disguise for our inability to give a rational explanation of an action or an event. When the historian, as is often the case, speaks of an event as fortuitous or accidental, he simply means that its occurrence falls outside of the particular causal sequence that at the moment engages his attention. The web of history is woven of multitudinous strands, each of which constitutes a distinguishable causal series. When one such series x cuts across another y, we have an effect, the cause of which must be sought, not in prior events in series y, but in an alien series x; whose intrusion into y strikes the mind as a coincidence. Thus Alexander's death in 323 by infection from a bacillus seems fortuitous, though an expert in tropical medicine, had he been on the spot, might easily have diagnosed the malady and prevented death by scientific treatment. Again the causal

---

[1] On this question of the extension of the deterministic hypothesis to cover human actions, science speaks to-day less dogmatically than even half a century ago. But the reader should be on his guard against construing its recent provisional hesitations as implying a decisive verdict in favour of the libertarian alternative.

factor, though alien to series x, may well be due to purposive volition, just as Cæsar's murder, though an accident as regards Cæsar's own actions, was due to deliberate purpose on the part of his republican enemies. In the case of Socrates' death, on the other hand, there is nothing that can be regarded as fortuitous; Socrates himself deliberately chose the course of action that led to the fatal issue. Further, just as there is no such thing as blind Chance, so there is no such thing as blind Necessity (ἀνάγκη) or Fate. History, which lives and moves in the world of concrete actuality, has no place for such hypostasised abstractions. They merely veil the obvious truth, that there are causes beyond the grasp of man's intelligence and the range of his control. " There's a divinity that shapes our ends, rough-hew them how we will." So is it, again, with the modern invocation of the *Zeit-geist*. No individual, however endowed with genius, is impervious to the ideas that dominate his world. Ideas are *idées-forces*, which tend to realisation; but they affect history solely through the medium of the characters and actions of individuals. The same is true also of the alleged dialectical laws of economics and politics.[1] These carry no mysterious prerogative of compulsion; in so far as they hold, it is as formulæ descriptive of the ways in which individuals and groups have been found to act. I make special reference to groups, not with any intention of affirming a doctrine of " corporate personality " or of ascribing to organised societies a real individuality of a higher order than that of their members,[2] but because the historian is directly concerned with the life of such societies— their growth, maturity and decay—as conditioning the lives of individuals. Realising that man is by nature a social being, he fixes his attention not on individuals in isolation (for none such can either be or be conceived), but on their acts as members of more or less civilized groups, exhibiting a relatively complex type of social structure. Below this somewhat arbitrarily selected level lies the province of pre-history, the special preserve of the anthropologist. I have here in mind not only states, but churches and confraternities, gilds and municipal corporations, universities and trade unions, as well as larger political federations, such as the United States of America, the Union of Soviet

---

[1] I have specially in mind Hegel's metaphysical dialectic, as expressed in the process of history, and that of Karl Marx in the special field of economic development.

[2] As for example does Bosanquet, following Hegel, in his *Theory of the State* and his Gifford lectures on *Individuality and Value*.

Socialist Republics and the British Commonwealth of Nations at the present day. We must be on our guard against the natural tendency to think of political organisation exclusively in terms of the nation-state. The nation-state is a modern growth, which saw its rise in the fifteenth and sixteenth centuries, and it already shows signs of yielding place to a different form of supra-national organisation. Looking ahead for a moment, we can envisage new types of political unification, embracing not only a plurality of nation-states, but even whole continents and hemispheres.[1] And there is another and even more consoling prospect. A graver menace to civilization even than international wars is that, the larger the political community, the more the individual citizen is swamped in the mass, and finds himself deprived of opportunity for the expression and development of his personality. He counts for little or nothing, even when in a democratic state he is registering his vote at an election. Against this peril, the smaller communities within the state offer a remedy. In his church, his university, his professional organisation or his trade union, he can not only exercise personal influence, and acquire training in affairs and skill in the handling of personal relationship with his fellows, but can play an effective part, if indirectly, in shaping the policy of the government. No government, if legislating, say, on public health, can afford to neglect the corporate opinion of the medical profession, or, on matters of education, that of universities and teachers, or, on labour questions, that of employers' federations and trade unions. Thus even to-day democracy functions in *concreto* less through direct constitutional machinery than through the active expression of the general thought of the community in the medium of non-political confraternities. To foster their vigour and independence is thus increasingly a main interest of the national or supra-national Commonwealth.[1]

§ 3. But our original question presses itself upon us from another angle. History is the record of the past acts of civilized mankind; but can we say that all civilization falls within its purview? With regard to the facts, there can be no question; the historian is concerned with them all, in their varying measure

[1] See above, c. xi.
[2] See Miss Ruth Follett's well-known book, *The New State*, with special application to the training furnished to American citizens in the New England township. The "corporative" principle advocated above has been recognised alike by Soviet Russia and in Fascist states. See Mr. Christopher Dawson on the Turkey reformed by Mustapha Kemal as the earliest and most instructive type of Fascist state.

of importance.   No fact is intrinsically too trivial for his notice;
a broken potsherd or a memorandum of personal expenditure
may at any moment throw a flood of light on his researches.
History has become democratic, like the rest of us; it is a crude
fallacy to suppose that the historian is solely interested in outstanding personalities rather than in the sentiments and behaviour
of ordinary human beings. So much for his concern with the
facts of civilization; but what about its ideals, which, as we
have seen, are integral to man's civilized life? With these also
the historian is concerned, not, however, in their timeless being,
but in their influence as motives determining human actions and
in their effects on man's cultural history. He will note, for
instance, how the Calvinistic conviction that all men are equally
sinful in the sight of God had its repercussion on secular politics
in fostering the principle of democratic equality at Geneva, in
the Scottish Lowlands, and in the Puritan settlements in New
England. So, again, St. Paul's missionary journeys and the
adoption, under Constantine, of Christianity as the official
religion of the Roman Empire, will hold in his eyes a greater
historical significance than the writing of the Fourth Gospel or
the martyrdom of Saints Felicitas and Perpetua. It is therefore
untrue to say that ideals lie altogether outside his province. No
one will question the legitimacy of extending the range of history
to include the history of art and literature, of philosophy and
religion, or of any of the innumerable specialised branches that,
with the ever-increasing accumulation of materials, have come
to be discriminated within the area of human civilization. But
what the historian takes note of is not the intrinsic worth of
æsthetic, ethical, religious or speculative ideals, so much as their
temporal effects on the cultural life of individuals and societies.[1]
He accounts for these effects by tracing them to their causal
antecedents, thus constructing an intelligible pattern, say, of the
rise of Christianity or of the Renaissance. With any causal
agency from beyond the scene of temporal events such as divine
intervention in the lives of individuals or communities, or with
any other-worldly purpose implied in such intervention, the
historian, *qua* historian, is not concerned. As a man and a
Christian he may acknowledge such agency, but to explain its
existence and its manner of operation falls outside his competence. For the historian as such, the supernatural is equivalent to the non-existent. In Bacon's phrase, *Deum semper*

[1] See Appendix II, pp. 477–479, for the historian's criterion of
" importance."

excipimus. In the traditional language of the schools, he confines his attention to secondary causes.[1] Where these fail to
account for the phenomena, his only resource is frankly to admit
his inability to offer a reasonable explanation. To have recourse
to the miraculous is to quit the ground of scientific history.
Only in so far as actual men have been inspired to act in certain
ways by their (real or supposed) vision of an other-worldly order
do such ideals come within his province.

§ 4. This is the reason why (as I have stated in the Preface,
p. ix. (ii), and at the opening of the chapter on Christianity)
I have contented myself with indicating the personality of Jesus
of Nazareth as the source from which the first disciples and the
Church as a corporate body drew the living energy that enabled
them to preach the Gospel and, in the course of four centuries,
to Christianise the civilized world. So it has been all down the
ages and so it still is to-day. All that has been achieved in
accordance with the divine purpose has its sole spring in the
abiding presence of Christ among men, inspiring individual
Christians and the Christian church by the indwelling in their
hearts of His Holy Spirit. The visible effects of this inspiration
are legitimate matter for the labours of the historian. But to
analyse the nature and activity of the divine Person who inspired
them lies beyond his scope. That is why, in writing a work on
history, I have purposely refrained from any such enquiry.

This must be my answer to the complaint of a fair-minded,
and even generous, reviewer in a notice of the first edition of the
present book, in the *British Weekly.* " It is unpardonable," he
writes, " in a work conceived on this scale that, although the
writer is convinced ' that the history of Christianity can only
be accounted for by the unique personality of its Founder,' he
applies infinitely more psychological insight in his estimate of
the personalities of Amos and Jeremiah than in the single page
[he might have said with truth, "the single sentence."] devoted
to the personality of Jesus of Nazareth. Our Lord's conception
of religious authority is assumed rather than defined." Was it

---

[1] See Aq. *S.c.G.*, iii. 71 (*ad fin.*). A difficult theological problem here
arises. God's causality extends to everything, and therefore is operative
concomitantly with instrumental and secondary causes. Moreover, it is
immanent in such secondary causes, not added to them *ab extra*. It is no
more possible to refer the effect partly to God, partly to natural causality
than to distinguish within the unitary Person of the Incarnate Christ those
features which exemplify His divinity from those which exemplify His
human nature. All is alike at once human and divine. The same applies
to God's immanence in the created universe as creating it and conserving it
in being.

not assumed rather than defined by our Lord Himself? He
claimed unique authority as the Son of God, leaving the task of
defining that doctrine to His followers, to whom He delegated
that authority. As for a psychological estimate of His personality, this depends for its possibility on the answer we give
to a simple question. Was Christ a mere man or was He God
incarnate? In the former case, his personality, like that of
Amos, Jeremiah, or any other man, allows of psychological
analysis. But if He was no mere man, but very God incarnate,
how can we dare, how can we claim the competence, to enter
upon such an undertaking? As a recent living Christian writer
has put it, " We are in no position to draw up maps of God's psychology." [1] We know indeed that on certain occasions Christ was
moved to pity or to anger and we can draw rough generalisations
from such cases; we know that His presence excited curiosity,
devotion, love, hatred and, most frequently, awe and astonishment, in His disciples; but what inference can we draw from
these broken lights as to what He was Himself? He was, on
occasion, such as this or that; but He was infinitely more than
this or that, and the " infinitely more " lies beyond our comprehension. We cannot, for instance, draw any clear line of
demarcation between those of Christ's actions which are due to
His divine and those which are due to His human nature. It
was the vain attempt to discriminate in this matter that entangled
Christendom in the Monophysite and Monothelete controversies
of the sixth century. Cyril of Alexandria, who, though not in
all respects an estimable character, was a supremely able theologian, rightly insisted on the presence of both natures in every
detail of Christ's life and character. It is the same with the
attempt to account for His acts in the light of their historical
antecedents. Much may be learnt by enquiry into Jewish thought
and practice before and at the time of His earthly sojourn; and
we know that His life and teaching were designed so as to bring
His revelation of the Gospel within the comprehension of His
hearers. But, again, our historical researches carry us only a
few steps towards the knowledge of God's infinite purpose in the
Incarnation and of the grounds for Christ's fulfilment of it in
His life and death. Nor is the significance of Christ's life and
the evidence for His divinity to be sought in the historical consequences or in its influence on civilization, however widespread

[1] Mr. C. S. Lewis, in an address in Southwark Cathedral, March 16,
1943.

and persistent in after times. Were that so, the absurd conclusion would have to be drawn, that the value of His Incarnation increased with each successive generation, in proportion to its historical effects on human culture. If Christ be truly God, His acts, though occurring in the time-process, transcend that process in their originating principle and, as proceeding from a supertemporal ἀρχή, defy explanation by the methods of the scientific historian.

§ 5. The futility of the attempt to prove Christ's divinity or to measure the significance of His life by appeal to historical consequences has been impressively exposed by Søren Kierkegaard in his *Training in Christianity*.[1] He contends that Christ's life was in-and-for itself infinitely noteworthy and that, even if it had had no historical consequences, its intrinsic value as the life of God on earth would have been unaltered. " From history,' he says, " one can learn nothing about Christ "; faith alone, implying contemporaneousness on the part of the believer with Christ's supertemporal presence, can reveal the truth. Kierkegaard presses over hard the rigid distinction of faith from reason, and his view that the history ruled out as irrelevant is secular, not sacred, history is not free from ambiguity. The following passage from a Catholic theologian [2] puts the main point with less obscurity and one-sidedness. Writing of the mystery of the *Parousia*, of Christ's coming in all ages to each individual, as a judgement (*krisis*), he insists that the decisive act of acceptance or rejection is not a temporal process but is complete in the moment of its occurrence. " It is the privilege of personal beings not to come to be, but to be themselves at any moment they will. . . . It is for this reason that, according to the traditional teaching, at any moment of our rational life (even *in articulo mortis*) we can sin grievously or win eternity by an act of love, be for God or against Him. So to think of ourselves is not to deny that we can grow and become more perfect. The truth for us lies in the special character of our development which is by means of a series of complete acts, of what Aristotle, in writing of acts of knowledge, called τελείαι, because they do not end a process." I suggest that it is in some such way as this that we should conceive the integration of God's eternal causal agency with temporal events in the course of human history.

[1] English translation by Lowrie, pp. 28 ff.
[2] Father M. C. D'Arcy, S.J., Master of Campion Hall, Oxford, in his Presidential address to the Oxford Society of Historical Theology (1938–9) on *The Christian View of History*.

§ 6. Leaving this difficult, yet all-important problem of the relation of the two worlds, the eternal and the temporal, to one another, there is one further point to be noted strictly relevant to a discussion of the historian's technical procedure. We remarked above that any fact, however trivial, is of potential interest for history. But this is not to suggest that all facts are equally important. The historian has to select from a vast mass of material the specific problems for his investigation, and for a given enquiry certain data will be more relevant than others and therefore, for his immediate purpose, more important. But, apart from this pragmatic and largely subjective criterion, can we not ascribe to certain events, say, Cæsar's murder or the outbreak of the Russian revolution, an objective significance, which others (say, the composition of this paragraph) do not possess ? What, then, is the criterion by which the objective importance of historical personalities and events is to be gauged ? The only standard available for the historian is the cultural achievement of his own race and age, including its acknowledged values, and enlarged by a generous recognition of achievements alien to his experience. Thus the Western European will be ready to ascribe value to the civilizations of India or China, however remote their outlook upon life may be from his own. But the standard remains this-worldly and humanistic. Judgement on other-worldly ideals will be strictly determined by their fruits as displayed within the framework of a historical civilization. For him, as for Protagoras of Abdera in the fifth century B.C., " man is the measure of all things." This is why the scales of historical greatness and of religious or moral excellence present such a disconcerting discrepancy. But this raises a large and difficult problem, requiring consideration in a separate Appendix.

ON HISTORICAL GREATNESS AND MORAL GOODNESS

I.

§ 1. THE problem referred to at the close of the preceding Appendix, of the distinction between the historian's valuations and those of the moralist, is one which most writers on the theory of value seem to have ignored. The usual practice is to treat of values under the threefold rubric of truth, beauty, and moral goodness. This threefold classification, grounded on the misleading eighteenth-century distinction of cognition, feeling, and will as mutually exclusive modes of consciousness, is not exhaustive. For one thing, it limits value to the sphere of rational consciousness, whereas we discern valuation, in some measure, at infrahuman levels; indeed, if Spinoza and Dr. Whitehead are in the right, it is present even below the plane of consciousness in every "actual entity." Among ideal values, again, there are other claimants to recognition; the religious life, for instance, though practical, is not, like morality, merely practical, but is inspired by theoretical vision, nor is its characteristic value, holiness—the *virtus infusa* of the saint, identifiable with moral virtue. Once more, within the domain of ethics, there is the distinction between the standards of right and of good, about which much has been written of late, especially by Oxford philosophers. In what follows I shall use the terms "moral" and "ethical" indiscriminately to cover both types of value, without prejudice to my convictions, which have been expressed elsewhere,[1] that rightness cannot be interpreted as due to intrinsic or consequential goodness, that an action is moral only when done for its intrinsic rightness, that action *sub ratione boni* is a type of action distinct from moral action, and that both types, the moral and the optimific, have ethical value. Further, in the field of æsthetic valuation, we discern a manifest qualitative difference between the sublime and the beautiful. All this shows the error of overhasty simplification. Value itself is a highly abstract term, which is bereft of significance when divorced from concrete experience. It implies compresence with a valuing subject, whose individuality is reflected in his acts of valuation. Moreover, standards of value are no bare formal unities, universals standing aloof from embodiment in particular instances and awaiting a content to be externally supplied from the realm of

[1] *From Morality to Religion*, c. I, pp. 4–5, cc. II and III.

empirical fact. The values are found in the facts, which would not be the facts without them, though it takes a living mind to find them; and when found they are pregnant with anticipatory inspiration of the novel response to the practical situation.[1] The ethical ideal of goodness, for example, is no empty rule or form, but a form *of life*, a synthetic principle of unification, which, however vaguely apprehended, is capable of generating, in relation to the changing current of events, schemes and purposes that are ever individual and new. So it is also with truth, beauty or holiness. When held apart from the concrete truths of the special sciences, from the artist's manifold intuitions, from the personal revelations of the religious life, these values degenerate into barren formulæ, as impotent as they are unmeaning.

§ 2. I come now to the problem. Everyone will agree that ethical valuation—whether the judgement be that of rightness or of goodness—is concerned with human character and conduct. Few, again, would question that in this practical sphere the ethical valuation is ultimate, even in regard to the pursuit of truth or beauty.[2] It is a moral duty for the philosopher to seek truth for truth's sake, and for the artist to seek beauty for the sake of beauty. Moral obligations control not only the choice of a vocation, but also its exercise in detail, as when a man is called upon to forgo the practice of his art or his science in order to serve his country, or, again, to be single-minded in his devotion, in the face of temptation to do inferior work for the sake of gain or popularity. Herein lies the primacy of the Practical Reason. Yet the historian habitually employs, in judgements upon human achievements, another and apparently a very different standard, that of eminence or greatness.[3] The two measures of

---

[1] As has repeatedly been pointed out in the course of this book (see esp. c. ix, xii, and Appendix I).

[2] I do not here discriminate between ethical and religious valuation. Where these fall apart, the religious valuation is final.

[3] The view that it is the philosopher's prerogative to value the facts recorded by the historian has already been rejected (see c. xii, p. 462, *note* 1). Hegel himself would have repudiated any such severance of fact from value; indeed, in the *Introduction* to the *Philosophy of History*, he poured contempt on the suggestion that the philosopher, " so far from leaving history as it is, should force it into conformity with an idea and construe it *a priori*." But Hegel's professions were not infrequently belied by his performance, as when he relegates to romance all that, in his judgement, is irrelevant to the manifestation of Spirit, declaring that " the essential characteristic of the Spirit . . . is always contained in great events " and that " all the particular facts which remain are a superfluous mass, which, when faithfully collected, only oppress and obscure the objects worthy of history." Such a doctrine as this is, as we have said, anathema to the historian.

value are not merely different; they can, and frequently do, conflict with one another. It is evident that great men are not necessarily good, or at any rate that their goodness is not proportioned to their greatness; also, happily for most of us, that it is possible to be good without being great. We recall the closing words of *Middlemarch* : " The growing good of the world is partly dependent on unhistoric acts; and that things are not so ill with you and me as they might have been, is half owing to the number who lived faithfully a hidden life, and rest in unvisited tombs." The day-labourer who gives his life to save a drowning child merits ethical approval, though his deed finds no place in history. The peoples of the civilized world showed a fine sense of this distinction when, at the close of the last war, they paid their tribute of honour, not only to famous generals and statesmen, but also to the " unknown warrior," recognizing thereby the moral value of a thousand unrecorded acts of sacrifice. On the other side, both imaginative literature and history afford numberless examples of great characters, whose ethical goodness or badness has little relevance for our estimate of their greatness. " Il y a des héros en mal comme en bien "; we admire Æschylus' Clytæmnestra, Dante's Farinata, Milton's Satan, as we admire Cæsar or Napoleon, by a valuation of a very different order from that of moral approval or disapprobation. Greatness, again, is ascribed on grounds that in the main are non-ethical, to societies and institutions, such as the Roman Senate or the English Parliament. Dante, following Augustine, saw in Pagan Rome a supreme example of imperial greatness, which went far to justify her selection by Divine providence as the secular instrument for the foundation of Christianity. Hers was not indeed the excellence of the *civitas Dei*, but that of the *civitas terrena*, the city of the world; yet she held, among reprobate principalities, an unquestioned primacy, on a valuation parted by an abyss from that of moral goodness.[1]

II.

§ 3. Surely there is here a serious problem, alike for the philosopher and for the historian. But, before addressing ourselves to its solution, we must show that it cannot be eluded by subordinating either of the two standards to the other, either (1) by interpreting historical greatness in terms of goodness, or (2)

[1] See above, c. xi, p. 418, and c. xii, pp. 458–61.

by restricting judgements of moral approbation to acts and persons whom the historian accounts " great."

(1) First, we may call in question the autonomy of the historian's valuation. The so-called great who are not good are, it may be said, not really great; and the sooner the historian recognises this and renounces his own standard for that of morality, the better will it be for history. Alexander and Napoleon were, like " Tamburlaine the Great," mere organisers of slaughter; historians, like the public, have simply been deluded by the glamour of successful ἀδικία on a grand scale. We may reply that the villainy, if villainy it be, is yet on a grand scale, and as such commands admiration by its sheer magnificence and splendour. Yet, even if we throw conquerors and tyrants to the lions, what are we to say of those morally bad men, like Henry II of England, whose claim to greatness rests on their achievements in the fields of government and law ? More deserving of consideration is the variant on this view which seeks the criterion of a man's greatness in the good effects of his work upon the world.[1] Socrates or St. Francis, it will be said, were great in themselves, for they were also good; but the Cæsars and Napoleons owe their greatness to the fact that what they achieved enabled good people to promote the moral welfare of mankind. I do not, however, think that this doctrine is satisfactory. In the first place, it makes greatness, at least, in the case of bad men, solely dependent on consequences for good, and in no wise intrinsic to its possessor. Secondly, the criterion proposed is beyond the historian's or anyone else's power of application. Who can gauge the moral issues of an act through a long course of history ? Even if moral goodness were determinable by causal laws, the laws are manifestly incalculable; while the knowledge of the effects has to be gathered from their overt expression, and is restricted to the rare instances where goodness emerges from its normal obscurity and is proclaimed upon the house-tops. Moreover, if by goodness we mean " moral goodness "—and this is certainly what is intended by the view in question—we throw the historian's estimate overboard and deny all value to achievement that cannot justify itself at the bar of ethics. The moralist may acquiesce—indeed, if I understand him aright, Dr. Ross has defended this position [2]—but is it seriously proposed that history should be rewritten on such a

---

[1] T. H. Green seems at times to approximate to this variant.
[2] *The Right and the Good*, pp. 152 f.

principle? Ethics cannot claim a right to question the canons of the historian within the bounds of his own enquiry. This admission, however, does not imply that his valuation is final beyond its own limits, or that his estimate of greatness and the ethical estimate of goodness stand on the same plane.

§ 4. (2) If greatness cannot be explained in terms of goodness, intrinsic or consequential, can moral goodness be explained in terms of greatness? This alternative method of evading the issue lands us in even wilder paradox. It would mean that a man's title to be called good rested solely on his own greatness or on his capacity to produce the conditions of greatness for others. It is true that moral excellence enters into the ideal of civilized life which, as we shall see, is the historian's criterion of greatness, but only as one cultural factor among many. Virtue can hardly be identified with the specific excellences of the artist or the philosopher. The two most serious objections, however, are the following. (a) If goodness is to be measured in terms of greatness, it will be limited by its possessor's ability to display it overtly in the public life of his generation, by shaping the thought and practice of society to ethical ends. Of the inward springs of moral action, as distinct from its expression in notable achievements, the historian takes no account. Whether Scott wrote his novels to get money for building Abbotsford or to pay Ballantyne's debts; whether Rembrandt painted in order to provide Saskia with a necklace or from pure joy in creative work; whether Cæsar conquered Ariovistus to win power for himself or to protect Roman territory from Teutonic invasion is irrelevant to the estimate of his greatness. What matters is that Ariovistus was conquered, and that by Cæsar's genius and his strong right arm. The estimate is based on the thing done, not upon the disposition of the man who does it; and the thing done must be on a memorable scale. But in judging goodness of character—whatever may be the case with the rightness of the action—motive is all-important. So, again, the problem of freedom, which the moral thinker is bound to take in earnest, simply does not exist for the historian. For him determinism has no terrors. "Ought implies can"; but the estimate of greatness rests on the thing done, not on the disposition of the man who does it. Greatness depends both on gifts of natural endowment and the presence of opportunity favourable to its display. With moral goodness it is otherwise. (b) Morality is very independent of circumstance; in every practical situation there is a duty to be done or a good to be realised, and the value hinges on the effort that the agent makes in willing it. If few achieve goodness, the possibility is there for all, and those who fail fail on their own responsibility. Herein lies the democratic appeal of morality, which impressed Kant so deeply, accounting for his admiration for Rousseau's writings, where it found eloquent expression. A man's goodness is never, like greatness, " thrust upon him "; he is master of his moral personality, whatever be his station or his talent. Greatness, on the other hand—and this holds also of *moral* greatness—is dependent both on rare gifts of natural endowment and on an exceptionally favourable environment. This is why genius so often strikes us as accidental, so that we can understand Napoleon's question in regard to candidates for high command : " Is he lucky ? " What from an other-worldly standpoint is the " cunning of reason " or the decree of divine providence, appears to the historian as the gift of Fortune. We have noted how the great man of action is often blind to the ends for which he is working and to the real significance of his achievements. Greatness, like pleasure, comes to him by the way. If he has flashes of clear vision at crucial moments in his career, his thought is for the most part concentrated on the solution of particular problems, each of which, taken in isolation, is trivial and monotonous. Great men lay themselves open at every turn to the charge of opportunism; for they know better than others that to act effectively they must wait on the ever-shifting movement of events. " There are sudden providences in things," said Cromwell; and a Cæsar or a Napoleon or a Bismarck, though they might discard the religious implication, wait with a like patience the signal from an agency not their own.

§ 5. Thus it is that great men seem conscious, when face to face with the critical opportunity, of being in the presence of an alien and overwhelming power. The situation, which calls their whole personality into action, is not of their own choosing. They see in it, according to their varying temperament, the hand of destiny or chance or God. Their response is felt by them as a response to something greater than themselves; they create, but with a sense of restricted freedom. This consciousness of the numinous—to use a hard-worked term—in history cannot be accounted for by any wiles of psychological analysis. The objective order of things—to employ the secular language proper to the historian—has in some mysterious and unfathomable manner given birth to a richly pregnant crisis, which breaks as a unique intrusion into the normal process of historical development. You may trace out in detail the genesis of the French or the Russian revolutions; but when all has been said and done, the issue defies resolution into its antecedents. The historian, like the actor in the drama, is confronted by what, from the standpoint of scientific method, he must confess to be irrational. It is the same with greatness in art or science, with the experiences that inspired Dante to compose the *Divina Commedia*, or Faraday to discover the hidden secrets of electro-magnetism. Now for the historian, as such, the presence of this disturbing factor in history furnishes no speculative problem. He probes into the story of its origin, notes the emergence of a new phenomenon and, if the action that ensues tallies with his criterion of human culture, pronounces the action or the agent " great." But the philosopher must go farther and ask questions that may well carry him beyond the bounds of human history. Is the mysterious power that of the spatio-temporal universe, sweeping onward in its totality towards a higher level of evolutionary development ? Or is it, as for Hegel, the " cunning of reason," overruling the petty interests and designs of mortals at the behest of the Absolute Idea ? Or, once more, is it that Power to which religion does obeisance, a supernatural Providence whose designs lie beyond the scope even of metaphysics, save in so far as metaphysics furnishes justification for religious faith ? It is noteworthy that in all ages greatness has been the form of value most commonly ascribed to the object of religious worship. " Allah alone is great." " Great is the Holy One of Israel in the midst of thee." Has not the philosopher defined God, when arguing to his existence as *id quo maius cogitari nequit* ? [1] Something of this numinous quality seems to attach to all forms of greatness. This is why some have been led to rank greatness above goodness and have striven to emancipate " world-historical individuals " from allegiance to the moral law.

These considerations seem to be conclusive against any attempt to evade the problem of the dualism of valuation by reducing moral goodness to historical greatness. Yet I cannot help suspecting that a good many writers on ethics, including all those who adopt a Naturalistic theory, are committed to this view by implication. I do not see how, if we identify the good with a form of civilization immanent in the temporal process, we can differentiate the moral ideal from the historian's criterion of great-

[1] Anselm: *Proslogion*, c. ii. "Than which nothing greater can be conceived."

R

ness. For that criterion, as we shall see presently, is nothing other than just such a form of social life, in which cultural values find scope for actualisation. Are not the advocates of humanism in ethics logically bound to renounce the claim of ethics to autonomy, and to accept the historian's standard of greatness as the measure of the moral life ?

III.

§ 6. Since, then, the difficulty cannot be side-tracked by reducing either greatness to terms of goodness, or goodness to terms of greatness, we must frankly recognise a divergence of standards of value. Let us first ask what the historian means when he calls a personality or an achievement "great." The following considerations will serve as an approach to an answer.

(i) Greatness, like goodness, has a variety of meanings, not all of which are relevant to our purpose. Its use, in popular speech, to signify mere quantitative magnitude, as when we talk of a great river or a great fortune, may be ruled out of account. It is as a qualitative factor that magnitude enters into the estimate of historical greatness. A university may be of smaller size than a big business corporation like Imperial Chemical Industries, but it is a greater thing. We recall Coleridge's saying about Milton : " If there be one character of genius, predominant in Milton, it is this, that he never passes off bigness for greatness." The late Professor Alexander, writing on " Beauty and Greatness in Art," points out that an analogous distinction arises also in science and morality. It is idle, he says, to ask, e.g., among works of art, whether one is more beautiful than another; for all alike are beautiful, as all truths alike are true, and all ethically good actions alike are virtuous. Whether this be so or not is another story; what is relevant to our purpose is his recognition that though there are no degrees of beauty, truth or goodness, there are degrees of greatness. Scott's novels, he holds, rank higher in the scale of greatness than Jane Austen's, the truth of the law of gravitation than that of a property of a botanical species. So with morals; " there is a double standard by which conduct is measured or judged. . . . Within virtuous action there is an order of greatness or smallness, an order of perfection." Now the greatness in each kind depends, according to Professor Alexander, on the subject-matter, the beauty, truth or goodness on the form. That which is great, he says, is great by virtue

of the "magnitude or splendour" of its theme—including
under or along with these its "complexity"; or, again—
though here surely form comes into play as well as subject-
matter—by virtue of the subject being handled "more exten-
sively, more profoundly and more subtly," with "deeper insight
and penetration." Greatness thus indicates a differentiation
within the wider areas of the beautiful, the true and the good,
great art being always also beautiful, great science true, great
virtue good; the differentiation being determined by the magnitude or splendour of the subject. This doctrine, that greatness
lies in the splendour of the theme of art, science or conduct, is,
I am sure, sound; with the addition, perhaps, of the mark of
completeness. Great works of art, like the *Divina Commedia* or
the *Fifth Symphony*, great philosophical constructions, like the
Republic or Spinoza's *Ethics*, feats of action like the battles of
Blenheim or Trafalgar, strike upon the mind with a finality
which no criticism, however conscious we may be of its validity,
can utterly destroy. In the moment of appreciation, they are
self-contained and satisfying; within the limits of the aesthetic
intellectual or practical situation—and, in the moment of appreciation, we do not look beyond—there is no more to be said or
done.[1]

§ 7. But, while thus indicating a generic property of greatness, Professor Alexander does not consider in his paper the
relation to goodness of the specific type of greatness that we
have called historical. He discusses the relation of *moral* great-

[1] The difference in the case of these other forms of greatness, e.g., in
art and science, lies in this, that here the historian accepts the estimate of
experts in other fields, the musicians' estimate of Beethoven's greatness,
the scientists' of Darwin's, the philosophers' of Aristotle's or Spinoza's. I
admit that the line is hard to draw; for the historian of art or philosophy
must understand his subject, as we say, from within. Conversely, an
adequate understanding needs some knowledge of the historical context.
Yet the activities are distinguishable; a given individual's capacity for
Kunstgeschichte is not proportionate to his capacity as an artist. Even in
philosophy, where the moments are least separable, the difference is discernible; Kant was but poorly instructed in the thought of the past, and
Zeller was a more erudite historian of philosophy than Hegel. The
historian's verdict in these matters is not autonomous; but he judges
Caesar or Napoleon great on his own authority, in the light of his own
standard of civilization. That standard embraces all cultural values,
while assigning primacy to the establishment and maintenance of social
organisation and law. That Richelieu composed a tragedy and founded
the French Academy, that Frederick of Prussia enjoyed intellectual
companionship with Voltaire, will condition the judgement as to their
historical greatness. So too with ethical values; it is equally obvious that
moral goodness enters as a factor into the historian's judgement, and that it
is not his sole or dominant criterion (see § 10, pp. 486-7).

484   THE LEGACY OF THE ANCIENT WORLD

ness to goodness, explaining that it is goodness *plus* the characters of magnitude and splendour, which add to the goodness
a distinctive value. But, as he points out, between *morally*
great action and action that is just good there can be no opposition, any more than between great art and art that is just beautiful, or between great philosophy and philosophy that is just
true. Hence his conclusions, acceptable as they are, scarcely
touch the root of our problem. Historically great action is not
good action, enriched by the distinctive value of greatness. It
is not necessarily good at all. It may be good, bad, or morally
indifferent. The question : How is it that within the field of
human action there have come to be two rival orders of valuation,
which are frequently found to conflict, and each of which claims
independence of the other ? remains unanswered. Unlike " good,"
which is often employed as a predicate, " great " is rarely used
except as a qualifying epithet, and never properly of abstracts ;
we say that pleasure is good and talk of good pleasures, but the
phrase " a great sincerity," though admissible, carries a suggestion of metaphor. The natural use of the term is (*a*) of persons,
and (*b*) of things or events as expressive of personal agency, as
when we speak of a great poem or discovery or, again, of a great
city, meaning one that has unique significance in human history.
Rome is a great city, not for its size—Athens too is great, while
Pekin and Chicago are not—but because it is the outcome and
embodiment of significant human activity and has profoundly
influenced the course of human activity both within and beyond
its bounds. But greatness cannot be measured simply by its
effects. While " good " is also applicable to what is not good in
itself, but merely conducive to a good result, greatness is a
quality intrinsic to its possessor. To judge an individual or an
institution great on the strength of its causal efficacy, and of that
alone, is to confound a property of greatness with its essence.
If offered as a definition, it lands us in a circle. For every
action, however trivial, has innumerable effects ; what is characteristic of great action is that its effects also are great. " Spirits
are not finely touched but to fine issues." True ; but this brings
us no nearer to an understanding of what greatness means.

§ 8. (ii) The view that the key to a man's greatness is to be
found in the fact that he is typical or representative of his age
has a certain *prima facie* plausibility. Great historical personages do seem, as Emerson noted in the case of Napoleon, to
sum up and embody, in their thought and actions, the dominant

pattern of their time. So is it with great works of art and literature and with great philosophy; Dante's *Divina Commedia* and
the *Summae* of St. Thomas, in their several ways, express in
encyclopædic form the spirit of mediæval culture. But here
again we are in danger of falling into a circle. Great men and
their works represent what is of high significance, patterns of
thought and life which are judged to be dominant, on the score
not merely of their prevalence, but of their greatness. Some
ages are moulded to patterns which are trivial and insignificant;
in these, greatness, if it appears at all, is revolutionary rather
than representative. There is a sense, again, in which every
individual represents his age, representing it indeed in inverse
proportion to his individuality. The great man stands rather for
the forward *nisus*, implicit, it may be, but not explicit, in the
life of his generation, for the pattern that is not yet, but thanks
to his creative genius is to be. Great men of action are as a
rule unaware of the full significance of their undertakings, which
becomes clear to the historian of a later generation only after long
lapse of time. They are aware only that the time is ripe for
new development, and are driven onwards by a dim but compelling sense of vast possibilities, to reshape their world to ends
that lie beyond their vision. Thus, so far from being typical of
the life and sentiment of their age, they are, as we say, "ahead
of their time," and liable to misrepresentation, obloquy or persecution from their contemporaries. To quote Hegel again, so
far from great men enjoying happiness, "their whole life is
labour and trouble. . . . When their object is attained, they fall
off like empty husks from the kernel." That this is so they are
themselves aware. Cromwell's words to his Parliament, "I
would have been glad to have lived under my woodside, to have
kept a flock of sheep rather than undertaken such a government
as this," can be paralleled in the case of many famous men in
history. For this reason the appeal to the social sentiment, the
"standardised mind," on which Professor Alexander lays so much
stress in his treatment of ethical value, fails alike in the case of
goodness and in that of greatness.

§ 9. (iii) Continuing this process of elimination, we must rule
out of account all attempts to make greatness dependent, solely
or mainly, on the formal character of the agent's will. It does
not consist in mere efficiency or in successful adaptation to the
practical situation. Efficiency, sheer force of will, is, as Croce
has shown, a condition *sine quâ non* of every action; if it be

not willed effectively, there is no action, but failure to act. What is willed—the matter of the action rather than its form— is the factor decisive of the greatness. So with successful adjustment, appropriateness, fitness; these are characteristics which may be exhibited in quite unhistoric situations, as when I " do the right thing " in guiding my car skilfully in a sudden and perilous emergency. Appropriateness for what ? is the relevant question, and the answer must be in terms, not of mere efficiency or fitness, but of specific ends. Nor does greatness lie in mere talent, however brilliantly displayed. Lord Brougham was called " prodigious " by his generation just on this account; but no historian would judge him great, for great purpose was lacking to his life and actions. Nor will the test of coherence of wills, for all its array of philosophic champions, avail us better. Every action demands a measure of coherence, as of efficiency, both inwardly among the agent's dispositions and outwardly in co-operation with his fellows. At the other extreme, perfect coherence of wills is an ideal assured only to moral and religious faith, and belongs to a realm of vision of which the historian at all events takes no account. Within his purview, conflict and incoherence are as evident as harmony and coherence; men and societies cohere for evil purposes as well as good, as when three of the leading states of Europe cohered to effect the partition of Poland. The lives of historically great men have been lives of ceaseless conflict, both within and without, and history goes far to justify religion in its relegation of ideal harmony to another world and in its characterisation of man's secular condition as a *militia*. At each stage in our search for the meaning of greatness we are led away from the formal characters of action to the consideration of its subject-matter and its purpose.

§ 10. (iv) Once more : The distinction between greatness and goodness is complicated by the fact of moral greatness, greatness, i.e., that is grounded upon goodness. A morally great character or action is also good, just as a great work of art is also beautiful; but the converse does not hold, though, given a practical situation which calls for a heroic solution, the action cannot be called good unless it solves the problem and is therefore, in this instance, great. Now, great goodness is also great historically, as are great art and science; for these have their histories, integral with that of man's action in society and recognised by the historian as legitimate branches of his science.

There is thus a wider sense of historical greatness, in which it covers the whole field of greatness, in addition to its more specific application to social and political action. Hence it is untrue to say that the historian in estimating greatness takes no account of ethical values. Even where the greatness is not greatness in goodness, moral qualities enter as factors into the life or action, which are judged great as unitary wholes. But the historian's judgement on these qualities differs from the ethical, in that he looks not to the agent's inward disposition, but to its overt expression. The achievement is largely dependent for its greatness on conditions that lie beyond the scope of the moral judgement. If, thanks to uncovenanted graces and opportunity, a man is enabled to display his goodness conspicuously in the public life of his generation, by shaping its thought and practice to his ethical ideal, he is entitled to be called not only good, but great. The same is true of religion. In so far as a St. Paul or a St. Augustine sets the stamp of his spiritual faith on the institutional life of secular or ecclesiastical societies, either by direct participation in their affairs or by influencing the beliefs and practice of those who govern them, he becomes significant in human history. But the inward springs of religious devotion, the ὁμοίωσις τῷ θεῷ, which is the be-all and end-all of the religious life, lie outside the historian's province. They win for their possessor the salvation of his soul and the enjoyment of the celestial kingdom; but they do not make him historically great. Thus it is with the mystics, save when, as in the case of St. Bernard, their vision prompts to effective action in public affairs, or when, as in the case of St. Francis, it finds expression in the establishment of an order that leavens the social life of their age. Thomas à Kempis, like the vast majority of morally good men, calls for scant notice from the historian.

§ 11. (v) It is at this point that Croce comes to our aid, with his distinction, within the field of the practical, of economic and moral activity. He is, I think, the one philosopher of our time who has clearly grasped the problem, though, for a reason to which I shall refer presently, I am unable to accept his answer. Economic volition or action—these are for Croce identical—is volition of the particular; moral volition or action is volition of the universal. The former embraces all material ends, the latter is, as moral, purely formal. Since the universal can only be effectively willed in willing particular ends, all action, including moral, is economic, i.e., the economic moment, though distinct, is present in every moral act of will. But not all economic action is moral; for the particular may be willed for its own sake, and not as an embodiment of the universal. Such purely economic action is neither moral nor immoral, but amoral. Moreover, each form of action has its own standard of value; we approve moral action for its goodness, or—in logical, Kantian, terms— for its universality; but we approve also economic action for its efficiency, quite apart from its moral worth. The two forms are not co-ordinate, nor is economic action a lower grade of moral action; they are distinct types of practical activity, the economic being capable of standing alone, while the moral necessarily presupposes the economic.

§ 12. We seem here to have found the clue to the nature of the distinction between historical greatness and goodness. For Croce not only recognises two distinct types of practical valuation, but grounds the distinction on that between two sorts of activity, each directed to a different end. The one is wholly immersed in the finite and temporal, the other, while immanent in the finite and temporal, works therein in the light of the infinite and the eternal. " The volitional act," he writes,[1] " *quâ* economic, satisfies us as individuals in a determinate point of time and space," but " unless it satisfies us at the same time as beings transcending time and space, our satisfaction will prove ephemeral and will be changed swiftly into dissatisfaction." And he goes on to show how purely economic volition, since it fails to satisfy, misses the mark that volition of the universal can alone attain. How this is consistent with his doctrine of the rationality and independent value of economic action, it is a little difficult to understand.[2] But in so far as Croce is faithful to the dualism of activities and ends, and to the distinction between the temporal and eternal on which it rests, his theory of economic action gives the clue to what the historian means by greatness. The historian's outlook is limited to an ideal construction, reached by an enlargement of the ascertained course of history. He recks nothing of timeless or absolute values, save in so far as such values—let us say, truth, beauty and goodness—find concrete exemplification within the temporal process.[3] He abstracts rigorously from any other-worldly reference. His estimate of historic achievement is made in the light of an ideal form of

---

[1] *Filosofia della Pratica*, p. 221.
[2] See my essay in *From Morality to Religion*, pp. 311–328, on *Croce's Theory of Economic Action*.
[3] See above, p. 476.

human civilization, which, while it transcends the *fait accompli*, lies strictly within the range of possible future attainment, and is filled out with detail drawn from man's actual attainment in the past. He is profoundly distrustful of visionary Utopias, knowing that all such, even the *Republic* of Plato, would, if realised, prove hells upon earth. Moreover, in judging the characters and actions of historic personalities, he keeps his eye fixed on the type of civilization realisable in a given age, e.g., on what was practicable for Alexander or Cæsar or Napoleon under the actual conditions in which they worked. His standard of judgement is no clear and distinct concept, cut to the measure of Cartesian Rationalism, but a form of desirable social life, shadowily envisaged and incapable of precise definition. Such an ideal is not a final or perfect state, but a phase, vaguely conjecturable on the basis of what has been realised in past experience, and itself a temporal process and a becoming. This is not to affirm uniform progress; epochs long past may exemplify details in the ideal type more perfectly than the present or recent times. It implies, certainly, an immanent *nisus* in human development, towards a goal that, however dimly apprehended, transcends actual attainment. But the transcendence falls wholly within the bounds of the spatio-temporal process. The ideal is purely secular and humanistic. From the mass of persons and events within this temporal process, all in their degree possessing historical interest and significance, those that bear the further qualities, in Professor Alexander's phrase, of " magnitude and splendour " are selected by the historian as " great."

§ 13. A further difference between the standards of greatness and goodness leads directly to our conclusion. The historian's valuation is relative, in that his measures of greatness have no finality, but grow with the growth of his knowledge and experience. The ideal, were it actualised, would cease to be an ideal and would yield place to a new ideal, as provisional as the former, and so on *ad indefinitum*. Moreover, it is a purely ideal standard, devoid of actuality save in the thought of the mind that thinks it. It is a light of man's own projection, that witnesses indeed to his unconquerable thirst for self-transcendence, yet, being temporal, ever recedes into the future, as he moves forward, he knows not whither, on its track.

With morality it is otherwise; the standard of valuation is both absolute and actual. Morality is a cheat, if moral obligation be not unconditional; and how can a standard that is dependent on the vague and ever-shifting apprehension of it by the human mind possess unconditional validity ? Many philosophers will, I know, question these assertions, and even among those who recognise the absoluteness of obligation many again will deny its actuality. Goodness, they will say, is real and has objective being; but its being is that not of existence, but of subsistence. I have no desire to quarrel over words, but the term " subsistence " seems to me to state a problem without answering it, and I fall back on the unambiguous doctrine of Dr. Whitehead, that universals and values—his " eternal objects " —are devoid of being save as ingredient in an actual entity.[1] This is not the place for a detailed discussion of this argument, familiar from Kant's time onwards. The point I wish to make is that, if we are prepared, as I am certainly prepared, to accept it, moral experience, when thought out, implies the belief in an other-worldly reality, transcendent of the world of spatio-temporal events; and that this implication furnishes a firm basis for the distinction between historical greatness and moral goodness. Human action is judged great by a standard relative to the temporal process; it is judged good by a standard that as absolute is super-temporal and super-human. This affirmation of transcendence is not a denial of immanence; indeed, immanence seems unmeaning unless that which is immanent transcends that which it informs. It is Croce's uncompromising refusal to admit any reality beyond possible historical experience, any reality save " l'umana e il terrena," that vitiates his solution of the problem of greatness and goodness. No answer to that problem is possible on purely humanistic ground.

§ 14. Our discussion has led us from a special difficulty in the theory of conduct into deep waters of metaphysics and the philosophy of religion. In speaking of the various meanings of greatness, I made no reference to its application to the object of religious worship. The being or beings which, in Dr. Otto's phrase, are charged with numinosity, excite in a supreme degree those impressions of magnitude and splendour and, above all, of finality, which we have seen to be the properties of greatness. We have here an exception to the rule that the term " great " is used only as an attribute, not predicatively; we do not say " the great God," but rather that " God is great." Such super-human greatness obviously implies transcendence and is very far removed from the greatness displayed in human history. Nor

[1] See my *From Morality to Religion*, pp. 182–186.

does it give rise to any problem of rival valuations. For in God, as revealed in religious experience, all values meet in unbroken unity. Moreover, for religious faith the temporal process, which the historian values on a purely immanent standard, appears as the scene for the manifestation of a transcendent purpose. Human history is transfigured into a theodicy; in events, which the historian finds fortuitous and irrational, religion sees the hand of Providence, overruling the unchancy and the evil for other-worldly ends.

This recognition of other-worldly value in no way abrogates the claim of history to form its independent valuation. Man is a creature of two worlds, the temporal and the eternal, the one a derivative, the other an original reality, the one the object of rational enquiry, the other of moral or religious faith.[1] Each world has its proper measure of value. The historian is fully justified in refusing to trespass beyond his own domain or to embark on the vain endeavour to decipher a pattern that lies beyond the scope of the methods of his science. But when, as in the problem I have been considering in this Appendix, we attempt to relate his valuations to those of morality or religion, it is only by reference to other-worldly value that a solution can be found. In no other way can we escape the *impasse* which gave the initial impulse to our enquiry. Either history must be rewritten in the light of ethics, or the historian's verdict of greatness must be accepted as the criterion of what is morally good. And, on either alternative, it is evident that—to quote the words of Browning's *Cleon*—

"The doctrine could be held by no sane man."

[1] I have not attempted in this Appendix to bridge the gulf between the consciousness of moral obligation as implying a super-historical reality and the identification of that reality with God. I know that any reference to other-worldliness and transcendence suggests a two-world metaphysic; and that no one who is serious about philosophy can rest satisfied in a final dualism. But such a dualism is very far from my thoughts. If it be urged that the " other world " is but " this world " fully understood, I readily assent; but on two conditions. Within " this world " must be found a place, not only for the ever incomplete stream of historical occurrences, but also for the abiding presence of a super-human and super-temporal power, whence the course of history derives its origin and its value; and the " right understanding " must not be restricted to what is clearly and distinctly known by inference and analysis, but must include therewith the assurances of a reasonable faith.

HUMANISM AND THE WORLD CRISIS

I.

§ 1. In the concluding chapter (XII) we quitted the proper terrain of the historian, viz., the record and interpretation of what has happened in the past, to consider how the legacy of antiquity has contributed to shape our contemporary world. This enlargement of our horizon brought into view speculative problems, which fall within the province of the philosopher as well as that of the historian. We were led to ask what light the study of past history casts on the meaning of human experience and, in particular, to what extent it supports the belief in the progress of civilization. Leaving on one side the pessimistic theories, widely prevalent in antiquity but alien to modern thought, of progressive deterioration and cyclical recurrence, we reached the conclusion that, while the last four centuries have witnessed a steady advance, in accord with a logical order of development, in the fields of pure, and even more markedly of applied, science, any wider generalisation as to the onward march of civilization can hardly be sustained. In particular, it remains highly questionable whether man's intellectual progress has been attended by any corresponding growth in his moral and other spiritual achievement.[1] This doubt has inevitably been intensified by the catastrophic events that have menaced the very foundations of our culture within our own life-time. Some reflections on the nature and import of these phenomena, written amid the stress of world-war, will form a fitting close to our survey of historic civilizations.

§ 2. Let us revert for a moment to the outline of historical movement, known as the Renaissance, traced in the concluding sections of the eleventh chapter. There we were primarily concerned with pointing the contrast between the life and thought of the Middle Ages and that of the new Humanism that followed their gradual disintegration. Here our attention will be fixed rather upon the characteristics of that new outlook and upon its issues from the epoch of the Renaissance up to the present day. The profound change that then revolutionised men's view of life was marked, first, (a) by the assertion of individuality, illustrated

[1] See c. xii, p. 446.

or exemplified; in religion, by the appeal to private judgement against the authority of the Church; in politics, by the rise (as already noted) [1] of nation-states swayed by separatist ambitions and rivalries; and in philosophy, by Descartes' insistence on the consciousness of the individual thinker as the basis for metaphysical construction.[2] Secondly, (b) it was marked by a vigorous rationalism, reason being construed, in accordance with mathematical and scientific procedure, as the faculty of logical ratiocination, which recognises only " clear and distinct " concepts and proportions, relegating all thinking that is vague, shadowy and mysterious to the limbo of irrational feeling and imagination. That was the " short way " taken with religion by the philosophers of the Enlightenment, save with such " natural theology " as could be hold to fall within the domain of reason as thus defined; all else, i.e., " revealed religion " generally, being regarded as matter for unreasoning faith. Thirdly, (c), as we have already seen, a this-worldliness of outlook, and the restriction of intellectual interest to spatio-temporal phenomena and their laws replaced the other-worldliness that had dominated mediæval thought. Hence the new Humanism, unlike that of the Middle Ages, was frankly secularist and anthropocentric. Man was the measure of all things. The God of Judaism and Christianity survived for a season, shorn of His revelational accretions, as the " Author of Nature," posited to account for the inexplicable fact of the existence of a universe, governed by " immutable laws " of Nature, which had been indeed imposed by the Creator, but which allowed of no further supernatural intervention. The faith that inspired the leading minds of Europe in the epoch of the so-called" Enlightenment," that reached its climax at the time of the French Revolution and persisted in the intelligentsia of the nineteenth century, especially in France (from Condorcet to Auguste Comte), and in England (William Godwin and the Utilitarian school of Bentham), and is still influential (witness the writings of Bertrand Russell and H. G. Wells), was centred in man, and in his power, thanks to the methods and achievements of the positive sciences, to control his own nature and the world in the service of human purposes. Its articles may be summarised as follows. First, its disciples had a touching confidence in the inborn excellence of human nature, in the per-

[1] See c. xi. § 23.
[2] He proceeded from the individual thinker to God (viâ the idea of God in the thinker's mind) and to the world (viâ God).

fectibility of man, and in the possibility of unlimited progress. The evils that block the way are due, not, as Christianity taught, to original sin, but to the bad organisation of society, and are curable by remedial legislation. Secondly, they championed individual liberty, dreaming of a millennium when each will achieve salvation by his own effort, and therewith the happiness of all other members of the community. Thirdly, this happiness,. the goal of all endeavour, was interpreted as economic welfare, the possession by each individual of a sufficiency, and something more, of this world's goods. Lastly, the way to this Utopia lay in rational enlightenment, dispelling the mists of superstition, above all in education in the sciences, which already gave promise to man of boundless mastery over nature.[1] If few serious thinkers to-day would endorse this creed without reserve, this is due rather to its practical failure to cope with the evils that beset the world than to a conviction of its theoretical deficiencies. But in truth the latter presents as serious an obstacle to its acceptance as the former. Both lines of criticism will be discussed in the ensuing pages, with the view of deciding the question, whether the secularist Gospel or its rival, Christianity, offers the more reasonable alternative, and one better adapted to man's nature and to his situation in the universe.

II. The Abuse of Knowledge.

§ 3. Readers of Plato's *Republic* must often have been startled by a question, put by Socrates at a critical turn of the argument : " How can the State handle philosophy without being ruined ? "[2] He was thinking of the use or abuse of knowledge and of the power that knowledge gives. The issue depends on the moral character of the rulers, on the end or good to which they dedicate their lives. By philosophy, he meant the reasoned enquiry into the intelligible realities that lie behind the show of sensible appearances; an enquiry culminating in the vision of the sovereign reality, the source of all being and of all value, the Idea or Form of the Good. Plato was convinced that only those whose intellectual efforts were grounded on a firm foundation of moral principle were privileged to achieve this vision.[3] In his view it was one of the most difficult problems to secure in the same individual both intellectual acuteness and moral stability

---

[1] See, for more detail, my book *Towards a Religious Philosophy*, c. xi and Conclusion.

[2] *Rep.*, vi. 497D.   [3] See above, c. v, §§ 19–24.

—clever men are so rarely good, and good people are so often stupid. That is why he insisted on moral discipline as the initial stage in the training of anyone who aspired to the know-ledge of the absolute Good. Unless philosophic studies were based on this foundation the State would be ruined. Men of intellectual power and force of will, lacking the vision of the true Good, would be dazzled and enchanted by finite, this-worldly, goods and would throw all their energies into the pursuit of them. They would be the victims of that ignorance of the true principle of goodness that Plato elsewhere calls "the lie in the soul," and would become the bane of society instead of its salva-tion. For knowledge is power, and the use or abuse of power determines the fate, for good or evil, of the entire community.

What Plato said more than two thousand years ago is as true now as it was then. The advance of modern science has outstripped man's competence to make right use of it. In their blindness to the vision of the true Good, men have set their affec-tions on this-worldly ends, forgetful of the things that are above. Their ambition has been centred on the transitory and mundane goods that science has placed within their grasp. In the language of Christianity they have chosen to live for the glory of man and not for the glory of God. I propose to trace the issues of this failure in modern civilization, and, particularly, to consider the severance that has come about between men's progress in knowledge and the development of their moral character.

§ 4. The term "progress" is in constant use, but few take thought as to its meaning. "Words," said Hobbes, "are wise men's counters, but the money of fools." We are apt to forget—though Hogarth's *Rake's Progress* is there to remind us—that advance may be towards evil as well as towards good; and that, even when we have in mind the process from a lower to a higher level of value, any significant assertion on the matter must be made under qualification. It is difficult to say any-thing with truth about the general progress of civilization. The question has to be considered under limitations of time and place, and with reference to specific fields of cultural activity. We have traced, for instance, among the Hebrew people from the ninth to the fifth century B.C., the advance under prophetic influence from a relatively primitive monolatry to a pure form of ethical monotheism. But this religious progress went hand in hand with the disruption of the Jewish state, and culminated in the hour of its political annihilation. We must be equally guarded in our characterisation of the intellectual progress of modern Europe in the centuries since the Revival of Learning and the Renaissance. The progress has been within a determinate field of knowledge, that of the sciences of man and nature. It may well be that the thinkers and poets and saints of the Middle Ages—Bernard and Anselm, Dante and Aquinas—possessed a deeper knowledge of God and of the things pertaining to God's service than any save a few of the philosophers and theologians of the last four hundred years. The knowledge distinctive of the modern period is of another order; being centred on nature, and on man as part of nature, the speculative outlook that it has brought to birth is essentially humanistic and this-worldly. But within these limitations it offers as fine an illustration of intellectual progress as can be found in history. In the first place, the process throughout is luminously intelligible to the mind of the observer. Science follows upon science in the natural order of development : at the outset the reasoned study of matter and motion (mechanical physics) in the century between Galileo and Newton, followed (especially in the nineteenth century) by the development of chemistry and of the biological sciences, and finally, in quite recent times, by the application of scientific method to mental processes and behaviour in psychology. At each stage, the new discoveries give occasion for efforts after philosophic synthesis, in the speculative systems of Descartes, Leibniz, Kant, and, in our own day, in those of Alexander and Whitehead. Moreover, the sciences which were first developed, far from yielding place in man's interest to those of later appearance, rather continued to progress with increased vigour ; Faraday and Clerk Maxwell were in physics the contemporaries of Lamarck and Darwin, as in our own generation Einstein is the contemporary of the psychologists Freud and Jung. In the second place, we may note how this advance in scientific knowledge has enlarged beyond belief the range of man's control over his environment. All knowledge gives power; as the knowledge of God gave power in things of the spirit to the saints of the Middle Ages, so has science given power over physical nature to the peoples of the modern world. The practical applications of science to the conditions of human life have, in the last few generations, revolutionised the face of nature and the whole order of social intercourse. Were an Englishman of the early sixteenth century wafted back four centuries into the past, he would still be able to thread his way in the England of the

Plantagenets. After the first shock of surprise was over he could make himself comparatively at home. But if we imagine him transported over an equal stretch of time into the England of to-day, he would feel a hopeless alien. Here and there, at the sight of a cathedral or village church (until he entered them), in the procedure of Parliament and of the Law Courts, and in the rites of the Roman church, he might, if gifted with exceptional intelligence, catch the echoes of the England he had known. But the more obtrusive sights and sounds of the factory, the railroad, the aeroplane, the wireless and the newspaper, would soon blot from his mind these scanty relics of antiquity. Now the knowledge that has thus enabled man to transform his physical and social surroundings and to adjust his behaviour and modes of life to the changed world is primarily, though not exclusively, a knowledge that gives power over things perceived by sense. All human knowledge and all human desire take their origin perforce from objects of sense-perception; prolonged effort of thought and will is needed, if man is to rise above what is obviously on a level with his capacities, so as to know and desire the spiritual world that lies beyond. To be beguiled by the lure of material things, and by pride in his mastery of nature into a this-worldly philosophy of life, is the temptation that besets the most gifted in the modern age, and, most of all, those who are marked out to be the leaders in their community. We are brought back to Socrates' searching question : whether such a philosophy, if it gains ascendancy, must not be ruinous to the state ?

§ 5. That there has been progress in knowledge, and in the power that knowledge gives, is beyond dispute, but has there been a corresponding progress in morality ? Are men the better, or the worse, for their intellectual achievements ? We have only to put the question to see that it admits of no cut and dried answer in terms of Yes or No. Let us consider only a single aspect of the problem, what we may call the ethics of public policy and public practice. Of course the public life of the community is inextricably interwoven with the private life of the individual members ; no man lives to himself, nor has the state any being apart from the citizens who compose it. Yet a distinction may surely be drawn between the use of the wireless by Smith in his drawing-room and by the government for purposes of propaganda, or between Jones's use of an aeroplane for a business visit to Amsterdam or Paris, and its employment as an engine of destruction in war. But even if we follow Plato's precedent and limit our discussion to morality as exhibited " in large letters " in the state, the verdict must still be a mixed one. On the one hand, there is undeniably less corruption and far more public spirit to-day in corporate bodies, such as parliaments, churches, trades unions and universities than at any period in the past. Above all, the troubles that have recently beset us have aroused in civilised peoples a widespread desire, not merely for security, but for a constructive peace, i.e., for effective co-operation in the establishment and maintenance of a stable and just international order. The League of Nations may have failed to realise the hopes of its founders, but the aims formulated in the Preamble to the Covenant are more alive in men's minds and hearts to-day than at any previous moment in its history. But it is to the other side of the picture that we must turn in our search for the sources of world-trouble. Over against the evidence for moral betterment we must set the evils that have spread in these last years with startling rapidity through the abuse by governments, both in peace and war, of the weapons that science has placed within their reach. I will give three examples.

§ 6. (1) Recent inventions have vastly increased the resources at the disposal of governments for sustaining and strengthening their power. Love of power is, as Plato remarked, one of the most potent forces in human nature; and its gratification acts as a stimulus to yet wider ambitions. Even in democratic countries the danger from the tyranny of public opinion, dreaded by so strong an advocate of representative government as John Stuart Mill, is far greater to-day then when he wrote his book on *Liberty*. In the totalitarian states, be they Fascist or National Socialist, tyranny stalks naked and unashamed. Such constitutional checks as have been suffered to survive seem impotent to curb the power of the dictators. *Plébiscites* have always lent themselves easily to manipulation from headquarters. It would be an error to suppose that the power thus concentrated in the rulers' hands is used to gratify purely personal ambitions; the personal aims of Mussolini and Hitler were identified with public causes, such as Italian imperialism, the dominance of the Aryan race, or the overthrow of capitalism. They pursued these ideals with a zeal religious in its intensity, and by the traditional methods of religious propaganda—giving and demanding from others a single-minded loyalty that is rightfully due to God alone. Whole peoples have been forced, under penalties of incarceration or even of death, to bow down in worship before these temporal and finite idols. The potent weapons of mass-suggestion by the controlled press and wireless have been utilised to stifle freedom of thought in the citizen from childhood onwards, and to bar the doors of his mind from a disinterested regard for truth. Napoleon threatened to dominate Europe a century and more ago; he, too, rose to greatness as the champion of a new order called into being by the French Revolution; but he lacked the scientific means of mastery—the telegraph, the telephone, the railroad, the aeroplane, and the mechanised army—that are at the disposal of our modern autocrats. The peril to-day is graver than it was then. Moreover, the likelihood of a successful revolution is greatly lessened by the government's monopoly of the instruments for its suppression. The rulers can strike at a distance and with a swiftness that allow to a popular rising little chance of victory.

§ 7. (2) My second example is of an evil that directly touches ourselves, viz., the increase of mechanisation, not only in industry but over the whole of life, menacing human personality with atrophy or asphyxiation. Think of the fate of a factory hand, doomed to pass eight hours of each day mechanically tapping eggs with the same gesture on the same spot! What chance has he for the expansion or development of individual character ? [1] This is one of the issues of man's application of science and the machines he has invented. I am not blaming the scientists or the employers who make use of their discoveries. I am pointing out a case of cause and effect. The effect is monotony and standardisation, in every walk in life, the clerk's, the teacher's, even that of a professor in a university. The worker on the land, whom hourly contact with Nature in her infinite variety has hitherto preserved from contamination, is now threatened by the tyranny of the machine. In each succeeding decade there is less scope in men's lives for originality, independence, freedom. We all desire workers in a mine or mill to have shorter hours and higher wages, that they may enjoy leisure for their soul's good; but what a confession of failure lies behind the desire ! We are at best tinkering—tinkering, if you will, generously and nobly—with the evil; like the doctor whose high calling would have no occasion for exercise were there no diseased

[1] See D. H. Lawrence's *Letters*, edited by Aldous Huxley (p. 771), for a passionate protest against this asphyxiation of personality.

bodies to be healed. In our modern industrial system the work is perforce so monotonous that the worker can find no joy in it. Fancy suggesting to St. Paul that he should preach the gospel for only eight hours a day, and seek his joy and peace at leisure in the time left over from his vocation : or to Beethoven that he would be branded as a blackleg if he spent more than eight hours a day at the keyboard. Ideally work should be a delight; yet it is becoming every year more of a drudgery. True, we educate the workers; but the very immensity of the task forces us to mechanise the education. There are millions of children to be taught, and heaven-born teachers are very few; teachers must therefore be manufactured, on standardised methods, as in a machine. You cannot help this, any more than you can help using machinery in the manufactory; it is better that all children should be taught, even at the cost of sacrificing quality to quantity in the teaching. But let us at least discern the evil, and be on our guard against its consequences. The young workers have been educated to self-consciousness; they are asking questions and pressing for a full share in determining their own and their country's future. The new gospels that have spread like wildfire over many European peoples, Communism, Fascism and National Socialism, draw their main strength from their appeal to youth. They have given to the youth of Russia, Italy and Germany an opportunity to play their part in remoulding the world after their heart's desire.

Let us be under no illusion. The war now smouldering to its close was not a war against Germany and the German people, but neither was it solely against Hitler and Hitler's government. The real enemy was and still is the Nazi youth. They can be counted by millions. Hitler could never have risen to power save for their enthusiastic response to his leadership. The Germans are a people of high intelligence though of a mentality different from our own, and they would never have been beguiled into loyalty towards a cause that had no grip on their personality. In Germany, as in Russia, youth saw its chance and took it; a chance—be it noted—that is denied to youth under the more monotonous, leisurely, conservative *régime* of our own land.

§ 8. (3) My third illustration is the most important, for it touches the source of our failure to use rightly the power placed in our hands by the applied sciences. The source, though not the responsibility, lies in large measure in science itself. As all know, physical research during the last century has resolved the

Newtonian conception of a universe of moving bodies into something that is scarcely distinguishable from pure motion. Atoms and particles of matter have gone by the board as physical ultimates; in their place we have centres of energy—electrons, protons and the like—eddying with incredible velocity and diffusing, each of them, its activity over all space. Under the influence of the new physics, philosophers, like M. Bergson and the late Professor Alexander, have rejected the traditional dogma that only the permanent can change, and have posited motion, without a *mobile*, at the very heart of reality. The same influence has set its stamp on the mind of the public. Just as all science has its roots in pre-scientific popular thinking, in the rough-and-ready generalisations of the plain man in presence of natural phenomena, so, at the other extreme, its conclusions, the fruit of mysterious processes of calculation and experiment that are " caviare to the general," are appropriated by the intelligent public and pass into the structure of ordinary thought. It has happened thus with the apotheosis of motion; only that, in this instance, the public has gone out to meet the new deity with willing worship. Speed records, moving pictures, swift transport, ceaseless change of occupation and amusement are the idols of the modern generation. The passion for movement has even invaded their religion; churches would be crowded if the preacher taught belief in a suffering and striving God, who looked to men for help in His effort for victory over evil. The older views of God as without variability or shadow of turning, and of man's heart as restless until it find rest in Him, are no longer congenial to the taste of the modern world. The effects of this changed outlook on morality are not far to seek. Not only has the traditional belief that the distinction between good and evil, right and wrong, rests on an immutable foundation— the will of God or the principles of natural reason—been relegated to the museum of speculative antiquities; even the mention of absolute and eternal values is apt to be greeted by serious thinkers with a smile of sceptical forbearance. Relativity holds the field, in ethics as in physics.

If secular moralists to-day still claim objective validity for moral ideals and are inspired, as is frequently the case, to acts of sacrifice and unselfish devotion in the cause of humanity and justice, this is not so much on account of any reasoned faith in an other-worldly absolute, a Platonic Form of Good or Kantian Moral Law, as because an aroma of sanctity still clings around those principles, long after their detachment from their original source in Christianity. My point is that if ethical standards express merely changing adaptations to the this-worldly requirements of a particular society in a particular epoch of its history, their pretensions to universal validity are null and void. Unless we are convinced of the reality of an other-worldly order, and of eternal and absolute principles of right and wrong, our criticism, for instance, of Hitler for saying one thing one day at Munich and contradicting it by his action a few days later, is devoid of any ethical justification. We may contend that he acted ill-advisedly—that is a matter of prudential calculation; but, save in the name of an other-worldly ideal, we have no right to pass moral condemnation on his conduct. A thorough-going ethical relativism, as Plato saw clearly, can find no place for morality; it knows only interests.

§ 9. Where, then, lies the remedy? How can the gulf be bridged between men's knowledge, with the power it has brought, and their halting moral endeavour in matters of public policy and conduct?

Obviously the remedy does not lie in barring the way to intellectual progress. Such a counsel of despair is neither possible nor desirable. The example of the very men who have most abused the instruments of public power is there to warn us. Intellectual progress is possible only where thought is free, and what freedom have men had, even to think, in present-day Germany? It is not the scientists who are to blame for the misuse of their inventions; the responsibility falls wholly on those who, from lack of moral vision, have perverted the knowledge that could have saved society into an engine for its ruin.

Nor can we look to the further promotion of knowledge for a remedy, tempting as is the suggestion, and one that in time past has had many advocates. It is a faith of long standing, dating back to Condorcet and the French revolutionary idealists, that universal education, especially in the sciences and their applications, would prove a panacea for all human maladies, and would banish all sin, sorrow and suffering from the earth. Bitter experience has taught us that this is not the case. Knowledge, as we learn from Plato, is a two-edged sword, that has power to make or mar the lives of those possessed of it, according as they use or abuse it, for weal or woe. The cure for our present ills can only lie in raising the level of moral character and conduct. The familiar cliché, " moral rearmament," is evidence that the need is widely felt. The phrase is a metaphor, and not a very happy one. It suggests that morality itself can furnish the means of moral regeneration. Those who use it will perhaps appeal in defence to a famous passage in St. Paul's *Epistle to the Philippians*. But the weapons of which St. Paul spoke were forged in the armoury, not of morality, but of religion. The armour he bade the Christian put on was the armour of God.

§ 10. Mere morality is not enough. I contend that progress in morality can only become possible if inspired by religious faith. What the world needs is to recover the conviction that moral distinctions are not relative, but absolute, independent of what you or I, or even the entire community, like to think. Men's changing moral valuations have never been mere adaptations to a historical environment; all down the ages, they have expressed his groping effort to grasp the vision of an other-worldly reality, of an abiding moral order that is at once transcendent of, and immanent in, the world in which we live. Secular morality, apart from religion, can hardly avail to inspire this saving faith. Yet without this faith we are plunged ever deeper into the maelstrom of relativity. There are two reasons why morality is unequal to this task of self-preservation. In the first place, its scope is limited to the field of human actions. There are other values beside the practical; the knowledge of the truth, for instance, that is the goal of the scientist, the historian and the philosopher, or, again, the expression of truth and beauty in the arts. There is a plurality of values, each with an absolute claim on our allegiance; when the claims conflict, no single claimant, not even morality, has the right to decide the issue. Religion alone can give a final judgement, for religion knows no departmental limits. It embraces the whole personality of the worshipper, his mind and heart and will; and God, the object of worship, is the Alpha and the Omega, the source of all being and of all value, compassing with His presence the whole universe of reality. There is a further reason why morality is incapable of healing its own sickness. It is true that reflection upon the nature of moral obligation lifts us, as Kant impressively showed, beyond the spatio-temporal processes of nature and history to the recognition of an other-worldly and eternal Moral Law. It is true also, as Plato showed, that reflection on finite goods lifts us to the vision of an other-worldly principle of goodness, in which alone the soul of man, with its

restless aspiration for the infinite, can find rest and final satisfaction. But both these objects of moral faith, the eternal
Moral Law and the eternal Form of Good, remain, for moral
vision, abstract and impersonal. I fully admit, what is in the
light of human history indisputable, that wise and strong natures,
such as are endowed with a wide culture and a lofty pride in
their own rectitude, are able to direct their lives aright by reliance
on such impersonal ideals. Stoicism is still a living power
among such men to-day. But it offers no solution to our main
problem. For one thing, I am convinced that reason cannot rest
satisfied with an other-world of self-supporting values. Absolute
goodness, absolute beauty and the rest are intelligible only if
integrated with the consciousness of an existing individual as
their bearer (*Träger*), in other words, with God. I have discussed the philosophical approach from ethics to theism elsewhere,[1]
and must content myself here with this bare statement of conviction. Moreover, even were the Stoic doctrine proved adequate
in philosophy, it could never be a gospel of salvation for the
multitude. Its appeal is to a moral aristocracy, to the cultured
few who are able by strength of will to stand four-square against
all winds that blow.[2] The rank and file—and it is these who in
this democratic age most need moral remarmament—will never
be stirred to sacrifice by an abstraction, not even though it be
Kant's transcendent Moral Law or Plato's transcendent Form of
Good. They must have an object of worship that can evoke
response, not only from the intellect and will, but from the
imagination and the heart. Of this the leaders of National
Socialism were well aware, when, in their contempt for rational
justification, they set in its place a battle-cry for victory.[3]
These false creeds with their false promises of a terrestrial millennium, must be combated by a living theistic faith. *In hoc signo
vinces.* The religion that sets its trust in man can only be conquered by a religion that sets its trust in God.

[1] See my Gifford Lectures, *From Morality to Religion.*
[2] I have in mind the teaching of Nietzsche, which many (erroneously)
hold responsible for the ideology of National Socialism. For the error,
see Father Copleston's discerning study, entitled *The Philosophy of
Friedrich Nietzsche.*
[3] It is matter of common knowledge that the adherents of such doctrines habitually decline to engage in speculative discussion of their
validity. They regard argument as irrelevant. Embrace the creed and
you will be assured by faith of its credibility. On the whole subject,
Georges Sorel's *Réflexions sur la violence*, one of the most significant books
of the last half-century, should be consulted (see especially, in the Introduction to the volume, on the application of Bergson's doctrine of the
" myth," the references to Pascal, and the analogy with early Christianity).

III. The Idol of Humanism.

§ 11. In the preceding sections of this Appendix, I have tried to show that the only hope for the world lies in the revival of faith in Christianity. I now proceed to reinforce the conviction from a different, though allied, standpoint.

The distinctive note of European thought in the last four centuries is the growth of Humanism. I am using the term in the sense hallowed by the Oxford English dictionary, where humanism is defined as " any system of thought or action which is concerned with merely human interests (as distinguished from divine), or with those of the human race in general." Thus understood, it implies an essentially this-worldly outlook, in contrast to that of the Middle Ages, when not only scientists and thinkers, but ordinary men in their rare moments of reflection never questioned that this earthly life was a transitory state of probation, the ante-room of heaven and hell. Not that such an other-worldly outlook is incompatible with the claims of humanism within the larger scheme. Indeed we shall see presently that it is only in subordination to a theocentric world-view that those claims can be realised without contradiction and disaster. But modern humanism is absolute, not relative, an end to be sought for its own sake, regardless of any other-worldly sanctions. That this should be so is at once strange and inevitable. It is strange that the scientific revolution which dethroned man and " this earth his habitation " from their central position in the universe should have led to the exaltation of human interests and welfare as the final aim of both thought and conduct. Yet it could not have been otherwise. The new science owed its triumphs to the exercise of man's natural powers of reason, independently of religious faith or supernatural illumination. Mathematical deduction and inductive generalisation from data of observation and experiment call for no intrusion on the part of divine grace. That Dr. Whitehead is a theist, Earl Russell an agnostic, is quite irrelevant to the value of their work in mathematics. Moreover, the objects on which the activity of reason was directed were events in space and time, to be explained solely in terms of their spatio-temporal antecedents. Reference to divine agency or, indeed, to any grounds outside the process of nature lies beyond the province of the scientist. Can we wonder, then, that men's thought should have been diverted more and more from the mediæval tradition, to be concentrated more and more on the promise of a humanistic millennium, to be achieved in the strength of their own powers of thought and will ? The uniform progress of civilization, the perfectibility of human nature, the eventual banishment, through rational enlightenment, of vice and suffering, the advent of an age when all men equally should enjoy material prosperity and social concord; such was the faith that inspired the reformers of the French Revolution, and that won classic expression in Condorcet's *Esquisse d'un tableau historique du progrès de l'esprit humain*, written in prison under the shadow of the guillotine. Half a century later Comte openly proclaimed the religion of humanity. The " idol of humanism " was set up for worship, the image of a Man-god in place of the God-man of Christianity.

§ 12. Comte, it is true, found few disciples; the apotheosis of man was too extravagant a demand to secure acknowledgement even from an age bewitched by the spell of humanism. Yet he did but draw the logical conclusion from the premises implicit in the dominant thought of his generation. That they still dominate the minds of multitudes to-day is evident from a moment's glance at the warring creeds which threaten our civilization. Mr. Michael Oakeshott, in his book entitled *The Social and Political Doctrines of Contemporary Europe*, has collected documents illustrative of the five main types of political and social theory, each of which commands the passionate loyalty of millions of our fellow human beings. Of these five, only one, the Catholic doctrine as embodied in the *Encyclicals* of Popes Leo XIII and Pius XI, is grounded on faith in an otherworldly order, within which the claims of human nature to temporal satisfaction are accorded their full measure of recognition.[1] All the other four types are, in their several ways, secularist and humanistic. Communism, as exemplified in the Marx–Engels–Lenin doctrines, is avowedly atheistic; its programme, the achievement of a classless society by means of a class war, is, if not wholly materialistic, at any rate wholly this-worldly. National Socialism, as the event has made tragically manifest, subjects religion, morality, and all other activities of the spirit, to the interests of the state, in its effort to secure an earthly hegemony for the peoples of Aryan race. Italian Fascism, despite its opportunist compromise with the papacy, is equally insistent in principle on the absolute claim of the state to unquestioning obedience from the citizens. " Mussolini,"

---

[1] The preamble to the constitution of Eire, included among Mr. Oakeshott's documents, is instructive in this connexion.

so ran the authoritative decalogue, " is always right." " The
Fascist state," wrote the Duce in his article on the doctrine of
Fascism, " the highest and most powerful form of personality, is
a force, but a spiritual force, which takes over all the forms of
the moral and intellectual life of man." When we pass to what
Mr. Oakeshott calls Representative Democracy, i.e., to the conception of society fostered, if not with religious zeal, at least
with resolute conviction, by the peoples of the British Commonwealth, France, the United States, and many other of the smaller
states of Europe, it is more difficult to pronounce judgement.
The view in question has a long history, during which it has
shown remarkable elasticity, nor have its principles ever received
precise formulation as have those of the other four types. Many
of them, such as the promotion of human welfare, the maintenance of liberty for each individual and nation to work out its
own salvation in its own way, the furtherance of social and
international justice—the aims, in fact, for which we now
contend—are consistent with loyalty to the Christian faith.
It is otherwise with the materialist interpretation of human
happiness, and the baneful economic and industrial doctrines
that have so often been held integral to it. But the link
between representative democracy and Christianity is, on
the side of the former, not essential but contingent. It is
true, as we shall see later, that Liberalism—I use the word in
its broadest sense—is impregnated with ideas of Christian origin.
But how many of its supporters would admit that their advocacy
was inspired by any but purely secularist motives ? When I
read in the *Church Times* that it is " matter of common consent
that the only hope of civilization is a return to the religion on
which it is based," I open my eyes in amazement. The truth is
rather, as we read in the same issue, that " nations will only be
Christian when the majority of their citizens are Christians."
In fact they are not; nor, I fear, are the majority of statesmen
in the self-governing democracies of to-day. They regard their
political principles as ends in themselves, not as attempts to
realise the Kingdom of God among men. They live and move
and have their being under the spell of secularist humanism.

§ 13. Is it not strange that this faith in man's ability to
achieve the aims of humanism by his own strength should have
persisted despite the tragic experiences of the last thirty years ?
One would have thought that if man had been endowed by
nature with the faculties requisite for the mastery of his environ-

ment, his progress in knowledge and in the power that knowledge brings would have proved more successful in effecting the desired result. One would have thought, for instance, that the resources now at his disposal for securing social unity—the steamship, the telegraph, the telephone, the aeroplane, the wireless—would have furthered, instead of hindered, inter-racial and international harmony. In the nineteenth century, when material prosperity was on the upward grade, the humanistic creed could offer a certain plausibility; but to-day in the light of the widespread disintegration of the bonds of human fellowship and social order, it is surely a paradox that it should retain its power to inspire thinking men. We are confronted with a practical *reductio ad absurdum* of the secularist faith. If this be so, is it not high time that we should set ourselves to question its foundations, and consider whether man's final goal can be found in a state where there is no finality, and not rather in an otherworldly reality, that embraces the temporal and human in integration with the eternal and the divine? I use the word "integration" designedly, with reference to M. Jacques Maritain's book, entitled *L'Humanisme Intégrale*. It means that the two realms, the kingdoms of nature and of grace, are not severed one from the other, or arbitrarily conjoined, but that the latter is "integral"·to the former, in that apart from God, nature can neither be, nor be conceived. I do not here raise the difficult question whether the world is as necessary to God as God is to the world, but content myself with the Christian answer, that the facts of experience level with our capacities reveal the necessary dependence of man and the world upon God. I want to show that to assert man's self-sufficiency is to imagine him to be other than he is, and that the recognition of his dependence, so far from belying the claims of humanism, is the primary condition of their realisation. To this end, I offer the following considerations.

§ 14. (1) If we analyse man's nature, as it unfolds itself in the course of his brief history, we find in it potentialities and desires that can never be satisfied under the conditions of earthly life. The contrast between these claims of his nature and the narrow limits that thwart their attainment gives rise, as consciousness develops, to an inward tension that serves at once to stimulate activity and to baffle it. In richly-endowed personalities, the tension may even be felt as intense agony; "as the hart longeth for the waterbrooks, so longeth my soul for the living God." All men, at some times and in some degree, experience a sense of shortcoming, an awareness that their reach exceeds their grasp. So in a pre-Christian age Socrates measured his advance towards wisdom by his growing consciousness of ignorance; so, again, the saints of the Church, realising more than ordinary men the gulf that parts their imperfect achievement from the infinite holiness of God, confess themselves with truth to be miserable sinners. Let me give two illustrations. In the *Summa contra Gentiles*, Aquinas grounds his argument to a future life on the fact that man's intellect, with its infinite desire for knowledge, a desire that defies fulfilment under this-worldly conditions, marks him out as designed by the very constitution of his nature for an other-worldly consummation. For "nature does nothing in vain." Implicit in man's finite intellectual capacity is an unrest which spurs him onwards from partial truth to partial truth, but which cannot be quieted by any knowledge short of a truth that is absolute and complete. The same holds of man's natural desire of good. In the magnificent passage with which Spinoza prefaces the *Tractatus de Intellectus Emendatione*, he tells how in youth and early manhood he vainly sought felicity in this-worldly goods, till he learnt how in the love of a *res infinita et aeterna* alone could he attain fruition. "A mere case of wish-fulfilment," as many in these latter days will protest; to draw from which an inference to an other-worldly reality is simply to offer men an opiate. Georges Sorel saw deeper in this matter than Marx and Lenin. He rejected, it is true, the Christian conclusion, but he recognised how deep-rooted in man's nature is the "tourment de l'infini," and how urgent is its claim for satisfaction. He sought to quench it in ardour for the "general strike" and the class-war against capitalism. Rather, as the event has proved, it is such temporal remedies that are the opiates. Butler's argument still holds its ground. If earthly happiness were man's proper end, the constitution of nature is very ill-adapted to its attainment. Whereas the world is admirably fitted to be the scene of his moral probation and discipline. There is no half-way house between passive acquiescence in a meaningless universe and faith in the sovereignty of an other-worldly order.

§ 15. (2) Let us, secondly, approach the question from the opposite pole, and, assuming the truth of the theocentric world-view, ask whether it allows full scope for man's this-worldly interests and aspirations. Here we find ourselves in presence of an apparent paradox. On the one hand, the claim of religion is all-embracing. There is nothing in the universe that does not draw its life and being from God. He demands the consecration of our whole personality to his service. " Whether ye eat or drink, or whatsoever ye do, do all to the glory of God." Ultimately, then, all human activities and all human knowledge fall within the province of religion. Yet, within this larger view of the religious life, there exists a real distinction between the religious and the secular. St. Paul's motive in tent-making was doubtless to earn the wherewithal to enable him to preach the gospel without being a burden on his converts. But when actually engaged on his craft, his attention must have been wholly concentrated on its exercise. Otherwise he would have made bad tents. A man's activity, in private prayer or in the reception of the Sacrament, is manifestly of an order different from his activity in solving a mathematical problem or playing a round of golf. The paradox, however, is but apparent; for— and this is the point of interest—the distinction between the religious and the secular has its roots in religion itself.[1] A God who is the object of religious worship must be transcendent of the world of his creation. Now between the being of the Creator and that of the creature there is a difference of kind, that can only be bridged *ex parte Dei* by God's revelation of Himself to man. For only God can truly create; man is never more than an architect working on given materials. If we talk loosely of the creative activity of the artist, it is to signify that, as the late Professor Alexander put it, the artist's mind is blended with the material in the product, which is therefore something genuinely new. It follows from this that the distinction between man's activities and knowledge, in so far as they are directed immediately upon God, and man's activities and knowledge, in so far as they are directed upon the world of God's creation, is not only sanctioned by religious experience, but is its necessary consequence. Thus the *Deum semper excipimus* of the scientist and the historian finds its secular justification. I do not know how science first had its birth from amid the rough and tumble of man's sense perceptions; but in any case it must sooner or later have arisen in obedience to the demands of the religious consciousness.

Thus we find (1) that not only do the facts of man's nature

---

[1] See Bowman, *Studies in The Philosophy of Religion* (c. xvi), and above, c. xi, § 15 (on Aquinas).

in his present state point on examination to his other-worldly destiny, but also (2) that the theocentric world-view—and, we may add, it alone—allows full scope and satisfaction for his humanistic aspirations.

§ 16. (3) If we consider the concepts most distinctive of modern humanism, we shall find that they not only have their source in Christianity, but that, when severed from their religious context, they are robbed of all intelligible meaning. The concepts I have chiefly in mind are those of *Fraternity* and *Personality*. Liberty and Equality, for the French Revolutionists, were terms of negative import, calling on men to sweep away the abuses of tyranny and privilege that marked the *Ancien Régime*. Their positive implications are ambiguous so long as our outlook is confined within this-worldly limits. What we want to be freed *from* is clear; but what we want freedom *for* is greatly dark. Men are not, and never can be, equal; " one to count as one and as one only " is a formula that has no relevance beyond the ballot-box; and " equality of opportunity " means merely that all alike should start at scratch in the race to achieve superiority. The only positive liberty is to be found in the service of God which is perfect freedom; the only positive equality in the status of all mankind as children of their heavenly Father. But in the concept of *Fraternity* we strike the nerve of the appeal of humanism to the modern world. The brotherhood of mankind is the clarion-note heralding the goal towards which the workers of all nations march as " comrades." That this conception had its birth in Christianity is beyond question. It was reached, not by progressive enlargement from love of kinsmen or fellow-citizens, but as the direct corollary of God's all-embracing love of man. " Beloved, if God so loved us, we ought also to love one another." " This commandment have we from him, that he who loveth God love his brother also." It was for their love, one for another, that the early followers of Christ were remarkable in the eyes of the pagan world. How far has the concept retained its force in the theory or the practice of modern secularism ? The word survives with its glamour scarcely dimmed; but in unnatural union with the gospels of class-war and racial antagonism. The contradiction thus avowed in theory is yet more evident in action. I am thinking not merely of the hatred *à l'outrance* displayed by Communists towards adherents of capitalism or heretics who question any detail in the authoritative doctrine, but rather the temper of suspicion that has spread within the fold, and threatens even the ranks of the orthodox with disintegration. What most appals me in the gospels of class-war and racial antagonism is the poisoning of the sources of personal friendship among the young, of that free intercourse that is the salt and savour, for instance, of life at a university between the youth of either sex—a thing to which we may surely apply Aristotle's great saying about justice, that it is " fairer than the morning or the evening star." " See how these comrades hate one another "—such surely will be the epitaph to be inscribed on the graves of the victims of the illusion of a terrestrial millennium. The concept of *Personality*—and we may add, the allied concept of humanity—tells the same tale. The " infinite worth of the individual " is a catchword on everyone's lips; but as signifying a truth of human nature it draws its meaning from the religion in which it had its origin. It has won its hold on modern thought chiefly through Kant's well-known formula : " Treat humanity, whether in thine own person or that of any other, always as an end withal, never merely as a means." But by " person " Kant meant not the empirical human self, as a phenomenon in space and time, but the noumenal ego, the purely rational selfhood by virtue of which every man is a member of the supersensible " kingdom of ends," the other-worldly community of which God is sovereign. What claim to infinite worth can be ascribed to any man, regarded purely as a denizen of the world of nature ? Even the greatest, when so regarded, has only relative and finite value; of the rest, there are many whose value is rather a minus quantity or disvalue, of whom it might be truly said that from the stand-point of this-worldly interests " it were better if this man had never been born." It is questionable whether, for instance, of men now living there is any that is of equal worth, as a creature in time, to a master-piece by Rembrandt. Can we then be surprised when we turn to the actual behaviour of those whose pretension it is to free men from " self-alienation " in bondage to religion to realise their true inherent personality, to find such an utter disregard for life as has led Nazi Germany to doom hordes of Jews, Czechs and Poles to wholesale torture and execution ? What again are we to think of the more subtle but equally disastrous wastage of individuality, in our own as well as in foreign lands, due to the growing mechanisation of industry.[1] " By their fruits ye shall know them." The bane of secularist humanism,

[1] See Appendix II, pp. 499–500.

and its *reductio ad absurdum,* is the appalling inhumanity of its performance. Nor can the advocates of Totalitarianism ride off triumphant by pointing to the dark record of animosity and persecution in the history of the Christian church. For by their own admission the crimes enacted are the logical outcome of the precepts of their respective gospels. These prescribe war as the necessary means to peace, hatred as the chosen instrument of love. Thus even the fair-sounding claims of fraternity and personality have been bereft of all concrete significance. In the mouth of the this-worldly humanist, they are no longer *verba,* words fraught with meaning, but mere *voces,* i.e., meaningless sounds.

The term *Humanity* itself, which in this last century and a half has stirred men to so much sacrifice and to so much crime; what significance does it retain apart from an other-worldly reference ? Does it mean our common human nature ? Man's spirit will hardly be touched to fine, or even to baser, issues by a conceptual abstraction. What is clearly intended by those who proclaim the service of humanity as our final goal is mankind as a collective whole of individuals, the totality of the human race. But where is such a totality to be found ? Can it even be conceived in imagination within the bounds of temporal history ? And what of the generations that are past ? How can they have part or lot in the love and service that claim to be offered to all mankind ? It is otherwise indeed if we lift our eyes above this earthly scene to the vision of the other-worldly community, where all men, past, present and future, are fellow-citizens in the kingdom of which God is King.

§ 17. There is but one remedy for this two-fold canker which for three centuries has been menacing the heart of European civilization—the lack of moral principle in the exercise of the power that knowledge brings, and the progressive secularisation of men's outlook—to wit, the restoration of faith in Christianity. That alone can effect moral regeneration ; that alone can establish humanistic culture on a sure foundation. For a world-view centred in sense there must be substituted a world-view centred in God. This in no way implies a sterile return to the tradition of mediævalism. History never repeats itself ; least of all, the history of a great religion. The task that has been laid upon the Christian in each succeeding age is to prepare the world for the coming of God's kingdom. But that kingdom is no mere temporal phenomenon, past, present or future. Though mani-

s

fested temporally alike in the past, the present and the future, it is an eternal reality, above the vicissitudes of time and change.

Thus there remains for Christian men the further problem, that of the application of the theocentric world-view to the ever changing situations of public life, and particularly to the present crisis in international history. The problem is one of special difficulty, in that Christ laid down no programmes or rules of policy; he laid down principles, leaving it to men's free judgement, to their enlightened consciences to apply them to the variable circumstances of this present life. To embark in any detail on a discussion of this further question is, of course, impossible here. But there are two points where our consideration of the general principles has already touched upon the manner of their application. Whenever a state pursues a policy directly contrary to Christ's religion, it is the Christian's duty to resist it. I do not see, for instance, how whole-hearted co-operation can be possible even within a Federated Europe, if any major power should persist in uncompromising hostility to the Christian faith. On the other hand, the question of the merits of Communism as an economist doctrine, or of the Totalitarian form of government, is one that is largely independent of considerations of religion. This brings me to my second point of contrast, the real, though relative, distinction between the religious and the secular. To prepare the way for God's kingdom does not mean to subordinate state to church or to set up in Europe the rule of the saints. The state has its legitimate autonomy, recognised by Christ himself. " Render unto Cæsar the things that are Cæsar's, and unto God the things that are God's." But the recognition of this relative distinction must never blind men to the ultimate universality of the divine sovereignty. In this sense we may say that the future of civilization lies in the hands of the conscientious objector.

Returning at the close to Plato's question with which we started, How can the state study philosophy without being ruined ?, we are now able to give the answer. The state can only survive and flourish if finite and temporal goods be acknowledged as dependent on the one good that is absolute and eternal, that is, on God.

IV. Conclusion.

§ 18. I wish in conclusion to guard against a possible misunderstanding of the views on Humanism expressed in the foregoing pages. We have seen how both philosophical reflection and a survey of the recent history of civilization point to the conclusion that a purely secularist humanism, such as is advocated in many quarters at the present time, is incompatible alike with the facts of human nature and the structure of the universe in which we are placed. Man is an animal, but not merely an animal; there are potencies in his nature, intellectual, moral and religious, which cannot achieve satisfaction within the bounds of temporal existence. Nor is the world, as it appears in time, intelligible without remainder as the historical fulfilment of the principle of order in the light of which science and philosophy seek to understand it. But it is an error to regard these two types of humanism, the anthropocentric and the theocentric, as co-ordinate species of a common genus. The position I am maintaining, is rather that a secularist humanism, since it is grounded on a mutilation of our nature and experience, is not to be regarded as humanism, but as a travesty of humanism; and that integration with a theocentric world-view, as in a Christian philosophy, is requisite even for the satisfaction of man's cultural aspirations. The Provost of King's, when addressing a meeting of the Classical Association at Cambridge, rightly deprecated the introduction of controversial *clichés* and party battle-cries. " The challenge to the validity of ancient standards must," he allowed, " be answered." But he added : " Let there be, however, no ' I am for the Classics,' ' I am for Religion,' ' I am for Science, sacred Science.' " [1] That the classics and the sciences both fall within humanistic culture, no serious thinker will now dispute ; but what about religion ? The pitting of religious and secularist humanism one against the other is a yet graver menace ; for it does violence alike to humanism and to religion. We can learn better from a study of the Christian philosophy which was the crowning glory of the Middle Ages, with its ever-memorable watch-word ; *gratia perficit naturam, non tollit*. Human nature, apart from supernatural grace, is doomed to imperfection and, being foiled of its

---

[1] Quoted from *The Times* report, April 16, 1943.

515

connatural end, to disillusionment and eventual despair; religion, unless grounded on man's nature, is, together with the entire supernatural economy, relegated to the limbo of irrationality. The worship of the Creator is bereft of its due homage. Nor, again, can there be any rivalry of " I am for Hebraism," and " I am for Hellenism." Here too, as we have seen,[1] the Christian philosophy of Aquinas offers a corrective, with its impressive synthesis of the Hebrew, Greek and Roman legacies. True, the Hebraic–Christian legacy is revelational, the Hellenic rational. Yet, for all the difference in their credentials, they present note-worthy affinities. Both affirm a cosmic teleology, grounded on an other-worldly reality, apprehended by an act, in the one case, of religion, in the other, of metaphysical faith. To neither was it granted to transcend the bounds of human reason, so as to comprehend in full detail how the rational purpose of the Creator is fulfilled in the temporal processes of nature and history, in the life whether of the individual or of the race. When we seek, as we needs must, to know the nature of this principle of cosmic order and its manner of working, there is a further affinity in the answers given by both traditions. The order, whether its source be in the nature of metaphysical reality or in the will of the Creator, is a moral order, so that, in ways that to men's finite intellect are greatly dark, the chequered course of history is at every point overruled for good.

> " All shall be well and
> All manner of things shall be well
> When the tongues of flame are in-folded
> Into the crowned knot of fire,
> And the fire and the rose (the purifactory suffering and its reward)
> are one." [2]

Once more—and here lies the relevance of this faith for man's life and destiny—both the Hebraic and the Hellenic traditions assert the paramount obligation binding men to rule their conduct in conformity to the order of the universe, and define sin as *hubris*, the temper of pride of self that prompts him to rebellion against the moral law. Both are at one in teaching that for sin, as thus defined, the law exacts inevitable retribution. He who, like Agamemnon, treads the purple, subjects himself to an inexorable doom. He sows the wind and reaps the whirl-wind. Where the traditions part company is in their respective doctrines of salvation. Whereas the Platonist taught salvation by philosophical wisdom and the Stoic salvation by self-sufficiency

---

[1] C. xi, above.   [2] T. S. Eliot, *Little Gidding*.

rooted in strength of will, the Christian preached the gospel of redemption through the Incarnate Christ. " God so loved the world." The gulf here is immeasurable. Of the love of God for His creation, and of the consequent obligations upon man to love God with his whole heart and his neighbour as himself, Greek philosophy knew nothing. These are revealed truths inaccessible to unaided reason ; but if we bear firmly in mind that the grace which perfects is *praeter*, not *contra naturam*, we can understand how a Christian philosophy, and it alone, enables man to realise his human capacities in full measure as a freeman of an other-worldly commonwealth.

BIBLIOGRAPHICAL APPENDIX

The list given below represents merely a selection of trustworthy English works, admittedly incomplete, but sufficient to start the reader on a closer study of the main topics handled in this volume. All the books should be accessible in a good public library. Excellent bibliographies will be found at the close of the principal articles in the " Encyclopaedia Britannica" and in the " Cambridge Ancient and Medieval Histories," to which the student is referred for fuller information throughout.

I. HISTORICAL ATLASES.

Kiepert's *Atlas Antiquus* (Williams and Norgate), W. R. Sheppard's *Historical Atlas* (Henry Holt), and the *Atlas of Ancient and Classical Geography* in the *Everyman* Series (the last less expensive).

II. CHAPTER I.

J. L. Myres : *The Dawn of History (Home University Library).*

III. CHAPTER II.

The articles on *Egypt, Babylonia and Assyria, Hittites, Aegean Civilization, Crete* and *Persia* in the 11th edition of the *Encyclopaedia Britannica*; and the *Cambridge Ancient History*, vols. i (Egypt and Babylonia to 1580 B.C.) and ii.

Breasted : *History of Egypt.*
Budge : *Egypt (Home University Library).*
Rogers : *History of Babylonia and Assyria.*
Maspero : *The Dawn of Civilization, Egypt and Chaldaea* (ed. Sayce).
Maspero : *The Struggle of the Nations* (ed. Sayce).
Maspero : *The Passing of the Empires* (ed. Sayce).
Woolley : *The Sumerians.*

The original documents are translated with introductions and comments in the series of volumes entitled *Ancient Records of Egypt* (ed. Breasted), *Ancient Records of Assyria and Babylonia* (ed. Harper), *Ancient Records of Palestine, Phoenicia and Syria* (ed. Harper), published by the University of Chicago.

On the religions, consult

Sayce: *Religions of Ancient Egypt and Babylonia* (Gifford Lectures, 1902).
Jastrow : *Religion of Assyria and Babylonia.*
King : *Babylonian Religion and Mythology.*
Pinches : *Religion of Babylonia and Assyria.*

On the laws of Khammurabi,

Johns : *The Oldest Code in the World.*
Handcock : *The Code of Hammurabi* (S.P.C.K. Texts for Students, cheap).
Cowley : *The Hittites* (Schweich Lectures, 1918).
Burrows : *The Discoveries in Crete.*
Hawes : *Crete, the Forerunner of Greece* (inexpensive).
Schuchhardt : *Schliemann's Excavations.*

Above all, the monuments in the British Museum should be visited, with the aid of the cheap and well-illustrated guide-books to the various collections. Parties are shown round by an admirable official guide.

IV.   CHAPTER III.

Consult the article *Bible* (*A. Old Testament*) in the *Encyclopaedia Britannica*; also those on *Hebrew literature, Hebrew religion, Jews*, etc.   Hastings' *Dictionary of the Bible* and the *Encyclopaedia Biblica* may be referred to; the latter represents the extreme of radical criticism.   The several Books of the Old Testament should be studied with the aid of the volumes in the *International Critical Commentary*.   Peake : *Commentary*; and the volumes of the *Cambridge Bible for Schools and Colleges* are also recommended. Driver's *Introduction to the Literature of the Old Testament* (9th edition, revised, 1913) is an invaluable guide to Old Testament study and contains full bibliographies.   See also the brief survey in Moore : *Literature of the Old Testament* (*Home University Library*).

F. C. Burkitt : *Jewish and Christian Apocalypses.*
R. H. Charles : *Eschatology.*
R. H. Charles : *Apocrypha and Pseudepigrapha.*
Klausner : *Jesus of Nazareth.*
Manson : *A Companion to the Bible* (with bibliographies).
G. F. Moore : *Judaism.*
Oesterley and Robinson · *History of Israel.*
Schürer : *History of the Jewish People in the Time of Jesus Christ.*
W. Robertson Smith : *The Religion of the Semites.*
W. Robertson Smith : *The Prophets of Israel*
W. Robertson Smith : *The Old Testament in the Jewish Church.*
The People and the Book (Essays, ed. Peake).
Record and Revelation (Essays, ed. Wheeler Robinson), with bibliographies.

V.   CHAPTERS IV–VI.

(A) **General.**—The best modern text-book of Greek history is Bury : *History of Greece.*   See also, *The Legacy of Greece* (ed. Livingstone), Holm : *History of Greece*, and the yet larger works of Grote and Thirlwall (for the seventh century onwards).

On Greek literature, Mackail : *Lectures on Greek Poetry*; Gilbert Murray : *History of Greek Literature.*   On Greek philosophy, the works of Zeller and Burnet; Gomperz, *Greek Thinkers*; and Adamson's *Development of Greek Philosophy*.   Translations of the Greek (and Latin) classics will be found in the *Loeb* and *Everyman* Series and in the *Temple Greek and Latin Classics.*   In the Loeb and Temple volumes the Greek (or Latin) text and the English translation face one another throughout.

(B) **Special Subjects.**—The following works are referred to the part of this book where they will first be found useful.   In many cases, they contain matter relevant to later sections.

(1) CH. IV : PART II.

Warde Fowler : *The City-State of the Greeks and Romans.*
Zimmern : *The Greek Commonwealth.*

PART III.
P. N. Ure : *The Greek Renaissance.*
P. N. Ure : *The Origin of Tyranny.*

PART IV.

Gilbert Murray : *Rise of the Greek Epic.*
Jebb : *Introduction to Homer.*
Leaf : *Companion to the Iliad* (in Lang, Leaf and Myers' translation).   Translations of the *Iliad* by Lang, Leaf and Myers, of the *Odyssey* by Butcher and Lang, and by Palmer.

PART V.

Burnet : *Early Greek Philosophy.*
Burnet : *Thales to Plato.*
Cornford : *Greek Religious Thought.*
Guthrie : *Orphism.*
Jane Harrison : *Prolegomena to the Study of Greek Religion.*
Jane Harrison : *Ancient Art and Ritual* (*Home University Library*).
Adam : *Religious Thoughts in Greece.*
Gilbert Murray : *Five Stages of Greek Religion.*
Nilsson : *A History of Greek Religion.*
A. E. Taylor : *Platonism and its Influence.*

(2) CH. V : PART I.

The student should not fail to read translations of *Herodotus* (in the *Everyman* and the *Loeb* Series, or by Macaulay) and *Thucydides* (in the *Everyman* Series, or by Jowett); also Plato's studies of democracy (with Athens in his mind) in Books VI and VIII of the *Republic*, and of timocracy (with Sparta in view) in Book VIII. The *Republic* is translated by Jowett (Clarendon Press) and by Davies and Vaughan in the *Golden Treasury* Series. Zimmern's book is excellent on the economic basis of Athenian public life.

PART II.

Greek art is far better studied in the galleries of the British Museum than in books about the subject. The cheap and excellent official guide-books will furnish the requisite assistance. A good general hand-book is Fowler and Wheeler : *Greek Archaeology.*

On the drama,

Haigh : *The Attic Theatre.*
Ridgeway : *The Origin of Tragedy.*
Gilbert Murray : *Euripides and His Age.*
Gilbert Norwood : *Greek Tragedy.*
Verrall : *Euripides the Rationalist.*

The following translations may be noted as of special value : *Aeschylus* by W. and C. E. S. Headlam, *Sophocles* by R. Whitelaw, *Euripides* (certain plays) by Gilbert Murray, *Aristophanes* by Rogers and (certain plays) by Hookham Frere. Aeschylus' *Oresteia* by E. D. A. Morshead, the *Agamemnon* by Gilbert Murray, Euripides' *Alcestis* by Robert Browning (in *Balaustion's Adventure*). If a selection is desired, the student is advised to begin with Aeschylus' trilogy (the *Oresteia*) and *Prometheus Bound*, Sophocles' *Antigone*, *Oedipus King* and *Philoctetes*, Euripides' *Medea*, *Hippolytus*, *Alcestis* and *Bacchae*, Aristophanes' *Frogs*, *Clouds*, *Acharnians*, *Birds* and *Wasps*.

On Thucydides, read Cornford : *Thucydides Mythistoricus.*

PART III.

On the Sophists and Socrates, Burnet : *Thales to Plato* and Gomperz (vol. ii). Xenophon's *Memorabilia* is well translated by Dakyns. All students should read Plato's *Apology*, *Crito and Phaedo*, which are translated in the Golden Treasury Series by Church, under the title *The Trial and Death of Socrates*, and by Jowett.

PART IV.

Plato's dialogues have been translated in their entirety by Jowett. In addition to the versions of separate dialogues referred to above, the *Symposium* has been translated by the poet Shelley, and the *Lysis, Phaedrus* and *Protagoras* by Wright (*Golden Treasury* Series). Several dialogues have been issued in English in the *Everyman* Library. It is much to be regretted that no cheap and good version of the *Gorgias* is obtainable.

On Plato's philosophy, see Burnet and Gomperz (vol. iii), A. E. Taylor's *Plato*, Grote's *Plato*, and the essay on *Plato's Theory of Goodness and the Good* in R. L. Nettleship's *Lectures and Remains* (vol. i). The best aids to the study of the *Republic* are the last-mentioned writer's *Lectures on the Republic* and his essay in *Hellenica* on *The Theory of Education in the Republic of Plato*. On Platonism and its history, see A. E. Taylor : *Platonism and its Influence* (*Our Debt to Greece and Rome* Series).

(3) CH. VI : PARTS I–II.

On Alexander, Hogarth : *Philip and Alexander*.

On Alexander's successors,

> Bevan : *House of Seleucus*.
> Tarn : *Hellenistic Civilisation*.
> Mahaffy : *The Progress of Hellenism in Alexander's Empire*,
> Holm : vols. iii, iv.

Theocritus is translated by Andrew Lang in the *Golden Treasury* Series.

PART III.

On Aristotle, Grote : *Aristotle*, Zeller : *Aristotle and the Aristotelian Schools*, Gomperz : vol. iv. Jaeger : *Aristotle*, Mure : *Aristotle*, J. L. Stocks : *Aristotelianism*.
A translation of the whole of Aristotle's works has been published by the Clarendon Press ; a volume of translated selections has been compiled by Sir D. Ross. Students are advised to approach the study of Aristotle through the *Ethics* (translated by Peters, and in the *Everyman* Series by Chase) and the *Politics* (Jowett's translation, ed. Davis—Clarendon Press). Muirhead's *Chapters from Aristotle's Ethics* and the introductory volume to Newman's edition of the *Politics* are also recommended. The beginner may well find in Dante the stimulus to an interest in Aristotle's philosophy, bearing in mind that Dante interpreted Aristotle in the light of many beliefs that were post-Aristotelian.

PART IV.

Zeller : *Epicureans and Stoics*, Bevan : *Stoics and Sceptics*, Wallace : *Epicureanism*, Dudley : *Cynics*.
Marcus Aurelius and *Epictetus* have been frequently translated (e.g., in the *Camelot* Series). The former has been translated by Rendall (*Golden Treasury* Series) with a useful Introduction. *Lucretius'* poem (*On the Nature of Things*) has been translated by Munro and by Bailey.

VI. CHAPTERS VII–VIII.

(A) **General.**—The best short text-book is Pelham : *Outline of Roman History* (a reprint of his article in the *Encyclopaedia Britannica*); among many others, those of Wells, of How and Leigh, and Warde Fowler's *Rome* (*Home University Library*) will be found useful. See also *The Legacy of Rome* (ed. C. Bailey) and H. Stuart Jones : *Companion to Roman History.* Of larger works, Mommsen's *History of Rome* is specially valuable for its interpretation of Roman institutions, law and civilization.   Greenidge :   *Roman Public Life,* Heitland : *Roman Republic* and T. Rice Holmes : *Roman Republic,* may also be mentioned.   Montesquieu's *Grandeur et décadence des Romains,* written in the first half of the eighteenth century, is full of acute and pregnant observations.

(B) **Special Subjects.**

(1) Ch. VII : Part I.

Warde Fowler : *City-State of the Greeks and Romans.*
Sohm : *Institutes of Roman Law* (tr. Ledlie).   This work should be consulted on the history and character of Roman law up to the time of Justinian.   See also the article *Roman Law* in the *Encyclopaedia Britannica* and Maine : *Ancient Law.*

Part III.

Bosworth Smith : *Carthage and the Carthaginians.*
Bosworth Smith : *Rome and Carthage* (*Epochs of Ancient History*).
Church and Gilman : *Carthage* (*Story of the Nations*).
Mabel Moore : *Carthage of the Phoenicians.*

There is much need for a new history of Carthage, and of the Phoenicians, that shall embody the results of recent research. Flaubert's novel *Salammbô,* the scene of which is laid in Carthage after the first Punic war, is based on a close study of the material available in the middle of the last century.   On Rome in the East, Bevan : *House of Seleucus.*

Part IV.

On Latin literature generally, Mackail : *Latin Literature* and, for fuller treatment of the poets, the works of W. Y. Sellar.

(2) Ch. VIII : Part I.

Greenidge : *History of Rome from 133 B.C.* (unfinished).
Warde Fowler : *Caesar* (*Heroes of the Nations*).
Warde Fowler : *Social Life at Rome in the Age of Cicero.*
E. S. Shuckburgh : *Augustus.*
Pelham : *Essays in Roman History* (and for the rest of this chapter).
G. Boissier : *The Opposition under the Caesars.*
Jeans : *Select Letters of Cicero* (an admirable translation, with brief explanatory introductions).
T. Rice Holmes : *Caesar's Conquest of Gaul.*

Caesar's narrative of the *Gallic War* can be read in Rice Holmes' translation.

Part II.

Mommsen : *Roman Provinces under the Empire* furnishes a brilliant survey up to the time of Diocletian, based largely on the evidence of contemporary inscriptions.

H. Stuart Jones : *Roman Empire (Story of the Nations).*
Capes : *The Early Roman Empire (Epochs of Ancient History).*
Capes : *The Roman Empire of the Second Century (Epochs of Ancient History).*
W. T. Arnold : *Roman Provincial Administration.*
W. T. Davis : *The Influence of Wealth in Imperial Rome.*
Haverfield : *Roman Britain* (a reprint of the article in the *Encyclopaedia Britannica*).
Haverfield : *The Romanisation of Roman Britain* (ed. Collingwood).

PART III.

The reader is advised to become acquainted with Cicero through his *Letters* (translated by Jeans) rather than through his speeches or other writings. Lucretius has been translated by Bailey and by Munro. The *Aeneid* may be read in Dryden's poetic version or in Mackail's prose translation. Tacitus has been translated by Church and Brodribb; Catullus, Ovid's *Metamorphooooo, Senoca, Quintilian, Pliny's Letters and Boethius' Consolation* in the *Loeb* Series; Plutarch by Langhorne. See also H. E. Butler : *Post-Augustan Poetry,* Boissier : *Tacitus and other Roman Studies.*

VII. CHAPTER IX.

PART I.

The literature dealing with the rise of Christianity is well-nigh inexhaustible, and the arbitrary nature of any brief selection is obvious. In the author's judgement, the most adequate history of the early church is by a French scholar, the late Mgr. Duchesne : *Histoire ancienne de l'Eglise* (translated). The following English works will serve as an introduction to the period :
Bp. A. C. Headlam : *The Life and Teaching of Jesus the Christ.*
Bigg : *Origins of Christianity.*
Bigg : *The Church's Task under the Roman Empire.*
Burkitt : *The Gospel History and its Transmission.*
Cochrane : *Christianity and Classical Culture.*
Dodd : *Apostolic Preaching.*
Moffatt : *An Introduction to the Literature of the New Testament.*
Stanton : *The Gospels as Historical Documents.*
Harnack : *The Expansion of Christianity in the First Three Centuries.*
Ramsay : *The Church in the Roman Empire.*
Döllinger : *The Gentile and the Jew.*
Hatch : *The Influence of Greek Ideas and Usages upon the Christian Church.*
Hatch : *The Organisation of the Early Christian Churches.*
And articles in Hastings' *Dictionary of the Bible, Encyclopaedia Biblica* and the *Cambridge Medieval History* vol. i. (esp. C. H. Turner on *The Organisation of the Church*). For the New Testament literature, consult the volumes in the *International Critical Commentary* and Lightfoot : *Epistles of Saint Paul;* for the literature of the subsequent epoch, Lightfoot : *Apostolic Fathers* and translations in the *Loeb* Series.

PART II.

Cumont : *The Mysteries of Mithra.*
Cumont : *Oriental Religions in Ancient Paganism.*

A. S. Geden : *Select Passages illustrating Mithraism* (S.P.C.K.).
Kennedy : *St. Paul and the Mystery Religions.*
S. Angus : *The Mystery Religions and Christianity.*
Warde Fowler : *The Religious Experience of the Roman People.*
Warde Fowler : *Roman Ideas of Deity.*
Dill : *Roman Society from Nero to Marcus Aurelius.*
Dill : *Roman Society in the Last Century of the Western Empire.*
On the philosophy of the period, see translations of Marcus
Aurelius and of Epictetus (as above) and Renan's volume on
Marcus Aurelius. Philostratus' *Life of Apollonius of Tyana*
is translated in the *Loeb* Series. There is a very interesting
translation of Plotinus by Stephen MacKenna. On Neo-
Platonism, Inge : *The Philosophy of Plotinus*, Whittaker : *The
Neo-Platonists*, Bigg : *Neo-Platonism*, E. R. Dodds : *Select
Passages illustrating Neo-Platonism* (S.P.C.K.). Webb's short
History of Philosophy (*Home University Library*) is admirable
on this period.

PART III.

Harnack : *History of Dogma.*
Hefele : *History of the Councils.*
Both these works are exhaustive studies of the history of
doctrine.
Bigg : *Christian Platonists of Alexandria.*
Gwatkin : *Studies of Arianism.*
Bright : *Age of the Fathers.*
Newman : *The Arians of the Fourth Century.*
Figgis : *The Political Aspects of St. Augustine's City of God.*

The articles in the *Dictionary of Christian Biography* may be
usefully consulted. Translations are to be found in the *Library
of Nicene and post-Nicene Fathers.*

VIII.   CHAPTER X.

(A) **General.**—On the Decline and Fall, the great work of Edward Gibbon
should form for all readers the basis of study. It has been re-edited
with notes by Bury. Students must bear in mind that it was
compiled mainly from the literary sources available in the later
eighteenth century, and that it reflects throughout the outlook and
temper of the age of Rationalism.

Bryce : *Holy Roman Empire.*
Davis : *Medieval Europe* (*Home University Library*).
The *Cambridge Medieval History*, vols. i and ii (with copious
bibliographies).

(B) **Special Subjects.**

PART II.

On ancient agriculture, Heitland : *Agricola.*

PART III.

Hodgkin : *Italy and Her Invaders.*
Davis : *Charlemagne* (*Heroes of the Nations*).
Bury : *History of the Later Roman Empire* (from 395).
On the life and times of Justinian see Procopius (*Loeb* transla-
tion in progress).

PART IV.

Bury : *op. cit.*; and *Eastern Roman Empire.*
Diehl : *History of the Byzantine Empire* (translated by G. B. Ives).
Finlay : *History of Greece* (written 1864).

On the Slavs, see the articles by Peisker in the *Cambridge Medieval History*, vol. ii.

On Mahomet and Islam, see the articles by Bevan and by Becker in the *Cambridge Medieval History*, vol. ii, Margoliouth : *Mohammed (Heroes of the Nations)* and *Mohammedanism (Home University Library)*, and translations of the *Koran* by E. H. Palmer, Rodwell and George Sale (ed. Ross, 1921).

PART V.

On Justinian's Code, see Gibbon (c. 44), the article in the *Cambridge Medieval History*, and Sohm. On the Monophysites, see Duchesne and Harnack ; on the Iconoclastic conflict, Bury : *Later Roman Empire*. On Byzantine civilization, see the *Encyclopaedia Britannica*, esp. the article by Krumbacher on *Greek Literature (Byzantine).*

IX. CHAPTER XI.

(A) **General.**—As this chapter is of the nature of a supplement to those which precede it, only a few of the most accessible works bearing on points of special significance are mentioned below. Davis : *Medieval Europe (Home University Library)*, gives a brief outline of the mediæval order of society and history. H. O. Taylor : *The Medieval Mind*, gives a useful and comprehensive survey. On classical learning in the Middle Ages, Sandys : *History of Classical Scholarship.* On the universities, Rashdall : *The Universities of the Middle Ages.*

(B) **Special Subjects.**

PART II.

Webb : *History of Philosophy (Home University Library)* contains an excellent chapter on the subject. No single large history of medieval philosophy with outstanding merits is available in English. De Wulf : *History of Scholastic Philosophy* is useful, as also is the medieval section in Ueberweg's *History of Philosophy.* R. L. Poole : *Illustrations of the History of Medieval Thought* should certainly be read. On Aquinas, see Wicksteed : *Reactions between Dogma and Philosophy (Hibbert Lectures*, 1916) and E. Gilson : *The Philosophy of S. Thomas* (translated). The *Summa Theologica* and the *Summa Contra Gentiles* have been translated by the English Dominicans.

On the Arabs, see Renan : *Averroës et l'Averroisme.* Dante should be read in the *Temple Classics* edition.

PART III.

Pollock and Maitland : *History of English Law*, vol. i.
Vinogradoff : *Roman Law in Medieval Europe.*
Gierke : *Political Theories of the Middle Age* (ed. Maitland, with Introduction).
Poole : *Essays in Medieval Thought.*

Carlyle : *A History of Medieval Political Theory in the West.*
Figgis : *Divine Right of Kings.*
Figgis : *Studies of Political Thought from Gerson to Grotius.*
Jenks : *Law and Politics in the Middle Ages.*

PART IV.

On Erasmus, Seebohm : *Oxford Reformers.*

Froude : *Erasmus.*
P. S. Allen : *The Age of Erasmus.*
P. S. Allen : *Selections from Erasmus.*

Mark Pattison's *Life of Casaubon* and *Essays*, Payne's *History of the New World called America* (vol. i) and Miss Haldane's *Life of Descartes* will serve to illustrate other aspects of this part of the chapter.

INDEX

NOTE.—Figures in heavier type indicate the most important of the passages referred to.

Passim = constantly mentioned : n. = note.

Where the reference is both to the text and to the notes on a given page, the page only is indicated, unless the note is of special importance.

INDEX